Danny Goodman's
HyperCard
Developer's Guide

Danny Goodman's HyperCard Developer's Guide

Danny Goodman

BANTAM BOOKS
TORONTO · NEW YORK · LONDON · SYDNEY · AUCKLAND

Danny Goodman's HyperCard Developer's Guide
A Bantam Book/July 1988

Apple, ImageWriter, LaserWriter, and MacPaint are registered trademarks of Apple
Computer, Inc.
Finder, HyperCard, HyperTalk, Macintosh, MultiFinder, and StackWare are trademarks
of Apple Computer, Inc.
APDA is a trademark of A.P.P.L.E. Co-op.
Turbo Pascal is a trademark of Borland International.
DiskTop is a trademark of C.E. Software.
MacRecorder, HyperSound and SoundEdit are trademarks of Farallon Computing, Inc.
SoundWave is a trademark of Impulse, Inc.
Stack Exchange is a trademark of Heizer Software.
Icon Factory is a trademark of HyperPress Publishing Corp.
VideoWorks is a trademark of Macromind, Inc.
Visual Interactive Programming is a trademark of Mainstay.
HyperDA is a trademark of Symmetry Corp.
LightSpeed C and LightSpeed Pascal are trademarks of Think Technologies.
VideoStack is a trademark of The Voyager Company.

NOTE

ISBN 0-553-34576-1

Published simultaneously in the United States and Canada

Bantam Books are published by Bantam Books, Inc. Its
trademark, consisting of the words "Bantam Books" and
the portrayal of a rooster, is registered in U.S. Patent and
Trademark Office and in other countries. Marca Regis-
trada. Bantam Books, Inc. 666 Fifth Avenue, New York,
New York 10103

PRINTED IN THE UNITED STATES OF AMERICA

0 9 8 7 6 5 4 3 2 1

Contents

PART ONE
Key Stack Developer Issues

Stacks • Customizing User Preferences • Inside the Preferences Card •
Button Customization • Inside the Button Customization

PART TWO

HyperTalk Techniques for Developers

String • Plain Sorting • Sorting By Field • "Dual Key" Sorts • Sorting Card Suites

PART THREE

Resources For Stack Developers

Acknowledgments

While the actual writing of a book is a lonely task, this particular volume had what Hollywood would call "a cast of thousands." Some I've had the pleasure of meeting in person; others I've met only through their electronic message questions or by exploring their HyperCard stacks. Hearing questions about stack design and implementation from the real world dramatically broadened my views.

Many of the opinions in this book, especially in Part One, came to life as a result of speaking engagements around North America since the release of HyperCard. The forums provided by local Apple offices in Portland, Pittsburgh, and Denver, Ellen Leanse of Apple's User Group Connection, the Software Entrepreneurs' Forum, and numerous Macintosh user groups helped me codify these ideas in what I believe is meaningful language.

I was fortunate to receive enormous technical help in areas that were new to me. Chris Knepper, who wrote the XCMDs in Part Three, went to the trouble of getting a half-dozen signatures (including Jean-Louis Gassée's) to allow him to write the code on his own time, on his own machine, in his own home. Mark Baumwell contributed heartily to the serial port XCMD, while Chris Derossi and Steve Maller offered many valuable suggestions for all three XCMDs.

Additional help in various forms from Apple Computer came from Mike Holm, Moira Cullen, Peggy Redpath, Lynn Knerr, Olivier Bouley, and Mimi Obinata.

Outside the halls of Apple, I received wonderful support from Darrell Leblanc at Think Technologies, David Intersimone at Borland International, and Tom Nalevanko at Mainstay.

I also wish to thank my aesthetic guiding spirit, David Smith, the finest Macintosh screen designer I've ever encountered.

Neither this book, nor the *Handbook* before it, would have been possible, of course, without Bill Atkinson's vision of what HyperCard would mean to personal computing. And Dan Winkler's teachings on HyperTalk have done me well.

Through it all, Linda again proved to be my greatest supporter, sharing my enthusiasm for HyperCard and its promise.

A Note to My Friends

I've written this book for readers of *The Complete HyperCard Handbook* who want to learn more about stack development.

If you're a *Handbook* reader, then you and I have already spent a good deal of time together—700+ pages is no quick read. We may have already met face-to-face at a Macworld Expo or user group meeting. In a way we're friends. And I'm glad you're here to renew our friendship.

This book is divided into three sections:

> Stack Development Issues
> HyperTalk Techniques
> Resources

You may jump around the book's chapters as you please, but I strongly recommend reading Part One before anything else. What I have to say about the 10 key development issues will influence how you apply what you'll learn in the rest of the book.

Many of the examples are taken from my first two commercial stack products, Business Class and Focal Point 1.0, both of which are published by Activision, Inc. In a few instances, I have updated some HyperTalk scripts for this book. Don't be alarmed if you examine a product and find a slight difference between scripts in the book and in the software. While it's not essential that you have these products at your side when reading the book, let me introduce each product to you.

Business Class comes packed with information for those who conduct business with people in other countries—whether by travel, telephone, or mail. It has lots of maps (which you click on to zoom into one of 63 countries covered in the product) and information cards for 13 categories. For instance, you can calculate what time and day it must be in your office to telephone someone in Tokyo at 11:00 am on Friday, Tokyo time. You can also get a rundown on visa and customs requirements for a country you plan to visit. It's a very graphic environment, and you browse through it almost entirely with the mouse.

Focal Point is quite different. It is an organizer and planner for appointments, to do items, clients, vendors, projects, proposals, expenses, names and addresses, telephone records, and several other items that are normally a nuisance to manage day-to-day. I wrote Focal Point initially for myself to help me manage the parts of my business that I don't like to worry about. There are a total of 18 stacks, into which you enter your information. Links among all the stacks automatically post important data where you expect it, and my guiding principle is that you should never have to retype anything. Thanks to HyperCard, you can customize Focal Point to any vertical business application you like.

As you'll see in this book, both products are treasure chests of HyperTalk structure and scripting examples (all scripts are unlocked), while being practical programs at the same time. They are living applications of my so-called "ten commandments" of stack design, which you'll learn about in Part One of this book. My greatest hope is that these two products serve as the baseline definition of quality stacks, and that your stacks will be even better.

I'd like to hear from you if you have questions or comments about the Handbook or this Developer's Guide. You may write to me in care of Bantam Books (666 Fifth Avenue, New York, NY 10103) or, for a much faster response, contact me electronically on CompuServe (address 75775,1731) or AppleLink (address X0576).

Welcome back.

Danny Goodman
May, 1988

When is HyperCard the Right Choice?

After hearing from many readers of *The Complete HyperCard Handbook*, I am especially sensitive to the diversity of expertise among active HyperCard users. By "active users" I mean those who actually make an effort to build stacks for themselves or others. For some, the *Handbook* represents a mountain of knowledge to be scaled slowly, sometimes presenting difficult passes toward the top. Others not only reach the top quickly, but wish to soar even higher. Fortunately, the vast majority find the content to be just the right combination of challenge and reward. Still, the fact remains that for many reasons, no two HyperCard users acquire identical facility with the program's powers and possibilities even after reading the same source material.

A Range of Developers

This holds very true for stack developers as well. In fact, the distance between the least and most knowledgeable stack developer is far greater than the same categories of everyday HyperCard user. At one end are those who bring to HyperCard expert knowledge about a business, academic, or real world situation, yet whose knowledge of HyperCard scripting and stack design is quite small. At the opposite end are truly experienced Macintosh programmers who wish to use HyperCard as a "front end" to complex systems developed in traditional Macintosh development environments. But people at both ends and everyone in between may be classified as serious HyperCard stack developers.

Interestingly, the success of a stack is not necessarily dependent upon technical expertise. Success, of course, is measured in several different ways. Success may be the financial reward of a stack in the commercial software marketplace; it may be a warm reception to a stack from the limited audience in a company or classroom to which it is directed; it may also be that hundreds or thousands of people use a stack you design for distribution in the public domain.

A successful stack needn't be a technical *tour de force* if it communicates its content well to the user. If the content is well illustrated and the organization is inviting, the stack's technical foundation may be built on little more than Go To commands and thoughtfully positioned visual effects.

Higher up the technical scale, developers can accomplish surprisingly remarkable applications using the HyperTalk scripting language built into HyperCard. Despite its simple vocabulary, the language is capable of performing enough "big time" software effects to suit many a stack developer. For example, with the exception of one command, everything you see taking place in the first releases of *Business Class* and *Focal Point* is written solely in HyperTalk. Spreadsheet-like calculations, world time conversions, creation of linked sets of cards, and pop-up lists of clients for selection and input by the mouse—they're all possible with HyperTalk alone.

At the very technical end of the stack development scale, you may extend the command and function vocabulary of HyperCard or even link HyperCard to powerful freestanding software engines by adding external code resources to a stack. Commonly called X-Commands (a name derived from the XCMD and XFCN resource types for external commands and external functions), these add-on chunks of computer code may be written in any traditional programming language and development environment of your choice—Pascal, C, Assembler, or any language capable of being compiled into a Macintosh resource (we've reserved Part III of the book for the subject of resources).

"Developer" Defined

When I talk about a stack developer, the definition includes a variety of people in the HyperCard community. Basically, a stack developer is anyone who designs a HyperCard stack that one or more other people will be using. That includes corporate stacks developed for in-house use, perhaps as training vehicles or as the basis for departmental information management services. In academic circles, a stack developer may be a student who writes a stack for other students in class or an instructor who develops teaching and simulation tools for students. A stack developer is a computer consultant whose charter is to create information tools for clients, whether the tools be for time and money management or a freestanding kiosk of trade show exhibitors and products. Many individuals who have identified information needs or wish to share their expertise with others of similar interests are joining the ranks of stack developers every day. Finally, some traditional software developers look at HyperCard as a way to involve more Macintosh users in a customizable environment for accessing their software and as a vehicle for on-line help systems and tutorials for their products.

Stack Categories

In the brief history of HyperCard development, four categories of stack products have emerged: information publishing, information management, external device control, and utilities. Let's examine each one.

Information Publishing

A potentially huge category of stacks is one in which the stacks come jam-packed with information. *Business Class* is one example, in that it comes loaded with travel-related information for 63 countries. The user browses through the information by clicking on maps and buttons. Figures i-1a through i-1f demonstrate a typical browsing sequence to find information about Japan. But *Business Class* represents only a tiny fraction of the possibilities of using HyperCard stacks as an information publishing medium.

Taking the "publishing" term seriously, some HyperCard entrepreneurs have begun stack-based magazines, like *HyperNews* (Figure i-2). With good design behind it, this medium offers an enjoyable experience for the user. *HyperNews*, for instance, offers several different subject sections, just like a magazine—features, interviews, reviews, and so on. Even *MacWeek*, the weekly tabloid magazine, started offering a stack version of the publication in early 1988, although its purpose is primarily for reference. The printed

Figure i-1a *A typical browsing sequence in Activision's Business Class stack product. Starting at the world view, you work your way toward information cards about a specific country.*

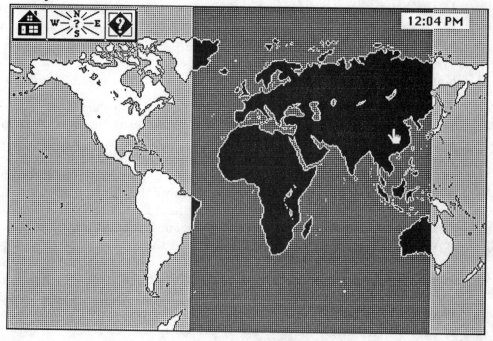

Figure i-1b

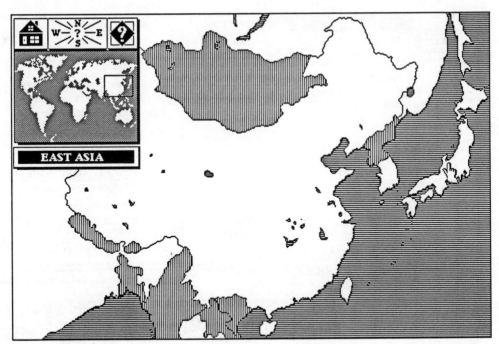

Figure i-1c

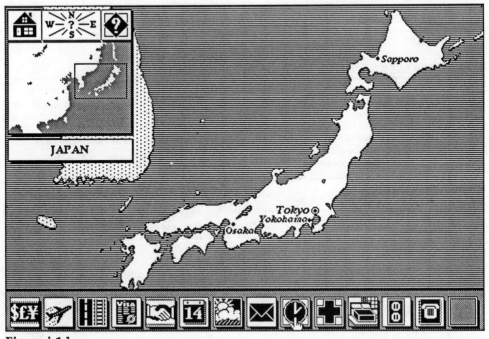

Figure i-1d

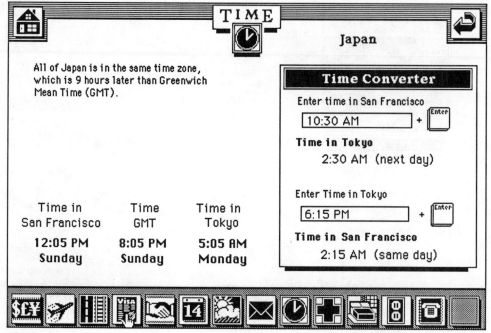

Figure i-1e

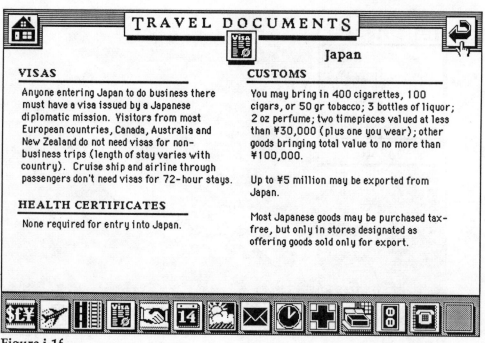

Figure i-1f

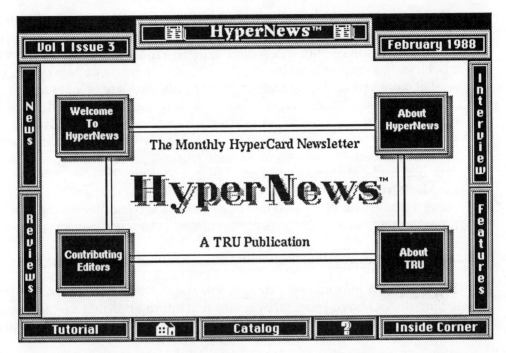

Figure i-2 *HyperNews is an information publishing stack that comes loaded with Hyper-Card-related news and information.*

magazine is still the primary information delivery vehicle.

Any kind of instructional stacks also falls in this category. This is where a number of stack opportunities lie. With the proliferation of Macintoshes on college campuses, the possibilities for classroom instruction are endless. Self-help programs for language instruction are already available. In-house corporate training is another important stack subject. Interactive tutorials for new employees can describe the various policies and benefits packages available to them. A new hire may select the package that best suits his needs, right on the stack. And, because the HyperCard environment is so much easier to manipulate than traditional programming environments, the job of updating a corporate training stack can be handled in-house by the people who know the subject matter. Updates can be made quickly and efficiently.

Informational stacks for the general public are also good candidates. An early stack on the AIDS disease has been well received and widely circulated. Freestanding kiosks for public access of information are a natural for Hyper-Card stacks. For example, scattered throughout the exhibit halls at Macworld Expos in Boston and San Francisco are Macintosh SE computers set up to help attendees locate booths for particular products and vendors. Running on the Macs is an information stack that entertainingly brings you to a menu of information about the event, including places to eat and sights to see outside the show. Figures i-3a to f show excerpts from the opening screen sequence. There's no reason such an idea should be limited to a trade show. Information machines in a corporate lobby, at information points on a college campus, in a retail store and shopping mall, or other public sites are great ideas.

Within the computer industry, we're already seeing product demonstrations, tutorials, and on-line help systems being built as HyperCard stacks. Because of the potentially interactive nature of a HyperCard stack, these stack applications usually turn out to be more engaging and meaningful than the previous read-only formats of demos, help, and tutorials. Now, too, those in the Macintosh community with good instructional skills have the power to convert those skills into a program that runs on the computer. In the past, the programming barrier held many great ideas hostage.

Information Management

To distinguish information management stacks from the information publishing stacks, above, I start off by saying that information management stacks come "empty." Empty of information, yes, but not empty of power or content.

Figure i-3a *The MacWorld Expos feature a helpful HyperCard stack with this engaging opening sequence (excerpt).*

Figure i-3b

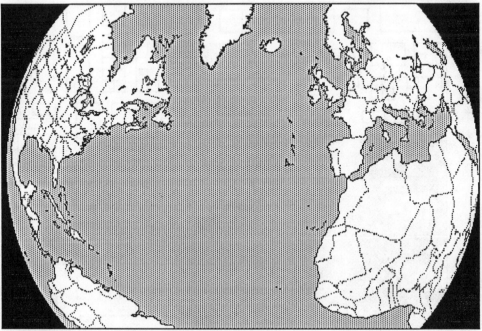

Figure i-3c

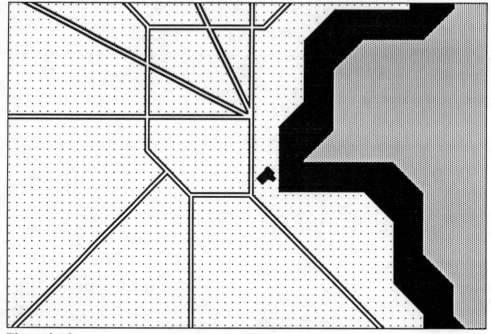

Figure i-3d

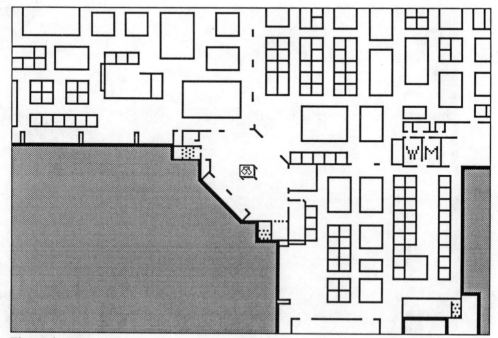

Figure i-3e

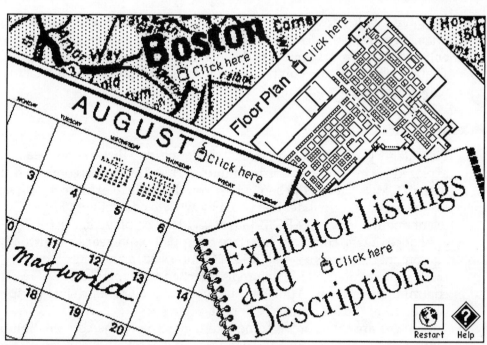

Figure i-3f

Well-conceived information management stacks provide powerful frame-works within which the user stores, manipulates, and accesses his or her own information. The framework contains intelligently planned connections or links between information that the user enters into the system. In *Focal Point,* for instance, the To Do List stack is preprogrammed so that when you select a person's name in the list of people to call and then click on the Outgoing Phone Log button with the Option key pressed, *Focal Point* automatically looks up the person's name in the Directory stack, dials the phone number, and generates a time-and-date-stamped call log card. All the links are there. All you do is provide your own information. Then the preprogrammed framework does its wonders on your information.

Other styles of information management stacks include various kinds of record keeping for business and personal use. Macintosh consultants and in-house corporate stack developers are building such stacks daily. They're in use in hospital emergency rooms, on retail sales floors, and on secretaries' desks.

Information management stacks lend themselves particularly well to vertical market applications, in which expertise in a discipline or knowledge about a company's *modus operandi* is more valuable than Macintosh programming experience. When you identify a problem in your work that no one has yet solved with software, HyperCard often provides an avenue to a solution. Then, if you keep the design of the stack versatile, it may become a marketable entity to the narrow segment of the business universe with similar problems. That's how a software company often starts: computerizing a system originally developed on paper.

External Device Control

The category of controlling external devices is one that has not been widely explored yet in the HyperCard community, but its time has come (in fact, one of the XCMDs later in the book gives you the tools to explore it yourself).

Among the external devices you may wish to control with HyperCard are telephone modems, CD-ROM players, videodisc players, electric light and appliance timers, computer interface equipped radio gear, and virtually any equipment that offers a serial (RS-232C) interface for computer control. With more sophisticated interfacing tools attached to HyperCard, it is feasible to control devices on an AppleTalk network as well as hardware peripherals connected to the Macintosh SCSI port.

Chances are that you've come into contact with the combination of the HyperCard Dial command and a modem to dial telephone numbers from an address stack. But with a more powerful link between a HyperCard stack and the serial port (as offered by the Comm XCMD in Chapter 29), you can use HyperCard to build user-friendly "front ends" to on-line commercial tele-communications services or corporate mainframe computers. There is an enormous opportunity for this type of stack to help inexperienced computer users overcome the genuinely complex aspects of linking two computers over the telephone and gaining access to computer-based information.

CD-ROM (Compact Disc-Read Only Memory) is a relatively new method of storing and distributing information. Identical in appearance to the compact digital audio discs, CD-ROMs can hold more than 500 megabytes of data (equivalent to 25 Apple HD-20SC hard disks), but the data must be stamped into the disks at a compact disk pressing plant. In other words, the disks are for reading only (hence the ROM part of its name), and the disks require a special CD-ROM disk drive to work with your Macintosh. When a stack developer places a read-only stack on a CD-ROM disk in the HyperCard stack file format, there is no special requirement for controlling the CD-ROM disk player—HyperCard "sees" the disk as if it were a very large, locked floppy disk. But in those cases in which a stack developer wishes to use HyperCard as a front end to an existing CD-ROM database and indexing (searching) scheme, then the developer must include an XCMD that acts as a bridge between the HyperCard front end stack and the player hardware. It's a control issue completely separate from the information content of the disk.

Several HyperCard developers have already had experience with joining HyperCard to a videodisc player (Figure i-4). As the stack screen offers interactive computer "play," the stack is also controlling high-quality still and motion laser disc video on a standard color television screen. A pioneer in linking HyperCard and laser discs, The Voyager Company, now offers a developer's toolkit, called *VideoStack*. With help like this there will surely be more development in this area. Together, the computer and video media can create a strong instructional environment, each greatly enhancing the other.

Any other device that can be controlled through a serial interface, including the possibility of factory process controls, are potential targets for HyperCard stacks in this category. That includes exporting stack data directly from your Macintosh to a laptop computer (even an MS-DOS laptop) via a serial cable linking the two machines.

If external device control appeals to you for potential development, be smart in the way you use HyperCard to perform the controlling. There is nothing more wasteful of an opportunity than to use HyperCard merely as an expensive remote control panel for a laser disc player or other device. A user needn't spend a couple thousand dollars for the privilege of clicking on screen buttons replicating the handheld remote control.

Cats

16941	Lioness, Panthera leo; feeding	
16940	Lioness, Panthera leo; feeding	
16937	Mountain lion, Felis concolor	
18581	Mountain lion, Felis concolor	
18582	Mountain lion, Felis concolor	
16835	African wild cat, Felis lybica	
16939	Cheetahs, Acinonyx jubatus; feeding	
16938	Cheetah, Acinonyx jubatus; feeding	
16832	Cheetah, Acinonyx jubatus	
16833	Leopard, Panthera pardus	
16834	Tiger, Panthera tigris	
16935 ➡	Bobcat, Lynx rufus; feeding	
16936	Bobcat, Lynx rufus; feeding	

SearchWords: Vertebrate, mammal, warmblooded, fur-bearing, carnivorous

KINGDOM:
Animalia
sub: Eumetazoa
PHYLUM:
Chordata
sub: Vertebrata
CLASS:
super: Tetrapoda
Mammalia
sub: Eutheria
ORDER:
Carnivora
FAMILY:
Felidae

Classification
About Cats...

? FIND
RETRACE   Topics Animals Plants Low Life Biomes
Notes LOCATE AGAIN
Go✓ SHOW SLIDES

Figure i-4 *A Stack by The Voyager Company interacts with a videodisc player to display high-quality video on a nearby television screen.*

Instead, design a stack or card that engages the user or supplements what is happening on the external device with interactive material on the Hyper-Card/Macintosh screen. This is especially true of laser disc control. Capture the attention and imagination of the user on the HyperCard screen. Then let the control part of the stack work miracles behind the scenes, almost magically causing things to happen on the external device. If the external device is presenting instructional material, add value to that material by engaging the user within the stack, questioning or challenging the user to use the knowledge gained from the other device.

Utility Stacks

The final category of HyperCard stacks we see today is called utilities. This term goes way back to the early days of computing, when programmers had little programs that helped them do their programming jobs. That's still the case with HyperCard utilities—they're stacks that make the life of an active HyperCard user much easier.

My favorite example of a quality utility stack is *Script Report*, written by Eric Alderman (Figure i-5). This stack systematically goes through the

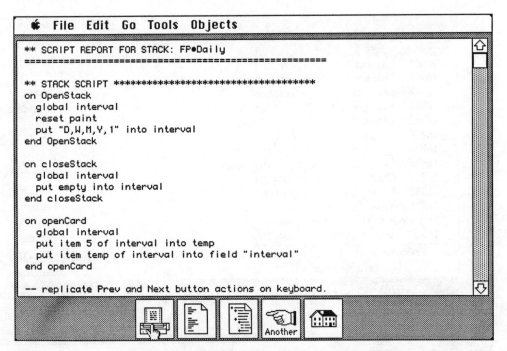

Figure i-5 *Script Report is an excellent example of a HyperCard utility stack product. It retrieves, formats, displays, and prints scripts from your stack for review and analysis.*

HyperTalk scripts in every nook and cranny of a HyperCard stack, gathering a long list of the scripts and the names of the objects to which they are attached. You may then print the listings or view them in an outline format with Living Videotext's *MORE* program. *Script Report* is invaluable to the serious stack developer (who may, of course, write his own version or adapt the canonical edition). Since part of creating a complex stack is experimenting with various methods, it's very possible to leave handlers and experimental objects scattered throughout a stack. *Script Report* is like an X-ray photo of the stack that reveals if you've left any instruments in the patient before you sew it up.

Other Than HyperCard

It is easy to get caught up in the hullabaloo about HyperCard to the exclusion of other development systems available on the Macintosh. HyperCard is not the do-all, end-all development system, despite its built-in powers. You still have the choice of developing in a flat file manager type of database program, a high-end relational database environment or in a traditional programming language. There are cases in which these other environments are better suited to a task than HyperCard is. Knowing when to use a database program instead of HyperCard—and vice versa—is crucial to developing an application that lives up to your expectations.

Flat File Databases

All too often HyperCard is defined as a database program. I suppose this comes largely from the fact that cards have fields on them, just like database program screens have fields for text and numeric information. The more you try to stretch the database paradigm by saying that cards are equivalent to database records and that stacks are equivalent to database files, the farther away from HyperCard you roam.

While a HyperCard on-screen card and a database entry form may look alike, the way each treats the information you enter into fields is quite different—a difference that points up the reasons for choosing one environment over the other. Each time you enter information into a HyperCard card field, the text is stored as data accompanying the card. In other words, the entire card is stored on the disk. Of course, shared background graphics and other attributes aren't stored with each card—just those items that distinguish one card from the next, like its name, id number, HyperTalk script, text, and so on.

In most databases, there aren't on-screen cards, but rather an entry format that acts like a template for information you enter or recall for display. The template forms remind me of the carnival attraction in which you have your picture taken when you poke your head through a hole from behind a painted picture. All during the day, the body in the painting stays the same, but different faces fill the hole.

When you type data into the fields of an entry form and "enter" the data by pressing the Enter key, the data is saved in the database file in a list-like format. A good way to visualize a database file on the disk is to think of it as stored in a columnar list, much like a spreadsheet (Figure i-6 top). The fields of information from a single entry form are kept together as a record (one row of the list). When it comes time to look at that data in the same screen format as that in which it was entered, a recordful of data is fetched from the database file, and each field's data is plugged into the screen template of fields (Figure i-6, bottom).

There is an inherent advantage to storing information this way if you need to view your data in selected lists on the screen—something HyperCard cannot do on its own. For instance, in a database program, you can design an on-screen (and printed) report format that reveals only some of the fields associated with a record, like only the name, city, state, and telephone numbers of a detailed name and address database. In the report, therefore, there are "holes" in the template to view only some of the fields of each record. Using the selection capabilities of the database program, you may then request to view a specific selection of records from the entire database—all records whose ZIP code field contains numbers ranging from 60600 to 60699, for example, to list those people in the city of Chicago.

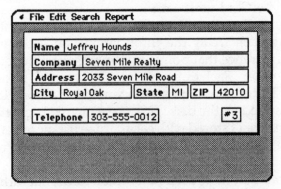

	Name	Company	Address	City	State	ZIP	Telephone
1	Andrew Foobar	Foobar Associates	300 Main St.	Cleveland	OH	49255	513-555-5821
2	Sally Rhodes	National Air Corporat	5000 Industrial Blvd.	Bayonne	NJ	01443	201-555-2000
3	Jeffrey Hounds	Seven Mile Realty	2033 Seven Mile Road	Royal Oak	MI	42010	303-555-0012

Figure i-6 *Databases store information in lists. You view the data through a template.*

Relational Databases

HyperCard is also often compared to relational databases, such as the high-end packages *Omnis 3* (Blyth Software), *Double Helix* (Odesta), *dBase Mac* (Ashton-Tate), and *Fourth Dimension* (ACIUS). While HyperCard can perform relation-like actions, it is not intended to replace relational databases, any more than it is meant to replace simpler database programs.

Relational Basics

If you're not familiar with relational databases, let me provide you with a simple example of how such a system works. The underlying structure of a relational database system is a method of connecting largely distinct databases. For instance, a company might keep all customer information (name, address, phone number, credit rating, etc.) in a customer database. A separate database would be used for order entry: Each order submitted by a customer is typed into an Order Form (Figure i-7).

The relational part comes into play when the order entry keyboard operator needs to input the customer's name, billing address, and so on. With a relational database, the entry operator can type a customer's ID number into

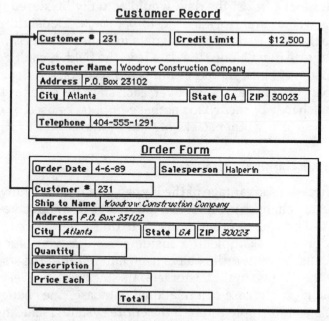

Figure i-7 *A relational database may be structured to retrieve data from its primary location, and display copies in other templates when needed. The information, however, is stored only in its primary location.*

one field of the order entry form. Pre-established links between the order entry form and the customer database automatically use the ID number as a way to look up pertinent customer data in the customer database, and insert that data into the order entry form for the operator. In Figure i-7, for instance, when the user types "231" into the Order Form field for customer number, the database retrieves several fields of data from the record of customer 231. That data is automatically entered into their corresponding fields in the Order Form.

What makes this operation different in a relational database than in a HyperCard equivalent (HyperCard can imitate the above action without any difficulty) is the manner in which the information is stored among the files. In most relational database implementations of this order entry system, the customer data (except for the ID number) does not get stored with the order information. Customer data remains solely in the customer database. Whenever a form appears on the screen that needs the customer data, the relational database looks up the data and inserts it into the appropriate fields on the form. Relational databases are optimized for these kinds of lookups and insertions.

Things are different in HyperCard. If your order entry HyperCard stack were to look up the customer data in a customer stack and display the data in the order entry fields, the data would actually be stored in the order entry stack, as well as in the original customer stack. Depending on the design of your stack systems, the storage of data in multiple places may have a distinct advantage. After all, once the data is in the field, it can't get damaged, even if the customer stack should be damaged. No stack is dependent on another for display of field data. Moreover, each stack becomes a standalone bank of data, which may be carried to another computer or used by others who do not have access to any other stacks of your system.

HyperCard vs. Relational Databases

The primary disadvantage of the HyperCard method, however, is that if the information changes in one stack, the change does not take effect in the other stacks, unless you've programmed it to do so. For instance, in the customer and order entry example, if a customer notifies you of a shipping address change after several orders have been entered into the stack, you'd have to change the address in the customer data stack and on every pending order in the system. In the case of a relational database, one change in the customer database would ripple through the entire system, including other databases or reports that generate shipping labels, invoices, and so on. Since the address data is not summoned except when needed for display or printing, the most current data is guaranteed to be available for output.

In a highly structured HyperCard stack environment, a change like the one just mentioned can be accommodated by a carefully planned script that goes into action when important fields in the customer database change. But since HyperCard stacks are likely candidates for customization by the user, a stack developer cannot assume that the structure imposed at the outset will survive. Moreover, the tendency in developing a HyperCard stack should be to free the developer and the user from the kind of rigid on-screen structure that formal databases have forced us to use for years. We'll go deeper into how structure affects design later in the book.

Limitations imposed by the comparatively rigid structure of relational database environments open the way for one of HyperCard's great strengths: its ability to establish rather arbitrary links between bases of data. When building a relational database model, you need to exercise care in establishing the way one database section will look up information in another. How a database is to be accessed often dictates how it is structured, like whether the customer ID number is the ruling feature that distinguishes one record from another within that collection. If you later determine that you need another way of accessing that database, such as looking up a customer name based on a telephone number, you may be out of luck (or require very sophisticated programming within the database's procedural language). With HyperCard, however, there are no structures that dictate how a stack of cards must be organized. You may retrieve data from a stack by searching for text in any field; you may post data into a specific card in another stack based on any lookup or search criteria you wish, even after multiple links to that stack have been established from other stacks.

Focal Point is an example of the preference for the unstructured approach to linking information. After failing to implement a system like *Focal Point* on one of the high-end relational databases, I found HyperCard to offer the kind of flexibility that my ideas required. For example, the Deadlines stack, which collates all unfinished to-do items from proposals and projects records, fetches data from those two stacks, some of which originally came from yet another stack, the Client stack (Figure i-8). Because the design of the *Focal Point* system called for client data to be posted to projects and proposals records, the lookup tasks of the Deadlines stack were simplified, and let me focus on the direct link, rather than trying to establish some multistepped link through several stacks. Operation is not only simpler, but faster as well. At the same time, I established other links in the reverse direction, so that if the user checks off a Deadline item as being completed, its line item in the Proposal or Projects stack is checked off, and other parts of those stacks are updated accordingly. Also, by selecting the text of the deadline item, the user may go directly to the detail card in the Project or Proposals stack by clicking

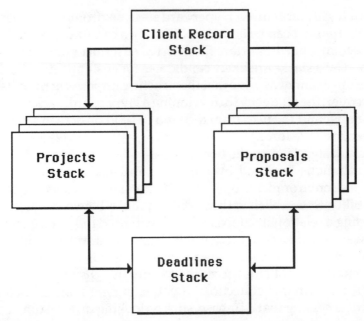

Figure i-8 *Information flows among HyperCard stacks may be arbitrary, and are not limited by a relational structure.*

on a single button. And, despite the complex network of linkages among these stacks, the stage is still set for yet other links as the user cares to expand the system to meet specific needs his or her business requires.

Database or HyperCard?

Databases of any kind are primarily list-oriented. HyperCard, on the other hand, is a browsing environment, in which the data is best served by residing in on-screen cards and in which it is comfortable to access these cards in a linear, sequential order or in a non-linear, hop-skip-and-jump order. Oddly enough, the same body of information may be suited to either the traditional database or HyperCard based not on its content, but on the manner in which the user must interact with the information.

For example, consider HyperCard and Omnis 3 versions of a form designed to hold customer information. In addition to the standard name, address, and telephone fields, there is also a field that contains a running total of the orders made by that customer during the year (the mechanics for keeping this total would be built into a separate order form stack). Except for visual characteristics inherent in both HyperCard and Omnis 3, the screens would look very similar, especially since both have the same field structure.

Before going any further, however, please note that the running total field in the Omnis database would not be stored with the customer information, but would be calculated by a formula in that field. The job of that formula is to retrieve from the order entry database all order totals for the customer whose number appears in the Customer ID field.

You should favor putting this application in HyperCard if access to the information is through browsing—sequential searching or using HyperCard's very fast Find command. Since it's a trivial matter to place a dialing button on the HyperCard version, the person who uses this stack might use it like a rolodex. Searching first for the customer's name, the person clicks on the dialing button to dial the number in the telephone number field. The Find command may be used to browse quickly through all customer cards whose telephone numbers have the 212 area code. By typing Find "(212)" into the Message Box, the user may repeatedly press the Return or Enter key to view only those customers in that area code. More sophisticated, but slower, searching techniques may be built into a special button. The script for that button might, for instance, go to each card (with the screen locked), and test whether the last order date is 30 days or more prior to today's date. When the test proves true, the script ends, and the user may view a card meeting that criteria. To resume the search, the user presses that custom search button again.

The database version is preferable, however, if the user needed to view selections of the customer data in various on-screen and printed reports—usually in a list format. The key difference, however, is that a database program provides the user with the ability to perform "multiple selects" on the entire database. Therefore, the user may specify that he see only records whose telephone field contains 415 and 213, whose last name field begins with letters A through M, and whose last order date is earlier than March 1, 1988. Selecting search criteria like this is like masking all other data in the file. You probably won't be able to see other data in the file until you disable the selection criteria.

Where the database version shines is in obtaining on-screen and printed reports of the selected data. A salesperson about to leave on a trip for Boston could obtain a list of all customers in the 617 area code whose order level is above $5000. With that list, the salesperson can be sure to check up on the company's big customers while in their town.

In all fairness to HyperCard, report selection and printing is now available as an add-on product, called Reports, published by Activision, Inc. The gap between HyperCard and databases is closing.

Traditional Programming Environments

Publishers of traditional programming languages—the Lightspeed series from Think Technologies/Symantec, Turbo Pascal from Borland, TML Pascal, Consulair C, Apple's MPW series, and others—should have nothing to fear from HyperCard's programming prowess. In fact, I was amazed at the long-running furor coming from several of these companies over the release and bundling of HyperCard with all Macintosh hardware. They saw Hyper-Card as a threat to traditional programming languages and development systems. On the contrary, HyperCard actually opens up an entirely new market of future programmers in Pascal, C, and Assembler, as HyperCard developers seek to extend the power of HyperCard through external commands—commands that must be written and compiled in one of these language environments.

There's no way HyperCard will be the platform for the next word processor or desktop publishing system. Fundamental, high-powered applications programs, especially in the graphics and number crunching worlds, will continue to be developed in the traditional programming environments. Many types of programs simply don't fit well into the card metaphor of HyperCard.

But as anyone with experience in these programming areas will tell you, it's no simple part-time endeavor to program a Macintosh application from scratch. First, it takes a complete understanding of the five encyclopedic volumes of *Inside Macintosh*, Apple's bible of what goes on inside the Macintosh ROM Toolbox and system. Bill Atkinson, who is no slouch when it comes to learning a computer's inner capabilities, is quick to tell you that it takes a year to learn enough of *Inside Macintosh* to start serious programming. Then, of course, you also need to know one of the programming languages. All in all, it's an area best left to the professionals, or at least to those part-timers who have acquired extensive experience over the years.

Just the same, HyperCard and the traditional programming systems are a great team together. If you've wanted to get your feet wet in programming the Macintosh's ROM Toolbox, HyperCard is the perfect way to start, because you can begin writing small external commands in Pascal, C, or Assembler, and experiment with various parts of the Toolbox. Because you use Hyper-Card as the primary platform, you don't have to write an entire program from scratch to learn a small Toolbox point. HyperCard gets you right up to the point at which your external code can execute. Gradually you will gain experience with the Toolbox with far fewer problems than diving straight into writing an entire program.

Even though the HyperTalk language is very powerful on its own, I believe HyperCard will provide the gateway for many interested parties to work their way into full-fledged Macintosh programming. Later in this book, you'll see some examples of external code that should get you a long way into writing your own code.

The Final Choice

If there were a simple formula into which you could plug the variables of your intended application, it would be easy to see if HyperCard were the right environment. Of course, it's not that easy. But here are some questions to ask yourself:

1. *Can the application's information be conveniently divided into screen-sized cards?*

   While HyperCard offers scrolling fields, which may hold up to 32,000 text characters, I am not fond of putting long text blocks into these fields. First of all, it's boring for the user to scroll through fields. Second, the card metaphor of HyperCard works best when the user—who is often just a browser or simple typist—can see all pertinent information at one glance when a card appears on the screen. This is not to say that you should cram field after field of 9-point type onto each card. Just the opposite. Keep the amount of information on a card to a minimum. Break up related information into card-length packets and create intelligent links between them to ease the user's journey to various parts of the information. I'll have more to say about this in Chapter 6.

2. *Is the need for reporting limited or at least made manageable by external report-generating HyperCard add-ons?*

   Over time, this will become less of an issue as both HyperCard and outside programs assist in gathering data for printing and on-screen display of list-like reports. Activision's Reports is a breakthrough in that regard. Future releases of HyperCard may also improve reporting facilities. Don't forget, too, that HyperCard's fast search operation, with repeated Find command execution by pressing the Return key, is often faster and more inviting than a dull list of selected data.

3. *Do you want your application to be fun and inviting to use, especially for non-computer or non-Macintosh literate users?*

   Since HyperCard lets you design the entire screen interface, there are many opportunities to develop interesting applications, including those that non-Macintosh users can use without any training, as in freestanding kiosk locations (more about this in Chapter 3).

4. *Do you want the user to be able to customize the application?*
One of HyperCard's greatest strengths is that the "insides" of a stack are largely accessible to the user, if you so desire. Since it is rare for a developer to know exactly how each user performs the tasks covered by an application, the ability to customize a HyperCard stack makes it all the more marketable. Most high-end software written in traditional languages or developed by relational database consultants are not user-customizable. Stack applications are inherently democratic, in that they give the user control over his or her destiny. To paraphrase an Apple advertising slogan, HyperCard gives you "the power to be yourself."

If you answer "yes" to any of these questions, then HyperCard is the right choice to pursue the dream of the application in your mind, even if the potential audience is a small one.

The Next Step

Once you've decided on using HyperCard as the development environment, you still have much to think about in designing the application, before you write a handler for your first button. Part One, which follows, explores 10 issues you must face as you begin to lay out your application. The earlier you confront these issues in the design stage, the easier development will be in the home stretch.

PART ONE

Key Stack Developer Issues

1

How HyperCard Literate is the User?

I've got good new and bad news. The good news is that HyperCard is packaged in every Macintosh box out of the factory. The bad news is that not every new Macintosh owner knows what HyperCard is. The trouble is that a HyperCard developer might easily assume that anyone who makes an effort to look at a stack is HyperCard literate—HyperLiterate, if you will. This is wrong, wrong, wrong. You cannot assume that users of your stack are HyperLiterate. This obviously puts a much greater burden on your role as stack developer, but by following this rule you will attract a much wider audience than if you ignore it.

Difficult Concepts

Our jobs as HyperCard stack developers is to shield the user community from the parts of HyperCard that may confuse or bewilder the first-time Hyper-Card user. Here are some of the difficult concepts you should design around.

1. *Icon buttons on the Home Card.* If you're lucky, the person using your stacks is at least MacLiterate enough to recognize that an icon represents an application or document, as it does on the Macintosh desktop. But that user is in for a rude awakening when he looks at the HyperCard Home Card and tries to move the icons around as on the desktop. The idea that those icons are buttons takes some getting used to. Consequently, the last thing a new user will easily comprehend is that in order to have an icon on the Home Card that links to the stack, he'll have to copy the button from the stack and paste it into the Home Card.

2. *Stack, document, and application pathnames.* In a Macintosh desktop world of folders and icons, the three pathname cards in the Home Stack are as mysterious as an MS-DOS C> command prompt. If you never let the user get within sight of these cards while setting up your stack, all the better.

3. *Object hierarchy.* An inexperienced HyperCard user will have never heard of the object hierarchy, and will not know why you'd want to copy a resource or handler to the Home stack. For that matter, you should not even assume that a HyperCard user has the same kind of Home stack that you do. The customizable nature of HyperCard leads HyperLiterate folks to treat their Home stacks as personal playgrounds. It's not nice to fool with somebody's Home stack unless you're invited.

4. *Button scripts.* Just because you know that a HyperCard button generally has a button script attached to it doesn't mean that your user will know a script from a ROM routine. If actions in your stack entail the creation of buttons that tailor the operation of the stack to the user's wishes, don't expect the user to know how to write such a script. Provide user-friendly front ends to such things. HyperTalk gives you the power in one script to write the script of another object (or even the same object).

5. *Stack structure and stack-to-stack delays.* After designing a few Hyper-Card stacks that rely on data in other stacks, you soon learn to accept the delays inherent in stack-to-stack lookups. Perhaps for you the sound of the disk drive is enough to soothe the impatience that normally pervades com-

puter use. But an inexperienced user may hear the disk drive whirring, while seeing nothing happening on the screen and thus panic in thinking something in the computer is "hung up." Before you know it, the user turns off the computer in the middle of file access, probably trashing the stack file forever.

These are the major concepts to plan around. Now, let's look at examples of how you can make the user feel as much at home in your stack as in a standalone Macintosh application.

Installation Routines

Since the Home Card acts as a desktop to other HyperCard stacks, you provide a good service to your users by supplying an installation routine with your stack that does two things: 1) copies an icon button to the person's Home Card; and 2) enters the proper pathname listings in the "look for stacks" card of the Home stack.

Figure 1-1 shows the installation card that comes with *Business Class*. I chose to place this installation routine in its own one-card stack. That way, the user could discard the installation function once the installation was complete.

Note that several key points appear about this card. First, there are some simple instructions on the card. They tell the user what will happen during installation. There are no surprises for the experienced user. For the novice, there is an air of authority that leads him to believe that whatever goes on here must be the right way to do things.

Next, a sample of the button appears on the card. This, too, is a kind of preconditioning. The user knows before returning to the Home card what the button will look like. In fact, the placement of the sample button in that location on the card was no accident. Midway through the installation procedure, a copy of this button will appear on the Home Card—in exactly the same spot. From there, the user may adjust its location.

Notice that there is a Cancel button on this card. As you certainly must know from poking around new parts of software, you expect a way to back out of a procedure that looks like it may be irreversible. Perhaps you're not ready to go through with the installation because you're previewing the software on someone else's computer; or perhaps you want to set up your folders differently before carrying out the full installation. Whatever the reason, offer a Cancel button for any significant action. In the case of the *Business Class* Installer, the Cancel button brings the user back to the Home Card, from which the Installer stack was most likely opened.

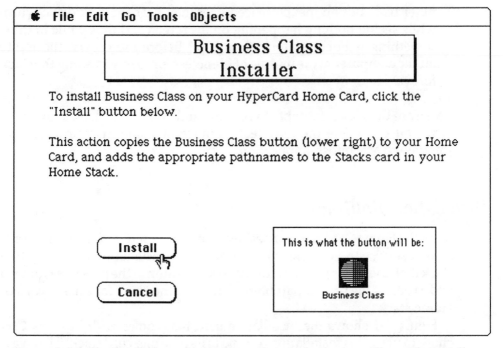

Figure 1-1 *The installation screen (a one-card stack) for Business Class. The Install button contains a script to copy the Business Class button and modify the Home stack's pathnames list.*

When you click on the Install button, an answer-style HyperCard dialog box appears, asking whether you wish to install the stack in a hard disk or floppy disk system (Figure 1-2). Again, there is another Cancel opportunity to back out, returning you to the instant before you clicked on the Install button.

Pathnames Settings

Offering two choices for installation has to do with the pathname part of installation. Due to the structure of *Business Class'* stack files, the installer stack must write two lines to the stack pathnames card in the Home stack (covered in more detail in Chapter 5 on stack structure). Running the stacks from floppy disks entails an entirely different pathname than running them from a hard disk. The answer from this dialog box determines how the text lines that eventually go into the stacks list are assembled.

The installation routine, contained entirely in the mouseUp handler of the Install button, is relatively simple. Its basic structure is shown below (this is

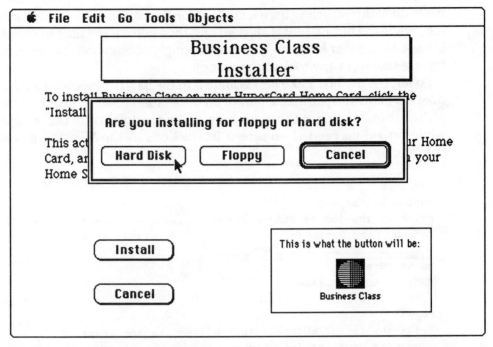

Figure 1-2 *Pathnames may be different for hard disk and floppy disk installations. Business Class offers an easy way to select how the user wishes to use the product.*

not the actual script, but rather an outline of the actions taken in the handler):

```
on mouseUp
   display dialog requesting disk type
   if "Cancel" then exit this handler
   if "Floppy" then assemble floppy-based pathnames
   if "Hard Disk" then assemble hard disk pathnames
   select the sample button with the Button tool
   copy the button into the clipboard
   go to the "Look for stacks in..." card of the Home stack
   add the pathnames to the end of the list
   go to the Home Card
   paste the button from the clipboard
   display instruction in the Message Box to "drag the button to
      the desired location, and press Command-Tab" (to return
      to the Browse tool.
end mouseUp
```

Since writing the original routine, I've thought of improvements to smooth out what I consider a rough edge at the tail end of the handler. The rough edge has to do with instructing the user to position the button while it is still selected (i.e., while the button tool is chosen) and then getting the user to choose the browse tool, either knowingly or unknowingly (Command-Tab restores the browse tool from any tool you're using).

So far, the method I like best is shown in the handler below. This handler does not show the pathname part of an installation routine, just the handling of the button copying, pasting, positioning, and restoration of the browse tool, while providing needed on-screen instructions in the Message Box at the crucial moment.

```
on mouseUp
   choose button tool
   click at the loc of button "Stack Button" -- selects the button
   doMenu "Copy Button"                    -- puts it in clipboard

   go to "Home"
   doMenu "Paste Button"

   repeat
      set the loc of button "Stack Button" to the mouseLoc
      put the mouseLoc into oldLoc

      put "Position the button where you'd like it, and then click."

      wait until the mouseLoc ≠ oldLoc -- hide msg at first movement
      put empty into msg
      hide msg

      repeat until the mouseClick        -- drag without clicking
         set the loc of button "Stack Button" to the mouseLoc
      end repeat

      choose browse tool            -- see the button as it will be

      answer "Is it at the desired location?" with "No" or "Yes"
      if it is "Yes" then exit repeat
      else choose button tool

   end repeat
end mouseUp
```

The handler begins by choosing the button tool to perform some button maneuvers, such as clicking on it to select it and copying it to the clipboard. Then the handler takes you to the Home Card and pastes the button in the same spot from which it was copied on the installation card.

In the outermost repeat loop that follows, the button (still selected after the paste command) zips to the location of the cursor. That location is temporarily stored in a local variable, oldLoc, for use a couple lines later. Instructions about positioning the pointer and clicking are then placed into the Message Box to guide the user along with the installation. A Wait command suspends execution of the handler until you move the mouse—the location of the mouse not being equal to the original mouse position. At that point, presumably you have read the instructions and are ready to position the button. Thus, the instructions are removed from the Message Box (so you won't see them again if another stack should show the Message Box upon opening) and the box is hidden from sight.

The small repeat loop that follows simply places the center of the selected button at the location of the mouse. As you move the mouse around the screen, the selected button tracks the pointer. It does this until you click the mouse button (a click being equivalent to a mouseDown, not a mouseUp). To see how the button looks in its new position, the handler chooses the browse tool to remove the rectangle around the button's icon. But an answer dialog also gives you another chance, in case the position is not quite right or you didn't get the instructions the first time around. If you click on the No button of the answer dialog, the entire outer repeat loop starts over, giving you another opportunity to read the directions and carefully place the button. Once you are sure that the location is right, and you click the Yes button in the answer dialog, the handler ends, and you're all set.

Inside the Stack Button

Installation routines for multistack HyperCard applications, like *Business Class* and *Focal Point*, serve another important function. The button installed on the Home Card should be preloaded with a handler that brings the user to the correct startup stack in the system. If your stack system requires the setting of certain global variables based on user preferences, then it is imperative that you direct the user to start your stack system in the prescribed manner. By installing the preloaded button on the Home Card for the user, you assure that each time he goes to your stack from Home, the operation will run as you designed it. Figure 1-3, for example, shows the *Focal Point* stack button's script, which performs interesting visual effects on the way to a specific stack. An openStack handler in stack FP•Startup gathers the global variables and moves onto the first productive stack, the Daily Appointment stack.

Fortunately, too, when you copy and paste a button from the installation

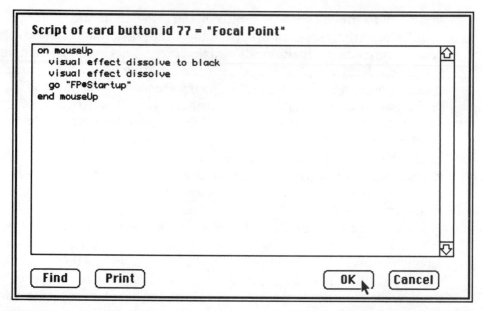

Figure 1-3 *The Home Card button that is installed for Focal Point contains a script with special visual effects.*

stack to the Home stack, HyperCard also copies and pastes the ICON resource. Art attached to the button follows the button wherever it goes. The user may then copy and paste your button from his Home stack to any other stack on his hard disk, in case he wants instant access to your stack from something he's developed or otherwise incorporated into his daily Macintosh work.

Hands Off the Home Stack

Outside of installing a stack button and adding pathnames to the Home stack—items that are visible to even the browser-level HyperCard user—I avoid modifying the user's Home stack at all cost. Certainly, there are advantages for the developer to put often-called handlers, functions, and resources into the Home stack, but I believe it's inviting trouble to do so, unless you offer sufficient warnings.

Perhaps the biggest hazard to modifying the user's Home stack is that any modification you make may impinge on a modification that either the user or another, less friendly application has made. For instance, if your stack's installation routine appends a custom handler called printWeek (the handler would begin on printWeek), it is conceivable that the user or another stack has also added a handler with the same name. When that happens, your stack will expect to find the one you designed. But since HyperCard executes the first handler it finds in a script with a matching name, HyperCard will never find your handler. Instead, it will execute the earlier handler with that name, causing, well, unpredictable (if not disastrous) results.

Conversely, if your handler is the first one with that name in the Home card stack script, it preempts the user from writing a handler with that name for his stack script. If he doesn't know that you've "reserved" that handler name, it will make for a frustrating debugging session. Therefore, I believe it's unfair to make changes to scripts in the Home stack without warning, since such changes won't be obvious to the user and could interfere with the user's own stack development. These kinds of changes to the Home stack also presume the user fully understands the hierarchy of objects and message passing within HyperCard—something you cannot assume.

I don't even like the idea of secretly copying resources, like icons, sounds, fonts, and XCMDs to the user's Home stack. For example, if you have many custom-made icon buttons in your stack, and you copy them to the Home stack at installation time, then every time the knowledgeable user creates a new icon button for his or her own stack, all your icons will appear in the icon dialog box, ripe for the picking. You may quickly lose control over the art you so carefully crafted for your stack application, as the user, thinking the icons are part of HyperCard, freely plugs them into stacks that may go anywhere.

This means, of course, that all stacks in a multiple stack HyperCard system, like *Business Class* and *Focal Point*, have identical sets of icon resources for all the buttons that permeate the system. It's true that they take up extra disk space, but keeping the resources local to the stack means that the icons will always be in those stacks, even if the user transfers the stacks to a new computer running a virgin copy of HyperCard and a fresh Home Stack.

That's not to say that the Home stack should be kept squeaky clean as it comes out of the HyperCard box. On the contrary, the Home stack should be the repository of all kinds of resources and handlers that you, personally, use within your own stacks or during stack development. I'll have several examples of Home stack tidbits you should add in Chapter 21 on debugging HyperTalk scripts.

User-Friendly Front Ends

If you assume that a potential user of your stack is not HyperLiterate, you must also realize that he will not understand anything about HyperTalk commands, scripts or objects containing scripts. Therefore, if your stack features operations that usually entail writing scripts or issuing commands from the Message Box, then you should design a simple front end to those features. Here are three examples derived from *Business Class* and *Focal Point*.

Printing Cards

Printing individual cards from a variety of stacks is relatively simple when doing the job manually from the Message Box. You start by typing `open printing with dialog`, and adjusting the Print dialog box settings for the number of cards you wish to print on a page. Then navigate through the stack as you normally do to reach the cards you wish to print. Each time you reach a card you wish to send to the printer, type `print this card` into the Message Box. Actually, you only have to type this command once. Since it stays in the Message Box (until you type something else there or a script puts text there), you can use the mouse to navigate to each card and then simply press the Return or Enter keys to print the card. When you've sent all cards to the printer, then type `close printing`. That's all there is to it. Not much for an experienced stack writer. But for inexperienced users, this is a terrifying ordeal. The good news is that a good stack will cover up all vestiges of HyperTalk commands and present the printing concepts in an easy-to-understand context.

Figure 1-4 illustrates the printing card from *Business Class*. The card gives the user the option of selecting individual information cards for a given country or one click to select all cards. The interface to selecting information categories is the familiar check box style button.

Attached to the OK button is a handler that looks through all the checkbox buttons to see which ones' highlight properties are set to true. Armed with that knowledge, and the name of the country from the pseudo-scrolling field of country names, the handler goes to the country's map card and begins electronically clicking on subject buttons (using the `send mouseUp to button x` command) and issuing the `print this card` command upon reaching the desired cards. Once all cards have been sent to the printer, the handler issues the `close printing` command and returns the user to the view of the printing card.

Script-Writing Scripts

A second example, derived from *Focal Point*, demonstrates how to soften the blow of writing button scripts for the non-HyperLiterate user. One of *Focal Point's* stacks, the Document Launcher, offers two ways to group Macintosh documents from any application and then lets the user open those documents directly from *Focal Point* (Figure 1-5). The tricky part is that a button opening

Figure 1-4 *A friendly front end to complex printing of information cards is recommended. This is the one that is built into Business Class*

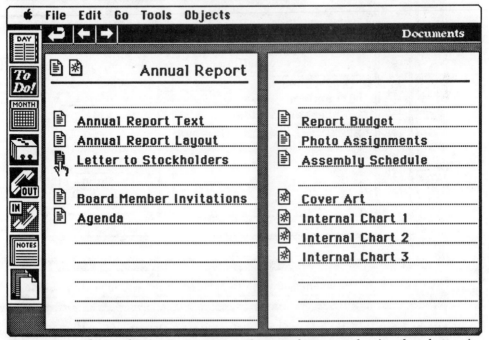

Figure 1-5 *The Focal Point Documents stack creates buttons and writes those buttons' scripts without the user even having to see the Script Editor.*

a document must have a mouseUp handler written for it, bearing the name of the document and the application program.

In the early design stages of this application, I was very concerned that the only way to get the user to create these button handlers was to actually open up the script editor for a new button and modify a template of the command, which I'd present there. The script would also contain substantial commentary about how to go about entering the document and application names into the script. This would be all the more complicated for application names that used special characters like the bullet, trademark and copyright symbols, which, while available on the Macintosh keyboard, are not standard characters everyone knows how to access.

Fortunately, the application (or rather the sanity of potential users) was rescued by an external function written by Steve Maller of Apple Computer. Called *filename*, this public domain function presents a Standard File Dialog Box—something with which all Macintosh users are familiar—that lets the user select a file name in an acceptable manner (Figure 1-6). That function provided the stack's button creation handlers with all the necessary information to create those document launching buttons all behind the scenes. A

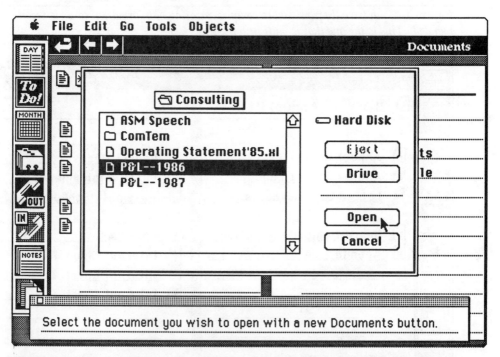

Figure 1-6 *With the help of Steve Maller's filename() external function (XFCN), the user sees familiar Macintosh surroundings to select documents and applications for the button scripts.*

script from one of these new buttons looks like this:

```
on mouseUp
  if the ShiftKey is down then clearButton
  else open "HD-20:Correspondence:envelope"¬
  with "HD-20:Applications:MS-Word"
end mouseUp
```

The user never knows that those buttons are gaining custom scripts crafted from their clicked responses in the standard file dialog boxes. Suddenly a new button appears on the screen, and they can position it where they want. It's an appealing kind of magic added to the stack.

Customization Front End

The third example of a friendly front end also comes from *Focal Point*. In this case, it's the part of the help system that lets the user customize the array of application buttons that flank the screens in the applications. *Focal Point* ships with 16 of its 18 applications pre-installed as shown in Figure 1-7. Since user customization was to be a top feature of the program, there had to be provision for changing the order of buttons or swapping one or two of the pre-installed buttons for buttons to the other stacks that come with the package.

Given the fact that some *Focal Point* stacks have as many as six different backgrounds, the idea of changing the order of buttons among all the stacks "mounted" into *Focal Point* would surely scare away users. Not only were there a lot of buttons to copy and paste into their right holes, but the script attached to a particular icon button changed, depending on which stack that button was in. For example, when you are in the Daily Appointment stack and you click on the To Do list button, the To Do List button not only goes to that stack, but it also searches for the card whose date matches the date on the Daily Appointment card you were viewing. The handler for the To Do List button is different from the Document Launcher. It simply goes to the To Do List stack and searches for today's card.

So there you have it: the need to change as many as 11 buttons (the first five buttons are hard wired into all stacks) in each of 22 possible backgrounds, and not all buttons are the same for all backgrounds. Trying to make a change to these buttons by hand would be a nightmare, sure to cause the hapless user to make some mistakes along the way.

To head off possible consternation among *Focal Point* users, I created a front end to the entire process (Figure 1-8). With this button installation card, the user clicks on a button and holds the mouse button as all possible *Focal Point* button icons and stack descriptions appear in the button location. The user

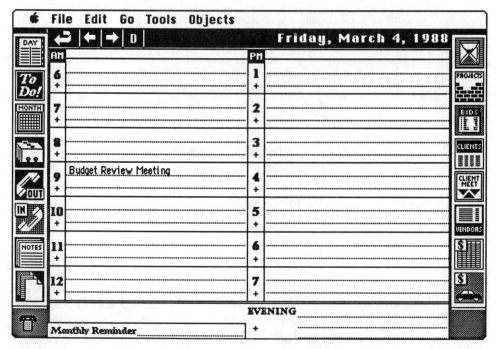

Figure 1-7 *The standard alignment of 16 applications in Focal Point. Each button on the left and right edges links to a different application.*

releases the mouse button when the target application appears in that button location. Once all the buttons are in the desired order, the user clicks on the Install Buttons button. Inside of three minutes (less on a Macintosh II), the substantial handler behind that button copies icon numbers and scripts (the scripts are in a series of cards at the end of this stack) for pasting into the buttons situated in all the stacks of the *Focal Point* system.

These kinds of front ends to HyperCard's inner workings are essential if you wish the masses to adopt your stack.

Front End Visuals

Our final discussion on the subject has much to do with the hardware you use to design and run your stacks, so we'll save most of the discussion for the next chapter. But in the meantime, if you design a system of stacks that rely heavily on stack-to-stack communication, do something to entertain the user while time marches on without any apparent action taking place.

In one sense, things should look like they're frozen, at least as the screen display goes. I believe it is very confusing for a user to see stack screens flash

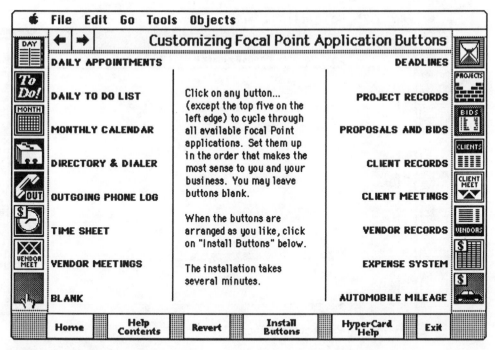

Figure 1-8 *The most complex script in Focal Point is devoted to letting the user choose a different application button alignment and then installing the icons and scripts in all the Focal Point stacks.*

for a second or two as a handler goes to another stack, looks up a card, gets the data, and returns to the original stack. Those kinds of distractions are inexcusable, in light of HyperCard's ability to lock the screen (set lockScreen to true). Not only will locking the screen reduce screen confusion, but it also speeds the process, because writing information to the screen takes valuable fractions of seconds. Add up the time devoted to refreshing the screen in a stack-to-stack exchange, and the net result is quite noticeable.

If extensive stack-to-stack exchanges take place in your stack system, then be sure to offer visual feedback to the user that something is going on, even if the screen doesn't seem to change.

For very slow operations, I find it useful to use the Message Box or a temporary card field to communicate the steps taking place while operation seems to be at a standstill. A case in point is the Deadlines stack of *Focal Point*. A handler in that stack goes to all the Follow Ups cards of each unfinished project and proposal. As the handler performs such functions as retrieving all the deadline dates from the projects, it displays a message in the Message Box to that effect (Figure 1-9). In fact, as each Follow Ups card is read, an extra arrow appears in the Message Box. The user sees telling action of some kind,

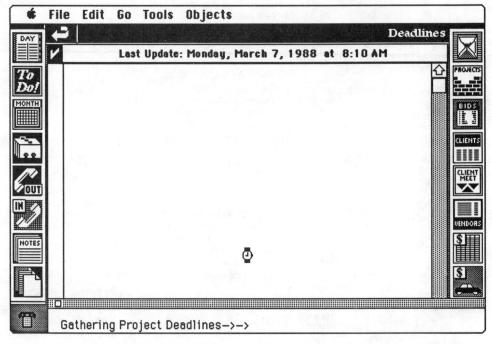

Figure 1-9 *To let users know that a long handler is at work, the Focal Point Deadlines stack provides a progress report in the Message Box.*

even though the screen is frozen. Messages during the procedure are:

```
Gathering Projects Records
Gathering Proposals Records
Sorting Deadlines
Merging Deadlines
```

You must exercise care, however, when designing messages like this, because the need for such messages depends very much on the hardware the stack will be running (see Chapter 2 for more details).

The Watch Cursor

One very important element you can add to a handler that involves much stack-to-stack transfer of heavy duty number and text crunching is to change the screen cursor to the watch cursor while the handler is running (Figure 1-10). There's something psychologically soothing about seeing the watch cursor when the Mac is churning away. We suddenly become much more patient with a comparatively slow procedure as long as the watch cursor is on

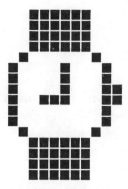

Figure 1-10 *The Watch cursor (set cursor to 4) is a good psychological tool to help the user be patient with a time-consuming operation.*

the screen. I suppose it means that the Macintosh is working as fast as it can, and it will let you know when control has returned to you.

Many of my more involved handlers have a common start to them. First they change the cursor to the watch and then lock the screen, as in:

```
on mouseUp
  set cursor to 4        -- the watch cursor number
  set lockScreen to true  -- freeze on-screen action
  ...
end mouseUp
```

You don't have to reset either the cursor or lockScreen properties, because when the handler ends, and HyperCard begins sending idle messages again, the cursor returns to the appropriate HyperCard cursor (either the browse tool or the text entry tool) and the lockScreen property returns to false.

The Beachball Cursor

Starting with HyperCard version 1.2, you may program your stack to display the rotating beachball cursor when a long handler is working. The nature of the beachball is such that it should be used primarily inside repeat loops.

Fortunately, the mechanism for rotating the beachball is built into Hyper-Card. All your script needs to do is set the cursor to "busy" inside the loop. Each time the loop repeats, the beachball advances 45 degrees (one-eighth of a complete rotation). Thus, you'd put the beachball to work in a loop like this:

```
on mouseUp
  repeat with x = 1 to 100
    set cursor to busy
```

```
    [your other work within the loop]
  end repeat
end mouseUp
```

If your repeat loops are complex scripts, you, as stack author, can recognize each 45-degree rotation as a spin through the repeat loop. If you can see the ball turning rather slowly, the repeat loop's performance may need to be improved (discussions about improving performance will come later).

Anticipating Macintosh Literacy

One last note about HyperLiteracy. While you can't expect the user to be HyperLiterate, you can expect the user to be Macintosh literate (even if some are not). This means that you must anticipate some of the Macintosh-like things that a Mac-literate is inclined to do. Take the double click, for instance.

The Macintosh desktop and many applications have put us in the habit of double-clicking the mouse pointer on things to get some operation going. Double-clicking on an application icon in the desktop starts the program without having to choose Open from the File menu. In many dialog boxes in Microsoft Excel, if you double click on a radio button to select a preference, it is the same as clicking once to select an option and then clicking on the OK button to make the option effective.

After you've used HyperCard for awhile, especially as a developer, you feel secure that single clicks are sufficient to initiate action. After all, they are the only kinds of actions your button and locked field mouseUp handlers recognize. But a non-HyperLiterate Macintosh user will tend to double click on icon buttons and certain other buttons that set action in motion.

In Chapter 3 you'll see how to trap for double clicks when they produce unwanted results with background buttons. But for now bear in mind that HyperCard and Macintosh literacy are two different disciplines. You can't expect the former, and you may have to guard against the latter.

One complaint that often caused fumbling for HyperCard stack users of all literacy levels has been repaired. Prior to HyperCard version 1.2, the only way to advance the text pointer from field to field from the keyboard was with the Tab key. While experienced database users might be comfortable with that, it was a cause for concern when a user pressed the Return key in a single-line field. Instead of moving the cursor to the next field, the Return key advanced the cursor to the next line of the first field—out of view.

The autoTab field property, which premiered in version 1.2, lets the Return key be used to advance the cursor to the next field. If less than one-half the height of the next line of a field is visible, the Return key acts identically to the

Tab key—otherwise it advances the cursor to the next line, which you'd expect of multiple line fields. For database-style HyperCard cards, I recommend turning on autoTab for all fields. Your users, however, must be using HyperCard 1.2 or later for this to work.

By now I hope you have a good idea of what it means to design your stack around the non-HyperLiterate individual. It certainly requires more planning than writing for stackheads, but it also means you're getting good experience at designing small parts of man-machine interfaces. Your users will appreciate the effort.

2

Designing for all Macintosh Models

In the early days of Macintosh (they're not quite "the old days"), it was relatively easy for a software designer to map out one interface for every machine out there. He could count on a fixed execution speed and a fixed screen size. But that comfort is now gone. Software must run on a Macintosh Plus, Mac SE, and Mac II. The designer must be prepared to have his programs operate on the standard 9-inch internal monochrome monitors, as well as gigantic color monitors. HyperCard developers have these same concerns.

When you work on a particular Macintosh hardware configuration, it is very easy to become myopic about the hardware that other folks are using. As a result, you tend to design for the machine you use and forget that others are running faster or slower computers, or have larger or smaller screens. These two factors—speed and screen size—impact the design of HyperCard stacks. If you know for sure that your stacks will be run or demonstrated only on one hardware configuration for time immemorial, then you can afford to be nearsighted in your design. I doubt, however, that many of us have that luxury.

Execution Speed Concerns

Stack execution speed in HyperCard is dependent upon three hardware elements: the microprocessor, the ROM, and the disk drive. Let's see how these elements affect each of the three main Macintosh models.

Macintosh Plus

The oldest Macintosh computer capable of running HyperCard is the Macintosh Plus (or equivalent upgrade). This machine contains a Motorola 68000 microprocessor and a ROM chip set that represented the first major ROM upgrade for the Macintosh line. While this is not the forum to debate the relative speed or slowness of the 68000 in the microprocessor world, suffice it to say that the 68000 in the Mac Plus is the slowest microprocessor chip inside any Macintosh. The ROMs, too, are the slowest of current Macs in the way they execute a number of important time-consuming duties, like refreshing the screen. Despite this, execution speed of the Mac Plus is acceptable when running typical (but not all) HyperCard stacks.

Because HyperCard is so disk intensive—text entered into a field of a typical stack is immediately saved—the speed of disk drive access becomes a critical factor in the perceived execution speed of HyperCard and stacks running on HyperCard. Since the Mac Plus has been around the longest, it is likely there are still many in use today that have hard disks connected via either the serial port (the first generation of hard disks, actually predating the Mac Plus) or the floppy disk port (like Apple's original HD-20 hard disk). Between the two styles, the HD-20 style is probably the more prevalent in these older systems.

With the advent of the Mac Plus, however, the Macintosh gained the SCSI (Small Computer Systems Interface) port that allowed much faster data transfer between the Macintosh and external devices, such as hard disks. In fact, soon after the release of the Mac Plus Apple changed over from the floppy disk ported HD-20 to the SCSI ported HD-20SC to take advantage of this extra speed. Many third-party hard disk drive manufacturers also produced SCSI hard disks, and that's the standard today.

Among hard disk drives, as you're probably aware, there are noticeable differences in access speed. Typically, the greater the hard disk capacity (up to about 150 megabytes), the faster the access, due largely to the manner in which data is spread across multiple disk platters in high-capacity drives. HyperCard users, therefore, will get greater perceived performance from a Mac Plus with a high-capacity SCSI hard disk drive than with the original HD-20. But in fairness to potential users of your stack whose hardware configuration may be held in check at the Mac Plus/HD-20 level, you should consider these users in your stack design.

On the screen side of the Mac Plus, the machine comes with its own built-in 9-inch, 512 x 342 pixel monochrome monitor. Since this is the smallest screen size you'll have to address, make sure that if you design your stack on a large screen it works the way you expect it does—graphically—on a 9-inch screen. I'll have more to say about this later in the chapter.

The Macintosh SE

While the Mac SE runs the same 68000 microprocessor as the Mac Plus, its ROMs are of a newer design, which, among other things, refreshes the screen more quickly. That accounts for a noticeable improvement in speed when running any kind of Macintosh program on the SE versus the Mac Plus. HyperCard stacks, which also do a lot of refreshing of the screen (as in going from card to card), run faster on the SE than on the Plus.

Most SEs also have built-in hard disks. Whether the user has an internal or external SCSI hard disk, expect your stacks to run approximately 25% faster on an SE than on a Plus.

It's safe to say that most SE users have the single, built-in 9-inch monochrome display, but the availability of the expansion slot inside the computer tempts owners to add large screens, like those from Radius, E-Machines, Micrographics, and others. The expansion slot also accepts one of several accelerator boards now available. Such boards include a faster microprocessor, which may be just a faster version of the SE's 68000 (running twice as fast and maintaining software compatibility) or a version of the Mac II's 68020 that runs at twice Mac II speed (but may also present software compatibility problems with non-Mac II-friendly software). Many accelerator boards also contain sockets for other chips that speed up calculations and other operations even further. Owners of the fast 68020 accelerator boards claim that their Macintosh SEs run faster than the Mac II.

All this speed, however, can affect the design of your stack, as we'll see later in the chapter.

The Macintosh II

At the top of the heap is the dream machine of many Macintosh owners, the Macintosh II. Dave Winer of Living Videotext once described the Mac II as the "infinity machine," because it can be expanded to do great things we haven't even thought of.

At the core of the Mac II is an 8-MHz Motorola 68020 microprocessor, a speedy chip compared to the 68000 chips running in the other Macs. Coming to a Mac II from either the Plus or standard SE, the speed improvement is remarkable. Conversely, if you work all day on a Mac II and then have to sit before a Plus or SE at home, execution speed seems interminably slow on the smaller machines. As such, I believe it is a real hazard to develop stacks on a Mac II, and use its execution speed of intensive stack-to-stack manipulations as an acceptable benchmark. If an operation takes "just the right amount" of time on a Mac II, it may be unacceptably slow on other machines.

Screen sizes on the Mac II vary widely, but one thing you can count on for sure: No Mac II user has anything smaller than the 640 x 480 pixel screen of the low-end Apple monitors. That means that the HyperCard window will be a free-floating entity on the screen, not taking up the entire screen. The menubar stretches across the top of the monitor, outside the HyperCard window. And the user sees the title bar of the HyperCard window, including changes in the stack name being accessed in a stack-to-stack exchange, even when the screen is locked (Figure 2-1).

You can also count on hard disks for the Mac II to be fast. It's rare to find a Mac II out there with anything smaller than a 40-megabyte hard disk, while the average hard disk size in the community will grow very quickly as 80-megabyte and larger hard disks become the norm in the Macintosh II environment.

What About Floppies?

Word amid the Macintosh community is that approximately 70 percent of the Macintoshes in use today are linked up with a hard disk of some kind. Despite that penetration, there are enough floppy disk-only users in the world to make you think twice about designing a stack system strictly for hard disk owners. In some fashion, you'll have to accommodate those who have two 800K floppy disk drives on their Mac Plus or Mac SE.

There will be more specifically about structuring your stacks for floppy disks in Chapter 5, but it's important to realize that stacks distributed on magnetic disk media (as opposed to optical CD-ROM or streaming tape media) must be organized carefully for ease of installation on a hard disk and ease of use when used strictly from floppy disk drives.

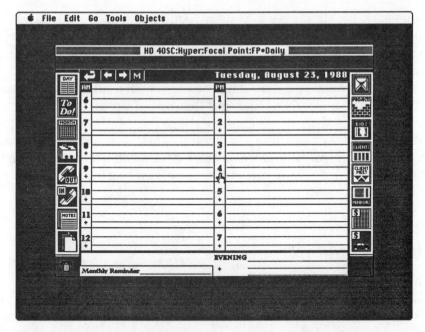

Figure 2-1 *In large monitors, HyperCard appears as a window on the desktop. The menubar is located at the top of the screen, detached from the stack window.*

Multimegabytes of RAM

The near simultaneous release of HyperCard and MultiFinder presented a seductive software pair. On the one hand, HyperCard can be used as a repository of every bit of information you need at your fingertips during the day. On the other hand, MultiFinder lets you access that HyperCard treasure chest in its entirety even while another application is running—provided, of course, that you have enough RAM in your Macintosh to accommodate it all.

Since HyperCard likes to have 750K of RAM all to itself, you need a minimum of 2 megabytes of RAM to use HyperCard along with MultiFinder and another application. If your suite of hour-by-hour applications contains a few applications programs, then even 2 or 2.5 megabytes won't do. It's 4 or more megabytes for you.

MultiFinder is an attractive setting for doing stack development, particularly if your stack creation draws on artistic tools of outside graphics programs or you are testing text importing and exporting. But since most Macintoshes are still equipped with only 1 megabyte of memory, you cannot assume that a wide audience for your stack has MultiFinder capability while running HyperCard (unless you are doing an in-house stack for a specific bank of multimegabyte Macs). You are free, of course, to limit the appeal of your stack by stating as a system requirement that your stack requires MultiFinder. In fact, there are certainly cases where this will be true. But for mass appeal stacks, assume the user has 1 megabyte of RAM and no concurrent operation of HyperCard and MultiFinder.

That's not to say you should ignore those with multiple megabytes. Their ranks will grow slowly at first, but then speed up as 2 or more megabytes become standard memory configurations for Macintoshes and the high-capacity memory modules (1 megabit SIMMs) resume the customary price cuts of RAM chips. Therefore, in stack documentation and on-line help, be sure to acknowledge how your stack can be used best in a multiple application environment.

Screen and Card Size

Through version 1.2 of HyperCard, card size has been limited to the standard 512 x 342 pixel Macintosh Plus and Macintosh SE screen. What users of those computers don't see, however, was that the active area of the card is actually inside a fixed size Macintosh window. The title bar is positioned "above" the top of the screen, out of view. When viewed on a larger screen, like the 640 x 480 pixel color and monochrome monitors Apple offers for the Macintosh II, the idea that a card is a Macintosh window hits home, since you can see the title bar, and the HyperCard window sort of floats in mid-air on the screen, unless you drag it around.

Bill Atkinson's original rationale for restricting the HyperCard card size to 512 x 342 pixels was that a card designed on any Mac model would be completely visible on every other machine. That makes perfect sense to me. It would be a significant inconvenience to the user who came to a 9-inch screen Macintosh and had to scroll around in search of buttons or fields on a larger card.

A future release of HyperCard will probably give the stack developer the freedom to make cards larger than 512 x 342. Power-hungry developers will probably disagree with me, but I feel strongly that stacks intended for a wide Macintosh audience should be no larger than the 512 x 342 pixel size of the original HyperCard card. I also believe you do yourself a disservice by laying out huge cards whose design integrity is lost on the majority of users, who have small screens.

The time to take advantage of the larger card size is when you know the stack will be used on a very specific hardware setup. For example, if you are designing a stack for a freestanding kiosk situation, you have control over the screen size at these stations. If the screen is a 640 x 480 pixel monitor, then it's safe, if not preferable, to design the stack with cards of that size. My advice, therefore, is to be conservative in expanding your card sizes.

You'll also probably be able to make cards smaller than the 512 x 342 screen size. When used on large monitors, there is a distinct advantage to having stacks appear in small windows if the information content doesn't normally fill the standard card size. Small cards can prove very helpful in a MultiFinder environment when the user has a 640 x 480 monitor. Since that monitor is too small to display a typical application window and a standard HyperCard window side by side, a smaller HyperCard stack window could clean up what normally looks like a hodgepodge of overlapping windows.

Screens and Menus

One design element you must always be sensitive to is the interaction of the menubar and your card design on various size monitors. If your application leaves the menubar showing, it covers the topmost 20 rows of pixels on a 9-inch internal Macintosh monitor. On a larger screen, the menubar appears distinct from the HyperCard window, at the top of whatever size monitor you're using. Very often, you can tell what kind of monitor the stack author has by trying out the stack on both the internal and the external, larger monitor.

Figure 2-2 shows the result of a stack designed on a large monitor when displayed on an internal 9-inch monitor. My guess is that because the menubar never impinged on the card layout area on the stack author's large screen, he never expected the menubar to cover any of the card. Consequently, there is no Hide Menubar command in the openStack handler of this stack. But on a 9-inch monitor, the menubar covers part of the intended full-screen design.

In designing *Focal Point*, which has the menubar showing throughout, I discovered the opposite effect. The screens had been laid out on an internal 9-inch monitor. Below the menubar is a black bar, which contains navigation buttons and the name of the stack (Figure 2-3a). When I first demonstrated a prerelease version of the product on a Macintosh II and its 640 x 480 pixel monitor, I was astonished to see a blank white band between the HyperCard window's title bar and the black bar of the card (Figure 2-3b). Not only that, but the top of the black bar looked unfinished because the bottom black row of pixels of the menubar had given the appearance of a border between the black bar and the menubar. I had forgotten to take into account the area under the menubar, because on the monitors that my screen artist and I were using, the menubar was always there, eating into the active area of each card design.

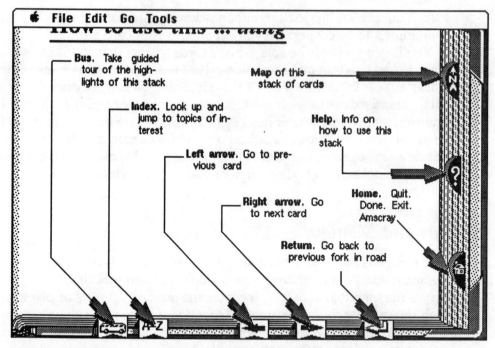

Figure 2-2 *An obvious case of a stack being designed on a large-screen display. The menubar should have been hidden upon opening the stack to let the full screen art show through.*

Knowing that my audience would be using all monitor sizes, I added some art to the background underneath the menubar. First, I balanced the top border of the black bar to match the bottom border. Then I filled in the top blank space with a gray fill pattern. The gray would be less distracting that an empty space under the window's title bar (Figure 2-3c).

The lesson learned from this experience, therefore, is that if you intend to use the HyperCard menubar, you must plan for its presence and absence in your card design. Don't design with active elements in the area that goes underneath the menubar on a 9-inch monitor. But don't leave the big monitor folks with a gaping hole where the menubar appears on small screens.

I believe we will see HyperCard applications that generate their own menubars (via XCMDs), probably within the stack window. They will, in one sense, be easier to design, because the screen designer can count on the menus being there, no matter what size monitor the user has connected to his Macintosh.

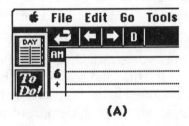

(A)

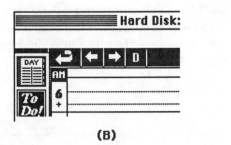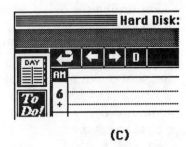

(B)   (C)

Figure 2-3   *Focal Point was designed on a 9-inch monitor (A). When viewing it on a large screen for the first time, the area under the menubar looked unfinished (B). Some additional artwork gives the card a more finished look when viewed on a large screen (C).*

Timing

My first demonstration of a development version of *Focal Point* on a Macintosh II held another surprise for me. A data manipulation handler in one stack was taking so long on my Mac Plus that I displayed a message in the Message Box about what was going on. This, I figured, would put the user's mind to rest that the program was, indeed, working, and had not frozen. But when I ran that operation on a Mac II, the Message Box came and went so fast that I couldn't even read the message. On the Mac II there was little reason to tell the user to be patient if the operation was going to be completed before they could read the patience message.

That experience caused me to dig deeper into that handler and the operations it was performing to find a more efficient way so that the user on the Mac Plus would not need a patience message. In one case, however, I left the message in because the operations took long enough on a Mac II to make the message meaningful. The situation is in the Deadlines stack of *Focal Point*, which updates its listing by going through many different cards in the Projects and Proposals stacks, performs some bubble sorts, and then formats the text so it is readable in the destination field. Messages that appear in the Message Box do more than simply tell the user to wait a moment. They describe the progress the handler is making in extracting, sorting, and formatting the data, as detailed in the previous chapter.

Ticks, Seconds and Delays

In designing *Business Class* and *Focal Point*, I had built in a brief delay at the opening of each product's title card. On the Mac Plus it was just about the right amount of time to see the title and scan the author and artist credits. From there, the program continued to the first screen of the active programs. I was in for a shock, however, when I first demonstrated the product on a Mac II. The title screens went by way too fast.

For timing the delay, I had used the Wait command, specifying a number of ticks to delay. My first inclination was to think that the Mac II counted ticks differently than the Mac Plus or SE—more than the specified 60 ticks per second. Upon further investigation that proved wrong. Here is the handler that shot down my original thesis:

```
on mouseUp
  get the ticks
  wait 1 second
  put the ticks - it
end mouseUp
```

No matter on which machine I ran this handler, the indication was that there are 60 ticks to the second universally.

The difference in delay speeds was due, it turns out, to the fact that all other operations in a handler are much faster on the Mac II. What I thought was a part of the programmed delay on the Mac Plus was more a factor of comparatively slow screen refresh and handler execution. On a Mac II, the actual delay is just as long as on a Mac Plus, but all the handler and screen action getting to that delay is nearly twice as fast.

What I also discovered is that the longer you make the delay (on the order of several seconds), the less the apparent disparity between Mac Plus and Mac II. The reason, obviously, is that the fixed delay becomes a larger percentage of the total execution time for the handler. But that leads to another question: Is a delay something you should program into a stack?

When Delays Are Necessary

Wait loops are hotly contested among experienced HyperTalk programmers. Some hate them, others use them sparingly. I fall into the second category. Still, I'll never use a Wait command to intentionally slow things down. A wait loop like this:

```
wait 5 seconds
```

can be frustrating for the user, because the only way to break out of the waiting period is to interrupt the handler by typing Command-Period. If you need to build a delay of some kind, like showing a title screen for a short time, then make it possible for the user to break out of the delay by some action, like clicking the mouse. Here, for example, is part of the openStack handler for *Focal Point* that shows the title card for five seconds or until the user clicks the mouse anywhere on the screen:

```
on openStack
  ...
  put the seconds into mark
  repeat until the mouseClick or the seconds - mark > 5
  end repeat
  ...
end openStack
```

Note that this timing loop does not even use the Wait command. Instead, it puts the current clock setting into a local variable, mark. The repeat loop keeps whirling around either until the user clicks the mouse or until the difference between the clock's seconds and the number of seconds just put into the mark variable is greater than five—meaning five seconds have elapsed. Even though a Mac II may go through the repeat loop more than three times as often as a Mac Plus, the effect on all Macintosh hardware is identical.

Animation

If you've ever seen Bill Atkinson's standard HyperCard demonstration, you were probably amazed at the near animation quality survey through his clip art stack. His demo has a couple of things working in his favor. First, he's running on a Mac II. Second, he pre-caches the clip art stack into his multimegabyte RAM before showing the audience (to pre-cache the images, he shows all cards without anyone looking).

Regardless of how he does it, you can't help but think of the possibilities of using HyperCard to create animation sequences in a stack. If you have a Mac II and lots of memory, you can do it. But the moment you try the stack on a Mac Plus or unaccelerated SE, the results will be disappointing. The primary reason is that screen refresh rates are slower on the smaller machines. Unfortunately, there is no simple way to make animation run at the same speed on all Mac models.

The hard way is to use an XCMD to find out which machine the stack is running on, and branch to a slide show handler tailored to that machine's speed. But that presupposes that you'd allow the Mac II animation to be artificially slowed to make it work at the same speed as a Mac Plus. That's unlikely—you should always want the fastest animation possible.

If your animation is of the variety that uses HyperTalk scripts to control HyperCard painting tools, then HyperCard version 1.2 will speed things up for you on all machines. HyperCard now switches between painting tools much faster. You will still experience different execution speeds on different hardware models, but at least now some of your ideas may be feasible on the Macintosh Plus.

An alternative to HyperCard-only animation is to employ an animation program driver. MacroMind, creators of VideoWorks II, offers a driver and XCMD that lets your stack display VideoWorks animations inside a stack—even in color on a color monitor. *Play VideoWorks*, as the system is called, is more reliable across all machine speeds and all the art rests in a VideoWorks file, rather than in your stack. This is the preferred method of including high-quality animation in your stacks.

To distribute a stack that plays VideoWorks movies, you'll have to license the driver from MacroMind. The company has a sliding scale of one-time licensing fees to include the driver with your product. The user of your stack must copy the drive file to the same folder level as your HyperCard application, but the animation files may be nested in other folders as you please.

In summary, then, be sure to test your stacks on machines from both ends of the speed and screen spectrum. You'll learn a lot about your stacks in the process, and probably find ways to make them work better on all machines.

3

What About the Macintosh User Interface?

HyperCard created a kind of furor among many experienced Macintosh program designers and users because, they claimed, HyperCard did not adhere to the User Interface Guidelines. The basic elements of the Macintosh user interface—elements such as pull down menus, windows, and click-and-drag text selection—date back to an Apple document written in 1982 for early Macintosh developers. So when Bill Atkinson appeared to throw away the manual, some in the community felt it was like fooling with Mother Nature.

I don't agree with the purists who decry HyperCard's abandonment of the user interface guidelines. As a Macintosh program, HyperCard does adhere quite closely to the guidelines. It has pull-down menus. Its dialog boxes and buttons inside dialog boxes behave like any Macintosh dialog box and button. It even introduces a new interface extension about which few people quibble: the tear-off menu.

Interface purists expect all Macintosh programs to be displayed in grow-able, scrolling windows. While HyperCard does use a standard window for its display (you don't realize this unless you see it on a large-screen monitor), the user may not resize the window at will, because there is no grow box at the bottom right corner of the window. Most programs, other than HyperCard applications, tend to revolve around documents that may be larger than the standard 512 x 342 pixel Macintosh internal monitor. These documents are on-screen replicas of the kinds of paper documents from the physical world, whether they be filled with words, numbers, or drawings. But because the on-screen metaphor of HyperCard's information unit is a card, it makes sense to me that the window to the HyperCard applications should be the size of that card. A "card" also conveys a finite, tight information package, which should be seen at a single glance. You shouldn't have to scroll around a card to find a button or field—a card's content should be obvious in one visual scan of the card. That being the case, growable windows and scroll bars aren't required. And non-growable windows are a predefined window type in the Macintosh toolbox. There's nothing special going on in that regard.

No, HyperCard, itself, does not wander far from the guidelines. But admittedly the applications you can create with HyperCard can appear to toss the guidelines into the wastebasket. This becomes, then, an important issue that any stack developer must address before setting out on a stack project.

Let's look first at the kinds of deviations from the user interface guidelines that HyperCard allows. Then we'll see where deviating from the guidelines might be okay.

The Menubar

Except for some game programs, virtually every Macintosh program pro-vides a menubar across the top of the screen. Even the simplest programs offer the Apple, File, and Edit menus. The Apple menu, of course, lists the desk accessories installed on the current System File you're running. The File menu, at least, offers such basic items as Open, Save, Print, and Quit. The Edit menu, as prescribed by the guidelines, offers selections for copying, cutting, and pasting selected items in the document, plus a selection for undoing a cut or paste.

As we've come to expect in Macintosh applications, the menubar is where we turn to initiate some action, whether it be to open a document, start a spelling checker, or change the outline thickness of a graphic object. In a

HyperCard stack, however, the tendency is to initiate action by clicking on screen buttons. You even have the choice of hiding the menubar from view in an application. In its current stage of evolution, HyperCard does not provide for a custom menubar to replace the HyperCard menubar.

How you handle the menubar issue in your stack often has a lot to do with the Macintosh and HyperCard literacy of your audience. There are two issues here: whether to show the menubar at all and, if so, how much of it to show.

If the intended audience for your stack is guaranteed not to be Macintosh literate, as in freestanding information stations available to the public, then pull-down menus probably won't mean anything to them. In fact, the user probably wouldn't know how to use the mouse to pull down a menu or what to do with that menu once it was pulled down. To experienced Macintosh users, menus are second nature; to non-computer folks, a menubar can be mysterious. Such stacks, then, should hide the HyperCard menubar and create on-screen buttons that look like things you should press (even clicking on a button won't be natural at first, but a simple on-screen instruction is all that's needed). A button should both look inviting and be clearly labeled as to the action resulting from a press of that button.

Inapplicable Menus

The difficulty with leaving HyperCard menus showing for Macintosh-literate, HyperCard-illiterate users is that some of the menu items may not apply to your stack. To help reduce the confusion, the menus change as you adjust the user level of the stack. Therefore, in a browsing or typing level, only three menus (plus the Apple menu) appear on the menubar. And, while these menus are shorter than they are at higher levels, they still might contain menu items that don't apply to your stack. For example, if your stack is not meant for printing of any kind, the application still appears to offer three printing options—Print Stack, Print Card, and Print Report. Even though you can use HyperTalk to trap for these menu items so they never execute, it is still unfair to the user to have items on the menu that don't do anything. How frustrated do *you* get when you go to a restaurant and order something listed on the menu, only to learn from the waiter that the item is not available that evening? It's the same for a stack user.

If you are creating a browse-only stack, several items in the Edit menu makes no sense. By setting the user level to 1, there is no chance that the browser will be able to select text (except in the Message Box), graphics, or any object to cut, copy, or paste. The Go menu, too, may be a problem for users, especially if you, as stack designer, would prefer they not have access to the Message Box or to the Find command in the Message Box. Again, you'd have to trap for these menu items. You could successfully intercept the Find menu item and put up an Answer dialog box to prompt the user for a search string, but the Message item in the Go menu would produce either nothing or a dialog that states the item is not available. Yet the navigation items in the Go menu may be incredibly useful to your design.

Showing the full menubar (as when the user level is set to 4 or 5) presents even more potential confusion for the user, unless you know the audience has an appreciation for HyperCard and needs access to the object and scripting tools to customize the application. *Focal Point* 1.0 shipped with all menus showing, because the user is invited to customize the look and actions of everything in the stack system. At the same time, the initial audience for this application was largely HyperLiterate and thus was eager to investigate the internal machinery. Future releases, however, will not display the Hyper-Card menu automatically, because a greater percentage of new *Focal Point* customers will be less HyperLiterate. The profusion of irrelevant menus and menu items will only confuse this audience (but the application will still maintain its previous level of customizability and accessibility for the Hyper-Literate).

The point of this discussion is that the menus appearing on the HyperCard menubar—at any level—are HyperCard menus, not menus for your stack. That makes a big difference in the way the menus are perceived by the user. The "HyperCard-ness" of the application starts to show through, and may distract attention from your application content. I believe the application should be the center of attention, not the fact that it is running on HyperCard.

When to Show Menus

As long as the audience for your stack is Macintosh literate, then pull-down menus make excellent sense. In particular, they let you place the equivalent of many buttons in a convenient, yet uncluttered place in your application. The tendency to clutter screens with buttons for the most trifling, infrequent action is something to be avoided. Those kinds of actions should be hidden until needed—hidden in a pull-down menu. Therefore, I believe we'll see more HyperCard applications coming along with their own menus, whether they be in the traditional menubar format or as pop-up menus in the middle of screens. For either type of menu to behave with the same speed and interface as Macintosh menus, they must be created as external commands and functions. In Chapter 28, we show you how to create an external function to generate pop-up menus.

If you develop an XCMD to display traditional menus, however, the burden falls on you as the stack designer to make sure that custom menus adhere as closely as possible to the Macintosh User Interface Guidelines. If you are making a stack look like a Macintosh application, then the users of that stack will expect it to behave like a true Macintosh product. Keep menu items short. Group menu items logically, separating groups of related functions by dotted lines. If you are doing your own menubar, then be sure it has an Apple menu listing installed desk accessories, and that other menubar conventions are followed, like putting the Quit item in the File menu.

Buttons, Icons, and Clicking

I can just about guarantee that every experienced Macintosh user wrinkled his or her brow (as I did) when working with the HyperCard Home Card for the first time. First of all, we assume that the Home Card is like a desktop to other HyperCard applications, and those little snippets of art are icons representing those applications. But clicking on one of those "icons" does not select it visually—it does not invert. In fact, a single click causes the application to start, not a double click as in the Finder. And then, how do you select an icon and drag it around the card? It was a mind-bending experience. To make things even worse, we learn later that what we believe are icons connected to applications are nothing more than bit-mapped art drawn on the card, covered by transparent buttons. Wild stuff.

This, I believe, is where the user interface critics of the Macintosh world come down hard on HyperCard for violating the rules. Frankly, I can't disagree with them that the familiar feel of the Finder and double-clicking icons are not here. It troubled me at first. But then other questions arise— questions that must be answered with a broader view than that of an experienced Macintosh user.

Of Mice and Clicks

Macintosh experience counts for a lot when it comes to knowing how to use the mouse and act on things appearing on the screen. Experienced Macintosh users think in terms of single clicks and double clicks. For example, consider this inconsistency that most of us don't even realize exists.

When the cursor is the text insertion pointer, we know that a single click plants the flashing text cursor in the spot at which we click. A double click selects the entire word surrounding the location of the click. One click insert; double click select. In other situations, such as in the Finder, a single click selects an item, while a double click causes some major action. One click select; double click act. Selecting text occurs with a double click; selecting an object occurs with a single click. But that doesn't bother us. We know how this all works, so it's no big deal.

What stack developers must remember, however, is that not all stack users—especially users of information publishing kinds of stacks—will be familiar with the concepts of selecting or double-clicking on something to cause an action. Think about it. How intuitive is a double click? Not very. Yet experienced Mac users rely on the double click for initiating all kinds of action. In fact, having learned the power of double clicking in the Finder and in other applications, many users tend to double click before even trying a single click (we'll talk about this more in a moment).

Single Clicks Do All

HyperTalk is largely responsible for the "single click-ness" of HyperCard. Recall that when you press the mouse button, HyperCard sends a mouseDown message; while the button is held down, HyperCard sends mouseStillDown messages; and when you release the button, HyperCard sends the mouseUp message. There is no collective "click" message, much less a "doubleClick" message when you press and release the mouse button (the mouseClick function simply lets you test for the action of pressing the mouse button, but no message is generated as a result).

As noted in the *Handbook*, the distinction among the three mouse-related messages gives you added flexibility in the kinds of mouse response you wish to build into your stack, plus it corresponds to the way the mouse works in traditional Macintosh toolbox-based programs. A click, like on an OK button, takes effect only when you release the mouse button with the pointer atop the same button over which you pressed the mouse button. Thus, you can press and hold the mouse button atop a button (Figure 3-1b), drag the mouse pointer away from the screen button and release the mouse button without activating that OK (Figure 3-1c). It's a subtle but important user interface point that lets us retract an erroneous mouse action before it's too late.

Trapping Double Clicks

The norm in HyperCard is the single click. That doesn't sit well with everyone, but for simplicity's sake, a single click is a good solution, especially for non-Macintosh-literate users. What you, as stack developer, must remember is that experienced Mac users may double click on buttons. HyperCard, itself, discards the second click of a double click on card layer buttons, but not on background buttons (this may change in a future release). In some cases, that can be disastrous, or at least cause unexpected results. For example, if you double click on the right arrow navigational button on a card, the button gets the first mouseUp message, acts on it according to instructions in its mouseUp handler, then gets the second mouseUp message, and handles it again. In other words, click twice on the right arrow button, and you advance two cards

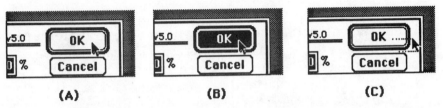

Figure 3-1 *In the Macintosh User Interface, when you click on a button, it highlights (B). If you then drag the cursor out of a highlighted button, the button returns to normal (C).*

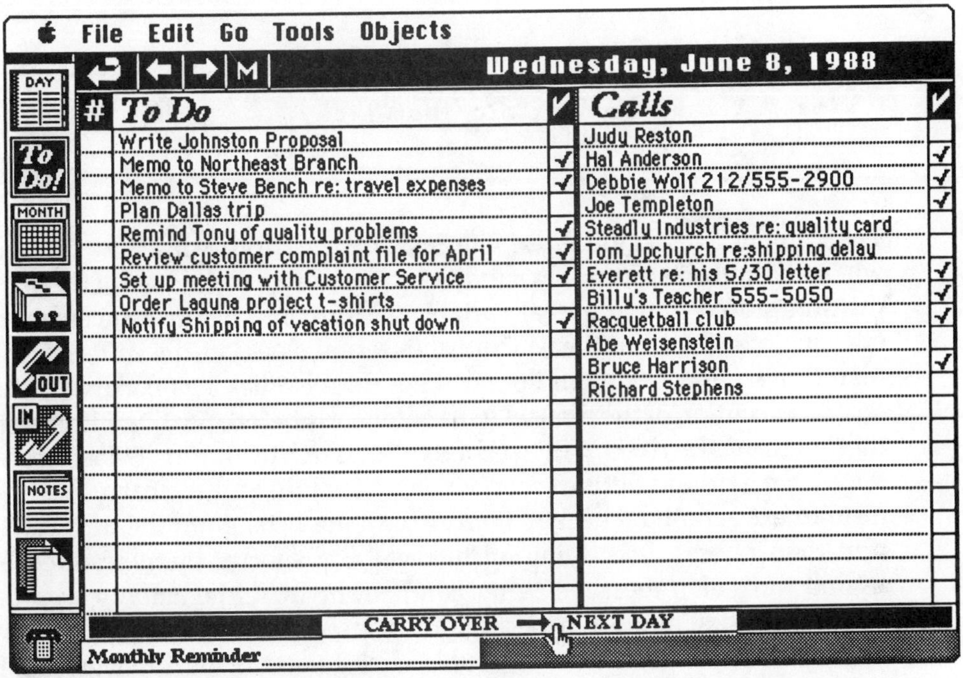

Figure 3-2 *Double-clicking on the Carry Over button (bottom) would cause data to be copied to each of the next two days' To Do cards. The handler had to trap for double clicks, ignoring the second click.*

in the stack.

It's not too serious if a navigation button doesn't intercept double clicks. If the user double clicks on a left or right arrow button, then the damage can be undone with one click of the opposite arrow or a press of the Back (tilde) or arrow key. But when data is being manipulated as the result of a click, then a double click can be more of a nuisance. For instance, in the To Do list stack of *Focal Point*, there is a button near the bottom of the screen that automatically posts unfinished to-do items to the next day's card (Figure 3-2). In testing, I discovered that new *Focal Point* users sometimes double clicked on this button. When they did, the unfinished items were posted to the next two days' cards, because the Carry Over button acted if it had been clicked twice: once on the starting card, and once again on the second day's card. Since undoing the posting of data to the third day was an undesirable job, the button had to include a timing scheme to make sure that double clicks would not inadvertently double post items. Here's an excerpt from that button's script:

```
on mouseUp
   global lastClick

   -- trap inadvertent double clicks
   if the seconds - lastClick < 5 then exit mouseUp
   else put the seconds into lastClick
   ...
end mouseUp
```

The script utilizes a global variable, lastClick, to capture the time (in seconds) when this button's mouseUp handler last ran. Then at the start of this handler, the time stored in that global variable is compared against the current time (also in seconds) from the Macintosh internal clock. If the difference is less than five seconds, the handler senses a double click has occurred, and the second execution of the mouseUp handler ends before posting information to the third card. I arrived at five seconds after much testing on a Macintosh Plus. It took a maximum of five seconds (on a Mac Plus) for the carryover mechanism to extract all unchecked items from long lists, go to the next card, and post them there. Specifying an interval any shorter often resulted in the second mouseUp message being handled, because the actual elapsed time between the first mouseUp message and the reception of the second mouseUp message was longer than the double click interval. In other words, if the specification called for a second mouseUp message to be ignored if it occurred within two seconds of the first, and it took three seconds to execute the works of the first mouseUp handler, the button would figure it's okay to process the second time, which it definitely was not.

Icon Buttons

One of the interface shocks to the experienced Macintosh user is the fact that you cannot simply drag what appear to be icons around the screen like you can on the desktop. To drag a button, you must first select the button tool. First-time HyperCard users are not likely to discover that right away, especially since HyperCard comes out of the box set to user level 2, which hides the existence of a tool palette. But even if the novice user learns about the button tool, there is yet one more shock: The art behind the buttons on the Home Card is not attached to any of the buttons. The buttons aren't icon buttons at all, but transparent buttons atop card layer graphics. To move a button and its art requires two different moves, with two different tools.

Given the cut-and-paste ability of true HyperCard icon buttons, in one sense I was amazed at the decision to make those buttons transparent atop background art. In defense of that decision, the button art was both unique (i.e., not part of the library of icons pre-installed into HyperCard's Home stack) and larger than the 32-pixel square limit on true icons. I have no problem with the quality of the art, but I felt that the concept of buttons separated from their art might be a little much for the newcomer.

If that experience taught me anything, it was that whenever possible, art-based buttons on customizable stacks should be icon buttons. It makes it easier for the user to adjust the location of the button to suit personal tastes. For details on creating icons for icon buttons, see Chapter 24.

Button Feedback

Something else that may surprise new users of the HyperCard Home Card is that when they click on one of the buttons, nothing happens to the button to indicate that it has been clicked. Were it not for the disk activity associated with going to the stack linked to that button, the user might think that the button was a fake or the mouse click didn't register.

Typically, buttons in other Macintosh environments, including dialog boxes, offer some kind of visual feedback that you are clicking on them. The most common feedback is an inversion of the pixels of that button. Black turns white and white turns black (Figure 3-1b). From a user's point of view, it's very comforting to see something happen on the screen as the mouse button is pressed.

HyperCard button settings give the author a choice between providing visual feedback—it's called auto-highlighting. Figure 3-3 shows the setting checkbox of the Button Info dialog box. The default setting for a new button (either by choosing New Button from the Objects menu or by dragging a new button with the button tool) is for auto-highlighting to be turned off—no feedback.

Turning auto-highlighting on for some styles of buttons may present unexpected results. Therefore, while I strongly endorse visual feedback for buttons, it is not always wise or possible to do it every time you wish.

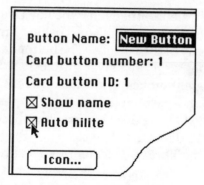

Figure 3-3   *Setting a button's auto-hilite property to true causes buttons to invert when clicked.*

When to HighLight

Auto-highlighting works best on button styles *other* than transparent buttons that encompass background or card layer graphics. Here's why.

When you size a transparent button's rectangle (all buttons except round rectangle buttons are rectangles), the entire rectangular area inverts when you click on it with auto-highlighting turned on. That differs greatly from the same kind of button assigned icon art. Assigning an icon to a transparent button restricts inversion to the art of the icon (see Figure 3-4 for a comparison of four button styles). Inversion of the icon art mimics the kind of feedback you get by clicking once (selecting) an icon in the Desktop. While inversion of the rectangle around non-icon art does invert the art, the extra inversion area may be distracting, if not surprising to someone expecting feedback from an icon-like situation.

Most other button styles should have auto-highlighting turned on, especially those styles derived directly from the Macintosh treasure chest: round rectangle, radio button, and check box styles. But the last two have special auto-highlighting behavior that differs slightly from other button styles.

Radio and Check Box Button Highlighting

Auto-highlighting for radio buttons causes part of the interior area of the button to highlight, as it does on radio buttons you'd find in a dialog box. This does not, however, cause the black dot inside the button to appear when you release the mouse button. It is up to you to install HyperTalk scripts in the group of radio buttons to handle the highlighting of the chosen button and unhighlighting of the others. Remember, radio buttons are used to make a single choice from among two or more choices. Only one radio button in an associated group may be highlighted at one time.

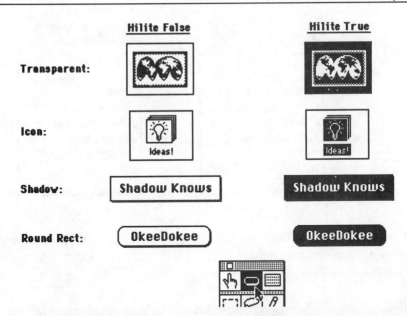

Figure 3-4 *Different button styles react differently to highlighting. Transparent buttons invert their entire rectangle, while icon buttons invert only the icon art and the button name. Shadow and Round Rect buttons invert in their entirety (but not their drop shadows).*

Check boxes behave differently. With auto-highlighting turned on, a click of the mouse button places an "X" inside the check box. A subsequent click of the mouse button removes that "X". That's good news, because it removes the responsibility from the stack author of writing handlers for all the check box buttons to turn highlighting on and off in response to mouseUp messages. The button, itself, handles it all. That's fine for the standard application of the checkbox user interface, too, because check box buttons allow you to choose more than one item from two or more check box items. Another button, like an "OK" button, then checks the condition of all the check box buttons to see which ones have their hilite properties set to true. The handler in the OK button proceeds based on that information.

Feedback Problem

Unfortunately, now that I've carried the banner for button visual feedback, there's some bad news that complicates the issue. In early versions of HyperCard, clicking on an auto-highlighted button causes any text selection in a field to become deselected (Figure 3-5). For example, if you write a button mouseUp handler to get the selection, go to another stack, and find the text that had been selected, that handler will work as planned only if the button

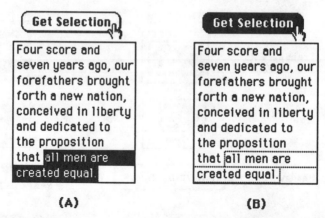

(A)   **(B)**

Figure 3-5   *Auto-hiliting is not always desirable. HyperCard de-selects any selected text when you click on a button that highlights. This will be repaired in some future release of HyperCard.*

does not highlight when you click on it. If the button's auto-highlight is turned on, and you click on that button, the inverted, selected text in any text field on the card will become instantly deselected. The handler, when it tries to get the selection, finds that the selection is empty, and thus cannot perform the search in the other stack as you expected.

If you have even one handler in your stack or stack system that relies on a text selection as source material for further execution, you must give serious thought to the button highlighting you set up for the entire application. It is important to be as consistent as possible. I don't believe it makes sense for some icon buttons to have auto-highlighting turned on because they don't utilize selected text, and others to have it turned off because their handlers act on selected text. Inconsistency like this can make for a very confusing time for the user, for if he or she sees one icon button highlight, and another not, then the thought that something is wrong with the application will be quite prominent. Therefore, if even one icon button depends on a text selection, then none of your icon buttons should have auto-highlighting turned on.

That's not to say that all buttons should be have auto-highlighting turned off, but be logical about it. If a series of buttons perform similar operations and stands by itself (and doesn't rely on selected text), then it's permissible to turn on auto-highlighting for those buttons. Figure 3-6 shows a card from the Outgoing Phone Log stack of *Focal Point*. Because all the icon buttons along the left edge of the card work with selected text, none of those buttons have auto-highlighting turned on. But the buttons at the right edge, which close out a call, all perform similar tasks, and appear nowhere else in the *Focal Point* system except here. These buttons have auto-highlighting turned on. Note,

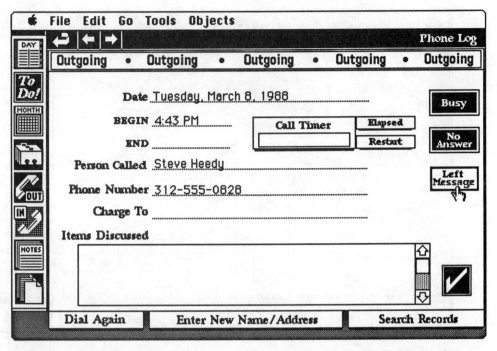

Figure 3-6 *None of the icon buttons on the left edge invert when clicked, because their actions are dependent on selected text. The related group of buttons on the right, however, highlight when clicked.*

too, that the buttons are transparent atop rectangular art in the background graphics layer. By carefully positioning the rectangle of the transparent button atop the rectangle of the art, the illusion is one of a rectangle button that shows its name. But by using background art, the font of the button is one that few Macintosh systems might have (Garamond), yet the text of the button appears the same on all systems.

Choose the Correct Button Style

HyperCard gives the author enough latitude to go far afield in conceiving button designs, especially when you consider transparent buttons atop any kind of bit-mapped art in a graphic layer. Even a part of a map may be a button, as shown in the excerpt from *Business Class* in Figure 3-7. Therefore, you are not obligated in any way to use standard buttons in your stacks. But— and this is a big BUT—if you use standard Macintosh buttons, you had better use them as they were meant to be.

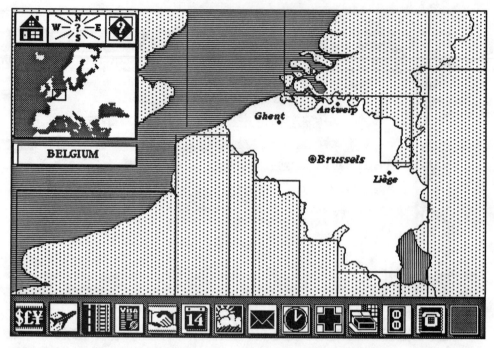

Figure 3-7 *Sometimes it takes several rectangular buttons (each with the same handler or button name) to cover an irregular area. Transparent buttons, like those in the Business Class maps, turn any region into an active button area.*

The biggest button sins I've seen committed in early HyperCard stacks revolve around improper use of radio buttons and check box buttons. I've seen examples of both styles being used to initiate actions. That's not how they are used in traditional Macintosh situations, and that's not how they should be used in a HyperCard application. Both styles of buttons are for establishing settings of some kind: only one of a group of radio buttons; any combination of check boxes. These kinds of buttons must be accompanied by some other button or action starter, which, in turn, acts according to the selections made with the radio or check box buttons. What this comes down to is a rule—one of the few hard and fast rules about HyperCard design which you must follow:

If you use Macintosh user interface objects, then those objects must behave the same way in your stack product as they do in other Macintosh products.

The best way to learn how these items work in traditional Macintosh products is to observe them in action. A good playground for buttons is any fully featured dialog box, including the dialog boxes within HyperCard. The font dialog box shows examples of correct usage of check box and radio buttons (Figure 3-8). Additional commentary on button interfaces may be found in *Inside Macintosh*, Volume 1, amid other discussions about the Macintosh User Interface Guidelines—good reading for any stack designer.

Taking a Stand

As you can see, the question of user interface in HyperCard is a complex one, primarily because HyperCard lets you be as free-form or as rigid as you like.

What it all means, however, is that no matter which way you go—even if you choose a middle ground—you have to be very aware of how you intend to adopt or shun the Macintosh User Interface Guidelines in your stack product. There is nothing in the rulebooks saying you must "toe the line" in stack design. In fact, as pointed out earlier, the standard user interface means nothing to some audiences for stacks. For them the interface may be more confusing than an interface you devise from scratch.

If you decide to hide the menubar completely in your stack, then make sure the user has ample instruction or other visual clues on the screen to help him navigate through the stack. Make buttons (or other "click-me" areas on the screen) inviting and intuitive.

If, on the other hand, you prefer to adhere more closely to the Macintosh interface guidelines in an attempt to give the impression of a free-standing Mac application, then don't blow it by careless application of the guidelines.

Figure 3-8 *The font dialog box demonstrates proper usage of checkbox and radio buttons in Macintosh applications. Their behaviors should be emulated in a HyperCard stack.*

Above all, when you use tried and true interface elements, like radio buttons, make sure they behave the way an experienced Macintosh user would expect them to work.

Finally, you may also strike a balance between something completely new and the familiar. As long as you don't misuse accepted interface elements, there's no reason you cannot create your own interface extensions that work best in your application. I believe there is a genuine opportunity in Hyper-Card for creative people to develop valuable extensions to the Macintosh user interface. Had we not had HyperCard, the Mac interface might have re-mained stagnant or in the hands of just a few. Now we all have a say in it. Successful implementations will be imitated by others, perhaps working their way into the accepted Macintosh user interface of tomorrow.

4

Screen Aesthetics

Aesthetics is a philosophy about the concept of beauty. It may sound odd, then, to be discussing such things in a book concerned with computer programs and programming. But in the HyperCard development environment, the subject of aesthetics is vitally important if you expect others to perceive value in your work.

My 80/20 Aesthetics Rule

Early in my experience with HyperCard, I had the opportunity to watch the results of talented Macintosh artists like Kristee Kreitman and Marge Boots as they designed prototypes for a number of HyperCard applications. They were taking full advantage of the bit-map painting tools in HyperCard and creating wonderful metaphors of real world objects on the screen—flip charts, note pads, open books, and so on.

Then I got the idea to work on what eventually became *Business Class* and *Focal Point*. The basic concepts—what information would be on the screen, how the user would interact with it, how the user would navigate through the information—were pretty firm in my mind after awhile. When it came time to mock up these applications, however, it was clear that as a non-artist, I was not equipped to make them look like "real" applications. Very early in the development process, at a time when there were no real stack developers, I recognized an 80/20 rule that still holds true today:

A user will want to use a stack 80% for its information content or information handling ability and 20% for its visual appeal, but the initial perceived value of the stack will be 80% predicated on its visual appeal and 20% on its information abilities.

In other words, a person will be in search of a solution for a particular information problem. Finding that solution is the primary motivation for searching out an application. But when taking first looks at several stacks of comparable information handling prowess, the most visually pleasing stack will make the best impression in the mind of the potential user. The prettier face will look to be the best value.

You should stop short, however, of calling a stack's aesthetic appeal a "glitz" factor, because the underlying information handling characteristics must be in the product. If the functionality is not sound, then the pretty face of the product will be seen as the thin facade it was probably intended to be.

HyperCard stacks are inherently graphic, or at least they encourage developers to think in graphic terms. The fact that adding bit-mapped graphics to a stack is so easy is certainly an important factor. Whereas traditional Macintosh productivity applications tend to look a bit "dry" on the screen, it's rare to find any kind of HyperCard stack that hasn't been embellished in some fashion with the author's flair for incorporating original or derivative graphics.

Even buttons tend to be graphic. The ease of adding icon art from the built-in library of button icons encourages this universal, visual approach to stack screen design.

All this flexibility, however, can also create a serious problem for the stack developer. Unless care is given to the graphic design of a stack—whether information publishing, information management, external device control, or HyperCard utility—the screens can become barren, overcrowded, overpowering, barely readable, unfinished, non-intuitive, or any combination of these.

Macintosh Artists and Screen Artists

Since the release of HyperCard, I have met many artistically inclined individuals who were pursuing stack development. That, to me, is exciting, because they may bring new levels of artistic brilliance to Macintosh program design. But that talent is rare. More typically, a stack developer is someone who has a great idea for an application because his or her expertise is in some specialized business or academic area—not in screen design. That was clearly my case.

In my search for an artist, I discovered something unexpected. While there are many qualified people who justifiably claim to be Macintosh artists, they are not all qualified to design Macintosh screens. That may seem like a crazy distinction, but it is very true.

The majority of Macintosh artists these days started their art careers in other artistic media. Enamored by the graphics abilities of the Mac, they use the Macintosh as another artistic tool, like they use pen and ink as a tool. In the vast majority of cases, these artists use the Macintosh to produce works that ultimately show up in printed media, such as newspaper charts and graphs, magazine and book illustrations, posters, calendars, restaurant menus, annual reports, concert programs, and so on. Quite often, these artists are successful, if not swamped with work, thanks to the sophisticated products coming from their Macintoshes and laser printers.

Designing for the Macintosh screen, however, is an entirely different discipline—a discipline that, today, very few Macintosh artists practice with success. When a program's art is not tailored to the screen, the result can be less pleasing, even though the quality of the basic art is good. For example, there is a shareware HyperCard-based entertainment product, called Tilt. Based on jousting sport of days gone by, the screens included very elaborate Arthurian bit-mapped art (Figure 4-1). While the art, in and of itself, is very good, to me much of it seems out of place on the Macintosh screen, even within the context of the game.

Icon Design

Good screen design also encompasses good icon design, if your program plans call for icon buttons. Icons are bit maps that fit inside a 32 x 32 pixel square. For an artist, that can be a very confining chunk of screen real estate, but the opportunity to tell a long story in such a small space should be worth the challenge. I personally prefer icon buttons over named buttons when given the choice. Named buttons in any of the typical button styles (rectangle,

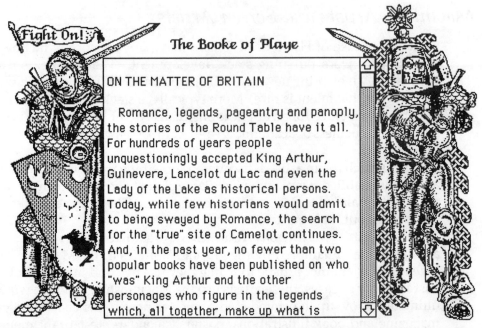

Figure 4-1 *Art should be appropriate and in scale to the information of a card. Even high quality art can seem inappropriate for a screen design, as in this game screen.*

shadow, round rectangle) often take up more room on the card than an icon does. Moreover, an icon can convey a lot of meaning with a tiny picture. Figure 4-2, for instance, shows the icon buttons in *Business Class* and the names of the categories to which they lead. Imagine having named buttons with all 13 categories on the card. There would be little room left for the map, and the card would end up looking like a mess of buttons. The user would be overwhelmed at first sight.

The point is, the artist who works on your stacks should feel comfortable working within the confines of the icon format. It's not necessary to create the icons in an icon design utility program. As long as the icons come to you in bit-mapped form—created in MacPaint, SuperPaint, FullPaint, or whatever— you will be able to transform them into icon resources (see Chapter 24) for inclusion into your stack. Three excellent sources of inspiration for icons are:

The Symbol Sourcebook by Henry Dreyfuss (Van Nostrand, Reinhold, 1972)
Trademarks and Symbols by Yasaburo Kuwayama (Van Nostrand, Reinhold, 1973)
Handbook of Pictorial Symbols by Rudolf Modley (Dover, 1976).

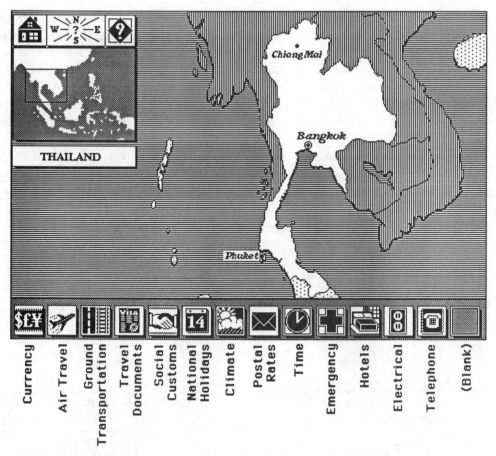

Currency | Air Travel | Ground Transportation | Travel Documents | Social Customs | National Holidays | Climate | Postal Rates | Time | Emergency | Hotels | Electrical | Telephone | (Blank)

Figure 4-2   *Icon buttons can convey a lot of information in a 32-pixel-square area. Had named buttons been used in Business Class, there'd be little room left for the maps.*

Finding an Artist

Locating Macintosh artists to interview for your stack project may not be an easy task in many parts of the country. This is particularly true if you want to find someone who has experience doing screen designs for other products. Such artists tend to be located in the areas populated by software companies, predominantly in major metropolitan areas like Boston, New York, Chicago, San Francisco, and Los Angeles. A good place to start looking is at a local Macintosh user group. While it's not likely that many artists will be active in these user groups, their friends and acquaintances will be. You've got to get the word out that you're in search of a Macintosh screen designer. Another way of contacting potential artists is through local desktop publishing service bureaus, which seem to be popping up all over the country, even in smaller cities. Again, the artists might not be on staff, but the firm probably knows of free-lance Macintosh artists who have done other art and design work.

It's important when you interview a potential artist that you explain as fully as possible what you have in mind for the artist to do. It may be that the thought of designing what looks to be a series of business-oriented database forms is just too dull a prospect for the artist, so be honest about the work ahead. Ask to see examples of the artist's Macintosh screen design work. Examples from other media are of less value to you, even if they're of excellent quality. Of course, you may wish to help a talented Macintosh artist get started in screen design, but prepare yourself to be more critical if the artist's first attempts aren't to your liking. Also be supportive of those pieces that you do like as you both learn screen design skills. You might even stage a small competition in which you give the same instructions to all candidates for the design of a simple screen and an icon or two. Then compare the results and base your decision on that. Just don't use the competition as a way to get free art. That's simply unfair.

Paying for Art

Financial arrangements with an artist can vary. The two most common methods of payment are flat fee or an advance and royalty. In the flat fee method, both of you agree on an amount for the entire project or an hourly rate (perhaps with a ceiling).

The other method is more like an author-publisher arrangement, in which you pay the artist an amount while work is in progress (the advance—payable in installments at various milestones during production). The advance is a payment made against future royalties, the rate of which is calculated as an agreed percentage of the revenues you collect in the sale of the product. For example, if you pay the artist a $2500 advance against a 15% royalty, the first $2500 of royalty payments earned from sales of the software go toward paying you back for the advance. Once the $2500 advance is earned, the artist then gets 15% of your revenues. In a royalty arrangement, you are liable for issuing royalty statements and payments at a fixed interval (quarterly or semi-annually are common terms) for the life of the product. All such details should be spelled out clearly in a written agreement between you and the artist.

Whichever financial arrangement you agree to with the artist, it is important for you, as stack developer, to acquire exclusive rights to the artwork. By assuming all rights to the artwork, the copyright of the entire stack product will be yours. If your stack is eventually published or distributed by a software publisher, the agreement you sign with the publisher will probably insist that you have sole rights to all pieces of the product anyway.

Although it's up to you, it is a gesture of good faith and cooperation to credit the artist (and other contributors) somewhere in your product. If your stack has an About box or title screen, give credit to the artist there. If a printed manual accompanies the product, then acknowledge the artist there, too. Keep reminding yourself about the 80/20 rule, and you shouldn't have trouble remembering to mention the artist prominently.

Working With the Artist

The old maxim, "form follows function," is as true for HyperCard card design as it is for any other kind of product. As stack creator, it is your job to define the function; leave it to the artist to define the form based on the function.

That's not to say that the developer shouldn't try his hand at laying out elements on a card. There must be a draft or sketch of at least the elements—fields, buttons, graphics content—from which to start. It would be virtually impossible to start designing the function of a stack without such a sketch, either on paper or as a trial run on the screen within HyperCard. Once you have a skeleton of functionality working, it's time to bring in the artist.

Explain to the artist how the various elements work together: what happens when you click on every button; what the most important textual or graphic information is on the card; what kind of impression the user should get when opening a card; what the user and information flow is through the stack; which buttons the user is likely to click the most often. I don't believe it is critical that the artist be fluent in HyperCard, but it is essential that the artist fully understand the stack application: who uses it; when they are most likely to use it; how they will use it in the course of a day; how the stack interacts with other Macintosh applications. The artist must share the same vision and have the same enthusiasm for the product as its creator does. That commitment will show through the product—as will a lack of commitment.

Don't be surprised if your artist makes suggestions about the functionality of the product. Often an artist can be a good early tester of a program idea or functional detail. He or she will probably be one of the first testers of the product you'll encounter. You may even be challenged to explain why a certain feature works the way it does. Guard against becoming strictly defensive about your "child." If the artist questions something, it could be that your intended audience may question the same feature. Listen carefully to criticism—not just the criticism, but the basis for it. Solicit solutions. Even if you don't like the one presented right away, it might stimulate other ideas for a better implementation of a feature.

When to Hire the Artist

The timing factor—when to bring in the artist—is an interesting point. I was once asked to consult with a software company to offer my suggestions about a series of HyperCard stacks it was developing to support a series of its standalone Macintosh software products. This company had hired a first-rate Macintosh screen designer to be the Creative Director of the entire project. At the same time, it hired individual writers to develop each of the handful of stacks in the series. At the one meeting I attended, I couldn't believe what I was seeing.

The company essentially wanted the Creative Director to specify a form, which each of the authors would follow to create the functionality of the stacks. There was no agreement on the stack structure. Each author had his or her own idea about what the stack presentation should be. Around all this, the artist was supposed to develop a common "look" to the series. That, simply put, was an impossible task. The company was asking function to follow form—a form that had no explicit direction. The artist was not equipped to define the form, because there was no functionality to design around. Needless to say, the project languished and the artist left the project. Eventually the stacks made it out, but not until after a reappraisal of the methodology of developing the stacks and specifying the art.

Perhaps I was lucky, but the artist I found for my stack products (David Smith of David Smith Design, Sausalito, California) turned out to be a valuable asset in the development of both *Business Class* and *Focal Point*. It took me several months to find him, and that occurred only after interviews with almost a dozen Macintosh artists. Once we agreed to work together, we didn't always see eye to eye on issues, and sometimes each of us felt like we were talking to stone walls. But the intellectual exchanges were excellent, and now we both believe the results are far better than if each of us had worked independently—it was synergism in action. The key ingredient for our teamwork, I believe, was respect for the other's talents. We also shared the same visions in creating what we believed were useful and fun products.

Key Design Guidelines

Remember, however, that the visual formulas that worked for us in *Business Class* and *Focal Point* may not work in your stacks. A different kind of stack structure (see Chapter 5) will probably call for different visual elements. And for me to impose design guidelines on you or your artist is risky business, because the HyperCard environment is too new to burden it with aesthetic design rules. Acknowledging that risk, here are a few general comments that might help direct the design team for your stack (that includes you):

1. *Keep screens as simple as possible.* Occasionally, I see information management stack screens composed of so many buttons and scrolling fields that I get too confused to figure out what I'm supposed to do next. If a screen requires supplemental information, find ways of nesting the extra data (covered in detail in Chapter 18).

2. *Let the information be the star.* Since your stack more than likely stores and displays information, the center of the screen should be devoted to that information. Place buttons that perform ancillary actions or link to other stacks at the periphery of the screen. That lets the user's eye focus on the information. Just as Macintosh users tend to forget about the menubar until it is needed, buttons at the edges of the screen fall outside the view of a person concentrating on the information content.

3. *Choose screen fonts carefully.* While some of this discussion might seem better suited to desktop publishing, the selection of fonts on a HyperCard screen is equally important. If your card has fields the user types text into, make sure the fields are of a different font than the field labels, which most likely will be in the background or card graphics layer. Anticipate a very low common denominator of field fonts in the user's System File for editable fields. Just because you have Palatino in your System File doesn't mean that everyone does. Play it safe with standard fonts, like Geneva, New York, Monaco and Chicago. Field labels, generated as bit-mapped characters in the graphics layer, may be of more exotic fonts if appropriate, because the user need not have those fonts installed for them to appear as you designed them. Also exercise care in specifying font sizes. Not everyone who uses the Mac has an easy time reading 9-point, closely leaded fonts. Either choose a large enough font for the original design, or leave enough space in the field for the user to adjust the font up a size or two.

4. *Make the graphics appropriate to the subject.* Unless the stack is designed to show off some special art, avoid overpowering the viewer with art that does not contribute to the stack's information content. A little ornamentation on an otherwise simple card may be alright, but don't overdo it.

5. *Be consistent.* If cards of one background or one stack of a stack system have navigation buttons in one place, then make sure similar buttons on other backgrounds or other stacks are in the same place. I've seen cases in

which the arrow navigation buttons were shoehorned into places around different art on cards. This is utterly confusing. The user will never feel at home in the stack.

6. *Remind the user where he is.* Information cards usually need titles of some kind to let the user know what he's looking at. A particular background or card style may be obvious to the stack designer, but not to the first-time user of the stack. And, harkening back to item 5, above, be consistent in the location of the card title. Figures 4-3 through 4-5 demonstrate the title conventions used in *Business Class*, *Focal Point* and the *Focal Point* help stack, respectively.

7. *Label all fields.* As the user tabs through data entry fields on a card, there must be a title next to each one to indicate what kind of information goes in there. In an information publishing stack, the card title may suffice, provided there is only one field of information on the card. If there are multiple fields, then some rationale for their distinction must be evident from the titles of the fields.

8. *Make best use of precious screen real estate.* A number of the backgrounds that come on the HyperCard Ideas disk (in the HyperCard package) have a vertical format to them, like an open book lying flat on a table, binding

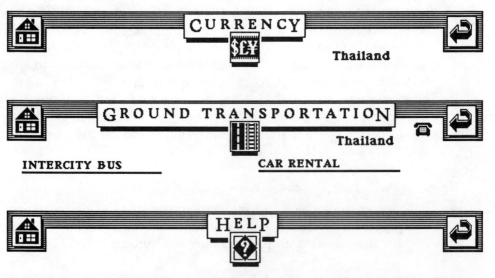

Figure 4-3 *A consistent style and card titles help the user maintain spatial bearings in a large stack system. These titles are from the information cards of Business Class.*

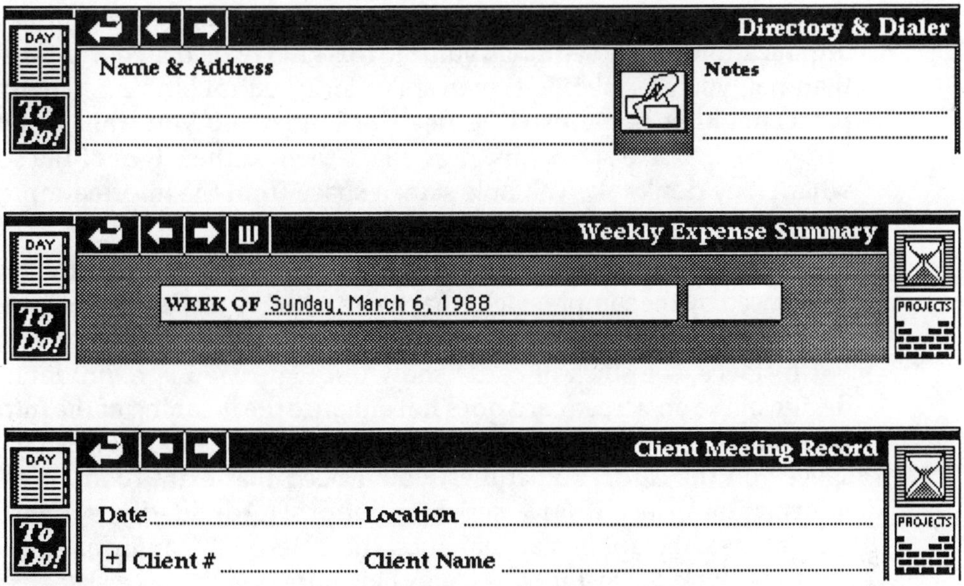

Figure 4-4 *A similar layout and card titles keep the many applications of Focal Point in order.*

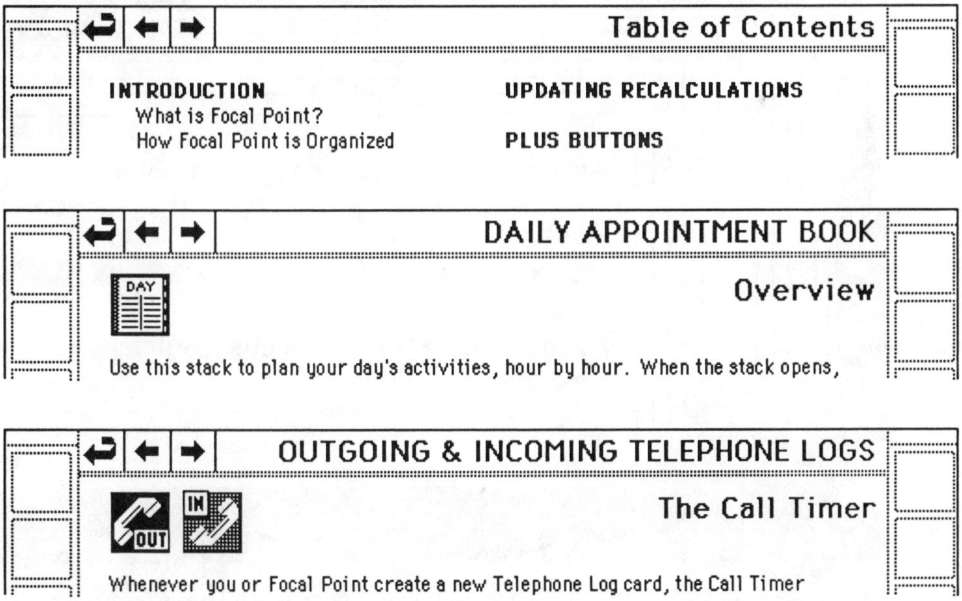

Figure 4-5 *The Help stack of Focal Point has a look derivative of the main program, yet a strong consistency within this 97-card stack.*

down the middle of the screen. Except for very specialized information organization, I don't see much value to this kind of field layout. More often than not, you are robbing screen space for a central binding, when those pixels might be better used for fields or buttons. If you want to employ visual devices like spiral bindings, place them at the edges of the screen, where they don't take valuable screen space from the information.

9. *Use the full screen.* I believe a number of stack designs are unduly influenced by the sample stacks that come with HyperCard in the way they display a card metaphor atop the underlying HyperCard card metaphor. For instance, the stack of cards shown in Figure 4-6 is redundant. The design of the on-screen card does not enhance the meaning of the information or the collection of data. In the meantime, there is a lot of wasted "gray space" on the card. Sometimes, you'll need that extra room to convey information or use it for a series of buttons. Admittedly, sometimes a screen card metaphor can enhance the role of the information. The Address stack, for instance, is a good introduction to the card concepts of

Figure 4-6 *A double metaphor—a graphic stack of cards in a HyperCard stack of cards— serves little purpose here. Some graphic cards, like the rolo-style Address stack cards, do convey the functionality of the stack.*

HyperCard because of its rolo-like metaphor. Still, once the fundamental card concept is understood, the screen metaphor is often unnecessary.

10. *Be original.* Use material in the HyperCard Ideas disk stacks for your own use—like when you're mocking up a stack to test functionality. Aside from the legal implications of redistributing artistic material copyrighted by someone else, borrowed art looks borrowed. Figure 4-7a shows a screen from a commercial stack, and Figure 4-7b shows a card from a stack that comes with HyperCard. To my way of thinking, it's hard to charge money for a design that is so unoriginal.

From the realm of screen aesthetics, we next go to the concepts of stack structure, where the talents of a stack developer show through with blinding clarity.

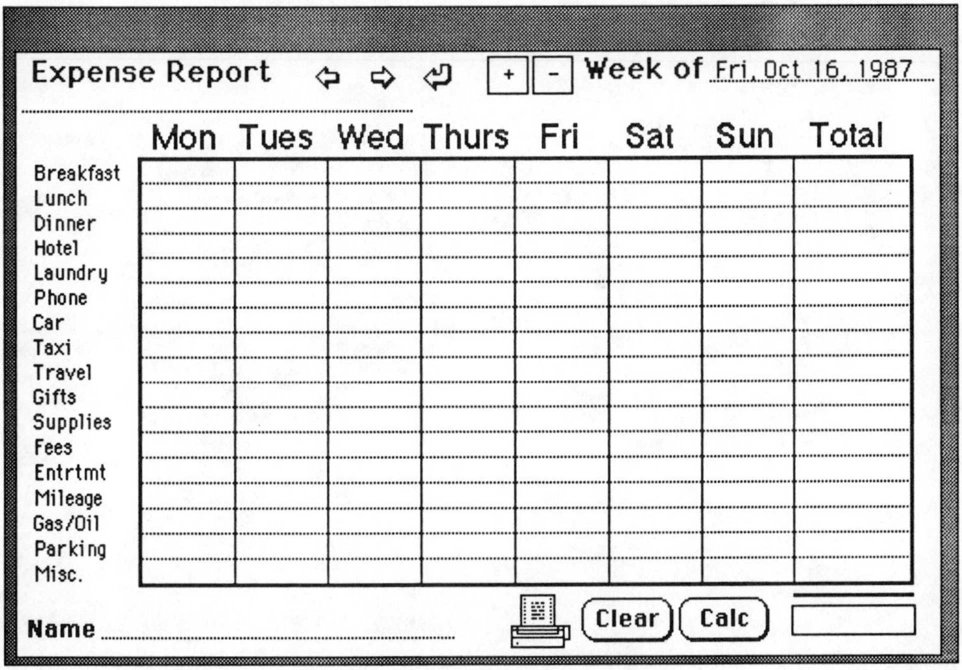

Expense Report ⇦ ⇨ ↵ [+][-] Week of Fri, Oct 16, 1987								
	Mon	Tues	Wed	Thurs	Fri	Sat	Sun	Total
Breakfast								
Lunch								
Dinner								
Hotel								
Laundry								
Phone								
Car								
Taxi								
Travel								
Gifts								
Supplies								
Fees								
Entrtmt								
Mileage								
Gas/Oil								
Parking								
Misc.								

Name _____   [Clear](Calc)

Figure 4-7a   *A glaring example of unoriginality: a card from a commercial stack (A) and a card with almost identical look and function from the HyperCard ideas stacks (B).*

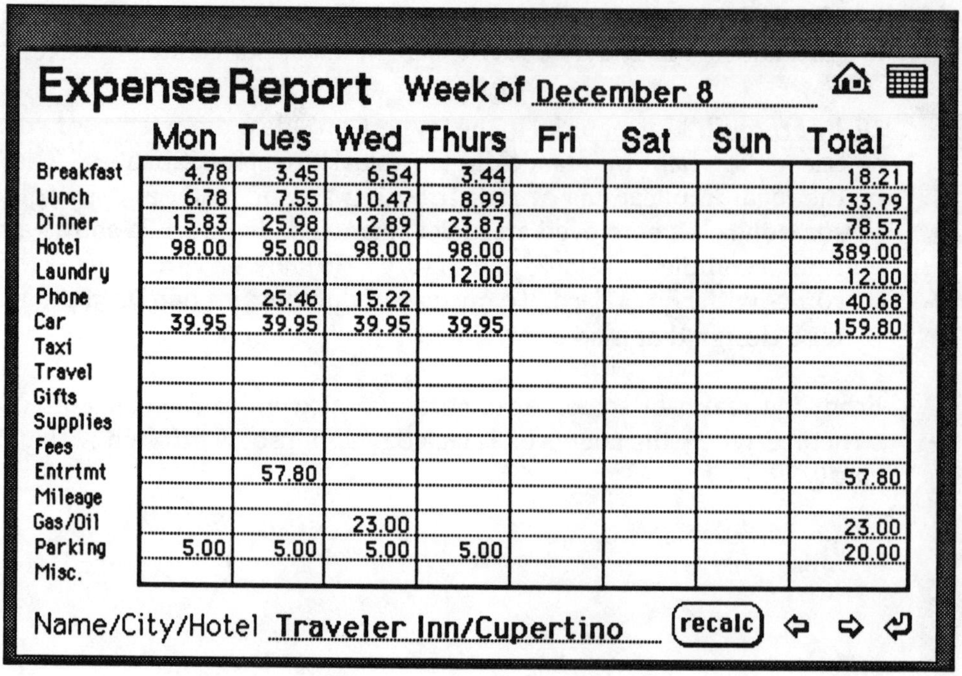

Expense Report Week of December 8

	Mon	Tues	Wed	Thurs	Fri	Sat	Sun	Total
Breakfast	4.78	3.45	6.54	3.44				18.21
Lunch	6.78	7.55	10.47	8.99				33.79
Dinner	15.83	25.98	12.89	23.87				78.57
Hotel	98.00	95.00	98.00	98.00				389.00
Laundry				12.00				12.00
Phone		25.46	15.22					40.68
Car	39.95	39.95	39.95	39.95				159.80
Taxi								
Travel								
Gifts								
Supplies								
Fees								
Entrtmt		57.80						57.80
Mileage								
Gas/Oil			23.00					23.00
Parking	5.00	5.00	5.00	5.00				20.00
Misc.								

Name/City/Hotel Traveler Inn/Cupertino   (recalc)

Figure 4-7b

5

Stack Structure

Laying out the structure of your stack is one of the most important steps in developing the product. This is where substantial planning takes place to determine the organization of cards, backgrounds and, if it's a large system, stacks.

Internal and External Structures

Structure applies to two distinct organizational issues about a stack: internal and external structures. Internal structure is the one that involves decisions such as whether to keep all cards in one heterogeneous stack of several backgrounds, divide the system up into several homogeneous stacks, or perhaps do a combination of both. Internal structure also pertains to the way cards and backgrounds in a stack are linked—how the user flows through the stack. Not all link structures apply to all types of stacks, as we'll see shortly.

External structure is often not considered until too late. It doesn't apply to single stack applications, provided the stack is small enough to fit on one floppy disk. But as any author of a large stack system can tell you, the distribution of multiple, linked stacks on floppy disk and their potential use on that format by the user community cause problems that need addressing in the design stage. While the majority of Macintosh owners have hard disks, not everyone does. If your stack product is going into the world, you must prepare your product for use on floppy disk-based systems.

Homogeneous and Heterogeneous Stacks

Introduced in the *Handbook*, the concept of homogeneous and heterogeneous stacks has caught on. Briefly, a *homogeneous* stack is one in which all cards share a single background. The stack might be one card (like a calculator card) or thousands of cards (like a well-stocked address stack). From beginning to end, there is only one style of card. A *heterogeneous* stack, on the other hand, contains more than one background. Usually, the information contained in the different backgrounds of a stack have some common bond. While a heterogeneous stack has multiple backgrounds, the stack should still have a central theme running through it. For example, the Datebook stack that comes with HyperCard has three backgrounds in it: a to-do list, a weekly appointment calendar and a six-month calendar (Figure 5-1). All three have the common thread of time and task management.

Another organizational concept you should consider is that of a stack system. By this I mean a group of linked stacks, which, together, make up a complete application. Both *Business Class* and *Focal Point* are stack systems. Sometimes, as we'll see later in the chapter, it makes sense to divide one large heterogeneous stack into several homogeneous or heterogeneous stacks to form a stack system. Stack systems have their disadvantages, too, as we'll see later.

Navigation Flow

Regardless of the homogeneity or heterogeneity of your stacks, you'll have to consider the navigational flow the user follows through the stack. I've seen some developers plan a stack by way of elaborate block diagrams of flows,

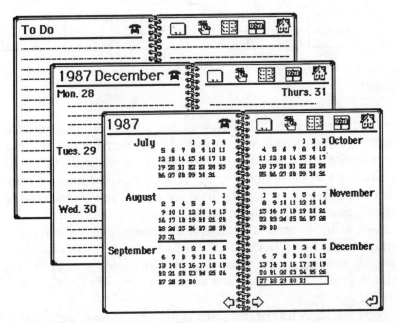

Figure 5-1 *A stack may consist of multiple backgrounds, each of which is perceived as a distinct application. HyperCard's Datebook sample stack demonstrates this quite well. Three buttons on the Home card link to different backgrounds of this stack, as do the buttons at the top right of each card.*

almost card by card. If that helps you visualize your stack, then go ahead and do it. But basically there are only four ways to organize the user flow within a stack: as a straight line, as a tree, as a cobweb and as a combination of two or three of the others. In many cases, the kind of application you have in mind dictates which flow model your stack will follow.

The Straight Line

Homogeneous information management stacks, such as the Address stack that comes with HyperCard, are organized in straight lines—a linear format. In a typical browsing environment for such a stack, you open the stack to reach the first card, and then go through each card, one after the other, from beginning to end (Figure 5-2). Fortunately, HyperCard's Find command lets you transcend this linearity and skip ahead to a desired card, but the underlying stack structure is linear.

Information publishing stacks of a homogeneous nature may also be linear. HyperCard's association with Ted Nelson's hypertext concept is at times unfortunate. It often leads developers of information publishing stacks to go

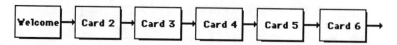

Figure 5-2   *A straight line structure leads the user from start to finish down a prescribed pathway.*

out of their way to break free of linearity. While HyperCard seems to encourage the linking of data outside rigid structures, there are still times when a linear approach makes the most sense, particularly if your information publishing stack is telling a story. A story has a beginning, middle, and end. If breaking free of the story's linearity means you'll reach the end before the middle, then the break harms the storyteller's intention.

Even a linear organization can be interesting and diverse. One of the earliest stacks in public circulation was a children's story called Inigo Gets Out (Inigo is pronounced "eye-nee'-go"). This stack was the first of a series of extraordinarily well-conceived stacks by Amanda Goodenough (AmandaStories).

The basic story line of this stack is the adventure of a cat, named Inigo, who slips out of the house and is confronted by various opportunities to get into trouble (Figure 5-3). The user determines where Inigo explores by clicking on various areas of the screen. Even as you explore what might appear to be branches off the main story line, the branches are small, linear units of their own, which always bring you back to the decision spot on the main story line. The diversions are more like loops hanging on the main line (Figure 5-4). Because you always come back to familiar territory, you never get the feeling of being or becoming lost in the stack, and that's important. You quickly gain confidence that the stack designer will take care of you on your journey.

Product demonstrations and tutorials are good candidates for information publishing versions of linear stacks. They are much like storytelling in that they should have a beginning, middle and end, and the stack developer should be the guiding spirit while the user makes his way through the cards. Allowing for occasional looping detours might help break the tedium, just as a sidebar does for a long magazine article. But unlike Inigo's story, you probably want the user to experience a definite series of cards to get your message across in its entirety. Don't be afraid of linearity in stack design. Let interesting visual effects, graphic elements on cards and engaging content hold the user's attention in an otherwise straightforward format.

The Tree Structure

A common structure for reference information stacks is the tree structure. As its name implies, a tree structured stack has a trunk and branches. Typically,

Figure 5-3a *Inigo Gets Out (excerpts shown here) demonstrates that a basically linear stack structure can be anything but boring.*

Figure 5-3b

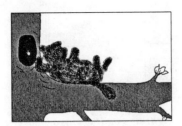

Figure 5-3c

Figure 5-3d

Figure 5-3e

Figure 5-3f

the branches lead to a dead end—that is, a point from which you can go no farther than back to the trunk. In a reference stack this kind of structure is fine, because the user typically is looking for a single piece of information that may be anywhere on the tree. Through one or more cards at key junctures, the user gradually finds his way to the desired information (Figure 5-5). These junctures are decision points.

The large HyperCard Help stack system (written by Apple's Carol Kaehler) is a good example of a tree-structured stack. The title card presents several tabs at the bottom of the screen—decision points to branch you to more specific information (Figure 5-6). Click on the HyperTalk button, for instance,

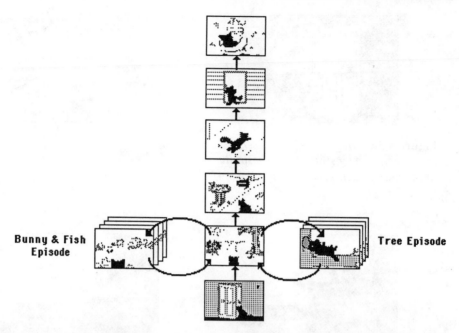

Figure 5-4 *Short, linear detours from the straight line path of Inigo Gets Out always return the browser to a familiar screen. There's no chance of getting disoriented.*

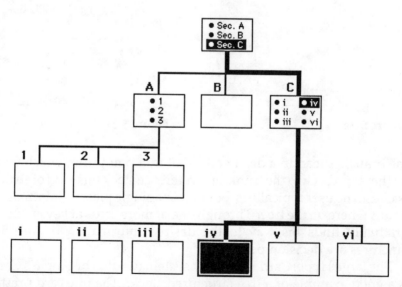

Figure 5-5 *A tree structure is useful when the information lies at the end of a series of decision paths. From that final information card, you usually exit the stack or return to the top card to follow a different path.*

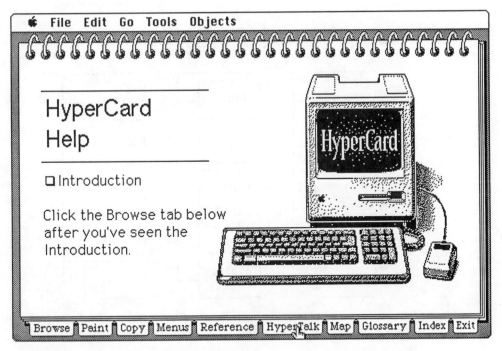

Figure 5-6 *The HyperCard Help stack is a fine example of a predominantly tree-structured stack.*

and you arrive at the beginning of the HyperTalk branch. Once there, you may choose to see more detail about a specific command by clicking on its word. While in the HyperTalk section, you may move linearly if you want to get an overview of all the commands. But more typically, as a reference, you find the information you're looking for at the end of a branch, and you're done. From there, you return to the command summary, the beginning of the Help stack, or back to the stack from which you originally came.

Information management stacks may also be tree structured, if the information requires it. For instance, the Projects stack (the stack name is FP•Projects) in *Focal Point* has an unusual way of linking cards into branches (Figure 5-7). There are six backgrounds for information cards in the Projects stack. One background is a summary card, through which the user typically moves in a linear fashion (or bypasses linearity with the Find command). In fact, I encourage the user to flip through the summary cards one by one to get an overview of the status of all current projects.

The other five backgrounds are detail cards that support the information on the summary card. Instead of the internal structure branching off to a linear collection of each of the backgrounds, the stack tightly links one of each style of background card to one summary card. From a summary card, you click

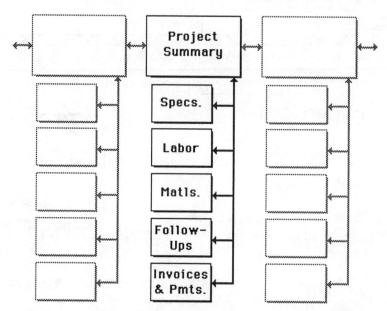

Figure 5-7 *Information stacks, like Focal Point's Project stack, may also be tree-structured. From any detail card, the only way out is back to the summary card.*

on a button that takes you to that project's specifications, labor worksheet, materials worksheet, followup schedule and financials cards. When you view one of these supporting cards, you may not navigate linearly to any other project's supporting cards, because you'd soon get lost. It is better to focus your perusal through supporting cards all within the realm of a single project. In fact, each of the supporting cards gives you only one navigation option within the Projects stack: to return to the summary card. You might also visualize this branch as a star, rather than a hierarchy (Figure 5-8). The HyperTalk links that make this possible are maintained in hidden fields on each of the cards. Details about this structure are featured in Chapter 18.

A genuine hazard within extended tree structure stacks, like the Hyper-Card Help stack, is that unless you design the stack carefully, the user can become lost. A kind of spatial disorientation can occur, and the user is left with no hope but to return to the starting point or exit the stack altogether and return to the Home Card. I believe the Help stack is a good example of a tree structure, because no matter how deeply you roam through the system, there are enough navigation buttons (tabs and arrows primarily) to get you back to familiar territory in a flash. That was not the case, however, with the first attempt at writing a HyperCard stack to supplement the 1987 Annual Report of none other than Apple Computer, Inc. (Figure 5-9). I'll save a detailed examination of this stack for Chapter 7, where you'll learn about making an

Specs.
Invoices & Pmts.
Project Summary
Labor
Matls.
Follow-Ups

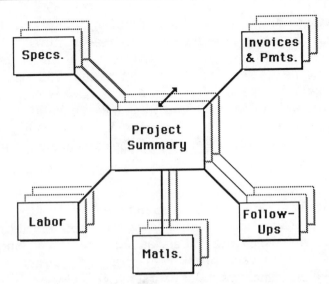

Figure 5-8 *Another way to visualize the tree structure of the Projects stack. Linear browsing is accomplished in the Summary card.*

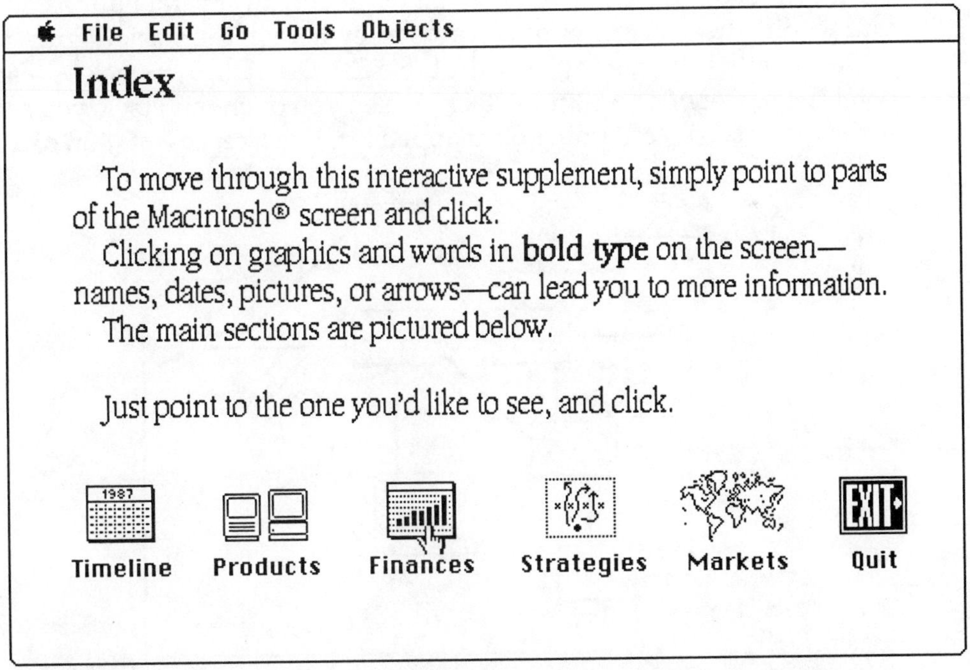

File Edit Go Tools Objects
Index
To move through this interactive supplement, simply point to parts of the Macintosh® screen and click.
Clicking on graphics and words in bold type on the screen—names, dates, pictures, or arrows—can lead you to more information.
The main sections are pictured below.
Just point to the one you'd like to see, and click.
1987
Timeline
Products
Finances
Strategies
Markets
EXIT
Quit

Figure 5-9 *A stack designed to supplement an Apple annual report was tree-structured, although it should have been less restrictive in movement across information areas. You must come back to this Index card to go from subject to subject.*

information publishing stack inviting and engaging—which this stack should have been. Suffice it to say, the stack was tree-structured but made me feel like I was falling through a time-and-space warp at times. I could not get my bearings. The problem, I think, was that instead of telling a more linear story, the stack designers made this standalone stack a reference, without enough clues as to what to do next. Something tells me that this stack started out as a block diagram on a white board in an Apple meeting room. The team got too caught up in structure and forgot the content along the way.

The Cobweb

I specifically avoided the term "spider web" for this third, non-linear stack structure, because that term may actually connote a well-defined, symmetrical structure, which the spiders outside my office window occasionally weave. But a cobweb, appearing magically in a corner of the ceiling, looks more like the visualizations of neural networks inside the brain—a severely intertwined ("intertwinkled," Ted Nelson would say) network of links.

HyperCard stacks can take on this structure, but there aren't many examples of it so far. In such a stack, there would be no particular beginning, middle, or end. In fact, it would be all middle, with several buttons on each card leading to a variety of other cards elsewhere in the stack (Figure 5-10).

One of the stacks that comes with HyperCard, the ClipArt stack, reveals the potential power of a non-linear stack. When you open this stack, you see one of the many cards containing bit-mapped art, like a representation of a huge

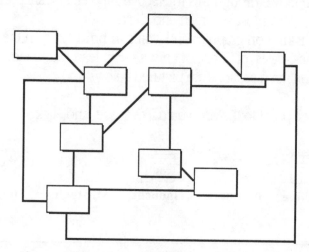

Figure 5-10   *A non-linear, cobweb-style stack may have a beginning, but from there, navigation can go in several directions from any card. Extreme care must go into preventing the user from becoming spatially disoriented.*

clip art library. When you click on the eye of the fish, the transparent button atop that eye takes you to the nearest card in the stack that also has an eye on it (Figure 5-11). Click on the wheel of the horse-drawn carriage, and you zip to another card with the picture of a wheel on it.

There is no special magic in this stack, although viewers seeing Bill Atkinson demonstrate this stack gasp at what's going on here. In reality, there is a field on each card with key words about major elements in the card's art—eye, wheel, hat, and so on. The button atop the fish's eye has a simple command in it that says:

```
Find "eye"
```

This summons HyperCard's search abilities to find the next occurrence of the word "eye" in that field, completely disregarding any structure (or lack thereof) in the stack. The links that join the few cards in this sample stack run all over the place, like the silky threads of a dense cobweb.

A stack like this is quite an adventure to follow. The paradigm of text

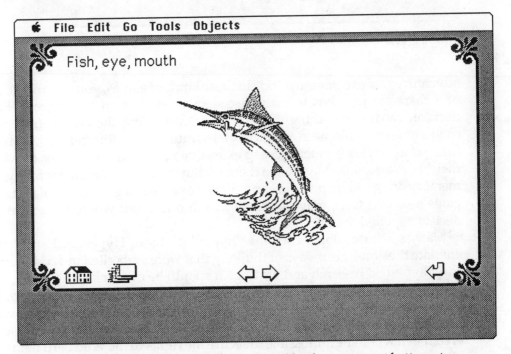

Figure 5-11a   *Perceived non-linearity is achieved by the transparent buttons atop various parts of the graphics in the Clip Art stack. From the fish (A) you may go to one of several cards, depending on what element you click. If it's the eye, then you'll go to the man (B), who also has eyes.*

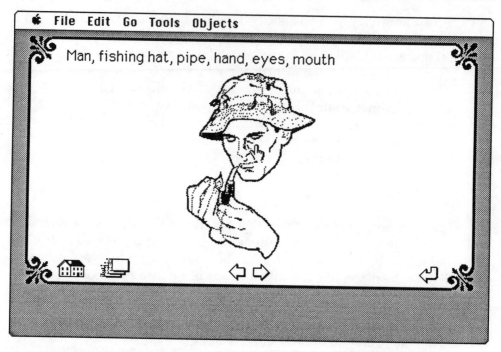

Figure 5-11b

adventure games comes to mind. In these kinds of games, you control the fate of a character who has to make decisions at every step of the way. Each decision causes something to happen, often leading the character to new rooms or level of rooms in a complex labyrinth (often subterranean). Adventure game players frequently keep extensive notes and make maps of where they believe the links have taken them within the maze. Were it not for a good memory or a good map, the user might be hopelessly lost or, upon playing the game a second time, may not be able to find the spot where the erroneous decision spelled disaster.

Many stack developers see the "hyper" prefix to HyperCard and try to emulate the non-linear ways of thinking that were embodied in Ted Nelson's early hypertext research and writing. It should be made clear, however, that the HyperCard name was attached to the product in the last two weeks of the product's three-year development. All during its gestation period, it went under Bill Atkinson's name for it, WildCard. When Apple Computer discovered that it would be impossible to secure the rights to the WildCard name, an alternate was sought. HyperCard was one of dozens considered. It wasn't everyone's favorite name, but it was clear for copyright purposes, and the product did allow non-linear constructions, so "HyperCard" it was.

I mention this as a reminder that while HyperCard empowers us to construct completely non-linear environments, non-linearity is not a prerequisite for a good stack, especially if the non-linearity is included at the expense of the user's logistical senses. There will certainly be some fabulous, entirely non-linear stacks coming from creative people—and I encourage research into such stacks—but be prudent in employing non-linear structures.

Hybrid Structures

Few stacks maintain a single structure throughout. More typically, a stack will contain elements of two or three structures. A tree-structured stack will very likely contain stretches of linearity, as the HyperCard Help stack does. It's almost impossible to avoid. Again, don't feel that you have to be "cute" in your card links. Linearity is the proper choice for some stacks in their entirety or for parts of more elaborate stacks.

Experimenting with non-linear, cobweb-style structures within a hybrid stack might be appropriate, provided you give the user some idea of where the current card fits within the cosmos of the stack. Perhaps a schematic map of the overall structure and the current card or card group highlighted on the map will help provide an orientation for the user.

Stack Systems and Non-linearity

Despite my cautions about creating non-linear stacks above, there is ample room to apply non-linear thinking to HyperCard applications. The best situation I've discovered so far is to link multiple stacks together in a non-linear fashion. *Focal Point* provides an excellent example.

In a typical *Focal Point* screen, the current stack is the center of attention. Most *Focal Point* stacks are entirely linear, with a few of them being hybrids of linear and tree-structure stacks. Yet the stack system provides for non-linear links between the current stack and any stack for which a button is visible. Here's an example.

While viewing a card in the To Do stack, you may select the text of someone's name and click on the button linked to the Directory and Dialer stack (Figure 5-12). By clicking that button, *Focal Point* immediately jumps to the Directory and Dialer stack and then searches for that person's name (Figure 5-13). The user sees nothing in between the Daily Appointment card and the Directory card with that person's name on it. The jump did not follow any predefined tree structure, because the button doesn't know where it will end up each time it performs the find. The destination is solely dependent on the name selected in the Daily Appointment card.

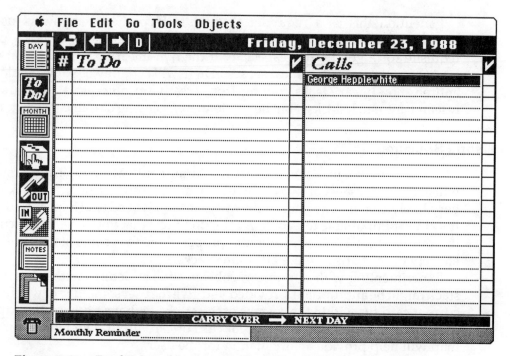

Figure 5-12 *Focal Point achieves practical non-linearity by linking all stacks with text selections. If you select text in one stack, and click on an icon button to another stack, the button takes you to that stack and the first instance of that selected text (see Figure 5-13).*

This select-and-find non-linearity pervades *Focal Point*. In any stack, you can select text and click on another stack's button to jump to the first matching instance of that selected text. Yet the user does not get lost in any way, because the destination stack—which is usually a simple linear stack—is well-defined in the user's mind by the act of clicking on its button. After the button's script has run, the user knows where he is and where he's been.

Had this feature not been built into *Focal Point*, the process of finding someone's name in another stack would have required a comparatively tedious passage through more structure. The easiest method would have been for the user to choose Find from the Edit menu, hold down the Command key while dragging over the person's name (to put the name into the find string), click on the button for the Directory Stack (which brings you to the first card of the stack), and then press the Enter or Return key to issue the Find command that is sitting in the Message Box.

The non-linearity introduced by the select-and-find instructions could also have been executed within a heterogeneous stack, except that the Go To part of the command would lead to the first card of a specific background, instead of a separate stack. Either way, this is one method to add productive non-

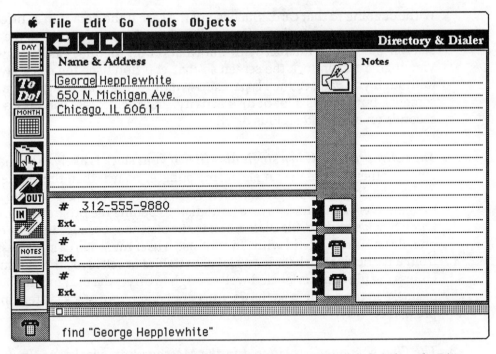

Figure 5-13 *Having selected text in one stack (Figure 5-12) and clicked on the Directory & Dialer button, Focal Point goes directly to the card that matches that selected text.*

linearity to a HyperCard stack or stack system.

Deciding Stack Structure

Once you've settled on your stack idea and you see that it requires two or more active backgrounds (i.e., more than just a title card and the rest of the cards in a single background), you have a big decision to make about structuring the product as a heterogeneous stack or a stack system. While each case is different, here are advantages and disadvantages of each method.

Heterogeneous Stack Advantages

1. *Access to information stored on any card in the stack is faster than if the cards are in separate stacks.* In fact, you are probably aware that you can retrieve information from a field on a particular card in the same stack

without going to that card. Such is not the case if the data is in a different stack—you must go to that other stack, get the data, and return to the first stack if the results interact with information on the first card you were viewing. You can lock the screen so that you don't see the stack switch (although you can see the HyperCard window title bar change on larger screens), but there is a lot of disk activity, and the process can take a few seconds on a Macintosh Plus or SE.

2. *The entire program is in a single disk file.* If your stack is likely to be shared among other people via an electronic bulletin board, then the single file makes sharing of the program easier. A single file is also easier for the user to maneuver within folders on a hard disk. Opening the program from the Open Stack standard file dialog box is simpler, too, because there is only one file name to contend with. In contrast, a user must start a stack system from a particular stack (to load global variables or retrieve other settings). Unless the file name is labeled well enough to direct the user to it in the list of stacks in the dialog box, the user may not enter your stack system in the prescribed way.

3. *The Find command, as entered in the Message Box, works for the entire program.* Because the Find command works only on the current stack, it doesn't know how to continue the search through other related stacks. You may script a search path through several stacks in a search button handler, but the script will have to be different for each stack in the system, because the sequence is different from each stack's perspective.

4. *It is easy to divide a heterogeneous stack into a stack system later.* By making copies of your heterogeneous stack and deleting all cards except those of a specific background, you can create a stack system from a heterogeneous stack. Combining a stack system into a heterogeneous stack is possible, but rather tedious (involving copying individual cards from the other stacks and pasting them into the one stack designated as the heterogeneous one).

5. *Debugging scripts is simpler.* Interaction among linked stacks can be a source of difficulty until you get the bugs worked out. For instance, if some of your stacks show the Message Box in an openStack handler, but you don't want it to show in others, you have to be careful to hide the Message Box with a closeStack handler. More complex openStack, openBackground, and openCard handlers may interfere with stack-to-stack information retrieval even when the screen is locked.

6. *There is no duplication of scripting effort.* If a heterogeneous version of a stack has stack scripts that maintain watch over the user's application of the arrow keys, or traps for certain menu commands, these will all have to be duplicated in the stack or background scripts of each of the individual stacks of a stack system.

7. *Compacting is more convenient.* Particularly during development, but also in the course of using a stack, you should occasionally choose Compact Stack from the File menu. You can squish a heterogeneous stack with one menu choice. A stack system requires either the manual method of going to each stack and compacting it, or writing a script that does it for you. Some users of *Focal Point*, for instance, wished the first release of the program had included a command or button to compact the entire stack system. I should have recognized that need because I had devised and frequently used such a script during *Focal Point's* development .

8. *The overall size of a single stack will be smaller than the same stack divided.* A completely empty stack takes up about 5K on the disk. That means that for every new stack you make for a stack system, you add 5K to the total disk space occupied by the system. In practice, that extra space grows even more. HyperCard, as you're well aware, likes to reserve disk space for stack growth if you type any information into a field. On a hard disk, it grabs a chunk out to the nearest 8K multiple. It is conceivable (although unlikely) that every stack in the system could be holding 6K or 7K of disk space in reserve until you compact the stacks. In a 10-stack system, that's a lot of disk space unavailable for other uses.

Now for advantages to dividing a HyperCard stack into multiple, linked stacks.

1. *Each stack can be dedicated to a finite subject.* In *Focal Point*, for instance, there is a separate stack for each of the 18 possible applications that come with the program, plus some help and utility stacks. I believe knowing that each application is its own stack helps the user maintain a concept of space within the entire system: "I'm in the Expenses stack now, so that's all I have to worry about." Just because the system is divided into multiple stacks doesn't mean that some or all of the stacks cannot be heterogeneous. On the contrary. The Projects, Proposals, and Expenses stacks are all heterogeneous (with 6, 5, and 4 backgrounds, respectively). Thus, some of the advantages of heterogeneous stacks can still apply to your system.

2. *Each stack is a separate file.* The advantage for many stack systems is that the user may decide not to use all the stacks and thus can reduce the amount of disk space occupied by the program. If there is an application or background in a heterogeneous stack that the user doesn't use, he or she may be hesitant about deleting those cards from the stack.

3. *Archiving of stack information is simpler.* Some stacks in a stack system may fill up faster than others or may contain information that should be saved as an archived stack. When applications are in separate stacks, the user can save a filled stack with a new name, and bring in a blank stack to start storing new information. This is particularly useful for stacks containing cards bearing daily dates. If a daily appointment book were part of a heterogeneous stack, the stack would continue to grow, year after year, with hundreds of outdated cards going along for the ride, needlessly filling up your hard disk. It's far simpler to remove the filled stack from the system, rename it, and drag into the folder a newly built stack for the next year.

4. *Adding to the system is easier.* Because of the inherently modular nature of a stack system, the user will probably find it easier to customize the system by removing unwanted stacks that come with the product and adding stacks that link back to the others in the system. Entry points to the existing stacks will be much easier for the user to locate than if they were buried in a 14-background heterogeneous stack.

5. *Restricting text searches is easier.* As many HyperCard authors have discovered, HyperCard's Find command is often difficult to work with when the search needs to be confined to only one background. In fact, at least through version 1.2, you cannot explicitly limit text searches to a particular background. If a search script button limits the find to a particular field named in the current background, HyperCard continues its search in the field with the same field number in the other backgrounds of the same stack. That can spell disaster if you are trying to keep some reference cards hidden from the casual browser. A Find command might display that card, causing all kinds of confusion. But if your stacks are separate and homogeneous (or only lightly heterogeneous), you can better control the way HyperCard will search for text in one or more fields.

6. *Sorting is easier.* Trying to sort a heavily heterogeneous stack can be difficult, perhaps resulting in a jumbled mess. But, again, with a system of

linked homogeneous stacks, the outcome of a Sort command can be better anticipated.

7. ***The risk of disaster is spread across more stack files.*** It's happened to a lot of us: Something went awry when HyperCard was writing information to the disk, and the stack went that-a-way. The stack became damaged beyond repair, or, rather, beyond opening. If that happens to a massive heterogeneous stack that contains tons of information, it's enough to make your heart stop. If it happens to one stack amid 10, then the loss won't be as great. I have no technical evidence to back up the following statement, but I always feel safer with several smaller files on my disk than one enormous one. You do back up your hard disk, don't you?

You see, there are many points in favor of both heterogeneous stacks and stack systems. Most often I find that the application dictates which method works best. A guideline I use is this: If the application involves two or more very distinct bodies of information, I'll go with the stack system method. If the application has one major group of cards supported by setup cards or other ancillary information cards, then I'll put everything into a heterogeneous stack, with as many backgrounds as necessary.

In all honesty, there are some cases in which the decision could go either way, as was the case of *Business Class*. But the ultimate decision about internal structure was heavily influenced by the necessities of external structure.

External Structure

So far we've been discussing the way you might collect or distribute information in stacks. But what we haven't said much about was how to physically distribute stacks to others and how a user's disk drive situation influences organization. These concerns—essentially how your stack product fits on floppy disks—are all part of the external structure of a stack.

One thing you can count on when distributing HyperCard stacks on floppy disk is that every HyperCard owner has at least one 800K floppy disk drive. HyperCard, as you're probably aware, requires at least the 128K ROM chips, which were initially designed for the release of the Macintosh Plus. These are also the same chips that are installed in upgrade kits that convert older 128K and 512K Macintoshes to the 512KE and Mac Plus equivalents. Part of that upgrade included an internal 800K double-sided disk drive, which is also the standard disk drive on all other Macintosh models.

Floppy Disk Concerns

An 800K disk doesn't really give you a full 800K of stack space, however. First of all, the Macintosh operating system grabs about 7K for the disk directory and other information it needs to consider the disk a Macintosh-formatted diskette. But more importantly, HyperCard stacks need room to breathe, no matter what medium they are stored on. If the user is allowed to enter information into fields, add buttons or fields, make new cards, adjust the graphics layers, or modify scripts, the stack will need to grow. If the stack is being used on a practically full diskette, HyperCard may not allow some entries to take place.

Interestingly, HyperCard is more considerate with tight floppy disk space than with a wide open disk. As soon as the available disk space on a disk drops below 64K, HyperCard grows stacks in 1K increments, instead of the usual 8K increments. Therefore, in the Stack Info dialog box, you'll see no more than 1K free in a stack's allocated disk space when the disk starts to fill up. Still, you must leave room on the disk for expansion if your stack accepts information input.

If your stack application is larger than 800K to begin with, then you have to make some tough decisions about dividing your application among disks. Both *Business Class* and *Focal Point* come on two diskettes, but the strategy in dividing the systems across the disks were very different due to the nature of the products. Here's what happened with each.

Focal Point Strategy

The "basic" *Focal Point* comes with 18 stack applications, plus a startup stack that contains the title screen and a couple of global variables used in some other stacks. From an internal structure viewpoint, the startup stack was maintained as a separate stack even though it automatically sends the user to the Daily Appointment stack after a brief delay of viewing the title card. By keeping the title card and global variables in a separate stack, however, the system is left open to change so the user may adjust the stack script to go to a stack other than the Daily Appointment stack if he deems another one more important to see first. Other *Focal Point* stacks that round out the system are the Help stack, a Setup stack (for customizing button locations and building or extending stacks consisting of daily cards) and an Import stack, which contains buttons to aid importing existing database data into the Directory and Dialer stack. Together, these stacks more than filled a single 800K disk.

Another factor came into play. If the program were shipped entirely empty, it would mean that a new owner would have to build the Daily Appointment, To Do, and one or two other daily stacks if desired. While the Setup stack simplified the process, it meant that the user would not be able to use the product immediately out of the box. The setup time—making all those cards by script—could be an hour or more, if the user decided to make a couple of years' worth of cards in the stacks. I knew that I wouldn't put up with such a delay if I had bought the product, so the dated stacks had to be pre-installed for at least a practical, realistic amount of time.

By putting the Help, Setup, and Import stacks on the second disk, enough room opened up on the first disk for an eight-month collection of daily cards for the Daily Appointment, To Do, Expenses, and Time Sheet stacks. Thus, on a single disk, a user had all the necessary stacks to get started. There was even enough room on the disk for someone using a floppy disk system to start entering data on a working copy of the original disk. In practice, many users found that they entered more data than there was space on a single disk, so they had to offload unused and infrequently used stacks to a third disk. With as many as 16 growing stacks vying for what was left on the original 800K disk, this wasn't surprising.

On the second *Focal Point* disk, there was now enough space to include a blank set of the dated stacks so users could build their own, as well as a set with 14 months in them, encompassing the end of 1987 and all of 1988 (Figure 5-14). The range of months included in these stacks and on the first disk are adjusted periodically so that new buyers have stacks with relevant dates in them.

For ease of installation on a hard disk, all the *Focal Point* stacks on disk 1 are placed in a Focal Point folder. All the user need do is drag the folder from disk 1 to the hard disk. To get help on the line, the user then drags the Help and Setup stacks from disk 2 to the Focal Point folder already on the hard disk. Stack systems can get messy when they consist of dozens of stacks, so it's incumbent upon the stack designer to make it easy for users to install the system on a hard disk without the possibility of missing stacks in the transfer.

Business Class Strategy

Business Class presented very different structure problems during its development. It started out as a single, heterogeneous stack, complete with maps and information cards for the top 60 or so trading countries of the world. While researching the information, it became clear that for purposes of maintaining potentially volatile information stacks, it would be better to break up the monster stack into smaller units—one for all the maps, and one each for the information categories. Until all the maps were drawn and all the information was gathered, I could only estimate the total disk space required for this stack. The maps soon grew much larger than I had anticipated. Unlike certain other graphics, which have large areas of repetitive patterns for greater bit-map compression, these maps were very rich in their detail. The degree of

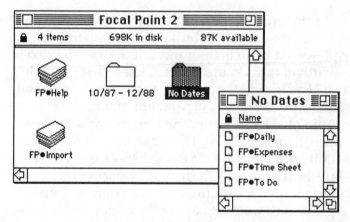

Figure 5-14   *Disk 2 of Focal Point had room for the Help system, text importing stack, and two complete sets of dated stacks. External structure influenced what files could go on each of the two disks.*

compression was less per picture than originally expected. Space required for the information cards was reasonable, but with 13 categories (and backgrounds) times 63 countries, a single disk was quickly overshot.

Rather than reduce the coverage of the world, I divided the system across two diskettes. By this time, I had one rather large map stack (about 650K) and 13 information stacks (ranging in size from 30 to 75K). The easy way out would have been to put the map stack on disk 1 and the information stacks on disk 2. Ah, but there's the rub.

Imagine a floppy disk-based *Business Class* user journeying through the maps, settling on Uruguay as a destination (remember, HyperCard and the System are in the internal drive, and only one *Business Class* disk is in the external drive). Clicking on any one of the information buttons would prompt the user to insert another disk (with that dreaded disk swap dialog box). Not only that, HyperCard may ask for a couple of swaps before finally reaching the desired information card. Now, from the information card, the user could access any other information card for Uruguay without any swapping. But to return to the map would require more disk swaps. That just doesn't work.

To solve this problem, I divided each of the stacks into two broad geographic regions. I placed the maps and information stacks for Europe and the Middle East on disk 1; the maps and information cards for the rest of the world went on disk 2. Thus, a user may browse through Europe or the contiguous Middle East—maps and information cards—without swapping a disk.

Making those divisions entailed extra work, of course, and also extra disk overhead for the entire system, because there were now two map stacks, two currency stacks, and so on. But the result was that the entire system fitted comfortably on two disks, which floppy disk based users could operate with the least possible inconvenience.

At the same time, it was important to organize these stacks on the two disks so that hard disk users would not be aware of the geographical divisions of the original disks. All the stacks for disk 1, for instance, are in a folder called Business Class 1; stacks on disk 2 are in a folder called Business Class 2. To install *Business Class* on a hard disk, the user must create a new folder called, simply, Business Class, and then drag the folders from each of the floppy disks into the new folder on the hard disk (Figure 5-15).

Regardless of the user's disk medium, division of the system into two geographical areas also placed a greater burden on the HyperTalk programming aspects of locating maps of countries in the other area. For instance, if you use the Business Class *Search* box to find a country or capital city by name, *Business Class* performs a HyperTalk Find on the string you type into the dialog box. The handler that performs that find must know which geographic group you're in, and then must search both map stacks for the name you typed. Additionally, when you click on an area of a map that is in the other geographic stack, *Business Class* must know that the desired card is in the other stack. To see how this was done at the HyperTalk level, see Chapter 30.

The point of this *Business Class* detail is that restrictions of external structure had a large impact on the internal structure of the stack system. To make the system easy for the user to navigate, the author had to put much more thought and effort into the system's structure and execution. Be prepared for this if your stack system grows large.

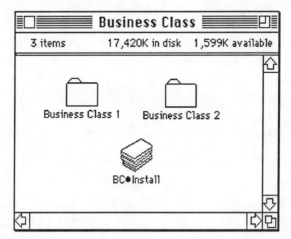

Figure 5-15 *External structure considerations caused Business Class to be divided geographically, with maps and information cards for certain regions of the world being included in the Business Class 1 disk. On a hard disk, the two folders are copied to an inclusive Business Class folder.*

CD-ROM Structure

With the advent of CD-ROM connections for HyperCard, the stack structure questions become a little different. First of all, CD-ROM stacks are read-only, meaning that they will most likely be the information publishing variety. The stacks won't be posting information in other stacks, but there is the possibility that one stack might rely on information retrieved from another stack on the CD-ROM disk.

Access time on a CD-ROM is slower than what you expect on a hard disk, so it may make more sense to keep information in one large heterogeneous stack than divide data into separate stacks. If I were to put *Business Class* on CD-ROM, I'd probably combine all stacks into one large one to assure the fastest possible access to information. And, because of the nature of this durable read-only medium, I wouldn't be too concerned about corruption of a stack file. HyperCard never tries to write data to stacks on a CD-ROM disk, so even a power outage in the middle of disk drive activity can't harm the file.

The potential of CD-ROM based stacks occupying perhaps hundreds of megabytes is a bit mind-boggling at this early stage of development. Most of the CD-ROM activity, I believe, will be in the business and academic environments, in which the CD-ROM drive will be a shared resource on workgroup or larger networks. HyperCard's forte at handling large amounts of information will certainly be a boost for CD-ROM and other high-capacity storage media. We may yet face new challenges to stack structure that we can't foresee until large-capacity media are more prevalent.

6

Converting Existing Databases to HyperCard

HyperCard attracted many people who had already assembled databases with the help of other programs. Between the fast full-text search and user customizability, HyperCard often appears to be a friendly place to move existing database applications. Before you do such a transformation, however, there are several issues you must consider. Among the most important questions you must ask yourself are whether the application is right for HyperCard, how fields should be rearranged, how reporting will be affected, and what to do with long text chunks.

Is HyperCard the Right Environment?

Deciding whether HyperCard is an acceptable environment for an existing database digs deeply into the discussion of whether HyperCard is, in fact, a database program. Perhaps because of the layout of text fields, which resembles database programs, many HyperCard reviewers and commentators classify the environment as a database environment. I disagree with that classification, even though you can create database-like applications with HyperCard.

Just as we discussed in the Introduction to this book, not all data-intensive applications are right for HyperCard. Moreover, it is not just the function of the information, but rather what you intend to do with the information that counts. When a database is designed to provide you with on-screen selected lists of information culled from the database, then a HyperCard version won't be of much help to you, even if it is faster in searching for information. Also, if the database is heavily relational, in that is relies on data from other data collections to display information, then it is better left in the database. Trying to replicate densely relational systems on HyperCard will not likely prove worthwhile from a performance point of view.

As a rule, then, follow the same guidelines laid down earlier for deciding which method—database program or HyperCard—is best for your database.

If your database is a read-only environment, such as an encyclopedia on CD-ROM or a large database available via on-line telecommunications networks, you'll have to examine your information's organization to decide if it will fit within the card-based environment of HyperCard. We'll have more to say about this later in the chapter.

Field Structure

By their very nature, true database systems are very field intensive. Typically, a database author defines a separate field for every possible chunk of information that may be later indexed, sorted, or reported. It is not uncommon, for example, to find someone's name and address book stored in a database set up in the manner shown in Figure 6-1. Each element has its own field, including two address lines and two telephone numbers. Often the two-line situation is caused by the database program's inability to allow multiple line information—each field can be one line only. I have even seen databases in which the author has created separate fields for each area code and each phone number for voice, modem, and facsimile telephone lines.

In a traditional database environment, individual fields let someone using the database perform selections and sorts on those fields. For instance, if you

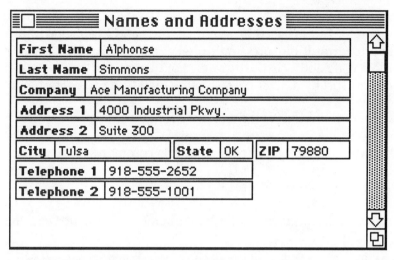

Figure 6-1 *A typical name-and-address database form, which you may wish to bring into HyperCard.*

needed to sort a mailing list by ZIP code to obtain a presorted first class mail discount, you would instruct the database to sort all the records by the ZIP field in ascending order. Then you could print out the address labels from the database in that order. To sort by names, you would specify the Last Name field as the primary sort "key" and the First Name field as the secondary sort "key," so that the resulting list shows all names alphabetically. If there were two Johnsons in the database, then the one whose first name comes first in the alphabet would appear before the other. So, given the sorting and selecting powers of databases, the individual field setup makes sense.

To an experienced database user, the intensive field nature of the database seems natural. But to those who are more used to word processors or to no computers at all, individual fields seem very restrictive. Thus, the Address stack that comes with HyperCard seems natural to many new users, because it replicates the field-less nature of the typical rolo-style card: You type in the name and address information in one clump, then put the telephone number in a separate spot on the card to make it easy to find.

When you decide to move an existing database to HyperCard, you should give serious thought to modifying the field structure to a less field-intensive layout, particularly if there is information that can be naturally grouped together, such as the name and address data, above.

Replicating Narrow Sorts

Combining database fields into single HyperCard fields does not take away the sorting powers you had in the database. Because you can specify HyperCard sorts based on specific words and/or lines within a field, as well as perform multiple sorts (multiple-key sorts in database terms), you shouldn't be losing flexibility in the transfer. For instance, in the Address book example, you can sort by a person's last name by issuing the command:

```
sort by last word of line 1 of field 1
```

Or you may sort by ZIP code with this command:

```
sort by last word of field 1
```

To sort by last and first names at the same time, the sort command would be:

```
sort by last word of line 1 of field 1 and first word of field 1
```

This last script, however, points up a potential problem for freeform fields, like the one in the Address stack. If someone enters a name in the first line of the name field and appends a degree, like "M.D.," then the sort fails its original intent, because the last word of the first line is "D," regardless of the doctor's real last name. Putting the "doctor" part at the front of the line won't help either. Unless you put a title in front of each name in the stack, such as "Dr. This" and "Mrs. That," in which case you'd perform the secondary sort on the second word of the first line, "Dr. Emily Jones" will be sorted after "Brian Jones," because "Dr." sorts after "Brian."

To Combine or Not To Combine Fields

It should be clear, therefore, that it is not always the right idea to combine database fields into single, multiple line fields in HyperCard. What you intend to do with the information rules how your fields should be organized. If the alphabetical sorting of your address stack is critical (it's not permissible for the occasional Ph.D to be out of sync with the rest), then you might want to have a more rigid field setup in your HyperCard cards. But, on the other hand, if you frequently copy the name and address from your HyperCard address stack into your word processing letters (assuming you're using Symmetry's *HyperDA* desk accessory or MultiFinder to view both your address stack and a word processing document at the same time), then it will be more convenient to put all name and address data in a single field. You use the Find command to locate a card, select the entire field, Copy, and then Paste into your document. Imagine having to copy and paste six or seven fields to get the data into the letter.

Another reason to maintain the original field organization is that field labels often help users enter the correct information—and all information—into the card, just as they do on a database form. When the fields of a card are not intuitive, then the field labels act as prompts for the user: The name goes here, the street address goes here, and so on. While the Address stack's rolo-like card lets you use that form not just for names and addresses, but for anything you might want to put on a rolo file, not many forms have that characteristic. Most cards have very specific purposes, depending on the fields that define that card.

Multiple-Lined Fields

That's not to say you should go overboard, like the stack I saw that had separate fields for area codes and phone numbers. For the sake of card performance, you should try to keep the number of fields to a minimum (early HyperCard versions had a maximum of about 128 fields—a lot, but sometimes not enough in spreadsheet-like applications). Remember, too, that HyperCard lets you use multiple line fields freely. There is no penalty for defining a text entry area as a multiple line field. In fact, it works to your performance advantage to reduce several distinct fields to one multiple lined field.

The decision to use multiple lined fields must also be predicated on how you intend to use the information. A potential problem with multiple lined fields is that the user may not put information in a specific line, as you expected when you laid out the card. Therefore, if another operation or procedure expects to find information in line 3 of a particular field, and the person who entered the information accidentally added or omitted a line, then the retrieved information may not be there or may be the wrong information.

A Case for Single Fields

As an example of how this might come up, look at the Client Record card in *Focal Point* (Figure 6-2). Notice that there are separate fields for the names and phone numbers of the three main contacts at the client company. If the information were not used in any other place, it could have been combined into one three-line field, with appropriate field labels identifying the information in each line (e.g., "Contact 1").

But a procedure in the Proposal stack summons this information. When you click on the Plus button next to the Client fields of a Proposal Summary card (Figure 6-3), you see a scrolling list of clients, a list derived from the Client Record stack. Clicking on a client from the list first pastes the client's name, client number, and billing rate into appropriate places on the five cards

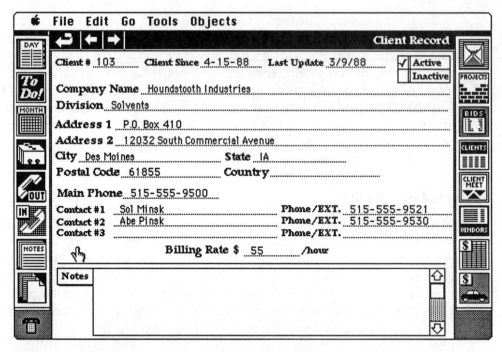

Figure 6-2 *The Contact and Phone/EXT. fields of Focal Point's Client stack were maintained as separate fields. Another stack had to make sure the information was always in the same spot for each client (see Figures 6-3 and 6-4).*

associated with the proposal. The action also goes back to the Client stack, finds the client's card, and copies the first two contacts and their phone numbers for insertion into the corresponding fields in the Proposal card (Figure 6-4). The procedure relies on the correct information being in the correct field. If there were any deviation from that format during data entry in the Client record, the Proposal record card could be out of sync. In the field-intensive nature of the Proposal record card, the separate fields for the contacts and phone numbers look right.

Remember, too, that HyperCard version 1.2 makes single-line fields a bit more friendly when the autoTab field property is set to true. A press of either the Tab or Return keys advances the text cursor to the next field

Field Design Tricks

At the same time, you can design around a single, multiple-lined field when it's appropriate, even tricking the eye into believing there are many fields in a section of a card, when a single field is better from the author's point of view. The *Focal Point* Directory stack is a case in point.

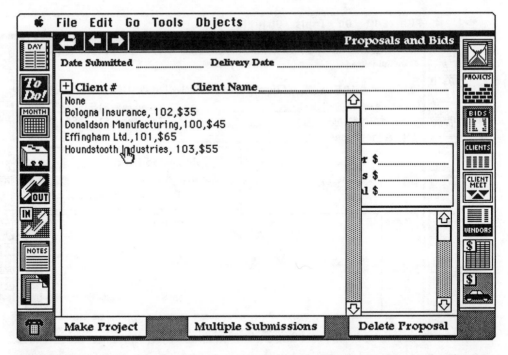

Figure 6-3 *In the Proposals stack, when you click on the Plus button next to the Client #
field, a scrolling list of clients (from the Client stack) appears. You insert one by clicking
on the name.*

Assuming that *Focal Point* owners very likely started putting information
into the Address stack that comes with HyperCard (it's one of the readily
usable stacks), I carefully designed the Directory stack so that data could be
transferred from the Address stack to the Directory with as little trouble as
possible. Therefore, despite appearances, which make it look like the telephone number section has three fields in it, all telephone numbers are stored
in one field, just as they are in the HyperCard Address stack (Figure 6-5). All
the user need do is click on a special Export/Import button in the *Focal Point*
Help system to watch all data being extracted from the Address stack and then
inserted, card by card, into the *Focal Point* Directory.

To make this work within the confines of a single field, two design elements
were called to work.

First, the positions for three telephone numbers had to be separated
graphically. The darker lines separating the three sections give the visual
sense of three distinct regions in that part of the screen. The lines had to fit
within the spacing decreed by the line height setting of the font used for that
one telephone number field.

Second, there had to be an easy way for the user to dial just one of the

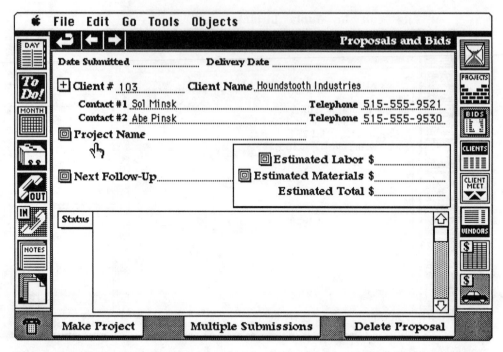

Figure 6-4 *Contact and phone number data is retrieved from specific fields in the Client card and inserted into the Proposals card. Because of the field structure, the information will always be correct.*

numbers, even if there were three in the field. In the HyperCard Address stack, if there is more than one phone number in the field, you must select it before clicking on the dial button—far too many manual actions for my taste. Thus, in *Focal Point* the three dialing buttons were attached to the three sections of the field. Not only do they add to the sense that there are three distinct telephone numbers, but they simplify the dialing. Their scripts are identical except for specifying which line number of the field they should dial—1, 3 or 5.

The net result of this design tactic is ease of importing and a distinct perception that there are three phone numbers possible for each card.

Importing Database Data

In converting an information publishing database to a stack, you will be responsible for bringing the data to HyperCard. The more you alter the field arrangement between the original database and the HyperCard version, the more complex the import script will be, but don't be put off by this.

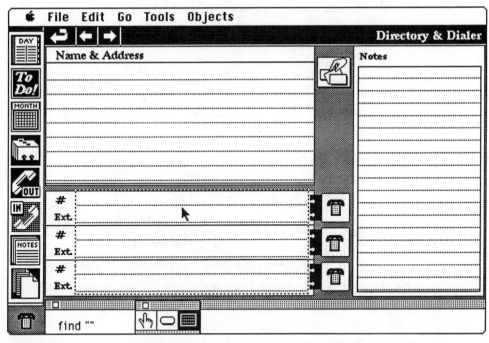

Figure 6-5 *With careful alignment of background artwork, the single telephone number field looks like it is three fields.*

Preparing the Data

The first task in importing database data is preparing the data in the database program. Regardless of the program, the desired outcome is a text-only file containing the information that is to go into HyperCard. Some database programs give you amazing flexibility in this regard, while others have only one option.

In a simple case, like a Microsoft Works database (this also applies to Microsoft File and other databases that let you save a database as a text-only document), the Save As dialog box gives you the choice of saving the data as an export file (Figure 6-6). What this means is that Works saves the data to a file separate from the file you normally use with Works. Information from your form is written to the file so that tab characters are placed between information from each field, and a return (like a press of the Return key) character is placed after the last field on the form. All the data filling one form is called a record. Thus, you can say that Works saves data in a text-only format as a tab-delimited field, return-delimited record file (Figure 6-7). Data from all fields in the form are saved to the disk file.

More sophisticated databases, like Omnis 3, Double Helix and 4th Dimen-

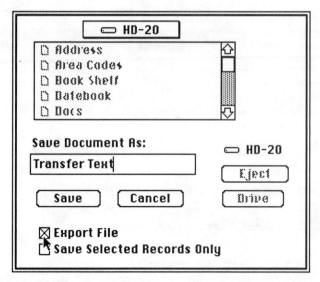

Figure 6-6 *Nearly every Macintosh database program lets you save information as a text file. This is the format HyperCard needs to import the data into a stack.*

sion, provide more powerful exporting capabilities. For instance, in Omnis you may specify which fields are to be exported, in which order they should be written to the text file, and what special characters should be used as delimiters between fields and records (Figure 6-8). The results are the same as the simpler databases, except you have much more control over which data you export (in case you don't want to take every field along).

The Script

Once the data is saved as a text-only file, you need an importing script whose job it is to read the information from the file and put it into the desired fields on the HyperCard card. Typically, the script is assigned as a mouseUp handler to a button you place (temporarily) in the new stack you're building. If your HyperCard field structure is identical to that of the original database, the import script is quite simple. Given a tab-delimited field, return-delimited record file, and a one-for-one field alignment, the following script should work nicely:

```
on mouseUp
  ask "Which file do you wish to import?" with "Transfer Text"
  if it is empty then exit mouseUp
  put it into fileName
  open file fileName
  go to last card
```

```
repeat forever
  doMenu "New Card"

    -- Read entire record into "it" at once
    read from file fileName until return

    -- If the record is empty, then get out of this loop
    -- otherwise, make the last field look like another
    -- tab-delimited field.
    if it is empty then
      go to first card
      close file fileName
      exit mouseUp
    else put tab into last char of it

    repeat with x = 1 to the number of fields
      put char 1 to (offset (tab,it)-1) of it into field x
      delete char 1 to offset (tab,it) of it
    end repeat
  end repeat
end mouseUp
```

Here's what the script does for you. First it presents a dialog box asking you for the name of the text file you wish to import. It displays a default file name, Transfer Text. If you saved your database export file with this name, you may just click the OK button. Otherwise, type in the file name and click OK. If you

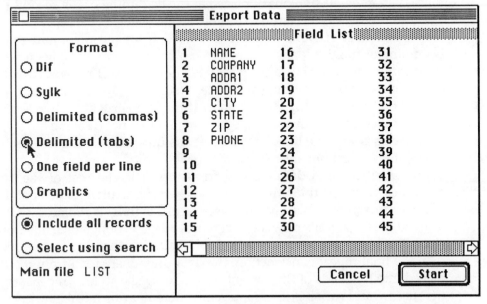

Figure 6-8 *Advanced database programs, like Omnis 3, offer you options about saving only certain fields and which characters are inserted as delimiters in the exported text file.*

click the Cancel button or delete the name in the dialog box, then the handler quits. If you click OK, the handler uses the name in the dialog box as the name of the text file to open. The handler then goes to the last card in the stack, so that new cards with imported data are added at the end of the stack.

The major repeat loop is the main action of this handler. It says "repeat forever" because there is a built-in stopper within the repeat construction, as we'll see in a moment. The first command the handler gives is to make a new card. Then it reads information from the disk until it encounters a return character—the end of the first record as saved by your database program. If you have a database program like Omnis or Double Helix and specified a different character to mark the end of a record prior to exporting the data, then that character should be used here instead of the "return." Be very careful, however, in specifying the record delimiter: It must not be a character that might be in your database text; it must be a unique character that will appear only at the end of records and nowhere else.

As you may recall from your explorations with the Read command (see Chapter 27 of the *Handbook*), the information HyperCard retrieves from the disk goes into the special local variable, It. Therefore, after the first Read command, the entire first record is in It. The Macintosh keeps track of where in the file the Read command gets its information, and holds a metaphorical thumb in the spot of the last Read. Therefore, after the first Read command, there is an invisible bookmark placed at the beginning of the second record. The next time the Read command comes around (within the repeat structure), HyperCard will retrieve the second record from the disk, and mark the beginning of the third, and so on. After all the records have been read, the Read command won't be able to go any further, because the bookmark doesn't cycle around to the beginning of the file. Instead, the Read command will put an empty string into It. Thus, a short if-then construction always tests for whether the Read command pulled in any data. If not (It being empty), then the file closes, and the handler quits—it has finished reading in all the data. That's the way out for the "forever" repeat loop.

But when there is data coming from the disk, the rest of the handler continues. The next thing that happens is that the return character at the end of the record (remember, the complete record is in It) is replaced with a tab character. This will simplify the next repeat construction, which relies on a tab character being at the end of every field, including the last one of a record.

In the final repeat construction, the data previously read from the disk is placed into the fields of the current (new) card. The style of repeat structure here uses a local variable, x, as a gradually incrementing number to refer to the HyperCard field number, corresponding to the number of the database field. The first time through the repeat loop, for example, all the characters from the first character of It to the character just before the first tab are placed into the HyperCard card's first field. Then the entire first field, including the tab character at its end, is deleted from It. That leaves the second field at the head of the queue, so to speak. The second time through the loop, x takes on the value 2. The second database field (in It) is placed into field 2, deleted from It, and so on until all the fields of the card are full.

You must preplan the field structure carefully, because if the HyperCard stack has one fewer field than tab-delimited fields saved by the database program, the data for the last field will not get into the HyperCard stack. It will still be safe in the text-only file, but you'll have a more difficult time trying to get that data into a newly created field once the cards have all been created and filled. It may be easier to do the entire import over again with the corrected HyperCard field arrangement.

Changing the Field Structure

Importing data into a different field arrangement, as mentioned earlier, requires a more complex import script. There is no way I can show you the precise script you'll need to accomplish the modified import you need, because I don't know the field setup of your database nor the field setup of your HyperCard stack and how you wish to combine previously separate fields into multiple line fields.

What I can do, however, is show you an example of a name and address database that is to go into *Focal Point*. The sample database looks like the one in Figure 6-9, complete with 11 different fields, which will be combined into three in the *Focal Point* Directory and Dialer stack, as shown in Figure 6-10. Here's the script:

```
on mouseUp
  global oneRecord
  ask "Which file do you wish to import?" with "Transfer Text"
  if it is empty then exit mouseUp
  put it into fileName
  open file fileName
  go to last card

  repeat forever
    doMenu "New Card"

    read from file fileName until return

    if it is not empty then
      put tab into last char of it
      put it into oneRecord
    else
      doMenu "Delete Card"
```

```
         go to first card
         close file fileName
         exit mouseUp
      end if

      put dataExtract() && dataExtract() into holder
      put dataExtract() into line 2 of holder
      put dataExtract() into line 3 of holder
      put dataExtract() & return & dataExtract()¬
      into line 4 of holder

      get dataExtract() & ", " & dataExtract() && dataExtract()
      if line 5 of holder is tab
      then put it into line 5 of holder
      else put it into line 6 of holder
      put holder into field 1

      put dataExtract() & return & return & dataExtract()¬
      into field 2
      put dataExtract() into field 3

   end repeat
end mouseUp



function dataExtract
  global oneRecord
  get char 1 to (offset(tab,oneRecord)-1) of oneRecord
  delete char 1 to offset(tab,oneRecord) of oneRecord
  return it
end dataExtract
```

The opening of this script is identical to the one just before it, except that it declares a global variable, oneRecord, which will be used by the dataExtract function, which is a second handler within the import button's script. After the Read command, the script differs markedly from the earlier script.

An if-then-else construction tests for the contents of It—that is, the data read in from the text-only file. If It is not empty, meaning that HyperCard was able to retrieve data from the disk, then the return character at the end of the record is replaced by a tab character, and the entire record is placed into the global variable, oneRecord. As with the previous script, if there is no more data in the file, the file closes, and the handler ends.

The balance of the handler must dissect the record and place various pieces of it in very specific spots on the Directory card, sometimes in specific lines of a field or even in a specific order on a single line, as when combining the first and last name fields into one line. To assist in this dissection and recombination, there is a separate function (a user-definable function, in HyperCard terms) that extracts one field from the record and deletes that field from the record in preparation for the next extraction. The decision to make this

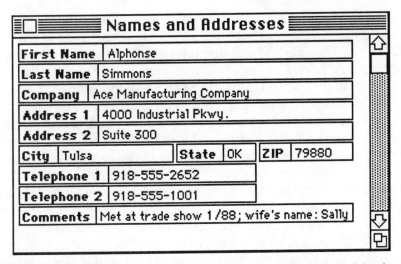

Figure 6-9 *For our example, we'll use this typical database. In traditional database style, each item is in its own field.*

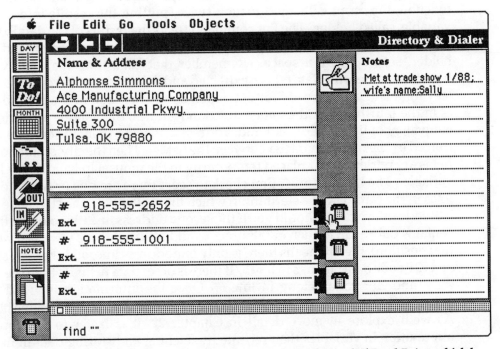

Figure 6-10 *The destination card is the Directory & Dialer card of Focal Point, which has the same three-field arrangement as HyperCard's Address stack (although the third field is larger here).*

extract-and-delete activity a function was predicated on the fact that we would have to call these operations once for every field of data in the record. Extracting the data and deleting it for each field would add at least two lines of HyperTalk code for each field in the record. By turning this operation into a function, the mouseUp handler can reuse those lines over and over, thus making the entire import procedure more compact and faster.

Because the record is read in the mouseUp handler and then extracted and chopped away in the function, the record data must be placed in a global variable—one that can be accessed by both the mouseUp handler and the dataExtract function handler. The action performed within the dataExtract function is identical to the action taken in the repeat loop of the earlier import script, with one slight modification. Instead of putting the extracted data directly into the field on the Directory card, the function extracts the data with a Get command, which, in turn, places the field data into the function's local variable, It. Then the function returns the value of It. Thus, whenever we use the dataExtract() function in the mouseUp handler (user-definable functions must have a set of parentheses after the function name), the function plugs in the field data.

Therefore, in the first line of the mouseUp handler to use the dataExtract function, the script calls the function twice, putting the results into a local variable, called holder. The Put command treats the results of the dataExtract functions just like containers, putting the first field and the second field into holder, separated by a space. Remember that each time the dataExtract function is called, the data is both extracted and deleted from the entire record, leaving the next field ready for extraction by the next call of the function.

In the fourth line of the data extraction routines, the handler extracts the equivalent of fields Address 1 and Address 2, placing them in separate lines (forced by the return character between the fields). Then the city, state and ZIP fields are retrieved, but placed temporarily in the mouseUp handler's It local variable. The handler must first check to see if there are one or two address lines in the card before determining which line of the field the city, state and ZIP code information should go. If the second address line (line 5 of the field) contains only a tab (which dataExtract would return if there were no data in that position), then it means there is only one address line, and the city, state, and ZIP code data belongs in line 5. If there is other data in line 5, then the city, state, and ZIP code belong in line 6. Once the information for field 1 is assembled in the holder variable, the data is placed into the field in one blow. As we'll explore in more detail in Chapter 22, it is faster to manipulate information in variables than repeatedly fetching and storing data in fields. The remaining two command lines of the mouseUp handler place the telephone numbers into field 2, separated by a blank line (two return characters), and the Comments field into field 3 of the card.

These two examples should give you plenty of guidance in importing database information into a HyperCard version of a database. Importing a collection of word processing text is a slightly different matter. It may be moved into HyperCard in two ways: by script or manually. But either way, you should give some thought as to the text's organization in the card style format of HyperCard stacks.

Importing Word Processing Data

One of the best examples of why you might wish to convert a word processed set of data into HyperCard would be to create a card system based on boilerplate text. For example, a lawyer might place various clauses and paragraphs of contracts into separate cards in a stack. With the help of a button on the cards, the attorney or legal secretary could assemble the text of a contract by finding the desired segments' cards and letting a script build the entire document, ready for printing or exporting to a text file for printing by a word processor. The point of having the boilerplate segments in HyperCard is to make it easy and quick to assemble the final document without typing a key.

Many other databases, especially those that contain excerpts, abstracts, or even full documents, are stored today in word processing formats. The allure of HyperCard for organizing and finding desired data is quite real.

Handling Long Text Blocks

A potential difficulty with creating a stack of this nature, is that the chunks of text may be very large—certainly larger than a single card on a 9-inch Macintosh screen can handle. That means, of course, that the text would probably go into a scrolling text field.

When the design of a stack assumes that the user will be browsing through the stack, card by card, then scrolling fields are not particularly appealing, especially if the browsing is to be not by card title, but by the content of the large field. Long text that is intended for reading should be divided into card-sized chunks, with ample navigation buttons around to facilitate moving through the text. Card-by-card browsing implies that the user can see an entire card's contents just by going to that card. Scrolling is inconvenient for reading. I also believe that scrolling fields are just plain unattractive and end up being less well-integrated into a card design than other types of fields.

From a functional standpoint, scrolling fields are permissible when the data in them is not meant for card-by-card reading. If access to the textual data in a long field is by the Find command, then its location in a long, scrolling field is not critical. When HyperCard finds the text, it automatically sets the scroll of the field so that the matching text appears at once—no scrolling necessary.

You should also feel free to use scrolling fields when the user will not see the fields. For example, in the legal contract boilerplate example, cited earlier, if the stack designer created a friendly front end to the stack that lets the person assembling a contract click on buttons corresponding to names of the components, the user may never need to look at the actual content of each component, at least not on a regular basis. The stack would then fetch the long chunks of text from their scrolling fields, even though the screen is locked, and the user doesn't see the cards from which the data comes.

Long Text Import Scripts

The methodology for importing word processing data by script depends largely on how the information is divided in the first place. Of course, before you could import it into a HyperCard stack, the text must be saved as a text-only file from the word processing program used to create the file.

Probably the only time a script-based import routine would be worthwhile is if the text you want to import needs to be divided from one large text file into a number of stack cards. If that's the case, then using the word processing program (before saving it as a text-only file) you will have to place some unique text character at the end of each chunk that is to go on a single card. Let's say, for instance, that the character you wish to use as a delimiter is the bullet (Option-8 on the Macintosh keyboard). Go through the original text and insert the bullets between what will become each card's text, and save the file in the text-only format. In your HyperCard stack, create a temporary button with the following script:

```
on mouseUp
  ask "Which file do you wish to import?" with "Transfer Text"
  if it is empty then exit mouseUp
  put it into fileName
  open file fileName
  go to last card

  repeat forever
    doMenu "New Card"
    read from file fileName until "•"

    if it is empty then
      go to first card
      close file fileName
```

```
      exit mouseUp
    else delete last char of it
    put it into field "mainText"
  end repeat
end mouseUp
```

This simple handler reads each bullet-delimited chunk one at a time from the disk and puts it into the main text field you've designed for the card.

Another method of importing word processing text involves the use of any desk accessory text editor, like MockWrite (CE Software). You may open up the text-only file (as saved by your word processing program) in an editing window atop the HyperCard card. Then select and copy the desired section into the Clipboard. Click on the HyperCard card, position the text insertion pointer to the desired spot, and paste the text into the field. If your boilerplate sections are scattered about in many different fields, then this method may actually be faster than trying to import the text by script, even though you need to invoke the desk accessory each time you want to open a text-only file (this isn't necessary on large screens, however, because the editor window will remain open behind the HyperCard window—position the two windows so you can click on one or the other, as you need each window).

A HyperCard text field can hold up to 32,000 characters. Unless the field or card is generally hidden from view, avoid placing large chunks of text into a text field. It makes it difficult to read and inconvenient to browse. If you find it impossible to divide large text blocks into card-sized chunks, then either the database shouldn't be converted to HyperCard or the HyperCard version will offer an incentive to create a user-friendly front end to a huge bank of textual data. The latter would certainly be more interesting to pursue.

7

Stack Protection

One of the biggest differences between the HyperTalk language and other Macintosh programming environments is that HyperTalk is very much an open system. HyperTalk program code is stored on disk in a relatively easily accessible format—straight ASCII text. Therefore, even if you believe the stack protection facilities built into HyperCard will prevent lurkers from prowling through your scripts (and it's impossible to keep them out anyway), they'll be available to anyone with a file editing tool, like John Mitchel's FEdit disk utility.

Why Protect?

In the early days of personal computers, it was very common for enthusiasts to share their experiences and hard work with others in computer clubs. Since a lot of the activity was the result of a hobby interest in computing, there was little to lose by revealing the program listings to friends and colleagues. In fact, it was more like show-and-tell, or even a bit of a boast to show others how you conquered the machine for a particular application or operation.

As the computer industry matured, programming became more of a business, and programmers started to be protective about their code. They didn't want someone lifting an idea that had taken much time and effort to create, and turn it into a commercial product before the originator could. Commercial competition, sometimes even within the same company, has created a generation of programmers who jealously guard the contents of their programs—the source code listings that are compiled into freestanding programs.

Along comes HyperCard, designed by a gentle spirit who still recalls "the old days" of sharing and openness. He designs a product with the idea that when people share ideas about creating stacks that the effect will be like compounded interest—users' facility with the program will increase dramatically in a short time. Only when existing software companies received prerelease copies of HyperCard to explore commercial product possibilities did the request—make that "demand"—for stack protection come loud and strong. Let's examine in detail the kind of protection available in HyperCard.

Private Access Protection

One method of protecting a stack is to forbid entry into the stack, unless the user knows a password. When you choose Protect Stack from the File menu, the resulting dialog box offers several choices about how the stack should be protected (Figure 7-1). The option we're considering here is Private Access. With this check box selected, you may then click on the Set Password button to assign a password to the stack. To test out the password, you'll have to quit HyperCard and then try to re-open the stack. You'll be prompted for the password. An incorrect password won't allow you access to the stack. A correct password lets you in. As long as you don't quit HyperCard after entering the correct password, you will be given instant access to that stack without having to enter the password.

Private access protection is not a good solution when running HyperCard on a multi-user network. If an authorized user successfully opens the password protected stack, then anyone on the network will be able to open

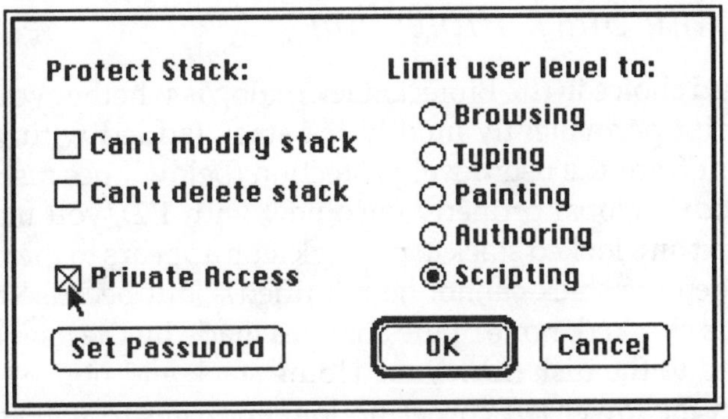

Figure 7-1 *The Protect Stack dialog box lets you adjust a stack's user level as well as request a password when opening for the first time within a HyperCard session.*

that stack thereafter, until someone quits HyperCard (presuming HyperCard is running on the file server).

Incidentally, the first release of HyperCard reportedly presented difficulties for some users who had protected their stacks for private access. A handful of users who had assigned passwords were unable to open their stacks, even with the correct password. HyperCard 1.1 supposedly solved that problem.

Stack Delete Protection

Another checkbox in the Protection dialog box lets you set whether the user will be able to delete the stack. Deletion, then, is password protected. Only people who know the password would be allowed to delete the stack.

In tightly controlled circumstances, such as in a network situation or in-house distributed processing system, this protection might be advisable, because the stack author won't want anyone to "accidentally" delete a valuable stack. But for a stack that is to be distributed to the world as public domain, shareware, or commercial product, this kind of protection is not advisable. Remember, too, that even though you use a password to protect a stack against deletion, the file may be dragged to the Trash in the Finder. And, while you can prevent a user from quitting HyperCard via the Quit Hyper-Card menu item (see below), the resourceful HyperCard snooper will know how to restart the Macintosh and bypass any Set Startup setting you've created to automatically go into the stack.

Can't Modify Stack Protection

The third choice in the Protect Stack dialog is whether you want to let the user or a script permanently modify the stack (added with version 1.2). This is different from the user level protection (below), because in concert with the userModify global property (also new with 1.2), you may let users paint or enter text on a locked stack (a padlock icon appears to the right of the last menu title when the stack cannot be modified). But because the checkbox in this dialog is checked, none of the changes made by the user or by any script will be saved to the disk (lock your Home stack and notice that the idle handler clock in the lower left corner no longer writes to your hard disk with each advancing minute).

This setting and the userModify global property are primarily of interest to those running HyperCard stacks on locked media (like CD-ROM) or in networked environments in which stacks might be locked to allow multiple access to the stack. Any changes you type into fields or make with painting tools may help in navigation or printing (HyperCard prints what's on the screen when you do a Print Card), but as a tool to keep snoopers out of your stack, it won't be any more effective than other HyperCard protection schemes.

User Level Protection

A stack author may set the user level of a stack, independent of the user level setting of the user's own HyperCard Home stack. Thus, if the user of your stack has the user level setting in the Home stack set to level 5 (scripting), you can still reduce the level in your stack by setting the user level to, say, 2 in the Protect dialog box. If you choose to password protect that setting, then the user will need to know two things: 1) the trick about holding down the Command key (at user levels 1 and 2) to access the Protect Stack item in the File menu; and 2) the password to access the Protect dialog box.

At first, the prospect of locking the user to a low user level sounds attractive if you want to keep your scripts to yourself. If you set the level to anything less than 5, then the user won't be able to summon the Script Editor for any object. Your scripts are safe from prying eyes, right? Well, no, they're not.

It turns out that even though you cannot see a script in the Script Editor with these settings, you may still access the script via another script. In other words, if you have a script that retrieves the script of a button (the script of any object is a property), then you can put the retrieved script into a container, like a field in a different stack, and print it out from there. That, in fact, is how utility products like Script Report work. They go into a stack, lift copies of each object's script, and then reassemble the scripts for printing or viewing. One script can also write the script for another object (e.g., set the script of a button), so even though you thought you locked down your scripts, a knowledgeable HyperCard user can dissect and modify the stack, difficult though it may be, without using the Script Editor.

Protection Problem

Locking the user level with the Protect dialog box can present a big problem for some stacks. The problem will surface early on provided you test your stack with the user level set to the low level.

Whenever a script in a stack needs to utilize a tool that is at a level higher than that set in the Protect dialog box, the script won't be able to access that tool. For example, in the Daily Appointment book of *Focal Point*, there is a script that summons a painting tool to literally draw a small box around the plus mark of an hour's label to indicate that there is text hidden in an associated field (Figure 7-2). For the script to draw that box, it needs the rectangle tool in the painting tool palette. The only way the script may use that tool is if the user level is set to 3 (painting) or higher. If the Protect dialog limits the user level to 1 or 2, then the script will produce an error dialog, indicating that the desired tool is not available at the current user level setting (Figure 7-3). Moreover, the nature of the Protect dialog setting is such that it overrides any change of the user level your script may command. Therefore, to try to set the user level to 3 in the drawing script would be useless if the Protect dialog setting had been set to 1 or 2. The same is true when your scripts need access to either the button or text tools. For access to those tools, the user level needs to be at 4 or 5.

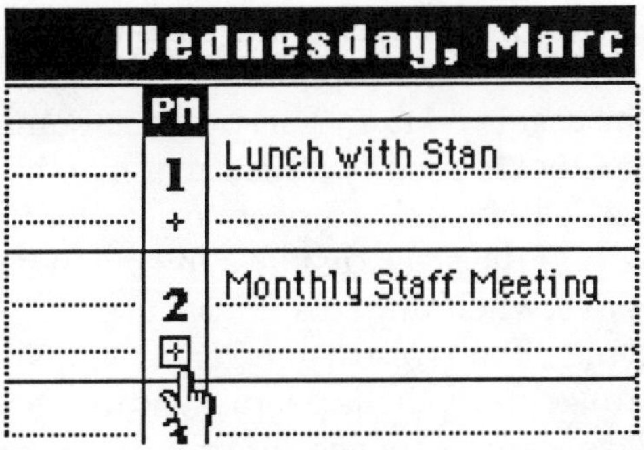

Figure 7-2 *In Focal Point's Daily Appointment stack, you may add information to a normally hidden field by clicking on the hour's number. If any data is in that field, the stack draws a square around the plus mark to remind you date is in there.*

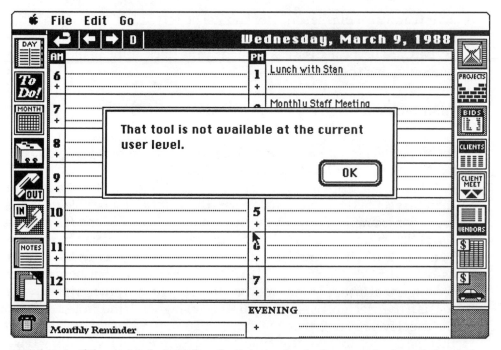

Figure 7-3 *If the stack is locked below the Painting level when it needs the painting tool, the script is interrupted by an alert box. You may not use HyperTalk script to change a user level set in the Protect Stack dialog box.*

When to Lock the User Level

Even though it looks as if it may be futile to password protect the user level setting, those user levels are there for a reason, and they make sense for certain kinds of stacks in special environments. Here are some examples.

Locking the user level prevents inadvertent modifications to stacks. Therefore, in a stack that might be used in a freestanding kiosk location, at which users are invited to browse through read-only material, it would be advantageous to lock the user level to 1. This prevents someone from accessing even the text insertion tool to modify a field that may have been left unlocked. It also prevents casual HyperCard users from modifying the painting layers, buttons, or fields. If the stack displays the menu bar, its choices are limited, thus being less overwhelming to a novice user.

The reduced menubar is also a good environment in an in-house corporate or academic setting, in which the people who use the stacks day in, day out are using the stack as a browsing and information entry system. By locking the user level to 2 (typing), the user won't be burdened by any more than the three main menu items (plus the Apple desk accessory menu), and the menus that do appear are shorter than usual.

When NOT to Lock the User Level

Whenever I talk about stack protection with experienced HyperCard users, the prevailing sentiment is that locked stacks are a nuisance, if not frustrating. HyperTalk-literate users seem to be forever curious about how a stack author structured various parts of the stack and how the scripts scattered throughout the stack are built. Moreover, if a user finds that the stack is useful enough to keep around on the hard disk, chances are that he or she will want to make some modifications to the stack. Typical modifications might be the addition of buttons that link to existing stacks in the user's collection. Many users also have established ways of going from stack to stack, which may entail changing visual effects. Useful stacks may also be blended into an existing stack system, so the user needs access to your stack's scripts to effect the necessary links between your stack and the rest.

To me the supreme advantage of using HyperCard applications is that the stack or stack system can be customized or enhanced to suit my needs. That's the essence of democratization that HyperCard brings to personal computing. No other applications give you that flexibility. For an author to restrict the addition of fields and buttons, or otherwise prevent the user from tailoring the application to his or her way of work is simply not in the spirit of HyperCard. That is one big reason why both *Business Class* and *Focal Point* come out of the box already set to user level 5. I even go overboard a bit, because I invite everyone to look at and learn from the scripts scattered about the stack systems. As a result, I often hear back from users about the ways they've modified the stacks for themselves, providing ideas for future enhancements to both products.

Something psychological also affects users of general audience stacks who encounter password protection to the scripts. It reminds me of two nearly identical houses in a suburban subdivision. One house stands there, like your basic house. The one next door has floodlights lighting the grounds, iron gates and brick walls surrounding the house, and intimidating signs about an alarm system that summons the county sheriff if an intruder should sneeze in the wrong direction. While the casual burglar would choose the unguarded house as the path of least resistance, the experienced burglar suspects that there must be something really worth stealing inside the fully armed house. Thus, when I start poking around a stack and find a request for a password to change the user level, I figure the author must be hiding something really neat or is perhaps ashamed of sloppy scripting. In either case, the lockout only peaks my curiosity and determination further. Instead of a casual glance at a few handlers, I'll be sure to take apart the entire stack and inspect every

HyperTalk word. I'm not alone, either.

Even if you get a kick out of slowing down entry into protected stacks, be aware that the public domain already contains utility stacks that disengage stack passwords. Where there's a will, there's a way.

The entire discussion about protecting HyperTalk scripts really comes down to one question: why bother? Since there is no secure way to keep determined eyes out of your stacks, it doesn't seem to make sense to protect stacks that go out to the world. On in-house stacks, as mentioned earlier, where casual users are the target audience, you can protect the stack primarily to save the users from accidentally getting into trouble. But that's about the only reason I can see to password protect the scripts of a HyperCard stack.

Commercial Proprietary Secrets

When I make statements like the one above, most traditional software developers and publishers shudder. They envision their works being dissected like a biology class frog. An open stack is like an invitation for others to steal scripts and scripting techniques for their own stacks. This is a legitimate concern.

One protection that developers have in this regard is the copyright law that protects original intellectual property. While there is no stopping an individual from incorporating your script in a stack for his or her own use, it is illegal for that person to use your scripts in a product that is redistributed, unless you have agreed to the arrangement. This is just like the copyright protection that covers printed material in books and magazines. If an author wishes to excerpt a selection from a book in another book, then that author must get permission from the original copyright holder to reprint that material. Sometimes the right to reprint entails payment of a licensing fee; other times the original copyright holder agrees to it in return for the proper credit line attached to the excerpt (in hopes that the excerpt will convince readers to buy the original work).

There's no question this still leaves a gray area. Can a stack developer modify someone else's script and claim its his own for publication in a new product? How many changes to the script's characters does it take before the original is no longer the original. And what about stack artwork? How many pixels can be changed to make it no longer a copy of the original?

Purists in the legal profession would say that if a work is derived from the original, then the second work infringes on the copyright of the original work. Truly original work must be just that: original. At the same time, some scripts will surely be copied and modified to such an extent that there is little trace of the original script, even though everything was derived from a copyrighted work. And in other cases, there may be only one elegant way to perform a certain operation. Two or two hundred stack developers may come up with the idea independently. How can you say or prove that one developer copied that script from another?

Unfortunately, the realm of copyright protection in stacks, as it is in software, will probably be tested in litigation before long. The safest way to avoid problems is to be original. If you contract out for artwork or HyperTalk programming, make sure that the agreement between you and the vendor states that the work is to be original (and that the contractor warrants such). HyperCard makes it inviting to borrow liberally, for not only are there scripts, card art, and icon art, but there are external commands, external functions, and sounds to worry about. Unscrupulous stack developers will try to "borrow" copyrighted work. If you're concerned about your scripts or other stack elements being ripped off, then it is up to you to monitor the stacks that reach the market through various channels and pursue those developers and publishers who use your work without permission.

True Protection

While I've made it clear that there is no way to protect scripts or other open elements of a HyperCard stack, you can still protect important algorithms that you design. If a portion of the operations taking place in a HyperCard stack are in the form of external commands or functions, that code is as protected from view as you can get.

As you'll learn more in Part III, external commands and functions (XCMDs for short) are written in Pascal, C, or Assembler and then compiled into a resource that attaches to your stack. These compiled chunks of code are in the same form as standalone programs written in these languages. For someone to decipher what is in an XCMD, he must disassemble the code, which generally provides an assembly language equivalent of the program. Disassembly, incidentally, is how engineers investigate programs in search of ways to defeat copy protection or learn how a computer's operating system performs certain operations. The first thing many seasoned hackers do when they get a new computer is to disassemble the ROM to look for clues to undocumented features or possible enhancements. In any case, I believe if someone is smart enough to disassemble an XCMD, they're entitled to the knowledge (although not entitled to copy it and re-sell it themselves).

Rest assured that disassembly of compiled code is not for the faint hearted. The typical Pascal and C programmers, who might want to see how you accomplished operations in an XCMD, are not likely to disassemble your code unless they're desperate and determined. An XCMD is a relatively safe place to put algorithms that you'd prefer not be in the hands of the world.

Fortunately, XCMDs can communicate with fields and objects in a Hyper-Card stack, so you could practically write the equivalent of a HyperTalk script in an XCMD. If much of the functionality relies on HyperTalk commands (instead of doing the information manipulation yourself in the XCMD), the performance may not be what you'd expect. But if you can replicate the functionality in an XCMD and keep communication with the card to a minimum, you may actually see a performance improvement—such as in a large math calculation.

Therefore, when a prospective stack developer asks me about protecting scripts, my advice is twofold. First I ask the reasons for protecting the scripts. If the response discloses a general feeling that no one should be able to look inside, I try to counsel against protecting the scripts. Second, if the developer has unique algorithms that should be protected, then I strongly suggest they be written as XCMDs for attachment to the stack. Do the bulk of the simple work in open HyperTalk; do the secret stuff in the compiled XCMD.

Buying and "Borrowing" XCMDs

If you're not yet into programming XCMDs in those other languages, then you can obtain XCMDs in two legitimate ways: get permission to use existing code; and contract the work for new code.

It's so easy to incorporate an XCMD into a stack, that it is often tempting to "borrow" a resource that is attached to someone else's stack or is offered for everyone's use in the public domain. Remember that copyright protection applies even to work distributed in the public domain. For you to incorporate such an XCMD in a stack for distribution to others, you must obtain the permission of the copyright holder. That's what I did in *Focal Point*. When I needed the standard file dialog box in the Document Launcher stack to make button creation simple, I found the filename XFCN written by Steve Maller. Even though Steve worked for Apple, he received permission to distribute the work in the public domain. I wrote to him, explaining why I would like to use the function and how I would credit the work within the product. Steve was happy to oblige, giving me permission to include the function in a commercial product.

If you cannot find a public domain or shareware XCMD that meets your needs, then it may be worthwhile finding someone who can write an XCMD for you. User groups often have knowledgeable Macintosh programmers who are capable of writing short snippets of code that go into XCMDs. As with an artist, negotiate a price based on the time it takes for the programmer to write the XCMD, or come up with a flat fee. If the XCMDs represent a major part of the product, you and the programmer may agree on a royalty agreement. As with working with an artist for graphics, be sure you obtain all rights to the source code of the XCMD. This will simplify matters if your stack product is marketed by a publisher or if someone wishes to license the XCMD from you.

I believe the future of commercial HyperCard stacks will depend on creative XCMDs made a part of creative stacks. That means that the talents of good artists, traditional programmers, and people with expertise in special interests will make for coming generations of outstanding HyperCard applications for narrow and broad audiences. As XCMDs begin holding more of the "gold" of a HyperCard stack, the worries about stack protection will diminish. It's better to spend more creative energy on the stack than on ways of keeping people out of it.

8

Engaging the Couch Potato

An information stack assumes a burden from the very outset. It must invite the user to start browsing, hold the user's interest, and leave the user with the feeling that the journey through the information was rewarding. The value of an information stack is directly proportional to the user's desire to return to the stack—to retrieve or store additional information.

In many respects, an information stack is like a television show. A good program captures its viewers with some kind of "grabber" in the first minute or two, prevents viewers from changing channels midstream, and then leaves the viewers with a good enough feeling to make them want to come back next week for more. In the world of HyperCard stack production, the developer is the producer and director (and writer), while the information is the star. It's the job of the director to make the star look good, to shape it into something that viewers—make that "users"—enjoy.

Make Stacks Inviting

To that end, I believe a good guideline to follow when building a stack is to make the stack inviting enough to interest people who would normally not get involved with computers—computer couch potatoes. Not to be confused with television couch potatoes, computer couch potatoes either have a predisposition against computers or simply have not been exposed to them. They're a tough audience. But if you can engage such a person enough to click the mouse button even once, then you stand a chance of converting a computer couch potato to a computer user.

As computer software designers target products for the computer couch potato, the rest of the computer community will benefit. The Macintosh started out as being "the computer for the rest of us." Its primary goal, although not stated in these terms, was to engage a new generation of computer users who were intimidated by the likes of MS-DOS computers and computer toys. A lot of that early Macintosh simplicity is now gone, but its original idea helped bring many people into computing who might never have made it before, at least not with the same enthusiasm and reward as the Macintosh community. Computing, in general, benefited from the underlying concepts of Macintosh's design. The same can happen from a stack written to engage a new type of user.

HyperCard and the Macintosh are well positioned for advances in couch-potato-friendly software, because the HyperCard developer community consists of a much more diverse group than what I call the programming priesthood. People in the arts, humanities, social sciences, and other disciplines now have access to a programming tool—a tool on a sophisticated computer. The results can be sophisticated software, bearing the expertise of its creators. That expertise would never find an outlet without a development environment like HyperCard. The people who know best how to engage computer couch potatoes are now in control of program design. There's huge potential in that.

Articles of Engagement

As much as we'd all like some easy formula to follow, it's not that easy. So much depends on the kind of information you're publishing or managing, how the art treatment blends with the information, the complexity of your structure, and other intangible elements, including the tone of the language in an information publishing stack. The challenge of making a stack inviting is where many of the points covered in previous chapters come together. Here are some suggestions to help make a stack inviting and engaging:

1. *Present an opening screen or sequence.* Tell the user right away what your stack is, who wrote it, and perhaps what it's for, if the stack is meant to attract passersby at a freestanding kiosk. The title screen or sequence should be a visual masterpiece, because it sets the tone for the rest of the stack. In the few seconds the title screen or sequence displays, you can grab or lose your audience. If it's inviting enough, the user will hang in there for more.

   An excellent opening sequence example is the one used for the Macworld Expo stacks (refer to Figure i-3 in the Introduction). If you want to view them, they are available from many user group stack collections. In the one for Boston 1987 and San Francisco 1988, the first six cards begin looping in sequence to present an effect that a small globe on the card is spinning. If you're walking down the aisle past one of the machines, the spinning globe cannot help but draw you into it. Then, when you click on the world, a series of 22 more cards zoom you in from outer space to the location of the exhibition hall.

   Focal Point and *Business Class*, as examples of commercial stacks, present the user with title screens, which announce the name of the stack system the user is about to enter (Figure 8-1). Since these stacks, especially *Focal Point*, are intended for daily business use, the opening sequence was maintained as a single screen (although with interesting dissolve visual effects) that can be bypassed quickly by a click of the mouse. To force the user to sit through a 5 or 10-second flashy intro several times a day would not endear the user to the product after long.

2. *Use visual effects wisely.* Even in a business software environment, users prefer to be intelligently entertained, as long as the entertainment value does not overpower the informational task of the program. HyperCard's visual effects add a great deal of entertainment value, even when the effects are there to help the user gain some spatial perception of what action a button incites. Those users who may have experience on the Macintosh but little in HyperCard will be "wowed" by quality visual effects in the right spot.

Figure 8-1 *An opening screen, like the one for Focal Point, helps orient the user about the stack or stack system he is about to enter.*

For instance, while the title cards of *Focal Point* and *Business Class* are single cards, they come to life for the user because of a special combination of two dissolve visual effects—a dissolve to black followed by a normal dissolve. By adding the dissolve to black, the dissolve is much stronger because the black sets up a more distinct divider between the previous screen (usually the Home Card) and the *Focal Point* system. A regular dissolve by itself may actually be confusing, because it might imply a transition between two related screens, rather than two very dissimilar screens. I've seen one *Focal Point* user also attach a sound resource to his Home stack so that when you click on the *Focal Point* button, the computer issues the Star Trek Transporter sound. Just like the Transporter dissolves a person in one place and reassembles the molecules in another, so does the *Focal Point* button bring you into a different domain. Within a stack, visual effects can play a big role in a person's enjoyment. Selecting the right visual effect is not a task to take lightly. It should be done only with extensive experimentation and comparative testing on users. Turning pages, for example, can be accomplished with a few different visual effects—scrolling, wiping, and zooming. On some cards, the effect of scrolling is not as dramatic as you may first think, especially if the information content in fields is sparse. The change from one card to the next may not be big enough for the scrolling to be visually effective. Wipes usually work best for going to next or previous cards. But when you use them, remember that the wipe direction is opposite to the direction the user is progressing through the stack. For example, when the user clicks on a right-facing arrow to go to the next card, the wipe direction is to the left, just like turning the page of a book to the left to advance to the next page (Figure 8-2).

Zooming is an effect that must be used carefully. HyperCard acknowledges the location of the mouse click that triggers a Zoom Open visual effect. The zoom action emanates from the click location. This is what you probably want. But be aware that when the Zoom Close visual effect occurs, it zooms back toward the center of the screen. There is no connection to the spot from which the last Zoom Open visual effect took place. This might be confusing to the user, depending on your screen design. If the card designs are different enough, the user probably won't recognize that the zoom closing is focused on the center of the card, because the Zoom Open made a significant spatial impression in the first place.

Barn doors and irises are useful effects when changing levels within a tree structure. Use the Open parameter to these visual effects when diving down a level; use Close when resurfacing to a higher level.

So far I have yet to see a respectable example of either the checkerboard or venetian blind effects, but there must be good stacks out there somewhere that put these effects to good use. I believe with a carefully planned series of cards designed especially for these effects, some striking visuals are possible. You can also expect to see additional visual effects added to

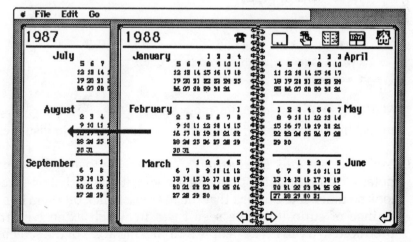

Figure 8-2 *When clicking on the right arrow to advance through a stack, the visual effect should go to the left.*

HyperCard as it evolves, primarily to aid the effects of flipping from card to card in a linear sequence.

Also be sure to exploit the Lock Screen and Unlock Screen commands that are new to HyperCard version 1.2. Because these commands (which are different from setting the lockScreen property) may be used in concert with visual effects, you can create interesting ways of hiding and showing objects on a single card. For example, a background button might trigger a dissolve effect that shows a card layer graphic and a button:

```
on mouseUp
  lock screen
  set the visible of card field "Instructions"¬
  to not the visible of card field "Instructions"
  unlock screen with dissolve
end mouseUp
```

The effect that used to take two cards may now be done in one. You may even combine visual effects for going to a card and visual effects for hiding or showing an object in the same script. For example:

```
--Version 1.2 has four new script shortcuts for objects:
--  bg   =   background
--  cd   =   card
--  fld  =   field
--  pict =   picture
on mouseUp
  visual effect iris open
  go to card 1 of bg "Detail"
  lock screen
  show cd pict
  show cd fld "Timer"
  unlock screen with barn door open
end mouseUp
```

Notice that the visual effect for showing the objects comes with the unlocking of the screen, and is independent of the Go visual effect.

3. *Make buttons look like buttons.* When trying to attract computer couch potatoes to information publishing stacks, it is vital that on-screen buttons look so much like buttons that the user *must* click on them to satisfy even a tinge of curiosity. I've seen cases in which extensive artwork was produced to try to invite people into clicking areas of the screen, but to my eye the attempt failed. Figure 8-3, for instance, shows a screen from the

Megacorp demonstration stack that Apple commissioned for the release of HyperCard. The huge bars may be attractive in their three-dimensionality, but are they buttons? To some users perhaps, but not to everyone.

That's not to say every button must look like a round rectangle button (which only experienced Macintosh users would recognize as a button). Skillfully crafted icon art attached to buttons invite clicking. So do on-screen representations of buttons from machines or common electrical and electronic devices.

On this subject, I'll have to admit that the opening screen of *Business Class*, which shows a world map, is not intuitive enough to invite the first-time user into the system. Is it natural for someone to want to click on a region of the world? To anyone who has used the system even once, the answer is "yes." But to someone seeing *Business Class* in a freestanding display, say at a travel agency, I'm not sure the need to click on a part of the world is compelling enough. Perhaps a simple message of some kind or even blocks around the possible regions would be more inviting. These two possibilities are shown in Figures 8-4 and 8-5. Which do you think would be more inviting to the person walking by the machine? Or is there yet a better way?

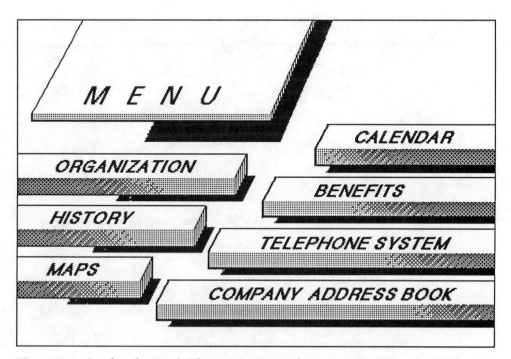

Figure 8-3 *Are these buttons? The art overpowers the message that these should be clicked by the mouse.*

4. *Use the appropriate structure.* By all means don't be so clever in your stack structure that the uninitiated HyperCard user will get lost within myriad backgrounds, tree branches, and non-linear extensions. If the stack is being designed to help a user find a particular piece of information, simplify the pathway to that information. If the stack is telling a story, don't let the user wander far afield from your linear track.

As noted earlier, one of the most highly visible stacks yet with one of the worst examples of appropriate structure was the HyperCard supplement to Apple's 1987 Annual Report. I feel as though it leads me down dead end paths, and I never know when I've seen the whole stack.

5. *Transform data entry into mouse clicks.* A welcome technique for data entry kinds of stacks is to find a way to codify the entries that fields require. The more you can limit the information in very specific fields, the easier it is to create pull-down lists or selections of buttons that enter data into the fields with a click of the mouse. Figure 8-6 shows two methods of simplifying this kind of data entry. In one, a HyperTalk generated list of options and radio buttons lets a user select one choice for entry into the field. The list appears whenever the user clicks on the field title. In the

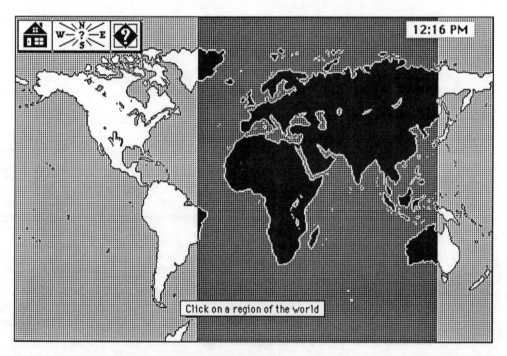

Figure 8-4 *Perhaps the opening map-menu of Business Class should have had an instruction on it about what to do...*

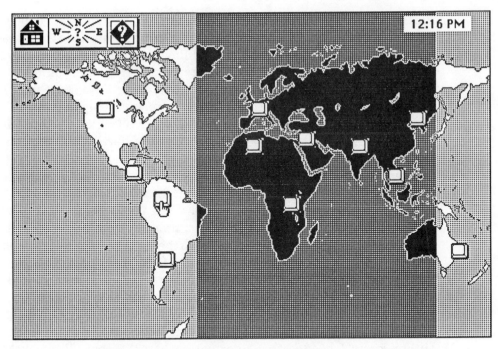

Figure 8-5 *...or things that looked like buttons to press.*

second example, an XCMD (described in Chapter 28) presents a pop-up menu of items when the user clicks and holds the mouse button on the field title. Choosing an item for entry into the field is done the same way you choose an item in a pull-down menu.

No matter how you do it, if you can eliminate typing of data into fields, then the users of your stack will be more likely to adopt the application, and feel like they're getting more work done with less energy.

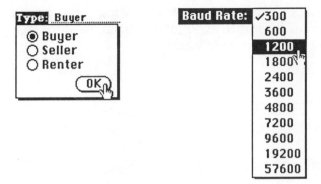

Figure 8-6 *Reducing the fear of typing is possible by making date entry the result of clicking on buttons (left) or with the help of XCMD-manufactured pop-up menus (right).*

6. *Build magic into the application.* When I think about the concept of putting magic in a stack, the first visions to come to mind are the fantastically elaborate domino toppling exhibitions that appear in the television news from time to time. That's where the push of one domino sets in motion the most amazing display of gravity in action you've ever seen. These displays can run for 20 minutes or more, involving literally millions of dominos that form multicolor mosaics, set off toy rockets, "climb" stairs, and much more. All of that is magic because it starts with the press of a single domino.

Therefore, a stack that contains magic has lots of activity connected to some simple operations, whether they be triggered by closing a field or by clicking a button. Magic, of course, can come in many guises, depending on the stack application. It could be as simple as triggering a recalculation of an on-screen spreadsheet replica, with the totals filling in one by one. It may involve information entered into one field being posted in a related, linked stack that doesn't even appear on the screen—all the user knows is that the information will be in the other stack when it's needed.

One of the tests I use to determine the amount of magic in a stack is whether I ask myself, "How did the author do that?" or "How did the author know I needed that information here?" That Ol' Stack Magic requires extra work and planning on the author's part. Anticipation of the user's needs is critical. Thus, it helps that the author be a user of the application, not just a distant designer of someone else's basic idea. When the author designs a stack for his own use, the fine touches, the anticipated features, the convenience—the magic—usually find their way into the application.

These are the elements that make stacks inviting and engaging. How well does your design measure up?

Another part of the magic that becomes more magic for fellow stack authors than for the user is building customizability into your stacks. Users will come to expect it, but it's not always so easy to accommodate, as we see in the next chapter.

9

Making Stacks Customizable

Someone once asked me whether I'd prefer to have *Focal Point* programmed in a traditional programming environment instead of Hyper-Card. Presumably he was concerned by some intensive arithmetic operations which were relatively slow with HyperCard 1.1 and earlier, perhaps about the extra second or two that it takes to go from one stack to another, and perhaps about the limited report printing abilities inherent in HyperCard. While I'd like to see all these improved (as they will be in future releases of *Focal Point* and HyperCard), nothing could sway me from keeping this organizational system riding on top of HyperCard.

The reason is that such systems must be customizable by the user, and HyperCard opens the door to the widest possible customizing pathways anyone can imagine.

When you design a stack for general consumption, a stack that will become the repository of the user's information, it would be presumptuous on your part to impose a card layout that every user *must* use. This kind of stack has two potential customers: 1) those who already do what your stack does (either on paper or in another program); and 2) those who adopt your stack to organize previously unorganized information.

To appeal to the group that already has a notion of working with the information in an organized fashion, your stack must first of all offer some vast improvement over existing systems. From a marketing perspective, your product must be different enough to draw the interest of those who already know what the product should be doing. If the differences and improvements are compelling enough, you will turn many tire-kickers into buyers.

But new owners already have a way of handling the information that may be slightly different from the system that works perfectly for you. For example, if their previous system includes a client database, they may have a field for a category code. Some client database designers prefer a two-character code number to distinguish categories, while others prefer fuller descriptions. If you design the database around a two-character number, then the user should have the option of lengthening the field to accommodate his or her longer coding system.

Leaving Clues

While adding or extending the length of a field on a card is not particularly difficult to do, more detailed modifications may require deep investigations into the scripts of your stacks. Have a heart, and place comments in critical areas of your scripts to help modifying users find their way through your handlers.

Documenting your stack internally is especially important when the handlers that react to the major mouse and field messages (mouseUp, mouseDown, mouseDown, closeField, openField) are in the background. For example, in the Monthly calendar stack of *Focal Point*, one background handler responds to the closeField message, which is initially sent to any of the two-line fields in a day's box. The handler copies the short text typed into a day's box and transfers it to the Monthly Reminder fields of the corresponding day's Daily Appointment and To Do list cards. Rather than have virtually identical handlers in each of the two-line fields of the card (there are 37 in anticipation of all possible combinations of date locations in a month), the one background closeField handler figures out which day of the month is connected to the text entered into a field. The fields have no handlers at all. To help the user figure out what's going on, there is a brief comment at the top of the background closeField handler to identify its purpose within the stack (Figure 9-1). The same is true for the mouseUp handler, which responds to clicks of the day's numbers on the calendar to go to the Daily Appointment or To Do cards for that date. We'll have more to say about positioning handlers in backgrounds and commenting style later in the book.

Customizing Front Ends

In Chapter 1, we looked briefly at the button customization card that lets *Focal Point* users define which applications buttons should be on their cards. Even for HyperLiterate users, certain customizing chores are tedious at best. Therefore, I strongly favor including friendly front ends to complex customizing tasks.

Building a friendly front end is not always simple, but the long term benefits far outweigh the work that goes into it. To give you a better idea of what can be involved in creating a front end to stack customization, we'll look closely

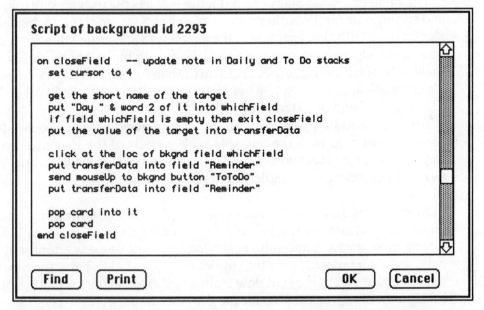

```
Script of background id 2293

on closeField    -- update note in Daily and To Do stacks
  set cursor to 4

  get the short name of the target
  put "Day " & word 2 of it into whichField
  if field whichField is empty then exit closeField
  put the value of the target into transferData

  click at the loc of bkgnd field whichField
  put transferData into field "Reminder"
  send mouseUp to bkgnd button "ToToDo"
  put transferData into field "Reminder"

  pop card into it
  pop card
end closeField
```

Find   Print   OK   Cancel

Figure 9-1 *Label scripts that are in odd places—like this closeField handler attached to a background—so that script readers and customizers will understand who does what.*

at the two customizing front ends built into *Focal Point* and one built into *Business Class*. The simpler of the two *Focal Point* front ends lets the user build or extend stacks that have a card for each day of the year. From *Business Class* comes a front end to setting the user's local time zone so that all time conversions work correctly. Then we'll take a closer look at the *Focal Point* button customization system, since it represents one of the most complex customizing routines you're likely to encounter.

Building and Extending Dated Stacks

Among the 18 *Focal Point* stacks are four that have cards for each day of the year: Daily Appointment, To Do, Expenses, and Time Sheet. Of these four stacks, three are homogeneous, while the Expenses stack has four backgrounds. As noted earlier, these stacks come in three different configurations: empty, filled to 8 months, and filled to 14 months. In typical use, the *Focal Point* user will start putting data into the 8-month stacks, because they're the ones that come to the screen without any special manipulation of the stack files. When the user reaches the end of the 8-month section, he has the option of archiving the existing files and building new ones, or simply extending the current files. In either case the process of filling out the dated stacks is best handled automatically by HyperTalk scripts, which are part of the *Focal Point* help system.

The Build or Extend Stacks card (Figure 9-2) lets the user specify a starting and ending date for the build process, as well as a way to signify which stacks should be so built. For example, if the user does not use the Time Sheet stack, then it would be a waste of time and disk space to build that stack. To select the stacks for building, the user clicks on the name of each desired stack so that a checkmark appears next to its name. Those that are checked will be built. Clicking the Build or Extend button starts the procedure.

All stack building is conducted by a long handler, plus some special handlers that help with the multiple backgrounds of the Expenses system. Depending on the condition of the checked fields atop the stack names in the Build/Extend card, the handler carries out commands for only the selected stacks.

After the stacks are built, the handler adds one more finishing touch to make the system more friendly for the next time the user needs to build or extend these stacks. The handler calculates the date one day after the ending date, and then puts that date into the starting date field. Thus, the next time stacks need building, the start date is already there, and the user need not look back on the stacks to see how far the previous build went.

The Expenses stack needs special treatment. While the other stacks have one day per card, and the long date plugged into a field on each card, the

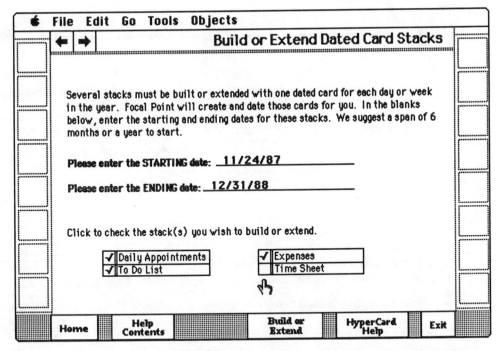

Figure 9-2 *Building or extending dated stacks in Focal Point is greatly simplfied with this front end. Type two dates and click on a couple stack names. The Build or Extend button (bottom) does the rest.*

Expenses stack has a weekly summary card, which must be dated with the Sunday of each week, and daily cards, which carry their own dates. Moreover, the stack building handler must establish hard links between each week's summary card and the daily cards for that week (and vice versa). Doing this kind of stack creation manually would be a nightmare, even for an experienced HyperCard user. The front end to this stack building was essential.

Customizing User Preferences

The first time you start *Business Class*, you come to the stack system's Preferences card (Figure 9-3). In this card, the user must make several settings that affect other parts of the system. By far the most important is the time zone in which the user's Macintosh is operating. *Business Class* must know this to accurately display the day/night lines in the main menu card showing the world map, as well as calculate foreign times in the often-used time conversion cards.

Time zones are mysterious subjects to many people, including frequent globe-trotters, so it was important to design a front end to setting the time zone

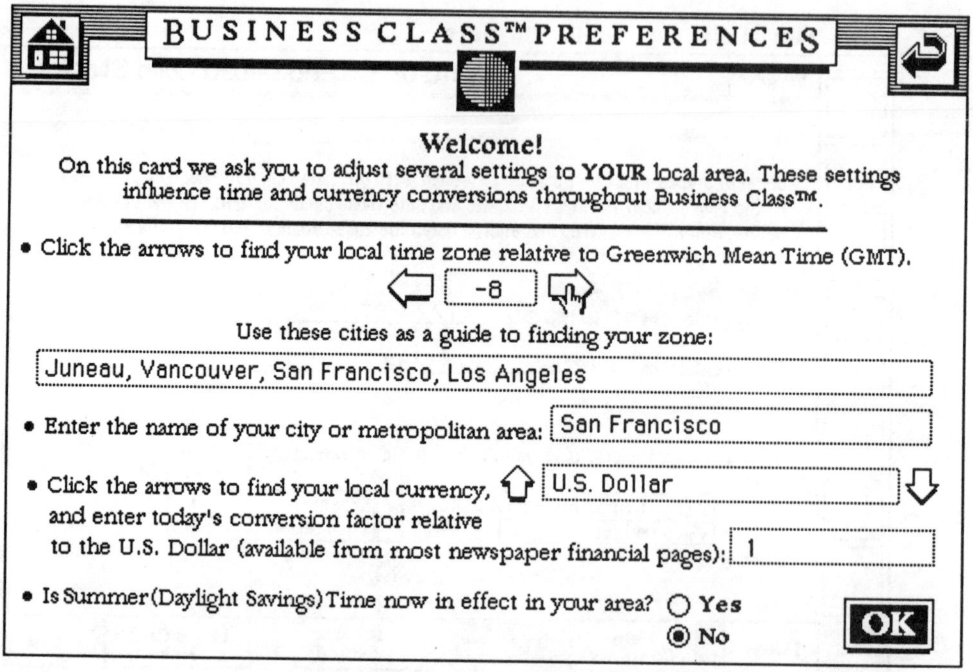

Figure 9-3 *Adjusting user preferences should be made simple, as in the time zone setting of Business Class. A list of large cities in each time zone helps the user pick the right offset from GMT.*

so that the user didn't have to know anything more about time zones than the time zone of the nearest large city, anyplace in the world.

Two fields on the card offer help in setting the local time zone. Both fields change as you click on the left or right arrow buttons on either side of the top field. Clicking on the right button summons time zones east of Greenwich Mean Time (GMT); a click on the left button increments through time zones west of GMT. The top time field shows the actual number of hours difference there is between any time zone in the world and the world standard time zone, Greenwich Mean Time. In other words, the time zone in the United Kingdom is plus zero hours from GMT. Eastern Standard Time in North and South America is minus five hours, meaning that it is five hours earlier in, say, New York City than it is in the United Kingdom (Chapter 19 goes into these calculations in detail).

All this plus and minus stuff can get confusing, however, especially when dealing with time in Australasia. To simplify matters for non-time-zone fanatics, there is a second field in the Preferences card that displays sample major cities as reference points to help out. Therefore, if you know that the city you're located is in the same time zone as Denver, then you've found the correct setting when you see "Denver" in the cities field.

Inside the Preferences Card

For those who want to know how this front end is constructed, all the data that appears in the two time zone setting fields is contained in a hidden field in the Preferences card. That field is displayed for you in Figure 9-4. Each line of the field contains many items: the offset from GMT; the sample cities (each of which is an item because of the commas separating them); and an index number representing the number of the line on which the first two items are located. Item 1 is displayed in the time zone offset field, while all other items, including the last item—the index number—are shown in the long field. Extra spaces are placed in the names of the cities to make sure that the third item, the index number, does not appear within the "window" of the long field on the card.

When a user clicks on the right arrow button next to the time zone offset field, the handler for that button looks to the index number to see which line

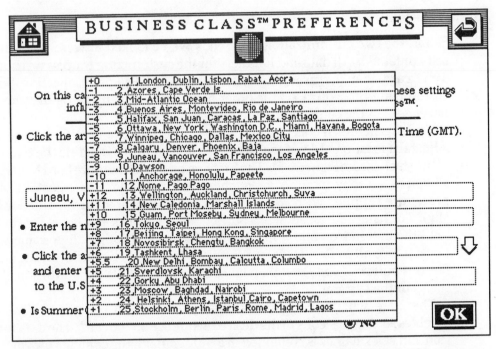

Figure 9-4 *A large hidden field contains all the information that drives the time zone settings. Items 1 and 2 of a line are put into the small field (between the arrows), while the city names go into the long field. The second item, an index number of the line, heops keep the arrows working correctly.*

item is currently displayed. Then it retrieves the items in the next line and deposits them in the appropriate fields on the card. The left arrow does the same, except it looks for the items in the line previous to the one currently displayed.

Internally, *Business Class* keeps track of the number of hours difference from GMT (plus or minus). When needed, the program uses that information and the current setting of the Macintosh's internal clock to calculate the location of the light and dark areas on the world map and to calculate the current time at GMT and in the capital city of the country you're inspecting. All that goes on behind the scenes, and once you set the Preferences card, you don't have to come back unless you change time zones or when you shift to or from daylight savings time in your area.

A similar front end is also provided for setting the local currency of the Macintosh owner. Another hidden field lists 40 different currencies in alphabetical order. Clicking on the arrow buttons to either side of the currency name cycles through all available currencies in the list. The currency name reappears when the user goes to any currency information card.

Button Customization

So far, the two customization front ends we've looked at were pretty much self-contained. All data and handlers for the customizing process were on the same card that the user interacts with. *Focal Point's* application button customizing procedure, on the other hand, entails many cards that the user never sees in the course of customizing the system.

To refresh your recollection of what goes on here, a *Focal Point* user may adjust the location of 11 of the 16 applications buttons that line the two sides of the stack cards (Figure 9-5). The first five on the left side are hard-wired into all stacks, so they may not be changed with the automatic customization procedure supplied with *Focal Point* (although they may be modified manually). To change the location of a button, the user clicks and holds on a button until the button icon and application name cycle through all possible selections. Once all button icons are as the user wishes, he clicks on the Install Buttons button. *Focal Point* then takes over and installs the buttons in all the stacks of the system.

There are actually two parts to this customization procedure. The first involves setting the icons in the desired sequence on the card. The data for the icon and stack names is contained in a hidden field, the contents of which are shown in Figure 9-6. There are also hidden fields connected with each of the 11 customizable buttons on this card. Here's how it all works.

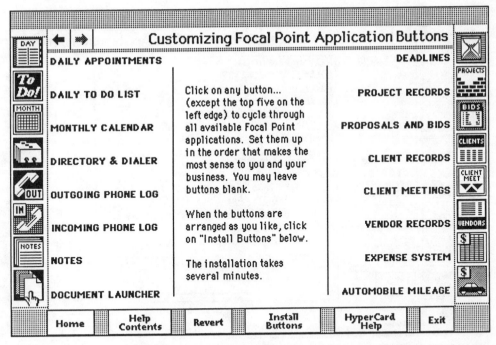

Figure 9-5 *Focal Point allows you to adjust the location of all icon buttons except the top left five. Just click and hold on any button, while the icons and stack names cycle through the list.*

Inside the Button Customization

When a user clicks on one of the prototype buttons, the handler begins to cycle through the icons and *Focal Point* applications names as listed in the large hidden field. The methodology of using an index number is very similar to the way the time zone system works in *Business Class*. In this case, the icon button, itself, is the trigger button. It works its way down the list when you click on the button, or works its way up the list when you hold the Shift key and click on the button.

Each time a new icon and application name appear in one of the button locations, the index to the line of the large field is inserted into item 1 of the small hidden field attached to that button. Item 2 of that field contains the index to the data before you clicked on the button to look for other icons. That second item, incidentally, is used to recreate your original setup with the Revert button, in case you change your mind about modifying the buttons. Clicking on the Install Buttons button really gets things going.

At the heart of the button installation routines is a series of cards in this setup stack that contain scripts for each of the possible buttons that might go

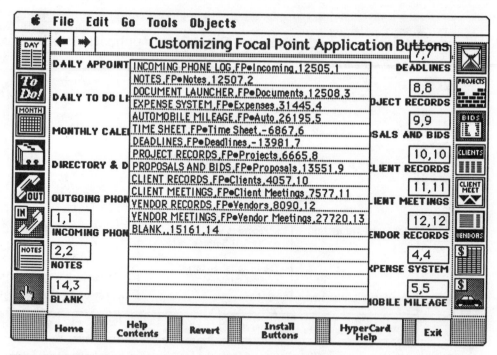

Figure 9-6 *The list is maintained in a hidden field, along with icon numbers, stack names and index numbers to the lines. Smaller hidden fields next to each icon hold the current setting of the stacks (item 2) and the proposed setting made by clicking and cycling through buttons (item 1).*

into each of the stacks of the *Focal Point* system. The cards look like the one in Figure 9-7, which contains all possible scripts that can go into stack buttons on the Projects stack. Cards bear the names of the stack (without the "FP•" prefix), and each scrolling field on the card contains the script that belongs to buttons linked to the other *Focal Point* applications. For example, in the field under "Outgoing" is the script that goes into the Outgoing stack's button within the Projects stack.

The massive handler that runs this installation routine first determines which stack buttons you want installed. Then it goes to each of the hidden script cards whose stacks you've selected, picks up the scripts to only those stacks you want installed, goes to the first stack of your system, sets the icons and scripts accordingly, and then repeats the procedure for each of the stacks in your system. Those *Focal Point* stacks not installed are ignored. And when a stack has multiple backgrounds, the installation procedure sets the icons and scripts for the buttons in all the backgrounds.

Finally, when all the button icons and scripts are set, the handler returns to the installation card and updates the small hidden fields attached to each

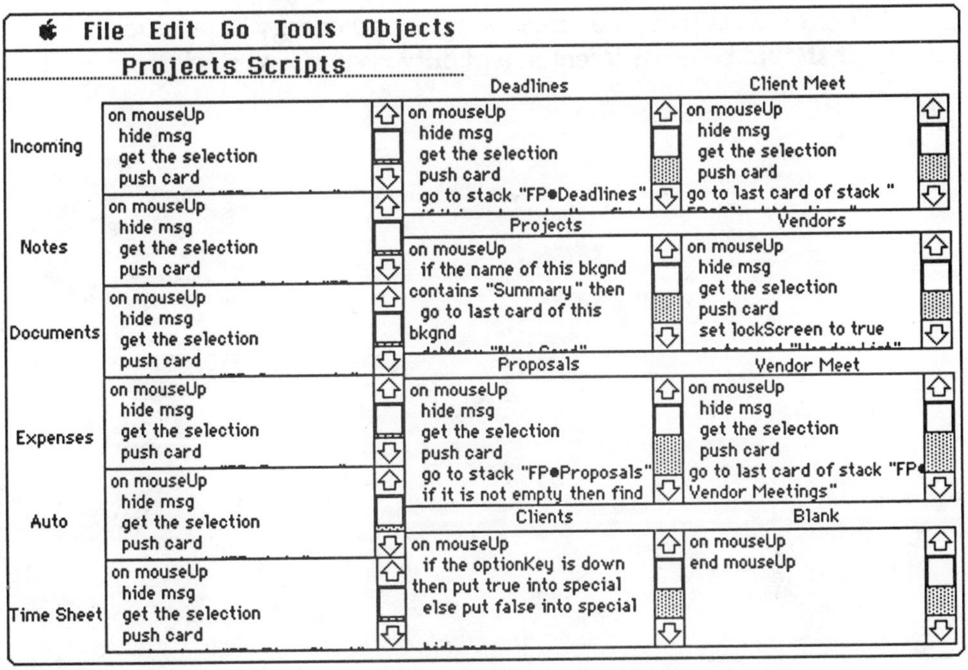

```
 ¢  File  Edit  Go  Tools  Objects
        Projects Scripts
                                          Deadlines                Client Meet
            on mouseUp            ⬆ on mouseUp            ⬆ on mouseUp            ⬆
            hide msg                hide msg                hide msg
Incoming    get the selection       get the selection       get the selection
            push card             ⬇ push card             ⬇ push card
                                    go to stack "FP●Deadlines" go to last card of stack "  ⬇
            on mouseUp            ⬆
            hide msg                           Projects                Vendors
Notes       get the selection       on mouseUp            ⬆ on mouseUp            ⬆
            push card             ⬇ if the name of this bkgnd  hide msg
                                    contains "Summary" then   get the selection
            on mouseUp            ⬆ go to last card of this   push card
            hide msg                bkgnd                   set lockScreen to true ⬇
Documents   get the selection
            push card             ⬇           Proposals                Vendor Meet
            on mouseUp            ⬆ on mouseUp            ⬆ on mouseUp            ⬆
            hide msg                hide msg                hide msg
Expenses    get the selection       get the selection       get the selection
            push card             ⬇ push card             ⬇ go to last card of stack "FP●
                                    go to stack "FP●Proposals" Vendor Meetings"        ⬇
            on mouseUp            ⬆ if it is not empty then find⬇
            hide msg                           Clients                  Blank
Auto        get the selection       on mouseUp            ⬆ on mouseUp            ⬆
            push card             ⬇ if the optionKey is down  end mouseUp
            on mouseUp            ⬆ then put true into special
            hide msg                else put false into special
Time Sheet  get the selection                             ⬇                        ⬇
            push card             ⬇
```

Figure 9-7 *The button customization script looks up a card like this for precise scripts to assign to installed buttons on each stack. Each field contains the script to a particular stack from the stack whose name is listed in the large field at the top.*

button. The index number (item 2 of each field) is set to the same as item 1.

While it may take a bit longer to show all the cards as the installation procedure progresses (i.e., not locking the screen), it is fun to watch and shows the user that something is really happening. If it appears that nothing is happening all this time, the user may believe the computer is frozen and will turn off the machine. Doing that may permanently damage the current stack the routine was in.

This button installation facility is without question the most complex part of *Focal Point*. Yet it has nothing to do with the day-to-day operation of the program. Without it, however, the fanfare of customization would have been subject to criticism, because one of the most difficult personalization aspects of the product would have been almost impossible for the non-HyperLiterate user. The relative complexity of this front end does not surprise me. In fact it reminds me of the difficulty that Macintosh software, in general, presents its authors. For a program to honestly claim ease of use, user friendliness, and all the other advertising catch phrases, much more work must go into the program—work that doesn't necessarily touch on the basic functionality of the program. It's the fine touches of user interface and front ends to typically complex tasks that take time, thought, and energy to produce. It should be no different in a quality HyperCard stack.

10

Stackware is Software

From the first day of HyperCard's release to the world, the marching cry of the HyperCard community was its ease of programming. There were even fully functional prototypes of applications running at the Boston Macworld Expo where HyperCard greeted the public in August of 1987. Still, it took another three months for the first commercial programs in retail distribution (*Business Class* and *Focal Point*) to ship. Other commercial packages written in and around HyperCard took another several months to ship. In critics' minds, there was a legitimate question about how easy HyperCard was to program. Having been on the inside of the stack development process, I learned an important lesson about creating stack products good enough to release to the general public. While HyperTalk coding and debugging is simpler than in other programming environments, all other facets of producing software apply equally to a stack product. In this chapter, we'll look at the non-HyperCard issues that affect your stack production.

Software Design

Just because a HyperCard stack can be whipped into a functional prototype in as little as a few hours (for a simple application), that doesn't mean that a HyperCard stack can be slapped together one day, packaged the next, and shipped the third. Before that first prototype, a lot of planning and thought should go into the design of the product.

One disadvantage that the legions of new HyperCard developers have is that they have not gone through the process of planning a software product in the same manner as the "big boys" have with mainstream commercial products. The first real life example I ever saw of what a major software company does to plan a product was watching Aldus develop PageMaker. As a contributing editor to *Macworld*, I was able to see an early prototype of PageMaker before its name had even been determined. After the private demonstration, the Aldus president, Paul Brainerd, supplied me with a hefty document that was labeled a "functional specification" for the product.

A Functional Specification

As its name implies, the functional specification described how the program worked, what the screens looked like, how the user interacted with the various parts of the program and tools, and other factors. This document evolved over several months, getting bigger and more specific with each revision. It served as an example to follow when I started specifying a standalone software product for myself in 1985—a product that ultimately became *Focal Point*.

The product specification I developed for the product gave an overview of the entire system—like *Focal Point*, it was many applications linked together—plus sample screens showing what information went into the system and descriptions of the actions taken by menu items. An important lesson I learned was that writing a specification for a product forces you to think through how the program is to work. It forces you to account for every piece of information, each menu item, each button on the screen.

When you start thinking about a stack application, often several ideas float around in your head, and you may have an intuitive hunch that things are going to work out the way you hope. But until you can set down on paper exactly how that program is going to work, the ideas tend to be ephemeral. They're sort of there, but not really.

Because HyperTalk coding of most applications is relatively simple, more time and effort should probably go into planning and design than into the coding. As you start programming, of course, you may run into snags or come upon other ideas that change the original specification. There's nothing wrong with that at all. In fact it's rare that the final product will look identical to the very first functional specification you draw up. Your ideas for the product must evolve with it.

Prototypical Focal Point

As mentioned earlier, originality is an important element in a stack's design. You can produce a specification for a program long before you bring in an artist to make the product pretty. For example, in writing the design specification for *Focal Point* I modified one of the stack backgrounds that were a part of prototypical HyperCard, as shown in Figure 10-1 (you may laugh at any time). While the overall design is not very exciting, it was enough to give all people involved with the project (the publisher, the artist, and myself) a sufficient idea of the product's functionality. Even at that early stage, the

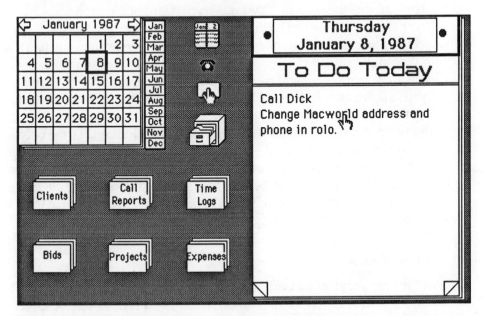

Figure 10-1 *A prototype screen of Focal Point served as a tool to flesh out the idea and explain it to publishers and artists.*

direction toward one stack per application was well entrenched. For the sake of the product specification document, designs for cards were temporarily lifted from the card designs that Kristee Kreitman had worked up as examples of HyperCard's possibilities.

With the functional specification well in hand, it was then easier for everyone to do his part in developing *Focal Point* further. The publisher was able to develop marketing ideas; David Smith, the artist, was able to get an overall picture of the entire product while working on individual pieces, and I was able to identify spots where better linking and front ends could be added to improve the product.

Writing a functional specification for a proposed stack product—even if it is one that is to be used in an in-house corporate environment—should be the first formal stage of designing a stack. And it takes just as long to specify a quality stack as it does quality software, because stackware is software.

Provide On-Line Help

Every self-respecting software publisher these days includes some form of instructions or other help that the user can access while in the program. Since HyperCard, itself, will probably be used quite often in the future for on-line help systems in standalone commercial products, there is no excuse for omitting an on-line help facility for a HyperCard stack product.

The help system should be tailored to the complexity of the stack. In other words, if the stack is a simple one, then the help might be no more than a single card that highlights the basic operation of the stack. More complex stacks, of course, may require several cards or, perhaps, a separate stack that is practically an application in itself. Remember that users are more likely to start using your product immediately, without reading any manual that comes with the product. In fact, there is even the good chance that the user won't reach for your on-line help if the product is exceptionally intuitive. But not all users are up to the same level of intuition, so if there is a chance that the user can get confused, there must be help available. If it's only one click or menu selection away, there's a good chance the person in search of "what to do next" will find your help system long before he reaches for the manual.

Help In Context

This idea of "what to do next" brings up a point about on-line help that not many stack developers have paid attention to so far. In any stack that has multiple backgrounds or multiple stacks, the user is probably faced with different tasks "to do next" based on the background of the card currently on the screen. It is very disruptive to the user to ask for help about a certain kind of card only to discover that he must now search the help cards or stack for clues about "what to do next."

The correct way to handle help in a multibackground or multistack environment is to design the help system so it is "context sensitive." This means that when the user asks for help, the assistance is directly relevant to the background card style currently on the screen. Let's look at *Focal Point's* help system to see one way to handle context sensitivity.

From any stack within *Focal Point*, you summon help by choosing Help in the Go menu. Normally, this menu command brings you to HyperCard Help, but all the *Focal Point* stacks intercept the Help message before it reaches HyperCard.

Focal Point maintains the bulk of its on-line help in a separate stack. Some setup functions, namely the button customization and dated stack building or extending, are in yet a different stack file. The Help stack has a title card, a four-card table of contents, and 97 cards of help, divided into groups according to each *Focal Point* application.

Interestingly, the only time you see the title card is when you open the stack via the Open Stack choice of the File menu or when casually browsing through the stack and you happen upon the first card of the stack (Figure 10-2). While it's an attractive card—note that the art is a subtle replica of the typical *Focal Point* card, but with the feeling you're diving underneath the facade—it's not terribly important that the user sees it, because it takes a deliberate call for help to reach this stack in the first place. Yet if someone opens the stack with the Open Stack menu item, the title card plainly describes what the stack is all about.

The Table of Contents (Figure 10-3) lists the *Focal Point* applications in bold face and the names of the cards (and the names of the help on the cards) in each section. These table of content cards are covered with transparent buttons that contain hard links directly to the help cards bearing the names. Therefore, when you click on the "Menus" selection under the Navigating Focal Point heading, you go directly to the "Menus" card (Figure 10-4).

Introduction and Stack Overview

Note that the first section of this stack is an introduction to *Focal Point*. This section is written as a short tutorial. It presents an overview of the entire system and then describes in detail the user interface points that all stacks share, particularly navigation and information entry. This introduction provides yet a different "entry point" for the user to the set of printed and on-line help supplied with the product.

In the event that a user wishes to print out the help stack, I had to make sure

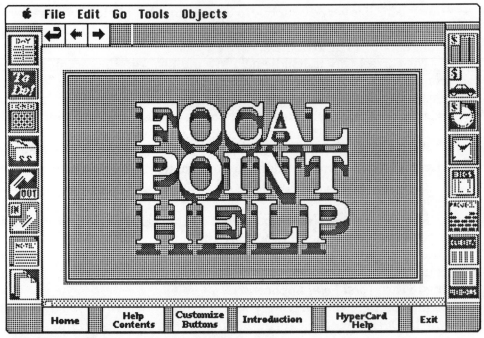

Figure 10-2 *The lead card of the Focal Point Help System.*

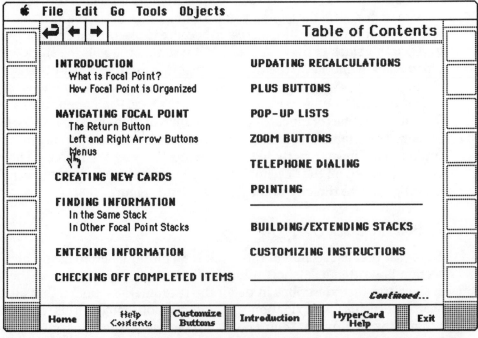

Figure 10-3 *One of four Table of Contents pages from the Focal Point help system. The user clicks on any title or subject to go directly to that card.*

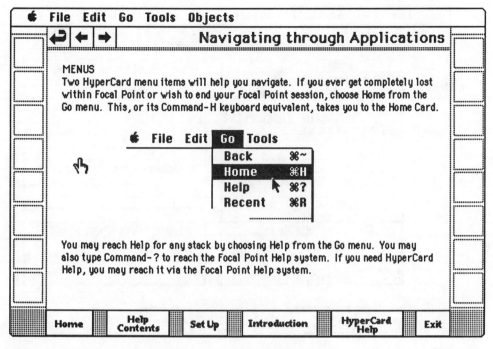

Figure 10-4 *A subject card in the Focal Point help system.*

that all text was in fields, rather than bit-mapped text. Thus, when printing on a LaserWriter, the fonts would print as high quality laser fonts. Since the version of HyperCard used to design *Focal Point* did not allow mixed text styles in a field, the effect of bold faced headlines and plain text subheads (indented) had to be done with two transparent fields for each column (Figure 10-5). Keeping the text in fields also makes maintenance and modification of the table of contents cards much simpler.

Intercepting Help

Whenever you are in a stack and choose Help from the Go menu, a stack or background script intercepts the Help message (which HyperCard sends when this menu item is chosen) and directs you to the first card of the help stack section for that *Focal Point* application. Where appropriate, the Help menu item brings you even more closely to the desired information. For example, the Expense stack is linked to three different cards in the Help stack. If you are viewing the Weekly Summary card of the Expense stack, the Weekly Summary help card is what you see after choosing Help; the Daily Expense cards are linked to the corresponding help card; and so on. Wherever possible, the stack anticipates where the user will need help, and directs the link

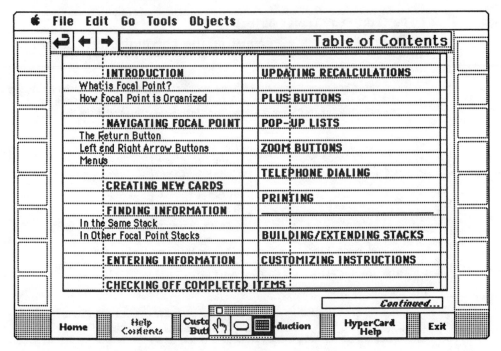

Figure 10-5 *To effect mixed plain and bold text in the Table of Contents (and elsewhere), there are two fields per column: one for boldface text, one for plain text.*

accordingly.

Once at any help stack card, the user may return directly to the card in *Focal Point* from which help was sought (by clicking on the Exit button or the Return button at the top left corner). Other options include going to the table of contents to search further for help; an introduction to *Focal Point*; either of the two sections of the setup stack (button customization or dated stack building/extending); or HyperCard Help (provided it's on the user's disk).

At 180K, the *Focal Point* Help stack is not particularly small in disk space. While there is a lot of text, the bulk of the space is taken up by artwork that is interspersed throughout the stack. By illustrating the help cards, the user can usually bypass the printed manual for quick help. Illustrations also make the Help stack inviting enough to encourage the user to browse through (Figure 10-6). Anytime you can get the user to read any part of your documentation—printed or on-line—you help reduce the need for product support of simple problems that are already well covered. That's a goal you should reach for because stackware is software.

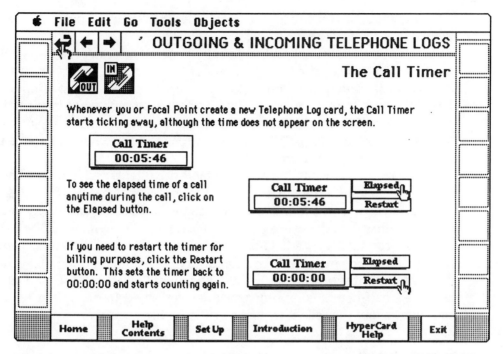

Figure 10-6 *A help system is more enjoyable when the text is punctuated with graphics from the stack.*

Include a Good Manual

Because so much of the early stack products to appear in the universe were distributed via shareware and the public domain, there may be the erroneous perception that stacks don't need manuals. Wrong! If you rate your stack product on the same level as software, then the user will insist on a good manual.

Who Reads It?

Computer hardware and software documentation is a study unto itself. Many people earn their livelihoods writing documentation and nothing else. Despite the personal reward of feeling you've written a good manual, documentation writing is most often a thankless task. I think that's because good documentation is virtually invisible to the user, while bad documentation shows up like an ugly weed on a golf course's 18th-hole green. In a product review by a magazine, a good manual will pass by barely noticed; a bad manual will be ripped to shreds in severe detail. Add to this the fact that users—especially Macintosh users—report that they seldom read manuals.

So if the user doesn't read manuals, why does the user insist on a good manual?

I believe that while the user community generally doesn't read manuals, I take that to mean they don't read manuals like you read a novel—from cover to cover. Instead, they insert the disk and fire up the program before removing the shrink wrap from the manual. But very few programs are so intuitive that every nuance of the program is self-evident or even described in sufficient detail within the on-line help. When questions arise or when the user is in a jam, the first thing to reach for is the manual.

A good manual will have an excellent table of contents and index so that the user can focus on finding an answer to the problem at hand. If the desired information is not in the manual, impossible to find, or explained in any language other than the user's native tongue, then the manual will be tossed across the room to the verbal abuse of its owner. A bad manual is clearly visible. It reminds me of the electrical utility. We think nothing of it during the day for months on end. But when the power flickers for a second, and it costs us a half-hour's computer work not yet saved to disk, then we hurl invectives about the reliability of a so-called utility.

Who Should Write It?

The greatest temptation for a stack developer—especially one who comes from outside the programming priesthood—is to write the manual after finishing the product. I believe that is bad methodology on several counts.

First, it is not good policy for the same person to develop a product and write the manual for it. A program creator develops an attachment to the product just as any creative person does: a sculptor for his sculpture; a writer for his writing; a musician for his music. The creator approaches the work from an angle that has been molded and defined over a long period of time. What the creator deems "simple" and "intuitive" may be something quite different to a new user trying to learn the program. A manual needs the perspective of a third party—a qualified documentation writer—to present the work to the user audience.

That's not to say that the creator should have no input on the content of the manual. Hardly. The documentation writer will likely prefer to see an outline for the manual from the creator, whether the outline be the formal product specification or a separate document. The developer must teach the writer everything he knows about the product. But then he must let the writer develop a formal method for teaching the user about the product and providing appropriate reference material.

When to Write It

Manual writing should begin before the product is finished. Too often—this has happened so many times in the industry, the world has lost count—the manual is begun only after the product is nearly finished. Disks are ready to ship, but manual production is holding up delivery. To get product out the door, the manual is rushed through with errors or sloppy design. In short, the manual looks cheap and thus cheapens the product.

By starting the manual process earlier, the documentation writer and program creator can work more closely together in producing a complete package. The documentation writer must work through every feature of the product and will often uncover bugs in the program that regular testing does not find. Moreover, if the writer gets in the project early enough, he or she may uncover inconsistencies in the way things work, based on the inconsistent ways procedures have to be explained in writing (I've seen this happen in the development of major Macintosh applications programs currently on the market). The documentation writer, therefore, can be an important member of the development team. The earlier on board, the better.

It is the obligation of the documentation writer, of course, to submit drafts of the manual to the creator and others on the team. The program creator must recognize the importance of the manual and should therefore take the time to review drafts as they come in, and recommend corrections as needed. An open line of communication between manual writer and creator is essential.

How Should It Look?

Documentation production varies with the channels of stack product distribution. For public domain and shareware products, which typically find their ways onto the disks of users via electronic bulletin boards, manuals may be text of MacWrite documents included with the stack product. To reduce downloading time via telecommunications services such as CompuServe, Delphi, GEnie, MacNet and others, multiple files may be packed together into one compressed file using one of two popular packing utility programs, called Pack-It and Stuff-It. These products, themselves, are available as shareware programs on the bulletin boards.

When you receive a packed file, either via a bulletin board, on a user group disk, or directly from a shareware publisher, the icon of the file is a descendant of the packing program used to pack the files together in the first place. The icons for Pack-It, Stuff-It, and the packed files they create are shown in Figure 10-7.

To show you what it's like to pack files with Stuff-It, Figure 10-8 shows a typical grouping of files into one Stuff-It Archive file, as it's called. You first

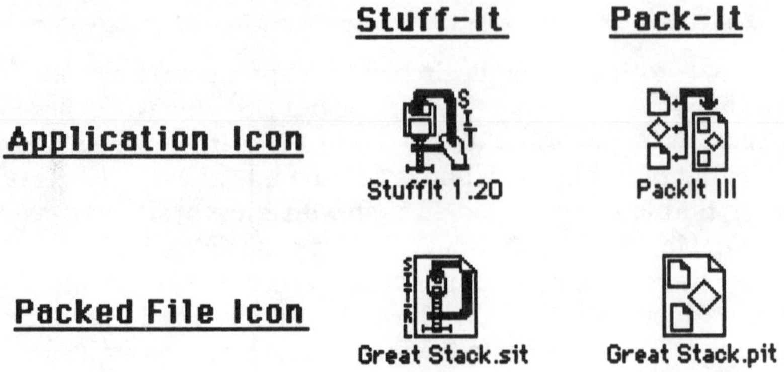

Stuff-It   **Pack-It**

Application Icon

Stufflt 1.20   Packlt III

Packed File Icon

Great Stack.sit   Great Stack.pit

Figure 10-7 *If you download a stack from a bulletin board, it may be "stuffed" or "packed." These files need to be unstuffed or unpacked with the corresponding compression program, Stuff-It or Pack-It.*

Figure 10-8 *Stuff-It compresses files so that they may be transmitted over telephone lines more quickly. Here, a stack and MacWrite documentation files are combined into one Stuff-It archive, called Great Stack. sit.*

provide a name for the Archive file, and then select the files from your disk that you wish packed into the archive. The original files are left intact. Packing typically reduces the size of files by a third or more. Thus, you can cram more than a megabyte of standard files on one 800K diskette.

MacWrite files are more desirable than standard text files, because the MacWrite format lets you be more creative with the layout of the pages and include graphics pasted from the clipboard. Text files are bland, single-font files that are pretty dull to read when displayed on the screen or printed out. Moreover, just about every Macintosh word processor can accept and convert MacWrite files. Therefore, as long as the user has a word processing program, the manual can be printed out with the same formatting and graphics you designed in originally.

In-house stack manuals needn't be as finished as a commercial product's manual. Some care should go into the formatting of pages to make the information pleasing to read. Distribution as a bound booklet or in a loose-leaf binder is essential. The more durable the packaging, the less you'll have to worry about replacing or repairing manuals damaged by excessive use or, at the other end of the spectrum, by neglect.

Finally, commercial programs need commercial-quality documentation. Text should be of typeset quality. That means that unless you or your printer has mastered the photo reduction of LaserWriter printed output for increased resolution, you should produce the master pages with traditional typesetting or output from a high-resolution PostScript-compatible phototypesetting machine (such as the Linotronic 100). Imagewriter output is a sign of a quick job, without much attendant care to the manual.

In a commercial product especially, the quality of the product on the disk is often linked to the quality of the manual in the box. It's no coincidence that expensive software programs have expensive-looking documentation. The design and layout of the manual carries a lot of weight in the user's sense of value and in validating the purchase. All this holds very true for stack products, because stackware is software.

Provide Data Importing

Genuine Macintosh programs that rely on textual information almost always allow for the importation of existing text data. A text-intensive stack product should be no exception. And, although HyperTalk gives ample flexibility in adjusting the data in a text-only file before planting it in various fields on a card, the possibilities make for potentially difficult times.

If there is a strong likelihood that the user of your stack has been accumulating in his own stack the same kind of data your stack uses, then it's up to you, the developer, to smooth the way for your customers into your stack. Recall that it's unfair to assume your users will know how to whip up an importing script on their own.

In chapter 6 we've already covered the difficulties in trying to design a universal importing script that will work for all comers. Because you don't know the field makeup of the original stack, and because your stack may combine previously distinct fields into one large field, it's rare that you can include a universal script, short of something like Steve Michel's Port Authority (Heizer Software).

One kind of help you can provide is a well-documented script that the user can use as a model for a script of his own. In *Focal Point*, for instance, I was faced with the possibility of users wishing to import their rolodex data from one of three sources: 1) the Address stack that comes with HyperCard; 2) Borland's SideKick address book application; and 3) any Macintosh database program, like FileMaker, Microsoft File, or one of the high-end relational databases.

To meet these three requirements, *Focal Point* provides three import scripts. The first one is a double-duty script, exporting data from the HyperCard Address stack to a text file and then importing that text file into the *Focal Point* Directory stack (Figure 10-9). The second one is specially tailored for SideKick files. Because SideKick exports its data in a pre-ordained format, it was easy for me to design a script that massages the fields just the way the *Focal Point*

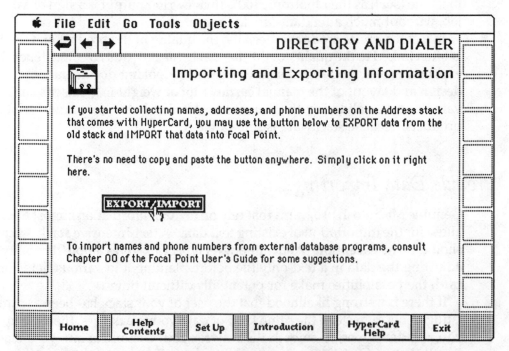

Figure 10-9 *Focal Point offers three ways to import data into the Directory stack. Here, a click of one button copies all data from the HyperCard Address stack into the Focal Point.*

Directory stack likes them.

The third script was a model script for those who have to import from their own databases. In addition to comments within the script, there are explanations about the way databases need to be exported and how the script needs to be modified based on the set up of the fields in the original database. This information is located both in the Import stack and in the manual.

Just as all Macintosh word processing programs let you read MacWrite files and all databases let you import and export field data, stacks that rely on text data should provide for text importing because stackware is software.

Test, Test, and Test

HyperTalk is a simple language compared to most, but it is often deceptively simple. The more complex the stack, especially with multiple backgrounds or multiple stacks in a stack system, the more chance there is for certain scripts to collide with each other as you begin building the script. That's why stack products need just as much testing as any software product. Nearly everyone in the personal computer user community has witnessed standalone software products that are announced by their publishers, only to be delayed many months due to bugs found during testing. It's hazardous to release a product without sufficient testing, only to let customers uncover all kinds of bugs. Computer magazines and newspapers are rife with these kinds of stories from time to time.

Start Testing Early

Software testing should begin the minute you have a working prototype, or even one section of the program. Early testing like this is not the same as formalized testing later in development. Rather, early testing should be conducted to discover if there are major conceptual difficulties or flaws in your basic design. Show your design to people who would understand the subject area of the stack (under a written non-disclosure agreement, if you deem it necessary), and watch very carefully how they interact with the product. Listen closely to their questions about what something on the screen means or where they feel they're getting lost. These are important clues for you. If enough comments come through along the same design elements, then you probably have a design problem, and should devote energy to improve it. It's easy to let your creative ego dismiss negative comments with sayings like, "you don't understand the application." If enough people don't understand the application, then your potential users or customers won't get it either.

Once the product is functionally complete—there are no new features you intend to add—it's time to begin formal testing for bugs. Hopefully, you and others have been using the program while still in development to uncover the more serious bugs, but formal testing will help find even more.

Testing Procedures

Formal testing procedures vary from developer to developer. Some delineate two major stages of the testing procedure with the names "alpha" and "beta." These terms, and the version numbers often associated with them (e.g., release Beta 7) are very imprecise, usually reflecting more the wishes of the developer to be done with the project than the solidity of the code. Other program developers avoid the alpha and beta notation entirely by releasing new versions bearing dates of their release.

Ideal testers are those who would normally use the product on a day-to-day basis. They're the ones who will start applying real data in real quantities to the stack or who will be browsing through the stack in ways you may have not anticipated. All of that kind of testing is important. It's also a good idea to get the product into the hands of a HyperCard fanatic, who will try to trip up your scripts by testing all kinds of key and mouse operations you know to avoid when you use it—but operations that untrained users are likely to do.

Gather written reports from testers on a regular basis (at least weekly). Then work to fix the bugs. When you feel you've made substantial progress in treating bugs (or even tweaking features that testers indicate they'd like), provide all testers with a new release. Accompany each release with a written set of release notes. These notes should itemize the bugs you have repaired so testers can return to their previous test reports and double-check your repairs.

Eventually, you should reach a point at which the testers no longer find new bugs. Unfortunately, by this time the testers usually have a methodology to testing the product, and are not likely to try new torture tests for it. That means that there may still be bugs in the program, but the most likely and potentially most damaging ones have probably been caught. In traditional software publishing houses, the in-house testers are the last ones to sign off on a product before releasing it for disk duplication. If you are producing a product in that environment, the program will not be truly complete until the testers find no more bugs.

The model of the traditional software houses is a good one to follow for testing, because stackware is software.

Be Smart About Marketing

HyperCard and the HyperTalk language dramatically lower the barrier between a person's dreams for a Macintosh application and the implementation of the dream. But as we've seen in this chapter, the other parts of developing software are no different. That includes the marketing end of developing a software product.

Determining the distribution channel is one of the most important decisions you can make as your stack idea comes into focus. The market for stack products is still very new, and there are few rules set in stone. But a little common sense is also in order.

The Retail Channel

The most romantic of the marketing channels for stack products is in retail stores and mail order channels. Let's face it, it's exciting to see a product of yours on the shelf at the corner software shop. Gaining a foothold in the retail channel without the help of an established publisher is very difficult and costly. It requires in-depth knowledge by someone on your staff of the pricing strategies, promotion requirements and distributor relationships that exist in the retail channel. It's not impossible to achieve, but it takes a sincere commitment and healthy financial backing to break into that channel on your own. The financial rewards are substantially higher if you become the publisher and achieve widespread distribution, but so are the risks and initial investment.

Getting help into the retail and mail order channel by way of mainstream publishers is another opportunity. Be aware, however, that such publishers are looking for high-volume products that appeal to a wide audience. Vertical market applications are not likely prospects for the likes of Activision, Electronic Arts, and others. Their dealers need to know that the products will attract a vast crowd and appeal to a wide audience. Of course, that means that if you can produce a broad-based tool that may be customized for individual needs, then that would be a likely candidate for submitting to a mainstream publisher for consideration.

In the meantime, I believe the trend for the bulk of HyperCard based products will, indeed, be directed more toward vertical market applications. That's where HyperCard's strengths lie, in my estimation. That leaves a number of other distribution strategies open to you.

Low Cost Publishing

One of the best opportunities would be to offer the stack product through a publisher like Heizer Software. Heizer offers its products (HyperCard stacks, Microsoft Works and Excel templates) through a direct mail catalog targeted at Macintosh owners. The catalog, called the Stack Exchange, currently boasts many vertical market applications for dozens of industries. As customers place orders for various products, Heizer copies the files to as many disks are needed to fill the order. In other words, your product does not have its own diskette and label, nor does it have a printed manual. You supply the manual in the form of a HyperCard stack or word processing file.

Heizer software generally sells at a lower price than retail packages—a $25 vertical market package is typical—but the author generally receives a much higher royalty percentage of the selling price than a product sold through a mainstream publisher. A supreme advantage to the Heizer approach is that other than your development costs, there are no further costs to get your product to market. Heizer does its own promotion and catalogs based on its cut from the sale of products.

Self-Publishing

Another option for a vertical market stack application is to market the program yourself via mail order or one-on-one selling, setting yourself up as a software publisher. One benefit of selling to a vertical market is that it is comparatively easy to find mailing lists and other advertising vehicles that target the market. You should get more mileage for your promotional dollars, because the vast majority of the people receiving your message will have an interest in what you offer.

Selling software directly to the end user offers the most potential for profit per unit sold. Since you sell the product at a price that is representative of its value, you don't have to worry about discounts to distributors or retailers. On the other hand, you are your own sales force, and you must keep promoting the product to find new customers. Promotion takes capital. Many a new business has failed by expecting early sales to finance operations. Becoming a software publisher means creating a business plan, seeking relationships with bankers, and perhaps seeking venture capital to get started. It's a commitment, to be sure, but perhaps one worth making if you believe in your product and have other ideas just waiting to turn into stack products.

Open Channels

The last two channels are often spoken of together, but they are really two very different channels: shareware and public domain.

Shareware is a concept made popular by the late Andrew Fluegelman, who wrote PC-Talk III, an early telecommunications program for the fledgling

IBM PC. The concept is simple: Try the software for awhile and pay the author if you decide to use it. The amount you pay is comparatively small for software, ranging from $5 to perhaps $35. It obviously depends on the honor system, but for Andrew and several others since then, it has worked.

It doesn't always work, however. For every successful shareware author—success being measured by turning a pastime into a software business—there are hundreds of unsuccessful ones. There is no magic formula that can make a successful program, but the ones that have succeeded have been just plain great programs that filled a need when nothing else was out there. The authors also made the commitment to support those folks who sent in their shareware fees by providing a printed manual, periodic free updates of the program, and telephone support. If shareware sounds a lot like the real software business, well, it is if you plan to make a go of it.

For a shareware program to have a real chance at making money, it must not only be a great program, but it must be one that people use very frequently. It must be one of those programs that the user can't be without. This is partly due to the fact that guilt often enters into the shareware formula. When users feel that a program is very useful to them, they just might feel guilty enough to send in the shareware fee. Some have even dubbed shareware "guiltware."

There are also examples of good shareware stacks that didn't bring in the bucks for the author, even though the user community adopted it almost as a standard. Eric Alderman's Script Report utility (described in chapter 2) started out as a shareware product with a $15 fee. Despite the stack's ready acceptance and consummate practicality, only a handful of users sent in their checks. While that experience may have completely soured some authors, Eric now distributes the product via the Heizer Software catalog.

There is another shareware story you must hear about—a HyperCard shareware strategy that was doomed from the outset. Someone had created a utility stack that imported SideKick address data into the HyperCard Address stack. Distributing it on a major bulletin board, he requested a $5 shareware fee if the user liked the program. Now, five bucks is not a lot of money, to be sure, but a person is probably going to use this stack only once, just enough to transfer data from SideKick into HyperCard. By trying the program out (which shareware encourages), you're already done with it. You have no further use for the program. How guilty will you be about having used a program once? Probably not at all. I don't decry the author trying to recoup the time he spent on the stack, but I think it was unrealistic of him to expect anyone to submit a fee for a one-time use shareware product. The concept violates the "repeated functionality" rule of shareware. That stack should have been distributed strictly as public domain software.

New stack authors may have suspicions about the public domain method of distribution due to concerns about copyright. The impression one gets from the term "public domain" is that there is no copyright protection for the author. That's not true. Provided the author clearly states copyright owner- ship in the product, an author maintains copyright on the product. As such, no one may resell or redistribute that product or parts of the product (like scripts, icons, background art, or XCMD resources) without the author's permission. Technically, a public domain stack uploaded to an electronic bulletin board may not be carried to another board or distributed on disk by user groups unless the author says it's okay on the stack. But a good stack will make its way around the boards and user groups on its own in short order.

Choosing the Channel

Determining which method of distribution applies best to your program is something you should do early in the stack development process. When the decision is to pursue distribution through a mainstream publisher or set yourself up as a publisher, the marketing planning then becomes as important as product planning. It can take many months to put all the marketing pieces in order. Don't forget, too, that if you plan to run ads in any of the monthly Macintosh magazines that their deadlines can run two and three months ahead of publication date. You may not be able to afford that lag time after the product is finished. Somehow, you have to bring the product and marketing together so every element of the package is on the same timetable.

Making these important marketing decisions may be new to you, but they're no different than what traditional software developers go through. Don't get caught in a trap by thinking that you can be more casual because you're dealing with a HyperCard stack, because stackware is software.

11

How to Build a Stack

Deep within the preceding 10 chapters are many techniques about the process of designing and building a HyperCard stack. In this chapter, we'll bring those elements together and present some new ideas while offering suggestions about how stacks come into being. Much of what is described in this chapter is the result of building two commercial stacks, many personal stacks, and helping others build their stacks. The procedures detailed here applied to the projects I was working on, but they probably don't apply to everyone's *modus operandi*. But if you fret over where to begin and how to proceed from there, then use this chapter as a guide to get you started. As you work on more stack projects, you'll develop your own strategies and timetables that work best for you.

Different Methods

In one way or another, I've participated in the creation of stacks for three categories: information publishing, information management and control of external devices. Designing a stack for each of these categories is significantly different, especially in the planning stages. Therefore, we'll approach the "how to" aspect of stack design separately for each type of stack. The primary difference is in the way you approach the stack structure, as you'll see. Then there are technical factors that distinguish each of the three types of stacks.

Information Publishing Stacks

The most typical applications for information publishing stacks are:

- Training and Education
- Reference Works
- Product Demonstrations
- Catalogs
- Paper Publication Substitutes

These are almost entirely browse-only kinds of stacks, in which you provide all the information that the application requires. It is up to you to organize, present and help users navigate through the information.

The supreme advantage in designing an information publishing stack is that the author has complete control over every text character and every graphics pixel that appears in the stack. You know from the outset what kind of reference data, message or story the stack is to convey. The idea for creating the stack in the first place comes as a result of an existing body of information that you want to make accessible in an inviting and enjoyable way.

Stack structure must fit the information like a hand-tailored suit fits its owner. Just like you don't have a suit made for you and then adjust your body to it, so would it be a mistake to devise a stack structure and then come up with the information to fit that structure.

Drawing a schematic diagram of the basic structure of your information is one of the best ways to start picturing an information publishing stack. The diagram should resemble a map to the entire stack. For example, the map to the HyperCard Help system, shown in Figure 11-1, is one way to draw such a diagram. As a reference work, this stack system is best treated as a tree-structure stack.

In your first draft of a structural map, of course, you needn't be so literal

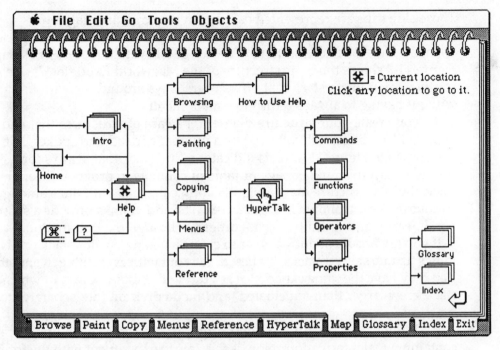

Figure 11-1 *Mapping out the proposed structure of a stack system is an important early step. Here's the map to Hypercard's Help stacks.*

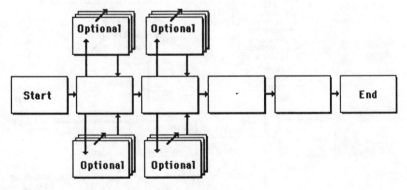

Figure 11-2 *The structure map of Inigo Gets Out.*

with the card metaphor in your diagram. For instance, Figure 11-2 demonstrates how I envision the structure of Inigo Gets Out (this is not necessarily the way the author designed the stack). In chapter 5, you'll recall, we saw how linear the structure of this story is, with occasional side trips off the main path.

Those side trips are represented as loops in the structure diagram.

Non-linear stack structure can become difficult to sketch out, especially when the links to various sections of a stack go all over the place. For example, Figure 11-3 shows the basic structure of the Macworld Expo stack system, a relatively non-linear stack that offers users ways around the various stacks without having to always return to a main menu.

As you create your structure diagram, beware of structures that end up looking like a single hub followed by a number of dead-end spokes, like the one shown in Figure 11-4. This indicates a dull stack that always forces the user to return to an index page or table of contents to progress through the stack. Such a structure may be significantly enhanced with links among the various spokes, as shown in Figure 11-5. The added links provide a sense of non-linearity and speed the user's progress through the information.

If you are unsure about whether to create a heterogeneous stack or divide things up into several stacks, it's best to start out with everything in one stack. You may have the same experience as I did with *Business Class*, in which the stack grew larger than anticipated, and made division into separate stacks practical.

With the stack structure in good order, create some mock-ups of cards containing real information. Now is the time to experiment with the format-

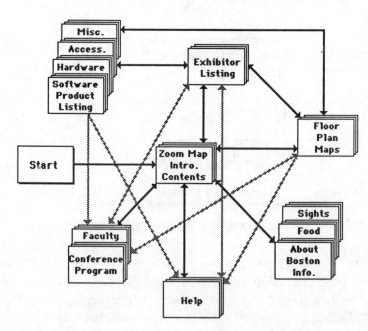

Figure 11-3 *The structure map of a non-linear stack system, the Boston MacWorld program.*

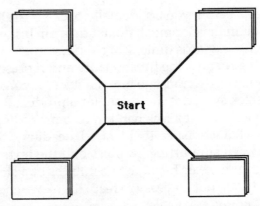

Figure 11-4 *The makings of dull stack are revealed by this map. A single start card is the only avenue to several other sections.*

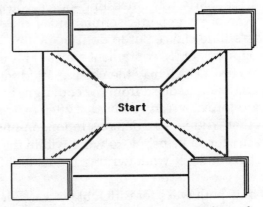

Figure 11-5 *By increasing the number of links across stack lines, the new map reveals a more inviting stack.*

ting of text and division of long text chunks to see how much information you intend to put on each card. The exact "look" of the card is not critical at this stage, but the information content should reflect what the final data will be on any given card. If you plan to add graphics to the cards, make sure you leave adequate room for them.

Once you have a notion of the stack structure and sample cards, it's time to write the functional specification for the product. For an information publishing stack, it is important that you explain how the browser progresses through a stack, noting what options are available at every kind of card or background. Understanding the flow through the stack is critical. As noted in Chapter 10, writing the functional specification will help you find loose ends in your design concepts before you accidentally back yourself into a corner.

At this point in development, do not delay in bringing in an artist to help with the look for the cards (unless, of course, you are the artist). Acquaint the artist with the structure, the functionality and representative samples of the textual information that must go into the stack. A consistent look throughout the stack or stack system is important for a product to exude quality design. Be sure to give the artist a free hand in recommending fonts, font sizes, line spacing, text characteristics (bold faced headlines, for instance), and the interplay between supporting graphics and the text. Formatting of textual information can make or break the usefulness of a stack. If the information isn't pleasantly laid out and easy to read, the experience of browsing through the stack will not be enjoyable.

As soon as the formatting of the screens is completed, it's then time for the most tedious part of assembling an information publishing stack: entering the textual data. If the data is from an existing source, you may be able to automate its input by way of an importer script. But if the source is from printed material, there's little choice but to do it manually. In some cases, optical character recognition (OCR) equipment may be able to scan printed material and turn it into text, which may then be imported into your stacks, but you must have permission to do so from the copyright holder.

With the card format already defined, it often makes it easier to input fresh data, such as that written for a demonstration, on-line help, or instructional stack. It is easier for some people to write within the confines of the format rather than envisioning it while writing the material in a word processing system.

I've input data both ways for different stacks. For *Business Class* data, in which the data came largely from questionnaires received from embassies and tourist bureaus, it was more convenient entering the data into the preformatted forms of the cards. At the same time, the data was arriving at random, so the preformatted cards also helped indicate where the holes in the information were. On the other hand, I wrote the help cards for *Focal Point* in a word processor, particularly because the content had to drive the card layout. Once I had drafted the text (indicating how much was to go on each card), I handed the text to the artist, who came up with not only the formatting scheme, but also the idea of inserting graphics to illustrate the points. With the card design back in my machine, I was then able to import the text of the cards via an importing script.

Be prepared for one surprise. No matter how carefully you anticipate oddball chunks of information in an otherwise smooth series of information cards, some non-standard data will come along to challenge the design you've established. It seems that even if you plan for a worst-case data scenario, when you start inputting real data, you encounter something "worse than the worst." The most typical example is when one card needs to contain more text data than there's room for in the format. Unfortunately, there is no magic incantation that makes the problem go away. Occasionally, you can make slight modifications to the width or depth of a text field to accommodate the weird text. Other times, you'll have to truncate the text data to make it all fit. Whatever you do, however, do not compromise consistency to make room for one oddball data event.

All during the data entry time period, you and others should be testing the program, making sure that the browsing flow is natural and intuitive. Find reviewers who will be candid and unafraid to criticize your work if they think some improvement is needed. Watch people work with your product, especially early in the development cycle to see where they stumble or seem confused. Even if they're polite in their comments, their uneasiness with parts of the program should be clear signals to you that changes are needed.

Information Management Stacks

Unlike information publishing stacks, information management stacks generally count on the author creating a framework in which the user will store and access his own information. The initial design phases are different, because the author does not always know the extent of information to be stored in the stack.

The idea for a stack in this category generally grows out of a frustration in trying to access or manage information on a regular basis. In your business, for instance, there are perhaps dozens of information tasks that are not being covered well by existing software or by a larger computer in the company. You intuitively feel that your Macintosh should be able to help you with managing the data, so you turn to HyperCard as a possible solution. If the need is broad based enough, you may decide to turn your idea into a product that you and others can benefit from.

From my experience developing *Focal Point*, I found it very valuable to work first in perfecting the information content of each card style, then the links between the stacks. Only after the functionality was stabilized did I call in David Smith to work on the art. I preferred this route because there was a great deal of experimentation going on as to what fields to place on each card and how extensive the links would be between applications. Testing began long before the stacks looked pretty. It was more important to get feedback on the functionality, which was under my direct control.

Since the development of *Focal Point*, I have also been involved in the design of other information management stacks, and have been more conscious of the design methodology at the very early stages. Here's the way I generally approach a stack of this type.

The first order of business for me is to establish the stack structure. For most applications of any substance, the need for multiple stacks in a unified stack system is omnipresent. Flexibility and archivability usually demand the division of information into separate stacks. Deciding on the division is not always easy. In a case like *Focal Point*, each application deserves its own stack largely because each one is, indeed, an individual application. The To Do List and Project database are not two stacks you'd consider related enough to place in the same stack file.

In another case, however, the situation called for numerous departments to fill out forms that were similar to each other. The content of the forms was created partially by a different stack, which, in a sense, created templates for the other stacks. Once the departments filled out their forms, the data was then pulled together into yet a different stack for reporting purposes. Figure 11-6 demonstrates the work flow.

Because of the number of departments, and the fact that a "set" of forms for each department consisted of as many as a dozen linked cards (and there could be 30 or 40 sets active within a department at any time), I thought it best to devote a separate stack to each department. A division of labor like this also

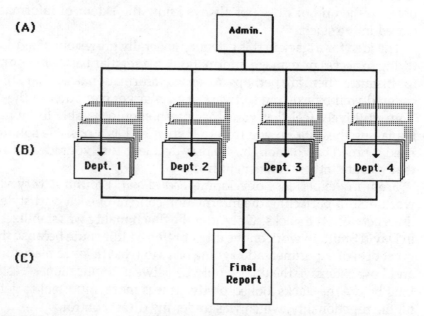

Figure 11-6 *A map of an information management stack that starts with one administrator, whose stack creates cards in other departments' stacks. Information from the department stacks is retrieved for a final report.*

reduces the possibility of data loss for the entire company if the forms were in one stack that somehow became corrupted. In fact, a damaged stack could be restored manually from the data posted elsewhere in the system. The tradeoff, however, was that stack-to-stack communications made the entire system slower than if everything were in one stack. Still, the safety and archivability of dividing the system overrode the speed factor. As HyperCard evolves, it can only get faster; but if the company loses all its data in one crash, then it doesn't matter how fast the system is.

After determining the underlying stack structure, I continue by sketching on paper what the major screens of each stack will look like. These are not necessarily suggestions for the artist, but rather an overview of what fields and buttons each card needs, and where information passes along the continuum of use—when data is to be fetched from one stack or posted to another. As I sketch and review these cards, I mentally walk through the work flow, imagining where I'd like to branch from each card I see, and what should happen when I branch.

From the sketches I start making a prototype for each stack, building in all the functionality required of the basic system. Buttons tend to be text buttons for identification purposes (leaving icons for later), and fields are generally Geneva font. Sometimes the reality of a stack differs from the dream on paper, and adjustments are necessary to the design from the sketches. Also, working with the real thing sometimes causes additional ideas to pop up in my head, adding new functions or reducing the work of the ultimate user of the stack. With a working prototype in hand, it's then time to write the formal functional specification, using the screens that have been patched together so far. The point is that you'll be able to explain the functionality from experience, knowing that the pieces do, in fact, work together.

Once your prototype is working as specified—all fields are active, all links are working, all data is being posted or retrieved from other stacks correctly—then it's time to bring in the artist to make your cards inviting. As with any kind of stack, the written product specification should help guide the artist, who may not fully understand the inner workings of the stack. Be as specific as possible as to the amount of data various fields will be holding. If various buttons on your prototype screens should be physically grouped together for ease of use, then make sure the artist knows that. Ask for suggestions as to where icon button art would be appropriate. And let the artist recommend font specifications, as noted above in the information publishing stacks.

More so in information management stacks than anywhere, it is vitally important that the program be put into the hands of typical users (after the artwork treatment) for strenuous testing. While you may think you know what kind of information people should be putting into various fields, your users will surprise you with the ways they'll interpret your intentions. You may discover that a field is inappropriately labeled or that it isn't large enough to display the data some people use in the real world. You also want to make sure that real world users agree with your estimation of needs for links you've established throughout the system. Typically called "beta testing," this testing method can prove to be both enlightening and helpful in preventing what users consider obvious errors or omissions to slip out with the product.

While the product is in beta testing, it's a good time to put a script utility to work on your stack system. I recommend *Script Report*. Print out all the scripts from all your stacks and look for inconsistencies or handlers that you made obsolete with newer code. Also use this time to annotate the code in your scripts. Add comments wherever you believe the user may need help in understanding what you're up to. If your HyperTalk code is open to the user—as I hope it is—then it should be clear how to customize it. Jot down the comments on the script printout, then go back into the stacks and add the comments to the actual scripts.

External Device Control Stacks

The steps involved in assembling a stack that controls external devices are similar to those for information management stacks, just mentioned. The main difference is that for a control stack, you must precede development with a bit of experimentation and research to make sure the control you have in mind will actually work.

First of all, controlling external devices will require the assistance of one or more XCMDs that give you access to the serial or SCSI ports of the Macintosh. Serial port controllers are more common so far, and we show you how to make one in Chapter 29.

Not all serial controller XCMDs work the same. Some let you set up an interactive terminal within HyperCard, so that you can communicate with a remote computer or device just like you would with a dedicated telecommunications program. One window (HyperCard card) displays incoming information as well as the information you type on your keyboard to send out. Other types, including the one in this book, are used primarily as components of a "front end" to an external device. It lets a HyperTalk script examine incoming data for specific key words, like "Enter Password: " or store incoming data into fields on cards for archiving purposes. HyperTalk can also send information out to the remote device.

Long before you start designing screens or building functional prototypes, you will probably create a "dummy" stack and start working somewhat manually with the serial XCMD. If the device you're communicating with sends and receives data, you will check out how the incoming data can be tested by a HyperTalk script and how the script can respond to various messages the device sends. If the device primarily accepts serial commands from your stack, you'll need to become familiar with the command language of the device so you can work them into HyperTalk scripts. For instance, one device I control with a HyperCard stack is a shortwave communications receiver that has a serial interface as an option. It accepts about a dozen commands that do things such as change the frequency, load frequencies into memories, and so on. The command to set the frequency to 9515 kilohertz (one of the frequencies for the BBC in London) is

FA0009515000;

which means that the command must be constructed out of the frequency field and several characters appended before and after the characters in the frequency field. To design a stack around this receiver's commands, I had to be fluent in the command language (including the series of confusing parameters for each command).

Only by knowing how you can communicate with the device or service at the other end of the serial connector can you begin sketching screens and assembling a prototype, just as you would for an information management stack, as noted earlier. Testing during development is particularly important when the stack is acting as a front end to another computer or communications service. Your scripts must anticipate a wide number of possible errors caused by the other computer, delays in the network linking your machine with the other, and general communications errors between your computer and the local telecommunications phone number. Telecommunications front ends are supposed to be invisible to the user, which means your stack has to be ready for the worst, and handle it gracefully. The only way you'll discover where the traps are is to test the front end often, thus adding to the probability that communications or other external errors will try to trip up your stack.

For this kind of stack I proceed through the rest of development as outlined for information management stacks, above.

How to Go Wrong

The worst way to start developing a stack is to jump in and start designing willy-nilly. I've seen stacks that started that way, and it's very evident if you start examining the stack from front to back. A haphazard construction usually forces you to navigate through the stack with buttons rather than keyboard arrows, because a sequential foray through the stack will reveal how much of a hodge-podge it is. When that happens, you spend too much of your scripting time figuring out how to keep the organization straight, while the stack grows in peculiar directions.

The more planning you do before diving into the background, field and button making—tempting though it may be—the better off you'll be in creating and maintaining your stack in the long run. Have patience, and plan ahead.

PART TWO

HyperTalk for Stack Developers

12

A Different Approach To HyperTalk

About one-half of *The Complete HyperCard Handbook* is devoted to the HyperTalk language. Because the book is both an introduction and ready reference to the various commands, functions, and properties of HyperTalk and HyperCard, most of the HyperTalk discussions are organized around the pieces of the language. Thus, there are separate chapters on action commands, arithmetic commands, functions, and so on. To help keep you focused on the meaning of a particular word of the HyperTalk language, the discussions had to operate in a kind of vacuum. Only with the application examples in the last part of the book is there an attempt to bring the pieces of the languages together.In this part of the *Developer's Guide*, we approach the HyperTalk language— including messages, commands, functions, properties, constants, and control (if-then-else and repeat) structures—from a different direction. As a HyperCard developer, you may fully understand the inner workings of numerous individual commands, but encounter difficulty in drawing together your knowledge of several related aspects of HyperTalk in a real application. Therefore, the subjects in this part of the book come from programming questions I've heard since the release of HyperCard and from problems I've seen in scripts within stacks from a variety of sources. Even if you're comfortable with HyperTalk, a number of the following chapters will offer some insights and suggestions you may not have heard before. At the same time, I don't assume that the following chapters will tackle absolutely every problem you've encountered. These are the predominant ones that I've heard about or inferred from scripts I've seen.

Throughout these HyperTalk chapters, I will be stressing compactness of scripts—making as few lines as possible do the most work as possible. Dan Winkler, the person most responsible for the syntax and inner workings of HyperTalk, believes a good HyperTalk script should look and sound like poetry. Of course, if you set two poets before the same sunset, the poems that each writes will be quite different. Similarly, two HyperTalk programmers pursuing the same functionality will likely code the solution differently. In few cases is there "the one best way" to write a HyperTalk handler, so it's difficult to pursue perfection in that manner. But if you can refine a handler so that it works faster in fewer lines, then the second generation is much better than the first. It is unfair to you and your stack to slap together a script and ignore it thereafter. Go back to it later, study it, and look for ways to make it simpler, more elegant, more like poetry. The following chapters should help you do that.

A Working Laboratory

To fully understand many of the concepts presented in this part of the book, it is essential that you try out the scripts and simple stacks that will be presented to you. It's a hands-on way of learning that cannot be beat. Simply watching static screens on the pages and trying to imagine what happens when you click a button won't bring the ideas home.

Because you'll be writing a lot of handlers and creating a lot of buttons in the following chapters, I've devised a two-background sample stack that will be used in all hands-on demonstrations. The stack is not a real application. The subjects covered in this part are too diverse to appear in a single application. Rather than forcing demonstrations into either an information publishing or management stack—or worse yet, trying to contrive a "real" application that encompasses both types—we'll make copies of the original stack in various chapters to work on numerous HyperTalk programming problems and opportunities.

Before we can get started, however, you'll have to build the original stack. The raw material for the stack are in the Stack Ideas stack that comes on the HyperCard Ideas disk of HyperCard. Here's how to make the stack:

1. ***Open the Stack Ideas stack.*** There is a button on the original Home Card that links directly to this stack. Or you may open it via the Open Stack choice in the File menu.

2. ***Click on the right-hand pointer until you see card four of the index (Figure 12-1).***

3. ***Click on the miniature card labeled "Divided Card."*** This card is named in the stack, so you may also type

```
go to card "divided card"
```

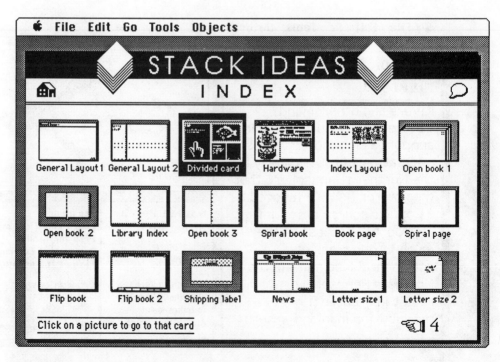

Figure 12-1 *The fourth card of the Stack Ideas index.*

in the Message Box.

This card (Figure 12-2) will be good for demonstrations, because it has five background fields (with which to test various text handling abilities of HyperTalk) and only four standard background buttons. The box at the upper right corner holding the fish picture will be a good work area for experimenting with buttons.

4. *Choose New Stack from the File menu.*

5. *Type the name "Developers Guide Master" into the file name field.* Be sure the check box, "Copy current background," is checked (Figure 12-3).

6. *Click the OK button or press the Return key.*

The new stack is created, and you are brought to that stack. All card-specific information stored in the prototype card from the Ideas stack disappears, leaving blank text fields and an empty box at the top right. The buttons and their scripts carry over, as does the background script that

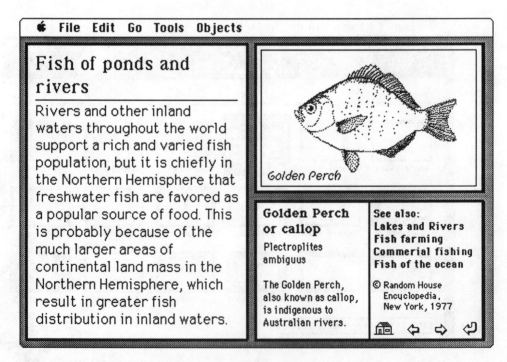

Figure 12-2 *This is the card layout that we'll use for all experiments.*

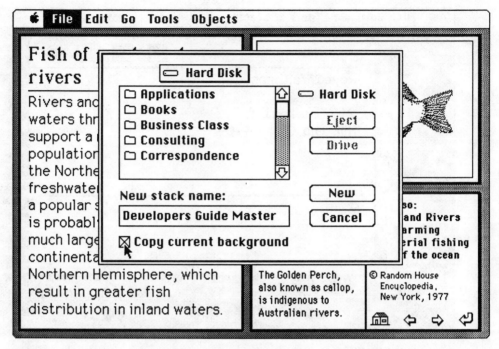

Figure 12-3 *Create a new stack, using this background, and call it Developers Guide Master.*

was in the original.

7. *Press the Tilde key or choose Back from the Go menu to return to the Ideas stack.*

8. *Type Command-1 or choose First from the Go menu to return to the first card of the Ideas stack.*

9. *Locate the miniature card labeled Address Card 3, and click on that mini-card (Figure 12-4).*

    This address card will become the second background in the new stack you're creating. The card comes with 10 background buttons, three background fields and one hidden card field.

10. *Choose Copy Card from the Edit menu.*

11. *Choose Open Stack from the File menu and open the "Developers Guide Master" stack you just made.*

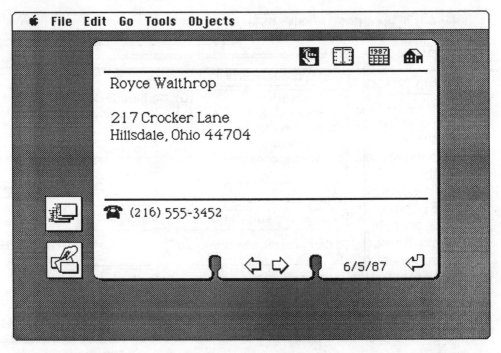

Figure 12-4 *The sample stack will also have a new background–the rolo-style card from the Stack Ideas stack.*

12. ***Choose Paste Card from the Edit menu.***

This pastes the copy of the address card into the stack. Because we copied the entire card, its card-specific data comes along with it, including the text in fields and the hidden card field. If you want to see that hidden field, type

```
show card field 1
```

into the message box. When you're finished with the field, type

```
hide card field 1
```

into the message box.

13. ***Remove the text from the two large fields.***

The script that is part of this card's background automatically inserts today's date into the third field. Leaves this script in place for now.

In most of the chapters of this part, you'll be making a copy of this master stack and modifying it to demonstrate and experiment with various HyperCard concepts and techniques. Let's get started with the subject of the HyperCard hierarchy, and determining where to put handlers, how to use target names and how I turned literally hundreds of mouse handlers into just one.

13

Scripts and the Object Hierarchy

Perhaps the single most perplexing concept facing stack developers has to do with where along HyperCard's object hierarchy various scripts belong. The thought first comes, I believe, when you design a stack and realize that two or more buttons have the same or nearly the same scripts behind them. Intuitively, you believe there must be a better way, but it may not be easy to discover the method that solves the problem. In this chapter, we'll dissect the object hierarchy and play a bit with the way messages work their way through the hierarchy. We'll also examine how you can detect information about an object in another hierarchy level—using the Target function—for tremendous flexibility in your script placement.

The Hierarchy—Two Perspectives

It is vital that you fully understand the object hierarchy of HyperCard if you hope to design efficient stacks. While a full knowledge of the hierarchy doesn't necessarily show through in a stack, a lack of knowledge sticks out like a sore thumb.

HyperCard's hierarchy consists of seven distinctly different objects, each of which has its own place within the hierarchy. The objects are arranged as shown in Figure 13-1. I prefer to show the hierarchy with HyperCard at the top and other objects below it. I'll alert you that this perspective is different than the way outlined in Apple's HyperCard technical documentation and by other authors. In many of those documents, the hierarchy is illustrated with HyperCard at the very bottom, and other objects above it.

It's important enough to describe both perspectives, because they may help more people understand the concept. I prefer the organization with Hyper-Card at the top, because I conceive of the objects in the order in which I encounter them in working with HyperCard. When I start HyperCard, HyperCard itself is the first object to take charge, then the Home Stack, then the current stack, and so on, down to the most nested object, either a field or button. When you click the mouse button atop a screen button, I prefer to envision the mouseUp message taking an active role in search of a matching handler in objects on its way to HyperCard. The matching handler, then, traps the message before it gets any higher up the hierarchy.

From the other point of view, messages go in the other direction. Rather than imagining a message actively in search of a handler, you may think of a

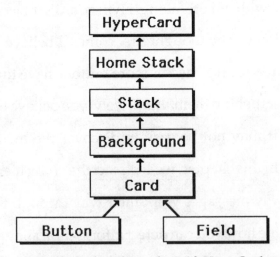

Figure 13-1 *The basic HyperTalk object hierarchy, with HyperCard at the top.*

message using "gravity" to makes its way through the hierarchy. If a mouseUp message doesn't find a matching handler in the current button, then the message "falls through" to the next level of the hierarchy, the card, and so on toward the very bottom, HyperCard. You can still say that a message handler traps a message, but here it's before the message reaches the bottom. Perhaps, too, this perspective sees HyperCard as the foundation upon which other objects rely: backgrounds rely on stacks; cards rely on backgrounds; fields and buttons rely on cards.

Now that you've seen both perspectives, be aware that I prefer the one with HyperCard at the top, and will use this perspective throughout the book, as I did in the *Handbook*. Messages in my "system" work their way *up* the hierarchy.

Making the Chapter's Stack

Before we go on, it's time to make the stack we'll be using as a working laboratory for this chapter's concepts. We'll also add two general purpose handlers to your Home stack, which will come in handy not only for this chapter, but in your stack development, as well.

First, make the stack:

1. *Open the Developer's Guide Master stack.*

2. *Choose Save a Copy from the File menu.*

3. *Type "Chapter 13 Stack" into the file dialog box.*
    This makes the copy, but leaves you in the original master stack.

4. *Open the Chapter 13 Stack using the Open item of the File menu.*

5. *To distinguish this stack from the master and others to be created throughout this book, choose the text tool from the Paint tools palette.*

6. *Choose Background from the Edit menu, or type Command-B.*

7. *Type "Chap. 13" into the upper right corner of the bordered box on the card (Figure 13-2).*

8. *While still in the background editing mode, go to the second card in the stack, the address card.*

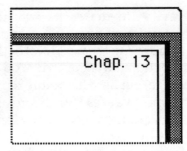

Figure 13-2 *Type "Chap. 13" into the background graphics layer of the first background.*

9. Type "Chap. 13" into the upper right corner, as shown in Figure 13-3.

10. Chooe the Browse tool.
This also removes you from background editing mode.

11. Go to the Home card.

We're now ready to enter two small Home stack handlers you'll find useful throughout your HyperCard days. Choose Stack Info from the Objects menu and click on the Script button. Scroll down to the bottom of the script editing window and type in the following handlers:

```
on lockFields
  repeat with x = 1 to the number of bkgnd fields
    set lockText of bkgnd field x to true
  end repeat

  repeat with x = 1 to the number of card fields
    set lockText of card field x to true
  end repeat
end lockFields


on unLockFields
  repeat with x = 1 to the number of bkgnd fields
    set lockText of bkgnd field x to false
  end repeat

  repeat with x = 1 to the number of card fields
    set lockText of card field x to false
  end repeat
end unLockFields
```

Figure 13-3 *Type "Chap. 13" into the background graphics layer of the second background.*

With these two handlers in your Home stack script, you may type the message names, lockFields and unLockFields, into the Message Box of any stack you're in (you may also include the messages in scripts you write for your own stacks). The handlers let you quickly lock and unlock all fields on the card, no matter how many or how few fields you have. Developing information publishing stacks, in particular, is quickened by these handlers for editing errors in cards with locked fields.

As an alternate, you could combine these two handlers into one, provided you pass along a "true" or "false" along with the message. That handler would look like this:

```
on lockFields setting
  repeat with x = 1 to the number of bkgnd fields
    set lockText of bkgnd field x to setting
  end repeat

  repeat with x = 1 to the number of card fields
    set lockText of card field x to setting
  end repeat
end lockFields
```

The message you would type into the Message Box to lock all fields would be lockFields true; to unlock all fields, you'd type lockFields false. While the second example is more compact, if you cannot remember that you need to type the parameter along with the message name, then it may be better to leave the handlers separate, since their names clearly indicate what you're trying to accomplish. In a couple of chapters from now, we'll have more to say about the concepts surrounding custom messages and handlers, plus the passing of parameters, like the true and false, above.

The Target and Me

Two of the most helpful terms in understanding the fine points of hierarchy and message passing are the function, *the target*, and a special word, *me*. Of the two words, the Target is more useful in streamlining the way one or two handlers can be in charge of many objects, while Me is understood best by the way it differs from the Target.

(We'll be discussing the Target and Me primarily as functions. With HyperCard version 1.2, both words may be used as containers referring to their objects. For example, a closeField handler could examine the new contents of a field and report back in the field if the number entered is out of range, by saying `put "Out of range" into me`. The text goes into the field referred to by Me. Target may be used the same way.)

As a function, the Target returns a value of some kind. What it returns is the name of the object to which a message is originally sent. There is an example from the business world to illustrate the concept.

Let's say a soap manufacturer has a Consumer Affairs department, where customer complaints are handled. An angry customer may not know that such a department exists, but instead goes to the library and finds the name of the company president. The customer writes a letter to the president, who reads it and passes it along to the Consumer Affairs department to handle. The people in Consumer Affairs see that the letter was originally addressed to the big boss, so the letter gets prompt attention. The president, then, was the target of the letter, and the Consumer Affairs department could see who the target was. If another dissatisfied customer sees the name of a regional sales manager in a local newspaper, that second customer may write a complaint letter to the local manager, since it's better to write to a name than a company. When that manager passes the complaint to the Consumer Affairs department at headquarters, chances are that the folks in the department will not act quite so promptly because the target of the letter is less important than the target of the first letter.

Two important things are going on in the above illustration. First, each recipient of a letter is a target—the one to whom a letter was originally directed. Second, the only place real action occurs to remedy the complaint is in the Consumer Affairs department, which was set up just for that purpose.

Now let's see how this applies to HyperCard.

The first inclination when designing a stack is to put a mouseUp handler in each button on the card. The same goes for closeField handlers when some action is to occur as the result of entering text into a field. This is natural, because HyperCard tends to be very modular, and you usually design one button or field action at a time. But when you recognize that several buttons are doing the same or similar kind of action, you can put the handler for that action in a higher level, like the background, and reduce the total number of handlers in your stack.

For one handler in the background to perform the work of several buttons, the handler must be able to identify which button was clicked. A handler uses the Target function to find out which button needs the action. Let's play a bit with the target function.

1. ***Open the Chapter 13 Stack***

2. ***Show the Message Box, and reposition it on the screen so you can see the four buttons at the lower right corner (Figure 13-4).***

3. ***Type the message that locks all fields (if you followed the directions above, it will be either*** `lockFields` ***or*** `lockFields true`***).***

4. ***Hold down the Shift key while choosing Background Info from the Objects menu.***
    This whisks you right to the script editor for the current background.

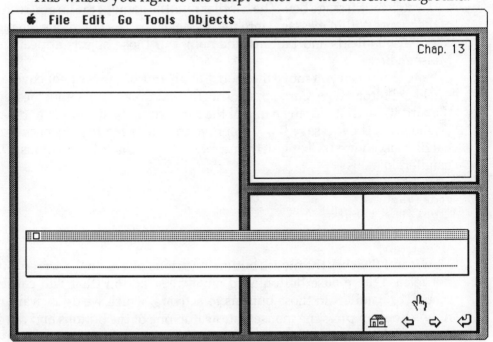

Figure 13-4 *Position the Message Box so you have access to the four buttons at the lower right.*

5. *Remove the openBackground handler, which was carried over from the original background found in the Ideas stacks.*

6. *Enter the following handler into the background script:*

```
on mouseWithin
   put the target
end mouseWithin
```

7. *Click OK or press Enter to close the Script Editor.*

The handler you just entered traps the mouseWithin message, which Hyper-Card sends whenever the screen cursor is inside the confines of a button or field. Remember that HyperCard sends the mouseWithin message to the button or field under the cursor. The recipient of the message is the target, and the Target function returns the name of the object that last received the message of the current handler (mouseWithin in this case).

Move the cursor around the screen slowly (don't press the mouse button), and watch the Message Box. The handler puts the name of the target (recipient of the mouseWithin message) into the Message Box. As you move the mouse over various fields and buttons, the names of those objects appear in the Message Box.

Note that when you move the mouse to an area of the card not covered by a field or button HyperCard appears not to send the mouseWithin message to the card itself. If it did, the name of the card would be the target and would be shown in the Message Box. To prove that, let's modify the background handler just entered. Change it from a mouseWithin handler to a mouseDown handler, like this:

```
on mouseDown
   put the target
end mouseDown
```

Now, carefully click the mouse button in various places on the screen, but do not release the mouse button atop any screen button (that will cause the mouseUp handlers in those buttons to activate, which we don't want right now). You can press the mouse button atop one of the buttons and drag the cursor away from the button to avoid triggering the button's mouseUp handlers. Note here that the card receives a mouseDown message from HyperCard, as evidenced by the card id showing up in the Message Box.

Short, Medium, and Long Target Names

As you experiment with the mouseDown background handler, pay special attention to the form in which the target names are displayed in the Message Box. When a card has no name, as is the case here, the target returns

```
card id 3071
```

which identifies the card's id number (it may be different in your stack) within this stack. The same goes for the background fields, which are identified as

```
bkgnd field id 2
```

or whatever number field you click on.

The buttons, however, return something slightly different. Because these buttons have names attached to them, the target function returns the type of object it is and its given name, as in

```
bkgnd button "Home"
```

when you trigger a mouseDown message on the Home icon button. The same would be true for any object, including fields and cards, when they have names. If, for instance, the first field at the top left of the card was named "Title," the target function would return

```
bkgnd field "Title"
```

in the identical manner to the named buttons in the current stack.

Incidentally, when you send a message from the Message Box, it goes straight to the current card, instead of any buttons or fields. Therefore, if you type

```
the target
```

into the Message Box, HyperCard sees that the last message (the command in the Message Box) was sent to the current card. Thus, the target of the last message is, again, the current card.

The Target function returns a kind of medium strength detail about the object that received the current message. In other words, from the Target function, you know whether an object is a card, a background field or a card button. You can also obtain more information about the place of that object within your HyperCard world by asking for the long name of the target. This version of the target function returns not only the name of the object, but the name of the stack, complete with its complete hard disk path name. Try this yourself. Type

```
the long name of the target
```

into the Message Box. You'll see a long string of characters identifying the precise object in terms of everything stored on your disk. If you have your stack deeply nested within several levels of folders, the full name of the target may extend beyond the right edge of the Message Box. Change the mouseDown handler in the background to

```
on mouseDown
   put the long name of the target
end mouseDown
```

and watch your Message Box fill with huge names of objects each time you trigger a mouseDown message in them.

Just as there is a long name of the target, there is also a short name. The short name, however, is different from the plain target only when the object has a name given to it. For instance, when you type

```
the short name of the target
```

into the Message Box, the short name of an unnamed card (or other object) is strictly its ID number. You cannot shorten that name and expect to know what kind of object it is. If you have a card, field and button that all have the same ID number (this is theoretically possible), you need the identification like "card" or "field" to tell them apart.

Retrieving only the short name of the target is useful when the object has a name. In that case, the short name returns only the name you've given the object, and no other data information about it. For instance, the Home button would return just the word, Home, and nothing else. To experiment with this, change the mouseDown handler in the background to

```
on mouseDown
   put the short name of the target
end mouseDown
```

and press the mouse button atop several objects. Notice that the card and fields (all unnamed) return the same as the plain target function. All four buttons, however, return just their given names.

Target Decisions

When you name an object, you can extract that name with the Target function, and use it for many different purposes. In other words, a handler higher up the hierarchy can test the name of the object (as derived from the Target function) and perform actions accordingly.

To begin our experiments in extracting target names, replace the mouseDown background handler with the following:

```
on mouseUp
  if the target is "bkgnd field id 1"
  then put the time into field 5
  else put empty into field 5
  pass mouseUp
end mouseUp
```

A simple if-then-else construction here tests for the results of the target function. If you click on the locked field whose id is 1 (that's the first field at the top left of the card), then the handler places the time into field 5 (Figure 13-5). If the target is anything but "bkgnd field id 1" then the handler clears the field. Note that each of the four buttons on the card has its own mouseUp handler, which traps the mouseUp message before it reaches the background. Therefore, the background handler responds only when you click on the locked fields or on a spot that has a clear shot to the card.

That means, however, that if you click on the card (outside of any field or button), the time is removed from the card, because the target is the card, not any field or button. You can let the handler respond only to mouseUp messages sent to the locked fields by limiting the actions taken in those cases. To ignore mouseUp messages that come from the card, another if-then-else construction is needed, as follows:

```
on mouseUp
  get the target     -- puts the target into 'it'
  if it contains "field" then
    if it contains 1
    then put the time into field 5
    else put empty into field 5
  end if
  pass mouseUp
end mouseUp
```

When you click on the card, the target returns "card id 3707." If the target name doesn't contain the word "field" then nothing happens to field 5. Only

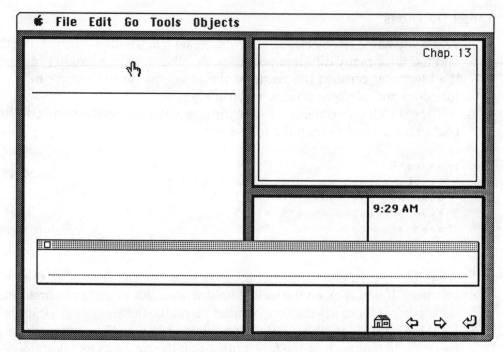

Figure 13-5 *Clicking in the first field (bkgnd field ID 1) causes the time to appear in field 5.*

when the target is, in fact, a field does anything further happen to the card. At that point, the second if-then-else construction looks to see if the target name contains a "1," which the target of bkgnd field id 1 does. If so, then the date goes into field 5; otherwise, the field is emptied. Please note, however, that with this specific example, I knew ahead of time that of all the background fields of this card, only one of them had a "1" in its ID number. If another of the ID numbers had been "12," the test for whether the target contained a "1" would proven true both for field ID 1 and field ID 12.

Naming Objects and Target Names

How you name an object can have a great impact on the elegance of your scripts, especially when handlers make decisions based on target names. More importantly, you can use the names, themselves, to supply information about what the handler should be doing with the message.

The best way to see what we mean is to create a series of four round rectangle buttons in the upper corner workspace of our card. Name each of them "Blinker" along with a number, ranging from 1 to 4, as shown in Figure

13-6. Do not enter any handlers in the buttons' scripts. Now insert three script lines into the background handler as shown below:

```
on mouseUp
  get the target     -- puts the target into 'it'
  if it contains "field" then
    if it contains 1
    then put the time into field 5
    else put empty into field 5
  else
    if it contains "blinker"
    then flash last word of it
  end if
  pass mouseUp
end mouseUp
```

The additional lines to the mouseUp handler look for mouseUp messages that come from any object whose target name contains "blinker." Since all messages from all fields are trapped earlier in the handler (by the first part of

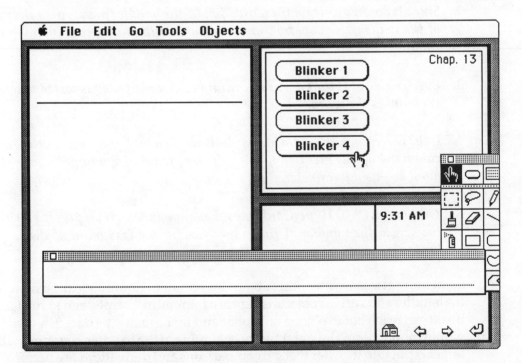

Figure 13-6 *A handler can derive information from the names of targets, like numbers from the Blinker buttons.*

the if-then-else construction), the only possible objects that could send the mouseUp message would be the card or a button. Only blinker-named objects get trapped here, however.

The key principle of this demonstration is that part of the object name is used as part of the Flash command, which is an external command (XCMD) that comes attached to HyperCard. The Flash command takes a number as a parameter, indicating how many times the entire screen should invert black and white pixels (actually invert and invert again to return it to normal viewing). Thus, a flash 1 command causes the entire screen to invert for a brief instant—a flash. You can tell the Flash command to invert the screen as often as you wish, by specifying a different number as a parameter to the Flash command. In the handler, however, instead of a fixed number as a parameter, the parameter is determined from the name of the target of the blinker button. Let's follow this through step-by-step:

1. *The name of the target is placed into the local variable, It.*
    In the case of the Blinker 3 button, the name of the target ("card button 'Blinker 3'") is placed into It.

2. *Since It doesn't contain the word "field," the handler passes over the part of the if-then-else construction concerned with putting or removing the time.*

3. *Every value of It that does **not** contain the word "field" is tested whether It contains the word "blinker."*

4. *If the target was, indeed, a blinker button, then the handler sends the Flash command up the hierarchy, using the last word of the target name—the number—as a parameter.*

5. *The Flash XCMD HyperCard traps the command, and executes it, flashing the screen the number of times specified by the last word of the target button's name.*

Something else is worth noting about this handler. Communication between the handler and various objects is kept at a minimum. Scripts tend to run faster if you can reach out to objects only once and manipulate the data in a variable within the handler. Thus, at the very beginning of the handler, the name of the target is put into It. After that, all comparisons and derivations are performed from the copy of the name in It, rather than going to fetch the target each time. The shorter variable name is also much easier to read on script lines than longer, multiple-word phrases.

You can take this idea of applying target names to other purposes one step further. For instance, if you change the names of the blinker buttons to flash buttons, as shown in Figure 13-7, then you can use the short name of the button targets as commands in themselves. The handler to take care of this would be:

```
on mouseUp
  get the short name of the target    -- puts the target into 'It'
  if it contains "field" then
    if it contains 1
    then put the time into field 5
    else put empty into field 5
  else
    if it contains "flash"
    then do it                        -- e.g., do "flash 3"
  end if
  pass mouseUp
end mouseUp
```

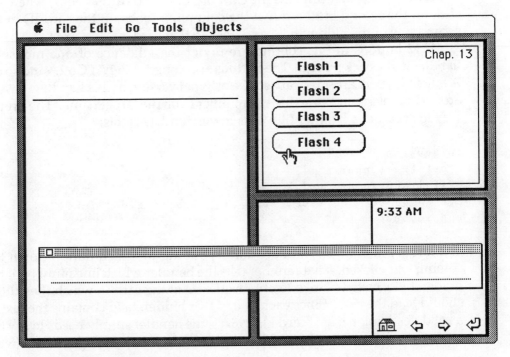

Figure 13-7 *Object names themselves may be used as commands, when retrieved with the short name of the Target function.*

Because the fields in this card are not named, the short names of those targets still contain the word "field," so the first part of the if-then-else construction is unchanged. The big difference is in the button part. Since the short name of the target of, say, button Flash 1 is "Flash 1," the handler must test for the presence of the word "flash" to see if it is one of the four flash buttons. Then, since the short name of the target is a valid command (including parameter), the handler sends the contents of It as a command up the hierarchy. The flash XCMD doesn't care where the command came from or how it was constructed—it carries out the command anyway.

When to Use the Target

As mentioned earlier, the initial tendency in building a stack application is to put a mouseUp handler in each button on the screen. You can also plan ahead for cases in which a thoughtful series of button or field names can be instituted from the outset. For instance in an application I wrote for an article in *Macworld*, there is a card in a stack that has a series of 12 identical-looking buttons adjacent to a multiple-lined field (Figure 13-8). A click of each button triggers a Go command in the mouseUp handler, using the corresponding line of a hidden field that contains the card IDs of linked cards. Thus, when you click on the second button down the column, it looks up the card ID in the second line of the hidden field and goes to that card.

All 12 buttons in this column are under the guidance of one mouseUp handler in the background. The buttons are named "Go 1," "Go 2," and so on. A bug in HyperCard 1.0.1 caused the original version of this handler to work around problems in extracting the number from the target name. The proper way to set up this handler (it works in version 1.1) is this:

```
on mouseUp
  get the target
  if it contains "go"
  then go to line (last word of it) of field "Links"
end mouseUp
```

The last word of It is a number corresponding to which button down the column was clicked. That number tells the handler which line number of the hidden field, called "Links," contains the ID of the card to which the button should lead the user. Since each line of that hidden field contains the text of a valid destination (e.g., "card id 32987"), the handler simply needs to say the equivalent of "go to line 2 of field Links" to initiate the jump to that card (we'll

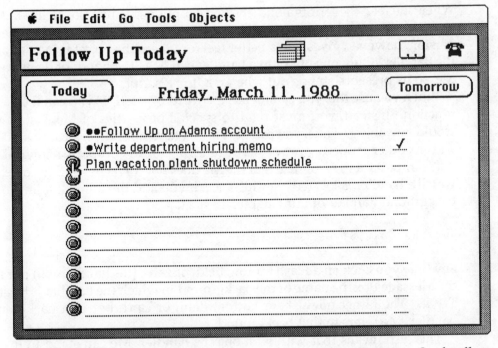

Figure 13-8 *Each of the round button's names is used to direct navigation. One handler, using the target function, does the job for all 12 buttons. This stack, the Tickler, originally appeared in Macworld magazine.*

see more examples of this kind of linking in Chapter 18).

The Target and Me

HyperTalk has a shortcut word you can use in a handler to refer to the object in which a handler is located: Me. It's not exactly a function, because it doesn't return a value. But you can use it in some ways as you would use the Target function when referring to the very same object that contains the handler.

Let's say you assign a handler in the Flash 1 button that must retrieve the hilite property of that button. In such a situation, the following two handlers yield the same results:

```
on mouseUp
   put the hilite of button "Flash 1"
end mouseUp

on mouseUp
   put the hilite of me
end mouseUp
```

When you read the scripts aloud, the first sounds very impersonal, like talking to a friend in the third person: "How is Theodore Cleaver today?" The Me version, however, gives you a better feel for where the object is in relation to the handler. Only one object in a handler can have the honor of being called Me, so its presence stands out when reading a script.

When you use Me, you cannot use the word by itself, as you can the Target function. Instead, you must refer to specific properties of Me, just as you would any object. Thus, you can get and set text properties, locations, styles, and any other property of an object by referring to the <property name> of me.

It's important to recognize that the Me does not travel beyond the object in which a handler is located. For instance, if you add the following line to the background handler of our Chapter 13 stack

```
put the name of me
```

any time you click on a Flash button, field, or card, this handler will put into the Message Box the name of the background in which the handler is located. Try it. The target might be a button, field, or card, but in a background handler, Me refers to that background.

This also means that within an object's handler, Me can stand in for the target, provided you specify the property you're looking for. Here's a table to help you understand the correlation between Me and the Target within a handler of the target object:

```
the name of me              the target
                            the name of the target
the long name of me         the long name of the target
the short name of me        the short name of the target
```

Therefore, my recommendation is to use the Target function whenever a handler needs information about an object other than the one containing the handler; use Me when working on an object's properties from a handler attached to that object.

Choosing the Appropriate Level

Now that you've seen some tricks of the trade, it's time to examine where the best place is in the hierarchy to put various handlers. It's difficult to generalize on such matters, because the organization of a stack often has much influence on the placement of common handlers. While many handlers have obvious locations (e.g., openStack in the stack script), we'll focus here on the more variable ones: mouse and field handlers.

Before getting too deep into handler placement, I should stress that it is often very appropriate to mix the location of handlers based on the actions that various buttons or fields instigate. In the Chapter 13 Stack we've been working with so far, we've said nothing about moving the locations of the mouseUp handlers attached to the four icon buttons that came with the stack. Each button has its own distinct visual effect and a single action command to either go some place or pop a card. Because the specific actions of these handlers are so different from each other, shifting them to a background or stack level mouseUp handler would be more trouble than its worth. In fact the resulting handler would have so many if-then-else constructions in it to direct the desired visual effect and action, that it could easily turn into a maintenance nightmare if some additional mouseUp action were added to the background. No, it's best to leave these short handlers inside the buttons.

Conversely, I don't often recommend putting mouseUp handlers at the stack script level. The primary reason for this is that even if a stack starts out in design as a homogeneous stack, with a single background, the likelihood of adding another background, even for a title card or group of index cards, is very high. Any other background you add will have a different set of buttons that do very different things. The chance that your mouseUp handler in the stack script will be valid for the buttons in the new background is small. By putting the handlers in the background to begin with, you leave yourself more open to an expanding stack without having to reposition your mouse handlers.

Reducing Handlers

It's very possible that a stack might have complex button handlers that share nothing with other button handlers. In such a case, it is most appropriate to keep all mouseUp handlers in their respective buttons. There's nothing wrong with that if the occasion calls for it. The situations to watch out for are when there is a series of similar buttons, as illustrated earlier in the Macworld stack, or when you notice that a number of buttons have nearly identical handlers.

To work with the second situation, I suggest placing the handler in the background level. About the only time I'd recommend putting a mouse handler in a card script is if the card is now and always will be a single card unto itself. Even then, if the card is the only card of a background, then I'd still tend to put the handler in the background just in case another card is added later to the background, sharing the same buttons.

When you recognize that several buttons have similar handlers, you should try to write a background mouseUp handler that uses the target names of the similar buttons to differentiate the actions of each button. Use numbers in concert with letters for button names (as in the Go 1, Go 2 series, above), or tie the name to the action that makes one button behave differently from another. For instance, if there are the same (or no) visual effects for going to the previous and next cards in a stack, consider using the names "Prev" and "Next" as button names. Then the handler would use the button names (short names of the target) to perform the action, as in the following script excerpt:

```
on mouseUp
   if the target contains "button" then
      get the short name of the target
      visual effect checkerboard
      go it
   end if
   pass mouseUp
end mouseUp
```

Here, the very name of the button dictates how the handler acts, by going to the previous or next card, as the case may be.

The Ultimate Handler Reduction

Now is as good a time as any to demonstrate the ultimate in reducing literally hundreds of individual mouseUp handlers to a single background mouseUp handler. It occurs in *Business Class*. The scheme that made this work was a careful system of naming cards and buttons to accommodate a wide variety of button choices on a *Business Class* card.

While *Business Class* was in development, I started putting individual mouseUp handlers into each button on every card or background. That meant that for a map card like the one in Figure 13-9 (which shows the button locations), there were dozens of mouseUp handlers for the card. Initially, the reasoning was sound, because the buttons on the map not only go to a particular country's map, but it also has a specific kind of visual effect—a wipe in one of four directions, depending on the relative location of the neighboring

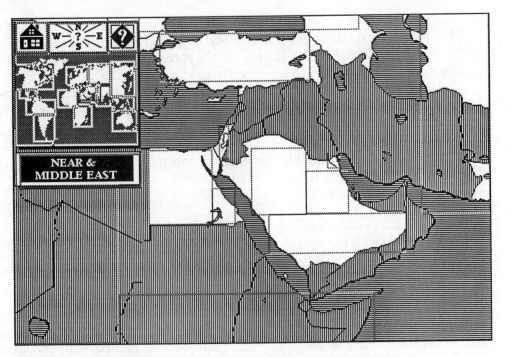

Figure 13-9 *One handler controls navigation on every transparent button in Business Class. The names of the buttons dictate the destination of a Go command.*

country you click on. A typical handler looked like this:

```
on mouseUp
   visual effect wipe down
   go to card "Belgium"
end mouseUp
```

Remember, too, that the *Business Class* maps are divided into two geographical groups. Stack names for these two groups are Business Class 1 and Business Class 2. Therefore, when you are viewing a map that has a button linked to a map located in the other stack, the handler would look like this:

```
on mouseUp
   visual effect wipe up
   go to card "Morocco" of stack "Business Class 2"
end mouseUp
```

Add to that the possibility that the user could click on the miniature regional map in the upper left corner that not only goes to the regional map, but also has a completely different visual effect, an Iris Close.

Finally, there is the row of buttons at the bottom of each country map. Those buttons must know which country's map you're viewing, and then go to that country's information card in the appropriate stack. To simplify this part of the operation, I had established very early in the creation process a global variable that was set to the country's name each time a country map card opened. That global variable, called currentCountry, played a big role in the background button scripts for each of the information buttons in early versions. A typical script looked like this:

```
on mouseUp
  global currentCountry
  go to card currentCountry of stack "BC1•Climate"
end mouseUp
```

Here, the stack name, "BC1•Climate," indicates the climate information cards for the countries whose maps are contained in the Business Class 1 portion of the world (Europe and the Middle East). As with the map cards, each information card within an information stack is named with the country name. Thus, there is a card named "France" in the Climate, Currency, Time, Travel Documents, and every other information stack in the *Business Class* stack system.

All in all, it meant that there were a lot of buttons, each with its own mouseUp handler. And I was running out of disk space, even with the division of the world into two sections. Intuitively, I knew I'd save a ton of disk bytes if I could combine all those buttons into far fewer handlers. In each of the map stacks, there are approximately 350 background and card buttons. Even at a conservative average of 75 handler characters per button, that meant the scripts were eating up more than 26K per disk.

One Handler Fits All

The supreme solution was to create a single background handler that took care of possibilities for any kind of button that could appear on a map card. While the handler isn't particularly complex, it helped to map out a strategy for naming the buttons so that the target names would assist in determining where the handler sends the user.

The scheme was as follows. Each transparent button on a map would be named with the name of the country to which the user would go when clicking on that button. The button name would also contain the direction of the wipe visual effect. If the visual effect part of the name is "close," that means that the effect is an iris, as opposed to a wipe. The handler was also to intercept mouseUp messages from buttons linked to information cards. The names of those buttons (they're background buttons, because they're the same for all country map cards) simply contained the name of the information card stack to which the user would go. All parts of the handler relied on the name of current country, which, as before, is automatically put into the global variable, currentCountry, when each map card opens.

Therefore, the handler must distinguish among three types of buttons: those with information stack names (all of which contain a bullet in their name), those with country names and wipe directions, and those with regional map names and iris close visual effects. The handler must also be prepared to switch stacks from Business Class 1 to Business Class 2, and vice versa, if the country button clicked on points to a country in the other geographic collection. In those cases, yet another character is added to the button name: the number 1 or 2, whichever is the other stack collection.

To demonstrate what some of these button names look like, consider the map of Spain card in Figure 13-10, which shows what the card looks like with the button tool selected. Note that Spain is in the map stack Business Class 1.

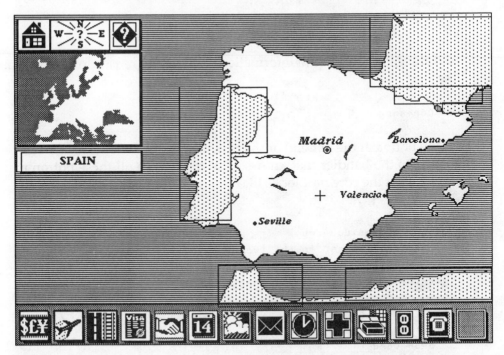

Figure 13-10 *Even adding the buttons to information cards didn't affect the single handler that controls navigation from every button (except Home and Help) in Business Class's map and information cards.*

Both of the rectangular buttons atop Portugal to the left of Spain have the button name

```
Portugal right
```

while the three buttons atop the corner of France are named

```
France down
```

The buttons covering the northern tip of Africa point to cards in the map stack Business Class 2. The name of the long button at the lower right is named

```
Algeria up 2
```

indicating that the wipe will be up, and that the handler must switch to the other map stack before going to the Algeria card.

It is difficult to see, but there is a transparent button on top of the miniature map of Europe in the upper left corner. When a user clicks on this map, he should zoom out to the Europe regional map. That button's name is

```
Europe close
```

And along the bottom row, information card buttons have informative names, like

```
BC1•Currency
```

for the button at the left end of the row.

Now to the handler that knows what to do with all these button names. Here's what the core of it looks like:

```
on mouseUp
  global currentCountry
  if "button" is not in the target then pass mouseUp

  get the short name of the target

  if it contains "•" then
    set cursor to 4
    push card
    visual effect wipe up
    go card currentCountry of stack it
  else
```

```
    if last word of it is "2" then
      put " of stack" && quote & "Business Class 2" & quote ¬
      into switch
      delete last word of it
    else put empty into switch

    if last word of it is "close" then put "iris close" into type
    else put "wipe" && (last word of it) into type
    visual effect type

    get "card" && quote & word 1 ¬
    to (number of words of it - 1) of it & quote
    put switch after it
    go it
  end if
end mouseUp
```

After declaring the global variable, currentCountry, the handler tests to make sure that it is handling button mouseUp messages only. All others are passed up the hierarchy. Next, the short name of the target—just the name you assign to the button—is put into to It.

The first test of the major if-then-else construction is whether the button name contains a bullet. If so, that means that the button is linked to an information card. That button name contains the name of the stack, and the visual effect to all information cards is a wipe up. All that's left is to go to the card bearing the name of the current country (from the global variable) in the stack.

All other buttons go to map cards either in the same stack or in the companion map stack. Thus, the first test for the rest of the buttons is whether the last word of the name contains a "2," which indicates that the map is in Business Class 2 (this handler in the Business Class 2 stack looks instead for a "1," which points to the Business Class 1 stack). If the "2" is part of the name, then the handler assembles the last part of the eventual Go command, which reads,

```
of stack "Business Class 2"
```

and places it into a local variable, called switch. Because the handler is finished with the "2," it deletes that last word of It, because the rest of the handler expects only two pieces of information: the visual effect and the name of the country.

The next few lines of the handler deal with the visual effect, which is the last word of It. If the effect is "close" then it means that the effect is an Iris Close.

Otherwise, the effect is added to the word "wipe" and placed into a local variable called type. This variable contains the visual effect, whether it be an Iris Close or Wipe with a modifier.

As we draw near the end of the handler, a comparatively long script line assembles the name of the card that the Go command will need. That name must include the word "card" and the name of the card. Some countries, button names, and country card names contain more than one word, so the name assembly includes word 1 through as many words as there are in It, less the one at the end containing the visual effect direction. For instance, if It contains "New Zealand left," then the card name the handler must prepare is

```
card "New Zealand"
```

with quotation marks and all. Note that by using the Get command, the handler reuses It by pulling the desired text from it and adding some fresh material to come up with the desired card name.

The switch variable, you'll recall, is either empty if there are no numbers after the button name, or contains the name of the other map stack. Thus, switch is added to the end of It to round out the destination. From the Spain map, for instance, if you clicked on the Morocco button, at this point of the handler It would contain

```
card "Morocco" of stack "Business Class 2"
```

It's now a simple matter to go to that card. The It variable contains the full "address" of the destination, even if it's in a different stack.

By replacing all those separate 350 handlers per map stack with one all-purpose mouseUp handler, *Business Class* was able to ship comfortably on two 800K diskettes as planned. Had the extra space not been found, the stack system would have been missing a couple of countries.

CloseField Handlers

Where you place closeField handlers is very dependent on your application. If you have any closeField handlers at all, you must evaluate how the ones you wish to control differ from the ones you don't care about. For instance, in the address card background of Chapter 13 Stack, a background level closeField handler puts today's date into the third field. Of the three fields on the card, only two are open for text editing. Appropriately enough, a change to either field should be reflected in an updated field 3.

There will be times, however, when a card has many fields on it, but only one or two fields' closing is of any consequence. In those cases, it is still not clear at which level the handlers belong. If the handlers are first placed in individual fields and they are significantly different, then they should stay in their fields. But if the actions of a few closeField handlers are the same or nearly so, then consider placing a closeField handler in the background. If closing every field causes the handler to execute—when you only want a couple fields to trigger the handler—you need a way to filter out the closeField messages. You should also do it quickly so that the normal tabbing progression isn't slowed by needless handler execution. To do this, name the action fields with at least one common element that only those field names share. Then, early in the background closeField handler test for that element in the target name. If it's not there, then pass the closeField message immediately, as in the following:

```
on closeField
  if "magic" is not in the target then pass closeField
  ...
  [do your stuff for the "magic" named fields]
  ...
end closeField
```

For one thing, you know for sure that closeField messages are sent only to fields, so your handler needn't test for whether the target contains "field," as you do for mouse messages.

As a living example of putting a closeField handler in the background that affects only certain fields, let's turn to the Daily Appointment stack of *Focal Point* (Figure 13-11). For each hour of the day, the card offers a two-line field to note appointments. When you need to write down some additional data about an appointment, you may click on the button to the left of the two-line field. This shows a large detail field. There is one large detail field for each hour of the day.

The design of the stack is such that when you hide the detail field, the stack checks to see if the content of the field has changed. If so, and if the field went from empty to not empty, then another handler draws a small box around the plus mark. Thus, the next time you come to the card, you get a visual clue that there is additional data one level below. While you can hide the field by clicking on the button again, I also allow the user to close the field by pressing the Enter key, which sends a closeField message to that field. None of those detail fields have closeField handlers in them. Instead, the message works its way up the hierarchy to the background closeField handler, which is:

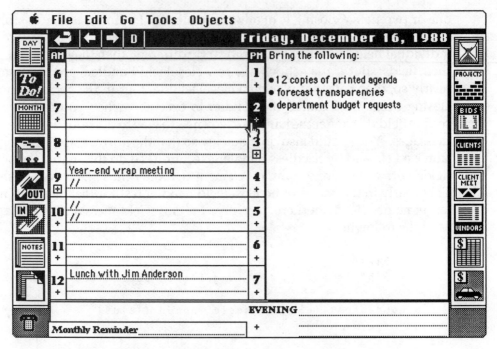

Figure 13-11 *By naming the hidden fields and the hourly buttons identically, it is a simple task to have a closeField message sent to the field trigger a mouseUp message in the button to hide the field.*

```
on closeField
  if "Zoom" is not in the target then exit closeField
  send mouseUp to bkgnd button (the short name of the target)
end closeField
```

What happens here is that the closure of one of those "Zoom" fields triggers the equivalent of clicking on the button for that hour, which, not coincidentally, has the same name as the Zoom field. Thus, the short name of the field (the target) becomes the name of the background button to which a mouseUp message gets sent. That mouseUp handler (which is also in the background) draws or erases the little square, depending on the contents of the Zoom field.

Lateral Hierarchy

In this section we cover an advanced topic, but one that is relevant to the subject of object hierarchy and the way in which messages are passed during the execution of a handler. There are two scenarios that we'll investigate:

executing a handler that takes you to a different background; and one that takes you to a different stack. What we'll be looking at in particular is what happens when a mouseUp handler that takes you to one of these places then sends a message. Because there may be two possible backgrounds or stacks, how does the message flow up the hierarchy?

For example, let's say that a stack consists of two quite different backgrounds. In each background, however, is a calculation handler that performs addition on various fields. The calculations are very different, so the decision is to keep the handlers in the backgrounds, rather than build them both into a single stack script handler. Now, let's say a button in Background A picks up a number in a field of the current Background A card, goes to a corresponding card in Background B, and then uses that number in a calculation together with data in the card in Background B. The button's handler would be

```
on mouseUp
   get field "Balance"          -- in a card of bkgnd A
   go to card "Final Invoice"   -- in bkgnd B
   put it into field "Balance Forward"
   calculate
end mouseUp
```

where "calculate" is the name of a handler in the background of the card "Final Invoice." If there is also a different calculate handler in the background of the original card (from which the Balance field was taken), which calculate handler prevails, considering that it is called by a button in the first card's background?

When a handler goes to another background or another stack and then sends a message of its own—whether it be a HyperCard command or a custom message—the traditional hierarchical order is slightly different than when all action takes place on a single card. The precise order varies, too, depending on whether the action is in a different stack or just in a different background. When the scene is in a different background, there are then two possible hierarchy orders. First, however, we'll look at what happens when changing stacks within a handler.

Stack-to-Stack Hierarchy

What we're about to describe is not simple, primarily because all the hierarchy rules you've learned so far get jumbled a bit the instant a handler jumps to another stack. For purposes of illustration, we'll use the calculation handler idea mentioned earlier. We'll assume that the mouseUp handler that gets things rolling also contains a calculate message. Here's the handler:

```
on mouseUp
  get field "Balance"  -- in stack "Details"
  go to card "Invoice Calculator" of stack "Invoices"
  put it into field "Balance Forward"
  calculate
end mouseUp
```

The button containing this handler is in the first stack, "Details." It picks up the value of a field ("Balance"), goes to a specific card in a second stack, inserts the value into a field in that other stack's card, and finally issues the Calculate message.

If there were no calculate handler anywhere in the hierarchy of either stack, the message would follow the hierarchical path illustrated in Figure 13-12 in search of the handler. Note that the message first exhausts all possibilities in the stack that contains the mouseUp handler, even though the handler has already brought you to the second stack. If nothing is found up through the stack script of the first stack, then the search starts at the card script level of the second stack. From there it works its way up the traditional hierarchy in the second stack, continuing to the Home stack as a last resort.

The importance of knowing this special hierarchy comes when you use identically named handlers in different stacks that do not perform identical

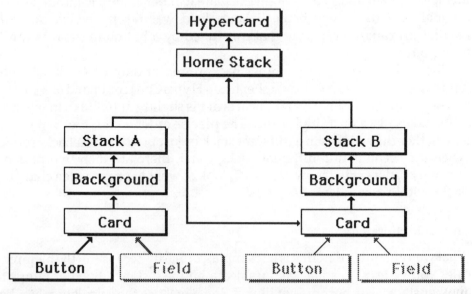

Figure 13-12 *The hierarchy is extended when your script takes you to another stack and sends you a message of its own. It first exhausts all possibilities in its own stack, then in the new stack before heading to the Home stack.*

operations. In the calculate message example, above, if you had a calculate handler in the background or stack script of the first stack, that's the handler that would be executed during the mouseUp handler, even though you may have expected the calculate handler in the second stack to be the operation. Duplicate handler naming may be intentional or accidental. Either way, you should understand that hierarchies behave a bit differently when switching stacks.

Background-to-Background Hierarchy

If a handler goes to a card in a different background in the same stack as the original handler, the hierarchy acts unexpectedly. If you have handlers of the same name in both backgrounds, you'll be headed for trouble. Here's what happens.

Using our earlier example of going to a card in a second background of the same stack, let's say that you have calculate handlers in both background scripts. When you run the mouseUp handler that sends the calculate message, the hierarchy runs like the one shown in Figure 13-13. In other words, if there is a calculate handler in any object belonging to the first background (button, field, card, or background script), or if the handler is in the stack script, the message never gets a chance to look for a match in the second background's scripts.

When no calculate handler is in the first background's objects or the stack script, then the message goes to the card and background scripts of the second background in search of a match. This is illustrated in Figure 13-14.

For the most part, you needn't worry much about these anomalies to the traditional object hierarchy of HyperCard, but you certainly should be aware of them in case you get some strange results. If you ever find the error message that the handler cannot find a certain field, click on the Script button to see exactly which object's script is causing the difficulty. You may discover that the handler is in one background or stack when you thought the handler in another should be at work.

Bypassing the Hierarchy

In addition to sending a HyperCard message along the various hierarchical paths—traditional and "lateral"—you can also be very specific if you want a message to go to a particular object that may be out of the ordinary order. For a demonstration, we can take a chapter out of *Focal Point*.

In the Projects stack, for example, a doMenu handler intercepts the New Card menu option, because generating a new card also entails generating a

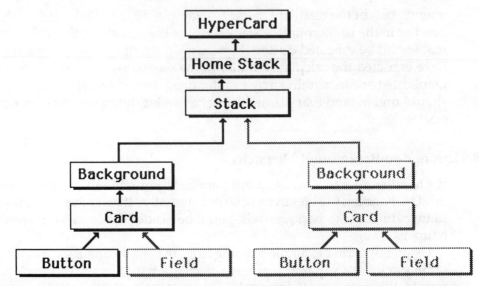

Figure 13-13 *When a handler goes to a card in another background and sends a message, it first looks all the way to the stack script for a match.*

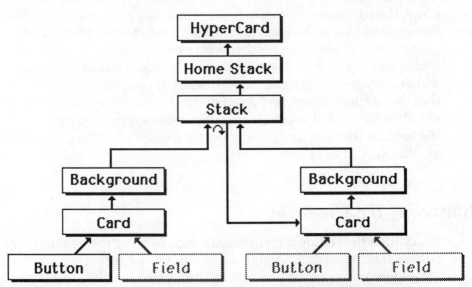

Figure 13-14 *If there is no matching handler in the stack script, then it looks in the card and background scripts of the second background before continuing up the hierarchy.*

number of linked cards. Therefore, whenever the user chooses New Card from the Edit menu (or types Command-N), a handler in the stack follows an involved sequence that generates new cards from each of the six backgrounds and maintains a system of hard links among the various cards (described in Chapter 18).

Within that handler, I must often generate a new card. If the handler simply sent the message,

```
doMenu "New Card"
```

that would be the same as choosing New Card from the Edit menu, which would start the handler again. Eventually the situation would get so recursive as to tie up the stack in a knot. To create the new cards, the handler must bypass the regular hierarchy and send the message directly to HyperCard. By sending the message to HyperCard, there is no way it will be intercepted by any other object along the way. Thus, the message becomes

```
send "doMenu New Card" to HyperCard
```

whenever the handler must create a new card in its magical workings.

"HyperCard" is a valid object name. If you send a message to any other kind of object, like a stack or background, be sure you use a valid name for the object, such as its ID number or its given name.

The discussions in this chapter should give you plenty to think about. How you treat the HyperCard hierarchy has much to do with the structure of your stacks and how handlers should be placed throughout. From here we can explore various HyperCard system messages to discover how the stack author can maintain control over such things as navigation through a heterogeneous stack, without the browser being aware of how much you're saving him from total confusion.

14

More About System Messages

System messages, you'll recall, are messages that HyperCard sends to various objects, usually as the result of some action. For instance, when you click the mouse button at an average down-and-up pace, Hyper-Card sends three messages to the screen button: mouseDown, mouseS-tillDown, and mouseUp. HyperCard has a vocabulary of 39 messages it sends at various times.

Who Gets Which Message

HyperCard sends messages to only three types of objects: buttons, fields, or cards. Precisely to which object the message goes depends largely on action the user takes. For example, the mouseUp message goes to a button when you click the mouse with the cursor atop a screen button. But if you click the mouse button with the cursor atop a locked text field, the mouseUp message goes to that field. And if you click the mouse button when the cursor "sees" the card—with no intervening field or button layers—then the mouseUp message goes to the card.

Table 14-1 lists all 39 HyperCard system messages and shows which objects may be the recipient of these messages. What may seem confusing at first is that several messages that relate to backgrounds and stacks are sent initially to the card level of the hierarchy. The card level is merely an "entry point" for HyperCard messages along the hierarchy. With the entry point at the card level, you may experiment with sending system messages from the Message Box, because anything you type into the Message Box goes to the current card first.

Table 14-1.

To Button: newButton, deleteButton, mouseDown,
            mouseStillDown, mouseUp, mouseEnter, mouseWithin,
            mouseLeave

To Field: newField, deleteField
            openField, closeField
            mouseDown, mouseStillDown, mouseUp
            mouseEnter, mouseWithin, mouseLeave
            returnInField, enterInField

To Card: newCard, deleteCard
            openCard, closeCard
            newBackground, deleteBackground
            openBackground, closeBackground
            newStack, deleteStack
            openStack, closeStack
            mouseDown, mouseStillDown, mouseUp
            returnKey, enterKey, tabKey, arrowKey
            suspend, resume, startup, quit
            help, idle, doMenu

As an example, let's say that you are at work on a handler that puts today's date into the first card of a stack when the stack opens. You need to trap for the openStack system message, which HyperCard sends immediately after opening the stack. The best place for an openStack handler (or any stack-related handler) is in the stack script.

While you're building an openStack handler, you certainly want to test it to make sure everything is working as planned. The hard way to test it would be to go to another stack and then reopen the stack you were working on. The fast way would be to send an openStack message manually from the keyboard. If you type

```
openStack
```

into the Message Box, that message first goes to the current card. From there it works its way up the hierarchy, until it finds the openStack handler in the stack script. You can use this technique to test any handler in stack, background, or card scripts.

While most other aspects of system messages are covered well in the *Handbook*, I've developed a number of strategies and techniques for using system messages in stacks. I've also seen cases in which system messages have been used improperly. In the following sections, we'll look at the finer points of system messages.

Mouse Messages

Perhaps the biggest misconception about mouseDown, mouseStillDown, and mouseUp messages is that they belong only in buttons. Far from it. Those three mouse messages may also be sent to fields and cards. Let's see how.

Text fields are often a puzzlement for new HyperCard authors, because the behavior of the cursor and HyperTalk is different for fields than for other objects. For instance, if you lock the field (check the locked text button in the Field Info dialog box), the cursor remains the Browse tool when drawn across the field. As long as you can see that little browsing hand, the field will respond to mouse clicks just as buttons do. Therefore, you may turn an entire text field into the equivalent of a button by locking the field. You may then put mouseUp or similar handlers into the field script, just as you would into a button script.

When a field is not locked, however, the cursor turns into an I-beam cursor, identical to the kind you find in word processing programs. A click of the mouse button plants the flashing text insertion pointer into the field, showing you where the next character you type will appear. That click, however, did not send a mouse message to that field. Yet the field is not inert when unlocked, for the act of planting the text insertion pointer into the field sent an openField message to that field. In a sense, you are opening the field for action. But any mouseDown, mouseStillDown, or mouseUp handlers you place in an unlocked field script will never be found.

All fields and buttons, however, may trap mouseEnter, mouseWithin, and mouseLeave messages, even if a field is unlocked. The sending of these messages is not dependent on clicking the mouse. I've seen a couple of stacks that use these messages in a potentially dangerous way. I suppose one author did not want the browser of a demonstration program to be burdened with clicking the mouse on screen buttons. With a mouseWithin handler in buttons, the user triggers actions simply by moving the cursor within the rectangle of the button. Perhaps this method is appropriate for some early learning and entertainment stacks, but I believe this can become very confusing for an unsuspecting user. If the novice user tries to accustom himself to using the mouse, he will probably draw the cursor all over the screen, including atop one of these mouseWithin buttons. When the screen shifts as the result of no apparent or deliberate action, I believe the user will think the stack is automated—acting on its own. A deliberate click of the mouse is a better trigger for action.

Also note that the card is a valid recipient of mouseDown, mouseStillDown, and mouseUp messages. That means that as long as no other objects on a card have those mouse handlers in them, you can place any of those handlers in the card script. This would be in lieu of drawing a full-card sized button and placing a mouse handler in the button. Such a button would be a waste of an object, and every object you add to a card slows the card's opening and closing time. To emphasize this point: There is no need to create a full-card-sized button, because you can put a mouseUp handler in the card's script.

Therefore, if you are creating an information publishing stack in which the user is supposed to click anywhere on the screen to continue, do these three things:

1. *Lock all text fields.*

2. *Make sure no buttons or fields have a mouseUp handler in them.*

3. *Put the mouseUp handler in the card script.*

Press-and-Hold Buttons

While we're on the subject of mouse handlers, there's a technique I developed for *Focal Point* to take the place of the traditional mouseUp handler in certain situations. The problem I had was that when in stacks like the Daily Appointment Book, in which you may need to click ahead several days, I found the repeated mouse clicking to be a nuisance. While clicking on the right arrow button, I felt that it would be more natural if I could click and hold the arrow button down, while the cards flashed by one at a time. The arrow would be more analogous to the arrows you find in scroll bars. When you click and hold those arrows, the scroll bar thumb continues to increment until you let up on the arrow.

While the problem of making a button continue to act while holding the mouse button down was not particularly difficult, it took a special combination of two handlers to also let single clicks act the way you'd expect. The two handlers are mouseStillDown and mouseDown handlers. Here's how they work.

The mouseStillDown handler is the handler that does all of the work that the arrow button should be doing, like going to the next card. In some *Focal Point* stacks, the actions are more complicated (like knowing how many cards to advance depending on the Daily, Weekly, Monthly, Yearly interval button setting), but the same basic handler structure applies. In a simpler stack, like the Notes stack, the mouseStillDown handler for the right arrow button is

```
on mouseStillDown
   go next
end mouseStillDown
```

That was the easy part.

Complicating matters is that on the slower machines, like the Macintosh Plus, or in stacks that have a large number of buttons, it was easy to click the mouse atop one of the arrow buttons—one complete mouseDown and mouseUp cycle—so quickly that HyperCard never had a chance to send a mouseStillDown message. That meant that the user might click on a button and get no response. That, of course, was unacceptable.

The solution was to force a mouseStillDown message every time the user pressed the button. In other words, inside a handler for one of the other two mouse click messages would be the message mouseStillDown. That message would be trapped by the mouseStillDown handler in the same button script. At first, I erroneously tried putting the mouseStillDown message in a mouseUp handler. While it worked fine for the slower machines (although there was a very slight hesitation before jumping into action), it was disastrous on the Mac II. Since the Mac II responds so fast, and is able to squeeze more messages per second, it sent a mouseStillDown message within a medium-length click. Then the mouseUp handler sent another mouseStillDown message, triggering another "go next." It was like a runaway train that always overshot the desired station by one.

The final answer was to put the mouseStillDown message into a mouseDown handler. Even on a Macintosh II, as long as you release the mouse button as the next card scrolls into view, HyperCard won't send a mouseStillDown message to trigger another scroll. Thus, the entire script for a right arrow button in the Notes stack of *Focal Point* is

```
on mouseStillDown
  go next
end mouseStillDown

on mouseDown
  mouseStillDown
end mouseDown
```

There is no mouseUp handler of any kind in the button.

Remote Control of Buttons

In multiple-stack systems, you may need access to button scripts to perform operations by remote control. For instance, the Deadlines stack in *Focal Point* is linked to the Projects stack so that if you check off a deadline item as being finished in the Deadlines stack, its corresponding listing in the Projects stack is also checked off as being completed (Figure 14-1). But when that happens, some updating in the Projects stack is also necessary. While the user does not see this interaction with the Projects stack (the screen is locked the entire time), someone must click on an Update button in the Projects stack to take care of housekeeping.

The operation that is performed by the Update button could have been incorporated into the handler that posts the check mark in the Projects stack, but why duplicate efforts? The procedure works fine when you manually click the Update button in the Projects stack. All you need is a way to click that button, even though you're doing it from a handler in the Deadlines stack.

The way you do it is to send a mouseUp message to that button, like this:

```
send "mouseUp" to bkgnd button "Update"
```

Like we discussed in the last chapter, the Send command traverses the rules of hierarchy. But, as you see here, it can do even more.

Sending mouseUp messages to specific buttons is a common occurrence in *Focal Point*, especially in the scripts attached to the various applications buttons along the card's left and right edges. For instance, when you are in the

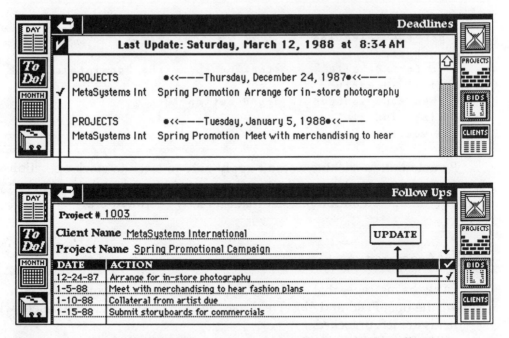

Figure 14-1 *Checking off a follow-up item in the Deadlines stack eventually triggers a remote control pressing of the Update button in the Projects or Proposals stack.*

Daily Appointment stack, its own icon button contains a script that finds today's card. When coming to this stack from most other *Focal Point* stacks, the system presumes that you want to see (or at least start with) today's appointment card. But when coming from the To Do or Monthly Calendar stacks, it is more likely that the destination appointment card is some day other than today. As a result, I could not place an openStack handler that automatically finds today's cards—it would not apply to every opening of the Stack. Instead, I placed the message

```
send mouseUp to bkgnd button "Day"
```

in the scripts of the Daily Appointment stack icon button in most of the other stacks. Importantly, those buttons send the message only if there is no text selected in the original card to be searched for in the Daily Appointment stack. For example, the script of the Daily Appointment book icon button from the Directory and Dialer stack is

```
on mouseUp
  get the selection
  push card
  go to "FP•Daily"  -- stack name for the Appointment book
  if it is empty
  then send mouseUp to bkgnd button "Day"
  else find it
end mouseUp
```

Remote button clicking doesn't apply only to stack-to-stack operations. It works just as well in any situation, even card-to-card operations, when you can call upon a button handler that's already been written.

Field Messages

Of all the messages that apply to fields, the ones we'll be concerned with here are the openField and closeField messages. These messages are sent when fields are left unlocked.

The openField message is always sent to the field that you tab to or click on with the I-Beam cursor. The message is always sent, regardless of the content, or lack thereof, of the field.

The closeField message is a bit peculiar in the manner it gets sent. First of all, the only time a closeField message could ever possibly be sent is when the contents of the field are different when it closes (i.e., when you tab, press the Enter key, or click outside the field). If you modify the text after opening it, and then restore the contents to its exact original state before closing, no closeField message gets sent to the field.

CloseField messages don't always come when you expect them, however. Through HyperCard version 1.2, the closeField message exhibits what appears to be anomalous behavior. To see if your current version of HyperCard behaves this way, or to see for yourself how it works, let's make a new stack for this chapter and experiment away.

To make the stack:

1. *Open the Developer's Guide Master stack, created in Chapter 12.*

2. *Choose Save a Copy from the File menu.*

3. *Type "Chapter 14 Stack" into the file dialog box.*

4. *Open Chapter 14 Stack via the Open Stack choice of the File menu.*

5. With the text painting tool, type "Chap. 14" into the card graphics layer of the first card.

To help with the experiments, name the five fields of this card. You can be as cute and clever as you see fit. For the purposes of this demonstration, however, we'll name them "theFirst," "theSecond," and so on.

You'll also need two new buttons (they may be in the card or background layers).

1. Choose New Button from the Objects menu.

2. Drag the selected new button to the upper right box, and, in the Button Info dialog box, rename it "No Hilite."

3. Clone that button by holding down the Option key and dragging a copy of that button directly below the first.

4. In the Button Info dialog box, name the button "Hilite" and check the Auto Hilite check box (Figure 14-2).

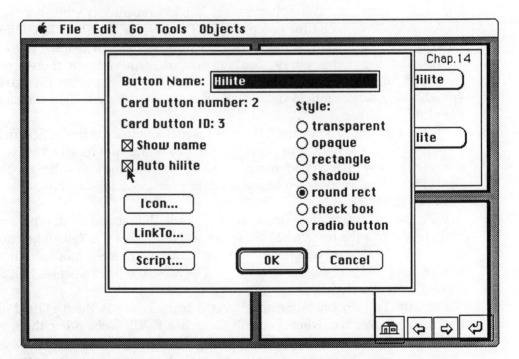

Figure 14-2 *The second experimental button should have auto-hiliting turned on.*

The last instruments we need for this experiment are two handlers that should go into the stack script of Chapter 14 Stack. The handlers are:

```
on openField
  put the target && "opened"
end openField

on closeField
  put the target && "closed"
end closeField
```

These two handlers will put the name of the field into the Message Box, along with a description of what happened to that field (if anything). Thus, when you open the first field, the Message Box will show

```
bkgnd field "theFirst" opened
```

to tell you what's going on.

A "Field" Experiment

For the first experiment, simply press the Tab key repeatedly while watching the Message Box. Each time you press the Tab key, the text insertion pointer moves to the next field in the field order, opening the field for action. Note that because nothing changes in the fields as you tab through them, there are no closeField messages being sent. If you click the mouse with the cursor anywhere outside of a field (including on a button), no closeField messages are sent then either.

Next, press the Tab key until the text insertion pointer is in the first field. Type a word in the field, and press the Tab key while watching the Message Box very closely. For a brief instant, the Message Box indicates that the first field closed. You've just seen how the Tab key can close a field whose content has been changed.

With the text insertion pointer still flashing in the second field, type some more text. Press the Return key a few times. Notice that the Return key does not trigger the closure of a field (see later in this chapter for more about the Return key). Now press the Enter key. The Message Box indicates that the second field was closed.

Press the Tab key once. Because there is text already in the first field, the entire text is selected when you tab to such a field. Remember the exact spelling of the word you typed into this field and press the Backspace key to remove the text. Without clicking the mouse button or pressing the Enter key, retype the word into that first field exactly as it was before. Now press the Enter key to close the field. Because the text of the field did not change from the instant it opened, there is no closeField message sent to the field.

Now press the Tab key twice to select the text in field 2. Press the Backspace key, followed by the Enter key. Because you removed the text and changed the contents of the field, the Message Box indicates that a closeField message was sent to that field.

Now onto what I perceive to be anomalous closeField behavior.

To Close Or Not To Close

Make a change to the first field contents and leave the text insertion pointer flashing in the field. Now click anywhere in the upper right box except on either of the two buttons. Note that clicking on the card caused a closeField to be sent to the first field, as you'd expect. The same would be true if you locked one of the other fields and clicked on it. The closeField message would still be sent to the changed field.

Things are different when clicking on buttons, however. Change the text again in the first field. Then click on the No Hilite button. Not only is there no closeField message sent to the field, but the text insertion pointer is still flashing there. This is not necessarily a bug, since there is utility in having access to the text insertion point when clicking on a button, such as using the button to insert boilerplate text into key points in a field. So, the field stays open until you press the Tab or Enter keys, or click on the card. That's easy enough to remember, I suppose, especially with the insertion pointer still flashing away.

The problem occurs, however, when you click on a button whose autoHilite property is set to true. Change the text in the field again, and click on the Hilite button. The text insertion pointer goes away. It just doesn't become invisible, still in the field, for if you start typing, the text from the keyboard goes into the Message Box, as it would whenever no field is open. So did the field close when you clicked the highlighted button? According to HyperCard, no. No closeField message was sent to the field, yet every other indication is that the field closed. I believe this problem is related to the one in which a text selection becomes de-selected when you click on an auto-hilite button. A future version of HyperCard will probably resolve the problem, but the field will probably remain open, as it does when clicking on a non-auto-hiliting button.

If your stack design is such that you're concerned about users clicking on buttons when you need a closeField message sent to a particular field, you can trigger a closeField message artificially with the help of a global variable and a few short handlers. The first handlers go in the stack script:

```
on openField
  global fieldOpened
  put the target into fieldOpened
end openField

on closeField
  global fieldOpened
  put empty into fieldOpened
end closeField
```

At the beginning of every mouseUp handler, then, you need to add the following script lines:

```
on mouseUp
  global fieldOpened
  if fieldOpened is not empty
  then send closeField to fieldOpened
  ...
```

This series of handlers uses a global variable to hold the name of the field last opened by any method. The additions to the mouseUp handler check to see if a field is currently open when the mouseUp message was sent by Hyper-Card. If so, then a closeField message is sent to that opened field. Presuming your field needs that closeField message for a closeField handler, that closeField handler must also pass closeField so that the stack script closeField handler, shown above, sets the global variable to empty—meaning that no field is open.

Taxing Returns

As long as we have our field message laboratory operating, let's look at one other point that may cause some headscratching. First, clear the contents of the second field on the card and close the field. You'll see the corresponding open and close notices in the Message box. Now, click the mouse button with the I-Beam cursor somewhere near the middle of the field. Then click with the browse tool somewhere in the upper right box, but not on one of the buttons. You may wonder why the Message Box indicates that the second field closed, even though you don't see anything in there, and the field was empty to start with.

The reason is that there are text characters in that field, even though you cannot see them. To prove it, type

```
the number of chars of field 2
```

into the Message Box. You'll see that there are around six characters in the field. Those characters are carriage return (end of line) characters, automatically entered into the field when you clicked in its middle.

These invisible return characters are cause for concern in a design issue I encounter in some stacks. When I create a stack that has pop-up fields attached to buttons, I like to make some graphic change to the button whenever there is text in one of those hidden, pop-up fields. That way, a browser knows that there is something buried there, and where to click to get it. As an example, the Daily Appointment stack in *Focal Point* provides pop-up note fields for each of the day's hours. When you click on the button containing the hour number, the corresponding notes field pops into view (Figure 14-3). During testing, it occurred that users sometimes clicked in the middle of the pop-up fields (sometimes accidentally), because it wasn't clear where to start typing. The user might then type a few characters in the middle of the field, backspace to get rid of them, and click the number button to hide what was supposed to be an empty field. Yet a few return characters were still in the field. Upon hiding the field, the script noticed that the field was not empty, and therefore drew a small box around the plus mark, signifying that there was a note there.

Figure 14-3 *If a user clicks the text pointer in the middle of a blank detail field (when not hidden), he unknowingly inserts Return characters. Upon closing the field, Focal Point thinks there's text in the field, and draws a square around the plus symbol. But the user would see no characters when showing the field.*

One way I used to prevent most accidental insertions of return characters was to insert a Click At command each time the field pops up. As coordinates for the Click At command, I used the top left corner of the rectangle of the field. That always places the flashing text insertion pointer at the left margin of the first line of the field (Figure 14-4). Then, if a user wants to experiment by typing in text, he or she must press the Return key a few times to move the cursor lower in the field. To remove the text, the tendency will then be to keep backspacing until the cursor is back at the top left corner.

Open and Close Object Messages

Cards, backgrounds and stacks all receive open and close messages when they, well, open and close. Opening and closing does not necessarily mean that you see one of these objects on the screen. If you lock the screen to go to another background or another stack and then return to the original spot, many open and close messages are sent. For instance, in the following mouseUp handler from a hypothetical stack named "Table of Contents"

```
on mouseUp
   set lockScreen to true
   push card
   go to card "Index 1" of stack "Art History"
   get field "Last Update"
   pop card
   put it into field "AH Update"
end mouseUp
```

look at how many open and close messages are sent:

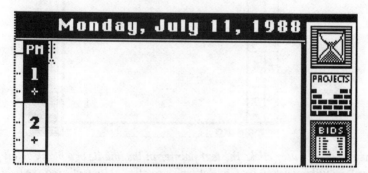

Figure 14-4 *By the script clicking at the top left corner of the hidden field when the field is shown, the tendency is to backspace all the way to the top to remove accidental characters.*

message	location
closeCard	current card with button in it
closeBackground	current background
closeStack	stack "Table of Contents"
openStack	stack "Art History"
openBackground	background containing card "Index 1"
openCard	card "Index 1"
closeCard	card "Index 1"
closeBackground	background containing card "Index 1"
closeStack	stack "Art History"
openStack	stack "Table of Contents"
openBackground	background containing original card
openCard	card with button on it

That's 12 open and close messages just to fetch a field in another stack. If the screen is locked or unlocked, the same messages still fly.

While it's true that all these open and close messages go to the card level first, it makes the most sense to place open and close stack handlers in the stack script and open and close background handlers in the background script. Card handlers, however, may be best placed at levels other than the card. About the only time you'd consider placing an openCard or closeCard handler in the card script was if the handler pertained to that single card only. More likely, you write an openCard or closeCard handler to control the opening and closing of a series of cards, either in the same background of a heterogeneous stack (in which case the handlers would go into the background script) or in the stack of a homogeneous stack (in which case the handler could go in either the background or stack script).

It's particularly important to recognize that open and close object messages are sent even with the screen locked, because these messages could adversely affect the posting or retrieval of information in a card, background, or stack other than the one locked on the screen. For example, if a mouseUp handler in one stack needs to retrieve data from a card in another stack, the openStack or openBackground handler of that other stack could perform some updating or other housekeeping tasks that may interfere or slow down the information retrieval. Fortunately, there is a way around these messages.

When you wish to bypass open and close object handlers in an information posting/retrieval situation, you can set the lockMessages property to true, as in

```
set lockMessages to true
```

at the start of the handler that fetches the data. When this global property is set to true, HyperCard suspends all system messages (except idle) until you set lockMessages to false or the current handler ends and HyperCard sends an idle message.

Keyboard Messages

There are just eight keyboard messages, of which only six make any sense in a stack product that will be distributed widely. This is because two keyboard messages, functionKey and controlKey, require keyboards other than the lowest common denominator keyboard of the Macintosh Plus. Both newer keyboards for the Macintosh SE and II have a Control key, while only the Macintosh Extended Keyboard has function keys. Before we get to these special key messages, let's take care of the four common ones.

Three keyboard messages, returnKey, enterKey, and tabKey, are rather straightforward. Each time you press those keys (Return, Enter, and Tab, respectively) while no field is open, their corresponding messages go to the current card. The only caution is that when you are editing text in a field—when the text insertion pointer is flashing in a field—these keys do not send their messages to the current card. Instead, while in text editing mode, these keys have very different functions, such as inserting a return character in a line of text, or closing a field. Fortunately, you can still trap for the Return and Enter keys when editing a text field.

Keyboard Trapping in Fields

Early HyperCard stack developers desired a way to trap for the user's pressing of the Return or Enter keys while editing a field. Beginning with version 1.2, HyperCard sends two system messages, returnInField and enterInField, whenever the user presses the Return and Enter key while the text cursor is flashing in the field (i.e., when the field is open). You can use these messages in two very different ways, depending on the nature of the fields and how you want the user to enter data into them.

If your only goal is to prevent the text cursor from jumping to a line below the last visible line of the field, then you'll be better served by turning on the Auto-Tab property in the field's info dialog box. For one-line fields, therefore, the Auto-Tab property may be all you'll need to prevent the user from adding text below the visible field area.

In a multiple-line field, you may wish to prevent the user from adding more than a single HyperCard line of text. Recall that a HyperCard line of text begins at a left margin and continues until it encounters a return character, even if the line wraps within the field. To restrict the text to one line you must not allow the user to type a return character into the field. To do that, you'd trap for the returnInField system message in a field script like this:

```
on returnInField
end returnInField
```

No return character will ever reach this field. But it also means that Auto-Tab (which requires the return key) will not work for this field, nor will pressing the Return key close the field.

❧

Field Entry Validation

One clear advantage of being able to trap for Return and Enter key presses within a field is to perform tests on the text within a field to make sure the entry consists of valid information. For instance, if you want to make sure that a user enters only numbers into a field, then you can create a returnInField handler for that field to test the contents of the field before allowing the user to proceed to the next field.

Here is an example of a returnInField handler that compares each character of a text field against a list of all numbers plus a decimal:

```
on returnInField
   repeat with x = 1 to the length of me
      if not (char x of me is in "0123456789.") then
         beep
         answer "Entry must be a number only."
         select text of me
         exit returnInField
      end if
   end repeat
   pass returnInField
end returnInField
```

If one of the characters is not a number or decimal point, then the handler beeps, presents an answer dialog box with a clue about what's wrong with the entry, selects the text in the field for quick re-entry of the data, and exits the handler. Only if all characters in the field are valid does the returnInField message get passed to HyperCard. Be sure to pass the message if you have Auto-Tab turned on—if HyperCard doesn't see the returnInField message, the cursor won't "tab" to the next field.

In the above situation, and in any situation in which you modify the action of the returnInField system message, it is generally desirable to make a press of the Enter key perform the same action as the Return key. Given a returnInField handler like the one above, you can mimic its action with the Enter key by adding this simple handler to the field script:

```
on enterInField
   returnInField
end enterInField
```

If you plan to offer different actions for each key, consider this move carefully. I'm not sure how intuitive this setup will be for the user. Some database programs use this system to advance the cursor through fields with the Return key, and advance to the next record ("card" in HyperCard terminology) with the Enter key. What works in a database program, however, may not be appropriate for a HyperCard stack.

The Text Arrows Property

Our discussion about arrowKey messages must be preceded by a discussion of a global property added to HyperCard 1.1—textArrows. When this property is set to false, as it essentially was in HyperCard version 1.0.1, the arrow keys are strictly stack navigation keys (except in the Script Editor, where they move the text cursor). Adding the textArrows property, and setting it to true turns the arrow keys into text cursor movers, rather than navigation keys. Even with textArrows turned on, you can use the arrow keys as navigation aids by holding the Option key at the same time.

I have mixed feelings about this property. On the one hand, I've grown accustomed to reaching for the arrow keys to navigate through many stacks. Having to hold down the Option key means a change of habit. On the other hand, I fully appreciate the desire to move the text insertion cursor in a field via the arrow keys, as you can in most word processors. Word processors, of course, also let you move the cursor in word jumps, which HyperCard does not. There is a tradeoff.

Perhaps the most disturbing part of textArrows being turned on is that the arrow keys are dead unless a text cursor is flashing somewhere in a field or the Message Box. They do nothing.

The way I treat this property in my stacks is to ignore it. When necessary, my scripts trap for arrow keys as navigation aids. I leave it up to the user and the Home stack preferences setting to figure out how the arrow keys work.

ArrowKey Messages

The arrowKey message is often a source of confusion for new HyperTalk programmers, because it's one of very few messages that comes with a parameter (left, right, up, or down). Any handler that is to trap for an arrow key press must be written to accommodate the parameter.

By way of explanation, you should remember that a press of the left arrow key actually sends the two-word message

```
arrowKey left
```

The word left is a parameter to the arrowKey message. The handler that is to trap for the arrowKey message must present a variable name into which the message parameter goes. Therefore, in the handler

```
on arrowKey whichKey
    if whichKey is "right" then
       visual effect wipe left
       go to next card
    else if whichKey is "left" then
       visual effect wipe right
       go to previous card
    end if
end arrowKey
```

the arrowKey message parameter is placed in a local variable, called which-Key. That variable may then be used within the handler to be tested against specific directions you're looking for. Note, too, that in the above handler, since the arrowKey message is not passed beyond the handler, the up and down arrow keys will be inert on the keyboard. Only the left and right arrow keys will do anything in this stack.

The Control Key

The Control key on the new keyboards (for the Macintosh SE and Macintosh II only) is there largely for the purpose of being compatible with IBM keyboards, just in case you use your Macintosh to emulate an IBM PC with co-processor boards or as a terminal to a mainframe computer. The Control key is nothing more than another modifier key, like the Option and Command keys on all Macintosh keyboards. In other words, you use the Control key in concert with one or more keys on the keyboard to issue some kind of command.

Unlike the Option and Command keys, however, the Control key issues a HyperCard system message to the current card when it is pressed. The Option and Command keys, you'll recall, may be tested by way of functions (the optionKey and the commandKey) to see if they're being held down while a handler is running, but you cannot trap for someone typing Command-Q, for instance. With the Control key, however, you can issue commands of any kind from the keyboard, because you can trap for a press of the Control key and another character.

The controlKey message is different than most messages, because not only does it send a parameter along with it, but the parameter is a code number for a character accessible from the keyboard. The code number is the character's ASCII code. There is an ASCII code for each character you can type from the Macintosh keyboard, including special characters accessed only with the Option key. To find the ASCII code for a particular character, you can look it up in an ASCII table or uncover it the more fun way by using HyperTalk in the Message Box. Just type the CharToNum function and the character whose code you wish to look up. Here are several functions you can try in the Message Box:

```
the charToNum of "C"
the charToNum of "c"
the charToNum of "•"    -- Option-8
the charToNum of "Ç"    -- Option-Shift-C
```

You may wish to set up some Control-key equivalents to summon various painting tools from the tools palette, like a quick way to summon the button tool without pulling down or showing the palette. Here's a controlKey handler you could use in that instance:

```
on controlKey whichKey
   if whichKey is 98           -- "b"
   then choose button tool
   else if whichKey is 102     -- "f"
   then choose field tool
   pass controlKey
end controlKey
```

Importantly, the parameter passed along with the controlKey message is case-sensitive. In other words, the ASCII codes for "a" and "A" are different numbers. If there is the chance that a user will issue the Control key sequence with the CapsLock key down, then your handler had better test for both upper and lower case instances of the parameter. A handler that tests for many

Control-key sequences might have a conversion routine at the beginning that converts the case of characters to all lower case or all upper case.

Function Keys

The Apple Extended Keyboard has a row of 12 function keys across the top of the keyboard. These keys are there to emulate IBM AT keyboards. Each key is labeled with its number. Each time you press one of these keys, HyperCard sends a functionKey message to the current card, along with a parameter consisting of the number of the key. Keys 1 through 4 are preset to take care of the four common editing functions: Undo, Cut, Copy and Paste, so if you like these functions on those keys, you can leave them. Apple's user interface guidelines would prefer it that way.

You have full license to program the actions of all 12 keys, including the preprogrammed ones. All it takes is to write a functionKey handler that traps for the desired key numbers. A typical functionKey handler might be

```
on functionKey whichKey
   if whichKey < 6 then pass functionKey
   else if whichKey is 6 then doMenu "New Card"
   else if whichKey is 7 then doMenu "Delete Card"
   else if whichKey is 8 then lockFields
   else if whichKey is 9 then unLockFields
   else if whichKey is 11 then doMenu "Compact Stack"
end functionKey
```

In the above example, you'll notice that you can use a function key to trigger any kind of action, like the locking and unlocking of fields, whose handlers you may have in your Home stack.

Unless you know for sure that every user of your stack will have new Apple keyboards, it's not wise to program the controlKey or functionKey handlers into your stack or rely on those keys alone to trigger key operations. These keys do, however, let you program many stack development shortcuts for yourself. For additional tips on authoring shortcuts and debugging tools, see Chapter 21.

DoMenu

A very powerful message that HyperCard sends—and therefore lets you trap for—is the doMenu message. Each time you choose an item in a menu, HyperCard sends the doMenu message along with the exact text of the menu item as a parameter. When I say "exact text," I mean it. If a menu item has an ellipsis (three periods) after it, then the parameter has three periods at the end of it (they're three periods, not the ellipsis character, Option-semicolon, found in some fonts).

The reason trapping for menu items is so important is that your stacks can let the user make menu choices from the HyperCard menus, but you can modify or amplify the operations triggered by certain menu choices. For example, in several *Focal Point* stacks, I intercept the New Card menu command because that operation entails creating several cards (from different backgrounds) and establishing links among them. Rather than trap for the newCard message, which comes only after one card has been created, my handler keeps me in complete control of the new card (series) creation process. It also means, as demonstrated in the previous chapter, that when I need a real new card, the handler must send a doMenu New Card message to Hyper-Card, itself, thus bypassing my own doMenu handler.

Another example of why you'd like to trap for menu items is the navigation choices in the Go menu. In a heterogeneous stack, you usually don't want the user to keep going to the next card until he breaks into the next background. That could really confuse the user. Better to restrict navigation to a particular background. This you can do by trapping for the Previous and Next items in the Go menu and modifying their action. Thus, the handler would be

```
on doMenu whichItem
   if whichItem is "Prev"
   then go to previous card of this bkgnd
   else if whichItem is "Next"
   then go to next card of this bkgnd
   else pass doMenu
end doMenu
```

This is just a hint of what's to come later in the chapter, when we examine how you stay in navigation control of the stack.

One facet of the doMenu message and associated handler cannot be overemphasized. Your handler must pass doMenu for all menu choices other than the ones you're trapping for. If you fail to pass the message, you'll be locked out of all menu items, including Quit HyperCard or getting the Info boxes for the background or stack. If you've placed a doMenu handler in your background or stack and find that the pass doMenu line is not working properly (thus preventing you from using the menus), then there is a last resort. If the Message Box is showing, then type

```
edit script of bkgnd  -- if doMenu handler is in the background
```

or

```
edit script of stack  -- if the handler is in the stack script
```

This will bring up the Script Editor for the appropriate object, and you may repair the script.

If the Message Box is not showing, you won't be able to bring it into view by typing Command-M, because that's the menu equivalent of Message in the Go menu—and all menus are locked out. Make sure the Blind Typing property is set to true in your Home stack and blindly type

```
show msg
```

to bring the Message Box into view. Then you may type the appropriate edit script command, as shown above (or you may blindly type `edit script` if you're confident in your typing abilities).

Suspend and Resume

The `suspend` and `resume` messages are sent when HyperCard launches another application and returns from another application, respectively. Suspending is considered different than quitting HyperCard. That's because when you suspend HyperCard, the next time HyperCard opens, it comes to the card from which you suspended operation. But because HyperCard "goes away" when it suspends (when not using MultiFinder), no global variables are automatically saved. That's something you have to take care of in your HyperTalk scripts.

If your stack or stack system offers facilities for launching outside programs, chances are that it's done from a very specific place, like a special stack, background, or card. If so, consider using the suspend message as a trigger to save the state of various global variables and other settings into a field on that card. For instance, if the user has adjusted the location of the Message Box on the screen, your program should save that location in a hidden field when suspending the program. Upon resumption, the location of the Message Box should be set to the coordinates saved previously. Adding such a touch makes your stack seem much more intelligent than HyperCard itself. Because you know that upon resume HyperCard will open to the very card from which it left, a field is a safe place for the data to be carried over. The Document

Launcher of *Focal Point* saves several states prior to launching an external application, and restores them upon resume.

One key point to remember about a resume handler is that the Home stack contains a very important resume handler—itself. That handler sets key global variables for looking up pathnames and also sets several system-wide parameters (e.g., userLevel) to settings in the Home Stack. Therefore, always pass resume at the end of your resume handler.

StartUp and Quit

Somewhat analogous to the resume and suspend messages are startUp and quit. These messages, however, represent more drastic actions on the part of the user. The startUp message is the one HyperCard sends when the program starts up from the Finder, from scratch. Quit, at the opposite end, is the message HyperCard sends when you choose Quit HyperCard from the File menu.

In the Home stack is a startUp handler that calls a long handler, getSysInfo. This handler, alluded to in the last section, puts together the global variables for the stack, document, and application pathnames, as well as setting global properties of user level, power keys, text arrows and blind typing. In very tightly controlled circumstances, in which the author is in charge of stack pathnames within handlers, controls the user level and never lets the user have direct access to HyperCard, the startUp handler can omit the getSysInfo handler, but this is not generally recommended.

The startUp message goes to the current card first, so if you have a startUp script in your stack and launch the stack from the Finder by double-clicking on the stack icon, your stack will trap for the startUp message before the Home stack will. Therefore, it is important that any startup handler you include in your stack pass start up up the hierarchy so the Home stack can do its important getSysInfo tasks.

Help

The help message is the message HyperCard sends when you choose Help from the Go menu. Because help is its own message, you may trap for it by name, rather than by trapping for it under the guise of a doMenu handler.

Trapping for help is important if your stack contains on-line help cards. In stacks that show the HyperCard menu bar, a single Help menu item can provide access to the stack's help cards and HyperCard help (via a button in the stack's help system). Getting to a stack's own help system via the Help menu item makes the stack application feel more like a freestanding program, since the menu item seems to work within your own stack, and not just with HyperCard.

Idle

The `idle` message is a troublesome critter, because it can be both powerful and dangerous at the same time—powerful because it can make things happen with the computer unattended and; dangerous because it can rob the user of control over text editing. Therefore, idle handlers must be used with special care.

HyperCard sends idle messages over and over anytime nothing else is going on in the stack. It's like the HyperCard motor always running, with the gear in neutral. In the idle state—called "idle time"—HyperCard sets a number of properties to false, especially all the locks on screens, message passing, and painting of miniature cards into the Recent box. Also at idle time, any pending visual effects are flushed from the list. Idle time, therefore, is an important time for HyperCard.

One of the most common applications of the idle message is trapping for it and displaying a running timer in a field on a card. It's not a bad idea. Even the Home Card, as it ships from the factory, has just such an idle handler in it.

Difficulty arises, however, when authors attempt to combine idle handlers and cards that have user-accessible text fields in them. Specifically, the problem comes from the commands within the idle handler, commands which usually put the time into a specific field. If a user is trying to enter data into one field, and the idle handler puts the time into another field, the user loses the battle for the text insertion pointer. If the clock is updating the time every second, it will be virtually impossible for the user to enter anything into other fields. Even if the time being put into the field is from the Short Time function, the idle handler robs the user of the text insertion pointer once each minute. If you've tried to coexist with this arrangement, you quickly discover that it's a very frustrating experience. I've never encountered an idle handler in an interactive card that I've liked.

Idle handlers are useful, however, when placed in a proper environment. Specifically, any card that has click-only interactivity is a fine candidate for an idle handler, if one is necessary. I'll show you two diverse examples of how I've used idle handlers in *Business Class* and *Focal Point*.

Idle in Business Class

As an extension of the simple clock field, like the one in the Home card, Business Class puts the idle handler to even more time-keeping work. The main world map (Figure 14-5) uses two large highlighted buttons to track the location of nighttime (the time between 6 pm and 6 am). The location of those buttons shifts as the day progresses (sometimes you can't even see one of the buttons—its coordinates are set to off the screen).

While I could have settled on locating the buttons at the time the card opened and left them there, I made the card come to life. If you are watching this card as the hour changes, you'll see the night/day lines shift one time zone. An idle handler keeps track of this as well as the local clock in the upper right corner.

Idle in Focal Point

A very different problem confronted me in the Deadlines stack of *Focal Point* (Figure 14-6). Here there are two fields, both of which must scroll in synchronization with each other. One field is the skinny one at the left which

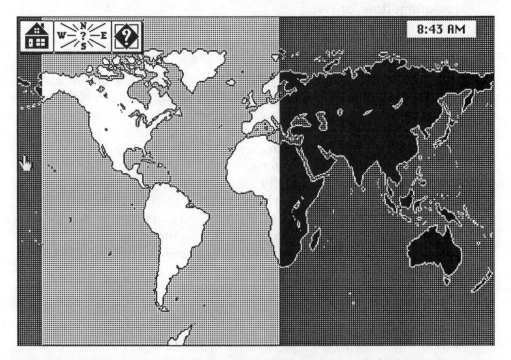

Figure 14-5 *With no text fields for data entry, the map menu card of Business Class is a suitable candidate for an idle handler to keep its clock and day/night lines "alive."*

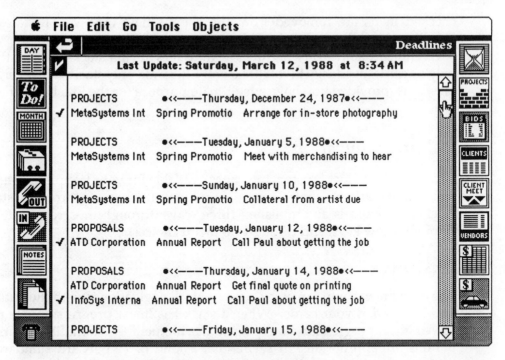

Figure 14-6 *An idle handler keeps the two fields of this card in sync (the checkoff field has a scroll bar, but it's hidden beneath the larger field).*

contains check marks inserted by clicking on the field next to an item you've completed. The other field contains the items due on all days listed in the Projects and Proposals stacks.

To make both fields scroll in sync, I first covered the scroll bar of the skinny field with the larger field, making sure the latter had a higher field number, and was thus in a layer closer to the viewer. Then an idle handler continually sets the scroll of the skinny field to the scroll of the larger field. The handler is simply:

```
on idle
  set the scroll of field 1 to the scroll of field 2
  pass idle
end idle
```

On slower Macintoshes, there is a slight delay between the scrolling of the two fields. In other words, the scroll of the second field doesn't adjust itself until the user lets up on the scroll bar of the larger field, thus allowing an idle message to makes its way up the hierarchy. Typically, however, the jerky look to the scrolling check marks in the left column aren't troublesome, because all checked items are removed from the list the next time you update the Deadlines list—they're rarely there.

Overall, my advice on inserting idle messages in your stacks is to use them only on cards that do not involve text entry. Browse-only stacks, however, are fair game, provided you have a legitimate purpose for the idle handler.

Controlling Navigation

Given the diversity of system messages available for your trapping, you can maintain remarkable control over the way your users move through a stack. Stack navigation is accomplished three ways: through on-screen buttons; through arrow keys; and through Go menu choices.

Button Navigation

The ultimate in control over your user's stack navigation is with the buttons you design into your cards. When a stack has linear progression—or perceived linear progression, as explained in a moment—then traditional arrow buttons are appropriate. It seems that a kind of HyperCard standard is evolving, in which the left and right arrows indicate previous and next cards, while a right angle arrow returns you to some previous stack or card. In some layouts, like flip card on-screen metaphors, a pair of up-down arrows also seems to be acceptable, with the down arrow signifying motion to the next card, the up arrow to the previous card.

In a homogeneous stack, linear navigation is pretty clear and simple. In a heterogeneous stack, however, you probably want to be in more control over how on-screen navigation buttons behave. One or more backgrounds of a heterogeneous stack should be perceived to be linear, even though they may be scattered a bit throughout the stack. The aforementioned commands to limit the navigation to cards of the same background come into play here. Thus, your right arrow handler may be:

```
on mouseUp
  visual effect wipe left
  go to next card of this background
end mouseUp
```

No matter how the user clicks on those screen buttons, he'll stay within that background. That gives the impression that cards of the same look are grouped together, as if banded together in the shoebox.

If the backgrounds of a heterogeneous stack are linked together, then there should also be navigation buttons pointing in the right direction and back again. For example, in the six-background Projects stack of *Focal Point,* the Summary card features what I call Zoom buttons that link to detail cards in a particular category (Figure 14-7). On the detail cards is a single navigation button, a return arrow, which takes the user back to the Summary card (Figure 14-8). The left and right arrow buttons on the Summary card restrict access to previous and next cards in the Summary card's background only.

Arrow Key Navigation

The keyboard arrow keys, in my opinion, should mimic the arrow keys on the screen. Therefore, if your main navigation buttons are left and right arrows, and they limit access to cards of a single background, then the left and right arrow keys should act identically. If you have up and down arrow buttons, then up and down arrow keys should mimic those buttons.

I believe the best way to handle this is for your arrowKey handler to send mouse messages to the navigation buttons on the screen. That way, if you

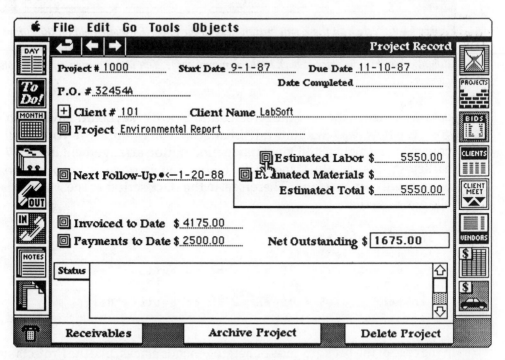

Figure 14-7 *Zoom buttons control navigation from summary cards to specific detail cards in the Projects stack of Focal Point.*

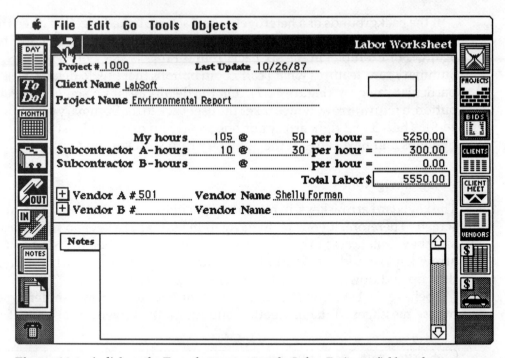

Figure 14-8 *A click on the Zoom button next to the Labor Estimate field on the summary card brings you to the Labor Worksheet card for the same project. From here the only navigation within the stack is back to the summay card. You may jump to any other stack, however.*

make a change in the way the screen buttons work, keyboard navigation will work the new way without any changes. For example, if you recall the mouseDown/mouseStillDown navigation button arrangement in *Focal Point* (earlier in this chapter), the main navigation is done in response to the mouseStillDown message. Therefore, in the stack scripts of most stacks is the following handler:

```
on arrowKey whichKey
  if whichKey is "left"
  then send mouseStillDown to bkgnd button "Prev"
  if whichKey is "right"
  then send mouseStillDown to bkgnd button "Next"
end arrowKey
```

In the case of the backgrounds of heterogeneous stacks, like the Projects stack, in which there are no left or right navigation buttons, a handler in the background script traps for all arrowKey messages, but does nothing with them:

```
on arrowKey
end arrowKey
```

This handler won't let the user navigate in any way with the arrow keys, which is exactly what I had in mind for these backgrounds. I wanted to direct the user back to the Summary card via the return arrow button on the screen. Note, too, that in the earlier arrowKey handler that I do not pass the arrowKey message. I trap the up and down arrowKey messages right there. The default actions of those keyboard keys (push card and pop card) is usually too confusing for novice users. A slip of the finger could cause great confusion. Better to disable the keys altogether.

Menu Navigation

The final way most users have access to stack navigation is through the Go menu. If you are overly concerned about the user getting out of line by using the Go menu choices, then you may also trap for the doMenu messages that those menu items send.

If you plan to trap for these menu items, then I suggest they act the same way the left and right arrow buttons and the left and right arrow keys operate. Again, the safest way to assure consistency is to send mouse messages to the arrow buttons.

Some information publishing stacks, like *Business Class,* do not have navigation buttons on their cards. All action is accomplished by clicking on maps or icon buttons on the screen. Since strictly linear access to the stack would not serve any purpose, I disabled the menu navigation items with this simple handler fragment:

```
on doMenu whichItem
   ...
   if "First,Last,Next,Prev" contains whichItem
   then exit doMenu
   pass doMenu
end doMenu
```

If any of those four menu items are chosen, the doMenu handler exits without passing the doMenu message up the hierarchy. You may use this technique to trap for any menu item or items in a single if-then construction, even if the menu items are in different menus.

Message Box Navigation

The last category of navigation—giving direct commands via the Message Box—is for the more experienced HyperCard user. In other words, even after you write limiting arrow button handlers, direct arrow key presses to imitate the button handlers, direct Go menu items to the same button handlers, or disable both the arrow keys and Go menu items, an experienced user may still type navigation commands into the Message Box. With Blind Typing enabled, the user may even do so without the Message Box showing on the screen.

For the most part, I've decided to leave this option available to experienced HyperCard users. No matter how I restrict or direct navigation through buttons, arrow keys, or the Go menu, I leave Message Box navigation open. I could always trap for command words, like Go, but I'd end up spending more time and script space trying to frustrate an experienced user than in working on the productive parts of the stack. Besides, why infuriate someone who might be a potential convert to your program?

One other advantage to leaving the Message Box navigation method open is that you can use it during stack development. After you've installed your carefully directed navigation system, you may still bypass it all by sending all kinds of Go messages via the Message Box.

Our discussion in this chapter does not exhaust all the possibilities of managing system messages or controlling navigation by message management. But there should be enough examples here to get you started thinking about others for your special needs. In the next chapter, we go into what is a mysterious area for many newcomers: writing your own messages and passing parameters to them.

15

Sending Your Own Messages

In previous chapters, we've already seen instances of writing custom handlers that respond to messages other than system messages. For instance, when you entered the handlers in your Home stack that locked and unlocked all fields on the screen, you wrote custom handlers. The messages you type into the Message Box to make those handlers work are for all practical purposes commands, just like the commands that make up the HyperTalk vocabulary. In this chapter, we'll look more closely at the rationale for writing your own handlers and messages, how to pass parameters to these handlers, and where such handlers belong in your stack product.

Commands and Messages

Everything that goes on in the course of HyperTalk execution is the result of messages flowing among various objects. System messages are those generated by HyperCard in response to some action, like opening a card or clicking the mouse atop a button. HyperTalk commands, too, are messages, except they usually originate within a handler.

A simple example would be the following handler

```
on mouseUp
  go to next card
end mouseUp
```

The command line in that handler, go to next card, starts with the Go command. That command is actually a message sent by this mouseUphandler. On its way up the hierarchy, the message starts looking for a Go handler in the button script. In most cases, HyperCard commands like this one reach HyperCard unimpeded. Only when you wish to intercept a command and modify it in some way would there be a handler ready to trap it along the way, as we'll see later.

Why a Custom Handler?

With so much of a HyperCard stack's activity driven by user interaction—tabbing through fields, clicking buttons, opening and closing cards or stacks—it may seem that all action in a stack would be adequately covered within handlers that respond to system messages. But there are times when it is more convenient to write a handler that responds to a message whose name *you* invent.

One case, like the Home stack handlers earlier, surfaces when you wish to initiate a particular string of actions that are independent of the stack. Stack developers commonly place utility handlers in the Home stack. By typing the message into the Message Box from any stack, that operation may be performed in the same manner as a standard HyperTalk command. Instead of the command reaching HyperCard, however, the command gets only as far as the Home stack handler of the same name. If that command should slip past the Home stack—perhaps you mistype the command in the Message Box—it will go all the way to HyperCard. But since that message is not in HyperCard's vocabulary, HyperCard will complain in a dialog box that it does not understand that message.

What you're doing, however, is essentially extending the command vocabulary of your version of HyperCard. Since the command is always available to you (by virtue of its location in the Home stack), you are adding to the HyperCard command language. But remember that because the handler is in your Home stack only, that command will not work in other people's stacks, unless they have the identical handler in their own Home stack or in the stack they're using.

Stack Commands

Another reason for writing your own messages and handlers is to add a command to a particular stack—a command that you may access by typing the message into the Message Box only in a certain stack. In the Monthly Calendar stack of *Focal Point* is a stack script handler that is available to those who wish to print out two adjacent months on a single sheet of paper. The handler is this

```
on twoPrint
    open printing
    print this card
    go to next card
    print this card
    close printing
end twoPrint
```

The way you use this handler is to navigate to the first month you wish printed. Show the Message Box (or type blindly if you're up to the task) and type

```
twoPrint
```

That message goes to the current card first, but eventually finds the twoPrint handler in the stack script, and carries out the command.

Convenience Handlers

Probably the most valuable way to use your own messages and handlers is to write small modules of code that many other handlers in your stack may use. Such a module acts as what programmers call a subroutine: a separate module that another module's execution takes a detour through, as illustrated in Figure 15-1.

The idea of modular construction has a lot of merit. For one thing, HyperCard itself is set up that way, dividing a stack's entire palette of actions into small handlers, rather than one giant program. Secondly, when you write

```
on mouseUp
   if field "Tax Rate" is empty
   then answer "Enter tax rate first."          ┌──► on calculate
   else calculate ─────────                     │    ...
   get field "Total" ◄──────────────────────────┤    [commands to calculate]
   go to card "History"                          │    ...
   put return & it after field "Invoices" ──────┘    end calculate
end mouseUp
```

Figure 15-1 *Your own handler is like a subroutine, to which another handler temporarily branches. When the custom handler is finished, the execution in the original handler picks up where it left off.*

small modules, they may often be reused in other stacks. After awhile, you may accumulate an impressive library of handlers that find their way into many of your stacks. The more you can make the modules generic—relying on parameters being passed instead of calling specific objects in a stack by name or ID—the more likely you'll be able to use the handlers "as is" in another stack.

As an example of how modular handler programming can be a convenience in writing a stack, let's look inside the Client Meeting Record stack of *Focal Point* (Figure 15-2). In this stack, a user creates a new card for each meeting he has with a client. The starting and ending times of the meetings are noted in their respective fields. When a client is selected from a pop-up list of clients, the billing rate is automatically posted to the Billing Rate field in the calculation box. The instant both starting and ending times are entered into their fields, a substantial handler, on calculate, figures out the elapsed time (in decimal number of hours) and calculates the total billing amount.

This calculate handler is called as the result of system messages being sent to various objects. For instance, whenever a closeField system message is sent to the Starting Time, Ending Time, and Billing Rate fields, it is necessary to recalculate the total amount. Thus, each of those fields has the following handler in it

```
on closeField
   calculate
end closeField
```

Closing any other fields on the card does not affect the calculation, so their closeField messages are not intercepted.

There is one more handler that sends the calculate message. Whenever you click on the Plus button next to the Client # field, a scrolling text field appears, listing all the clients stored in *Focal Point's* Client stack (Figure 15-3). That field is locked, and the user is to click on the name of the client with whom this meeting occurs. Among the various things that happen in that field's

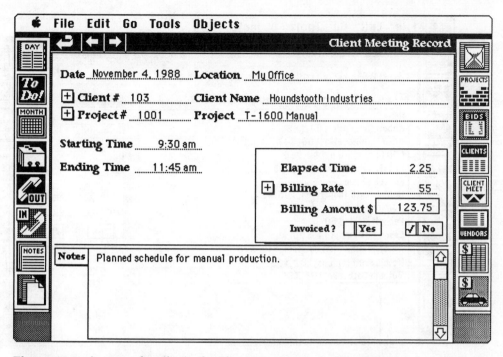

Figure 15-2 *A custom handler in the Client Meeting stack of Focal Point calculates the elapsed time and total billing amount. This handler is called by many different objects, making it convenient to have all calculations in a single handler.*

mouseUp handler is a check to make sure an elapsed time has been calculated, meaning that the starting and ending times have already been inserted into their respective fields. If the elapsed time has been calculated, then because this handler also enters the client's hourly billing rate into the Billing Rate field, there is sufficient information to calculate the total billing amount. Thus, the calculate message is also sent from that field's mouseUp handler.

Near the end of development of this stack, I added a plus button next to the Billing Rate field. Clicking on this button causes a kind of dialog to appear, revealing six radio button choices about the billing interval—how often the cash register rings, in a manner of speaking (Figure 15-4). Because it is possible that the user may adjust this setting after calculations have already been completed, it was necessary to trigger a recalculation when the OK button is pressed. That was a simple task, because I simply added the Calculate command to the handler (in the OK button) that hid the pop-up field and buttons.

The importance of putting the calculate handler in the background is that it is present in the stack only one time. Five different objects—four fields and one button—rely on that recalculation function, but it would have been very

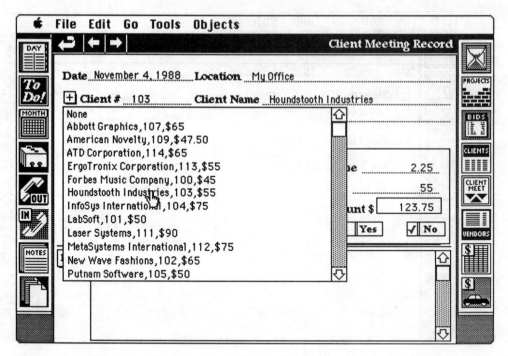

Figure 15-3 *Selecting a client (and its billing rate) is cause to trigger the calculate custom handler.*

wasteful to place that handler in the script of each object. Moreover, if the user wishes to customize the calculation card by adding another factor into the formula (and another field to the card), the adjustment to the recalculation operation is done in one place, not in the handlers of five or six objects.

This points to ways you can recognize the need for a separate handler that other objects call. If you notice that you are writing many of the same lines of HyperTalk code inside system message handlers of several objects in the same stack, that common code can probably be placed more conveniently in a handler of its own.

Convenience and Then Some

Remember that when you send a message from an object, such as a field or button, to a custom handler, all the concepts about the target function apply. As a result, information about the target is available to the custom handler.

To demonstrate what I mean, I'll show you a shortcut to programming the highlighting of a group of radio buttons on a card. Until I thought of this custom handler, programming radio buttons was a nuisance of setting hilite properties of various buttons in the group to true and false, depending on

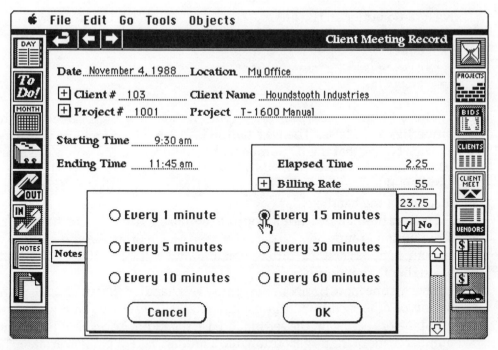

Figure 15-4 *Adjusting the billing increment also triggers the calculate handler. If the calculation handler needs changing, it doesn't have to be repaired in several places.*

which button was clicked. Now, one custom handler takes care of the entire group. And the good thing about this method is that it doesn't rely on the radio buttons being created in any particular order or even at the same time. If you decide to add a button to the group later, there is a simple change to the custom handler. If your design calls for it, you can even have multiple groups of radio buttons on the card, yet they won't interfere with each other.

The custom handler that takes care of a typical four-button group would be:

```
on radioGroup1
  put "49,50,51,52" into buttonList -- ID numbers of buttons
  repeat with x = 1 to the number of items of buttonList
    set hilite of bkgnd button id (item x of buttonList) to false
  end repeat

  set hilite of the target to true
end radioGroup1
```

Each radio button in the group, then, has as its mouseUp handler:

```
on mouseUp
   radioGroup1
end mouseUp
```

In the custom handler, all radio buttons in the group have their hilite properties set to false. Then the button just clicked has its hilite property set to true. Notice that the ID numbers of each button in the group are inserted into an itemized list within a local variable, called buttonList. If you add a button to this group, then simply add its ID number to the itemized list in the first line of the handler.

I named this handler radioGroup1 to emphasize that you can have as many radio button groups on a card as you need. Each group would have its own custom handler, with a different name and with the IDs of the buttons belonging to that group.

There is one more tip about how to use this handler effectively. Since an OK button or other action button usually checks the settings of a radio button group before acting on the setting, I'd use the radioGroup handler to put the number name of the target button into a hidden field or global variable. Thus, when the action button is clicked, the user won't have to wait while its handler checks the hilite properties of all buttons in the group. It can retrieve the current setting from the hidden field or global variable.

Naming Your Messages

You may assign virtually any name to your own message and handler, provided you follow two guidelines. First, unless you intend to trap a HyperTalk command and modify its execution, avoid assigning a word from the HyperTalk vocabulary to a message and handler. Consider all the commands, functions, properties, and constant names as "reserved words," which HyperTalk is best keeping to itself. If you use a property name, for instance, it might work today, whereas a future release of HyperCard may expect that word to work its way through the entire hierarchy.

Second, a message name must be a single text string, without any punctuation marks as part of the name. This may seem restrictive at first, because your message may require more than one word to describe its action fully—something a message name should do. You have two ways around it. The preferred method (preferred by folks like Dan Winkler and myself) is to combine multiple words into a single string with capital letters at the beginning of each interior word, much like the multiword system messages you've seen. Another valid way to link multiple words together in a single string is to join them with the underline character. Thus, the name `make_record` is an acceptable message name. Here are some examples of valid message names (including system messages you've already seen):

```
openCard
doMenu
update
updateCard
update_card  -- different from updateCard
convertCurrency
exportCardData
restore_settings
```

Note that you may use HyperTalk reserved words within a longer message name without fear of conflict. What you really must give some thought to is that the name mean something to you six months from now or that someone who may be customizing the stack for his own use can make sense out of your message naming scheme. I usually find it best to begin a message name with a verb of some kind, indicating some action that the handler does. Use a second and third word to help narrow the purpose, sender, or recipient of the action.

Modifying HyperTalk Commands

HyperTalk commands tend to be simple and generic. They perform basic operations that are generally quite useful on their own. But that's not to say they don't need help sometimes in being more specific or more powerful in their operation. You have the power to intercept those commands and modify them as you see fit.

An excellent example of how this works can be found in the Phone stack, which comes with HyperCard (Figure 15-5). At the core of the stack is HyperCard's Dial command, which lets you add some parameters about the telephone number, modem control, and modem commands. In an effort to simplify the need to specify a complex set of parameters, the Phone stack has a dial handler of its own, which can intercept any dial message that passes through the stack. The handler accepts the telephone number as one parameter. All other settings are established by radio button settings and the contents of a few fields on the Phone stack's dialing card.

Among the tasks that the enhanced dial handler takes care of is stripping out your own area code if it's attached to a number. It also makes sure that the

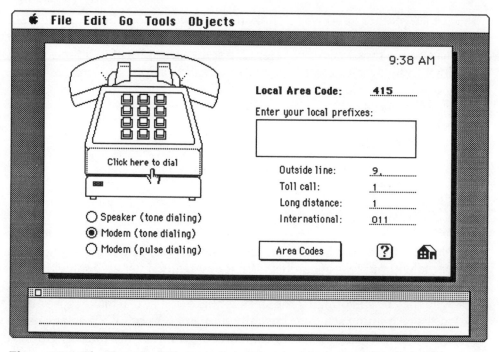

Figure 15-5 *The HyperCard Phone stack modifies the Dial message before it gets to HyperCard.*

rest of the number contains valid digits, stripping out unwanted characters before and after the telephone number. Any prefixes you specify, like dialing 9 to get an outside line, are inserted in front of the number. When the final telephone number is ready for dialing, the handler then summons the Hyper-Card Dial command again, but this time sending it directly to HyperCard. A fragment of the script appears in Figure 15-6. The handler can't send the Dial command to the current card, because it would be intercepted by the handler that sent it, causing too much recursion and an error.

Passing Parameters

HyperTalk provides a mechanism whereby one handler may pass values to another handler by tacking parameters onto a message name. We saw that effectively in the arrowKey system message. There, the direction of the arrow is always sent along with the arrowKey message when one of the arrow keys is pressed on the keyboard. The parameter is text, just like everything in HyperTalk, and is plugged into a local variable at the start of the handler.

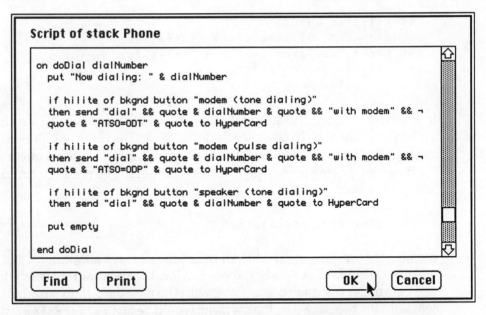

Script of stack Phone

```
on doDial dialNumber
  put "Now dialing: " & dialNumber

  if hilite of bkgnd button "modem (tone dialing)"
  then send "dial" && quote & dialNumber & quote && "with modem" && ¬
  quote & "ATSO=ODT" & quote to HyperCard

  if hilite of bkgnd button "modem (pulse dialing)"
  then send "dial" && quote & dialNumber & quote && "with modem" && ¬
  quote & "ATSO=ODP" & quote to HyperCard

  if hilite of bkgnd button "speaker (tone dialing)"
  then send "dial" && quote & dialNumber & quote to HyperCard

  put empty

end doDial
```

Find   Print   OK   Cancel

Figure 15-6 *In the stack's script is a handler (doDial) that is called by a dial handler that intercepts normal HyperTalk Dial commands. After much manipulation of the phone number, the handler sends a Dial command directly to HyperCard.*

Therefore, you press the right arrow key on the keyboard, and your stack has an arrowKey handler in it like this,

```
on arrowKey whichKey
  ...
end arrowKey
```

HyperCard places the word "right" into the local variable, whichKey, at the beginning of the handler. To find out which key has been pressed, the handler must compare the value of the whichKey variable against parameters it expects (e.g., `if whichKey is "right" then go next card`).

Generating a message with a parameter is simple, but perhaps examples you've seen have been confusing because of the way variables seem to pass from one variable name to another in the process. Let's take a simple (if not simplistic) example to see more precisely what's going on. Consider these two handlers:

```
on mouseUp
  get field "Subtotal"
  addSalesTax it
end mouseUp
```

```
on addSalesTax amount
  put amount * .05 into field "Sales Tax"
  put field "SubTotal" + field "Sales Tax" ¬
  into field "Grand Total"
end addSalesTax
```

In the first handler, the subtotal amount from a form is put into the local variable, It. Then the handler sends the addSalesTax message, along with the value of It. The name of the parameter is of absolutely no consequence while the message is being sent. Only the value matters. The message could just as easily have been

```
addSalesTax field "SubTotal"
```

because the value of the field is all the message cares about.

At the addSalesTax handler, there is a local variable sitting ready to catch one parameter that may come along with the message. If no parameter were sent with the message (i.e., the message would be just addSalesTax), then the local variable, amount, would be empty. If a value comes along as a parameter, then the value is plugged into the variable. Once that value is in the variable, the handler treats the variable as a kind of read-only variable. This is an important point: Do not adjust the content of a parameter variable, which holds a parameter passed with a message. If you need to change values, like converting a date to a different type before performing some calculation on it, put the contents of a parameter-holding variable into yet a different local variable. You are free to run endless comparisons (if-then-else constructions) against the variable parameter, but don't convert it, add anything to it, or in any way alter the contents of such a variable.

Passing Multiple Parameters

HyperTalk offers a syntax for passing more than one parameter at a time with a message. Both at the message sending end and at the handler end, the parameters are separated by commas. To illustrate, we'll present excerpts from the button script in *Focal Point* that builds and extends stacks for which there is a card for each day of the year.

To help you understand what's going on here, the card containing this button is shown in Figure 15-7. The button whose script we'll be describing is the one labeled "Build or Extend" along the bottom row of buttons. We won't go through the entire handler here, but suffice it to say that the first part of the handler calculates how many days there are between the starting and ending dates that the user types into the two fields. Then the handler checks

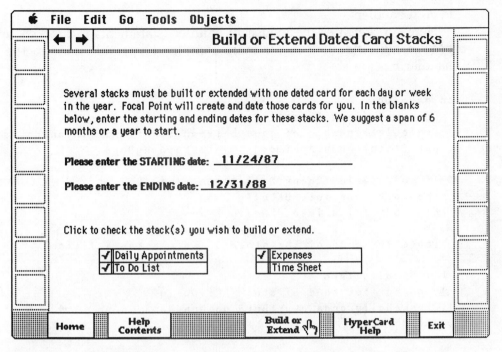

Figure 15-7 *A script in the Build or Extend button has custom handlers that pass multiple parameters.*

the state of each of the check marks next to the names of the four possible *Focal Point* stacks that need building or extending. If the user does not have all four installed in his system, then he need build or extend only those stack he's currently using. To select a stack for inclusion in the building process, the user clicks on the stack name, and a checkmark appears next to the name. The handler sets four local variables to true or false, depending on the check mark setting. If the user specifies that the Daily Appointment stack should be extended, then the local variable called OKDaily is set to true.

Three of the stacks, the Daily Appointment, To Do and Time Sheet stacks, all use the same stack building routine, a separate handler called makeDaily-Cards. This handler requires three parameters: the starting date, the number of days to build and a true or false setting as to whether some global information about the person's name and department should be inserted on each card (true only for the Time Sheets stack). The first two parameters are assigned to local variables in the mouseUp handler, and then passed as parameters. Those values are plugged into parameter variables in the makeDailyCards handler. One of the parameters happens to carry the same name, but that is only a convenience of a good name that serves the value well in both handlers.

Here's a sketch of the mouseUp handler (statements in brackets are in pseudo-code, standing in for more complex HyperTalk code in the real handler.):

```
on mouseUp
   put card field "Starting Date" into startDate
   [calculate number of days between start and finish dates]
   put [total number of days] into howManyDays

   if card field "Check Daily" contains "√"
   then put true into OKDaily
   else put false into OKDaily

   [same for each of the other three checkmark fields]

   If OKDaily then
      go to last card of stack "FP•Daily"
      makeDailyCards startDate,howManyDays,false
   end if

   If OKToDo then
      go to last card of stack "FP•To Do"
      makeDailyCards startDate,howManyDays,false
   end if

   [instructions for Expenses stack calls a different handler]

   If OKTimeSheets then
      go to last card of stack "FP•Time Sheet"
      makeDailyCards startDate,howManyDays,true
   end if

   [some other housekeeping tasks]

end mouseUp
```

In the same button script is this handler (simplified a bit for purposes of demonstration):

```
on makeDailyCards startDate,howMany,personalized
   global theName,theDepartment
   put startDate into theDate
   put startDate into dateCounter
```

```
repeat for howMany
   convert theDate to long date
     if personalized then
     put theName into field "Name"
     put theDepartment into field "Department"
   end if
   put theDate into field "Date"
   add (24*60*60) to dateCounter    -- add one day
   put dateCounter into theDate
   doMenu "New Card"
 end repeat
end makeDailyCards
```

While the fine points about handling dates will be covered in Chapter 19, a key element to note about this handler is that multiple parameters were received by the message in the same order in which the message was sent, and that parameters were separated by commas. Also note that the values assigned to the parameter variables were unchanged during execution of the handler, even though they were used many times in a read-only fashion. To accommodate arithmetic operations on the startDate value, it was handed off to other local variables, theDate and dateCounter.

Parameter Variables and the Param Function

HyperTalk actually gives you two ways to pass parameters to a handler. One way is as we've been describing here, in which you assign a parameter variable name in the opening line of a handler (e.g., `on makeCards howMany`). But if you don't declare a parameter variable name in your handler, you can also use the Param function to retrieve the value(s) passed with the message. This version would start like this:

```
on makeCards
   put param(1) into howMany
   . . .
end makeCards
```

My preference is for named parameter variables, because it's faster (in handler execution) to let values pass naturally than to add a Put statement to accomplish the same thing.

Parameters and Global Variables

Because parameter passing may be new to HyperTalk programmers, there is often a tendency to avoid them and pass data with global variables instead. Global variables, you'll recall, are containers that hold values (text or numbers) all during a HyperCard session. Once you set a global variable to hold a particular value, that value will remain there until a command in a handler alters the contents or you quit HyperCard. Even going from stack to stack does not alter the content of a global variable.

Using lots of global variables presents some potential difficulties. For one, if your stack system relies on several global variables, and the user makes a slight detour to another stack designed by someone else, it's possible that the second stack could use the same global variable name, and store entirely different data in that variable. Upon return to your stack, the variable may hold the wrong kind of information a handler expects. Second, I've seen some complex stacks using dozens and dozens of global variables. I don't know how the author kept track of them all. It would seem like a developmental nightmare to know where all those globals are at any given moment.

Quite often, one or more global variables are created and used when the data stored therein has a very short life. Yet the variable stays there until you quit HyperCard. If you find yourself declaring a large number of global variables, look for the possibility of passing parameters around during the execution of your handlers instead. Stack organizations and data requirements vary way too much for me to provide hard and fast rules about this, but passing parameters is a more efficient method of getting information from one handler to another. And you'll sleep better not having to worry about where your globals are.

Don't get me wrong about global variables. There are times when they are the right way to go. In fact, in the previous handler, you'll note that I use two globals to carry the name and department of the *Focal Point* user throughout the system. These globals are first declared and given their values while the user is looking at the *Focal Point* startup screen. This information is required by several different stacks at various times. Globals proved to be the most efficient way—in time—to handle this data among the 18 *Focal Point* stacks. The alternative was time-consuming, stack-to-stack information retrieval.

While we're on the subject of global variables, I've seen a disturbing tendency in some stacks to declare a raft of global variables without using them right away. Hear this: You don't need to declare a global variable unless you are using it in the same handler as the declaration. Even if you declare three globals together in one handler, like this

```
on mouseUp
  global startTime,interval,clientList
  ...
end mouseUp
```

you don't have to declare all of them again when another handler needs only one of them. Nor do they have to be in the same order (although for readability's sake it helps if they are). Therefore, in the same stack as the above handler, another button might start out this way:

```
on mouseUp
  global clientList,vendorList
  ...
end mouseUp
```

One other global variable tip for multiple stack systems. If you find that you need to keep a global variable alive just within individual stacks of the system but not from stack-to-stack, then feel free to reuse the global variable name in each of the stacks. Just be sure that the openStack handler of each stack stores appropriate data for the newly opened stack in the global variable. I do this in five similar stacks in *Focal Point:* the Daily, To Do, Monthly, Expenses and Time Sheet stacks. A global variable, called interval, remembers which next/ previous card interval is selected on the stack's navigation bar. When the stack opens, the smallest interval is automatically inserted (monthly for the Monthly calendar, daily for the rest). If you click on the interval button, say to change from daily to monthly interval, the new value is stored in the global variable. The next time you click the right or left arrow navigation buttons, the handlers check the contents of the interval global before figuring out which card to advance to.

In summary, be parsimonious with your global variables, and look for ways to pass parameters to your own handlers via custom messages of your own creation.

You'll have another opportunity to think creatively, as we next explore user-defined functions. Get ready for some more parameters, too.

16

User-Defined Functions

In your experimentation with designing stacks, I'm sure you've discovered that HyperTalk's built-in functions can be pretty powerful words in your scripts. Functions, as you'll recall, return values that commands may use in many ways.

Perhaps the most common function used in information management stacks is the Date, which reaches into the Macintosh internal clock and returns the date to which the clock is set. You then use the function within a command, like put the date into field "Date," HyperTalk offers functions and date, text manipulation, mouse and cursor locations, keyboard modifier key conditions and more. But as powerful as HyperTalk's built-in functions are, a HyperCard author has still more power available in the form of user-defined functions are, a HyperCard author has still more power available in the form of user-defined functions—functions that you design for your own script needs.

What User-Defined Functions Do

While most of the HyperTalk built-in functions return information about the system or a container (e.g., the length of a field), it may not be so clear why you'd want to define a function for yourself. After all, except by writing XCMDs, you don't have access to the Macintosh's "innards" to retrieve other system information. However, you may encounter situations in which you are repeating certain calculations. You may also wish to divide a long handler into modules that make the main module easy to read by you and others. Functions can help offload much of the technical details of the script's total execution, making the main handler a work of HyperTalk poetry.

Functions and the Hierarchy

The concept of message passing from object to object along the HyperCard hierarchy applies identically to functions. When a handler calls a function, that function name is sent up the hierarchy as a message, just like a command. That function message seeks a handler that starts, not with the word "on," but with the word "function." Because of its relative position in a command line, a function message with the same name as a command message will be intercepted only by function handlers (although for purposes of readability and debugging I don't recommend you use the same names for user-defined functions and commands in the same stack).

All rules about handlers intercepting messages on their way up the hierarchy apply to functions. That means that you could conceivably have two functions of the same name at different hierarchy levels—perhaps in one button script and in the background script. While it's not likely you'd do such a thing, it's comforting to know that you can pass a function just like you can pass a command. Therefore, if you call a function but need some slight modification for a particular button, the button script would look like this:

```
on mouseUp
  put myFunction() into field 3
end mouseUp

function myFunction
  [special processing for this button only]
```

```
pass myFunction
end myFunction
```

As you may have also guessed by now, you may also trap for HyperTalk's built-in functions before they reach HyperCard for execution. Be careful if you do this, because your modifications must not attempt to modify parameters passed along with the function. Leave the contents of parameter variables intact. One thing you cannot do with functions that you can with commands is send them to a particular level to jump the normal hierarchy.

Function Syntax

User-defined functions are slightly more restrictive in the way you can call them inside a command line. Whereas most HyperTalk built-in functions may be summoned in two ways, as in

```
the number of bkgnd buttons
```

or

```
number (bkgnd buttons)
```

user-defined functions must use the latter format, with parentheses surrounding any parameters that may be sent along with the function. When a function does not have any parameters, the parentheses must be there just the same, but with nothing between them. And user-defined functions are not preceded by the word, "the." Although you rarely see HyperTalk's built-in functions expressed with parentheses, the following functions are in valid formats:

```
long date()
mouseLoc()
numToChar(65)
seconds()
```

In thinking up names for your functions, it's still a good idea to consider the phraseology of HyperTalk's built-in functions. For example, when a function requires a parameter, it is common to say the phrase, "the numToChar of 66," where "66" is the parameter. Functions without parameters can be thought of as being preceded by the word "the." As you write the command line containing your function, say the line aloud, with and without "the." If either version sounds like good English and the function name makes sense in the context of the command line, then you've got a good function name.

Returned Values

All functions must have a Return command line in them. This line is typically the last one prior to the end of the function, although some functions might have several if more than one outcome is possible, as in the following:

```
function grade score
  if score < 75 then return "Fail"
  else if score < 80 then return "Fair"
  else if score < 90 then return "Good"
  else return "Excellent"
end grade
```

A function can return more than a single value, even though it looks as though the Return command allows only a single parameter. The key is to place multiple words, items, or lines of text into a single local variable within the function handler. Then return that variable. Whatever that variable would naturally evaluate to (e.g., a comma-separated, itemized HyperCard string), that's what gets sent back to the original handler that called the function. In a hypothetical example, here's how multiple return values would work in a button script:

```
on mouseUp
  get monthAndYear()
  put item 1 of it into field "Month"
  put item 2 of it into field "Year"
end mouseUp

function monthAndYear
  get the long date
  put word 2 of it into item 1 of monthYear
  put last word of it into item 2 of monthYear
  return monthYear
end monthAndYear
```

Because the words for the month and year were placed into an itemized list within a local variable, the contents of that variable were returned verbatim to the handler that called the function.

Function Modularity

Just as you may build a library of your own commands and handlers over time, you are equally likely to build a library of your own functions. If you design several stacks in the same category (e.g., information management), you'll probably find yourself attacking various organizational and operational problems with similar solutions across your stacks. Development time will be speeded up if you break out functions from your large handlers and reuse them in other stacks.

As you'll see later in this chapter, functions may call other functions. Therefore, it is advisable to keep function handlers as small and as modular as possible. You may be able to mix and match functions on different occasions. That means that you should try to make functions as generic as possible. Avoid calling objects by name; let the name be passed to the function as a parameter. And use parameter passing instead of global variables as the primary means of passing information to the function. You might not use the same global variable scheme in the next stack employing that function.

Simple Functions

The simplest kind of function is one similar to the non-parameter passing functions built into HyperCard, like date and mouse functions. A simple function returns a single value.

The best way to learn about functions is to test them out, so make a stack for this chapter, as you did for some of the previous chapters:

1. *Open the Developer's Guide Master stack, created in Chapter 12.*

2. *Choose Save a Copy from the File menu.*

3. *Type "Chapter 16 Stack" into the file dialog box.*

4. *Open Chapter 16 Stack via the Open Stack choice of the File menu.*

Name each of the five fields in the first card of the stack with the Field Info dialog box. The exact names you use won't make much difference for the purposes of the examples in this chapter. It's a good idea to get in the habit of naming objects, especially fields, buttons and backgrounds.

Our first function goes into the background script. Here it is:

```
function allFilled
  repeat with x = 1 to the number of bkgnd fields - 1
    if field x is empty then
      put false into filledOut
      exit repeat
    else put true into filledOut
  end repeat
  return filledOut
end allFilled
```

This function returns true if all fields have text in them. You might use a function like this in a background containing fields that undergo substantial math, like an invoice form. Before proceeding with the arithmetic, presumably as the result of a button press or a closeField message, you will want to make sure all fields except the Grand Total field (the last field in tabbing order) have numbers in them. If the math calculation handler should try the operation and encounter a blank field, the handler will stop and display a HyperCard error alert box, which could confuse the non-HyperLiterate user. A fine point about the if-then construction: It exits the entire repeat loop when a field shows empty, because if one field is empty then that's all the function needs to know to return false. There's no need to continue rounding the repeat loop any more.

To see this function in action, create a new button and place it in the upper right box. Assign the name Calculate to the button, and enter this handler:

```
on mouseUp
  if not allFilled()
  then answer "Sorry, some information is missing."
  else
    put zero into sum
    repeat with x = 1 to 4
      add field x to sum
    end repeat
    put sum into field 5
  end if
end mouseUp
```

This mouseUp handler depends entirely on a true or false result of the allFilled function. When the function returns false (i.e., not allFilled), then a warning box appears on the screen and no calculation takes place; otherwise, the first four fields are added together, their total placed in field 5. The best place for the allFilled function handler is in the background or stack script, because several objects may call this function. If objects in different backgrounds call this general purpose function, then it definitely belongs in the stack script.

Passing Parameters

Our next function demonstrates how you may pass a parameter along with a function. The example is another general purpose kind of function that would go in many information management stacks in which the user enters monetary numbers. Computer users who are familiar with spreadsheet programs are accustomed to setting a number format so that no matter what kind of number they type into the cell, the program always displays it as a number with two places to the right of the decimal—in dollars and cents.

The twoDecimal function, listed below, works in conjunction with a field or background level closeField handler. As soon as a user tabs or otherwise closes the field, the function returns the equivalent value with two digits to the right of the decimal. The closeField handler then replaces the value that the user typed with the correctly formatted version.

Here, then, are the closeField and twoDecimal function handlers. Type these into the background script of the first Chapter 16 Stack background.

```
on closeField
  get the short name of the target
  put twoDecimal (the value of the target) into field it
end closeField

function twoDecimal figure
  get figure
  set numberFormat to "0.00"
  add 0 to it
  return it
end twoDecimal
```

First, in the closeField handler, the parameter being passed with the function name is, itself, a function: the value of the target. Before HyperCard sends the twoDecimal function message on its way in search of a matching function handler, it evaluates the current function. In this case, it fetches the content of the field that generated the closeField message to begin with. Whatever the twoDecimal function returns will be going back into that very field.

Inside the function handler, the parameter variable is copied into the local variable, It. After the number format property of HyperCard is changed (remember, it resumes normal format at idle time), a harmless zero is added to the value. This is all HyperTalk needs to apply the new number format to the value. Then, the newly formatted value is returned to the calling handler.

Try this handler in the Chapter 16 stack. Enter values into any of the five fields on the card. As you press Tab or Enter, or click on the card, the value is converted into the dollars and cents format. If the dollar sign is important for your display, you could also add that to the function, or, better yet, write a different function with a more descriptive name for the currency symbol:

```
function dollarsAndCents figure
  get figure
  set numberFormat to "0.00"
  add 0 to it
  return "$" && it
end dollarsAndCents
```

Multiple Parameters

Our next example actually demonstrates two techniques at once: passing more than one parameter at a time, and calling one user-defined function from within another user-defined function. You'll also get a touch of date arithmetic thrown in for good measure.

The situation calling for these functions is a stack that needs to display the number of the day for today's date, like the 145th day of the year. While this could be written as a single function, the two modules turn out to be a logical approach, and each module becomes a piece of our function library. A function like this would probably be called from an openCard handler, so that the display of the day number would be automatic whenever the card came on the screen. Thus, the openCard handler would be

```
on openCard
  put dayOfYear() into field "Day Number"
end openCard
```

The main function, dayOfYear, does not pass any parameters, because it takes its cue from the internal Macintosh clock. But the dayOfYear function calls another user-defined function, called wholeMonthDays to offload some of the detail calculation to figure out how many days have elapsed in the completed months of the current year. Here are the two function handlers:

```
function dayOfYear
  get the date
  convert it to dateItems
  put wholeMonthDays (item 1 of it, item 2 of it) into amount
  add item 3 of it to amount
  return amount
end dayOfYear
```

```
function wholeMonthDays year,month
  if year mod 4 is zero then put true into leapYear
  else put false into leapYear
  put empty into total

  repeat with x = 0 to month - 1
    if x = 0 then next repeat
    if x = 2 then
      if leapYear then add 29 to total
      else add 28 to total
    else if "1,3,5,7,8,9,10,12" contains x
    then add 31 to total
    else add 30 to total
  end repeat

  return total
end wholeMonthDays
```

The first function handler extracts the year and month items (item 1 and item 2) from the dateItems version of today's date (see the Convert command discussion in the *Handbook* for a refresher on the dateItems format). Those two items are passed as parameters to the wholeMonthDays function. As in passing parameters with commands, the variable names assigned to parameters may change in the transition between caller and "callee," because only the values are passed. That's great news, because the two parameters to the wholeMonthDays function may be renamed to something more meaningful, year and month, instead of "item 1 of it" and "item 2 of it."

We needn't go into detail here about the inner workings of the wholeMonthDays function (we'll cover its command again in Chapter 19), but suffice it to say that the function checks for leap years, and accumulates a total of the days of completed months up to the previous month. The total number of days of completed months are then returned to the dayOfYear function, which adds the current month's date to that figure. The final total is what gets returned back to the calling openCard handler, and the correct number of the current day is ready for insertion into the specified field.

Using Your Function Library

As a stack developer, you will likely be gathering functions and adding them to your library. Because functions follow the HyperCard hierarchy, the temptation will be to place your library of functions in your Home stack. Thus, anytime you need the function, you know it's available for you in whatever stack you're working on.

The hazard with this methodology is that you may forget the function is in your Home stack, and not in your developmental stack. When someone tries to test your stack on a different Macintosh, it's unlikely that your function will be in that person's Home stack.

Now, I don't believe you should be so worried about this that you remove your functions from your Home stack. As it turns out, that's a pretty good place to store them. Just be sure you test your stack on a fresh Home stack or on other machines to make sure all your function handlers are within the stack itself. Otherwise it gets mighty embarrassing to demonstrate a stack on a strange machine and to see a "Can't understand..." error dialog box with your prized function's name on display. If you follow testing guidelines described in Chapter 21, then you'll find holes like this very early in development.

From functions we head into another subject that is a bit confusing for many first-time programmers: control structures. But experienced HyperCard authors should also be aware of the control structure performance issues explained in the next chapter.

17

Diving Deeper Into Control Structures

The term "control structure" comes from traditional programming environments in which a program usually consists of a long series of statements (commands, for instance). In such a program, a control structure influences the flow of program execution—down one of two or more paths or in a repetitive loop. In other words, a control structure alters the normal, linear flow of the program statements.

HyperTalk programs, if you can call them that, are not really long sequences of statements, but small modules triggered by messages passing up the object hierarchy. If it can be said there is any kind of program flow, it is predominantly within a given handler only. Unlike programs written in other traditional languages, when the program is at rest, there is usually no HyperTalk execution taking place (with the exception of idle handlers). Therefore, talking about control structures in HyperTalk stretches the definition, or at least the intent, of the term.

Control Basics

HyperTalk offers several ways of altering the execution flow of a handler. The two basic categories are if-then-else and repeat constructions.

If-then-else constructions perform a kind of simple decision making, presenting a programming equivalent to the fork in the road, when both paths eventually merge into one road again later. The author determines under which condition(s) the handler follows one path or the other. Additionally, each pathway may, itself, have another fork in it. No matter how many decisions the handler has to make, a control structure dictates that flow always returns to a single path. There are some exceptions. For example, in a roadway metaphor, let's say the decision to make one fork in the journey from point A to point B is whether to take the twisty, narrow mountain pass or the four-lane highway. The decision factor involved is the weather. If the weather is clear, then take the mountain pass, otherwise take the highway. While taking the mountain pass route of the fork, if a previous storm left the pass so muddy that your car gets stuck and damaged, then a helicopter airlifts you and your car out of the mountains, and the journey ends. We'll see more illustrations and examples of if-then-else constructions later.

Repeat constructions, although control structures, bear no resemblance to if-then-else constructions. Repeat constructions let you set up loops in the pathway of a handler's execution. Loops do just what they sound like they do: Execution goes round and round within a number of statements in the handler, sort of like driving into and getting caught in a traffic circle. Repeat loops are handy when you need to perform the same operation on a number of objects on a card. The Home stack handlers for locking and unlocking all fields on a card (Chapter 13) are a good example of that.

The handler author determines under what conditions execution may exit the repeat construction and what happens during each time through the loop. Loops may be executed a specific number of times or until a certain condition is met. Statements in the loop generally do something slightly different each time or at least modify the condition of some object or value during each loop. For example, statements in a loop might affect a different object during each time through the loop, as in the lock/unlock field handlers. If nothing changed during loop execution, and the loop was waiting for some condition to end the loop, then you'd have an infinite loop, which means that handler execution would never pass beyond the repeat construction. You obviously do not want an infinite loop in your handlers.

If-Then-Else Constructions

In case you're still not sure how if-then-else constructions work, this section should offer help. Because these constructions impact the flow of execution within a handler, I believe it may help to picture some of the possibilities with my version of what is called a "flow chart." Flow charting—a somewhat archaic concept these days in computing—illustrates the pathways that a program takes. Some programmers might take exception to illustrating HyperTalk's if-then-else constructions with flow charts, but they work for me, and I think they'll work for you, too.

The diagrams on the next few pages show five possible if-then-else constructions and the corresponding HyperTalk code. First, a few conventions used in the diagrams and program listings. As you should be aware by now, if-then-else constructions test for some condition at the very beginning. These tests usually involve a comparison of two numeric or text values, like whether the target contains the word "button" or whether field "Total" is greater than 10,000. Such comparisons always return either a true or false response. Therefore, immediately after the If statement in an if-then-else construction must be some comparison or other value that returns the HyperTalk constants True or False. In the diagrams, the If statement and its comparison is represented by a diamond. Two pathways branch from the diamond, one representing the path followed when the comparison yields true, the other for false. Then, squares represent HyperTalk statements that execute along various pathways. The statements are labeled with the letter "S" and a number to differentiate one statement from others. In the accompanying HyperTalk schematic example for each repeat structure, the statements are shown in their proper places with their numbers. Compare the S numbers in the code listing with their corresponding statement squares in the diagram to visualize how the HyperTalk handler treats various types of if-then-else constructions.

Figure 17-1 shows the simplest kind of if-then-else construction. It's so simple, in fact, that it is just an if-then construction. There is only one possible detour, S1. If the condition tested by the If statement proves false, then execution continues unchanged. In real life, a handler with this construction would look like this:

```
on mouseUp
   get the selection    -- put selected text into It
   go to stack "Address"
   if it is not empty then find it
end mouseUp
```

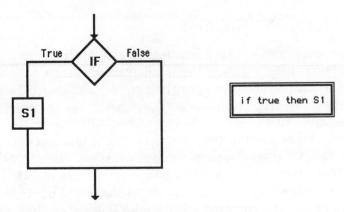

Figure 17-1 *The simplest if-then construction.*

In Figure 17-2, we add a second possible path to the construction, by adding an Else statement. This is how you produce two distinctly different paths, depending on the outcome of the If statement comparison. Notice that the HyperTalk version might give the impression to inexperienced control structure users that statement S2 gets executed after statement S1. The diagram shows how that is not true at all. Normal handler execution resumes after the else statement.

We've already seen one example of an if-then-else construction:

```
on mouseUp
    ...
    if card field "Check Daily" contains "√"
    then put true into OKDaily
    else put false into OKDaily
    ...
end mouseUp
```

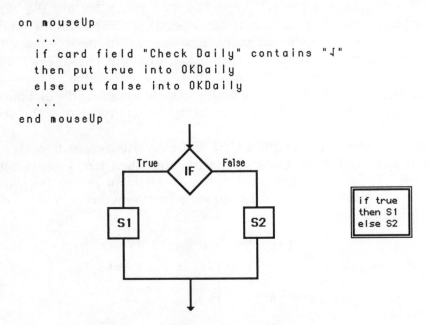

Figure 17-2 *The simplest if-then-else construction.*

By the time this if-then-else structure is complete, the handler will have gone through one path ("then") or the other ("else"). There is no possibility that the local variable OKDaily will be empty after this structure.

Going up one more rung in the ladder of complexity, Figure 17-3 shows our first nested if-then-else construction, which means you can place an if-then-else construction inside another one, as the logic of your decision making dictates. In the diagram, statement S1 executes only when the first ("outermost") If statement proves true. If that If statement is false, then it immediately encounters another If statement. If the second one is true, then statement S2 executes. Notice, that the only way for the handler execution path to reach statement S2 is for the first If test to come up false and the second one true. Earlier in the book, we trapped for the left and right arrow keys with this kind of if-then-else statement:

```
on arrowKey whichKey
   if whichKey is "left" then go to previous card
   else if whichKey is "right" then go to next card
end arrowKey
```

The only time the handler goes to the next card is when the arrow key pressed is NOT the left but IS the right. And, when the arrow key is up, for example, both If comparisons return false, and no statements execute in this handler when that key is pressed. Thus, the handler (intentionally) disables the up and

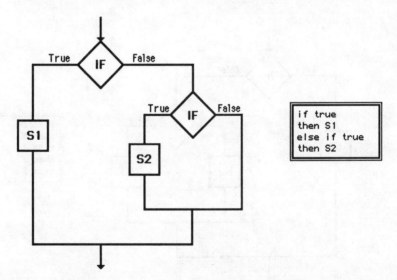

Figure 17-3 *Despite the look of the HyperTalk version, only one statement can be executed in this construction, and it's possible that no statement is executed (when both If tests return False).*

down arrow keys. To make the handler beep when any other arrow key is pressed, you'd add one more else statement at the bottom:

```
on arrowKey whichKey
  if whichKey is "left" then go to previous card
  else if whichKey is "right" then go to next card
  else beep
end arrowKey
```

This additional else statement is illustrated in the diagram of Figure 17-4. Of all three statements in the diagram, only one statement can be executed in the course of the if-then-else construction, depending solely on the results of the if statement comparisons.

The inverse of the structure illustrated in Figure 17-3 is worth showing in Figure 17-5, not because any different decision nesting is going on, but because the HyperTalk version looks different. You may nest an if statement directly beneath another if statement if the second decision point occurs along the TRUE path of the first decision point.

Our last if-then-else flow diagram is Figure 17-6, which shows one way to replicate in HyperCard what Pascal calls the CASE statement. When a particular variable or field might have one of several predefined values, and the operation of the handler is slightly different for each value, you can nest sequential else-if constructions. The diagram looks more complex than the

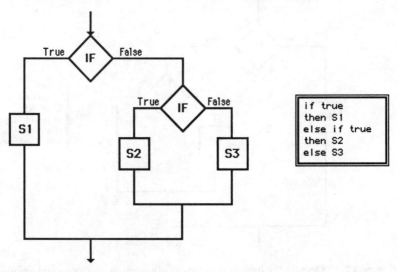

Figure 17-4 *One (and only one) statement will defintely be carried out in this construction.*

HyperTalk equivalent. The If statements down the chain would be testing the same variable or field against different values. For instance, here's a handler for a multiple-choice quiz that demonstrates the technique (psuedo-code in brackets):

```
on mouseUp
   get field "Answer"
   if it is "A" then [statement for A's answer]
   else if it is "B" then [statement for B's answer]
   else if it is "C" then [statement for C's answer]
   else answer "Sorry, invalid answer."
end mouseUp
```

As you've probably discovered in your own experimentation with if-then-else constructions, the possibilities are almost endless. Therefore, it's not feasible to show you more diagrams. It's better to understand the rules that govern handler execution within these constructions, and then build a structure around your particular needs.

If-Then-Else Style

If you are about to build a complex if-then-else construction, it may be helpful to fit a diagram similar to the ones above to your decision paths. The key

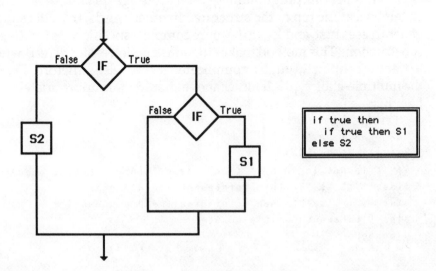

Figure 17-5 *The inverse of the construction in Figure 17-3.*

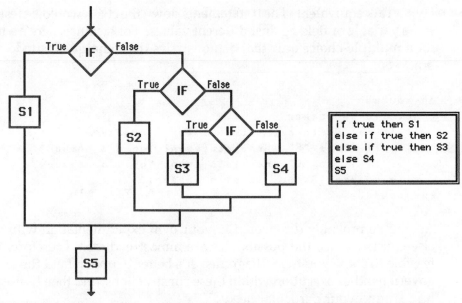

Figure 17-6 *You can replicate Pascal CASE statements in a series of nested if-then-else constructions*

technique is to carefully think through each possible path through the construction. Imagine what happens to various values or fields in the course of each path. Ask yourself if the results are what you expect for each outcome and whether there is a conflict or duplication between any paths.

Good HyperTalk programming style encourages placing the shortest nested statements at the top of the structure. In other words, treat the simple, most general cases first, and leave the more complex, specific ones for the end of the construction. This method makes the construction easier to read when trying to trace execution through a complicated if-then-else structure. For example, the multiple-choice quiz handler above should more appropriately be written like this:

```
on mouseUp
  get field "Answer"
  if it is not in "A,B,C" then answer "Sorry, invalid answer."
  else if it is "A" then [statement for A's answer]
  else if it is "B" then [statement for B's answer]
  else [statement for C's answer]
end mouseUp
```

Another major advantage to placing the general condition at the top of the structure is that it performs faster than when it is at the bottom of the structure. Each time the construction needs to perform another If statement, more time is added to the overall execution of the handler. Thus, those at the top finish their job faster, and the handler ends sooner.

If-Then-Else Reduction

This brings up an important subject about HyperTalk, especially within if-then-else constructions. If you are concerned about speed—and you should be—try to reduce the number of statements in a handler. That also means that you should try to combine a series of if-then constructions into a larger if-then-else construction.

Watching a handler makeover should be helpful to illustrate how you can streamline your if-then-else decisions. For example, buried deep within version 1.0 of *Focal Point* is the following absurd handler—written before I learned how to do it better. Warning: Do not attempt the following handler maneuver on your own—bad habits may accrue.

```
on mouseUp
  global interval
  if item 5 of interval is 1 then
    put 2 into item 5 of interval
    openCard
    exit mouseUp
  end if
  if item 5 of interval is 2 then
    put 3 into item 5 of interval
    openCard
    exit mouseUp
  end if
  if item 5 of interval is 3 then
    put 4 into item 5 of interval
    openCard
    exit mouseUp
  end if
  if item 5 of interval is 4 then
    put 1 into item 5 of interval
    openCard
  end if
end mouseUp
```

There is so much repetition in this handler, that it should be a dead giveaway something is amiss. Note that the If comparisons are all against the same thing: item 5 of the global variable called interval. The exit mouseUp statements had to be in this construction, otherwise the instant one If construction put another value into item 5 of interval, the next If statement might trap it, when the purpose of this handler was one adjustment per trip. No, this handler is far better served using nested if-then-else statements, as in the following:

```
on mouseUp
  global interval
  get item 5 of interval

  if it is 1 then put 2 into item 5 of interval
  else if it is 2 then put 3 into item 5 of interval
  else if it is 3 then put 4 into item 5 of interval
  else put 1 into item 5 of interval

  openCard
end mouseUp
```

There is no need to exit the mouseUp handler midway, because only one of those "put" statements can possibly be executed in the course of this handler. Then a single openCard statement concludes the handler, since all possible results lead to this statement anyway. The last Else statement omits an If comparison, because the only way execution would wind up down there would be for the value of it to be 4 in this very controlled environment. Why waste time testing for it if that's the only value it could be?

Incidentally, due to the arithmetical relationships among the various pieces in the above handler, it may be shortened even more:

```
on mouseUp
  global interval
  get item 5 of interval

  if it is 4 then put 1 into item 5 of interval
  else add 1 to item 5 of interval

  openCard
end mouseUp
```

Be on the lookout for repetition in your handlers as well as a series of two or more if-then constructions that rely on a comparison of a single object. There's a big clue there that you can condense the construction into a single structure, and perhaps enhance the performance of your handler at the same time.

One added tip, which also applies to the next discussions about repeat constructions, is that getting data out of, and putting data into, fields is a comparatively time-consuming task for HyperTalk. The same is true, but to a lesser degree, for getting and setting object properties. When you find repeated If statement comparisons (including else-ifs) revolving around the contents of a field, a property, or a chunk of a variable (e.g., "line 3 of bucket"), then do those manipulations only once. At the beginning of a handler or immediately preceding a control structure, retrieve whatever information you need and place the data in It or another local variable. On the other end of the handler, if you're assembling lines and words of text that ultimately go into a field, then assemble the text in a local variable first. When it's all set, then put the contents of that container into the field. We'll see some examples of how much this can improve performance later in this chapter.

Repeat Basics

If you've ever addressed Christmas cards or put stamps on envelopes to pay the monthly bills, then you have lived through a repeat loop. In a typical repeat loop in real life and in a HyperTalk handler, you go through the same steps more than once, but usually with some slight twist in execution each time. In addressing Christmas cards, it's writing a different name and address on each envelope; in a handler, it could be checking the condition of fields with different field names.

The number of times a HyperTalk repeat construction loops through its lines depends on the very first statement of the construction, the one with the word Repeat in it. Parameters to that statement indicate how many times to repeat. Sometimes it's for a fixed number of times, as in

```
repeat 10 times
```

When the repeat is based on a number of objects that may change over time, the author would best make the number of repetitions dependent on the number of objects:

```
repeat for the number of cards
```

Another indefinite repeat counter may be defined on comparisons of two values. In other words, the repeat construction should keep looping until a certain condition is met:

```
repeat until field "Date" is the long date
```

The opposite of the previous one is a repeat loop that continues to go round and round only while a certain condition is true:

```
repeat while the name of the background is "Summary"
```

It may also be helpful in your script for your handler to know how many times the loop is going around. You may set up a counting mechanism—a local variable, actually—that keeps a count along with each time through the loop. You may refer to that variable as often as you like within the repeat loop, and even use it to reference a sequence of buttons, fields, or chunk text expressions:

```
repeat with x = 1 to the number of bkgnd fields
```

Finally, you may set a repeat loop going on its own without any bounds. If there is no mechanism within the loop to stop it—to exit the repeat—the loop will go on forever. Normally in such situations, your handler is checking the condition of another object so it may break out of this potentially infinite loop. This structure is so infinite, it is even called

```
repeat forever
```

And we all know that forever is a long, long time.

Repeat constructions may be nested inside one another. There is no restriction on mixing repeat loop types in a nested construction.

Since the basic considerations about repeat constructions are well-covered in the *Handbook*, we'll spend time here focusing on more potentially confusing concepts: Repeat With constructions; nested loops; and Repeat Forever constructions.

Repeat With Constructions

In my experience building some heavy-duty stacks, I've found that the Repeat With construction has been more influential over stack design than perhaps any other HyperTalk command or construction. Whenever I am faced with a large calculation or data movement situation, I now look immediately to the Repeat With construction for ways of condensing what might otherwise be a massive operation.

You've already been exposed to a Repeat With loop in the utility handlers that lock and unlock fields (Chapter 13). Let's look at one of those handlers again and examine what's going on.

```
on lockFields
  repeat with x = 1 to the number of bkgnd fields
  set lockText of field x to true
  end repeat
end lockFields
```

The deciding factor about how many times the loop will execute is the range defined in the first line of the repeat loop. This loop uses a local variable, x, to maintain a count of the number of times through the loop. You may use any valid (i.e., single, non-reserved word) for a variable name in these repeat constructions. The first time through the loop, x will be assigned a value of 1. The loop will continue to run, invisibly adding 1 to the value of x each time, until the value of x is equal to that of the number of background fields. Therefore, if there are five background fields, this loop will run five times, with the value of x incrementing by one each time through. Note that the loop executes in its entirety five times—one for each increment of the variable. This setup also means that if the first line read

```
repeat with x = 3 to the number of bkgnd fields
```

then the repeat loop would execute only three times, as the value of x goes from 3 to 4 to 5.

We're not using this Repeat With construction just to figure out how many times to run the loop. If we just wanted to limit the number of repetitions, we'd use the Repeat For construction, as in

```
repeat for the number of bkgnd fields
```

or, in the case of wanting to do it two times fewer than the number of fields,

```
repeat for the number of bkgnd fields - 2
```

No, there is a very specific reason for using the Repeat With construction and assigning a variable to hold the counter. Our handler can use that variable to help it in its execution.

Follow the execution of the lockFields handler as its loop repeats five times. The first time through, the local variable is assigned the value of 1. In the next line, that x is used to help identify a background field. Because the value of x is 1, the field whose lockText property gets set to true is background field 1. The End Repeat statement tells HyperCard that it is to return to the top of the repeat construction and start again, but this time incrementing the value of x by 1, making it 2. The second time through the repeat loop, the lockText property of background field 2 is set. And so it goes until all five fields are set. At the end of the fifth time through the loop, the End Repeat statement sends execution back to the top once more. But since incrementing x one more (to 6) puts it over the number of background fields, the repeat loop is not executed again. Instead, flow returns to the statement immediately after the End Repeat statement.

Looping Through Object Names

While it's fine to refer to objects by their numbers when you don't know which specific objects are to be called in a handler (as in the lockFields case), you should play it safe by referring to objects within a stack by either their ID numbers or names. From a debugging and development point of view, referring to objects by names in repeat loops is a better strategy, because you are then free to add or subtract objects at any time without disturbing your handler more than by a couple of characters. If, on the other hand, you try using ID numbers in repeat loops, you must first be sure you create the fields or buttons in sequence so that the ID numbers come up in numeric order. If you wait until tomorrow to add another object in the series, its ID number will probably be out of the series, making your repeat construction practically worthless without a major overhaul.

While I have done some repeat handlers in which the controlling variable is used to reference ID numbers, as in

```
repeat with counter = 45 to 54
  get field id counter
  ...
end repeat
```

I'll show you how to name objects properly for this task, and how to call them from a repeat loop. There are a couple of non-intuitive tricks you have to play to pull this off properly.

Naming Sequential Objects

First of all, the names of the objects in a series must have a number as part of their names. HyperTalk may get very confused if you start the name of an object with a number. Therefore, it's best to start the name with a word or two, followed by a number. The number may be the last character of the name, or, for better readability, it may be separated from the name by a space. In Figure 17-7, you see the Materials Worksheet from *Focal Point's* Projects stack. Like a spreadsheet, each cell is its own field. The names of the fields in the leftmost column are named

Qty 1
Qty 2
Qty 3

and so on. All fields in the same row have the same number appended to them. Therefore, across the first row of the worksheet, the fields are named:

Qty 1   Item 1   Cost 1   Markup 1   Total 1

The handler that calculates extensions for each item is a Repeat For loop that uses the variable to address each row's cells. The schematic for that handler is

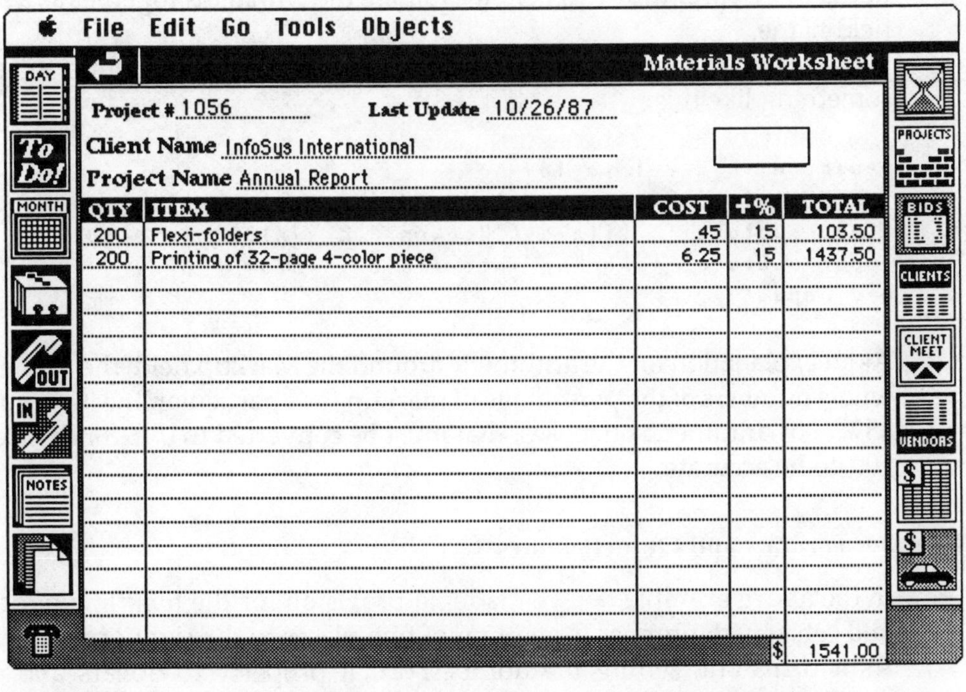

Figure 17-7 *Calculation of the spreadsheet in the Focal Point Materials Worksheet is done via a Repeat With construction. Field names were impacted by the numberFormat setting to accommodate dollars and cents (see text).*

```
on mouseUp
  repeat 18 times  -- the number of rows
    put Qty field * Cost field into subTotal
    put subTotal * Markup Field/100 into markUp
    put subTotal + markUp into Total field
  end repeat
end mouseUp
```

One difficulty you'll encounter with HyperTalk in assembling the actual working handler is that you cannot build the field names out of text and the variable as simply as you call an object by its number. In the lockFields handler, for instance, you referred to each field as "bkgnd field x" and that was that. Carrying the syntax over to a field name, you'd think, should be just as easy, as in "field Qty && x." But such is not the case. Field names containing a variable value must be build like this:

```
field ("Qty " & x)
```

that is, with the field name and variable within parentheses. HyperCard needs these parentheses to help it evaluate the two items together as a single field name.

Therefore, the repeat handler that takes care of the field names would be something like this:

```
repeat with x = 1 to 18
  put field ("Qty " & x) * field ("Cost " & x) into subtotal
  put subtotal * (field ("Markup " & x)/100) into markup
  put subtotal + markup into field ("Total " & x)
end repeat
```

As an explanation for the arithmetic around the Markup field, the user enters whole numbers of the percentage of markup for a particular line item, such as 15%. For arithmetic purposes, that must be converted to 0.15, or divided by 100, to be accurate.

Number Formats and Object Names

In the above example, we've made no provision for the handling of dollars and cents, with number formatting of two places to the right of the decimal. As it turns out, setting the numberFormat property to dollars and cents wreaks havoc with the scheme to create field names out of fixed text and a variable number. Here's what happens.

If you set the numberFormat to "0.00" and then build a field name with a variable counter, the number part of the name takes on the number format. Therefore, in the following version of the handler,

```
set numberFormat to "0.00"
repeat with x = 1 to 18
   put field ("Qty " & x) * field ("Cost " & x) into subtotal
   put subtotal * (field ("Markup " & x)/100) into markup
   put subtotal + markup into field ("Total " & x)
end repeat
```

the Qty field name would be assembled as "Qty. 1.00," with two digits to the right of the decimal. Because field names are treated very literally, the field "Qty 1.00" is different than the field's real name, "Qty 1." An error dialog box will tell you that the handler cannot find field Qty 1.00. Even if you try to reset the numberFormat property to empty for the first two lines of the repeat construction, you must set the format correctly before putting the total amount into the Total field, whose name would be called as "Total 1.00."

The way I usually work around this is to name all the fields just as the handler expects to find them, with numbers bearing two zeros to the right of the decimal. If you do the same, make sure you test other handlers that refer to those fields (or buttons in other applications) and be sure those handlers set the numberFormat to "0.00" before executing.

Nested Loops

To illustrate why we need nested repeat loops, here's a metaphorical example from daily life—not something you can program directly in HyperTalk. First of all, nested repeat loops have what is called an "outer loop" and an "inner loop" (for the case of one nested inside another). The outer loop works on a slower basis than the inner loop, because the inner loop must complete its round-and-round activity before the outer loop can start its next pass.

For instance, 12 times each year there are monthly bills to pay. Each month, there are the utility, phone, rent, car payment, and other bills for which checks must be written. In a HyperTalk-like environment, the nested loop of these actions would look like this:

```
repeat 12 times
  repeat with x = 1 to the number of bills
    write check for bill x
  end repeat
    mail payment envelopes
end repeat
```

In these very few lines of instructions, we've handled the writing of checks for perhaps hundreds of bills. The inner loop controls the writing of checks for one month, while that loop is, itself, repeated 12 times. Rather than have one repeat handler for each month of the year, the outer loop takes over.

Notice that even though the mailing of payments is usually done at the end of writing checks, that action does not belong in the inner loop, because it would be repeated for each of the checks you're writing. It belongs as part of the outer loop, because that action is repeated only 12 times—after each of the inner loops finishes execution.

For a real HyperTalk example, we go to *Focal Point*, where I customized the Expenses stack to print out as many weeks' worth of daily expense detail sheets as I need for a trip. The handler gets some assistance from a function (makeSunday) to be sure the entire week of forms is printed when I start the handler. Here is the entire script:

```
on printWeek howMany
  push card
  get makeSunday (line 2 of field "Date")
  convert it to long date
  find it
  open printing with dialog
  repeat howMany times
    repeat 7 times
      print this card
      go to next card
    end repeat
  end repeat
  close printing
  pop card
end printWeek

function makeSunday testDate
  get testDate
  convert it to dateItems
  put item 7 of it into dayOffset
  convert it to seconds
  subtract (24*60*60) * (dayOffset - 1) from it
```

```
    return it
end makeSunday
```

Briefly, the printWeek handler takes as a parameter the number of weeks I'd like printed. Assuming that I type this message into the Message Box while viewing any card from the starting week, the handler's first task is to determine the starting Sunday of that week. That's what the makeSunday function handler does. Upon returning the Sunday's date in seconds, the handler finds the Sunday card and opens printing.

There are two nested repeat loops here. The outer loop uses the howMany parameter to keep track of how many weeks of cards to print. The inner loop is repeated 7 times each time it's called, because it prints seven cards for each week. Therefore, if I specify 4 weeks of cards for printing, the inner loop is called 4 separate times, each time looping itself 7 times, for a total printing of 28 days' cards.

Repeat Forever

It might seem odd that you would intentionally set an infinite loop in motion, but the Repeat Forever construction does come in handy in very controlled circumstances. I first encountered it and still use it today in text importing scripts.

When importing from a text file, my scripts open the file, read from the file until a delimiter characters (tab or return) and then process the data that comes in as a result of the Read command. If there is no more data in the file—the entire file has already been read—then the Read command puts empty into It. The repeat loop that handles the reading can then test for when It is empty after a Read. When no more can be read, then the Exit Repeat statement bounces execution out of the repeat loop, and onto the statements below it.

A favorite importing script of mine, in which the data in the text file is set up identically to the field arrangement in the destination HyperCard card is as follows:

```
on mouseUp
    ask "Which file do you wish to import?" with "Transfer Text"
    if it is empty then exit mouseUp
    put it into fileName
    open file fileName
    go to last card
```

```
repeat forever
    doMenu "New Card"

    read from file fileName until return

    if it is empty then
        go to first card
        close file filename
        exit mouseUp
    else put tab into last char of it

    repeat with x = 1 to the number of fields
        put char 1 to offset (tab,it) - 1 of it into field x
        delete char 1 to offset (tab, it) of it
    end repeat
  end repeat
end mouseUp
```

The failsafe to this handler is that eventually the text file will be completely read into the stack, and any attempt to read from it will return empty into It. That's when the entire mouseUp handler exits (after housekeeping such as closing the file).

As long as we have another nested loop in the above handler, let's see how that's working. The outer loop reads an entire record (card) of data into It. The inner loop dissects It, pulling off field after field, and placing the data in appropriate HyperCard fields. The inner loop is executed as often as the outer loop is successful at bringing in a record from the text file.

Repeat Performance

As "neat" as nested loops may be, they can be performance hogs, making an involved handler very sluggish. Bear in mind that the statements that are part of the repeat loop itself, Repeat and End Repeat, take time to work. And when using repeat loops that perform evaluations at the very top (especially Repeat While, Repeat Until, and Repeat With), those evaluations take additional time to perform.

One speed stealer to be on the watch for in your repeat constructions is access to field data. At all cost you should avoid getting data from or putting data into the same field more than once per cycle. It will be faster to store intermediate results of repeated calculations in local variables, and then put the data into the field at the very end. In fact, if you can anticipate the getting of data outside the repeat loop entirely (and store the value in a local variable), then you'll do your stack's performance a big favor.

The warning about accessing fields also applies to reading and writing text file data. Thus, in the handler, above, an entire record is read into It at one time, instead of reading the data field by field.

Deeply nesting repeat constructions can sometimes bog down performance beyond acceptable limits. I encountered this in writing the *Focal Point* handler that customizes button icons and scripts among all the *Focal Point* stacks. My first attempts pushed nesting about three levels deep in an effort to keep the handler to a manageable size. Unhappy with the time it took to adjust all icons and scripts throughout the stack system, I experimented with a much less nested handler. Although the handler mushroomed in size, execution speed quickened by at least a factor of 5. It was a tough decision, but I sacrificed HyperTalk elegance for sheer speed of execution. I believed that non HyperLiterate users wouldn't care about the elegance, but they'd be disappointed at the performance. Therefore, the handler is no great example of HyperTalk style or poetry, but it does the job efficiently. Perhaps in further review of the handler at a later time, I'll find a golden mean between elegance and performance.

18

Setting Up Linked Cards

This chapter applies predominantly to information management stacks and some external device control stacks. We'll be dealing with heterogeneous stacks whose multiple backgrounds make up what I call "suites" of cards. For example, a suite of cards may consist of one summary card and five detail cards, each from a different background in the same stack. When a new summary card is created by the user, the script must not only create new cards from the other backgrounds, but also link all cards together, so that the user truly feels these cards are a single set.

In the organization of cards into suites, the "HyperCard-ness" of a stack begins to disappear for the user. The information suddenly takes precedence over concepts of stack structure, backgrounds, and hierarchy. These are still very strong concerns for the stack developer, but the user begins to see the application as an application and less as a HyperCard stack. If your goal is to produce more Macintosh-like applications, and less Hyper-Card-like applications, then this chapter is for you.

Suite Examples

From the HyperCard stack designs I've worked on that involved card suites, I've designed three different suite types. They'll be described in full throughout this chapter. These certainly do not exhaust the possibilities, but there should be enough ideas in the three descriptions to help you build your own suite arrangement if the ones here don't apply.

One type is like that used for both the Projects and the Proposals stacks in *Focal Point*. A Summary card has buttons that are hard linked to one card from four or five other backgrounds. For instance, in the Projects stack (Figure 18-1), if you click on what I call a Zoom button next to the Project field label, you

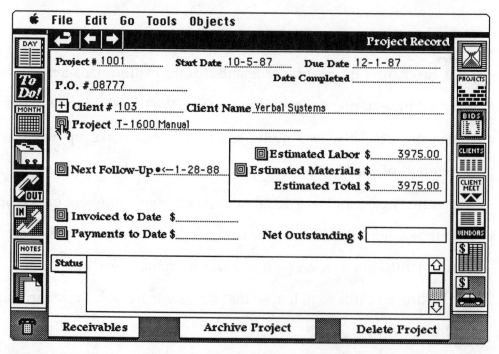

Figure 18-1 *The six cards in a Projects stack suite are tightly linked by way of a list of card IDs in a hidden field. A click of any Zoom button summons the card ID of the card to which navigation goes.*

zip to the Project Specifications card (Figure 18-2) for the project whose summary card you were viewing. From this card you have only one navigation possibility within the Projects stack: clicking on the return arrow button to go back to the Summary card. Each Zoom button is linked to a different detail card from one of six possible backgrounds (the two buttons next to the Invoiced and Payments labels link to the same card). To the user, the organization of the stack is by project, not by background style.

A second type, as demonstrated in *Focal Point's* Expenses stack, is a derivative of the first type. Here, a Weekly Summary card (Figure 18-3) has a row of buttons with day names (Mon, Tue, Wed, and so on) that are linked to Daily Expense Detail cards (Figure 18-4). Those day-name buttons are analogous to the Zoom buttons on the Projects stack Summary card. But when you reach the Daily Expense Detail, you find that you have full navigation powers within the background. You may move forward and backward in time by various increments. Even the Daily Expense Detail cards are linked to yet other cards, which I'll describe more fully later.

Third is a suite that operates with two backgrounds so that a Summary card links to detail cards, whose quantity is not known until they are generated.

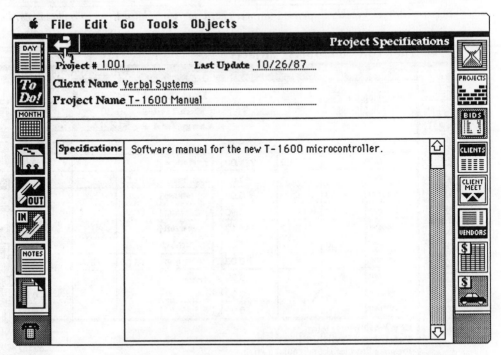

Figure 18-2 *A project's Zoom button next to the Project Specifications field of the summary card always goes to the Project Specifications card for that very client and project. The hard links make a mistake impossible.*

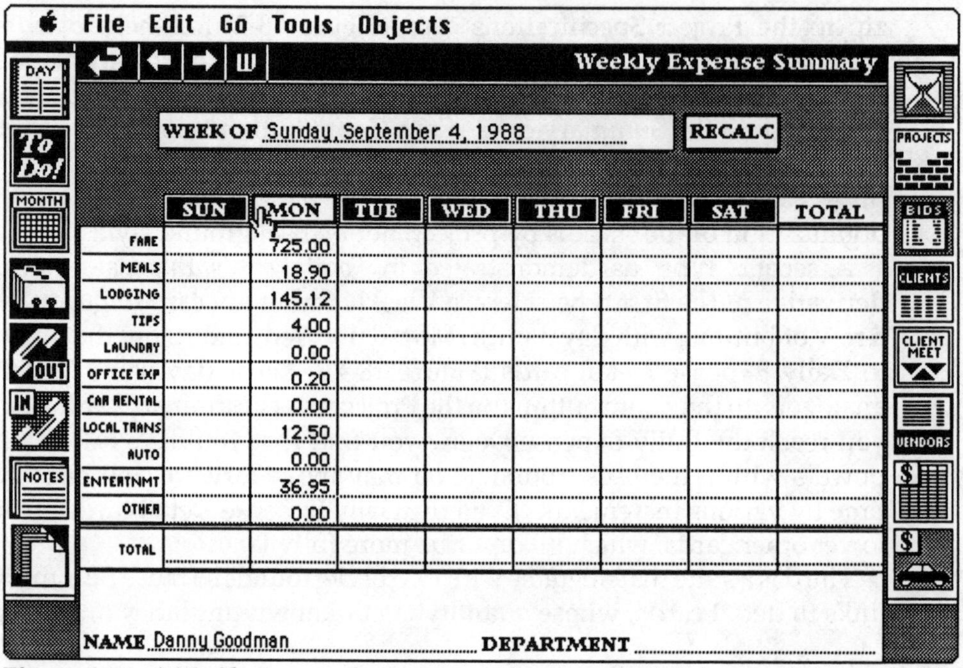

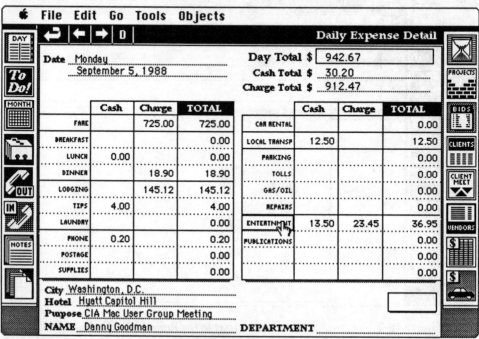

Figure 18-3 *A Weekly Expense Summary card has seven hard links to each day card of the week.*

Figure 18-4 *In a Daily Expense Detail card, you may go back to the week's summary (via a hard link) or navigate linearly through each day's detail.*

Within the detail cards is a linear connection between them, but only to the extent that you view detail cards linked to a single Summary card. Even after the detail cards are generated they may be deleted or added to, without affecting the flow between detail cards.

Multiple-Lined Containers—Arrays

At the root of all three suite types is one key concept: You may address any container—field or variable—by item or individual line of data. As you'll see, all linking information is maintained in a hidden field on every card of a suite. Every handler that creates a new suite of cards stores linked card addresses in various lines of a local variable. Each line has a specific duty in the scheme of things. Such containers usually have their contents placed into the hidden fields in the same multiline format when the creation process is finished.

You can practice the concept of placing text into different lines of a variable container from the Message Box. Type the following lines into the Message Box, and watch the results of the last three, which read the contents of the variable:

```
put "Four score" into line 1 of speech
put "and" into line 2 of speech
put "7" into line 3 of speech
put "years ago" into line 4 of speech
speech        -- you see only the first line in the Message Box
line 4 of speech
line 3 of speech && line 4 of speech
```

If you go to one of the stacks created in earlier chapters, you can see the entire contents of the variable by typing

```
put speech into field 2
```

in which case you'll see this:

```
Four score
and
7
years ago
```

just like you put the data into the variable.

Remembering that you can store data in a variable container and access it with the same text chunk expression tools as a field may make many card suite creation tasks much easier than imagined.

More About Arrays

You've also seen that HyperCard is, indeed, capable of creating what are known as *arrays*, or tables of information. You can build a one-dimensional array as many lines of single items or as one line of many comma-separated items like these:

line 1   item 1, item 2, item 3, item 4
line 2
line 3
line 4

When your array elements might contain commas, then it's best to use a "vertical" array, in which each element occupies its own line of a container. Conversely, if your data elements contain carriage returns, then use the "horizontal" form.

Two-dimensional arrays are possible by combining multiple lines and comma-separated items, like this:

line 1/item 1, line 1/item 2, line 1/item 3, line 1/item 4
line 2/item 1, line 2/item 2, line 2/item 3, line 2/item 4
line 3/item 1, line 3/item 2, line 3/item 3, line 3/item 4
line 4/item 1, line 4/item 2, line 4/item 3, line 4/item 4

You'd use HyperTalk chunk expressions to access a particular data element, such as "item 3 of line 2." Because you're using comma-separated items in the horizontal dimension, no data element may contain commas; and because you're using multiple lines in the array, no data element may have a return character in it.

By adding more fields with array data in them, you can create the effect of a three-dimensional array. Again, address an array element using chunk expressions, as in "item 2 of line 6 of field 3." Adding fields, by the way, is how you can also get around the carriage return or comma problem of a two-dimensional array. If your data elements have commas in them, then create a number of fields, each of which has a vertical array in it.

But let's get back to our card suites.

Type A Suite: Hub and Spokes

Since we'll be showing the handler that creates the card suites in Focal Point's Projects stack, we should get acquainted with the primary components, namely the background names. The six backgrounds are named:

Project Summary
Project Specs
Labor Worksheet
Materials Worksheet
Follow Ups
Financials

While HyperCard sees this stack as a collection of six backgrounds, each with an equal number of cards, the user sees a series of Project Summary cards with five other cards attached to each Summary card, as illustrated in Figure 18-5. The only place to go from any of the five detail cards is back to the associated Summary card.

Let's work through what kinds of links are needed for this suite of six cards. The Project Summary card needs a reference list of the five detail cards attached to it for a given project. Each of the detail cards needs a reference back to the summary card so it may return to the summary card when the return arrow button is pressed. I prefer hard links in all these cases, including the return button. While the push card/pop card or even the Go Back command would work, the hard link works every time, including when the user starts

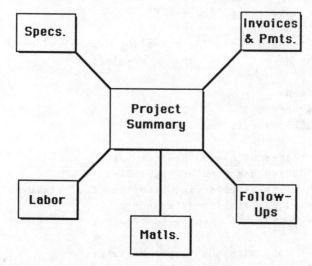

Figure 18-5 *The hub-and-spoke suite of the Projects stack in Focal Point.*

self-navigating with the Go menu commands, which are purposely not trapped in this stack. Whenever you view a detail card, and you click on the return arrow, you unequivocally go back to that detail card's summary card.

To accommodate the list of linked cards in the Project Summary card is a hidden background field, called "linkList." Each line of that field will eventually contain a card id of a specific linked card. For example, line 1 of field linkList has the card address of the Project Specifications card associated with this Project Summary card. In each of the detail cards is another hidden field, called mainCard, which holds the card id of the associated Project Summary card.

The basic action of creating a new suite is relatively simple. The handler goes to the last card of each background, creates a new card of that background, records the id of that card (in a local variable), and slowly builds a list of card IDs that go into the summary card's linkList field. Along the way, the handler also helps the user recognize the links among cards in a suite by posting the project number in all associated cards. Later, when the user inserts a project name and a client name, these bits of data are also posted to all linked cards (using the field linkList as a road map to all the cards).

Without further ado, here is the Projects stack newProject handler, which is intentionally left as a non-repeat handler so you can see the workings of setting up the suite card-by-card.

```
on newProject
    go to last card of bkgnd "Project Summary"
    send "doMenu New Card" to HyperCard  -- bypass doMenu handler
    get card field "Next Project Number" of card "Project List"
    put it into field "Project #"
    put it into projectNumber
    add 1 to card field "Next Project Number" of card "Project List"
    put the name of this card into mainCard

    push card
    set cursor to 4
    set lockScreen to true

    go last card of bkgnd "Project Specs"
    send "doMenu New Card" to HyperCard
    put the name of this card into line 1 of linkList
    put mainCard into field "mainCard"
    put projectNumber into field "Project #"

    go last card of bkgnd "Labor Worksheet"
    send "doMenu New Card" to HyperCard
```

```
put the name of this card into line 2 of linkList
put mainCard into field "mainCard"
put projectNumber into field "Project #"

go last card of bkgnd "Materials Worksheet"
send "doMenu New Card" to HyperCard
put the name of this card into line 3 of linkList
put mainCard into field "mainCard"
put projectNumber into field "Project #"

go last card of bkgnd "Follow Ups"
send "doMenu New Card" to HyperCard
put the name of this card into line 4 of linkList
put mainCard into field "mainCard"
put projectNumber into field "Project #"

go last card of bkgnd "Financials"
send "doMenu New Card" to HyperCard
put the name of this card into line 5 of linkList
put mainCard into field "mainCard"
put projectNumber into field "Project #"

pop card
put linkList into field "linkList"
type tab
end newProject
```

This handler is called by a doMenu handler, which traps for the New Card menu choice. In this stack, creating a new card means creating a new suite of cards to record a new project.

In the first group of statements, the new Project Summary card is appended to the end of the cards bearing the Project Summary background. Then, because the stack traps for the doMenu message, the handler bypasses the menu and sends a doMenu New Card message directly to HyperCard to actually create the card. The first card of the stack has a card field in it, called Next Project Number, which stores the number the next new project will be assigned. That figure is retrieved and inserted both into the Project # field of the new summary card and into a local variable, which will carry the figure to other new cards in the suite. One is added to the new project number field for the next time it is called.

An important line of this handler puts the name of the new card into a local variable, called mainCard. Since new cards in this stack are not given real names, this statement puts the full id of the card into the variable, in the form "card id xxxx," where "xxxx" is the id number assigned by HyperCard upon card creation.

The new summary card is pushed, because this where we will want to end up after all new cards are created. A counterbalancing pop card at the end of the handler will bring us back to the Summary card. To keep visual clutter to a minimum while alerting the user that the stack is still working, we set the cursor to 4 (the watch) and lock the screen.

In the next five 5-line groups comes the creation of the new associated cards. We'll follow the first group statement-by-statement.

The first order of business is to go to the last card of the background of one of the detail cards, Project Specs, and create a new card by sending the message directly to HyperCard. Now the name of the card (which reads like "card id 4070") is placed into line 1 of a local variable called linkList. This variable will be the cornerstone of the links between the summary card and detail cards at the end of the handler. In the meantime, the handler places the address of the summary card (stored in the local variable mainCard) into the hidden field, also called "mainCard." The project number is inserted into the Project # field.

This 5-line action is repeated four more times with one difference each time: The address of the newly created card is put into its own line of the linkList variable. Into each new card goes the address of the summary card and the project number.

Surprisingly, the end of the handler is quite simple. After returning to the summary card via a Pop Card statement, the content of the five-line linkList local variable is transferred to the hidden field of the same name. Then the handler types a tab to place the text insertion pointer into the first unlocked text field on the card, inviting the user to start entering data.

With the addresses of linked cards safely stored in the hidden field, linkList, the action of getting to those cards is left up to the short handlers in each of the Zoom buttons. For example, the handler for the Project Specifications Zoom button is this:

```
on mouseUp
  visual effect zoom open
  go line 1 of field "linkList"
end mouseUp
```

Because any of the first five lines of field "linkList" contains a valid card destination, the reference to the container chunk (line 1) is sufficient for HyperCard to know where to go next. Conversely, each of the return arrow buttons on the five detail cards have this handler:

```
on mouseUp
  visual effect zoom close
  go field "mainCard"
end mouseUp
```

Since only one address is in the field, the Go command simply summons the content of the entire field as a valid address. It is also important on the detail cards to control the user's navigation by keyboard arrow keys. On all detail cards, there are background handlers that trap for arrowKey messages, and do nothing with them, as in

```
on arrowKey
end arrowKey
```

Because there are no statements relying on the parameters sent with the arrowKey messages, there is no need to grasp the arrowKey message parameters for this handler.

Type B Suites: Rolling Hub and Spoke

You'll see a lot of similarity between the suite creation process of the Expenses stack and the Projects stack, above. Before we get to the script, however, look at Figure 18-6 to see the relationships between Weekly and Daily backgrounds, and then the navigational options available within each background.

Each Weekly Summary card has seven buttons on it, located at the top of columns of the worksheet. When you click on, say, the WED button, you go to the Daily Expense Detail card for the Wednesday of that week. Once you're at the Daily level, however, you may navigate through cards in the background as you wish, with the same flexibility as the Daily Appointment stack. Importantly, the return arrow button on the Daily Expense Detail cards

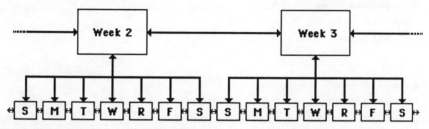

Figure 18-6 *The Expense stack demonstrates a rolling hub and spoke structure. Each week's card is hard linked to its daily cards. In the weekly or daily cards, however, the user is free to roam up and back in time as he wishes.*

always zooms you out to the Weekly Summary card for the corresponding week.

Just as with the Projects stack, the addresses of cards linked to the Weekly Summary card are maintained in a hidden field, called linkList. Of course, since there are seven cards linked to each summary card, the field is seven lines long. On the daily cards, a hidden field, called mainCard, holds the address of the week's summary card. In this stack the mainCard field also holds another number, between 1 and 7, indicating in which column of the weekly summary card all results from daily calculations should go.

Creation of links is done not at the stack level, but in the setup stack that builds and extends dated stacks. The handlers are modules called by the main build-and-extend handler. As you can imagine, there is a lot of date arithmetic and manipulation involved in building the Expenses stack. We won't get too deeply involved with those calculations in this chapter (see Chapter 19), so we'll focus, instead, on the linking parts of the handlers.

The process is divided into two handlers, one of which is repeatedly called by the other. One handler, makeCards, takes care of making each of the Weekly Summary cards. That handler calls another, makeDetail, which then creates the linked Daily cards and puts all the linking addresses in the right places. Here are the handlers:

```
on makeCards startDate,howMany
  global theName,theDepartment
  put makeSunday(startDate) into dateCounter
  repeat for howMany
    convert dateCounter to long date
    put dateCounter into field "Week"
    put theName into field "Name"
    put theDepartment into field "Department"
    makeDetail dateCounter          -- call the other handler
    convert dateCounter to seconds
    add 7 * (60*60*24) to dateCounter
    doMenu "New Card"
  end repeat
end makeCards


on makeDetail startDate
  global theName,theDepartment
  put id of this card into mainCard
  push card
```

```
repeat with y = 1 to 7
  go to last card of bkgnd "Daily"
  doMenu "New Card"
  put mainCard into field "mainCard" -- hidden field
  put y into item 2 of field "mainCard"
  put "D" into field "interval"

  get startDate
  convert it to seconds
  add (60*60*24) * (y - 1) to it
  convert it to long date
  put item 1 of it into line 1 of field "Date"
  put item 2 to 4 of it into line 2 of field "Date"

  put theName into field "Name"
  put theDepartment into field "Department"

  get the id of this card
  put it into line y of linkList
end repeat

pop card                                -- back to Summary card
put linkList into field "linkList"      -- hidden field
end makeDetail
```

The makeCards handler receives two parameters from the main handler: the starting date of the build and how many weeks it is supposed to build. The global variables contain data from the *Focal Point* startup card, data that automatically goes into the Name and Department fields at the bottom of every card in the stack. Next, the user-defined function, makeSunday (described in Chapter 16), returns the date, in seconds, of the Sunday of the week containing the starting date. The Expenses stack's week begins on Sunday, and the Sunday date goes into a field of the Weekly Summary card.

A repeat loop works primarily with the Weekly Summary card, putting the date into the week's date field, and inserting the global variables in their respective fields. At this point, the handler calls the second handler to create the seven detail cards for the current week.

Passing the Sunday date as a parameter, the call to the second handler is repeated for each week. If these two handlers had been combined into one, most of the actions of this handler would be in a nested (inner) repeat loop. While still at the Weekly Summary card, the handler grabs the ID of the card, placing it in a local variable, mainCard.

The repeat loop employs an incrementing variable, y, to help it along its seven times through. The loop begins by going to the last card of the Daily cards' background. This will ensure that all Daily cards are in chronological order, which future navigation will require. After making the new card, the id of the weekly summary card (stored in variable mainCard) goes into the hidden field on all daily cards, also called mainCard. Because the daily card needs to know in which column of the weekly summary card it should put all calculation results, the incrementing variable, y, is put into item two of the hidden field. It could just as easily have gone into line 2 of that field.

In the last line of the first group of statements, the letter D is placed into a field called interval. This field is the one that holds the letter representing the navigation interval, immediately to the right of the navigation arrow buttons. As you click on this locked field, the letters change to reflect other increments. "D" is for day; "W" is for week; "M" is for month; and "Y" is for year. As each daily card is created, the interval is preloaded with a D for daily navigation between cards.

The next group of statements takes care of date calculations to make sure the correct date appears on each daily card. We'll leave the details for our chapter on date and time arithmetic (Chapter 19). Two more lines implant the global variables on the card.

Two important lines of this handler follow. The id of the new card is placed into the line of variable linkList corresponding to the day of the week. Tuesday's card, for instance, would be created on the third time through the repeat loop. The value of y on that tour would be 3, placing the id of Tuesday's card into the third line of the variable.

Once all seven cards have been created for the week, the handler pops back to the weekly card, and puts a copy of the local variable into the hidden field, linkList. All the pieces are set. Now let's look at the buttons that navigate through and between these two sets of cards.

Navigation arrow buttons in the Weekly Summary card restrict the user to the previous or next cards of the same background. These buttons also use the mouseStillDown technique described earlier, allowing continuous scrolling through cards when you click and hold the mouse button. The script attached to the right arrow button is

```
on mouseStillDown
   if field "interval" is "W"
   then go next card of this background
   else go to card (number of this card + 4) of this bkgnd
end mouseStillDown

on mouseDown
   mouseStillDown
end mouseDown
```

```
on mouseUp
end mouseUp
```

Notice that this script traps for the mouseUp message. That's because there is an important mouseUp message in the background to handle the day buttons at the tops of the columns. Instead of filtering out the navigation buttons in that handler, we just prevent the mouseUp message sent to the navigation buttons from ever getting any higher up the hierarchy.

Each of the day buttons are named "To x," where "x" is the number of the day in the week. Thus, the WED button is named "To 4." All the handler really needs from the button name is the number, which indicates which line of the hidden linkList field should be accessed with a Go command. A single mouseUp handler in the background takes care of the seven days' buttons.

```
on mouseUp
  if "To" is not in the short name of the target
  then pass mouseUp
  else
    get word 2 of the short name of the target
    visual effect zoom open
    go to line it of field "linkList"
  end if
end mouseUp
```

First it passes any mouseUp message that may have been sent to the card or locked fields on the card. Then the handler retrieves the number from the button name (word 2 of the short name). That turns out to be the line number of field linkList that contains the desired daily card address.

Left and right navigation buttons in the Daily Expense Detail behave the same way as those in the weekly card, except they test for more possible letters in the interval field. The point is, navigation from this card is only within cards of the current background. No matter how the user works around the stack with these arrow buttons and their corresponding arrow keys, he will always stay within the current background. Lastly, the return arrow button on the daily card summons item 1 of the hidden mainCard field for the address of the weekly card to which this daily card belongs. Its script is similar to the return arrow script in the detail cards of the Project stack.

Linking On The Fly

What I haven't told you about the daily expense cards is that they, too, contain a hidden linkList field. When needed, the daily card can generate an entertainment expense detail card, which is linked directly to that day's card (Figure 18-7).

A third background of this stack, called "Entertainment," represents a card you'd use to record the details of an entertainment expense, as required by the I.R.S. You access it from the Daily Expense Detail by clicking on the Entertainment button in the second column labels. This card's place in the Expenses stack scheme of things is illustrated in Figure 18-8.

It would be a waste of disk space to generate this card for every day of the year when the stack is built or extended. Therefore, the button that links to the entertainment data builds the card (and establishes the two-way link) when you first click on the button of a day's detail. Once the card is created, you go straight to it at the click of that button.

All handlers for going to the card and creating the card (if it's not there to start) are located in that Entertainment button. There are two handlers:

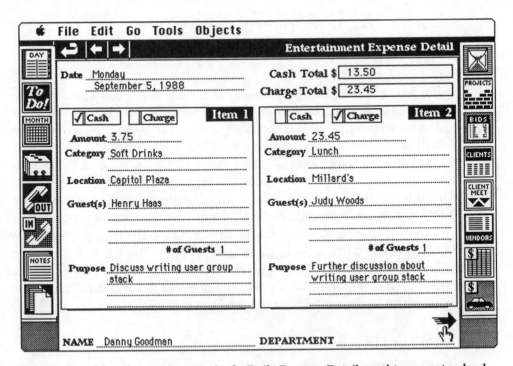

Figure 18-7 *The structure is set up in the Daily Expense Details card to generate a hard link to an Entertainment Expense Detail card for that day. This card is generated only when needed.*

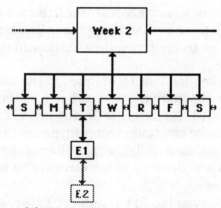

Figure 18-8 *The structure of the Expense stack when an entertainment card is linked to a daily card.*

```
on mouseUp
  visual effect zoom open
  if field "linkList" is not empty
  then go field "linkList"
  else makeEntertainment
end mouseUp

on makeEntertainment
  global theName,theDepartment
  set cursor to 4
  set lockScreen to true

  put field "Date" into theDate
  put the id of this card into mainCard

  go last card of bkgnd "Entertainment"
  doMenu "New Card"

  put theDate into field "Date"
  put theName into field "Name"
  put theDepartment into field "Department"
  put mainCard into field "mainCard"

  get the id of this card
  push card
  set lockScreen to true
  go field "mainCard"
  put it into field "linkList"

end makeEntertainment
```

The mouseUp handler first checks to see if there is a card address in the hidden linkList field. If there is, that means that a link has already been established, and it's safe to go there. If not, then it's time to make an entertainment card and link it here.

You'll see some familiar techniques in the makeEntertainment handler. Many of the lines pertain to passing data from fields in the daily card to the entertainment card. As far as the linking process, the daily card becomes the "mainCard" for the entertainment card, just as the weekly card is the "main-Card" for the daily card. All other handling of card addresses of the new card and main card are identical to the ways we've been working with them in other suite styles.

Interestingly, even the Entertainment Expense Detail card has a linkList field. That's because a user may need more than two entertainment reporting spaces for a given day. Thus, a fourth background of the stack looks like the third, but the item numbers are shown as 3 and 4 (Figure 18-9). Notice the fancy right arrow button near the lower right corner of the entertainment expense card (Figure 18-7). That's the button that looks for the contents of field linkList for an address of a second entertainment card. If the field is empty, then it creates a new card and links it back here. The handlers are identical to

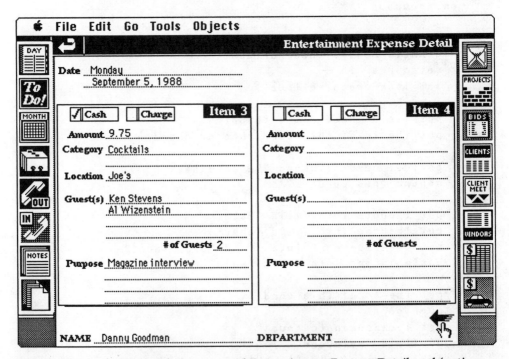

Figure 18-9 *An additional link to a second Entertainment Expense Detail card (notice items 3 and 4) is also possible when needed.*

those shown above for the Entertainment button, except the background name for the new card is called Extension.

Type C Suite: The Accordion

The last linked suite we'll look at is not found in *Focal Point*, so we'll be making up a scenario to illustrate the need. The setting is a medical patient stack. There is at least one card for each patient, listing key patient data, like patient name and number, attending physician, and so on. On that first card is also space to note one diagnosis requiring treatment. But if the patient comes into the hospital with more than one diagnosis, then the stack generates a supplemental card linked to the first. There may be several diagnoses at time of admission into the hospital; other diagnoses may be added during treatment or after tests; existing diagnoses may be deleted as incorrect or replaced by more accurate findings. The links among all these cards must be able to handle the dynamic life of the patient's record.

From a diagrammatic point of view, Figure 18-10 shows how the stack shapes up from the user's point of view. The physician has complete forward and backward navigation through the cards of the first background to allow browsing and searching for patient names. But in the supplementary cards for

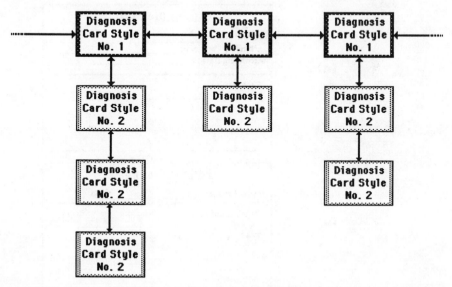

Figure 18-10 *An accordion suite consists of a lead card plus any number of cards that may be browsed in a linear fashion. The number of cards may vary during the life of the lead card. The structure must accommodate such changes.*

a given patient, the path is linear only within the cards for that patient. Because dozens of patients will be sharing the second background, it is not feasible to navigate through those cards just by limiting navigation to cards of that background only. Moreover, the cards in the second background may be added out of order for a given patient, especially when a diagnosis is added several days after the initial cards are made. Schematics of the two backgrounds of this system are shown in Figure 18-11.

The key to keeping all related cards attached to one another is maintaining a list in each card of the IDs of the card on either side of it according to the user's eye. Therefore, the first diagnosis card has a hidden linkList field that holds the address of the next card in the sequence. All subsequent cards have a two-line linkList field in them. Into the first line goes the address of the previous card in the patient sequence; into the second line goes the address of the next card in the patient sequence. As part of the handler that actually moves to the next card in the sequence, if line 2 of the linkList field is empty, then an answer dialog notes that there are no further diagnosis cards for that patient. This system is diagrammed in Figure 18-12.

To demonstrate the procedures involved in setting up a series of cards for a new patient, we offer the handler, below. This handler assumes several things. First, someone in admissions fills out information on a screen that

(A)

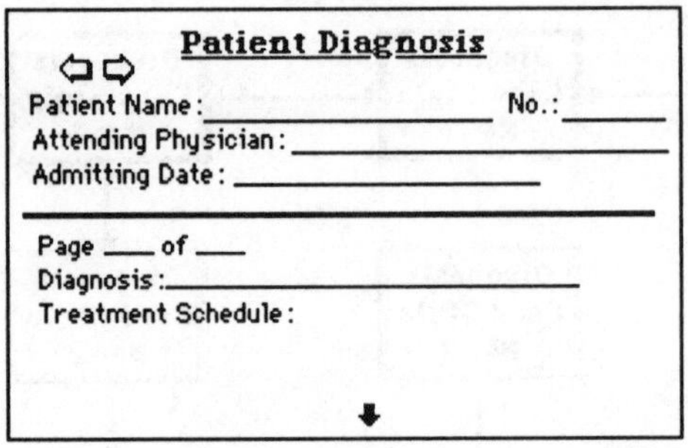

Patient Diagnosis

Patient Name : _____ No. : _____
Attending Physician : _____
Admitting Date : _____

Page ___ of ___
Diagnosis : _____
Treatment Schedule :

(B)

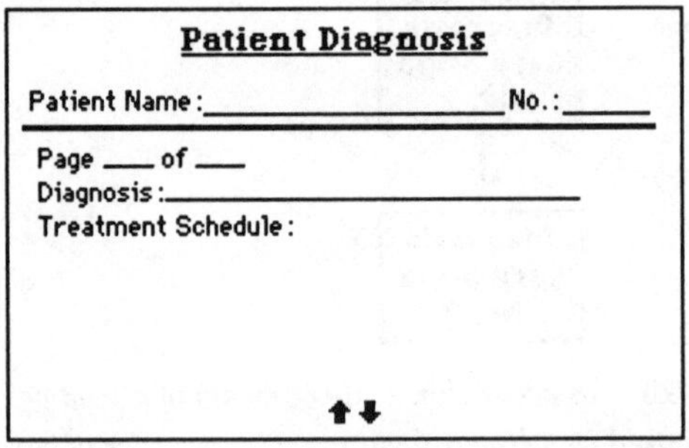

Patient Diagnosis

Patient Name : _____ No. : _____

Page ___ of ___
Diagnosis : _____
Treatment Schedule :

Figure 18-11 *A schematic of a lead card (A) and all subsequent cards (B) in the suite.*

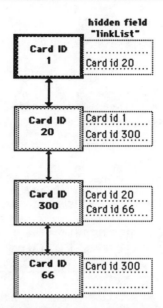

Figure 18-12 *Each card in the suite has a hidden field called "linkList." Line 1 of that field holds the ID of the previous card in the suite; line 2 holds the ID of the next card in the suite. Adding or deleting cards means shuffling these card references.*

gathers all patient data (name, number, physician, etc.) and a simple list of diagnoses. The purpose of the handler is to generate a detailed patient record for each patient, with a separate card for each diagnosis, which the physician uses to record progress and treatment.

The newPatient handler, below, also assumes that another handler (probably a mouseUp handler attached to a button in the admissions stack) assembles all the patient information in a five-line parameter, and that a list of diagnoses is assembled in a second parameter. The newPatient handler makes as many cards as there are diagnoses passed to it, starting with the first background, and adding more diagnoses to cards of the second background. Here's the handler:

```
on newPatient PatientData,diagnoses
   go to stack "Patient Records"
   go to last card of bkgnd "Diagnosis 1"

   repeat with y = 1 to the number of lines of diagnoses
      if y = 2 then go to last card of bkgnd "Diagnosis 2"

      doMenu "New Card"
      put the id of this card into line y of linkList
```

```
    repeat with x = 1 to 5
      put line x of patientData into field ("PData " & x)
    end repeat

    put y into field "page"
    put the number of lines of diagnoses into field "totalPages"
    put line y of diagnoses into field "Diagnosis"
  end repeat

  go to line 1 of linkList
  put line 2 of linkList into line 2 of field "LinkList"
  repeat with z = 2 to the number of lines of linkList
    go to line z of linkList
    put line z-1 of linkList into line 1 of field "linkList"
    put line z+1 of linkList into line 2 of field "linkList"
  end repeat
end newPatient
```

The handler starts by going to the appropriate stack and to the last card of the first background, Diagnosis 1. A repeat loop handles the creation of all cards associated with the patient. Since the suite needs only as many cards as there are diagnoses, the number of diagnoses (one per line) is the counting mechanism for the loop. When the counter reaches 2, it's time to shift to the second background, Diagnosis 2, and build onto the end of that background. Any subsequent new cards to this background for this patient will automatically be from the end of the background, so there's no need to go to the last card of the background except the first time.

Each time through the repeat loop, and after a new card is created, the id of that new card is added to its own line of local variable linkList. For each card the patient data, which passed to the handler as a five-line parameter, is put into the appropriate fields.

Each card has fields for both a page number and the total number of pages. Thus, when a physician is looking through a patient's record, he has some notion of how many diagnoses are there to be treated. This method of numbering pages is often very helpful for the user to get some bearing about where he is in the stack. The current page number is derived from the loop counter, while the total number of pages is derived from the number of lines of diagnoses. Finally, the name of the diagnosis, from the parameter, is placed into the diagnosis field of the card. This may be done at any time within the repeat loop.

Once all the cards are created, it's time to plant all the linked IDs in the hidden linkList fields in each card. By the end of card creation, the linkList local variable contains a complete list of all cards in the patient's record. The IDs just need to be distributed among the various cards.

To distribute the IDs, the handler returns to the first card of the patient's record and puts the ID of the second card into line 2 of field linkList. In keeping consistent with the line allocations of all linkList fields in this stack, the second line always carries the ID of the next card in the series.

Next, a repeat loop goes to each of the remaining cards in the list, and puts the IDs of the previous and next cards of the series into lines 1 and 2, respectively, of the hidden linkList field. In the case of the last card, when the handler tries to put line $z+1$ of linkList into line 2 of the field, that line of the field remains empty, as it should. The handler of the button that normally brings you to the next card in a patient series is this:

```
on mouseUp
  get line 2 of field "linkList"
  if it is empty
  then answer "No further diagnoses for this patient."
  else
    visual effect wipe up
    go to line 2 of it
  end if
end mouseUp
```

while the handler to go to the previous card in the series is, simply

```
on mouseUp
  visual effect wipe down
  go to line 1 of field "linkList"
end mouseUp
```

One of the distinctions between backgrounds 1 and 2 is that background 1 does not have a button pointing to previous cards in the series (but it does need buttons pointing to next and previous patient summary cards for browsing purposes).

Adding and Deleting From the Accordion Suite

This type of linked suite may need provisions for adding and deleting cards. Such adjustments are not difficult, but you must pay attention to details in your scripts. Not only do you have to adjust the linked card addresses surrounding a new or deleted card, but the page numbers and total number of pages must be adjusted for all cards in the suite. Because adding and deleting cards need the renumbering of all cards, I'd write that as a separate handler called by both the add and delete card handlers.

Assuming a new card may be added anywhere along the suite (i.e., not just at the end), the handler must obtain the ID of the new card, and place it into the linkList fields of the cards on either side of it, while putting the addresses of those old cards into its own linkList field. Here's one way to handle that:

```
on addDiagnosis
  set cursor to 4
  set lockScreen to true

  doMenu "New Card"
  put the id of this card into newCard

  go previous card     -- the one from which the new card was made
  put line 2 of field "linkList" into line 2 of linkList
  put newCard into line 2 of field "linkList"

  if line 2 of linkList is not empty then
    go to line 2 of linkList
    put line 1 of field "linkList" into line 1 of linkList
    put newCard into line 1 of field "linkList"
  end if

  go to newCard
  put linkList into field "linkList"

  renumberCards          -- call handler that renumbers cards

end addDiagnosis
```

The net effect of this handler is a reordering of card addresses in the linkList fields of the new card and the two cards on either side of it. The if-then construction is inserted to accommodate the situations in which the new card is the last card of the suite.

Deleting a card from the suite is just the reverse of adding one—addresses get shuffled in the other direction. Here's a handler to do it:

```
on deleteDiagnosis
  set cursor to 4
  set lockScreen to true

  get field "linkList"
```

```
      go to line 1 of it
      put line 2 of it into line 2 of field "linkList"

      if line 2 of it is not empty then
        go to line 2 of it
        put line 1 of it into line 1 of field "linkList"
      end if

      renumberCards

end deleteDiagnosis
```

Notice that this handler even accommodates the situation in which the card to be deleted is the first one of the second background. All the addresses are put in the right places, even if one of those places happens to be the very first card of the patient series.

As for renumbering the cards, you have many ways to accomplish it. The simplest (although not necessarily the fastest) way is shown in this handler:

```
on renumberCards
  push card
  repeat until the background is "Diagnosis 1"
    go to line 1 of field "linkList"
  end repeat

  put 1 into pageCount
  repeat until line 2 of field "linkList" is empty
    put pageCount into field "Page"
    add 1 to pageCount
    go to line 2 of field "linkList"
  end repeat

  put pageCount into field "totalPages"
  repeat pageCount - 1 times
    go back
    put pageCount into field "totalPages"
  end repeat
  pop card
end renumberCards
```

This handler first works its way back to the first card of the suite, no matter where a new card was added or an old one deleted. Once it's back at the first card, it starts going to each card in the suite, placing the page number in the appropriate field. The page number is maintained in a local variable, pageCount. By the time the numbering gets to the last card of the series, pageCount will contain the number of total pages for the patient. With that knowledge, the handler goes back (the same as pressing the tilde key or choosing Back from the Go menu) enough times to return it to the first card of the series, stopping at each card long enough to put the total page count into the field that displays the total number of pages for the patient.

The examples of linked suites presented in this chapter should cover a large percentage of situations in dynamic information management and external device control stacks. Of all the techniques shown here, the most important is that the user should not be aware of the internal stack organization. It is the job of the author and his scripts to let the user focus on the information and how the information is linked, rather than how various cards and backgrounds are linked. It goes a long way to helping the user get involved with the application, and distracting attention from the HyperCard engine beneath it.

19

Working With Date and Time

Although you'd think date and time calculations would be more predominant in information management and external device control kinds of applications, consider that *Business Class*, an information publishing stack, has just about as much time calculation going on as *Focal Point* has date calculation. So much of the information we work with from day to day is dependent upon time and date, there is no escaping a working knowledge of how HyperCard treats both.

HyperTalk Functions and Commands

Despite HyperTalk's substantial time and date calculation power, there are relatively few words in the language's vocabulary that pertain to the subject. The two major functions are the Date (four versions) and the Time (two versions) functions. A lesser used function is the seconds function. Aside from these, the only other HyperTalk word that affects time is Convert, a most valuable command that lets you convert dates and times into various formats.

Most time and date manipulations involve arithmetic of some kind. Perhaps your scripts need to know the date of next Wednesday, or calculate a half-dozen deadline dates prior to a project due date, or add two timings of music selections, or calculate the elapsed time of a meeting with a client, or figure out what time it is right now in Sydney, Australia. All these calculations are possible within HyperTalk's time and date vocabulary and a little arithmetic.

One of the fundamental building blocks of knowledge about working with time in HyperCard is that everything it does is based on the built-in clock of the Macintosh. That clock was "born" on January 1, 1904. If your date-keeping tasks take you back in history before this time, you'll have to perform some extra calculations to handle it. In other words, you wouldn't be able to calculate how many days the Civil War lasted, unless you modify the dates to the 20th century before calculation. You also won't be able to forecast past February 6, 2040, in HyperCard using straight, unmodified dates.

Seconds—The Common Thread

One element you'll see in common with just about every date or time calculation is a conversion to seconds. Here's why.

When you start working with time and dates, you quickly discover that the irregularities of the calendar work against you. For example, no matter how you try to calculate a date 42 days prior to today, the only sure method is to subtract 42 times the number of seconds per day from the number of seconds the Macintosh clock returns for today. When you reconvert the answer to a real date format, you can be assured the date is accurate, whether the month barriers crossed in the subtraction have 28, 29, 30, or 31 days in them.

Therefore, in searching for solutions to your time and date problems, look to the seconds as a common denominator.

Speaking of solutions, we'll present five different time and date problems and solutions in this chapter: 1) adding time; 2) calculating time zone differences; 3) calculating elapsed time; 4) calculating the number of days between dates; and 5) figuring the scheduling dates of milestones before a project deadline. For each problem, we'll establish a scenario from the real world.

Adding Time

The setting is a classical radio station that uses a HyperCard stack to figure out its play lists for each hour of the broadcast day. Each card is a worksheet on which the Program Director can juggle discs and selections to fill out the available music programming time within the hour (Figure 19-1).

The active fields in this background are:

Label	Field Name
Total Music Time Available	Total Available
Track Time (column of fields)	Track 1 to Track 8
Total Track Time	Track Total
Time Left	Track Left

These fields either trigger recalculation (with a background level closeField handler), adjust their own display (the Total Available field), or receive the results of calculations. All other fields merely store data.

One thing about time in HyperCard. When you type a time into a field, it must be in the form hh:mm:ss, as in 1:25:30 for one hour, 25 minutes and 30

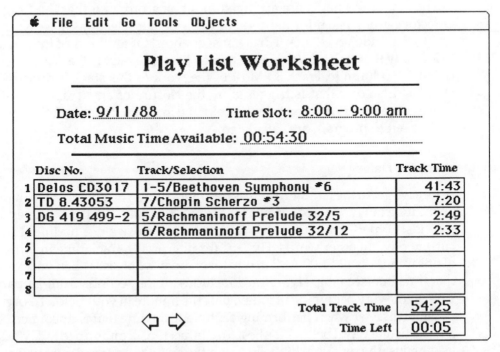

Figure 19-1 *A hypothetical application for a radio station requires adding up times of recordings to be played within a broadcast hour.*

seconds. If you enter a time with only one colon, HyperCard assumes it is time expressed as hh:mm, without any seconds. Therefore, if time is usually thought of in a particular application in terms of minutes and seconds (as it is here), then an extra "00:" must be stuck on the beginning of any time before it may be part of a calculation. At the same time, the handler may want to make allowances for time entries that include hours, minutes and seconds. To those entries, nothing should be added to the front.

That discussion served as an introduction to the closeField handler attached to the Total Available field. To aid calculations later, this handler preconditions the field's contents to be in the proper format immediately after you enter a time. Here's the handler:

```
on closeField
  if the length of (the value of the target) < 6
  then put "00:" before field "Total Available"
end closeField
```

If a time is entered as minutes and seconds (e.g., 25:30), the handler will turn it into the proper format (e.g., 00:25:30). But when the time is entered with an hour in it, nothing is added to the field.

The rest of the fields are arranged in tabbing order so that the Program Director can enter all information about a particular selection—Disc Number, Track/Selection and Track Time—in sequence. Of all the disc information fields, only the track time fields are named here, as Track 1, Track 2, and so on down the column to Track 8. Most of the work of this stack is done by the closeField handler that is triggered by the closure of any Track time field. Whenever a time is entered into the field, the total track time and the amount of time left to program are calculated.

Times Include Dates

Before we get to the handler, there is one more thing you should keep in mind about time in HyperCard. When you type a time in a field and convert it to seconds, HyperCard counts that as time on the clock since midnight of the current day. In other words, HyperCard interprets a track time in our stack of one minute as 12:01:00 AM on whatever today's date is. When you convert that time into seconds, HyperCard includes all the seconds from January 1, 1904, to the very beginning of today, plus the minute in your field. To prevent possible disaster when performing arithmetic on time that is unconnected to any particular day, I believe it's best to subtract the seconds up to today's date, leaving just the raw time in the field. In the script for our radio station stack, a function does just that.

At the back end of a time calculation, when the resulting seconds need to be converted back into recognizable time, HyperCard adds some text to the time that we don't need for the purpose of music track timings. First of all, when a time converts back to less than one hour, HyperCard shows that as being part of the 12:00 AM hour of the day (actually of January 1, 1904). For example, if you add one minute and three minutes together, after all the arithmetic and conversion, HyperCard shows "12:04:00 AM." That means any script must strip off excess data, like the "12:" for times under one hour, and the AM designation. In the script for the radio station stack, another function takes care of that.

The Handlers

Now we may proceed with the background script that handles the time arithmetic for adding the times:

```
on closeField
  if "Track" is not in the target then pass closeField
  set cursor to 4

  put empty into runningTotal
  put rawSeconds(field "Total Available") into available

  repeat with x = 1 to 8
    get field ("Track " & x)
    if it is empty then next repeat
    if the length of it < 6 then put "00:" before it
    add rawSeconds(it) to runningTotal
  end repeat

  put stripExcess(runningTotal) ¬
  into field "Track Total"
  put stripExcess(available - runningTotal) ¬
  into field "Track Left"

  if runningTotal > available
  then answer "There isn't that much available time"

end closeField


function rawSeconds input
  get input
  convert it to seconds
```

```
    put the date into history
    convert history to seconds
    return it - history
end rawSeconds


function stripExcess theTime
   get abs(theTime)
   convert it to long time

   if char 1 to 3 of it is "12:" then delete char 1 to 3 of it
   delete char offset("m",it) - 2 to offset("m",it) of it

   if theTime < 0 then return "-" & it
   else return it
end stripExcess
```

The closeField handler responds only to closeField messages initially sent to fields whose names contain "Track." Otherwise, the message is passed up the hierarchy. A local variable, runningTotal, is "initialized" by putting empty into it. This will allow values to be added to it later on. Next, the raw seconds of the time entered into the Total Available field are assigned to a local variable, called available, which will also be used later.

A repeat loop uses the counting variable, x, to retrieve the times in each of the 8 Track fields for summing to runningTotal. Early in the loop there is an if-then construction that short circuits the loop if a Track field is empty. This speeds loop execution, because several statements are not called for an empty Track field. For times entered as minutes and seconds (their lengths will be less than six characters), the obligatory "00:" characters are added to the beginning of that string. Then the raw seconds of that time are added to the runningTotal variable.

The next two statements call the stripExcess function on the way to putting the results of the time arithmetic into the two bottom fields of the card. Passing a seconds value as a parameter, this function performs the conversion back into regular time format, and removes a leading "12:" if it's there, and also removes the "AM" designation at the end of the reconverted time. The function also tracks whether a value passed to it is negative, which might be the case when the parameter is the difference between the available time and the running total. A negative time passed to the function forces the function to return the value preceded by a negative number sign.

One final touch of the handler is a test for whether the Program Director has overstepped the allotted time. An answer dialog box brings this to his attention in such situations.

World Time Conversion

If you've had a chance to see *Business Class*, then you know that the stack system has a few different world timekeeping and time calculating functions scattered about. Rather than reproduce that setting, let's make an entirely new card that a telephone globetrotting businessperson should have as part of his HyperCard-based set of desktop tools. On a single card will be listed the major cities that person frequently telephones. By going to that one card, the user can see at a glance what time and day it is in any of five cities and also whether the time in those cities is within the typical business hours of 9 a.m. to 5 p.m.

The best way I found to handle an array of world time conversions is to reference all times from the world standard time zone, Greenwich Mean Time (GMT). This is the time zone centered on Greenwich, England, and is also known as Coordinated Universal Time, or UTC, as well as Zulu when used with 24-hour time (0800Z).

Time conversion this way requires two figures for the number of hours (plus or minus) from GMT your own time zone is and also for the time zone of the target city. For example the Pacific Standard Time zone is eight hours earlier than GMT, so its offset is -8. Rome, on the other hand, is one hour later than GMT, so its offset is +1. Offset numbers are positive east of GMT all the way to the International Date Line, which runs down the middle of the Pacific Ocean; offset numbers run negative west of GMT to the date line. Table 19-1 shows offsets for many cities' time zones around the world (which you'll need for calculations).

Table 19-1.

Offset	Sample Cities
0	London, Dublin, Lisbon, Rabat, Accra
-1	Azores, Cape Verde Is.
-2	Mid-Atlantic Ocean
-3	Buenos Aires, Montevideo, Rio de Janeiro
-4	Halifax, San Juan, Caracas, La Paz, Santiago
-5	Ottawa, New York, Washington, D.C., Miami, Havana, Bogota
-6	Winnipeg, Chicago, Dallas, Mexico City
-7	Calgary, Denver, Phoenix, Baja
-8	Vancouver, San Francisco, Los Angeles
-9	Anchorage, Juneau, Dawson
-10	Honolulu, Papeete
-11	Pago Pago
+12	Wellington, Auckland, Christchurch, Suva
+11	New Caledonia, Marshall Islands

+10	Guam, Port Moseby, Sydney, Melbourne
+9	Tokyo, Seoul
+8	Beijing, Taipei, Hong Kong, Singapore
+7	Novosibirsk, Chengtu, Bangkok
+6	Tashkent, Lhasa
+5.5	New Delhi, Bombay, Calcutta, Columbo
+5	Sverdlovsk, Karachi
+4	Gorky, Abu Dhabi
+3	Moscow, Baghdad, Nairobi
+2	Helsinki, Athens, Istanbul, Cairo, Capetown
+1	Stockholm, Berlin, Paris, Rome, Madrid, Lagos

The basic calculation involves figuring GMT from your time zone and then figuring the time of the target city offset from GMT. GMT, in other words, becomes a kind of pivot point for the entire calculation.

One other factor that impacts the calculation is Daylight Saving Time (DST). In the United States and Canada, when DST is in effect (and not all areas of the countries observe DST), the offset difference between the time zone and GMT is one hour less. Therefore, while DST is in effect, the offset of Los Angeles to GMT is only -7 hours instead of -8. That part is easy to take care of in a conversion script.

The difficult part is knowing when or if a target city also observes its equivalent to Daylight Saving Time. It is not a universal adjustment, nor do those countries that observe it change their clocks on the same days. And don't forget, when countries in the southern hemisphere change their clocks for DST, it's in their summer months, while it's winter in the northern hemisphere. While the example stack does not take a target cities' DST setting, I'll suggest ways to accommodate that if you plan to replicate the stack for yourself.

Our example world time conversion is a one-card stack, shown in Figure 19-2. In the upper right corner are fields for the time and day of where your Macintosh is. In the center of the card are fields for you to enter up to five cities whose time and day you'd like to have available before making international telephone calls. Of all the fields on the card, the only ones you need to enter data are the ones in the City column (plus two hidden fields we'll see in a second). All other fields are calculated for you. Note, too, that the names of cities you type in are changed to italic text style when the current time in the target city is a time other than 9 a.m. to 5 p.m., meaning the offices in those places are probably closed. This card's calculation handler is triggered by an idle handler, so you can display the card on your screen and watch times, days, and city name text change. A checkbox at the bottom of the card lets you indicate whether Daylight Saving Time is currently in effect for where you are

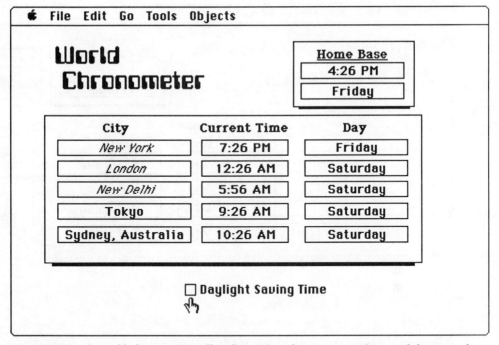

Figure 19-2 *A world chronometer offers five cities whose current times and days may be viewed at a glance. When the current time in a location is outside 9am and 5pm (business hours), the city's name is dimmed (italicized).*

in the world.

I keep referring to "where you are in the world," because this stack can be used anywhere in the world. It's not "hard-wired" for any particular country or time zone. That's because two hidden fields (Figure 19-3) hold time zone offset data for you and for the target cities. Using these numbers, the conversion handler figures out GMT and, from GMT, the times in the target cities. Each of the five lines of the larger field, called Offset List, corresponds to the city in each of the fields in the City column. Simply select the numbers from Table 19-1 for the cities, and type them in the corresponding line of the field. Then hide the field.

Here are the two handlers that go into the stack's background script:

```
on idle
  if field "Home Time" = the time then pass idle
  else updateTime
end idle
```

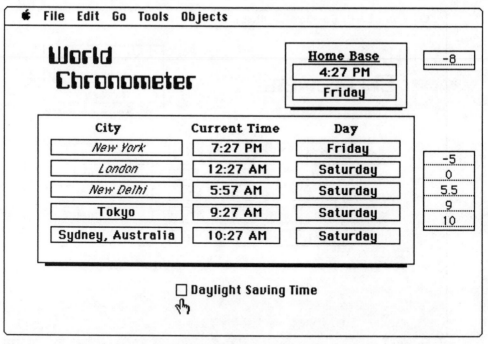

Figure 19-3 *Two hidden fields (right) hold important offset information. The top field is the offset between your Macintosh's time zone and GMT; the bottom field lists the offsets from GMT for each of the five cities.*

```
on updateTime
   set lockScreen to true
   put field "Offset List" into offsetList
   put 60*60 into oneHourSecs
   if the hilite of bkgnd button "Daylight Saving Time"
   then put true into SummerTime
   else put false into SummerTime

   put the time into MacTime
   convert MacTime to seconds
   put MacTime - field "Home Base Offset" * oneHourSecs ¬
   into GMTTime
   if SummerTime then subtract oneHourSecs from GMTTime

   convert MacTime to long date and time
   put word 5 to 6 of MacTime into field "Home Time"
   put item 1 of MacTime into field "Home Day"

   repeat with x = 1 to 5
```

```
put GMTTime + line x of offsetList * oneHourSecs ¬
into ForeignTime

convert ForeignTime to long date and time
put word 5 to 6 of ForeignTime ¬
   into field ("Foreign Time " & x)
put item 1 of ForeignTime ¬
   into field ("Foreign Day " & x)

convert ForeignTime to dateItems
get item 4 of ForeignTime
if it < 9 or it >16
then set textStyle of field ("Foreign City " & x) to italic
else set textStyle of field ("Foreign City " & x) to bold
end repeat

end updateTime
```

All updating is triggered by the idle handler. It checks to see when the time displayed in field Home Time (in the upper right of the card) is different from the time returned by the system. When the two don't match, then it is time to update the card.

The first group of statements of the updateTime handler perform preliminary work, like retrieving the entire five lines of field Offset List in one swoop (putting the field's contents into the variable, offsetList), setting the variable oneHourSecs we'll use as a kind of constant to represent the number of seconds in one hour, and then setting the variable SummerTime to true or false, depending on whether the Daylight Saving Time button is checked.

In the second group of statements, GMT time is calculated. The calculation is rather simple: the current Macintosh clock time (in seconds) minus the offset for your Macintosh's location (also in seconds). Note that this works no matter which side of GMT you're on. In the case of North and South America, for instance, subtracting the negative offset numbers actually adds time to your Macintosh clock reading to arrive at GMT. To the east of GMT, the offset is subtracted from the Macintosh time to arrive at GMT. If you've checked the DST box, then one hour is subtracted from GMT time to make the appropriate adjustment in the remaining calculations.

The two fields in the upper right corner, signifying the time and day of where you are, get filled in with the third group of statements. In one Convert command, the current time is converted both to a date and time. Then various words of that format are copied into the fields Home Time and Home Day.

It's in the repeat loop that all the foreign city times are calculated, using some of the data created previously in the handler. The repeat loop counter variable, x, acts as an index number to the line of variable offsetList and to each of the fields in columns. Calculation work is done on one row per repetition.

The time (in seconds) of the foreign city is calculated first, using GMT as the basis, plus whatever offset is in the appropriate line of the Offset List field (now in variable offsetList). Just as the Macintosh time was converted to the long date and time, so too is the foreign time for each city, with various words of the result going into fields for time and day. These fields are named Foreign Time 1, Foreign Time 2 and so on, making it easy for the repeat loop to fill them in row by row.

The last set of statements inside the repeat loop convert the foreign time for each city into the dateItems format to test whether the current hour is less than 9 or greater than 16—whether the current time is prior to 9 a.m. or after 5 p.m. If it's after business hours, then the textStyle property of the city field is changed to italic. A city whose time is within normal business hours is set to bold, just like the other text in the card.

Foreign Daylight Saving Time

As for accommodating Daylight Saving Time in the cities you list, you could provide a column of DST checkboxes to the left of the city names. When you know for sure that a city is observing DST, then check the box. In the updateTime handler, the group of statements calculating the foreign time would check the setting of that button (name the buttons with a name and number, like the fields), and add one hour's worth of seconds before converting the time to long date and time format. The modification would look like this:

```
if the hilite of bkgnd button ("DST " & x) is true
then add oneHourSecs to ForeignTime
convert ForeignTime to long date and time
  . . .
```

Automating the Daylight Saving Time for the other cities would be possible if you know the exact time change schedule. You could program those dates into the updateTime handler (probably using another hidden field to store the change dates) and not have to worry about it. Of course, some countries' time change systems are not so easy to program, such as the United States, which does it not by any particular date, but by the last Sundays in April and October. It's not simple, but it can be done in HyperTalk.

If you use this kind of time conversion application to complete a call to a distant land, you probably want to time the call. That's where an elapsed timer comes in handy.

Elapsed Time Counter

The following example is more of an exercise than a fully powered application. It consists of an electronic stopwatch that runs on the Macintosh clock. As such it is not accurate to fractions of a second, because the beginning of any time interval is based on the seconds counter of the Macintosh clock. But for many applications, such as timing a telephone call or a meeting, accuracy to within one second is more than adequate.

The electronic stopwatch we'll be using to demonstrate counting elapsed time is shown in Figure 19-4. It has two fields, one for the total elapsed time since the Start button was pressed, and one for a lap counter. When the Lap button is pressed, the time from the main field is copied into the lap field. A Stop button halts timekeeping.

This timer is designed around two global variables, which assure that the timer ticks away while the user goes off to another stack to look up or record other information. Of course, quitting HyperCard or launching an application will break the timer's sequence, since the value of the global variables will be lost. In a tightly controlled stack environment, you could save the variable values in hidden fields in the stack upon closing the stack, and retrieving them upon opening the stack. That would make it look like the timer was ticking away, even when the Macintosh was turned off.

We show the stopwatch as a small part of an entire HyperCard screen, because an elapsed timer is usually needed in another card, like a telephone log card. Unfortunately, for the elapsed timer to look like it's ticking through the seconds, and updating the display each second, the timer must be

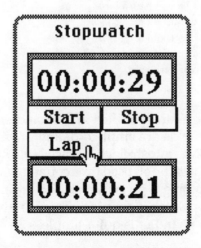

Figure 19-4 *A HyperCard stopwatch includes a lap timer. An idle handler keeps the displayed time ticking away on the screen.*

triggered by the idle system message. As mentioned earlier (Chapter 14), the idle message is troublesome if your card requires text input. Especially in the case of a timer that updates the display every second, the user would almost never have control over the text insertion pointer long enough to type more than a character or two. Therefore, I don't recommend this kind of time counter in a text-field-based stack. On the other hand, if the card has only buttons (or button-like objects) on it, then there's no apparent conflict between the idle handler and the buttons responding to mouse clicks.

To start looking at how the timer works, let's check out the handler in the stack script:

```
on openStack
  global running
  if running is empty
  then put false into running
end openStack
```

This handler is necessary for the first time you start this stack in a HyperCard session. Since the running global variable will not have been given a true or false attribution yet (and the idle handler, as it's written below, expects only one or the other), the variable is made false, keeping the fresh stopwatch turned off.

Now we can look at the handlers in each of the three buttons. First, the Start button's handler:

```
on mouseUp
  global startTime, running
  put empty into field "Timer"
  put empty into field "Lap"
  put the seconds into startTime
  put true into running
end mouseUp
```

Both global variables are modified in this handler, so they are declared at the beginning. Both fields are emptied of any previous contents. The seconds reading from the Macintosh clock is placed into startTime. This becomes the base time from which the elapsed time counter will be measuring. Finally, the variable called running is given the value of true. The idle handler will need to know if the stopwatch is running. This variable is the "switch."

The Stop button handler is quite simple:

```
on mouseUp
  global running
  put false into running
end mouseUp
```

The instant the next idle message is sent to the current card, the idle handler will bypass any further time counting. The button has, in essence, turned the timer off.

As any lap timer would, the Lap button merely takes a snapshot of the time in the main field and copies to the lap field:

```
on mouseUp
  put field "Timer" into field "Lap"
end mouseUp
```

In the background script of this application are two handlers:

```
on idle
  global running
  if running then updateTimer
  else pass idle
end idle
```

```
on updateTimer
  global startTime
  put the seconds - startTime into duration
  convert duration to long time
  delete char 9 to 11 of duration    -- delete "AM" or "PM"
  if char 1 to 2 of duration = 12
  then put "00" into char 1 to 2 of duration
  put duration into field "Time"
end updateTimer
```

The idle handler simply checks the running global variable whether the switch is on (true) or off (false). Whenever the switch is on, then it calls the updateTimer handler.

Using the startTime global variable as a base, the updateTimer handler finds the difference between the starting time and right now. Since these calculations are done in seconds, the number needs to be converted to the long time format, which provides hours, minutes, and seconds. Unfortunately, in 12-hour time it also appends an AM or PM to the time. Those letters are removed immediately after conversion.

As you'll recall from our discussion earlier in this chapter about dealing with raw seconds or time, HyperCard considers an amount of time such as 3 minutes to be 3 minutes after midnight. Therefore, the conversion to long time also inserts a leading "12" into the time (this occurs when the Control Panel is set to 12-hour time only). The next two lines of the handlers check to see if the first two digits are 12. If so, they're replaced with zeros. This means, of course, that this timer will never count past 11:59:59, because at 12 hours, the first two digits will be replaced with zeros. Finally, the correct elapsed time is put into the Timer field.

On a Macintosh II, the system messages and handlers run fast enough to display the time in what appears to be an even pace, advancing in step with each advancing second of the Macintosh internal clock. On a slower machine, like the Macintosh Plus, the increments are a bit uneven. This is due to the slower rate at which the idle message is sent, compounded by the comparatively slower execution of the updateTimer handler. Every second is displayed, but in a stutter-step fashion.

In *Focal Point*, I was faced with the problem of wanting to include a call timer in the Incoming and Outgoing telephone log cards. Because of the potential conflict with the text fields on the card, I chose a method other than constantly updating the timer display. Instead I installed buttons that let the user click to see the elapsed time of the call (Figure 19-5). When the call was completed, the total elapsed time was automatically inserted into the Timer field. The user could also restart the timer by clicking on yet a different button.

We'll now move from calculating time by itself to calculating dates.

Days Between Two Dates

A common business problem is figuring the number of days between any two calendar dates. As one solution to this problem, we'll create a user-defined function that performs this calculation, provided the two dates are passed to it as parameters. Since you can build this function into any kind of stack—or even experiment with it from the Message Box—we won't put it into any HyperCard application context.

The function handler is this:

```
function daysBetween dateOne,dateTwo
   put dateOne into firstDate
   convert firstDate to seconds
   put dateTwo into secondDate
   convert secondDate to seconds

   return abs(firstDate - secondDate)/(60*60*24)
end daysBetween
```

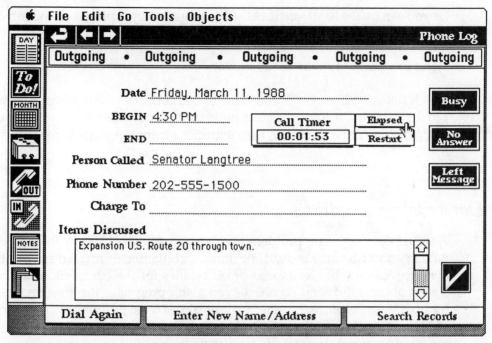

Figure 19-5 *Because of interference between an idle handler inserting new times into a counter field each second, Focal Point solved the elapsed timer problem by asking the user to click on the Elapsed button to peek at the elapsed time. When a call ends, the total time is automatically inserted into the field.*

It's so simple, it may seem hard to believe. Other than converting each of the incoming dates to seconds, the real action occurs in the return statement. There, the one date is subtracted from the other and divided by the number of seconds in one day. I use the 60*60*24 as a demonstration technique primarily. In practice, you'd use the number 86400 as the figure. The only somewhat tricky part of the statement is that it returns the absolute value of the subtraction and division. That's because you cannot anticipate in which order the user will enter the dates. If the earlier date is first or second, it doesn't matter when the absolute value (positive value only) is calculated and returned.

You might use this function in a mouseUp handler that reads dates from two fields, and puts the result into a third. For example:

```
on mouseUp
  put daysBetween (field "First Date",field "Second Date")¬
  into field "Difference"
end mouseUp
```

Or you can try the function from the Message Box by typing the function name and two dates as parameters, like this:

```
daysBetween ("6/3/88","10/4/88")
```

which returns 123 days. If you need to count the days inclusively, then add 1 to the value in the Return statement of the function. Conversely, if you don't wish to count either end day, then subtract 1 from the value before returning it.

Dates Before Deadlines

Another common date problem involves counting backward from a certain date to establish various deadline dates. Production of printed materials, for instance, usually has a number of milestones for the completion of various stages of copy, art, and so on. Given a shipping date for an item, and the number of days before that date various pieces must be finished, a HyperCard stack can calculate all the milestones—in effect, create a production schedule for the departments or people involved.

Figure 19-6 illustrates a skeleton of a card that can calculate the dates before a deadline. If a fixed list of production items is maintained for each project, then the only data entry will be the project name and the shipping date. A closeField handler attached to the Ship Date field triggers the calculations backward, based on the number of days before the ship date the items must be completed.

One extra consideration is that raw calculations of days before a particular date may mean that a deadline falls on a Saturday or Sunday. To be practical, the calculation should shift any weekend date back to the preceding Friday, to make sure the item is finished according to the set schedule.

In the sample Production Schedule stack, the important field names are those holding the number of days before a deadline a particular item is due, the due dates and the ship date. Because of the columnar arrangement of the Days and Due fields, they are named with numbers indicating their position down the column (e.g., field "Days 1"), so a repeat construction can loop through the calculations in relatively few HyperTalk lines of code.

The handler that performs the calculations is located in the background, and is triggered by the closeField handler of the Ship Date field. That small handler is:

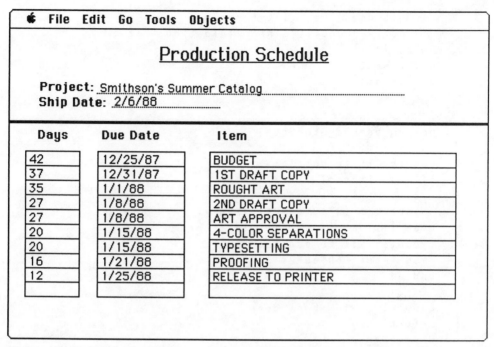

Figure 19-6 *Scheduling deadlines along a production schedule is simple when HyperCard calculates the dates based on the final shipping date. The handler even adjusts for weekends.*

```
on closeField
  calcDates
end closeField
```

which calls the calcDates handler in the background. The calcDates handler also calls a function, weekDay, which converts any Saturday or Sunday date to the preceding Friday. Here, then, is the background script for this stack:

```
on calcDates
  set cursor to 4

  put field "Ship Date" into deadline
  convert deadline to seconds
  put (60*60*24) into oneDay

  repeat with x = 1 to 10
    get field ("Days " & x)
    if it is empty then next repeat
    else
```

```
            get deadline - (it * oneDay)
            put weekDay(it) into field ("Due " & x)
        end if
    end repeat
end calcDates



function weekDay theDate
  get theDate
  convert it to dateItems
  if last item of it is 1 then
    convert it to seconds
    subtract (2*60*60*24) from it
  else if last item of it is 7 then
    convert it to seconds
    subtract (60*60*24) from it
  end if

  convert it to short date
  return it
end weekDay
```

Note that all calculations of dates are performed in seconds, the only reliable method. Thus, the date in the Ship Date field is converted to seconds (and into variable deadline), and all subtractions of dates are in intervals of one days' seconds.

Inside the repeat loop is where most of the action occurs. The number of days prior to deadline for each item is retrieved from fields in the Days column. Then its date (in seconds) is subtracted from the deadline variable. Before going into the Due field, the date is filtered through the weekDay function.

That function must check for the day of the week of the date. Fortunately, the dateItems version of any date includes the day of the week (numbered 1 through 7) as the last item. When that number is 1, that means the date is a Sunday, and two days' worth of seconds are chopped from the date; when the number is 7, then just one day need be subtracted from the Saturday. Before returning the value, it is once more converted, but this time into the short date format, which is what appears in the Due column fields.

International Dates

If you are developing a date- or time-intensive stack that will be used by Macintosh owners in other countries, you'll be in for a big surprise how differently times and dates are generated by Macintosh systems in other countries. These differences show through in HyperTalk's time and date functions. Localization of the System is handled by way of type itl resources, which specify such things as the order of date items, what kind of punctuation goes between items, how long and abbreviated versions are displayed, and so on.

Currently, non-U.S. editions of HyperCard have an extra resource attached to them. Called the "Date Zero" resource (it's a resource type DATE with an ID number of zero), it allows the HyperTalk Convert (to seconds) command to operate properly with most (but not all) localized Macintosh systems. You may convert a U.S. date to a localized date format by converting to seconds and then converting to long date. Seconds, once again, become the life preserver in a sea of format confusion.

Still, your scripts might have problems if they rely on elements of the time and date to be in certain locations in a field. For example, in the time calculation stacks in this chapter, we frequently add or remove characters connected to times in fields. But in localized versions, the time functions and conversions may not put "AM" or "PM" at the end of the string. The script would work incorrectly.

As an example of what the HyperTalk time and date functions do in localized systems, Table 19-2 demonstrates what several localized systems return.

Table 19-2.

Country	date	abbrev date	long date
Australian	27/3/88	Sun, 27 Mar 1988	Sunday, 27 March 1988
British	27/3/88	Sun, Mar 27, 1988	Sunday, March 27, 1988
Danish	27/03/1988	søn 27 mar 1988	søndag 27 marts 1988
French	27.03.88	Dim 27 Mar 1988	Dimanche 27 Mars 1988
French Canadian	27/03/88	Dima 27 mars 1988	Dimanche 27 mars 1988
German	27.3.1988	Son, 27. Mär 1988	Sonntag, 27. März 1988
International	3/27/88	Sun, Mar 27, 1988	Sunday, March 27, 1988
Norwegian	27-03-1988	søn 27 mar 1988	søndag 27 mars 1988
Spanish	27/3/88	dom, 27 mar 1988	domingo, 27 marzo 1988
Swedish	88-03-27	sön 27 mar 1988	söndag 27 mars 1988

Swiss French	27.3.1988	Dim, 27 mar 1988	Dimanche, 27 mars 1988
Swiss German	27.3.1988	Son, 27. Mär 1988	Sonntag, 27. März 1988
Turkish	27/3/88	Pazar, 27/ Mart/ 1988	Pazar, 27/ Mart/ 1988
United States	3/27/88	Sun, Mar 27, 1988	Sunday, March 27, 1988

Country	time	long time	dateItems
Australian	5:36 PM	5:36:48 PM	1988,3,27,17,36,0,1
British	5:36 pm	5:36:48 pm	1988,3,27,17,36,0,1
Danish	17:36	17:36:48	1988,3,27,17,36,0,1
French	17:36	17:36:48	1988,3,27,17,36,0,1
French Canadian	17:36	17:36:48	1988,3,27,17,36,0,1
German	17:36 Uhr	17:36:48 Uhr	1988,3,27,17,36,0,1
International	5:36 PM	5:36:48 PM	1988,3,27,17,36,0,1
Norwegian	17:36	17:36:48	1988,3,27,17,36,0,1
Spanish	17:36	17:36:48	1988,3,27,17,36,0,1
Swedish	17.36	17.36.48	1988,3,27,17,36,0,1
Swiss French	17:36	17:36:48	1988,3,27,17,36,0,1
Swiss German	17:36 Uhr	17:36:48 Uhr	1988,3,27,17,36,0,1
Turkish	17:36	17:36:48	1988,3,27,17,36,0,1
United States	5:36 PM	5:36:48 PM	1988,3,27,17,36,0,1

Apple's international group is in the process of documenting all the possibilities for time and date formats in all its localized versions. A commercial stack developer would be advised to get the latest information before releasing the product to the international market.

As you've probably seen throughout the demonstrations in this chapter, HyperTalk offers enough time and date functions and commands to handle just about every problem you're likely to encounter in stack development. Even when there doesn't seem to be a direct solution, a workaround usually isn't that complicated or sluggish. It's a tribute to the elegance of the language that you can do so much with so little.

20

Solving Searching and Sorting Mysteries

Among the most perplexing points of HyperCard facing stack authors are the fine points of calling Find and Sort from within scripts. The problems generally come from expectations that HyperCard's searching and sorting should be as complete as dedicated database programs. To the disappointment of many, that turns out not to be the case. But there are some techniques that are not obvious from descriptions of the two commands in HyperTalk language manuals. Additionally, stacks with more than one background have also proven troublesome to some authors. In this chapter, we'll attempt to demonstrate the ins and outs of advanced searching and sorting.

Workbook Stack

The best way to understand how Find and Sort work is to experiment in a controlled stack environment. For the purposes of this chapter, we'll clone the Master Developers Stack (Chapter 12) to provide a working laboratory for trying out various commands.

To make the stack:

1. *Open the Developer's Guide Master stack, created in Chapter 12.*

2. *Choose Save a Copy from the File menu.*

3. *Type "Chapter 20 Stack" into the file dialog box.*

4. *Open Chapter 20 Stack via the Open Stack choice of the File menu.*

We'll be using both backgrounds of this stack for demonstration. Several fields need names for the experiments. In the first background, name the first three fields in their Field Info dialog boxes as follows:

Last Name
Date
First Name

So you know which field is which, choose Background from the Edit menu. Then,

1. *Choose the Text tool from the painting tool palette.*

2. *As shown in Figure 20-1, type the names of the fields in the upper right corners of the fields on the card.*

3. *Choose the Browse tool to take yourself out of background editing mode.*

Now go to the second card, which looks like a rolo-style card. Open the Field Info dialog box for the first field and change the name of the field to "First Name." Change the name of the Phone field to "Last Name." Then, with the Text painting tool, type the names of the First Name and Last Name fields in the upper right corners of the fields, as shown in Figure 20-2.

One last setup task before entering sample data is to modify the closeField

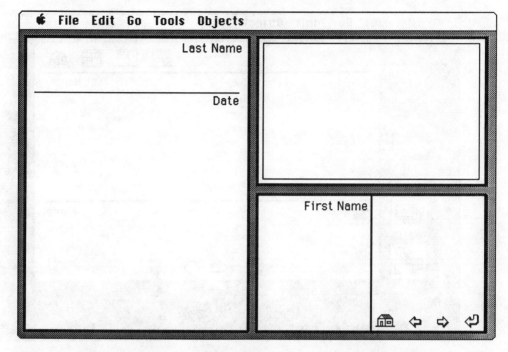

Figure 20-1 *For searching and sorting experiments, name and label (in the graphics layer) the fields of Chapter 20 Stacks. The field names are intentionally out of order.*

handler in the background script. This handler normally puts the short date into the third field of the card whenever one of the other two fields changes. For the purposes of sorting experiments later, the Date field needs to receive seconds counts instead of short dates. Therefore, change the handler to read:

```
on closeField
  put the seconds into field "Date"
end closeField
```

Now we're ready to create a few cards and enter some data to be searched for and sorted.

Entering Sample Data

As long as we're still in the rolo-style background, let's add some data and cards. The purpose of the data will be to test various methods of finding and sorting. As such, we'll put a first name in the first field, and a last name in the second field. Enter the following names into seven rolo-style cards:

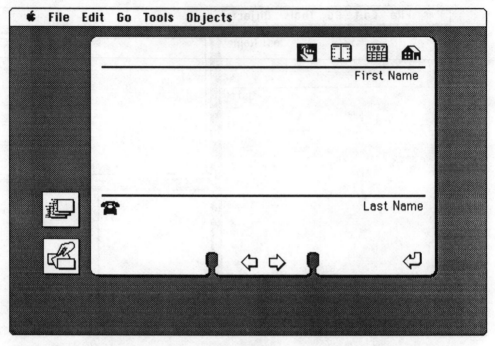

Figure 20-2 *Do the same with the second background in the Chapter 20 Stack for only the top two fields.*

Field "First Name"	Field "Last Name"
Bruce	Washington
Zelda	Washington
Charlie	Washington
Al	Washington
Morrie	Anderson
George	Anderson
Cecille	Anderson
George	Washington

Proceed to the first card of the stack, the single card of the first background. Into the topmost field, field "Last Name," type the name "Washington" (without the quotes).

We're all set for some tests.

Simple Finding

By now, you surely understand that searching for a chunk of text without any restrictions locates all instances of that text in a stack, even across background boundaries. Type

```
find "Washington"
```

into the Message Box, and keep pressing either the Return or Enter key. No matter where "Washington" appears in this stack, the Find command will stop on it.

Find works only on the beginning of words. Therefore, you could search for "Wash" and come up with the same searching results as searching for "Washington." However, if in this stack, you try to find "ton," there will be no apparent match.

You may, however, search for characters within a word by specifying "chars" as a parameter to the Find command. Type

```
find chars "ton"
```

into the Message Box. HyperCard will stop on each instance in which the letters occur in a word. Finding characters is much slower than the plain Find command.

If you try this on the Chapter 20 Stack, you may wonder why the Find command stops twice on the first card of the rolo-style card, yet you cannot see the rectangle surrounding the letters anywhere. The secret is that there is a hidden card field in the first card, and that field contains some text. To see its contents, type

```
show card field 1
```

into the Message Box. The word "button" is the word that stops the Find chars "ton" operation.

That Find locates words in hidden fields can sometimes wreak havoc with a stack you've created that holds hidden fields. This is something to remember when a Find command in a script goes awry.

Finding By Field

In a multiple field stack design, it is often desirable in a script to limit the Find command to one field. For example, in a stack that acts as a client database, you may set up a searching routine that prompts the user for a search string in an Ask dialog box, as shown in Figure 20-3. Then the script limits the search to the client name field. If you don't restrict the search, the Find command in

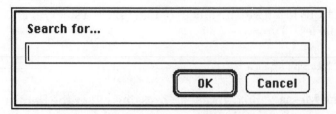

Figure 20-3 *Presenting a Search dialog box lets you control the extent of the search in a HyperTalk script, such as whether the search should be restricted to one field or should breach stack boundaries.*

your script may stop on an identically spelled word in a notes field of someone else's card. HyperCard, however, lets you specify a single field to search.

If you search for a text string limited to a particular field number, Hyper-Card will continue to search on that field number throughout the entire stack, even if there are multiple backgrounds, and those backgrounds' fields have an entirely different organization. Thus, the command,

```
find "Washington" in field 2
```

will locate all instances of "Washington" in field 2 of all cards of the stack.

Knowing this, many stack authors figure it should be possible to limit the search to a particular field of a background if the name of the field is specified, instead of the field number. Unfortunately, an unusual thing happens when you do this in a heterogeneous stack. If in the rolo-type background you type

```
find "Washington" in field "Last Name"
```

into the Message Box, you would expect HyperCard to find all instances of Washington in the Last Name field in the rolo card, and in the Last Name field of the first card of the stack. But when you try it, you discover that HyperCard does not find the instance in the first card, even though there is a field named "Last Name." What gives?

Inside HyperCard, the Find command starts its search in the current background on the field whose name you specify in the Find command. But from there the command is really keying in on a field number. The name becomes irrelevant. Therefore, when the other background comes into view, Find looks for the string in field 2, not some field called "Last Name."

Here's an experiment that will hammer this concept home. With the card setup specified earlier (make sure "Washington" is entered into the top field of the first card, as shown in Figure 20-1), type

```
find "Washington" in field "Last Name"
```

into the Message Box while viewing one of the rolo cards. Continue pressing the Return key until you have cycled through the cards at least once, to prove that you'll not stop on the first card with this Find restriction.

Next, navigate to the first card of the stack (type Command-1 as a shortcut). Duplicate "Washington" in both the Last Name and Date fields on the card. Now advance to any rolo card and issue the same Find command from the Message Box. Press the Return key slowly to watch what happens.

Eventually, you reach the first card of the stack, with HyperCard finding Washington in the second field (despite its name being "Date"). If you press Return again, HyperCard sends the command anew from this card. Since this card has a field named "Last Name," the command takes over, and finds the instance of "Washington" on this card in field "Last Name." But since this field is number 1 in tabbing order, any subsequent press of the Return key to find "Washington" in field Last Name will look for the text in the first field of other cards in this background or others within the stack. Try it. All you get is the first card of the stack.

Find in Field Workaround

This problem plagued one stack design I had. There was no question that the Find command that a script of mine issued had to limit search to one field in a particular background of a heterogeneous stack. Unfortunately, HyperCard does not let you limit a search to a single background. It's the whole stack or none.

I felt it was like cheating, but I ended up hiding a field in the other backgrounds so that the Find command would not stop on any cards in those backgrounds. I had to make sure that the empty, hidden fields in other backgrounds had the same field number (in tabbing order) as the field that was being searched for in the primary background. Because I discovered this late in the development cycle, the new field in each of the secondary backgrounds had to be pushed further into position. But once in place, the Find command from the primary background worked like a charm.

Incidentally, there seems to be a bug in all versions through 1.2 that makes Find unusable if you're trying to limit a search to card fields. The Find will stop on matches in background fields as well. Therefore, until this is fixed, avoid searches that must be restricted to card fields.

Boolean Finds

The plain Find command in HyperTalk, at least through version 1.2, allows only what is called AND searching, but not OR searching. AND searching means that if you specify two strings within the quotation marks as parameters to the plain Find command, HyperCard will stop only on those cards that contain BOTH strings somewhere in the fields of the card.

Some authors have asked about doing OR searches. An OR search would let you specify two strings, but HyperCard would find the incidence of *either* string on a card. So far, HyperCard does not allow that, nor have I seen any handlers that might replicate an OR search. Perhaps it's possible. I'd love to see it.

Find Whole and Find String

HyperCard got a boost in its Find capabilities with the release of version 1.2. Perhaps the most important addition is the Find Whole command (also activated from the keyboard by pressing Command-Shift-F). Whereas the plain Find command is sensitive only to word starts, the Find Whole command is sensitive to word starts and endings. Therefore, you may now search for the occurrence of two or more complete words when they appear together. For instance, if you wanted to find the state name "New Mexico," the simple Find command would stop on any card that had the words "new" and "Mexico" scattered anywhere on the card. But

```
find whole "New Mexico"
```

stops only on a card that has those two words separated by a space—just as it appears between the quote marks. Words in the Find Whole string must be the complete words you're looking for. If you try

```
find whole "New Mex"
```

HyperCard will not stop on "New Mexico," because the second word does not end "Mex." The good news, too, is that Find Whole uses the same fast searching technique of the plain Find command.

Find String, the second addition with 1.2, lets you search for any sequence of characters that span multiple words. Not sensitive to word starts or endings, the command

```
find string "w M"
```

would stop on "New Mexico" as well as on "how many." You would still use Find Chars when the characters are in one word.

To get the best performance out of the Find String command, specify at least three characters after the space. This triggers HyperCard's fast searching technique.

While HyperCard's Find has a number of quirks to it, its Sort is more straightforward.

Plain Sorting

HyperTalk's Sort command demands a parameter telling it what field or chunk within a field to sort on. For instance, in a rolo-style stack, you can enter peoples' names in the normal first and last name order, as they might appear on an envelope. Then you can sort the stack by the last word of the first line of the Names field. The Sort command is intelligent enough to use only the last words of the first line of that field to sort.

The Sort command also has other parameters to aid sorting. The one most often overlooked is the dateTime parameter. If you wish to sort cards according to dates or times in a particular field, you may specify dateTime as a parameter, instead of converting each time to seconds or some such weird thing. A command with this parameter would look like

```
sort dateTime by field "Date"
```

The *Handbook* spells out the workings of these parameters in detail.

Sorting by Field

Unlike searching, HyperCard sorting works the way you'd expect when sorting by named fields. Let's try it with Chapter 20 Stack.

If you followed directions to set up the stack earlier in the chapter, you have a few cards with the name "Washington" in the Last Name field, and some with "Anderson." You also have one other card in a different background, with the name "Washington" also in a field named Last Name. This Last Name, field, however, is field 1 in tabbing order, while all other cards place the Last Name field as 2 in the tabbing order. Type

```
sort by field "Last Name"
```

into the Message Box and press Return. An amazing thing happens. The lone card of the other background becomes mixed with the other cards based on the Washington value in the Last Name field. One of the Anderson cards is now the first card in the stack.

You may restore the stack to its original order by sorting on the Date field. In the rolo cards, this field contains the seconds values for the last updates to those cards. In the single card of the other background, that field is empty. Cards with empty fields in a field-specific sort are placed at the beginning of the stack. Try it now. Type

```
sort by field "Date"
```

into the Message Box. The single card of the first background comes to the front of the stack.

"Dual Key" Sorts

Database programs offer a facility to specify multiple "key fields" to sort a collection of data. In such a sort, the user specifies which fields are the primary and secondary key fields. For example, if you have a database with first and last names in separate fields and wish to sort the collection, you would specify the last name as a primary sort field, and the first name as the secondary sort field. That way, the database sorts initially by the last name. Then within records containing the same last name, the first names would be set in alphabetical order.

You can specify multiple value sorts in HyperTalk without much difficulty. While the slow way would be to sort the stack twice—once on the primary sort criteria, once again on the secondary—the Sort command allows multiple parameters.

To experiment with multiple sorts, let's be sure the Chapter 20 Stack is alphabetically mixed up. Type

```
sort by field "Date"
```

into the Message Box. This will put the stack in order based on the original entry order (unless you modified one or more cards since then), since the sort is on the seconds in the Date field.

Our goal with the next Sort command is to sort the rolo cards alphabetically so that all the Andersons are in front of the Washingtons, and each of the groups is alphabetized by first names. To do this, the Sort command needs two sort parameters, separated by an ampersand. Since according to logic the first sort we'd need would be on the last names, we'll pass field Last Name as the first parameter. Then we'll pass field First Name as the second parameter, because we want HyperCard to sort the first names after sorting the last names. Here's the command:

```
sort by field "Last Name" & field "First Name"
```

After that command executes, the cards are in a different order, with George Anderson's card at the front of the stack. As you flip through the stack, you'll notice that the lone card of the other background is sorted as the first card of the Washington group. That's because, you'll recall, the field First Name is empty on this card, and thus sorts first in the group.

You may also sort on multiple keys in reverse sort order by inserting the Descending parameter. To flip the order of the cards just sorted, type

```
sort descending by field "Last Name" & field "First Name"
```

into the Message Box. Zelda Washington's card is now the first card of the stack.

Sorting Card Suites

As we discussed in Chapter 18, you may organize a heterogeneous stack so that a very specific set of cards are linked together in a linked card suite. One of the supreme advantages of linking cards in this manner is that a sort does not harm the user's navigation to the cards. Links are hard-wired into the system, so sorting order is completely transparent to the user.

However, the author may wish to sort the cards for other purposes. For instance, you may want to collect an alphabetized list of clients from a heterogeneous client record stack for use elsewhere in your stack system. Such a sort would also keep the summary cards in alphabetical order for the user who wishes to browse through the summary cards for a client.

If you sort a card suite by a field name of the summary card, there is the danger that the first card of the stack after the sort will not be of the summary card background. This would happen if the other backgrounds do not have a field with the name of the sort key, or they have such a field, but the fields are empty.

When the other backgrounds have the same field name, it is incumbent upon the author to maintain control over the stack so that those fields are never empty prior to a sort, while the named field of the summary card has data in it. It probably requires posting of data from the summary card to the other backgrounds, but it must be done by the script to assure consistency and proper sorting.

Once a heterogeneous stack is sorted by field name, the cards could appear to be substantially jumbled if you were to do a sequential navigation through the stack. As long as your linked suite links are in good shape (and sorting doesn't touch them at all), then the linear order of the stack should be of no consequence. But if you need to retrieve data from a particular field in an alphabetical sequence of cards, use a repeat loop to go to the next card of the same background until you've made the entire circuit.

I hope that the above explanations and examples have cleared up the mystique surrounding HyperCard's Find and Sort commands. With any luck, I've also given you some organizational ideas for your next stack.

21

Authoring and Debugging Tools

While HyperCard does not have what other development environments would call a Debugger, HyperCard and the HyperTalk language provide many of the tools you need to debug troublesome scripts. Between a few error dialog boxes and the ability to display the contents of variables while a script is running, you have enough debugging tools to trace problems fairly quickly. Also, I mentioned earlier in the book that the Home stack may be used as a repository for a number of handlers that are of great value to stack developers. That's where we'll start this chapter.

Home Stack Tools

Building a stack, especially one that has lots of fields or buttons, can be very tedious at times. The layering of individual objects in either the background or card domains is great for HyperCard, but is occasionally a nuisance when you need to shift layers around.

A case in point is a background that has 20 fields on it. Then you suddenly realize that you need another field at the top of the tabbing order. In other words, when the user presses the Tab key, you need the text pointer to be flashing inside a new field you just added. Unfortunately, the new field is field number 21 in tabbing order. If the card also has a half-dozen buttons added to the stack after the fields, the new field is actually in layer 27. To get that field at the top of the tabbing order, you'd have to choose Send Farther from the Objects menu (or press Command-hyphen) 27 times.

The real difficulty here, aside from the tedium, is that you often don't know exactly how many layers exist between a new object and its desired location. The only clue to where the field is in the layered scheme of things is the Field Info dialog box, which shows you which field number it is. But this doesn't tell you how many button layers are also involved. Therefore, if six buttons were added after the 20 fields, you could choose Send Farther six times without adjusting the field number one iota. So, you keep checking the Field Info dialog box over and over.

A better way is to automate the process. I have four handlers in my Home Stack that let me adjust background fields and buttons in either direction. All I do is type the command into the Message Box, along with two parameters: the ID number of the object and the final number I'd like it to be among its peers. Those handlers are:

```
on sendButton idNo,final
  choose button tool
  click at the loc of bkgnd button id idNo
  repeat until number of bkgnd button id idNo is final
    doMenu "Send Farther"
  end repeat
  choose browse tool
end sendButton

on bringButton idNo,final
  choose button tool
  click at the loc of bkgnd button id idNo
  repeat until number of bkgnd button id idNo is final
    doMenu "Bring Closer"
  end repeat
```

```
      choose browse tool
end bringButton

on sendField idNo,final
   choose field tool
   click at the loc of bkgnd field id idNo
   repeat until number of bkgnd field id idNo is final
     doMenu "Send Farther"
   end repeat
   choose browse tool
end sendField

on bringField idNo,final
   choose field tool
   click at the loc of bkgnd field id idNo
   repeat until number of bkgnd field id idNo is final
     doMenu "Bring Closer"
   end repeat
   choose browse tool
end bringField
```

To push a new field (id 453) to be first in tabbing order, you type

```
sendField 453,1
```

You'll see the fields highlighted while the field tool is selected, and the cursor will flicker once for each time through the loop. When the fields are no longer highlighted (the browse tool is in effect), then the field is in the desired location.

Another Home stack development tool I use is the pair of handlers described in Chapter 13, which lock and unlock all the fields of a card. We won't repeat those handlers here. But there is another field utility I use quite often to prepare cards for tests of closeField handlers and clearing fields of sample data before releasing the product. It's a handler called clearEm (as in clear 'em), which empties all background fields in a card of their contents.

```
on clearEm
   repeat with x = 1 to the number of bkgnd fields
     put empty into field x
   end repeat
end clearEm
```

Not very complicated, but very helpful, especially when a card has hidden fields I needed cleared before my test or release. This handler should also be used with caution in the case of hidden fields. If a hidden field has some data that should not be removed, this handler will not be able to discriminate, so use it wisely.

Another development nightmare is testing a handler that creates a long series of cards in a stack. After the test, you may need to revise the script or just plain get rid of all the new cards. That's what the megaDelete handler does:

```
on megaDelete
  set lockScreen to true
  go to card 2
  repeat for the number of cards - 1
    doMenu "Delete Card"
  end repeat
end megaDelete
```

This works only for homogeneous stacks, because it deletes every card in the stack except the first one. Note that the handler never calls the Go command to go to the next card. That's because as you delete a card, the next one is front and center, ready to be deleted.

I frequently change a methodology for handling a certain operation or even stack organization, so that many scripts are affected by the change. It is periodically useful to peruse all your scripts. While I strongly recommend a script utility, like Eric Alderman's *Script Report* for printing out your scripts, you can put a handler in your Home stack that will show you the Script Editor for each object that has a script in it. At the same time, information about the object—which background or card it's in and the identification of the object— are displayed in the Message Box. It's a long handler, but modular enough that it shouldn't be too difficult to reproduce in your own Home stack.

```
on megaEdit
  push card
  edit script of this stack

  repeat with bg = 1 to the number of backgrounds
    go to card 1 of bkgnd bg
    put "Background " & bg
    get the script of bkgnd bg

    if it is not empty
    then edit script of bkgnd bg

    repeat with bbn = 1 to the number of bkgnd buttons
```

```
        get the script of bkgnd button bbn
        if it is not empty then
          put " Bkgnd Button " & bbn into word 3 to
          5 of msg
          edit script of bkgnd button bbn
        end if
      end repeat

      repeat with bfd = 1 to the number of bkgnd fields
        get the script of bkgnd field bfd
        if it is not empty then
          put " Bkgnd Field " & bfd into word 3 to 5
          of msg
          edit script of bkgnd field bfd
        end if
      end repeat
    end repeat

    repeat with c = 1 to the number of cards
      put "Card " & c
      go to card c
      get the script of card c

      if it is not empty
      then edit script of card c

      repeat with cbn = 1 to the number of card buttons
        get the script of card button cbn
        if it is not empty then
          put " Card Button " & cbn into word 3 to 5
          of msg
          edit script of card button cbn
        end if
      end repeat

      repeat with cfd = 1 to the number of card fields
        get the script of card field cfd
        if it is not empty then
          put " Card Field " & cfd into word 3 to 5
          of msg
          edit script of card field cfd
        end if
      end repeat

    end repeat
```

```
  pop card
  answer "We're Done!!"
end megaEdit
```

Not much that's remarkable happens in this handler. It consists of a series of repeat loops that open the Script Editor for each of the backgrounds, cards, fields and buttons that have something in their scripts. Since named objects have their names appear at the top of the Script Editor dialog box, the Message Box displays the number of the background, card, button, or field. Importantly, buttons and fields are identified by the background or field to which they belong.

Using this handler on a 9-inch internal Macintosh monitor places a tight squeeze on space to show the Message Box. I've found that by placing the box so that the dotted line of the Message Box text line is just below the edge of the screen, I can see the object designation in the available sliver of space (Figure 21-1). On a larger monitor, you may drag the Message Box anywhere in the clear.

Here's one last tangible idea that should help developers of stack systems.

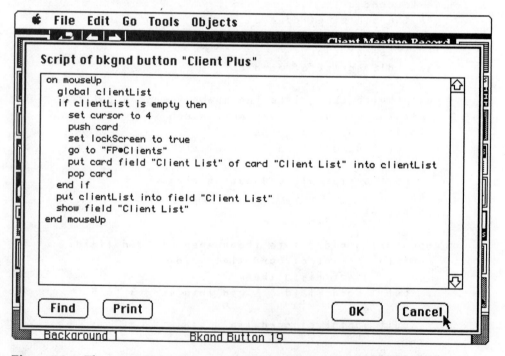

Figure 21-1 *The megaEdit handler opens the Script Editor of each object in a stack. Carefully position the Message Box so that you can see a sliver of text. The handler displays additional information about the object whose script appears on the screen.*

While in the process of modifying scripts, fields and buttons, your developmental stacks tend to grow quite large. Occasional compacting will free up space on your disk and often make your stack operate a little faster. But going to each stack in a stack system, choosing Compact Stack from the File menu and waiting for compaction to complete for each is a waste of time.

What I've done in this department is to create a handler for the Home Stack that goes to each stack in the system and compacts the stack (doMenu "Compact Stack"). I first got the idea for this while working on *Focal Point*, a 22-stack system on my hard disk. In the Home Stack I created a handler called megaCram, which compacted the whole system. Now, this does not speed up the compaction process necessarily, but it does automate it. I could leave the machine for a coffee break or a phone call, and come back to a tightly condensed stack system. Later, I added other "cram" handlers for other stack systems I was working on, building part of the product name into the handler name, as in BC•Cram for compacting all of *Business Class*.

These are only a few examples of the kind of generic handlers you can keep handy in your Home stack. You'll recognize the need for others when you notice tedious operations you perform over and over in developing a stack. For these kinds of handlers, make them as generic as possible, so you can reuse them in other stacks. If specific data is required, as in the case of the shifting of object layers, pass the details as parameters to the handler.

Author Tool Shortcut

If you have one of the new keyboards for the Mac SE or II, you can use Control-key sequences (and function keys on the Extended Keyboard) to launch some authoring tool scripts. For instance, you could write a Home stack handler that traps the Control-C keyboard message to compact your stack; or Control-L to lock all fields on the current card. For tools that require parameters (like sendField), the handler could present an ask dialog box to prompt you for the parameters.

You should also familiarize yourself with HyperCard's own tool shortcuts to help you move in and out of various object Script Editors. Many of these were added with HyperCard version 1.2.

While the Command-Option keyboard combo always let you peek at button locations, you may now also click on a particular button to zoom directly to that button's script. From the Script Editor, the same Command-Option-Click closes the Script Editor and chooses the browse tool—no more fumbling for the button tool and back. When you add the Shift key to this keyboard combo, you can peek at field locations and open their scripts by clicking on one of them.

You may also go directly to other object scripts by way of keyboard equivalents:

Command-Option-C —> card script
Command-Option-B —> background script
Command-Option-S —> stack script

Command-Option-clicking in the Script Editor of any of these objects closes the editor window and returns you to the browse tool.

And don't forget the two original shortcuts: Option-Tab to hide and show the tools palette; and Command-Tab to return to the browse tool from any other tool, including a painting tool.

Using Scripts to Build Stacks

As helpful as the Home stack utility scripts are in my stack development, I still find a need for writing little handlers to help me build a stack. These come in particularly handy when you change your mind about field and button properties after you've laid them out.

For example, in a card like the one shown in Figure 21-2, it is common to start cloning the rows and columns of fields before setting all the desired style and text properties of the original field. Or, you may have thought that a particular text size or text style would work, but change your mind when you see the completed card. Manually changing the text attributes of all those fields would be a nightmare of tedium, since you cannot select more than one field for change at a time. The most efficient way to handle the change is to write a custom handler that does the job. Since all these fields are in a contiguous tabbing order, their field numbers are in a linear series. That means we can use a Repeat With construction to make the changes in only a few lines of HyperTalk code.

Given that the top left field of the grid is field number 4, and the field at the bottom right of the grid is field 27, we can write a short handler for the current card that goes:

```
on changeText
  repeat with x = 4 to 27
    set textSize of bkgnd field x to 12
    set textStyle of bkgnd field x to condensed, bold
  end repeat
end changeText
```

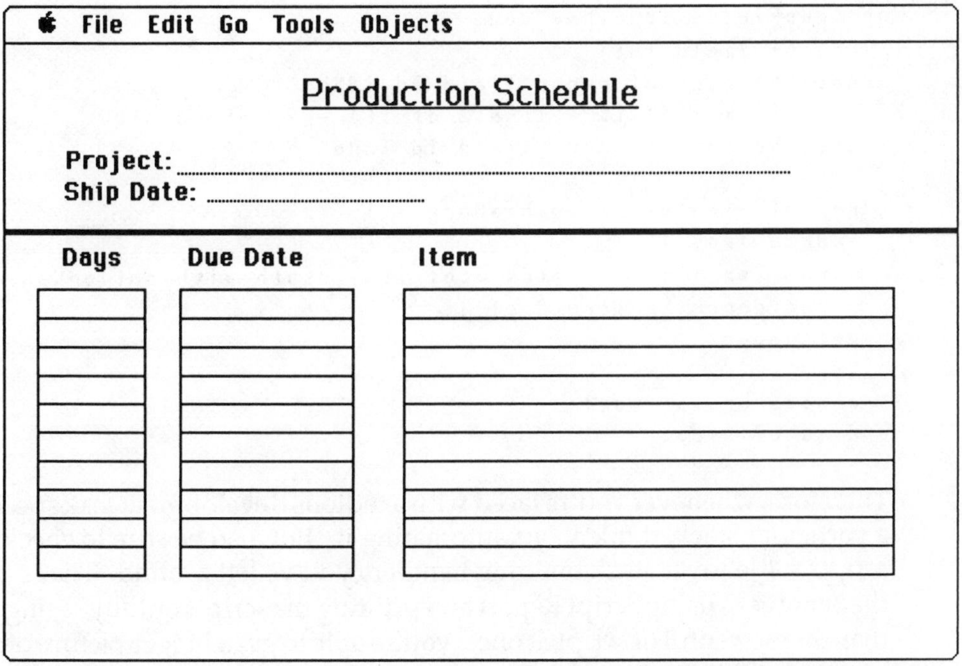

```
  🍎  File  Edit  Go  Tools  Objects
```

Production Schedule

Project: ....
Ship Date: ....

Days	Due Date	Item

Figure 21-2 *Laying out the background fields of a card like this can be automated with a HyperTalk script. When you've set the properties of a field at the top of a column, the script can clone the field as deep down the card as you need.*

Then, by typing changeText into the Message Box, all the fields are changed within a few seconds.

You can also name a series of fields or buttons with a similar kind of loop. Let's say you created 10 buttons whose names are to contain the word "Shift" and a number indicating its place in the series. A handler to do that for you would be

```
on nameButtons
  repeat with x = 1 to 10
    set name of bkgnd button x to ("Shift " & x)
  end repeat
end nameButtons
```

If your card has several columns of fields, the field-making process itself may be automated. To use the following stack-building utility, create one field at the top of the column. Assign all properties as you wish for text and style. Then type the name of the handler, specifying the ID number of the top field and the number of clones you'd like in the column as parameters.

```
on makeFields idNo,howMany
  choose field tool
  get the rect of bkgnd field id idNo
  put (item 4 of it - item 2 of it) - 1 into depth
  get the loc of bkgnd field id idNo

  repeat with x = 2 to howMany + 1
    drag from it ¬
    to item 1 of it, item 2 of it + depth with optionKey
    add depth to item 2 of it
  end repeat

  choose browse tool
end makeFields
```

Therefore, whenever you're faced with a tedious development task specific to a particular stack, think about automating it. But also be sure to check your scripts for leftover stack building handlers you've left around. That's one of the benefits of using Script Report and printing the scripts out. By seeing more than one screenful of script at once, you're able to get a bigger picture of more handlers. Those that don't belong seem to stand out better in print than in the Script Editor.

Debugging

There's nothing more satisfying than writing a handler and having it run the first time just as you expected it. Unfortunately, that doesn't always happen. When things don't go as planned, however, there are several things you can do to track down the source of the problem. Let's look at four debugging techniques I've picked up over the last year or more of scripting.

Check the Script Editor

While HyperTalk does not have much in the way of interactive debugging capabilities, it does let you know when you've made a major blunder before you run the script. Just press the Tab key, and look to make sure the final End statement hugs the left margin of the editing window. If it doesn't, several things may be wrong.

The first item to check is whether the handler name is the same in the first and last lines. If an Exit statement is nested in a handler, be sure the argument is either the handler name, If, or Repeat. Next, look down the handler until you find traditionally indented statements (such as if-then and repeat constructions) that are not indented properly. Make sure all repeats have balancing End Repeat statements and that those if-then-else constructions requiring End If statements have them.

I've noticed occasionally that inserting blank lines inside some repeat constructions causes the Script Editor to think that something is wrong. Try cinching up a non-formatting handler to see if that helps.

If all else fails, then insert an End statement in each line of the handler, starting with the second line. If, upon pressing the Tab key, the statement hugs the left edge of the script window, then all is well down to that line. Cut the line and paste it after the next line to try again until the script does not format correctly. The problem will be in the line just above. If you find that you must carry this out inside a control structure, you'll have to add the counterbalancing End statement for the structure as well. Eventually, you'll find the culprit line.

Heed the Error Dialogs

The error messages that come up in the form of dialog boxes tell you a lot about what your problem is. Moreover, they usually give you a chance to peek at that part of the script that trips HyperCard. What do the error dialogs mean?

Perhaps the most frequent one you'll get is warning that HyperCard cannot understand a particular word (Figure 21-3). Fortunately, HyperCard displays what the problem word is right in the dialog box. This error message means that the word in question is being used as a command or function, and that HyperCard cannot find a handler to match that word anywhere in the hierarchy. The best reason for this is that the word is misspelled in the location HyperCard has trouble with it. Either that, or you wrote the command or function correctly in one handler, but forgot to write the actual handler to trap that command, and the message went all the way to HyperCard. Occasion-

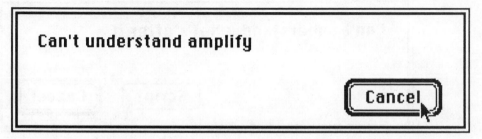

Figure 21-3 *The most common HyperTalk error message means that HyperCard received a message that it didn't know what to do with. The message may be mistyped or you forgot to write a handler to trap the message.*

ally, too, you may use a HyperTalk reserved word incorrectly in a statement. Click the Script button in the error dialog and let HyperCard point out the error. The text cursor will be positioned immediately before the word HyperTalk is stumbling over. Investigate why that word doesn't belong there.

Another kind of "misunderstanding" that HyperTalk can have is when a script tries to read the contents of a variable that has never had anything stored in it (including empty) prior to the erroneous statement. For instance, in the simple handler,

```
on test
  if fred then flash 1
end test
```

HyperTalk doesn't know fred from Adam. Therefore, it issues the error dialog in Figure 21-4, which indicates it doesn't understand "fred," which is the word after "if."

HyperTalk's internal error checking stops on the first error it finds in a handler. Therefore, if the above handler read

```
on test
  if fred then frobnitz 12
end test
```

and there was no handler called "frobnitz," then HyperTalk would display only the error referring to "fred." Once you solve the fred problem, Hyper-Talk will, on the next attempt at running this handler, complain that it cannot understand "frobnitz."

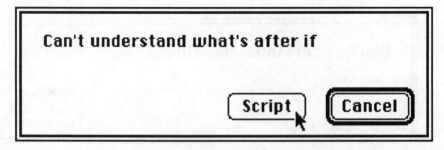

Figure 21-4 *HyperTalk often points the way to where in the script it balks at a message or construction. Whenever you see this error message, click the Script button to see where the problem is.*

Tracing Variable Values

Perhaps the biggest sources of bugs in developmental stacks are values of global and local variables not being what you thought they'd be when you drafted a handler. As the handler performs further calculations on the variable, things go from bad to worse, until nothing works right.

A nice feature of HyperTalk is that you can go into any line of a handler and display the value of a variable at any stage of its life. The window to these values is the Message Box, and the probe is the Put command.

Your script is most revealing about its variable disarray when a statement in the script puts a variable into a field; only the resulting display of data is incorrect. What you need to do at that point is trace the value of that variable through the handler. The method is simple: Insert a Put command, with the name of the variable as the argument, after the first line of the handler that calls the variable. If you're satisfied that the content of the variable is as you expected, then cut that Put command, and paste it after the next line of the handler that changes the value of that variable. Keep working your way down the handler until the value you see in the Message Box differs from what you expected at that stage of handler execution. That narrows the error to a particular line of your script—a breakthrough in debugging the script.

Sometimes a buggy script has more than one variable involved. If so, then modify the Put command to display the values of both commands, like this

```
put number && counter
```

Then keep shifting this statement down the handler until you find an unexpected value in one or both variables.

So far, we've been assuming that the variable contents fit on one line—the line of the Message Box. It's not uncommon for a variable to be more than one line, or even change its number of lines during execution of the handler (some field sorting routines in *Focal Point* use fields whose line counts change as the items sort).

Obviously, for these kinds of variables, the Message Box won't do. To accommodate these larger variables, you may have to create a temporary card-level field and put the intermediate results of the multilined variable in that card field, as in

```
put dataList into card field 1
```

If you need to investigate only one part of a handler without the rest executing, remember that you can enter a "decoy" End statement to the handler anywhere you want. That will stop the handler in its tracks, and give you a chance to see how various fields have responded to the handler thus far.

Another boost is to insert a number of pauses throughout the handler while it's undergoing debugging. One way to program a pause into the handler would be to enter this line in key spots in the handler:

```
wait until the mouseClick
```

This command gives you as much time to check out the condition of the card (and perhaps variable values displayed in the Message Box or the debugging card field) as you need. Click the mouse button to proceed to the next pause location. Unfortunately, there is no way to pause handler execution from the keyboard without preprogramming it for pauses. At most, you may halt the execution of a handler at any time (this includes what may be runaway handlers and infinite repeat loops) by pressing Command-Period. That is one unconditional HyperTalk halt command that no handler can trap for.

One other tip for testing the value of parameters sent to custom handlers or functions is to use the Params function. Since this function returns the name of the message plus the values of all parameters sent with it, you can temporarily insert the statement

```
put the params
```

into the top of your custom handler. You'll receive a snapshot of the complete message in the Message Box the next time you run the handler. If one of the parameters is not what you expected, then go back to the handler that sends the message and see why the values are being disturbed before sending the message.

Testing If-Then Constructions

It's sometimes difficult to tell when if-then-else constructions are working properly, because the results may not be apparent in fields on the card. The results do show up later, but the desire is to trap the problem at the source.

If you suspect an if-then construction is not doing what it should, you need another way to test which path through the construction handler execution is taking. A quick way to test this is to add a Flash or Beep command to both legs of the if-then construction. Use different parameters for the number of flashes or beeps so that you can tell immediately which pathway the handler took. There's a caution with using a beep as a testing device, however. If you've altered the beep sound of your Macintosh so that the digitized audio is longer than a traditional system beep, your system may not be able to distinguish between a single and double beep. If the signal for a second beep (of a double) occurs while the first beep is still playing, the second beep will pass through and never be heard. The flash, presenting a visual clue, is more reliable.

Once you're satisfied that your script is working as expected, be sure to remove all debugging code. As a rule, I place a comment after lines of debugging code as a reminder to delete the lines later. As you test your product, be on the lookout for sudden displays of numbers or text in the Message Box. You've probably left a debugging Put command in a handler somewhere.

Sometimes it feels that debugging never ends. In one sense that's true, because even after a stack has been released, you should return to it and find ways of doing things more efficiently, faster and with less HyperTalk code. And users will discover minor problems that even the best testing couldn't find. Don't despair, because it's bound to happen in software. Stack production, as we've said many times, is the same way.

22

HyperTalk Script Style and Practice

HyperTalk is a forgiving language. At times it offers you several ways to state the same thing. You can go to `card 3` or the `third card` of a stack, and HyperTalk will understand both. Precision capitalization of keywords or object names is not an issue at all. If-then-else constructions may be broken up into lines in a number of ways.

At the same time, HyperTalk has some straightforward rules of syntax. All lines in a handler begin with a command (either HyperTalk's or one of your own). Calls to functions have their specific way of passing parameters. Chunk text expressions must start from the most specific to the least specific (e.g., "char 3 of word 10 of line 2 of field "Data"). What all this means is that if you follow some basic syntax rules (HyperTalk will alert you if you fail to do so), and choose one of the allowable ways to perform tasks, you can get your handlers to work. Getting your handlers to work should be your first priority when writing HyperTalk code. After all, that's what you're there to do.

Practice and Style Guidelines

But after you've made the handler put all the right information in the right places, it's time to recheck the handler for three factors:

Readability
Efficiency
Comprehension

Readability, to my way of thinking about HyperTalk, is not about the content of a handler, but how easy it is to find the basic flow or modularity of a handler. If the stack you're developing will be open to modification by others, they must be able to see a pattern or flow in the handler to understand your methodology for an operation. Parts of a handler, like global variables, initial values for other variables, control structures, and other code snippets should be in expected places and with sufficient spacing to let a reader of your script get a quick overview of what's going on inside this handler.

Efficiency is more than just speed of execution. It also encompasses how many statements you use in a handler, how many calls you make to objects, how many variables (global or local) you use, and how often repetitive actions take place outside of repeat loops. While it's true that most of these affect execution speed, they also affect the overall number of lines of your handler, thus impacting readability. A shorter script—especially one you can see inside the confines of a single view of the Script Editor—is much easier to read than one you must scroll through to see.

Comprehension is a less tangible factor, but one that often makes the difference between spaghetti and poetry. And so, just as poetry should be read aloud, good HyperTalk code should also be read aloud (at least to yourself) with the intention of being able to understand what it's doing just by hearing the words. That means objects should have names. Variables and objects should carry names that truly identify themselves. Function names should accurately reflect the action they perform. All statements should be devoid of excess. And each line should contribute to the meaning of the handler, without needless repetition. Unlike some poetry styles, HyperTalk handlers do not need refrains ("quoth the Raven, 'exit mouseUp'").

Enough of generalities. Now onto specifics of turning a handler into a great handler.

Readability

Some handlers must set up certain variable values, or retrieve field data before the real action of the handler begins. In a long handler, the cursor may have to be changed to the watch, or the screen locked. All this preparatory stuff should go into a part of the handler I call the preamble. Not every handler needs a preamble, but those using global variables, assigning initial values to local variables, or setting the scene prior to the real action need preambles.

The Preamble

Taking a tip from other programming languages, it's a good idea to declare all global variables in the preamble. This lets a reader become familiar with non-HyperTalk words that will be used later in the handler. Whenever I'm reading a handler that has declared global variables in the preamble, I'm on my guard for those words, knowing I won't be surprised by some other globals creeping in later in the handle. Remember that you can declare many globals at once by separating the variable names with commas, rather than issuing one global command for each variable..

If your handler also uses local variables that must have some starting value before they may be used, then assign those values in the handler's preamble. For instance if a repeat loop later in the handler adds values to a local variable, you must warm up that variable by putting empty or a zero into it before anything may be added to it. Warm up that variable in the preamble.

The preamble is where you would set global properties that affect the entire handler. Thus, cursor, lockScreen, lockMessages, lockRecent, numberFormat, and userLevel would be the typical properties you'd set in the preamble, provided those settings apply to the entire handler. If they apply to only a small part, and the settings are altered again before the handler ends (like unlocking the screen to show the user some movement during the handler, or changing the number format to something else), then set those properties later in the handler so that the setting and resetting act as bookends to the code in between.

As you'll learn in a moment, it's best to fetch data from a field as few times as possible—once is best—in a handler. If the contents of that field are a prime object of the handler, then the preamble is a good place to do it, because that action will be setting a local variable (perhaps It) to the contents of that field. It makes the most sense to include that as a preamble operation.

Line Spacing

After filling up the preamble with preparatory commands, the rest of the handler should have ample line spacing between modules. For instance, leave a blank line between the preamble and what follows. A long handler tends to have various sections to it—sections that perform related actions on a variable or a property. It is best to separate any such section from the rest by a blank line on either side. I also tend to keep an outer repeat loop together by leaving a blank line before and after it. Breaking a long script into sections makes it much more readable. In a skimming of a handler so divided, a reader can get an overview of the basic structure of what's happening in the handler. It also helps the reader, when going through the handler in detail, to focus on one operation at a time.

Command Lines

It is also valuable to the reader to have individual lines of scripts that are as short as possible. Do not let a statement line run beyond the right margin of the Script Editor window. If a line is wider than the window, put a "soft carriage return" in the middle of a line (between HyperTalk words only) by typing Option-Return. A special character (¬) appears at the end of the physical line, indicating that the next line of text is part of the first.

Dividing long lines into two can be done with an eye toward readability. For example, in a long line involving a Put command, I usually divide the line so that the Put and the Into words are at the left margin of the handler. Therefore, the first physical line has the "what," while the second line has the "where." As the reader scans down the handler, the Put and Into words stand out, and the two-physical-line statement appears to be more of a whole. Such would not be the case if the line were split so that the left margin words were Put and Field.

Long if-then lines should always be broken so that the Then part starts on the second line. This is an accepted construction, so it is not necessary to place a soft carriage return at the end of the If line.

Efficiency

I have nicknamed Dan Winkler, "Mr. N-Minus-One," because it seems that every time he looks at a handler, including one he's written, he can find a way to make that handler perform in one less line than before. That kind of striving for maximum efficiency is something every stack author should emulate.

In previous chapters, we've already mentioned performance issues in a HyperTalk script. The most important one to remember is that getting data from and putting data into a field is perhaps the most sluggish action you can take in HyperCard. Fetch and post field data only once per field in a handler.

All other times you need to work with the information within the handler, put the field information into a local variable, and massage it to your heart's content. Only when you're finished making changes to the content, should you put the data into the field.

The same goes for getting and setting object properties, although the performance hit on these operations are not as serious as with fields. But the point is, if you test the state of an object property at the top of an if-then-else construction, and later act on that setting, avoid getting that property twice. For instance in the following handler

```
on mouseUp
  global allScripts
  if the script of the button "Calculate" is not empty
  then put the script of button "Calculate" after allScripts
end mouseUp
```

the script property of the button is retrieved twice. A more efficient way to write this handler would be

```
on mouseUp
  global allScripts
  get the script of button "Calculate"

  if it is not empty then put it after allScripts
end mouseUp
```

Since the entire text of the script is placed into It, you may test it, modify it, or post it anywhere you please without having to fetch the data from the object again. That's the basic principle to be applied to both properties and fields.

Another performance tip is to look for ways to combine statements into fewer statements. For example, it may be easier at first to map out a handler by making each operation a single statement line, like this

```
on mouseUp
  get field "SubTotal"
  multiply it by field "Tax Rate"
  put it into field "Total"
end mouseUp
```

But after closer inspection, you should notice that all three lines could be combined into one statement:

```
on mouseUp
  put field "SubTotal" * field "Tax Rate" into field "Total"
end mouseUp
```

In timing tests I ran on a Macintosh Plus, the second method ran almost 40 percent faster than the first. That's an impressive time saving, and probably will send you to your existing scripts right now to find where other lines may be condensed.

An adage that applies to writers also applies to HyperTalk authors: Write Tight.

Timing Tests

If you are unsure about which of two ways to code an operation is the faster, you should perform a timing test on the two handlers and compare the results.

Insert a statement at the opening of the handler that puts the current ticks reading (ticks are counted from the moment you power up your Macintosh) into a local variable. At the end of the handler, a statement displays the difference between the ticks reading at that point and the reading at the start of the handler. In the mouseUp handler, above, here's how the handlers looked with the timing tests built into them:

```
on mouseUp
  put the ticks into startTime
  get field "SubTotal"
  multiply it by field "Tax Rate"
  put it into field "Total"
  put the ticks - startTime
end mouseUp

on mouseUp
  put the ticks into startTime
  put field "SubTotal" * field "Tax Rate" into field "Total"
  put the ticks - startTime
end mouseUp
```

At the end of each handler's execution, the elapsed tick count appears in the Message Box. Note that the two additional statements do not interfere with the body of the handler we're testing. Thus, their own variable names are used (startTime). Also very important is to make sure that the timing statements are identical in both versions, so that the only difference in timing would be the execution of the body of the handler.

Occasionally, you'll want to compare the timings of two methods that execute too quickly to give you accurate results. In such cases, you may want to insert a repeat loop around the body of the handler. By repeating the operation 10 times, you increase your ability to discern differences in the results by a factor of 10.

It might also be worth keeping a log book (in a HyperCard stack, of course), of the various techniques you test for speed, and note those methods that are faster than others. And just because you compare two methods to find the faster one doesn't mean there isn't a still faster way to perform the operation. Keep an open mind, and keep exploring your scripts for greater efficiency.

Comprehension

After you've found the fastest ways to make your scripts cut through your stack and stack information, you should concern yourself with the comprehension of the stack. This is how understandable the handlers would be if a stranger were to read through your handlers. The real test would be how readable the script would be to someone who knows nothing about Hyper-Talk.

Comprehension is greatly linked to the way you name objects, variables, custom messages and user-defined functions. The names should have meaning, if not help the user draw a mental picture of the information stored in a container or of the action a message or function takes. In my early days of HyperTalk script writing, I didn't pay much attention to this factor, but the more I write handlers and the more I read other peoples' handlers, the more important this factor has become in my work.

The best guideline I use is literally reading aloud a handler I've written. But I also listen carefully to what I'm saying. Would someone else in the room get a picture of what I'm saying? Are the names clear enough to someone coming to the handler for the first time? Is there almost a sense of story line in a long handler?

These are important questions you should ask of every handler in a script that will be open to the world. Even if no one else sees your scripts, the practice you give yourself in making your stacks readable, efficient and comprehensible will add to your HyperTalk scripting abilities. Your stacks will run better, and they'll be much easier to maintain if you need to modify something a year from now.

So ends our tour of HyperTalk issues for stack developers. We now shift gears again, going into the subject of external resources you can add to your stacks to make them sound great, have great icons and do things that HyperTalk doesn't do.

PART THREE

Resources
for Stack
Developers

23

A Resource Crash Course

If you've been with HyperCard for any length of time, especially if you belong to a Macintosh user group or electronic bulletin board, you have probably heard the term "resources" bandied about freely. But unless you're an experienced Macintosh programmer, you probably wouldn't know a resource if it slapped you on your mouse hand. If that's the case, then this chapter will bring you up to speed quickly on the concept of Macintosh resources. You'll need to know what we say here if you hope to understand icons, sounds and external commands for HyperCard.

The Resource Concept

In typical computer programs for machines other than the Macintosh, most of the screen design elements, like menus, boxes, and so on, are defined within the program itself. A long program listing might be divided into several units which are compiled into one running application file.

To anyone who has used a compiler on a long program, the time it takes to compile—perhaps a minute for small programs to over one-half hour for big ones—feels like dead time, because there's nothing you can do while the computer is turning hundreds or thousands of lines of Pascal, C, or Assembler code into an executable program file. Therefore, you can see the frustration that might accrue in a very graphics-oriented environment like the Macintosh, in which very fine adjustments of elements such as dialog boxes, pull-down menu wording and art for an icon or other fixed graphic element, are necessary. Even changing the size of a dialog box by one pixel would mean recompiling the entire program again.

That also counts for the instances when a software program needs to be translated into another language for marketing in another country. Menu items, window titles, dialog and alert boxes—all these elements have to be translated into the native language of the target market. Even in English, spellings change, as in "color" and "colour." When the text for these items is buried within the program code, it makes translation—*localization*, it's called— difficult. And you must tamper with the program code to do it.

Recognizing these difficulties, the Macintosh design team came up with a brilliant solution: *resources*. The idea was to separate the specifications for these visual elements (or other elements that might change for localization) from the main program. In fact they're so separate that these elements may be modified without digging inside the program code or recompiling the program. Moreover, the Mac team designed resources in such a way that as long as you know the format for the information the elements need, you can write the resources without arcane programming code. Resources may also be added, deleted, copied and pasted to files by non-programmers, provided they have the right resource editing tools.

Macintosh Files—Data and Resources

When you see the representation of a Macintosh file on the Desktop, or see a file name in a standard file dialog box, you consider it as a single entity. An application or a document might have different purposes, but each appears as a single file on the disk.

That file, however, may consist of one or two pieces, called *forks*. One, the *data fork*, generally contains data that the user creates and saves, like the words you type into a word processing document. The other fork, called the *resource fork*, holds all the resource information and specifications for that file.

In line with this discussion, it is informative to see how different kinds of files contain data and resource forks, for a file may contain one, the other, or both forks. CE Software's DiskTop desk accessory lets you display disk directories with more detail than the Macintosh Finder. In addition to the file name and date, you can also see the name of the Creator and File Type (not important for this discussion), plus the sizes of each fork of a file (Figure 23-1).

A Macintosh application is usually all resource fork. That means that the main program code, as well as specifications for things like menus, dialog boxes, and so on, are considered resources. Resources for visual items are separate elements, and may be changed without accessing the main code. About the only time an application has a data fork is if it stores some user information (global settings that the program needs) when the program quits.

A document file, like a word processing file, a spreadsheet, or a fresh

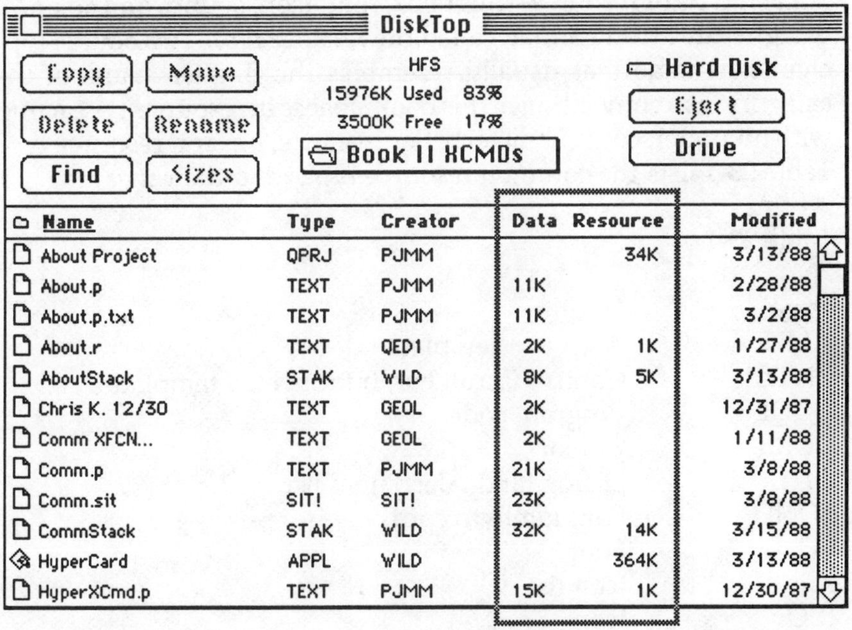

☐ **Name**	**Type**	**Creator**	**Data**	**Resource**	**Modified**
☐ About Project	QPRJ	PJMM		34K	3/13/88
☐ About.p	TEXT	PJMM	11K		2/28/88
☐ About.p.txt	TEXT	PJMM	11K		3/2/88
☐ About.r	TEXT	QED1	2K	1K	1/27/88
☐ AboutStack	STAK	WILD	8K	5K	3/13/88
☐ Chris K. 12/30	TEXT	GEOL	2K		12/31/87
☐ Comm XFCN...	TEXT	GEOL	2K		1/11/88
☐ Comm.p	TEXT	PJMM	21K		3/8/88
☐ Comm.sit	SIT!	SIT!	23K		3/8/88
☐ CommStack	STAK	WILD	32K	14K	3/15/88
☐ HyperCard	APPL	WILD		364K	3/13/88
☐ HyperXCmd.p	TEXT	PJMM	15K	1K	12/30/87

DiskTop window: Copy, Move, Delete, Rename, Find, Sizes buttons. HFS 15976K Used 83%, 3500K Free 17%, 📁 Book II HCMDs. ☐ Hard Disk, Eject, Drive.

Figure 23-1 *As this CE Software DiskTop display reveals, a Macintosh disk file may consist of data only, resources only, or a combination of the two. Application programs are usually completely resources, while documents are usually all data. HyperCard stacks frequently contain both.*

HyperCard stack is all data, and so has only a data fork in it. In HyperCard, everything you see on the screen of most stacks in the HyperCard Stacks folder consists of data forks only. All graphics, fields, buttons and information in fields are information that you bring to the game, so it is all stored as data in the data fork.

You'll learn in a moment that a HyperCard stack can also have resources attached to them. Thus, a HyperCard stack is a case in which a file has both a data and resource fork.

The mechanism that makes resources work is in the Macintosh Toolbox. The Toolbox consists of software built into ROM and the System File that a Macintosh program frequently summons for help in displaying common user interface elements, like windows, menus, and so on. When a program needs to display a dialog box, the program calls a built-in Toolbox routine, which, in turn, draws the dialog based on the specifications spelled out in a resource. Each dialog box has its own resource. A program needing an About dialog, for instance, asks the Toolbox to draw the dialog according to specification in the About box's resource. No matter how many times you adjust and fine tune that dialog box resource, the lines of code in the main program that call the resource never change.

Each type of resource—alert box, font, icon, sound, and so on—has a kind of signature attached to it, called the *resource type*. A resource type is a four-character name that usually resembles the English name of the resource category (as a convention in this book, spaces in resource-type names are filled with an underscore character). For instance, an icon resource type is ICON. Table 23-1 lists the common resource types and their meaning.

Table 23-1.

Type	Meaning
ALRT	Alert box template
CNTL	Control (scroll bar, button, etc.) template
CODE	Program code
CURS	Cursor
DITL	Dialog (and Alert) item list
FOND	Font family record
FONT	Font
ICN#	Icon list
ICON	Icon
MDEF	Menu definition procedure
MENU	Menu
PICT	Picture

WDEF	Window definition
WIND	Window template
snd_	Sound (there is a space after the "d")

Resource type names are case sensitive, meaning that the snd_ resource type must be in lower case letters, as shown in Table 23-1. Within a collection of resources of the same type, each resource must have a unique number (usually in the range of 128 to 32767 for resources created by programmers) and, optionally, a unique text name. The fact that the number and name must be unique only within a given resource type means that you may repeat the number and name in other resource types, even in the same Macintosh file. This comes in handy particularly when a resource of one type depends on specifications from a resource of another type—yes, resources may call other resources. It makes sense, then, to name and number the two related resources identically for ease of maintenance at a later date.

Anatomy of a Resource

It might be instructive at this point to see exactly what information goes into a typical resource. We'll look at what goes into specifying a simple dialog box, like the one shown in Figure 23-2.

There are actually two separate resources that specify a dialog box. One is called the Dialog Template (type DLOG), the other the Dialog Item List (type DITL). We'll take these one at a time.

The DLOG specifications have to do primarily with the overall appearance of the box outline. Therefore, the primary concern is the screen coordinates of the dialog box. Other data that goes into the specification of a dialog is the title of the dialog (although the title doesn't show in a standard dialog box), a reference constant (usually set to zero), a window type (from a library of predefined window styles in the Macintosh Toolbox) and the resource ID number of the DITL resource that has further specifications for this dialog. Figure 23-3 shows this information in an easy-to-use format from one of the

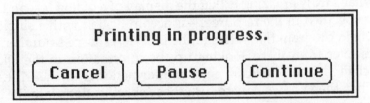

Figure 23-2 *This dialog box is created and displayed with the help of resources.*

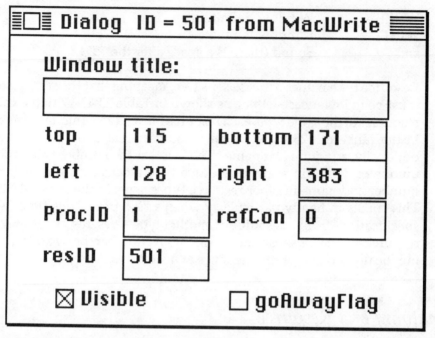

Figure 23-3 *Specifications for a dialog box's size and window style are maintained in a DLOG Template resource. ResEdit provides both a graphic and a textual display of the resource. This is the textual version.*

resource tools we'll be describing later.

All DLOG resources need to call a related DITL resource for information about what goes inside the dialog specified by the DLOG. As its name implies, the Dialog Item List is a list of all the text fields, buttons, and other items that appear in the dialog. Each different kind of item in the list has its own suite of specifications that the DLOG needs to display the box as desired. Round rectangle buttons have coordinates and interior text that are part of the item specification (Figure 23-4). In the case of text that appears in the dialog each time it shows on the screen, those words are part of the item list for a particular text field in the item list. So are the coordinates (within the dialog box) of the field (Figure 23-5).

What's truly amazing is that the display of a dialog box and its contents—once specified in the resources—is accomplished with a single statement in the main program that refers to the DLOG resource's number. The Toolbox takes over from there, looking up the information in the DLOG resource, which in turn automatically fetches information from the DITL resource. The Toolbox then knows how to turn those specifications into the dialog box we see on the screen. There is really very little programming involved for what

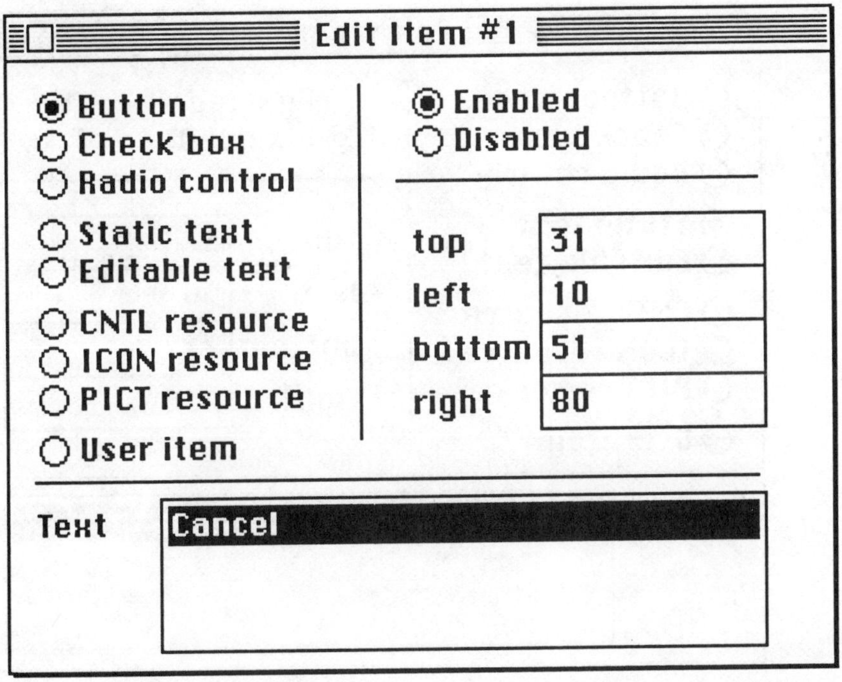

Figure 23-4 *A round rectangle button is one of several dialog items. Coordinates for the button within the dialog box are listed here in ResEdit, as is the text that goes inside the button.*

would be a complex chain of events without the help of the Toolbox.

If the dialog box doesn't turn out exactly the way you expected—perhaps it overlaps a fixed graphic element on an underlying window in an unpleasant manner—you simply use a resource editing tool to change the coordinates of the dialog template. Since the DITL resource items are arranged on the screen relative to the dialog window, those item coordinates needn't be changed when you change a DLOG's coordinates. DITL items will shift on the screen with the DLOG.

HyperCard Resources

If you start looking around your hard disk files with a resource editing tool, you'll notice that most of the resources are attached to application files, as opposed to document files. As you'll recall, document files are usually strictly data, with no resource forks as part of the files. But you can attach resources to document files, which is what all the excitement is about in HyperCard. By

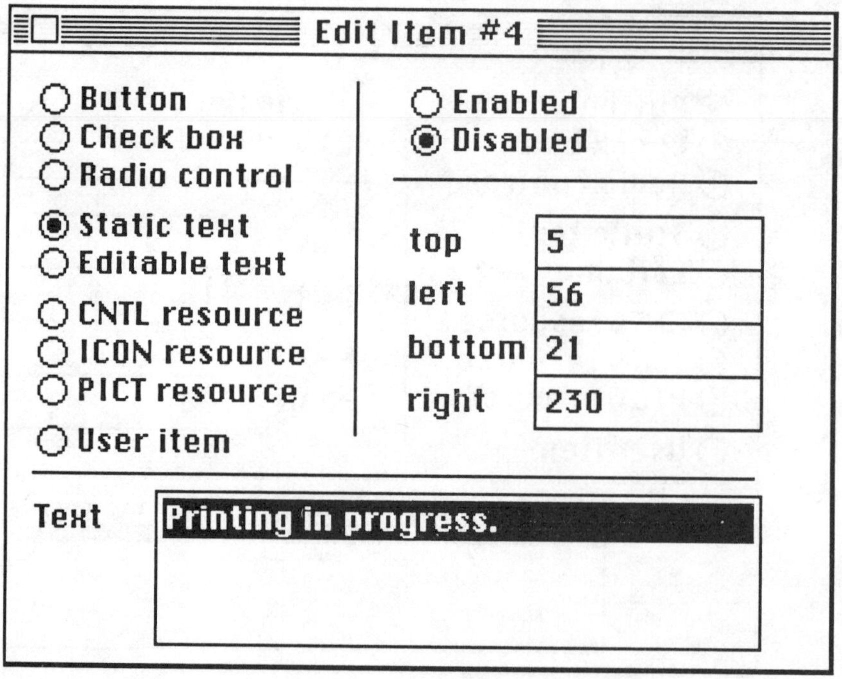

```
┌─────────────────────────────────────────────────┐
│ ▤□▤▤▤▤▤▤▤▤▤ Edit Item #4 ▤▤▤▤▤▤▤▤▤▤▤▤ │
├─────────────────────────────────────────────────┤
│  ○ Button           │  ○ Enabled                │
│  ○ Check box        │  ◉ Disabled               │
│  ○ Radio control    │ ─────────────────────     │
│                     │                           │
│  ◉ Static text      │  top     ┌──────────┐     │
│  ○ Editable text    │          │ 5        │     │
│                     │  left    │ 56       │     │
│  ○ CNTL resource    │          │          │     │
│  ○ ICON resource    │  bottom  │ 21       │     │
│  ○ PICT resource    │  right   │ 230      │     │
│                     │          └──────────┘     │
│  ○ User item        │                           │
│                                                 │
│  Text    ┌──────────────────────────────────┐  │
│          │ Printing in progress.            │  │
│          │                                  │  │
│          │                                  │  │
│          └──────────────────────────────────┘  │
└─────────────────────────────────────────────────┘
```

Figure 23-5 *In the printing dialog box, one field contains static text (i.e., it is not modifiable by the user in the course of running the program).*

attaching resources to HyperCard stacks, you can extend the capabilities of HyperCard.

The resource types you are most likely to add to your stacks are: ICON, CURS, FONT, snd_, XCMD and XFCN. Occasionally, an XCMD or XFCN will call upon one or more other resources, such as ALRT, DLOG, DITL, MENU and PICT types. That's because XCMD and XFCN resources are like small applications programs, which need alert and dialog boxes, menus (or menu derivatives) and bit-mapped pictures.

You are free, of course, to modify or add resources to the HyperCard application file, if you so desire. Like most applications, the HyperCard program file has more resource types than you'll normally wish to fool with, since the program code itself is contained in several resources. The Hyper-Card application already contains quite a few resources of the type you will want to work with. For instance, there are 101 icon resources—all the icons you see in the scrolling dialog box of icons when you specify an icon button. There are also three sound resources (Silence, Harpsichord and Boing) and one XCMD, the one that responds to the Flash command.

While there's nothing illegal about adding to the HyperCard application, it turns out not to be a great idea. First of all, when the time comes to update your HyperCard application to the next release (like going from 1.1 to 1.2), any resources you have in the old version of the application will not be automatically carried over to the new version. You'll have to move them with a resource editing program before you replace the application on your hard disk. If you forget to do this—you tend to forget about resources attached to a file—and you don't have a backup copy of your customized HyperCard file, you'll have lost those resources. Second, I prefer to keep application files in their pristine form on my hard disk. If something goes awry in the operation of the program, I'd hate to think it was the result of my tampering with the program.

Resources and the Hierarchy

You'd think that placing commonly used custom resources in the HyperCard application would assure that they'd be available no matter where you are in HyperCard. But fortunately, the HyperCard object hierarchy also applies to resources. Therefore, if you put ICON, snd_, or XCMD (or any valid type) resources in your Home stack, all other stacks will find those resources.

For example, if you add an ICON resource to your Home stack for a particular kind of icon button you like to use often —perhaps your version of a Home button—you can place the resource for that ICON art in the Home stack. Then, whenever you create a new button in another stack, and invoke the icon dialog box to assign an icon to the button, your own creation will appear in that window. HyperCard knows to get all ICON resources from the current stack, the Home stack and HyperCard itself in assembling that visual list of available icons. Summoning any resource works the same way: sounds, cursors, or XCMDs (note: Other resources called by XCMDs must be in the same file).

Resource Tools

Manipulating resources on HyperCard stacks is fun. They're even more fun when you can create some of the simpler resource types, like cursors and icons, without great trouble or programming expertise. One software tool that is essential in any HyperCard stack developer's library is a utility called ResEdit, which is short for Resource Editor. Produced by Apple Computer, this program is included in most Macintosh language products (at least those that compile code into executable programs), and is readily available from user groups and on-line electronic bulletin boards serving the Macintosh community.

Using ResEdit

Unfortunately, you probably won't get any documentation with ResEdit, unless you get it as part of Apple's Macintosh Programmers Workshop (MPW) development system. We'll get into details of some of the resource editing powers of ResEdit in later chapters, but for now, a quick tour is in order.

When you start up ResEdit (presuming you do so from your hard disk), you see a window in the upper left corner of the screen, with a list of all files and folders in the root directory of your hard disk (Figure 23-6). Miniature folder icons represent folders, while miniature document icons represent documents at the current directory level. You'll notice that there are two styles of document icon. The one with the short lines in it means that the document file has a resource fork in it. If you double-click on the mini-icon, you'll begin your journey through the file's resources. If you double-click on a file lacking a

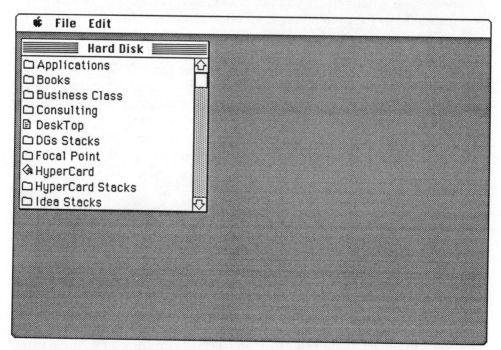

Figure 23-6 *ResEdit opens, revealing the files and folders in your hard disk. Document icons with small lines in them indicate they have resource forks already opened. You double click on a file or folder to open it.*

resource fork, you'll be asked whether you wish to create a such a fork. In succeeding chapters, we'll see how to do this.

Opening the resource fork of a file brings up an overlapping window that lists the resource types of all resources attached to the file (Figure 23-7). Double-clicking on one of the resource types then opens a third window, listing all the resources of that type in the file (Figure 23-8). For each resource, this listing shows the resource name (if one has been assigned) and the resource ID number, which all resources have.

At the level in which you can see listings of individual resources, you may click once on a resource to select it, and then copy it to the clipboard via the Edit menu. To bring that resource to another file, you open that file's resource fork, and paste the resource from the clipboard. That's all there is to moving an existing resource.

From the listing of individual resources, you may double click on a single resource to see what lies inside it. Many resource types are purely compiled computer code, and the resulting window won't mean much to you (Figure 23-9). But several resource types do provide additional windows—some of them graphic—to inspect, create, or modify a resource.

Let's follow the progression into a DLOG and DITL resource pair within

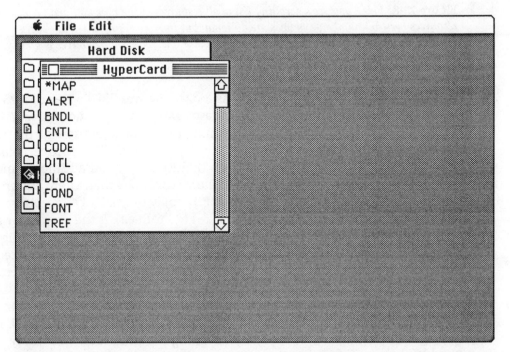

Figure 23-7 *Opening HyperCard, you find a scrolling list of all resource types attached to the application. Double click on one to open it.*

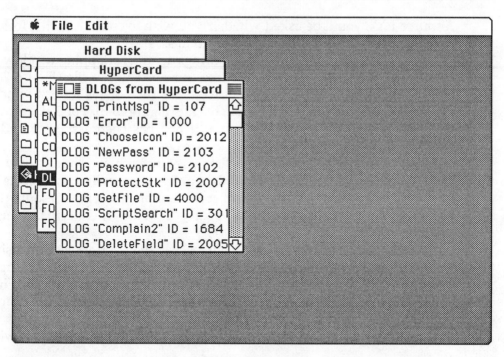

Figure 23-8 *Next, you see a scrolling list of all resources of the type you just opened. All resources have ID numbers. Names are optional, but in HyperCard, virtually every resource is named to make it easy to find a particular one. Naming resources is good practice.*

MacWrite (version 4.5) to see how this looks. Figures 23-10a through 23-10f show the sequence to the actual DLOG resource display for one of MacWrite's dialog boxes. The display shows a miniature representation of the final dialog, including the items from the corresponding DITL resource. Notice that when the DLOG resource appears (Figure 23-10e) an additional menu item, DLOG, appears in the menubar. There is only one menu item under this menu, which lets you change the graphic display of the DLOG resource to a text display, which is shown in Figure 23-11. From either the graphic or text display, you may double click on the window to see the DITL resource (Figure 23-10f). Actually, what you see is a representation of the dialog box sized to the specifications of the DLOG, and whatever items have been specified for the dialog—in this case one field and three buttons.

Clicking once on any item in the window selects the item, and puts a small grow box at the lower right corner of the object's rectangle (Figure 23-10f). You may graphically resize an object by dragging the grow box. You may also double click on any object to get yet another window, like the one shown earlier in Figure 23-4, to define that item. The object's rectangle coordinates

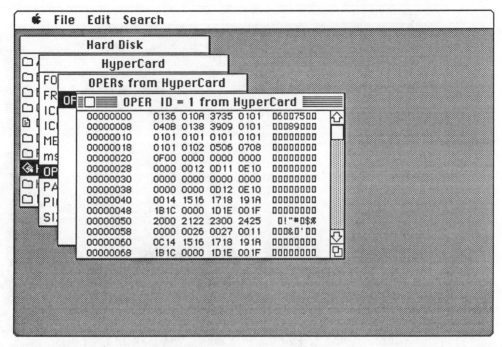

Figure 23-9 *Many resources are simply computer code, like this one. Numbers down the left column are memory addresses (counting from the beginning of the code); numbers in the four middle columns are hexadecimal equivalents of the code; numbers in the rightmost column are ASCII equivalents.*

may be fine tuned this way, and the fixed text may be modified.

To save any changes you make to a resource, you must work your way back up the windows (closing each one) or by closing the file's own window. ResEdit will prompt you on whether you wish to save changes. If you prefer to abandon the changes you've made, then click No. A click of the Yes button makes the changes permanent (until you change them again).

Important: I strongly recommend that you make resource changes to a file only if the file is safely backed up. If the power should dip or some other disaster befall your Mac while messing with resources, the file will likely be permanently damaged. Therefore, back up all files about to undergo resource surgery.

ResCopy

Another useful tool is a utility called ResCopy, written by Steve Maller of Apple Computer. This product is actually an XCMD, which you may therefore call from within HyperCard. It acts like the Font/DA Mover, except

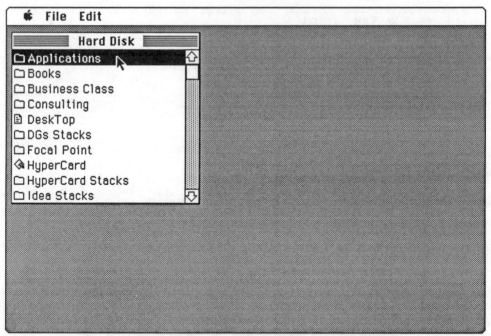

Figure 23-10a *A typical ResEdit sequence leading from the hard disk window to MacWrite's DLOG and DITL resources for a Printing In Progress dialog box.*

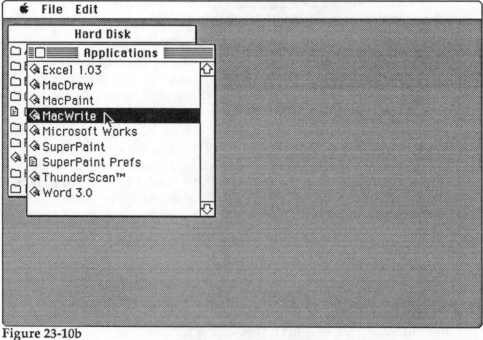

Figure 23-10b

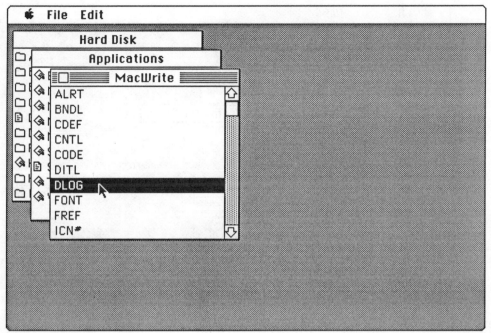

Figure 23-10c

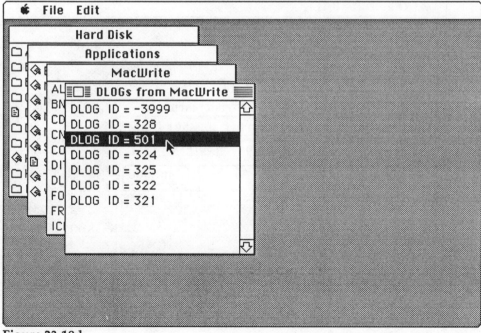

Figure 23-10d

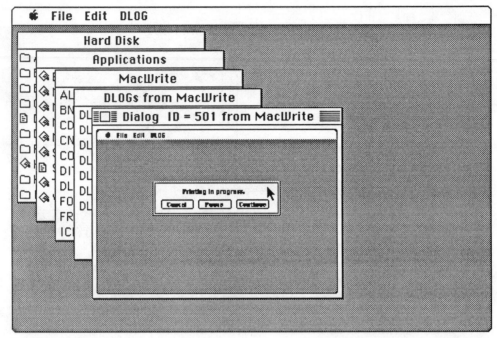

Figure 23-10e

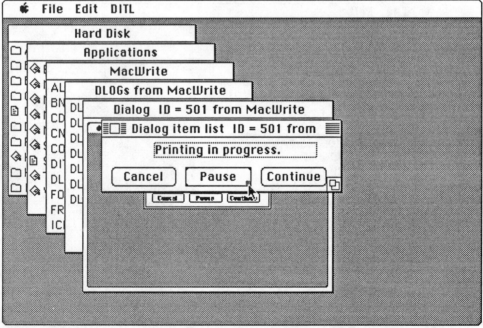

Figure 23-10f

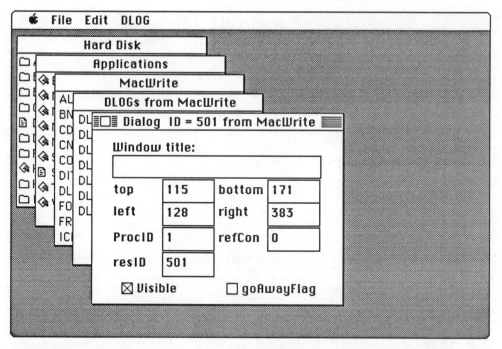

Figure 23-11 *You may inspect the DLOG resource graphically or in this text version. The DLOG menu appears when viewing the DLOG resource.*

that the items you're moving about are all kinds of resources (Figure 23-12). Though nearing completion as this is being written, ResCopy is already finding wide circulation of prerelease copies on bulletin boards and through user groups. It will probably be available through APDA as well.

ResCopy is aimed primarily at HyperCard stack authors, who need to shuffle resources among stacks. To transfer a resource between two stacks, you open two stack files. Each stack's resources appear in lists in their respective windows. Click on the resource you wish to copy (or Shift-click to select more than one), and then click the Copy button. In the blink of an eye, the resource(s) is copied. Each time you click on a resource, its size, in bytes, appears in the window to let you know how much you're adding to a stack file.

You also have a few other options. Aside from the ability to remove a resource from any stack, you may also play HyperCard-compatible sound resource, and both rename and renumber a resource to prevent conflicts with resources previously in the stack. One other nice touch, if you select an icon or cursor resource, is that ResCopy shows you the icon in its window or turns the current cursor to the one you selected. I like this latter feature, because you can try out a cursor from within ResCopy.

Because ResCopy is an XCMD, you can call it up by typing "ResCopy" into

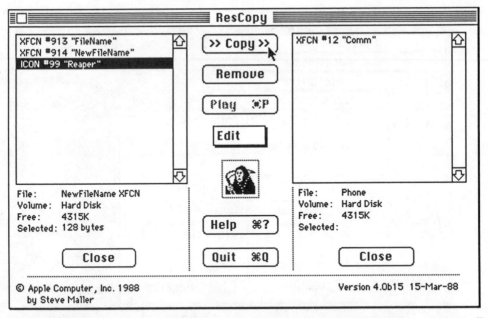

Figure 23-12 *ResCopy by Apple Computer's Steve Maller is an XCMD that you can call up anywhere while in HyperCard and shift resources from one stack to another. You may view icons and cursors, play sounds and rename or renumber resources.*

the Message Box. Its own window temporarily covers the stack card you're viewing, and suspends action on the card. The best place for this XCMD is in the Home stack. That way, no matter what stack you're viewing, you can call the ResCopy window by invoking it from the Message Box.

An additional power of ResCopy is that you can also transfer resources one by one within a script. As an XCMD, ResCopy is also a command. Steve Maller set up the XCMD so that if you pass a predefined set of parameters along with the command, the XCMD will transfer a resource from the current stack to any other stack you specify. Of course, unless you know for sure that the people using your stacks have ResCopy in their Home stacks, you cannot use that command as part of your stack's scripts.

We've flooded you with information about resources in this chapter, to be sure. But stack developers need to know how to incorporate resources into stacks, whether they be simple icons or complex XCMDs. Resources you bring to a stack become the avenues to distinctive stacks—stacks that don't look like they were thrown together using HyperCard's own icons and sounds. They add magic to a stack...a sense of wonder the first time through.

From here we can start getting specific about the kinds of resources you should be investigating for your stacks. We'll also look at additional resource tools designed for each of the key types: icons, sounds and XCMDs.

24

Icon Resources

It seems that one of the first attractions to resources by new HyperCard developers is the ability to create custom icon buttons. The library of 101 icons built into HyperCard have enough of the basics, but application-specific buttons have to be added by stack authors. Unfortunately, HyperCard does not include an icon utility for making and moving icon resources. On the other hand, ResEdit and other readily available icon tools make it possible for non-programmers to make icon resources.

Icon Basics

The first thing you need to know about an icon is that it may be no larger than 32 pixels square. Figure 24-1 shows enlargements of three familiar

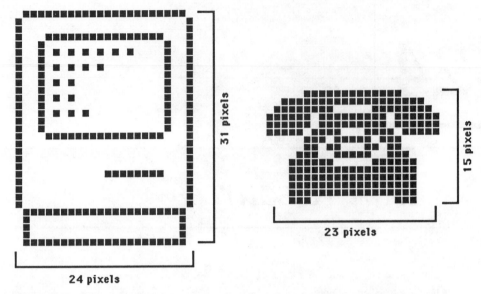

Figure 24-1a *Icons may be no more than 32 pixels square. These enlarged icons show you their pixel counts.*

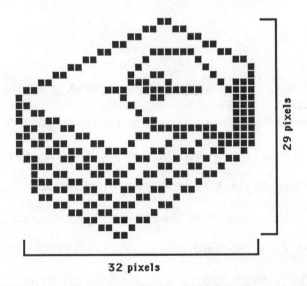

Figure 24-1b *Icons may be no more than 32 pixels square. These enlarged icons show you their pixel counts.*

icons and their pixel measurements. Depending on the message you wish the icon to convey, the area may be sufficiently large or extremely tight. A small telephone or arrow icon, for example, can fit nicely within that space. But in the case of buttons linked to applications (Focal Point, for example), those 1024 pixels must "say" a lot.

Of HyperCard's seven button styles, only the check box and radio button styles don't display an icon that you might specify for that button. But all the others—transparent, opaque, rectangle, shadow and round rectangle—display icons (Figure 24-2). When an icon button also displays the name of the button (Show Name is checked in the Button Info dialog box), the name appears in Geneva font. Only when a button is designated an icon button are you prevented from changing the font of the button. In fact, if you create a new button, assign an icon to it, and check Show Name, the button "thinks" its text font is the default style, Chicago, even though the display is genuinely Geneva. No amount of setting the textFont property of an icon button will change that.

As you create icon buttons and attach them to various stacks on your hard disk, icons like all resources, observe the object hierarchy of HyperCard. Thus, if you attach an icon resource to your Home stack, all stacks on your hard disk will have access to that icon. But if you give the stack to someone else who doesn't have that resource in their Home stack, the icon button in the stack will be blank. The stack can't find a matching icon resource for the one specified by the button.

In the real world of designing stack systems for others to use, you must include the icon resources in each stack of a stack system. In some controlled instances, such as in-house stack distribution in a business or academic environment, it may be permissible to include a routine in the stack system's installation routine to copy the resources to the Home stack's resources. But for stacks going out to the general public, I advise against modifying the Home stack. True, your installation program could ask for permission from the user to modify the stack by adding icon resources, but what if the user says "No?" The resources must be in every stack of a stack system, as they are in *Focal Point* and *Business Class*. It may add to the overhead on the distribution disks,

Icon Button Styles

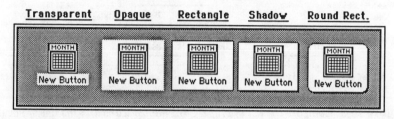

Figure 24-2 *Five of the seven button styles let you display an icon. Simply choose an icon from the Icon dialog box. Showing the name is optional.*

but it also eliminates possible product support headaches, since icon resources become a non-issue.

One other point you should be aware of. The first release of HyperDA (Symmetry Corp.), a desk accessory that lets you browse through HyperCard stacks from within any other application, does not check for a stack's resources. Thus, even if your icon resources are attached to each stack of a stack system (or to the Home stack, for that matter), HyperDA will not show those icons. The buttons will be active, but they'll be blank areas on the screen.

Creating an Icon Resource

Before we get to the nuts and bolts of creating icons, I must stress the importance of naming your icon resources. In the early days of HyperCard development, it was less important, because the ResEdit tool to move icons was graphical in nature. But with the advent of ResCopy, the shifting of resources from stack to stack is a much easier procedure, and resource names make it easier to find a specific button (or other resource) in a long list. For example, Figure 24-3 shows examples of the well-named icon resources built into HyperCard (left) and the unnamed icon resources in the first release of

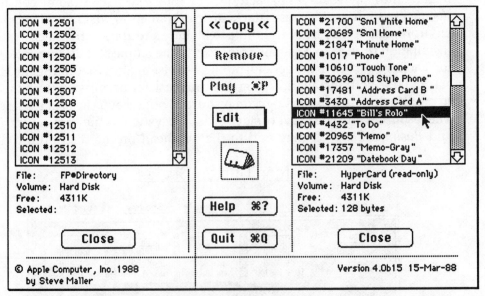

Figure 24-3 *Compare the list of HyperCard named icons and the list of Focal Point unnamed icons in ResCopy. With tools like ResCopy available, it makes sense to name all resources, like the ones in Focal Point should have been.*

Focal Point (right). While ResCopy lets me click on any icon resource and view the icon, having names as part of the resource specification certainly makes the job of identifying and copying icons much easier.

With that warning out of the way, we can focus on making icon resources from scratch. The software tools you need are rather simple, it turns out: HyperCard, the Scrapbook desk accessory and ResEdit.

Preparations

The overall sequence of events begins with creating the bit-mapped art for the icon with the painting tools of HyperCard. Next, you copy the art into the Scrapbook, where it automatically becomes a PICT resource in the Scrapbook file. Opening ResEdit, you create a new, blank icon resource in the stack file you wish the button to go. Then you copy the PICT from the Scrapbook and paste it into the ICON resource. All that's left is naming the resource and quitting ResEdit to save the resource to the stack file.

If you plan to do this kind of icon creation a lot, there are some preparations you can make to ease the way for future work. First, write a small handler in your Home stack that launches ResEdit from whichever stack you may be in. You can give it any message name you like. Here's what that handler looks like in my Home stack:

```
on resEdit
  open "Hard Disk:Programming:Utilities:ResEdit"
end resEdit
```

Now I can get to ResEdit by typing resEdit into the Message Box at any time.

A second preparation you can make is to create a small new stack that features a 32-pixel square template in which you may design your icon. The reason I like using HyperCard for this instead of MacPaint or similar bit-mapped paint program is that the background and card layering helps matters. The 32-pixel square template should go into the background layer, while you work with the icon art in the card layer.

Laying out the template requires a bit of care. First of all, it is the *internal* space that must be 32 pixels on each side. That means that you should start by drawing a square with 34 pixels on a side (Figure 24-4a). Because the solid lines of the template may interfere with your design, you can lighten the template outline by selecting the gray pattern from the Patterns menu and touching the tip of the Paint Bucket tool to the outline. Instantly the template becomes a less intrusive dotted line (Figure 24-4b).

A second part of this template goes into the card graphics layer. Using the dotted line template in the background as a guide, draw two straight lines to

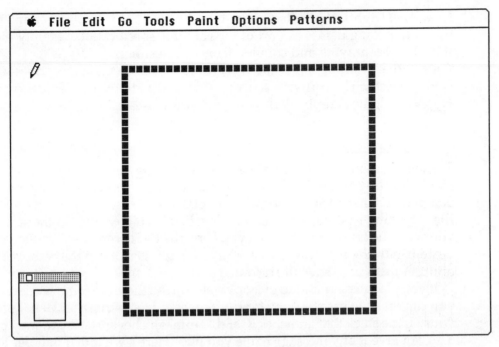

Figure 24-4a *Create a template for icon design by drawing a 34-square-pixel rectangle in the background graphics layer. Choose the gray fill pattern. Then touch the outer line of the square with the paint bucket tool to dim the outline (Figure 24-4b).*

cover the right and bottom sides of the template (Figure 24-5). Lasso the lines and drag them away from the template into a safe corner of the card. Verify that they are each a total of 34 pixels long (including the bottom right corner pixel).

Applying the Art

Now, in the card graphics layer, you may copy and paste art from any bit mapped art you like (desk accessories like Art Grabber or Artisto let you view and copy selections from MacPaint and FullPaint pictures without leaving your template card in HyperCard). Just make sure the art fits inside the dotted line (Figure 24-6). It is important that you center the art within the template as best you can.

The last stage of the HyperCard end of the process is to lasso and drag a copy (hold down the Option key before dragging) of the solid line template corner created earlier. Position the lines so they cover the dotted lines of the template (Figure 24-7). These lines will ensure that the location you specified for the art within the icon template will be the same location of the art in the

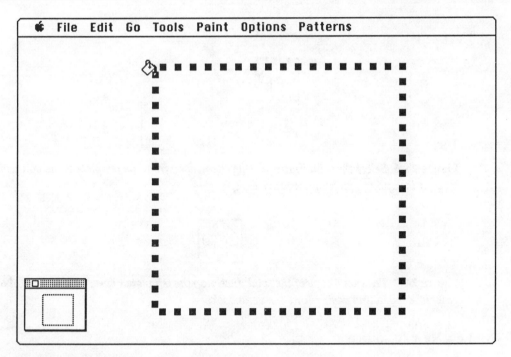

Figure 24-4b

icon resource.

To copy the art into the Scrapbook, choose the Selection tool, hold down the Option key and drag a marquee around the icon art. When you release the mouse button, the marquee will "snap to" the square of the icon art and corner lines. Choose Copy from the Edit menu (or type Command-C). Next, open the Scrapbook desk accessory, and choose Paste from the Edit menu (or type Command-V). Close the Scrapbook window.

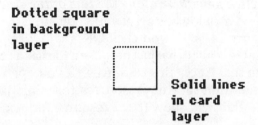

Figure 24-5 *Draw solid lines in the card graphics layer to cover the right and bottom lines of the icon template.*

Figure 24-6 *Select the solid lines and drag them away from the template while you work on your icon design with the painting tools.*

Figure 24-7 *Position a copy of the solid lines atop the template. Lasso the entire card layer graphic, copy it, and paste it into the Scrapbook.*

Make a New Resource

If you wrote a Home stack handler to launch ResEdit, then type that handler's message into the Message Box and press Return. Otherwise, do what you must to open ResEdit.

For purposes of instruction, we'll assume that the icon you just created is to be the first icon resource in a new stack. Thus, we will go through the process of creating a resource fork in a stack, as well as making the new resource.

1. *Open folders in succeeding ResEdit windows until you can see the listing for your stack.*
   If there is no resource fork for the stack, the miniature document icon will be blank inside.

2. *Double click anywhere along the line of the stack name.*
   A beep and a dialog box greet you, indicating that the file has no resource fork (Figure 24-8). If you click OK, that will open a resource fork. It's important to realize that just because a file has a resource fork opened does not mean that it contains resources. If you open the resource fork of this file and then don't add any resources, the miniature document icon for this file in ResEdit will show that a resource fork exists.

3. *Click the OK button to open the resource fork.*

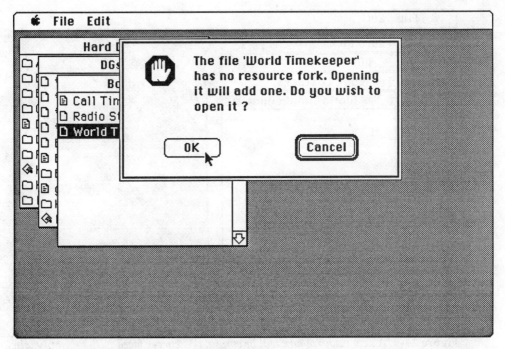

Figure 24-8 *If you open a document file whose resource fork is not yet created, you'll be alerted that you're about to create that fork.*

Another window opens, representing the resource fork for the file (Figure 24-9). It is empty.

4. *Choose New from the File menu to create a resource category.*
   A dialog box appears asking you to specify the name of the resource you wish to create (Figure 24-10). You may choose from the scrolling list of predefined resource names, or, for programmers who know how to do such things, type in a new resource name.

5. *Scroll until you see the ICON resource name and click on its name in the list.*
   "ICON" is typed into the little box for you.

6. *Click the OK button.*
   Yet another window appears. In a file that has icons already installed as resources, the icon art for each appears in this scrolling window. Since none have been installed for this file, the window is blank (Figure 24-11).

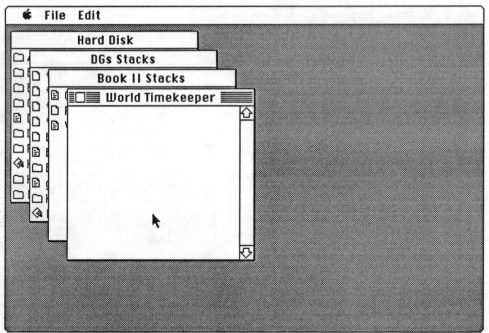

Figure 24-9 *A new resource fork will be empty. Whenever faced with an empty window in ResEdit, and you need to go deeper, choose New from the File menu.*

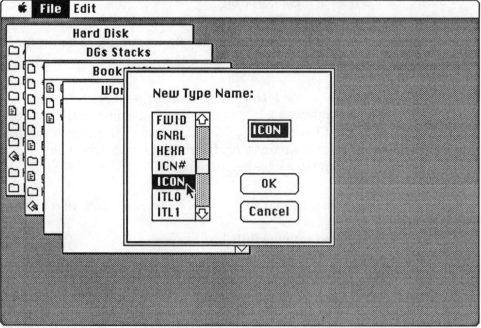

Figure 24-10 *To create a new resource, you may select from the list of common resource types presented in the dialog. Here we want an ICON resource type.*

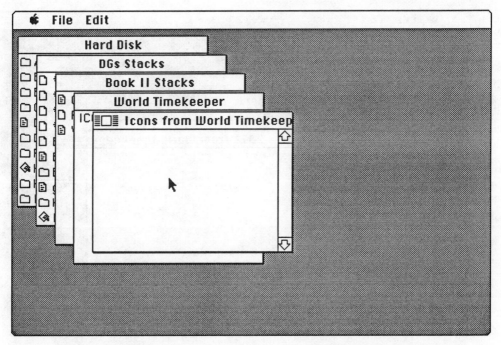

Figure 24-11 *This new, empty window will list all the icons (actually in graphical representations) installed on this stack. For now, choose New from the File menu.*

7. **Choose New from the File menu to open a new resource.**
   The next overlapping window that appears is blank (Figure 24-12). What you don't know by looking at this window is that it is a bit-mapped editing window. Click the mouse somewhere in the left two-thirds of the window. A Fat-bit dot appears under the cursor, while a life-size representation appears to the far right. Click and drag the cursor around the screen. It's just like working in Fatbits mode (Figure 24-13). If you're a good enough artist, you can actually create your icons in this window, rather than in HyperCard or another painting program.

8. **To transfer the Scrapbook picture to this window, first open the Scrapbook—you'll notice that the content of the page holding your art is noted as a PICT resource in the lower right corner—and copy the icon art you just put in there.**

9. **Close the Scrapbook.**
   Fortunately, ResEdit will convert the PICT resource, which you just copied from the Scrapbook, to art that the ICON resource can use.

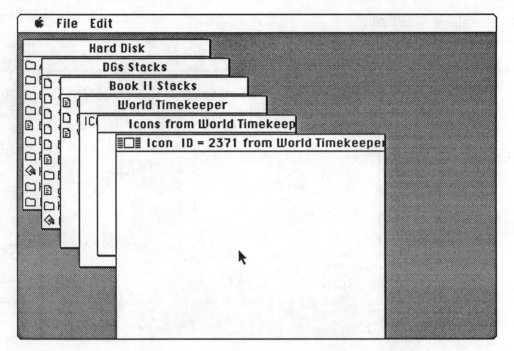

Figure 24-12 *Another blank window opens. But this is an icon editing window. A resource ID number has been automatically assigned by ResEdit. The number may be changed later.*

10. *Choose Paste from the Edit menu.*

Your icon art is now set, except for one thing: the name.

11. *Choose Get Info from the File menu.*

Yet another overlapping window appears (Figure 24-14). You can ignore most of the settings in this window. The ones of importance are the ID number and Name. The ID number in the box was assigned to the icon at random when the resource was created. You may change it now, if you like. Keep ICON resource numbers between a positive 128 and 32767.

12. *Type in the name you wish to know this icon by.*

13. *Close the topmost two windows.*

Note that the picture of the icon now shows in the window of icons for the file (Figure 24-15). The square around the icon art means that the icon is currently selected.

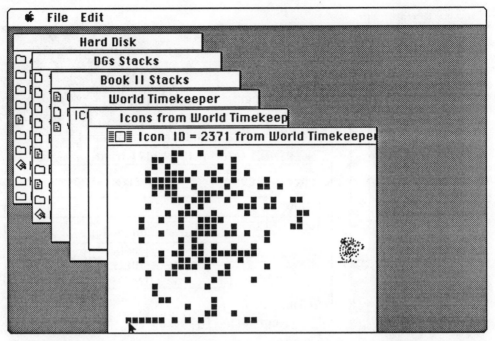

Figure 24-13 *Start dragging the mouse around the left three-quarters of the screen to see the Fatbit-style editing you have. A life-size replica of your drawing appears at the far right of the window. Copy your art from the Scrapbook and paste it into this window.*

14. Close two more windows.

You'll be prompted whether ResEdit should save the changes you made to the file (Figure 24-16). If the icon is as you like it, then click the Yes button. The icon resource is now a part of that file.

15. Quit ResEdit and open that HyperCard stack.

16. Create a new button and summon the list of icons.

Your icon will be in the list, ready to assign to any button in that stack (Figure 24-17).

The first couple of times you do this procedure, it seems like a lot of steps. But with practice, you find yourself whisking your way through ResEdit to get to the desired window for pasting the art into the resource and naming the resource.

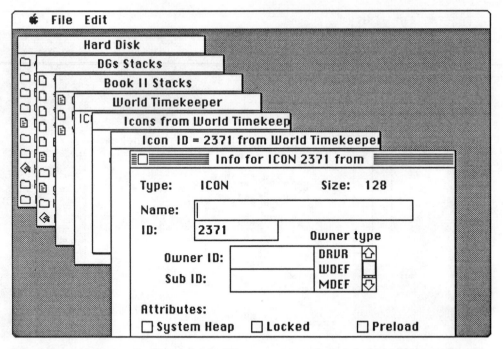

Figure 24-14 *Choose Get Info from the File menu to see the info box on this icon. You should type a name for the resource. If the ID number is between 128 and 32767, then you don't have to adjust the number now.*

Commercial Tools

A new icon creation tool, called Icon Factory (HyperPress Publishing), automates a lot of the process of creating an icon resource from an existing work of bit-mapped art. It also includes useful icon editing tools. Interestingly, the application is itself a HyperCard stack, albeit one loaded with some very sophisticated XCMDs.

The feature I like best about Icon Factory is its SnapShot option. When you click on the SnapShot button of the Icon Factory stack, a small window appears, letting you navigate to other stacks. The cursor becomes a square the size of an icon. Position the cursor atop any chunk of art you wish to turn into an icon and click the mouse button, such as the small organization chard in Figure 24-18. The art appears in the SnapShot window, showing you what the resulting icon would look like.

When you return to the Icon Factory stack, you can save it to an area on the

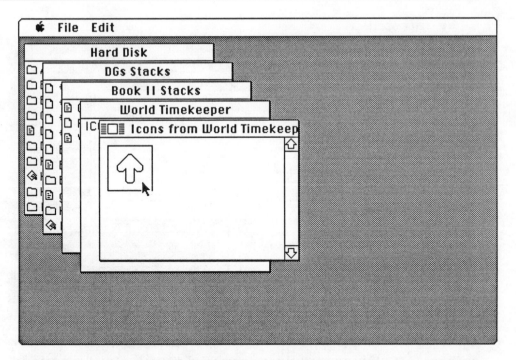

Figure 24-15 *After passing the art into the editing window and closing windows back to the Icons window, you now see the sole icon resource for this stack.*

screen called the Icon Editing Area. Here you can edit the art pixel by pixel in Fatbit mode (Figure 24-19). Several buttons surrounding the editing area let you shift the image one row or column of pixels at a time, flip and rotate the art, or reverse the art (turn white pixels to black and vice versa).

After the icon art is defined to your satisfaction, you may then use Icon Factory to save the icon as an ICON resource to whatever stack you like. No messing with ResEdit. If the ResEdit method of creating icon resources becomes tedious, then it might be a good idea to buy a copy of Icon Factory for your development arsenal.

Extracting Icons

Many exploring HyperCard authors have wanted to use the icons from applications programs within their own stacks. This is especially true for stacks written to act as Minifinders, launching other applications and documents. The problem has been that the icons you see in the Finder for an application and its documents are of a different icon resource type than the

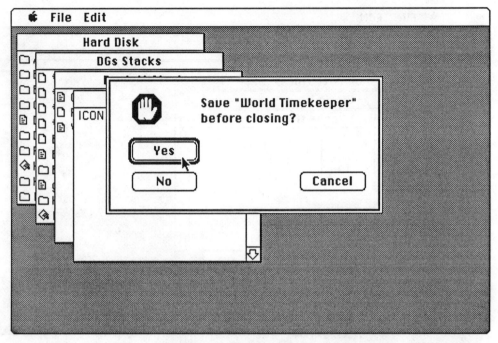

Figure 24-16 *When you try to close the stack's ResEdit window, you'll be asked whether you wish to save changes. Click Yes if you want to use the icon.*

ones used in HyperCard stacks. Icons you see in the Finder are of the ICN# type, which means Icon List (don't ask me how it means that, just take my word for it). Trying to copy an ICN# resource into the clipboard or Scrapbook and then pasting into a new ICON resource just doesn't work. Even though they look the same, they're really apples and oranges.

Icon Factory, mentioned above, lets you grab an ICN# resource from any file, bring it into the editing window, and then save the art as an ICON resource to any stack file you like. It's very simple to do.

The author of Icon Factory, James L. Paul, also wrote a separate application, called Icon Extractor, which was a precursor to a few features in Icon Factory. Icon Extractor was distributed as a shareware product (it's a standalone program), and is available on CompuServe and user groups that distribute public domain and shareware products on disk.

Icon Extractor is more of a "brute force" method of extracting all ICN# type resources from one file (like an application file) and tossing them all into a HyperCard stack file as ICON resources. The program pulls all ICN# resources from an application file at once, rather than selectively, as in Icon Factory. In any case, this extraction feature of Icon Factory just adds to the

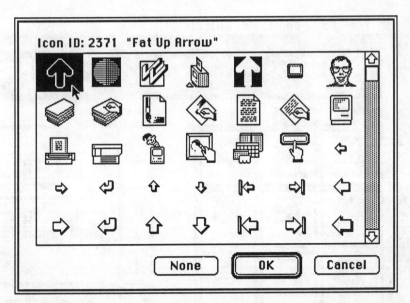

Figure 24-17 *The next time you specify an icon button for that stack, the new button will be in the icon list.*

Figure 24-18 *HyperPress' Icon Factory utility offers a SnapShot facility that lets you grab art from any HyperCard card and turn it into an icon. Here, it's grabbing the small organization chart from the Art Ideas stack.*

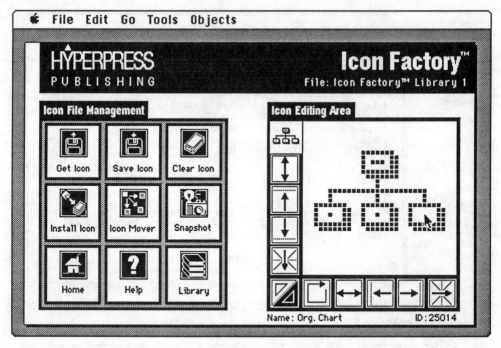

Figure 24-19 *Bringing the captured art back into Icon Factory, you may edit the art in a Fatbit mode. Buttons let you shift art one pixel at a time in any direction, rotate, or invert it. The program (which is a stack itself) automatically converts the art into an ICON resource.*

value of Icon Factory as a developer's tool.

Working with icons and icon buttons in HyperCard is fun. And since the tools needed to add icon resources to your stacks don't take a degree in computer science to use, everyone is encouraged to get creative in interesting button design.

25

Sound Resources

Icon buttons aroused early interest in HyperCard stack resources, but incorporating sound was a puzzle to many. While some developers immediately discovered the power of digitizing fresh sounds and turning them into resources, others had large sound libraries that they wanted to bring into their stacks. They could make some sounds work, but not others. Even sound resources that came with the Macintosh System (4.2) didn't work with HyperCard. It was very frustrating.

While fathoming the entire scope of Macintosh sounds (including startup sounds, beeps, and so on) is beyond the nature of the book, HyperCard sounds are not. This chapter will attempt to identify the problems facing sound conversion and then provide guidance in creating sounds for your HyperCard stacks.

Why Sounds?

Although the Macintosh has had a four-channel sound system built into the hardware since the very first machine rolled off the assembly line, most programmers have not given sound much attention (music software programmers notwithstanding). The fact is, sound is a new medium for the computing world, largely due to the sound playing abilities of HyperCard, and the improved sound hardware of the Macintosh II. Suddenly you can buy external hardware devices that record live sound for use within programs. And not just for beeps and startup sounds, but for meaningful additions to a product's user interface.

Because sound is such a new medium, there is little in the way of a standard in the way sound is to be used in applications. It wasn't until Volume 5 of *Inside Macintosh* that the User Interface Guidelines included a section on sound.

Using Sound in a Program

Sound, particularly in a HyperCard stack, can be used two ways. One is as a notification device for any number of program events: getting the user's attention after a long, automated procedure; highlighting an alert error message; or signifying the transition between operational modes in a program (analogous to going from card to background mode in HyperCard). In such uses, it is critical for the sanity of the user that the sounds chosen be short, non-melodic (how many times do you want to hear a little tune?) and not intrusive to the operation of the program. Most importantly, don't put in so many different sounds that the user thinks the Macintosh is a music machine, instead of a productivity machine.

The second application of sounds is when the sound itself is the information being stored and retrieved. For example, a series of HyperCard stacks written by Martin Rice teaches Russian language reading and pronunciation by including digitized voices of native speakers. A history stack may offer some background music from a period of time covered by the text and graphics on the screen.

With only a few exceptions, the applications of sound in HyperCard stacks thus far have been primitive. But it's a new medium for most of us, and we'll improve our sound skills over time, just as our graphics skills have improved from the early Macintosh days.

Digitized Sound

If you're new to the realm of computerized sound, then the terms "digitizing" and "sampling" might be foreign to you. Here are some of the basics of Macintosh sounds.

All sounds generated by the Macintosh are digital sounds, because they are stored as a long sequence of digital data—ones and zeros in their most basic construction. When sound is recorded by a digitizer, it takes thousands of audio snapshots of the sound each second (coming in through a microphone or audio line connected to a source such as a cassette tape or compact disc) and converts the sound into a digital representation of that slice. In other words, the sound is "sampled" thousands of times per second. The more often a sound is sampled, the greater the fidelity, just like the more animation frames you see per second, the smoother, more lifelike the motion is. The speed (number of times per second) at which the sound is sampled is called its *sampling rate*. The maximum sampling rate the Macintosh can handle is 22 kiloHertz—22,000 times per second. Many of the sounds you find in sound collections from user groups have been sampled at 11 kiloHertz, which provides fairly good sound on the Mac. The greater the sampling rate, the more disk storage space required for the sound. Unfortunately, sounds take up a huge amount of disk space per second.

Audio digitizers usually come with software to help you manipulate the sound once it has been recorded and stored in the Mac's memory. These programs generally present a graphic representation of the sound waves generated by the sound. If you know how to work with these sound waves or just like to experiment, you can modify the wave with the software or simply strip out unnecessary silence before and after the core sound you're after. Once you're satisfied with the sound, you save it to disk as a sound data file. These are the files that can be turned into startup and beep sounds with the help of utility programs available from most user groups. These sound files may not be used directly with HyperCard stacks, however.

Macintosh Sound Resources

The sounds used in programs other than music programs are generally stored as resources. This has not always been the case, nor has there always been a standard resource type that applications developers could count on. But today, the Macintosh system has settled on a resource of type snd_—lower case letters with an extra space at the end to make up a valid name of a four-character resource type.

There's nothing very visual about the content of a sound resource. After a little bit of information about the resource type at the beginning of the resource's code, the rest is predominantly code that represents the sound itself. But to make matters even more confusing, there are actually two different ways that snd_ resources can be formatted internally. These are known as Type 1 and Type 2 (also as Format 1 and Format 2). Type 2 resources assume that the sound is digitized, and thus only one Macintosh synthesizer channel (the one dedicated to sampled sound) is used for the sound; a Type 1 resource opens specific channels (of the four) for sound output. The formats of the two types are so different from each other that few programs can accept both.

Now, the real sad news is that you cannot tell from the name of the resource which type it is. In a resource utility like ResEdit or ResCopy, all such resources appear as snd_ resources, and that's it. It takes investigation into the actual resource code to figure out which is which.

HyperCard requires Type 2 snd_ resources (some sounds that come with HyperCard are erroneously labeled Type 1 resources internally, yet their data seems to be compatible with Type 2—thus Type 1 resources are not guaranteed to work with HyperCard, while Type 2 resources are). The snd_ resources delivered with System 4.2 are Type 1 snd_ resources (accessible only with a Macintosh II). Steve Maller's ResCopy XCMD not only copies sound resources from one file to another, but if it encounters a Type 1 snd_ resource in the source file, it will try to convert it to a Type 2 before depositing it into the HyperCard stack file. This isn't always successful, primarily due to the complexities of some sounds. Of the four Type 1 sounds in System 4.2, ResCopy can convert two of them—Monkey and Bong—into Type 2 resources that HyperCard can use. Just knowing that ResCopy tries to do the right thing with sound resources is reason enough for me to stick with ResCopy to move snd_ resources from non-HyperCard files to HyperCard stacks.

I've also encountered some sound resources that were not of type snd_. I'm not sure where these resources came from, but they are obviously resource types defined by early sound programs, whose designers were on the right track of storing sounds as resources.

Converting Existing Sounds

Many of the user group disks and electronic bulletin boards have libraries of sounds that Macintosh users have made with audio digitizers. These files for the most part have been created with sound software called *SoundCap* (for Sound Capture) or a later version of the program, called *SoundWave*. Sound-

Cap was packaged with an audio digitizer from a small company called MacNifty. *SoundWave* is part of the software package that today comes with a digitizer from Impulse Inc.

These two programs produce sound files that may be used as startup and beep sounds for the Macintosh. You'll recognize these files when you see them by their icons, as shown in Figure 25-1. If you check these files with ResEdit, you'll see that they are strictly data files, with no resource forks whatsoever. To use these sounds in HyperCard, then, you need to convert these sound files into Type 2 snd_ resources.

Fortunately, when HyperCard was released, a package of utility tools was also released by the Apple Programmers and Developers Association. The package included rather technical information on creating XCMDs, and also a sound conversion stack. This stack contained an XCMD, called SoundCap-ToRes, which extracted sound data from SoundCap files and created a Type 2 snd_ resource with that sound.

That XCMD is still valuable today, and is included with software from Impulse. A new stack, called Sound Convert 1.0 written by Kelly E. Major (also available from user groups and bulletin boards), simplifies the matter of choosing SoundCap or SoundWave files for conversion into snd_ resources (Figure 25-2). The utility, which puts a friendly front end on top of the original SoundCapToRes XCMD even places the new resources in a stack of your liking.

HyperSound

A newer audio digitizer, the MacRecorder from Farallon Computing, includes standalone software for manipulating sounds sampled by its digitizer, as well as a stack that lets you record and instantly save the sound as a HyperCard resource (Typed 2 snd_ resource), bypassing the conversion process (Figure 25-3). This program points in the direction that future sound tools for

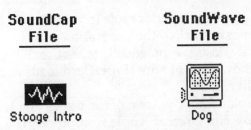

Figure 25-1 *Two common sound files and their icons: SoundCap and SoundWave. These sounds may be converted into HyperCard sounds.*

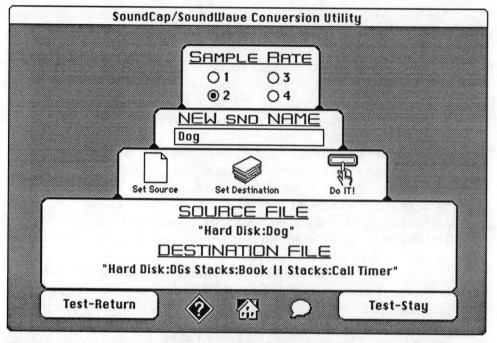

Figure 25-2 *Sound Convert 1.0 is a sound utility stack that lets you convert SoundCap or SoundWave files into HyperCard sound resources and attach the resources to specific stacks.*

HyperCard will be taking. Making the sound recording and editing process a HyperCard stack is a natural progression. The MacRecorder and Hyper-Sound stack are so simple to use (the handheld MacRecorder plugs into either of the Mac's serial ports) that it's the system I prefer for making HyperCard sounds.

Producing Sound Stacks

When sound plays an important role in your stack—primarily in information publishing types of stacks—the integration of sound into the graphic presentation is a critical issue. It practically takes the skill of a video producer with an intimate knowledge of how HyperCard loads and plays sounds to pull it off successfully.

The best explanation I've seen of the issues involved in such a production is the article by Tim Oren of Apple Computer. The article appeared in two installments in HyperAge magazine. The magazine has kindly granted

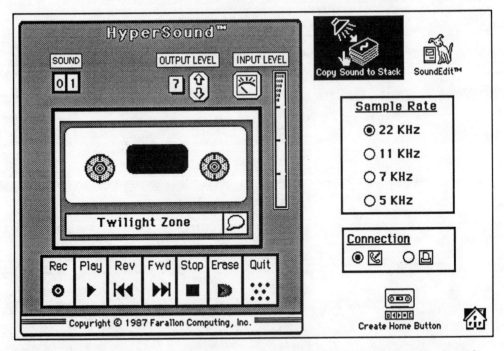

Figure 25-3 *Farallon Computing's HyperSound is a stack that works interactively with the company's MacRecorder sound digitizing hardware. You record sound directly into this stack, which, in turn, converts the sound into a HyperCard sound resource. This is a first-rate implementation.*

permission to reprint that article series as Appendix B. It is an important document that all sound-oriented stack developers must read. The article also provides hints on developing HyperTalk tools to help in the creation of a sound-and-graphics slide show presentation.

26

Introduction to XCMD and XFCN Resources

Adding an XCMD to a stack reminds me of adding a room to a house, especially if that room has a special purpose. For instance, if you like to do woodworking, at first you may try to stash some of your tools in the garage, and work around the car the best you can. No matter how you do it, though, using the garage for a wood shop is awkward. It's possible, but not practical or efficient. But add a room to the house to act as your wood shop, and suddenly you're a cabinetmaker. There's plenty of workspace, room for better power tools—just the right environment.

HyperCard and XCMDs are the same way. You may be able to perform certain complex operations with HyperTalk, but they perform slowly or don't measure up to the real goals you have in mind. But tack an XCMD onto the stack written for those operations, and suddenly the stack takes on the power of a real Macintosh application.

What Is An XCMD?

The term XCMD stands for "external command," while its counterpart, the XFCN, stands for "external function." As we have done throughout the book, we'll continue to lump both together under the term XCMD, unless stated otherwise. The four-letter names are actually four-character resource types (like ICON, MENU, etc.) because XCMDs, as you'll soon see, are strictly resources.

An XCMD is a subroutine, to which your HyperTalk script jumps. It's like detouring to a custom handler or user-defined function, except the XCMD or XFCN is not written in HyperTalk. Instead, it is written in Pascal, C, or Assembler and, after being processed through a compiler or assembler, attached to a stack as a resource.

A HyperTalk script calls the XCMD by sending a message with the name of the XCMD. In fact, it's as if you've added a word (either a command or a function) to the HyperTalk vocabulary. Thanks to the inner workings of HyperTalk, when a handler sends the message to start the XCMD, handler execution pauses until the XCMD is finished. When an XCMD is finished running its little program, it hands control back to HyperCard, which continues executing the original handler.

XCMD code is like a small program. Unlike HyperTalk, however, the XCMD code is compiled, meaning that all its instructions, originally written in languages like Pascal and C, have been converted to machine language by a language compiler. XCMDs, therefore, tend to run very fast, compared to HyperTalk (an interpreted language as of version 1.2). An XCMD that starts out as thousands of lines of Pascal or C statements can execute faster than 20 lines of HyperTalk code (depending, of course, on the nature of the XCMD and HyperTalk code).

XCMD code is compiled into what is called a code resource (most language compilers offer an option to compile code into a standalone program, a desk accessory, an Fkey, code resource, and so on). A code resource may then be attached to a file with a resource moving tool, just like icons and sounds. The contents of a code resource are gibberish to all but experienced programmers. Figure 26-1 shows the beginning of the code resource for the XCMD in the next chapter, as revealed by ResEdit.

XCMDs can communicate with the HyperCard stack, retrieving values of variables, fetching properties of objects, sending messages to the card, and so on. When you think about it, that's just what HyperCard does. An XCMD,

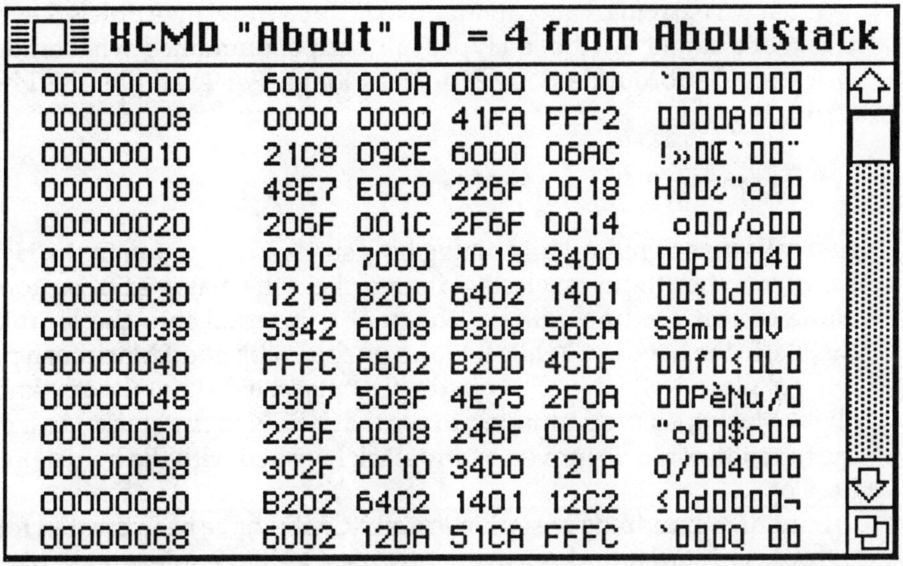

```
≡☐≡ XCMD "About" ID = 4 from AboutStack
00000000    6000 000A 0000 0000    `□□□□□□□    ⬆
00000008    0000 0000 41FA FFF2    □□□□A□□□
00000010    21C8 09CE 6000 06AC    !»□Œ`□□¨
00000018    48E7 E0C0 226F 0018    H□□¿"o□□
00000020    206F 001C 2F6F 0014    o□□/o□□
00000028    001C 7000 1018 3400    □□p□□04□
00000030    1219 B200 6402 1401    □□≤□d□□□
00000038    5342 6D08 B308 56CA    SBm□≥□V
00000040    FFFC 6602 B200 4CDF    □□f□≤□L□
00000048    0307 508F 4E75 2F0A    □□PèNu/□
00000050    226F 0008 246F 000C    "o□□$o□□
00000058    302F 0010 3400 121A    0/□04□□□
00000060    B202 6402 1401 12C2    ≤□d□□□□¬    ⬇
00000068    6002 12DA 51CA FFFC    `□□□Q □□    ▣
```

Figure 26-1 *ResEdit reveals that an XCMD is nothing but code. Hence, when you write an XCMD, the language compiler gives you an option to save the program as a "code resource."*

therefore, is a personal extension of HyperCard for your special purposes.

Why XCMDs?

HyperTalk is a powerful language in and of itself, and developers should not turn away from the language if a solution isn't obvious. You can accomplish a lot with HyperTalk alone. But HyperTalk does not do everything. If you are trying to emulate a standalone Macintosh program, a number of Macintosh system-level elements simply aren't available. I ran into that difficulty when developing *Focal Point*.

In the Document Launcher stack, I wanted a design that would let users create buttons that launched applications, but without forcing them to go inside a button script to write the Open command that did the job. The Macintosh way of doing it would be for a standard file dialog box to prompt the user to select a document and an application. Since HyperTalk by itself didn't have that facility, I turned to a public domain external function, called filename(), which did that for me. HyperTalk worked seamlessly with this function, by taking the data returned by the function (the text of the file's name) and assembling a script for the buttons created by the handler.

What was so remarkable about this XFCN (written by Apple's Steve Maller) was that a single word in a HyperTalk script summoned what amounted to an external subroutine dozens of lines long. For example, the HyperTalk script line

```
put filename() into theFile
```

first calls up a Standard File dialog box, suspending action in the HyperTalk handler. When the user selects a file and clicks the dialog's OK button, the full name of that file (including pathname) is inserted into the local variable, theFile, in the handler. While it took someone with good Macintosh programming skills to write the XFCN in the first place, it didn't take any knowledge about Macintosh programming to *use* that XFCN in my stack. As a resource, the function could be moved to any stack I wished with the help of ResEdit or ResCopy.

Similarly, hundreds of sophisticated XCMDs have been created for special purposes in stacks, and reused in other stacks by people who know nothing about Macintosh programming. All it takes is knowing how the resource works in a HyperTalk script and how to use a resource mover.

Writing Your Own XCMDs

When other peoples' XCMDs aren't enough, however, it may be time to write your own. While this is not a trivial matter for programming newcomers, it is far easier to write an XCMD than to recreate your entire HyperCard application as a standalone Macintosh application. Most of the program can be in HyperCard and HyperTalk, with an occasional jump out to an XCMD for a particular programming task that HyperTalk doesn't do or do well.

Writing an XCMD is not something a non-programmer can hope to learn overnight. It requires a working knowledge of a programming language like Pascal, C, or Assembler and a working knowledge of the Macintosh programming environment. All of that is a tall order, and requires a healthy time commitment. Therefore, while this book so far has not implied any foreknowledge of Macintosh programming, this chapter marks a departure.

Unfortunately, this is not the book to teach you Pascal or C. But once you have a basic understanding of either language, and have an appreciation for the issues involved in programming on the Macintosh, this chapter is where you may start your journey through XCMDs.

Learning Library

To those who are new to Macintosh programming, I suggest you look into the books listed below. One warning, however. The books on learning languages are devoted to specific versions of the language. For instance, one Pascal book is written for Macintosh Pascal, a precursor to LightSpeed Pascal, while the other is tailored to Borland's Turbo Pascal. The book on learning C is tailored to the Hippo C compiler, which, as far as I can tell, is no longer available. Still, the basic language concepts in these books apply to most compilers of the same language. Note, too, that learning the language is only one part of the process; learning to program in the Macintosh environment is another.

Learning Pascal:
> *Pascal Primer for the Macintosh* by Dan Shafer (New American Library)
> *Turbo Tutor* (Borland International)

Learning C:
> *Macintosh C Primer Plus* by Stephen Prata (Bantam Computer Books)

Programming the Macintosh:
> *How to Write Macintosh Software* by Scott Knaster (Hayden Books)
> *Macintosh Revealed*, Volumes 1 and 2 (Second Edition), by Stephen Chernicoff (Hayden Books)

Serious XCMD writers will also want to invest in the five-volume series, *Inside Macintosh* (Addison-Wesley), the reference bible for Macintosh programmers. The Chernicoff series, which is Pascal-based, has most of what's in the first three volumes of *Inside Macintosh*, but in a form that is highly readable and informative. Another worthwhile volume, especially if you're working in Macintosh II territory, is *Macintosh Programming* Secrets by Scott Knaster (Addison-Wesley).

What I particularly like about writing XCMDs is that unlike writing a complete Macintosh application, you don't have to devour all of *Inside Macintosh* (or an equivalent) to start writing XCMDs. Most of the hard stuff about an application is already handled by HyperCard. An XCMD is essentially just a small routine, for which you often don't have to worry about memory management, windows, menus, text editing, and the other interface issues that make Macintosh programming a difficult skill to learn.

I was amazed at the time HyperCard was delivered to see how defensive other language producers became about HyperCard. I believe they saw HyperCard as a threat to their existence, as if HyperCard were going to replace their products as development systems. Actually, the opposite was true. Instead of stealing potential customers from Pascal and C, HyperCard was likely to draw new customers to do XCMDs, who would not otherwise bother buying a Pascal or C compiler. Well, it took several months, but eventually the predominant language suppliers are now offering their versions of the routines that make XCMD creation simpler for their compilers. And that's good news for you if you're new to this.

Before You Go Off To Learn a Language

Pascal, C and Assembler programming environments are different from BASIC, in case you've had any experience there. A typical Pascal or C development environment consists of a text editor and a compiler. You type the actual Pascal or C language code into a text file, very much like a word processing file. The compiler then converts that text file—called the *source code*—into program code, whether it be a standalone program or a code resource for an XCMD. In general, you won't be able to test whether the code works until you compile it and try it. If you discover errors and modify the source code, you must recompile the program and move the resource to your stack to test it again. Fortunately, XCMDs are usually so small that compilation time is insignificant.

To help in compiling, the language producers include a series of "units" that are essentially prewritten source code modules that help your source code make the calls to the Macintosh Toolbox and operating system. During compilation, these units and your source code are combined into a single chunk of executable ("runable") code. A friendly compiler will look through the code being generated during compilation and alert the programmer to syntax errors in the source code. This helps track down errors in your source code before trying the XCMD in the stack and perhaps crashing the system.

Some language environments divide the tasks of compiling your source code and combining it with other libraries into two tasks, called *compiling* and *linking*. Others lump both activities together under the term *compiling*.

In Case You Know A Little Pascal

If you come to XCMDs with an exposure to Pascal, it is critical that you fully understand the concepts of pointers, handles and dereferencing. This is true for most Macintosh programming.

The source code you'll see in the following chapters is written in Light-Speed Pascal. Each compiler has a number of different conventions in the way other units are called and the way the XCMD source code begins. For example, in Macintosh Programmers Workshop Pascal (MPW Pascal), the name of the main XCMD procedure must be called EntryPoint. The Light-Speed Pascal compiler insists that it be called Main, while Turbo Pascal prefers the actual XCMD name. Some compilers require compiler directives (instructions to the compiler) at the top of their code (things like {$R} and {$S} plus the code segment name), while other compilers get their instructions in other ways. LightSpeed, for instance, lets you specify the equivalent of compiler directives in the Project window next to each segment's name (Figure 26-2). XCMD templates for LightSpeed Pascal, LightSpeed C, and Turbo Pascal are provided in Appendixes C, D and E as guides to overall structure.

Calling an XCMD—What Happens

When HyperCard sees that the message you send matches an XCMD or XFCN resource, HyperCard grabs a small chunk of memory to store what is called a parameter block. This *parameter block* acts as a staging area for information that goes back and forth between HyperCard and the resource's code. Here's what that information can consist of:

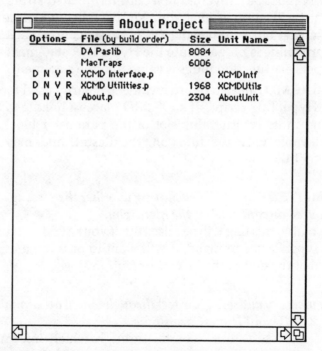

Figure 26-2 *LightSpeed Pascal puts the equivalent of compiler directives in the Project listing (under Options) rather than in the source code listing.*

1. *The number of arguments passed along with the XCMD message.*
For example, the message `flash 10` contains one parameter, 10, which rides along with the message name. Just as any HyperCard message, multiple parameters must be separated by commas.

2. *A list of handles to zero-terminated strings containing the actual arguments.*
On invoking the external code resource, HyperCard creates a handle for each argument and places the content of each argument in another location in memory, recording the handle to that location in an array (a list of handles) within the parameter block. HyperCard builds in space for a maximum of 16 handles to arguments, meaning that an XCMD or XFCN may have no more than 16 arguments that your code can access.

3. *A handle to the zero-terminated text to be returned to HyperCard after execution.*
XFCNs, for instance, usually return some kind of value, just like any HyperTalk function. Since all numbers or text of a returned value are considered as text strings by HyperTalk, the value to be returned from an XFCN must be converted to a zero-terminated string. A handle to that memory location is what your XFCN code must place in this part of the parameter block. When the XFCN passes control back to HyperCard, the return value is plugged into the HyperTalk statement in the same way a HyperTalk function plugs a value into the statement.

An XCMD can also return a value, primarily used for error detection in the HyperTalk script. If an XCMD places a handle to a zero-terminated string in its return value slot of the parameter block, that text will be retrievable with the function, the Result, and may be tested within HyperTalk.

4. *A flag (TRUE or FALSE) denoting whether the message should stop at the resource or continue up the hierarchy.*
Normally, this flag will be false. But if your XCMD is conditioning a built-in HyperCard command, it will want to pass the message up to Hyper-Card at the end of the XCMD execution.

5. *The memory address (pointer) through which all communication between the XCMD and HyperCard flows.*
This address is like a portal through which information flows from HyperCard to the parameter block. Your XCMD then retrieves information from, and posts information to the parameter block in order to communicate with the objects in a card or send messages to HyperCard.

6. **The code number of a request the XCMD wishes to make of HyperCard.**
   HyperCard responds to 29 different requests from an XCMD. Requests can be things like wanting to send a message to a card, obtaining the contents of a specific field or global variable, and so on. These request codes are assigned to constant names in one of the language units that get compiled along with your XCMD code. Your XCMD doesn't use the constant directly. Instead, your XCMD calls a procedure that is part of the glue routines (described below) compiled along with your XCMD code.

7. **A result code, signifying whether the call back to HyperCard was successful.**
   HyperCard sends back to your XCMD one of three possible result code integers (0, 1, 2) depending on whether the call back succeeded, failed, or isn't implemented (not every request has a result code implemented). These codes, too, are assigned constant names in the code unit compiled with your XCMD. A successful call back, for instance, returns the xresSucc ("external result successful") constant in both Pascal and C.

8. **A list of pointers to strings to be sent to HyperCard as arguments to requests.**
   Some requests expect arguments, such as which field's contents to retrieve. Those arguments are put in strings, whose pointers are placed in the parameter block's list of arguments going back into HyperCard (called InArgs). There is space in the parameter block for a total of eight argument pointers.

9. **A list of pointers to argument strings coming back from HyperCard after a request.**
   When a request to HyperCard yields an answer containing arguments, like the contents of a field, pointers to those arguments are stored in the parameter block's list of arguments coming back out from HyperCard (called OutArgs). There is space for four argument pointers.

Once the parameter block is created in memory, HyperCard passes to the actual XCMD code a pointer to the memory location of this block. That pointer is the only link between the XCMD and the parameter block and, in turn, HyperCard. In other words, all communication between your XCMD and HyperCard goes through the parameter block staging area.

Here's a look at how Pascal sees the parameter block:

```
XCmdPtr  =  ^XCmdBlock;
XCmdBlock =
  RECORD
    paramCount :    INTEGER;
    params:         ARRAY[1. .16] OF Handle;
    returnValue:    Handle;

    passFlag:       BOOLEAN;
    entryPoint:     ProcPtr;
    request:        INTEGER;
    result:         INTEGER;
    inArgs:         ARRAY[1. .8] OF LongInt;
    outArgs:        ARRAY[1. .4] OF LongInt;
  END;
```

The above type definitions (the XCmdPtr pointer and XCmdBlock record) are part of the units that must be compiled with your XCMD. That pointer, XCmdPtr, is the sole argument that gets passed to the XCMD code. Your XCMD then uses that pointer as a reference point to retrieve or put information into the various parts of the parameter block—for communicating back and forth with HyperCard.

For instance, to determine whether a call to an XCMD has three parameters sent with it, your XCMD needs to check the paramCount item in the parameter block. One way you'd get to it in LightSpeed Pascal would be as in the following sketch:

```
procedure  myProcedure  (paramPtr : XCmdPtr);
begin
  if (paramPtr^.paramCount = 3) then
    begin
        . . .
      end;
  end;
```

By deferencing the pointer to the parameter block, you have full access to all the items therein.

What You Need to Compile XCMDs

In addition to your XCMD source code and the compiler program (like LightSpeed Pascal or C), you need some additional units called *interfaces* or *glue*. The latter term comes from the fact that the information in these units forms the binding between your XCMD code and HyperCard. XCMD glue consists of two distinct parts: definitions and glue routines.

The definitions consist of the 29 constants for requests and three constants for results, plus the type definitions for the parameter block and the pointer to that block. Most compilers classify this unit as an Interface unit.

The glue routines are short functions and procedures that do the dirty work of communicating with HyperCard. They often condition the data in your XCMD code so that information is in the right spots of the parameter block before jumping back into HyperCard. Let's look at one of these routines in MPW Pascal:

```
PROCEDURE SendCardMessage (msg: Str255);
BEGIN
  WITH paramPtr^ DO
    BEGIN
      inArgs[1]  :=  ORD(@msg);
      request  := xreqSendCardMessage;
      DoJsr (entryPoint);
    END;
END;
```

In a Pascal XCMD statement, the above procedure would be called like this:

```
SendCardMessage(paramPtr, 'set cursor to 4');
```

with paramPtr having been defined in the XCMD as the name of the pointer to the parameter block (`"paramPtr : XCmdPtr"`). In other words, the statement calls the SendCardMessage procedure, passing the pointer to the parameter block as well as the actual string of the message as arguments. In the SendCardMessage procedure, two of the parameter block's blanks are filled in: one with the pointer to the message text, the other with the constant number assigned to the SendCardMessage request code. The DoJsr statement calls another glue routine which does the actual jump from the XCMD code back into HyperCard, by way of the entryPoint location placed into the parameter block when the block was created.

Typically, all the glue routines and definitions are compiled along with an XCMD, but that is not necessary. If there are only a couple of glue routines you need, you can also bring them into your XCMD source code listing, and treat the entire XCMD as one unit (plus the Macintosh Toolbox units that must be compiled with all XCMDs). For convenience, all XCMDs in the following three chapters were compiled with the complete library of definitions and glue routines.

What APDA Sends You

It is strongly recommended that anyone developing XCMDs for HyperCard stacks join the Apple Programmers and Developers Association (APDA) and obtain any available XCMD and XFCN reference material and disks. These include two example XCMDs each in Pascal and C, along with the definitions and glue routines written for MPW.

In MPW Pascal, for example, the compiler files included with the disk consist of a definitions file (HyperXCmd.p) and a file of all the glue routines (XCmdGlue.inc). Both files are provided as working samples, and are not the only way to handle communication between HyperCard and your XCMDs. Because each compiler uses different conventions for compiler instructions and formats for certain parts of the source code listing, these APDA files designed for MPW will not work directly with other compilers. Each compiler really needs its own version of these files, and they may be combined into a single unit.

If you are using LightSpeed Pascal, LightSpeed C, or Turbo Pascal, these compiler publishers have modified the MPW samples to work with their respective compilers. Interface and glue routines for these three compilers are listed in Appendixes C, D and E (and a disk with these files and samples is available from Bantam Books—see the information page in the back of the book).

Calling an XCMD—Object Hierarchy

In Chapter 13, we examined the traditional object hierarchy of HyperCard, showing the way messages are passed up the hierarchy in search of a matching handler name. Since a call to an XCMD is a message like any other, that message also works its way up the hierarchy. But what we didn't see in the earlier hierarchy description is that the pathway toward the HyperCard object includes searches in external resources attached to the current stack, the Home stack and HyperCard itself. The complete hierarchy is shown in Figure 26-3.

Notice one important element of this hierarchy arrangement. If you send a message, it exhausts all possible alternatives before reaching HyperCard. It checks for resources everywhere first. That means you can intercept one of HyperCard's built-in commands before it reaches HyperCard, in case you want to do something differently than HyperCard or wish to condition the command before it reaches HyperCard (you can pass the message to Hyper-Card after executing the XCMD). But most importantly, this arrangement demonstrates that if a future release of HyperCard should include a new built-

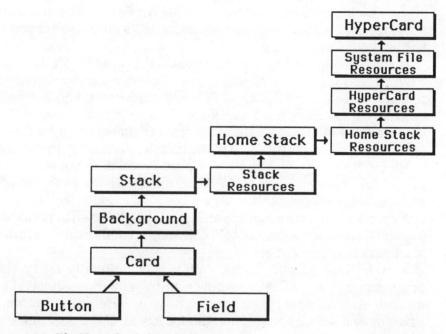

Figure 26-3 *The HyperCard object hierarchy is more complex when you consider resources, but the general flow is still the same. The only break is that System File resources are checked before a message reaches HyperCard.*

in command that is the same as one of your XCMDs, your XCMD will still work, without being clobbered by HyperCard's command. That should give you a bit of confidence about the longevity of your XCMD, regardless of the advances made to HyperCard.

About the Following XCMDs

The three XCMDs (acutally two XCMDs and one XFCN) in this book were written by Chris Knepper, a member of Apple's Macintosh Developer Technical Support (MacDTS) team. Chris obtained permission from Apple to work on this project, provided he do so on his own time and equipment at home. He also had some volunteer help from Chris DeRossi and Steve Maller, who took precious free time to offer suggestions for improvement.

These three XCMDs demonstrate a great deal about making your external code call Macintosh Toolbox routines and communicate back to HyperCard. While the subjects were chosen for their demonstration abilities, the three XCMDs—a real About box, a pop-up menu and a serial input/output driver—

are also examples of frequent requests that Apple's DTS team had from early stack developers. Our examples are intended as guides to get you started in writing your own XCMDs.

The decision to use LightSpeed Pascal as the compiler for the XCMDs was mine. It has long been a favorite of Pascal newcomers, is relatively inexpensive and is readily available. Both LightSpeed Pascal and Borland's Turbo Pascal are good entry-level compilers. General tips about XCMD structure plus the glue routines for both languages are detailed in Appendixes C and E.

Note to Pascal experts: You'll see an occasional Pascal goto statement in the following programs. Because LightSpeed Pascal does not support the Exit (procedure) statement, as MPW Pascal does, the goto is substituted to make printing possible on a narrow page.

Appendix D lists structual tips and glue for LightSpeed C, perhaps the most popular C compiler outside of MPW. It, too, is readily available through most Macintosh software outlets.

Because these XCMD chapters are written primarily for newcomers to programming and XCMDs, Apple's MPW environment (available only through APDA) doesn't get much attention here. It's a more complex environment, with language modules for Pascal, C and Assembler. It is also the environment of choice for most brand name software developers. Bill Atkinson, in case you're interested, uses MPW (mostly Pascal). Newcomers would do best to start with LightSpeed or Turbo and then perhaps graduate to MPW. But there's very little extra that MPW gives you in the way of programming power for the kinds of things you're likely to do in XCMDs. The other packages will take you a long way.

With these basics out of the way, we can proceed to the first of three XCMDs. It shows you how to write a resource that makes Dialog Manager toolbox calls, accepts parameters and centers a dialog window in the HyperCard window, even on a large monitor.

27

An About Box XCMD

For our first XCMD, we'll be adding an "About" box to a stack. One thing I've always wanted to do with a HyperCard stack was to show a traditional dialog box with information about the stack, just like About boxes in traditional programs. While there's no way for HyperTalk to short circuit the About HyperCard... menu item under the Apple menu so that it lists the name of your stack, you can still call a real-looking About box in any other fashion, such as clicking on a button.

The Stack

For this demonstration, we'll resurrect a stack used earlier in the book, the World Chronometer stack (Chapter 19). The only cosmetic change to the stack is the addition of a button in the upper left corner (Figure 27-1). This icon button is the same onethat is used on many HyperCard stacks to indicate that you can get information about the stack by clicking on it. In fact, the name of the button is "Tell About...," and comes in three sizes. The version in Figure 27-1 is the small one.

When you click on the button, it calls an XCMD, called "About." This XCMD draws a simple dialog box with four, single-line text items, one graphic and an OK button, as shown in Figure 27-2. If you're running this stack on a Macintosh II with a color monitor and you have color turned on, the text appears in red (or any color you wish to program into the XCMD).

This XCMD calls other resources, notably DLOG, DITL and PICT resources. All contents and specifications of the dialog box are determined by the resources, not the XCMD. Once you have the XCMD done, you can use ResEdit to fiddle with the size, text and other contents of the box. As we go through this XCMD, we'll also see how to create these three resources and include them in the XCMD.

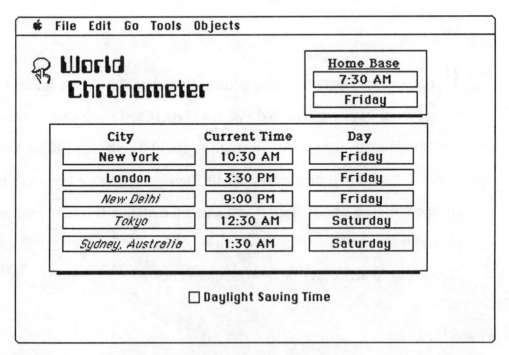

Figure 27-1 *Adding a balloon button at the upper left is the only cosmetic change to the World Chronometer stack.*

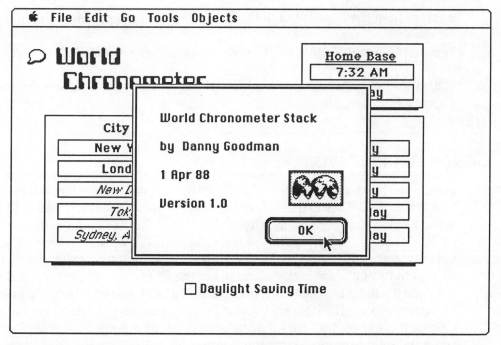

Figure 27-2 *That button's script calls the XCMD that displays a genuine About dialog box. All specifications for the text, button and graphic are in DITL resources linked to the About DLOG resource.*

Calling Conventions

The About XCMD requires at least one parameter, and as many as three parameters, depending on how much data you wish to feed to the text fields of the dialog box.

The one parameter that must be part of the command is the name of the DLOG resource for the box you wish to put on the screen. For example, if the DLOG resource for your box is called "My About," then the HyperTalk statement that would bring up that box would be

```
About "My About"
```

The DLOG resource then does the rest as far as retrieving the dialog items that go inside the box, including any pictures and buttons.

According to the way the About XCMD was written for this chapter, you have the option of changing the contents of the last two fields of the dialog box. The text for those fields may be passed as additional parameters to the About command. Therefore, if you wish to display a different date and version number than the ones listed in the DITL resource, the command would be

```
About "My About","25 September 1988","Version 1.4b"
```

With those parameters, the resulting dialog box would look like the one in Figure 27-3.

Design Assumptions

For the purposes of the sample XCMD in this chapter, we designed the About box so that field three is the slot for the release date of the stack, and field four is the version number. By modifying the XCMD source code, you can make all fields accessible by passing parameters with the About command. Conversely, you could remove the code that accepts parameters and force the XCMD to use only static text elements in the DITL resource for the dialog.

While it's not a big deal to change the text of a dialog box item, the passing of parameters for the date and version number items is a lazy man's way to change these specifications on prerelease versions of a stack. If you place the projected release date and version number (like "1.00") in the DITL resource, you can keep the prerelease date and version number up to date in the HyperTalk script. When the stack is ready to ship, then you simply remove the two extra parameters from the button that triggers the About dialog, and let the DITL data show through.

By showing an XCMD that performs both ways, you can see how an XCMD can accept parameters from a HyperTalk command (an important tidbit) and how to modify a resource "on the fly" once it's loaded into memory.

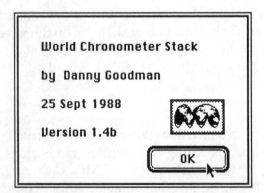

Figure 27-3 *The XCMD is written so that you may overwrite the date and version fields of the resource.*

The XCMD

Listing 27-1 contains Chris' LightSpeed Pascal source code the About XCMD. An important procedure in this code is the one called CenterPort. This is a useful routine that centers the About box in HyperCard's window, no matter where the HyperCard window is positioned on a large screen monitor. Without this procedure, the About dialog (like most dialogs in HyperCard) appear in relation to the upper left corner of the screen, regardless of monitor size.

Code resource units in LightSpeed Pascal do not need to be named, but the compiler expects a name of some kind at the top of the source file. Thus, in Listing 27-1, the placeholder is called AboutUnit. It could be any single word of your choice.

Compilers need the XCMD interfaces to make their callbacks to Hyper-Card. For LightSpeed Pascal, those units are called XCMDIntf and XCMDUtils. These two units are included in the compilation, as noted in the Uses section of the Interface.

The LightSpeed Pascal project for this XCMD consists of the bare minimum XCMD files:

DA PasLib
MacTraps
XCMD Interface.p
XCMD Utilities.p
About.p

the last file being the source code file for the About XCMD.

As with all single-unit XCMD code resources, the only public procedure that needs listing in the Interface section is the one referring to the main procedure of the Implementation section. In LightSpeed Pascal, that procedure must be named "Main." That procedure is the one that gets the pointer to the XCMD parameter block passed to it.

How the XCMD Works

The primary procedure, called About, has some local procedures and functions, so we'll start where the About procedure actually begins and look back at the functions and procedures when they're called. Pay particular attention to the instances when handles to the parameter block are locked (prior to access) and unlocked. Here are the basic steps in the main procedure:

1. *Check to be sure there are 1 or 3 parameters passed with the About command, sending an error message back to HyperCard if not.*

2. *Save the current state of HyperCard's grafport.* We'll be creating a new window (which has its own grafport) to draw the dialog box and its contents. When it closes, we'll have to restore the HyperCard grafport.

3. *Call the GetAboutDlog function, which performs a series of calls to set up the dialog box in memory.*
   a. Lock the handle to the name of the dialog box passed with the XCMD message.
   b. Make sure the name of the DLOG will become a valid Pascal string (i.e., is less than 255 characters long).
   c. Fetch the DLOG name from the XCMD parameter block and turn it into a Pascal string.
   d. Call the Toolbox GetNamedResource to open the DLOG and get the handle to it.
   e. Using the handle to the resource as a guide, get the resource ID number of the DLOG.
   f. Make sure a DITL with the same resource ID is available in the stack file.
   g. Create the dialog in memory.
   h. Unlock the handle to the parameter block.

4. *Call the CenterPort procedure to adjust the DLOG's coordinates to be centered in the HyperCard window.*

5. *If three parameters are passed with the About command, then call SetVersionInfo to plug parameters 2 and 3 into dialog items 5 and 6, respectively.*

6. *Show the dialog box.* The DLOG was set to invisible so the user doesn't see it move or change the text. All other changes, below, require a visible dialog.

7. *Call the OutlineOK function.*
   a. Store the current state of the QuickDraw graphics pen, because we're

about to change it for some drawing.

b   Using the rectangle coordinates of the "OK" button DITL resource, turn a plain OK button (the first dialog item) into an outlined button, meaning that it may be selected by pressing Enter or Return.

c. Restore the graphics pen to its original state.

8. *Turn the foreground color to red for text lettering.*

9. *Change the cursor from whatever it is to the northwest arrow.*

10. *Go ito a repeat loop that calls ModalDialog to handle user interaction with the About box. When the OK button is clicked, then the loop ends.*

11. *Dispose of the DLOG resource in memory.*

12. *Reset the current grafport to HyperCard's original grafport.*

13. *Release the handle to the DLOG resource.*

Error Handling

Within the XCMD there is a substantial amount of error handling, primarily there to let the stack author know that a piece of the About box mechanism is missing. For instance, at the very beginning of the main procedure there is a check for whether the number of parameters equals 1 or 3. If the count is neither, then execution branches to a HandleError procedure.

This HandleError procedure lets your XCMD pass a context-sensitive error message. In the case of the first error trap in the main procedure, the message is that the About command must have 1 or 3 parameters.

Importantly, the error message that comes back to your stack does so via an Alert box, just as a HyperCard error would. In fact, the XCMD uses a HyperCard ALRT resource (ALRT resource ID 3100), which has room for a two-line message, and provides an OK button to cancel. An Alert box (actually the function that displays the Alert) has its own trapping for the mouse click, so there's nothing that our XCMD needs to do other than display the Alert box.

The content of the single field of the 3100 Alert is set with the ParamText toolbox call. This routine stores up to four different strings for placement in future dialogs and alerts. The strings are assigned numbers 0 through 3.

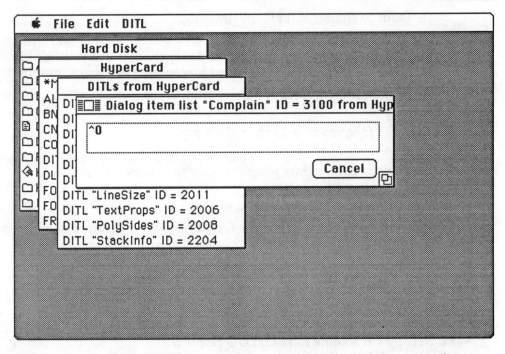

Figure 27-4 *The About XCMD even calls one of HyperCard's DLOG resources for error messages. The ^0 symbol in the DITL field is a placeholder for text that may vary when the dialog is called (see text).*

Placeholders for these strings are maintained in the DITL fields by a caret and the number, as in ^0. Therefore, if you open up the ALRT ID=3100 in HyperCard, you'll see that in the DITL field for the two-line field is the placeholder ^0 (Figure 27-4). Thus, in the XCMD code for error handling that uses that Alert, the first position is assigned the string of the error message with the ParamText call.

Even the HandleError procedure has a bit of error handling. If the procedure cannot find the ALRT 3100 resource, then the procedure produces a system beep. You may optionally add code that sends a HyperCard message to display an explanation of the error in the Message Box.

Elsewhere in the main procedure, the primary error checking is done on whether or not the XCMD was able to find the appropriate resources required to produce the About box. Chris uses a function of his own design, ErrOccurred, to take care of information that the Toolbox returns about attempts to load resources. After each attempt, the Toolbox returns an error code, which may be retrieved by the ResError toolbox function. If there were no error, then that function returns zero (equivalent to a constant called noErr). Otherwise, there are seven possible errors, each with a different number. For example, if the resource is not found, then the error number returned by the ResError function is -192.

The ErrOccurred function, then, takes as parameters the results of the ResError toolbox function and the literal string of the previous resource call (e.g., 'GetResInfo'). If the error is not zero, then the literal name of the Toolbox call and the returned error number are sent as text to the HandleError procedure. That text goes into the ALRT 3100 put up by that procedure. Finally, the ErrOccurred function returns a Boolean true to the main procedure.

All three XCMDs in this book use the same error handling technique, so we won't repeat it in those other code descriptions.

Creating the DLOG Resource

Since the About XCMD relies on DLOG and DITL resources, let's see how you can go about creating these resources with ResEdit. Experienced Macintosh programmers might prefer to build their resources "the old-fashioned way" by writing the specifications for them in an editor and running that text file through an early utility called RMaker. RMaker is, essentially, a resource compiler, turning source code listings of resource specifications into code resources for attachment to a file (that's what another utility, RMover, was for). But I find that for standard resources, ResEdit is quick and easy. Moreover, you can build the resource right in the file you intend it to go, like a particular HyperCard stack.

Before digging into the resource, however, let's pick out some graphics to include in the About box. In the Art Ideas stack is a picture of a map projection (Figure 27-5). To prepare it for inclusion in the About box, select it with the rectangle selection tool and copy it into the Scrapbook. That's all there is to it for now.

The steps for creating the DLOG and DITL resources start with getting the PICT resource in place for use later.

1. *Start ResEdit, and open the Scrapbook File until you can see its list of resource types (Figure 27-6).* The one we're interested in is the PICT type.

2. *Double click on it to reveal all the PICT resources stored in the Scrapbook.* All PICTs are in the resulting window, as if in a column. You may scroll vertically to see additional PICTs. The most recently added PICT, the map art in our case, is at the top (Figure 27-7).

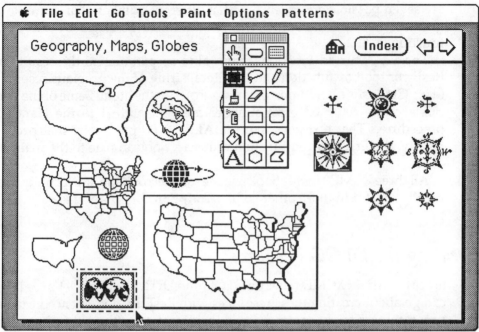

Figure 27-5 *To capture the art for the dialog, first copy and paste the art into the Scrapbook.*

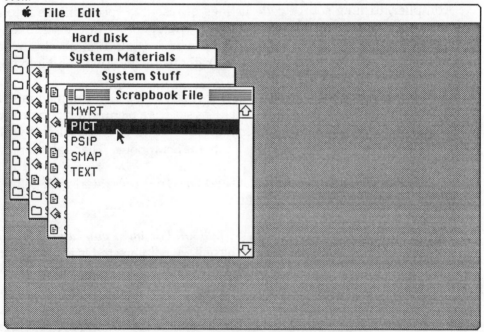

Figure 27-6 *Art that is pasted into the Scrapbook becomes a PICT resource. Here is the listing of my Scrapbook's resources.*

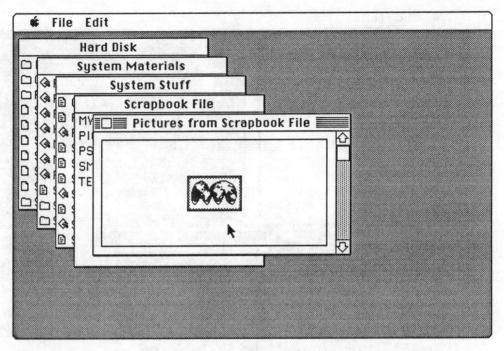

Figure 27-7 *Opening the PICT resources of the Scrapbook reveals a window that shows each PICT in the file. Since the map is the last one to be pasted into the Scrapbook, it is the top one. Copy this PICT resource.*

3. *Click once on the picture to select it, and choose Copy from the Edit menu.* Close all windows leading to the Scrapbook (but not the hard disk window).

4. *Open the file of the Chronometer stack (Figure 27-8).* If no resource fork has been created for this file (an alert box will tell you if that's the case) click OK to create the resource fork.

5. *Choose Paste from the Edit menu.* This pastes the PICT resource into the stack.

6. *Double click on the PICT listing in that window to show the picture in its own window (Figure 27-9).*

7. *Click once on the picture to select it, and choose Get Info from the File menu. You may enter a name for this resource, but it's optional.* Note the resource ID of the picture (Figure 27-10). You'll need this number in a

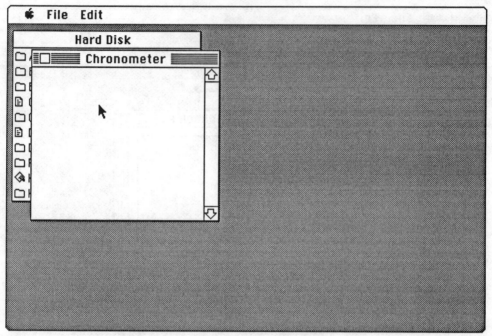

Figure 27-8 *Open the Chronometer stack file's resource fork.*

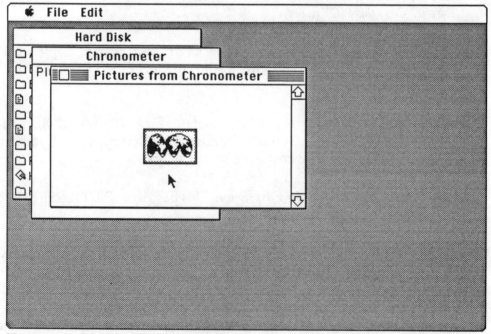

Figure 27-9 *Paste the PICT resource into the resource fork of the Chronometer stack.*

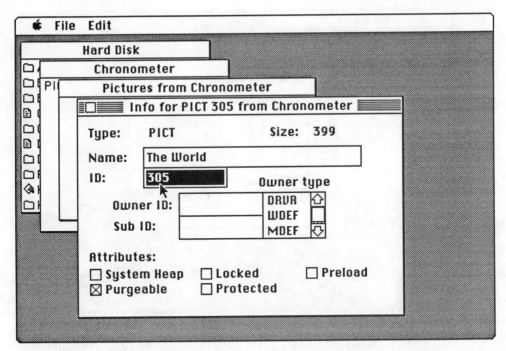

Figure 27-10 *Choose Get Info from the File menu to see the PICT's ID number. You'll need this later on.*

moment, so jot it down. Close the PICT resource window.

8. *With the Resource window of the Chronometer stack open (the same level as shown in Figure 27-8), choose new from the File menu to open a new resource type.*

9. *In the resulting dialog box, scroll the resource type list until DLOG is in sight and select it.* Its name is automatically inserted into the small edit window in the dialog (Figure 27-11). Click OK.

10. *With the resulting overlapping empty window in view (it normally lists all the DLOG resources for this file), choose New once again from the File menu to open a new DLOG resource.* ResEdit will generate a new window for the new DLOG and assign a random DLOG ID number to this resource (Figure 27-12).

11. *Choose Display As Text from the DLOG menu. In the text version of the*

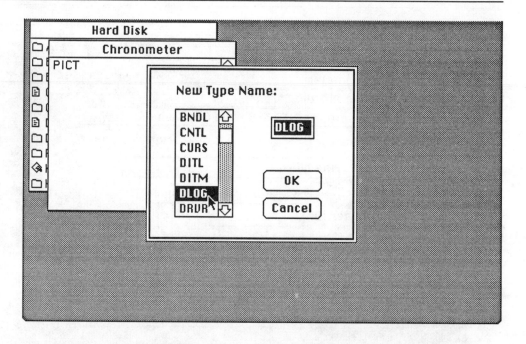

Figure 27-11 *Choose New from the File menu and open a new DLOG resource.*

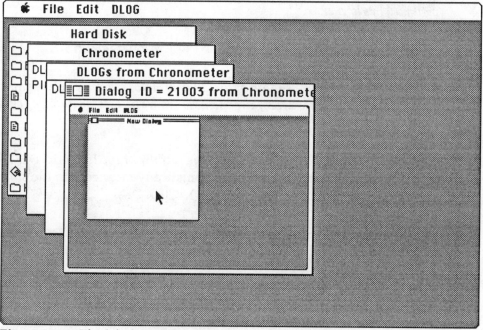

Figure 27-12 *The default DLOG resource has a title bar and close box, and is of the size shown.*

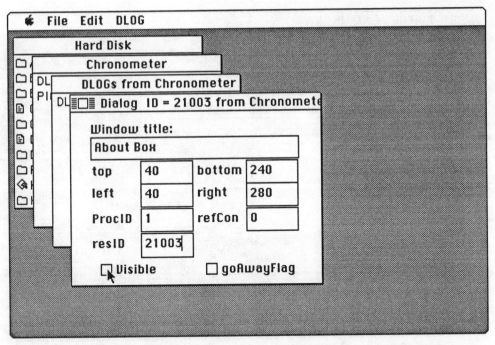

Figure 27-13 *Change the display to the text version. Change the ProcID to 1 (standard dialog box outline), type the DLOG ID number into the resID field and uncheck the two checkboxes at the bottom.*

> DLOG (Figure 27-13), uncheck the Visible and goAwayFlag checkbox items. Type a 1 in the ProcID box. This specifies the standard dialog box outline.

12. *Choose Display Graphically from the DLOG menu, and see that the window now looks like a dialog box style (Figure 27-14).*

13. *Double click anywhere inside the miniature dialog box.* This brings up another window, which shows the size of the default dialog box. There is where dialog items (DITLs) will be specified.

14. *Choose Get Info from the File menu. In the info dialog box, type the name you plan to give the dialog box, and enter the same ID number for the DITL that ResEdit assigned to the DLOG (you can see the DLOG's ID in the title bar of the DLOG window).* Also, check the Purgeable attribute button at the bottom, and close the window.

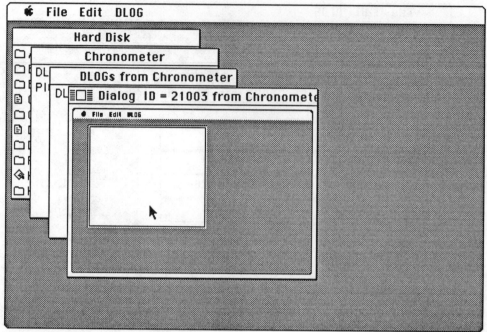

Figure 27-14 *Changing the view back to graphical, the dialog has changed its appearance to match our desires.*

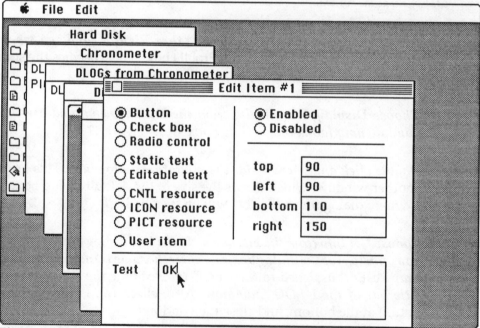

Figure 27-15 *Create the OK button as the first item in the DITL resource.*

15. *Choose New from the File menu to bring up an Edit Item window for the first item.* The OK button is the first item to be specified. Leave the specifications at their default settings except for the Text. Change it to read "OK" (Figure 27-15).

16. *Close the window. A selected button will appear in the center of the prototype dialog box.* Drag it to the lower right corner temporarily and drag the gray handle in the button's lower right corner to extend it slightly in the horizontal direction (Figure 27-16).

17. *Choose New from the File menu once more.* In the resulting Edit Item window, click the PICT button, and type the picture's ID number into the field at the bottom of the window (Figure 27-17)

18. *Close the Edit Item window.* A scrunched version of the art appears in the DITL window (Figure 27-18).

19. *Choose Use RSRC Rect from the DITL menu.* This restores the art to its

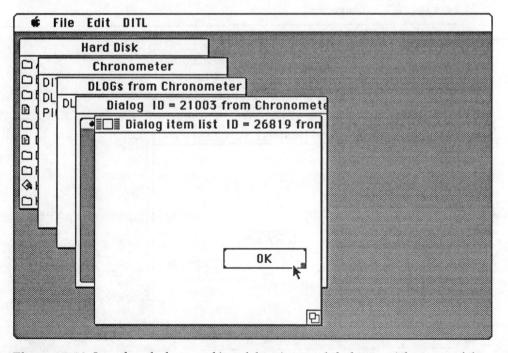

Figure 27-16 *Lengthen the button a bit and drag it toward the bottom right corner of the dialog.*

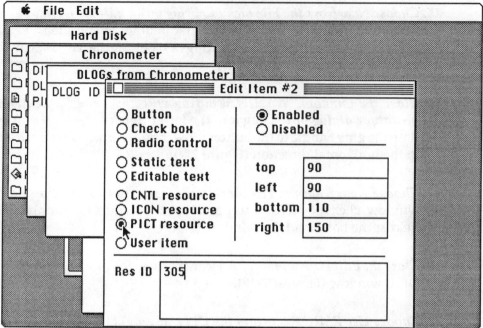

Figure 27-17 *Make the PICT resource the second item. Click the PICT button and enter the PICT's ID number.*

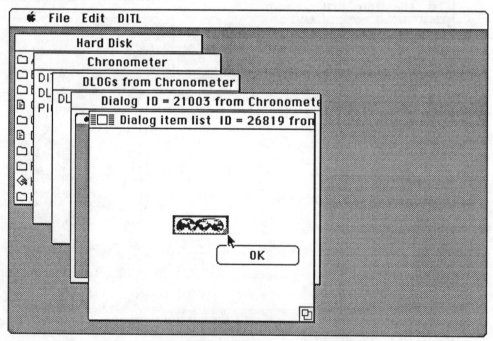

Figure 27-18 *At first, the PICT will be squished into a default size.*

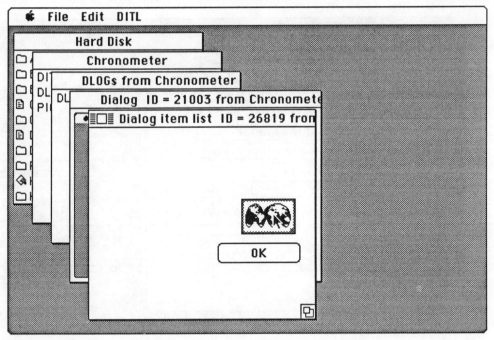

Figure 27-19 *Choose Use RSRC Rect from the DITL menu, and the art pops up to normal proportions. Drag it near the OK button.*

original size. You may now drag it to the desired location (Figure 27-19).

20. *For each of the text fields, choose New from the File menu.* In the resulting window, select the Static Text style and type the following text into the appropriate items:

Edit Item #3: [the name of the program]

Edit Item #4: [your name]

Edit Item #5: [a release date of your stack]

Edit Item #6: [a version number of your stack]

After filling in each window, close that window, drag the field to the desired location in the prototype dialog and grab the gray handle in the field's lower right corner to stretch it to the appropriate length for all the text to appear. You may adjust it as often as you need. Figure 27-20 shows the results after adjusting all four field items. If you need help aligning objects, turn on the Grid in the DITL menu.

21. *If the size of the dialog box is too big for the items you've placed in it,*

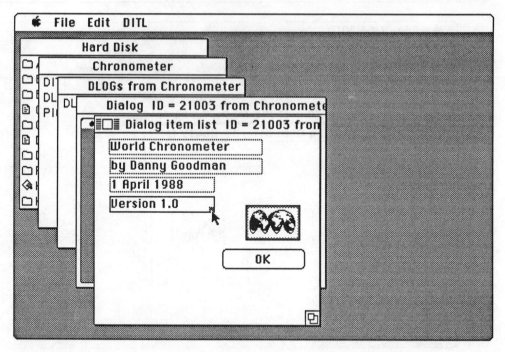

Figure 27-20 *After all four fields (DITL items 3 through 6) are added and resized, the DITL window should look like this.*

return to the Dialog window and drag the lower right corner of the miniature dialog to the desired size. You should double-click on the miniature box to see the DITL window once more, to make sure all items are fully visible after your adjustment.

22. *With the miniature dialog box showing in its window, choose Get Info from the File menu.* Enter the name you wish to give to this resource. This is the name that you'll pass to the XCMD with the About command.

23. *When you're all finished, close all Chronometer ResEdit windows.* When prompted to save changes, click Yes.

That's all there is to creating the supporting resources for the About box. If the results need some tweaking, then open ResEdit and adjust the size of the dialog or shift the location of text, button and picture elements. You can specify an icon as an artistic object, just as easily as a PICT resource.

Modifying the XCMD to address further fields, you can perhaps create a completely generic dialog box and pass as much text in as many fields as you see fit, using the same box all the time, but putting different text into it depending on the situation. That's how Alert boxes generally work, anyway.

Further Ideas

While the About box is one of the simplest methods of creating a dialog box, a study of dialog boxes in *Macintosh Revealed* should help you create even more interesting dialog boxes, including those that offer fields for text input and even controls, such as scroll bars, radio buttons and check boxes. Offloading some of these tasks to dialog boxes makes your stack much more Macintosh-like.

Listing 27-1

```
{   Title      :   About -- an XCMD to display an About box. }
{   Author     :   Chris Knepper }
{   Date       :   3/30/88 }
{   From       :   Danny Goodman's HyperCard Developer's Guide }
{   Publisher  :   Bantam Books, Inc. }
{   Copyright  © 1988 by Danny Goodman.  All rights reserved. }

unit AboutUnit;

interface

   uses
      XCMDIntf,      { the data structures for the XCMD }
      XCMDUtils;     { the glue for the HyperCard callbacks }

   procedure Main (paramPtr : XCmdPtr);        { the entrypoint to the XCMD }

implementation

   procedure About (paramPtr : XCmdPtr);
      label
         1;                 { The end of the About XCMD.  Jump here if errors occur. }
      const
         VERSIONDATE = 5;         { The DITL item of the version date -- a static text item. }
         VERSIONNUMBER = 6;       { The DITL item of the version number -- a static text item. }
      var
         pascalStr                { used to convert the parameters from zero-terminated strings }
           : Str255;
         myDlogHdl,               { Stores a handle to the DLOG resource. }
         myDitlHdl                { used in calls to GetDItem }
           : Handle;
         myItem,                  { item returned by ModalDialog }
         myKind                   { used in calls to GetDItem }
           : integer;
         myDialog                 { storage for the dialog pointer }
           : DialogPtr;
         myRect                   { used in calls to GetDItem }
           : Rect;
         savePen                  { to save and restore the pen while outlining the OK button }
           : PenState;
         savePort                 { to save and restore the graf port }
           : GrafPtr;
{-----------------------------------------------------------------------------------------------------}
   procedure CenterPort (whichPort, HCport : GrafPtr);
   { This procedure calls MoveWindow to center whichPort with respect to HyperCard's }
   { port.  CenterPort sets the port to whichPort when done. }
```

```
    var
      offset,                          { store the offset from the graf port }
      topLeftPt,                       { store the top and left items }
      botRightPt                       { store the bottom and right items }
      : point;
    begin
      SetPort(HCport);                 { HyperCard's port = "local" coordinate system. }
      with HCport^.portRect do         { Convert local coordinates to global. }
        begin
          topLeftPt.v := top;
          topLeftPt.h := left;
          LocalToGlobal(topLeftPt);    { make top,left global }
          botRightPt.v := bottom;
          botRightPt.h := right;
          LocalToGlobal(botRightPt);   { make bottom,right global }
        end;                           { with savePort^.portRect }
      with whichPort^.portRect do      { Calculate offsets. }
        begin
        { Compensate horizontally for the dialog. }
          offset.h := (botRightPt.h + topLeftPt.h) div 2 - (right - left) div 2;
        { Compensate vertically for the dialog. }
          offset.v := (botRightPt.v + topLeftPt.v) div 2 - (bottom + top) div 2;
        end;                           { with thisPort^.portRect }
      with offset do                   { Move the port. }
        MoveWindow(whichPort, h, v, TRUE);
      SetPort(whichPort);              { Set the port to the DLOG's port. }
    end;                               { Procedure CenterPort }
{-------------------------------------------------------------------------------------------}
    procedure HandleError (myStr : Str255);
    { HandleError sets the cursor to the arrow cursor and displays an error Alert }
    { informing the user of the error.  This procedure assumes that the ALRT & DITL }
    { resources with id = 3100 exist in HyperCard's resource fork, although this is a }
    { valid assumption in HyperCard versions 1.1 and 1.0.1.  Calls to GetResource() verify }
    { that these resources do, in fact, exist.  If they don't, this procedure produces a beep. }
      const
        ERROR = 3100;                  { use a HC ALRT for error messages. }
      var
        whichItem : integer;           { stores result of the Alert function }
      begin
        if (GetResource('ALRT', 3100) = nil) or (GetResource('DITL', 3100) = nil) then
          SysBeep(60)                  { beep if no ALRT or DITL resource }
        else
          begin
            InitCursor;                { set cursor to the arrow cursor }
            ParamText(myStr, '', '', '');  { specify the ALRT's text }
            whichItem := Alert(ERROR, nil);  { display and handle the ALRT }
            SendCardMessage(paramPtr, 'set cursor to 4');   { set back to watch cursor }
          end;
      end;                             { procedure HandleError }
```

```
{---------------------------------------------------------------------}
    function ErrOccurred (errNum : OSErr;
                      routineName : Str255) : Boolean;
    { ErrOccurred determines if an error occurred by comparing errNum with NoErr. }
    { If equal, ErrOccurred returns FALSE indicating that no error occurred.  Otherwise, }
    { it returns TRUE, indicating that an error occurred and creates a string from }
    { errNum and routineName which it then passes to HandleError. }
      var
        errStr                          { store error number as a Pascal string }
        : Str255;
      begin
        if (errNum = noErr) then
          ErrOccurred := FALSE          { no error occurred -- return FALSE }
        else
          begin
            ErrOccurred := TRUE;        { oops, error occurred -- return TRUE }
            NumToString(errNum, errStr);    { convert error number to a string }
            HandleError(Concat(routineName, ' returned ', errStr, '.')); { inform user }
          end;
      end;                              { function ErrOccurred }
{---------------------------------------------------------------------}
    function SetVersionInfo : boolean;
    { SetVersionInfo sets both the version date and the version number.  These should }
    { be passed in as the 2nd and 3rd parameters to About.  If errors occur, then }
    { SetVersionInfo returns FALSE, otherwise it returns TRUE. }
      label
        8;                              { the end of procedure SetVersionInfo }
      begin
        SetVersionInfo := TRUE;         { return TRUE indicates no errors }
        with paramPtr^ do
          begin
            HLock(params[2]);           { lock the handles, so the callbacks don't  }
            HLock(params[3]);           {    invalidate them }
            if (StringLength(paramPtr, params[2]^) > 255) then
              begin                     { it won't fit into a Pascal string! }
                HandleError('2nd parameter to About is too long.');
                SetVersionInfo := FALSE;     { return FALSE indicates function failed }
                goto 8;                 { exit SetVersionInfo }
              end;
            ZeroToPas(paramPtr, params[2]^, pascalStr);    { 2nd param is version date }
            if (result <> xresSucc) then     { test if ZeroToPas callback succeeded }
              begin
                HandleError('ZeroToPas callback on 2nd parameter failed.');
                SetVersionInfo := FALSE;     { return FALSE indicates function failed }
                goto 8;                 { exit SetVersionInfo }
              end;
```

```
        GetDItem(myDialog, VERSIONDATE, myKind, myDitlHdl, myRect);
        If (myDitlHdl = nil) then
          begin                            { GetDItem failed }
            HandleError('GetDItem failed on version date.');      { inform user }
            SetVersionInfo := FALSE;       { return FALSE indicates function failed }
            goto 8;                        { exit SetVersionInfo }
          end;
        SetIText(myDitlHdl, pascalStr);       { Set the version date. }
        If (StringLength(paramPtr, params[3]^) > 255) then
          begin                            { it won't fit into a Pascal string! }
            HandleError('3rd parameter to About is too long.');
            SetVersionInfo := FALSE;       { return FALSE indicates function failed }
            goto 8;                        { exit SetVersionInfo }
          end;
        ZeroToPas(paramPtr, params[3]^, pascalStr);     { 3rd param is version number }
        If (result <> xresSucc) then           { test if ZeroToPas callback succeeded }
          begin
            HandleError('ZeroToPas callback on 3rd parameter failed.');
            SetVersionInfo := FALSE;       { return FALSE indicates function failed }
            goto 8;                        { exit SetVersionInfo }
          end;
        GetDItem(myDialog, VERSIONNUMBER, myKind, myDitlHdl, myRect);
        If (myDitlHdl = nil) then
          begin                            { GetDItem failed }
            HandleError('GetDItem failed on the version number.');      { inform user }
            SetVersionInfo := FALSE;       { return FALSE indicates function failed }
            goto 8;                        { exit SetVersionInfo }
          end;
        SetIText(myDitlHdl, pascalStr);       { Set the version number. }
      end;                                 { with paramPtr^ }
8 :                                        { the end of procedure SetVersionInfo }
    HUnLock(paramPtr^.params[2]);          { unlock the handles before returning }
    HUnLock(paramPtr^.params[3]);          {     from SetVersionInfo }
  end;                                     { procedure SetVersionInfo }
{-------------------------------------------------------------------------------------}
  function GetAboutDlog : boolean;
  { The function GetAboutDlog gets the name of the About DLOG from the 1st param }
  { to About and gets the handle to the resource from the resource fork of the stack. }
  { If there is an error, then GetAboutDlog returns FALSE, else it returns TRUE. }
  { NOTE: GetAboutDlog assumes that the DLOG resource id and its corresponding }
  { DITL's id are the same. }
    label
      9;                                   { the end of function GetAboutDlog }
    var
      dlogID                               { Stores the id of the DLOG resource. }
        : integer;
      dlogType                             { Stores the type returned by GetResInfo. }
        : ResType;
```

```
begin
  GetAboutDlog := TRUE;                  { TRUE means no errors occurred }
  with paramPtr^ do
    begin
      HLock(params[1]);                  { locking the handle ensures it's valid }
      if (StringLength(paramPtr, params[1]^) > 255) then
        begin                            { it won't fit into a Pascal string! }
          HandleError('1st parameter to About is too long.');
          GetAboutDlog := FALSE;         { FALSE means error occurred }
          goto 9;                        { exit GetAboutDlog }
        end;
      ZeroToPas(paramPtr, params[1]^, pascalStr);      { 1st param is DLOG name }
      if (result <> xresSucc) then
        begin                            { ZeroToPas callback failed }
          HandleError('ZeroToPas callback on 1st parameter failed.');
          GetAboutDlog := FALSE;         { FALSE means error occurred }
          goto 9;                        { exit GetAboutDlog }
        end;
      myDlogHdl := GetNamedResource('DLOG', pascalStr);      { get hndl to DLOG }
      if (myDlogHdl = nil) then          { check for error }
        begin
          HandleError('GetNamedResource returned a nil handle.'); { inform user }
          GetAboutDlog := FALSE;         { FALSE means error occurred }
          goto 9;                        { exit GetAboutDlog }
        end;
      GetResInfo(myDlogHdl, dlogID, dlogType, pascalStr);    { get id of DLOG }
      if ErrOccurred(ResError, 'GetResInfo') then
        begin
          ReleaseResource(myDlogHdl);    { release handle to the DLOG }
          goto 9;                        { exit GetAboutDlog }
        end;
      if (GetResource('DITL', dlogID) = nil) then    { assume DLOG id = DITL id }
        begin
          HandleError('The DITL is not available.'); { inform user }
          GetAboutDlog := FALSE;         { FALSE means error occurred }
          ReleaseResource(myDlogHdl);    { release handle to the DLOG }
          goto 9;                        { exit GetAboutDlog }
        end;
      myDialog := GetNewDialog(dlogID, nil, WindowPtr(-1));   { create the dialog }
      if (myDlogHdl = nil) then          { check for error }
        begin
          HandleError('GetNewDialog returned a nil handle.');   { inform user }
          GetAboutDlog := FALSE;         { FALSE means error occurred }
          ReleaseResource(myDlogHdl);    { release handle to the DLOG }
        end;
    end;                                 { with paramPtr^ }
```

```
9 :                                          { the end of the function GetAboutDlog }
     HUnLock(paramPtr^.params[1]);           { unlock the handle before returning }
   end;                                       { function GetAboutDlog }
{-------------------------------------------------------------------------------------}
   function OutlineOK : boolean;
   { The function OutlineOK outlines the OK button in the About }
   { dialog and returns FALSE if an error occurs, otherwise it returns TRUE. }
     var
       savePen               { to save and restore the pen while outlining the OK button }
        : PenState;
   begin
     OutlineOK := TRUE;                        { TRUE indicates no error }
     GetDItem(myDialog, ok, myKind, myDitlHdl, myRect);     { get the OK button rect}
     if (myDitlHdl = nil) then
       begin                                   { GetDItem failed }
         HandleError('GetDItem failed on OK button.');        { inform user }
         OutlineOK := FALSE;                    { FALSE indicates error occurred }
       end
     else
       begin
         GetPenState(savePen);                 { save the old pen state }
         PenSize(3, 3);                        { make the pen fatter }
         InsetRect(myRect, -4, -4);            { make the rect a little bigger }
         FrameRoundRect(myRect, 16, 16);       { draw the outline }
         SetPenState(savePen);                 { restore the old pen state }
       end;
   end;                                        { function OutlineOK }
{-------------------------------------------------------------------------------------}
   begin                                       { procedure About begins here }
     { Check that either 1 parameter was passed in, or that 3 parameters were passed in. }
     with paramPtr^ do
       if (paramCount <> 1) and (paramCount <> 3) then
         begin                                 { Inform user of error. }
           HandleError('About expects either 1 or 3 parameters.');
           goto 1;                             { exit About }
         end;

     GetPort(savePort);                        { Save the old port. }
     if not GetAboutDlog then                  { Get the ABOUT dialog. }
       goto 1;                                 { exit About }
     CenterPort(myDialog, savePort);           { Center the dialog and set the port. }

     if (paramPtr^.paramCount = 3) then        { If 3 parameters are passed in, }
       if not SetVersionInfo then              { then set the version date and number. }
         begin
           DisposDialog(myDialog);             { get rid of the dialog }
           SetPort(savePort);                  { restore the port. }
```

```
            ReleaseResource(myDlogHdl);        { Release the handle to the DLOG resource. }
            goto 1;                            { exit About }
         end;

      ShowWindow(myDialog);                    { show the DLOG; the DLOG's invisible attribute is set }

      if not OutlineOK then                    { Outline the OK button. }
        begin
          DisposDialog(myDialog);              { get rid of the dialog }
          SetPort(savePort);                   { restore the port. }
          ReleaseResource(myDlogHdl);          { Release the handle to the DLOG resource. }
          goto 1;                              { exit About }
        end;

      { For fun, let's set the foreground color to red. }
      { This will display red text in the About box on a color monitor. }
      ForeColor(redColor);                     { set the fore color to red for drawing }

      { Display and handle the dialog. }
      InitCursor;                              { set cursor to the arrow cursor }
      repeat
        ModalDialog(nil, myItem);              { call ModalDialog to display and handle the dialog }
      until myItem = ok;                       { continue repeat loop until user chooses OK }
      SendCardMessage(paramPtr, 'set cursor to 4'); { Watch cursor. }

      { Clean up. }
      DisposDialog(myDialog);                  { get rid of the dialog }
      SetPort(savePort);                       { A last and very important step: restore the port. }
      ReleaseResource(myDlogHdl);              { Release the handle to the DLOG resource. }

   1:                                          { The end of the XCMD. }
     end;                                      { Procedure About }
{------------------------------------------------------------------------------}
  procedure Main;
{ procedure Main serves as the entrypoint for the XCMD.  All it does is call About. }
  begin
    About(paramPtr);                           { call About }
  end;
{------------------------------------------------------------------------------}
end.                                           { UNIT AboutUnit }
{------------------------------------------------------------------------------}
```

28

A Pop-up Menu XFCN

In Part One of this book, I suggested that a good stack designer makes the stack inviting and, well, fun to use. One way to accomplish this is to reduce or eliminate data entry that must be done by the keyboard. Typing is a loathesome task, which only a few computer users truly enjoy (I'm not one of them).

Therefore, I always look for ways in which I can lead a user to entering data by clicking the mouse. Thus, in the Preferences card of *Business Class* and several stacks of *Focal Point*, the user may select from a list of items strictly by clicking the mouse on arrows or text—the stack enters the data into appropriate fields automatically. I've also advocated the use of hidden fields and buttons which are brought into view when needed to make a selection from several options (see Figure 8-6 for an example). The problem with this is that, while things run strictly within HyperTalk, they may be slow on some machines, and take quite a bit of care in their programming to make sure all objects are shown and hidden at the right instant.

In this chapter, we look at an XFCN that produces a relatively new Macintosh user interface element, called the *pop-up menu*. Although its heritage is that of the pull-down menu, a pop-up menu is a slightly different animal. But the good news is that most of the hard work of the XFCN is already in the Macintosh Toolbox.

The Pop-Up Menu Interface

Since the pop-up menu is now a standard Macintosh interface item, it's important that you understand its designers' intent. Just as with check boxes and radio buttons, you should employ standard interface items in the same way as they would appear in standalone Macintosh software.

According to the Macintosh User Interface Guidelines (*Inside Macintosh*, Volume 5), a pop-up menu is one that appears someplace on the screen (other than on the menubar) when the user clicks on an indicated area of the screen. The example that Apple provides shows what look like shadow fields displaying the selected item in the menu list. Figure 28-1 is a replica of the example provided in the user guidelines.

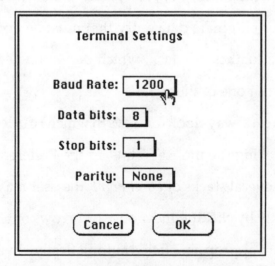

Figure 28-1 *A replica of the pop-up menu suggestion from Apple's user interface guidelines.*

Used primarily to make settings from a list of related items, a pop-up menu has some special properties that differentiate itself from a traditional menubar menu. First of all, the pop-up menu title is located to the left side of the field holding the value (Figure 28-2). Second, when you choose an item in a pop-up menu, it may be checked as a reference mark for the next time you pop the menu. In other words, in Figure 28-2, when you choose the 1200 item the first time, its value is placed in the shadow field. The next time you click on the field to display the menu, the pop-up menu already will have scrolled to the spot where the 1200 item is, displaying a checkmark next to it indicating that it was the most recent setting of that menu. The Macintosh Toolbox takes care of positioning the scrolled menu on the screen, based on the previously selected item.

Pop-ups and HyperCard

To accomplish the pop-up menu effect in HyperCard, we'll use Chris Knepper's PopUp XFCN (the function returns the currently selected item) in concert with a shadow field and a transparent button.

Figure 28-3 shows the breakout of the field and button items in a Hyper-Card replica of the dialog shown in Figure 28-1. Each field is locked and is programmed, so that a mouse click on either the field or the menu title button brings up the pop-up menu. The pop-up menu, when called, actually

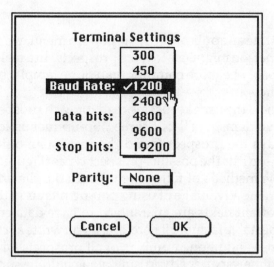

Figure 28-2 *Popping up a menu reveals that the last item selected in this menu is checked, and the menu is prescrolled to that spot.*

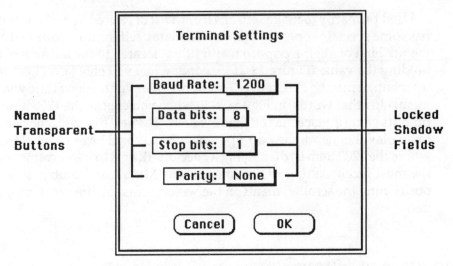

Figure 28-3 *Using the PopUp XFCN, we replicate the look of Macintosh pop-up menus with named transparent buttons and locked shadow fields.*

overlays the card while you hold down the mouse button. The XFCN is responsible for inverting the button's rectangle so that it looks just like the "real thing." A HyperTalk script, which calls the popUp XFCN is then responsible for placing the results of the menu call into the shadow field.

The Stack

To demonstrate an application of the pop-up menu, we'll use a stack that a real estate salesperson might use to track prospects. In a real-life situation, the card would probably be more complex than our example, but let's keep the stack simple for now.

In this stack, the user keeps one card for each prospect. To ease data entry for repetitive items, we'll put three pop-up menus to work. One lists the possible ways the prospect found the real estate office (Figure 28-4). The second pop-up lists the possible prospect types (Figure 28-5). And the last one lists possible methods of following up with the client (Figure 28-6).

One supreme advantage of using pop-up menus in the manner we are here is that important fields are guaranteed to have data entered into them in an orderly, repeatable fashion. Therefore, if you wrote a script that saves to a disk file the names and phone numbers of all prospects who came into the office as a result of newspaper advertising, you could be sure the Source field will have the words "Newspaper Ad" in it, and use that phrase to search for cards.

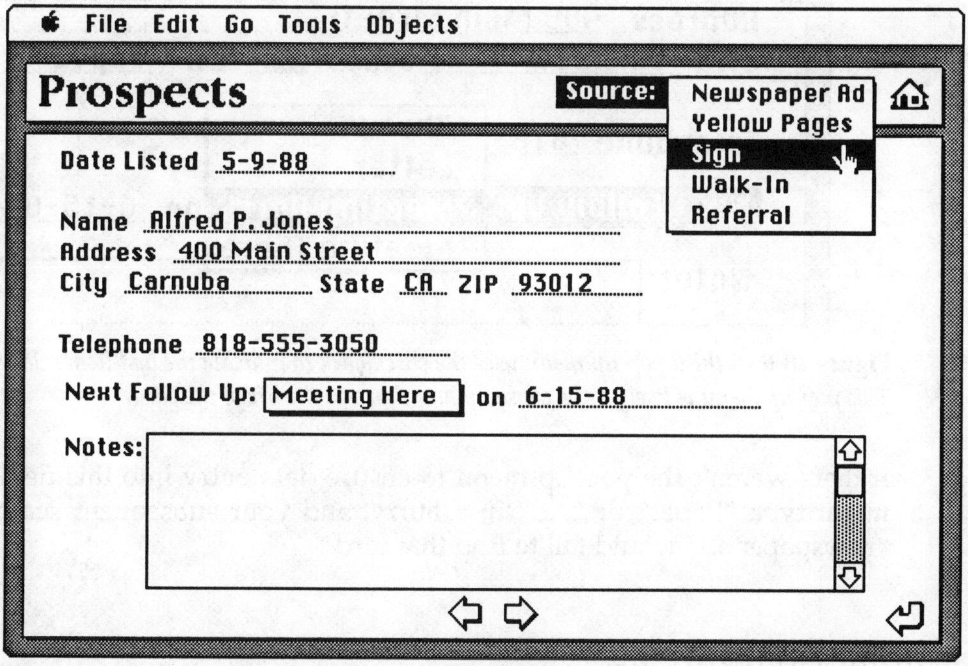

🍎 **File Edit Go Tools Objects**

Prospects

Source: | Newspaper Ad 🏠
           | Yellow Pages
           | **Sign**
           | Walk-In
           | Referral

Date Listed 5-9-88

Name Alfred P. Jones
Address 400 Main Street
City Carnuba   **State** CA **ZIP** 93012

Telephone 818-555-3050

Next Follow Up: | Meeting Here | **on** 6-15-88

Notes:

⬅ ➡   ↵

Figure 28-4 *In our sample stack, one pop-up menu provides a list of possible sources for a prospective client.*

Source: | Sign | 🏠

Type: | **Buyer**
         | **Seller**
         | Renter
         | Broker

012

Figure 28-5 *Another pop-up menu shows a list of prospect types.*

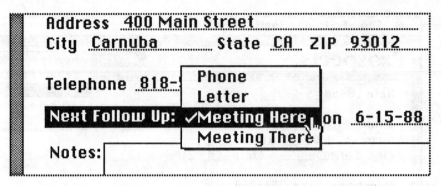

Figure 28-6 *A third pop-up menu uses the checkmark to indicate the last item selected. This pop-up menu is likely to be chosen many times in the life of the card.*

If there weren't the pop-up menu to ensure data entry into this field, you might type "Paper" or "Ad" in a hurry, and your subsequent search for "newspaper ad" would fail to find that card.

Calling Conventions

The PopUp function takes two or more parameters, resulting in three basically different ways to make the pop-up menu appear on the screen.

All calling methods require that the first parameter be a number corresponding to the item in the menu list that was last selected. This is the item that will have the checkmark displayed next to it and have the menu scrolled to its position. This "last item" parameter must be stored somewhere, like in a hidden field or on line 2 of the pop-up field (which is out of view), so that the next time you come to the stack or card with the pop-up menu, that parameter may be fed to the PopUp function. If you pass a zero as the last item parameter, the function does not place a checkmark next to any item, and the scrolling menu is set to the first item in the menu.

It's not a good idea to pass zero to this XFCN when the pop-up menu on a particular card may be called more than once. That checkmark and auto-scrolling to the currently chosen item provide important visual feedback for subsequent showing of the menu. For instance, in the Prospects stack, the Next Follow Up pop-up menu will probably be called several times in the card's lifetime. If you click on its button to show the menu, the checkmark next to the last selected item gives you instant feedback as to which item of the list is the currently selected one. If you drag the mouse away from the pop-up menu and release the mouse button, you know that the current item will stay in effect. Were that item not checked, you'd wonder if the top item of the list (which would automatically be highlighted if you clicked on the field part of the pop-up menu mechanism) would be inserted if you moved away from the menu and released the button. With the checkmark and auto-scroll, there is no ambiguity.

If, on the other hand, a pop-up menu is usually called only once, as in the Source and Type data entry items on the Prospects card, there is little reason to store a last item selected. Passing zero as the last item parameter lets the pop-up menu behave more like a traditional pull-down menu (in fact the XFCN is designed to be customized into doing just that).

Getting Items in the Menus

Additional parameters to the PopUp XFCN concern themselves with the text of the items that appear in the menu. You may pass that information in one of three ways: via a MENU resource, a HyperCard container of comma-separated text items, or a series of literal strings.

The pop-up menu mechanism in the Macintosh Toolbox is capable of calling traditional Macintosh menu resources to fetch the items that are to appear in the menu. These are the same MENU resource types that pull-down menus use. As a parameter, you pass the name of the MENU resource, as in:

```
get PopUp (field "Last Item","MyMenu")
```

where "MyMenu" is the name of the MENU resource containing the menu items for the pop-up menu. This XFCN is also compatible with HyperCard's own MENU resources. You may, therefore, specify the ShortFile MENU resource name to pop up a list of menu items identical to the File menu under Browsing and Typing user levels.

All attributes of pull-down menus, such as disabled items, changeable font styles, and so on, may be set as parameters in the MENU resource (as well as in the string parameters, below). Later in the chapter, we'll create a MENU resource from scratch to show you how it's done in ResEdit.

You may pass an itemized list of menu items either in a container (typically in a local or global variable consisting of items gathered from other sources in the stack) or as a literal list of comma- or semi-colon separated strings. For example, let's say that a personnel scheduler stack assembles an "item-ized" list of current store employees when the stack opens each day. That list, held in a global variable or field, may be passed as a parameter to the PopUp function. If the list is maintained in a card field called Roster, the call to the PopUp XFCN would be this:

```
get PopUp (0,card field "Roster")
```

As the content of field "Roster" changes, so does the menu change from day to day.

The other way to pass menu items is as literal strings. Thus, a call to PopUp that displays a menu of several cities would look like this:

```
get PopUp (field "Last Item",¬
"New York,Chicago,Dallas,Los Angeles")
```

To disable an item in a menu, simply place a left parenthesis before the item. Thus, if you wish to disable the Dallas item in the above menu, the statement would look like this:

```
get PopUp (field "Last Item",¬
"New York,Chicago,(Dallas,Los Angeles")
```

The menu would look like the one in Figure 28-7. A disabled item shows in the menu, but it is dimmed, and may not be selected with the mouse.

What the XFCN Returns

Because subsequent calls to PopUp require a parameter referring to the last item chosen in that menu, the PopUp function returns that information (in the form of a number), as well as the content of the menu item chosen. The string that PopUp XFCN returns is a two-item string. The first item is the full text of the menu item chosen. The second item is the number corresponding to that item. It's up to the HyperTalk script that calls this XFCN to put the menu and item number information into their respective fields or variables after the menu item has been chosen.

There is also one other piece of work that the HyperTalk script must take care of. If the user drags the mouse away from the popped menu and releases

Figure 28-7 *You may disable a menu item by preceding its text with a left parenthesis.*

the mouse button without selecting an item, the XFCN returns a zero as the item number and an empty string as the item text. The HyperTalk script must trap for that occasion and make sure the current content of the shadow field and any holder of that last item count are not touched when no item is chosen in the menu.

Design Assumptions

To replicate the action of Toolbox pop-up menus, the HyperCard shadow field and button must work in tandem. First of all, the XFCN is written with the assumption that the HyperCard object making the call is a transparent button (card or background) that contains the title of the menu. The title appears immediately to the left of where the pop-up menu appears and where the final item will display in a shadow field. The XFCN uses the coordinates of the button's rectangle to highlight the menu title.

If the button is the object that calls the PopUp XFCN, then that button may have to be pressed by remote control if the user clicks on the shadow field, as the pop-up menu interface guideline insists. Therefore, the locked shadow field has a mouseDown handler in it that sends a mouseDown message to the button. In the case of the Next Follow Up pop-up menu in our Prospects stack, the shadow field has this handler as its sole script:

```
on mouseDown
  send mouseDown to bkgnd button "Next Follow Up"
end mouseDown
```

The button, then, has its own mouseDown handler, which takes care of the entire pop-up menu and information handling:

```
on mouseDown
  get popUp (field "Last Type","Phone,Letter,Meeting Here",¬
  "Meeting There")
  if item 1 of it is not empty then
    put item 1 of it into field "Next Follow Up"
    put item 2 of it into field "Last Type"
  end if
end mouseDown
```

Notice two important things about this script. First, when a list of literal menu strings needs to be broken into two or more lines to be seen in the Script Editor window, you must break up the list by: a) closing the quote of a complete item; b) placing the comma separator at the end of the line; and c) after pressing

Option-Return to insert the soft carriage return (identified by the ¬character), starting the next line with a quotation mark. You may do this for as many lines as you need. Just be sure the comma separator at the end of each line is outside the end quote mark.

Secondly, notice how the handler traps for the instance when the user does not select an item in the menu. The function will return an empty string into item 1. When it is empty, then neither of the two fields is modified.

Because this XFCN behaves like any function, you could insert the function into a Put statement, like this:

```
put item 1 of popUp (0,"Larry,Moe,Curly,Shemp") ¬
into field "Stooge"
```

but that means that if the user doesn't select an item, the Stooge field will be set to empty, erasing previous contents. I believe it's better in virtually all cases to use the PopUp function in a Get statement, and then work with the returned values from the It local variable.

The XFCN Project

The LightSpeed Pascal project for this XFCN is the most complicated of the three in this book primarily because it makes a number of Toolbox calls that the other don't. The project file lineup is:

DA PasLib
MacTraps
ROM85Lib
XQuickDraw
XMenuMgr
ROM85
XCMD Interface.p
XCMD Utilities.p
PopUp.p

The file PopUp.p is the source code file for the XFCN.

How the XFCN Works

Listing 28-1 is Chris's LightSpeed Pascal source code for the PopUp XFCN.

The main PopUp procedure calls one local procedure (HandleError) and five local functions (ErrOccurred, GetTheTarget, CustomMenu, GetLastItem, and PopUpOK). The two error sections you've already met in the About box, so we won't repeat their discussion here. The GetTheTarget function finds the coordinates of the button that called the XFCN. With these coordinates the function knows where the rectangle on the screen is to invert (highlight) and where to display the pop-up menu. CustomMenu adds menu items to the menu when a MENU resource is not specified as a parameter. GetLastItem handles the first parameter of the PopUp message to set the checkmarked item in the menu. Again, pay attention to handle locking and unlocking. Also notice in PopUpOK how Chris checks whether pop-up menus are available in the system you're running. Since HyperCard is supposed to run on System 3.2 (on a Mac Plus), this XFCN has to as well without crashing.

Let's start with the main procedure. The basic steps are as follows:

1. *Save the current grafport so we can restore it after we're done with the pop-up menu.*

2. *Make sure that at least two parameters (the bare minimum) were passed along with the PopUp function call from HyperTalk.* If insufficient parameters were sent, then use the HandleError procedure to alert the user to the fact via the ALRT 3100 alert box.

3. *Call the PopUpOK function.* Pop-up menues were implemented in the Toolbox starting with System 4.0. If you're running System 3.2, the XFCN will not attempt a disastrous unimplemented call.

4. *Call the GetTheTarget function to load coordinates of the target button into appropriate variables.* The target name (i.e., the name of the button) must be less than about 30 characters, or else HyperCard's own menus may get confused later on—but menu titles should be short, anyway. This function, importantly, converts the coordinates (which come with reference to the HyperCard grafport) to global coordinates, which the PopUp Toolbox call will need to draw the menu in the right place on the screen. Note that just prior to locking handles that stay locked for some time, Chris calls MoveHHi. This puts the handle at the top of the heap, thus preventing heap fragmentation if HyperCard needs memory during a callback.

5. *Call the GetLastItem function.*
   a. Retrieve the first parameter (the number of the last checked item) and convert it to a Pascal string (using the ZeroToPas call, which is one of the glue routines).
   b. Test for the result of the HyperCard callback by comparing the result of the call to the xresSucc constant (one of the constants defined in the XCMD interface files compiled with the code).
   c. Convert the parameter (currently a Pascal string) to an integer and make sure it's not a negative number.

6. *If there are more than two parameters passed with the message, then create a new menu (with the CustomMenu function) and insert items from the container or the literal string list into the menu item list.* This is done in a loop that uses the number of items as a counter. Each time through the loop, the text of the next item is appended to the menu item list, whose handle is called popupMenuHdl.

7. *If there are only two parameters (meaning that the call either includes a MENU resource name or an itemized container), then first try to take care of the MENU resource instance.* If this fails, then call the CustomMenu function to make menu items out of the itemized container. This section uses a number of menu-related Toolbox calls, but most of the statements are devoted to error checking, making sure that the MENU resource is available and that various handles to the menu information are retrieved properly. Importantly, if there is an error in retrieving resource information, the handle to the MENU resource in memory is released, thus freeing up that part of memory for later use. The key part of this section, however, is to store the handle to the MENU items in a variable called popupMenuHdl.

8. *Invert the rectangular area of the button that called the XFCN.* We must use this route rather than simply set the hilite property of the button to true because of a quirk in HyperCard, mentioned earlier in the book. Setting that property to true will de-select any text selection on the card. If the pop-up menu relies on that selection being maintained throughout, the hilite version will not work the way you intend. By inverting just the rectangle of the button, the selection is maintained without any problem.

9. *If the last item parameter is something other than zero, then set the item marker of the pop-up menu to the numbered item passed along as a parameter with the PopUp function.* If the item is zero, then no menu item is so marked.

10. *Insert the menu items into the menu list in memory.* Pop-up menus are treated as hierarchical menus in the Toolbox, so the second parameter to the InsertMenu call is -1, the same as for hierarchical menus (see *Inside Macintosh*, Volume 5).

11. *Display the pop-up menu with a top left corner one pixel down and to the right from the top right coordinate of the button.* As long as the menu is showing (i.e., before you release the mouse button), the execution of this XFCN goes no further. When you release the button, then more things happen. The first is that the number of the item chosen in the menu is assigned to the variable *item*.

12. *Remove the menu from the menu list in memory.*

13. *Initialize to empty the string that will be sent back to HyperCard.*

14. *Retrieve the text of the menu item selected by referencing the item number against the list of text items.*

15. *Put the text of the menu item and the item number in a comma-separated variable, retStr.* In case you call the Apple MENU resource, this XFCN strips out the leading null byte (ASCII zero) that is invisibly refore each desk accessory name. A leading zero would wreak havoc in conversion back to a zero-terminated string.

16. *Invert the rectangle of the button again, to restore it to its original, unhighlighted state.*

17. *Release memory allocated to the menu only if a custom (non-resource) menu was created; otherwise, release the handle to the menu resource.*

18. *Put the returned value, retStr, into the parameter block (in the re-*

turnValue slot) as a zero-terminated string (converted from a Pascal string).

19. Restore the grafport to the original HyperCard grafport.

Now let's see what it takes to make a MENU resource.

Creating the MENU Resource

You can create the MENU resource that your PopUp XFCN can use to find text that goes into the pop-up menu. Using ResEdit, creating the resource is pretty simple. Here are the steps from scratch.

1. Start ResEdit, and open the file to which you wish to add the MENU resource. If you are prompted about creating a resource fork on a file, click OK.

2. Choose New from the File menu.
A dialog box will let you scroll through all the predefined resource types that ResEdit knows. Find MENU and click on it and the OK button. ResEdit will open a MENU resource and assign a resource ID number to it.

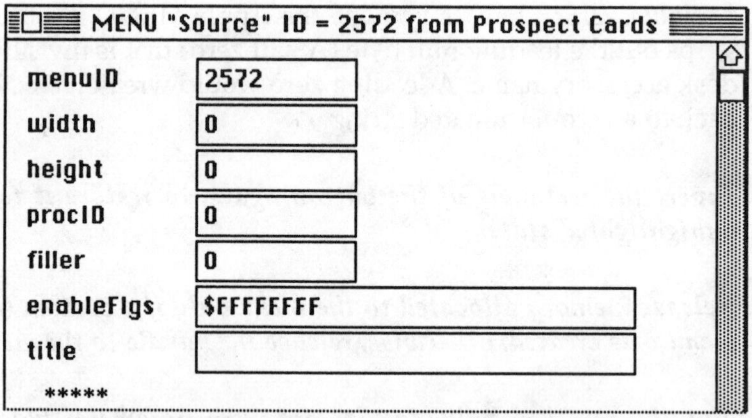

```
▦▢▤  MENU "Source" ID = 2572 from Prospect Cards ▦

    menuID       2572
    width        0
    height       0
    procID       0
    filler       0
    enableFlgs   $FFFFFFFF
    title
    *****
```

Figure 28-8 *Creating a menu resource starts with this ResEdit window. Make sure the enableFlags field looks like the one here. Most items are automatically taken care of by the Toolbox. To start entering menu items, double click on the row of asterisks at the bottom.*

3. *Choose Get Info from the File menu.*

4. *Type the name of the MENU resource, as you will be passing with your PopUp function call in your stack.*

5. *After you close the Get Info box, double click on the MENU resource listing in the window.*

6. *The new window is the one in which you enter the menu specifications.* Type the resource ID number into the menuID field.
Figure 28-8 shows how you should fill in the rest of the fields. Most are zeros, except for enableFlgs, which tells the Macintosh to enable all items in the menu, no matter how long the menu is (don't forget the dollar sign, signifying the hexadecimal numbering system). Enter the name of the menu you've assigned into the title field (although this information is not used in a pop-up menu).

7. *To start adding menu item names, double click on the row of asterisks at the bottom of the window.*
This creates a menu item, whose complete specification is shown in Figure

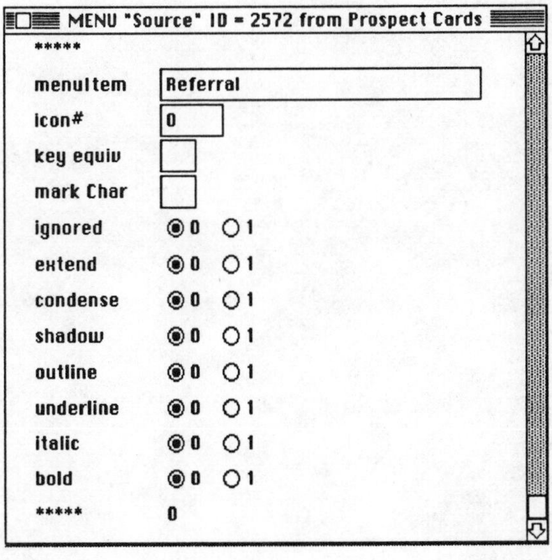

```
⊞▢▤  MENU "Source" ID = 2572 from Prospect Cards  ▤  ⇧
*****
menuItem       Referral
icon#          0
key equiv      ▢
mark Char      ▢
ignored        ⊙ 0   ○ 1
extend         ⊙ 0   ○ 1
condense       ⊙ 0   ○ 1
shadow         ⊙ 0   ○ 1
outline        ⊙ 0   ○ 1
underline      ⊙ 0   ○ 1
italic         ⊙ 0   ○ 1
bold           ⊙ 0   ○ 1
*****          0                                     ⇩
```

Figure 28-9 *A menu item for a pop-up menu needs little more than the item's text. All other settings are normally left at zero.*

28-9. The only information you need to set here are the menuItem name (the text of the item as it is to appear in the menu) and a zero for an icon number.

Listing 28-1

```
{    Title       :    PopUp -- an XFCN to handle a PopUp menu and return the item selected. }
{    Author      :    Chris Knepper }
{    Date        :    5/22/88 }
{    From        :    Danny Goodman's HyperCard Developer's Guide }
{    Publisher   :    Bantam Books, Inc. }
{    Copyright   ©  1988 by Danny Goodman.  All rights reserved. }

unit PopUpUnit;

interface

    uses
        ColorQuickDraw,                    { this library is necessary for ColorMenuMgr }
        ColorMenuMgr,                      { library for PopUpMenuSelect }
        ROM85, XCMDIntf,                   { the data structures for the XCMD }
        XCMDUtils;                         { the glue for the HyperCard callbacks }

    procedure Main (paramPtr : XCmdPtr);        { the entrypoint to the XFCN }

implementation

    procedure PopUp (paramPtr : XCmdPtr);
        label
            1;                             { This marks the end of PopUp so that when errors occur, }
                                           { the processing jumps here. }
        const
            MYPOPUP = 767;                 { the menu ID used in NewMenu (I like planes) }
        var
            savePort                       { stores the current port }
              : GrafPtr;
            myHdl                          { stores the results of calls to EvalExpr }
              : Handle;
            retStr,                        { sends a result back to HyperCard }
            pascalStr,                     { Used to convert zero-terminated strings to Pascal strings. }
            menuName,                      { stores the name of the menu. }
            theTarget                      { stores the target }
              : Str255;
            resourceID,                    { resource id returned by GetResInfo }
            menuID,                        { menu id derived from menu data structure }
            lastItem,                      { the last item selected by the user }
            count                          { for loop counter }
              : integer;
            popupMenuHdl                   { handle to the pop up menu }
              : MenuHandle;
            item                           { the result of PopUpMenuSelect }
              : longint;
```

```
    menuType                  { Stores the resource type for the call to GetResInfo. }
      : Restype;
    theRect                   { Stores the rect of the target. }
      : Rect;
    thePoint                  { Stores the point to pass to PopUpMenuSelect. }
      : Point;
    NewMenuWasCalled          { flag which indicates how to clean up }
      : Boolean;
{------------------------------------------------------------------------}
  procedure HandleError (myStr : Str255);
  { HandleError sets the cursor to the arrow cursor and displays an error Alert }
  { informing the user of the error.  This procedure assumes that the ALRT & DITL }
  { resources with id = 3100 exist in HyperCard's resource fork. Although this is a }
  { valid assumption in HyperCard versions 1.1 and 1.0.1.  Calls to GetResource() verify }
  { that these resources do, in fact, exist.  If they don't, this procedure produces a beep. }
    const
      ERROR = 3100;                         { use a HC ALRT for error messages. }
    var
      whichItem : integer;                  { stores result of the Alert function }
    begin
    if (GetResource('ALRT', 3100) = nil) or (GetResource('DITL', 3100) = nil) then
       SysBeep(60)                          { beep if no ALRT or DITL resource }
      else
       begin
         InitCursor;                        { set cursor to the arrow cursor }
         ParamText(myStr, '', '', '');      { specify the ALRT's text }
         whichItem := Alert(ERROR, nil);    { display and handle the ALRT }
         SendCardMessage(paramPtr, 'set cursor to 4');   { set cursor to watch }
       end;
    end;                                    { procedure HandleError }
{------------------------------------------------------------------------}
  function ErrOccurred (errNum : OSErr;
                 routineName : Str255) : Boolean;
  { ErrOccurred determines if an error occurred by comparing errNum with NoErr. }
  { If equal, ErrOccurred returns FALSE indicating that no error occurred.  Otherwise, }
  { it returns TRUE, indicating that an error occurred and creates a string from }
  { errNum and routineName which it then passes to HandleError. }
    var
      errStr                                { store error number as a Pascal string }
        : Str255;
    begin
    if (errNum = noErr) then
       ErrOccurred := FALSE                 { no error occurred -- return FALSE }
      else
       begin
         ErrOccurred := TRUE;               { oops, error occurred -- return TRUE }
         NumToString(errNum, errStr);       { convert error number to a string }
```

```
              HandleError(Concat(routineName, ' returned ', errStr, '.')); { inform user }
          end;
      end;                                      { function ErrOccurred }
{--------------------------------------------------------------------------}
   function GetTheTarget : boolean;
   { The function GetTheTarget gets and saves the target for future access.  If errors }
   { occur, GetTheTarget returns FALSE, otherwise it returns TRUE. }
      label
         8;                                     { The end of the function. }
      var
        myExpr                                  { stores an expression evaluated by HC }
         : Str255;
        count                                   { for loop counter }
         : Integer;
      begin
        GetTheTarget := TRUE;                   { return TRUE indicates no errors }
        myExpr := 'the target';                 { expression to evaluate }
        myHdl := EvalExpr(paramPtr, myExpr);    { evaluate the expression }
        with paramPtr^ do
          begin
            if ((myHdl = nil) or (myHdl^ = nil) or (result <> xresSucc)) then
              begin { inform user of error }
                HandleError('Can''t get the target.');   { inform user }
                GetTheTarget := FALSE;          { return FALSE indicates an error occurred }
                goto 8;                         { leave this function }
              end;
            MoveHHi(myHdl);                     { give HyperCard breathing room }
            HLock(myHdl);                       { lock the handle before calling ZeroToPas }
            ZeroToPas(paramPtr, myHdl^, theTarget);
            DisposHandle(myHdl);                { dispose of the storage allocated by EvalExpr }
            if (result <> xresSucc) then        { set as a result of ZeroToPas }
              begin
                HandleError('ZeroToPas failed on the target.');   { inform user }
                GetTheTarget := FALSE;          { return FALSE indicates an error occurred }
                goto 8;                         { leave this function }
              end;
            for count := 1 to 4 do              { Get the rect of theTarget. }
              begin
                NumToString(count, pascalStr);  { convert item to string }
                myExpr := Concat('item ', pascalStr, ' of the rect of ', theTarget);
                myHdl := EvalExpr(paramPtr, myExpr);   { evaluate the expression }
                if ((myHdl = nil) or (myHdl^ = nil) or (result <> xresSucc)) then
                  begin { inform user of error }
                    HandleError(Concat('Can''t get item ', pascalStr, ' of the rect of ', theTarget));
                    GetTheTarget := FALSE;      { returning FALSE indicates an error }
                    DisposHandle(myHdl);        { dispose of the storage allocated by EvalExpr }
                    goto 8;                     { leave this function }
                  end;
                MoveHHi(myHdl);                 { give HyperCard breathing room }
```

```
        HLock(myHdl);    { lock down the handle before calling ZeroToPas }
        ZeroToPas(paramPtr, myHdl^, pascalStr);
        DisposHandle(myHdl);              { dispose of the storage allocated by EvalExpr }
        if (result <> xresSucc) then      { set as a result of call to ZeroToPas }
          begin
            NumToString(count, pascalStr);  { convert item to string }
            pascalStr := Concat('Can"t convert item ', pascalStr);
            HandleError(Concat(pascalStr, ' of CommStorage to Pascal string.'));
            GetTheTarget := FALSE;         { returning FALSE indicates an error }
            goto 8;                        { leave this function }
          end;
        StringToNum(pascalStr, item);      { convert to a number }
        with theRect do                    { assign the items of the rect }
          case count of
            1 :                            { the first item is the left coordinate }
              left := item;
            2 :
              begin                        { the second item is the top coordinate }
                top := item;
                thePoint.v := item;        { Get the top item of the point. }
              end;
            3 :
              begin                        { the third item is the right coordinate }
                right := item;
                thePoint.h := item;        { Get the right item of the point. }
              end;
            4 :                            { the fourth item is the bottom coordinate }
              bottom := item;
          end;                             { case statement }
        end;                               { for loop }
      LocalToGlobal(thePoint);             { Convert thePoint to global coordinates }
    end;                                   { with paramPtr^ }
8 :                                        { The end of the function -- jump here if errors }
  end;                                     { function GetTheTarget }
{----------------------------------------------------------------------------}
  function CustomMenu : boolean;
  { The function CustomMenu creates a custom menu.  Now we know that either there }
  { are more than 2 parameters passed in or that the second parameter is a list of menu items. }
  { So, create a custom menu from the items passed in. }
    label
      9;                                   { the end of function CustomMenu }
    var
      count,                               { the for loop counter when getting the parameters }
      charCounter                          { the for loop counter when converting "," to ";" }
        : integer;
```

```
        scrLongint                        { scratch long integer used when calling NumToString }
        : longint;

    procedure CustomMenuError;
        { The subprocedure CustomMenuError handles errors in CustomMenu. }
    begin                                 { procedure CustomMenuError }
        HUnLock(paramPtr^.params[count]);   { unlock handle }
        scrLongint := count;              { convert to longint }
        NumToString(scrLongint, pascalStr);  { convert item to string }
        DisposeMenu(popupMenuHdl);         { release menu's memory }
    end;                                  { procedure CustomMenuError }


begin                                     { function CustomMenu }
    CustomMenu := FALSE;                  { default FALSE to indicate errors }
    popupMenuHdl := NewMenu(MYPOPUP, 'C.S.K.');    { allocate a menu handle }
    if (popupMenuHdl = nil) then
        HandleError('NewMenu returned a nil handle')   { inform user of error }
    else
    begin
        NewMenuWasCalled := TRUE;          { TRUE indicates that NewMenu was called }
        with paramPtr^ do
            for count := 2 to paramCount do   { Add items to the menu. }
            begin
                { Ensure that each item passed in will fit into a Pascal string. }
                MoveHHi(params[count]);    { give HyperCard breathing room }
                HLock(params[count]);      { lock the handle before dereferencing }
                if (StringLength(paramPtr, params[count]^) > 255) then
                    begin
                    CustomMenuError;
                    HandleError(Concat('PopUp parameter ', pascalStr, ' is too long.'));
                    goto 9;                { exit CustomMenu }
                    end;
                if (result <> xresSucc) then   { set as a result of StringLength }
                    begin
                    CustomMenuError;
                    HandleError(Concat('StringLength failed on parameter ', pascalStr));
                    goto 9;                { exit CustomMenu }
                    end;
                ZeroToPas(paramPtr, params[count]^, pascalStr);  { convert to pascal str }
                if (result <> xresSucc) then   { set as a result of ZeroToPas }
                    begin
                    CustomMenuError;
                    HandleError(Concat('ZeroToPas failed on parameter ', pascalStr));
                    goto 9;                { exit CustomMenu }
                    end;
```

```
            for charCounter := 1 to Length(pascalStr) do  { convert "," to ";" }
                if (pascalStr[charCounter] = ',') then { change "," to ";"... }
                    pascalStr[charCounter] := ';';            { ...before calling AppendMenu. }
            if (pascalStr = '') then          { Ensure item isn't empty. }
                begin
                    CustomMenuError;
                    HandleError(Concat('PopUp parameter ', pascalStr, ' is empty.'));
                    goto 9;                     { exit CustomMenu }
                end;
                HUnLock(params[count]);        { unlock handle }
                AppendMenu(popupMenuHdl, pascalStr);   { Add these items to pop up menu. }
            end;                               { for loop }
        CustomMenu := TRUE;                    { yay, no errors! }
    end;                                       { if popupMenuHdl=nil }
9 :                                            { end of function CustomMenu }
    end;                                       { function CustomMenu }
{-----------------------------------------------------------------------}
    function GetLastItem : boolean;
    { GetLastItem gets the first parameter to the XFCN, which is the last item chosen }
    { by the user.  If there is an error, GetLastItem returns FALSE, otherwise, it }
    { returns TRUE. }
    begin
        GetLastItem := TRUE;                   { TRUE means no errors }
        with paramPtr^ do
            begin
                HLock(params[1]);                       { lock handle before dereferencing }
                ZeroToPas(paramPtr, params[1]^, pascalStr);    { 1st parameter is last item }
                HUnLock(params[1]);                     { unlock handle }
                if (result <> xresSucc) then   { set as a result of call to ZeroToPas }
                    begin
                        HandleError('Can''t convert the 1st parameter to Pascal string.');
                        GetLastItem := FALSE;           { FALSE means errors occurred }
                    end
                else
                    begin
                        StringToNum(pascalStr, item);   { Convert to an integer and test later. }
                        lastItem := item;
                        if (lastItem < 0) then
                            begin
                                HandleError('The last item can''t be negative.');   { inform user of error }
                                GetLastItem := FALSE;   { FALSE means errors occurred }
                            end;
                    end;
            end;                               { with paramPtr^ }
    end;                                       { function GetLastItem }
{-----------------------------------------------------------------------}
    function PopUpOK : Boolean;
    { PopUpMenuSelect, implemented in System 4.0 and above, may not }
```

```
{ be available, since HyperCard runs on System 3.2 and above.  So, check if the }
{ trap is implemented using the NGetTrapAddress call.  Compare the results }
{ of NGetTrapAddress for the PopUpTrap and the UnImplTrapNum.  Return FALSE }
{ if not implemented, TRUE otherwise. }
  const
    PopUpTrap = $A80B;                      { trap number of PopUpMenuSelect }
    UnImplTrapNum = $9F;                    { trap number of "unimplemented trap" }
  var
    PopUpAddress,                           { address of PopUpMenuSelect trap }
    UnImplTrapAddress                       { address of UnImplementedTrap }
     : Longint;
  begin
    PopUpAddress := NGetTrapAddress(PopUpTrap, ToolTrap);
    UnImplTrapAddress := NGetTrapAddress(UnImplTrapNum, ToolTrap);
    if (PopUpAddress <> UnImplTrapAddress) then
      PopUpOK := TRUE                       { return TRUE if implemented }
    else
      begin
        PopUpOK := FALSE;                   { return FALSE if not implemented }
        HandleError('PopUpMenuSelect is not implemented.');    { inform user }
      end;
  end;                                      { function PopUpOK }
{-------------------------------------------------------------------}
  begin                                     { procedure PopUp }
    GetPort(savePort);                      { get and save the port }

    if (paramPtr^.paramCount < 2) then      { at least 2 parameters needed }
      begin                                 { inform user of error }
        HandleError('Call PopUp with: <Last Item>, <MENU name> | <container> | <Item List>');
        goto 1;                             { exit PopUp }
      end;

    if not PopUpOK then                     { is PopUpMenuSelect implemented? }
      goto 1;                               { exit PopUp }

    NewMenuWasCalled := FALSE;              { boolean flag indicates how to clean up }

    if not GetTheTarget then                { get and save the target & its rect }
      goto 1;                               { If there are errors , exit PopUp }
    if not GetLastItem then                 { get 1st parameter -- the last item }
      goto 1;                               { If there is an error, exit PopUp }

    with paramPtr^ do
      begin
        if (paramCount > 2) then            { if more than 2 parameters, create menu }
          begin
            if not CustomMenu then          { Create the menu from that list of items }
              goto 1;                       { If there is an error, exit PopUp }
          end
```

```
        else
          begin                              { 1st, assume that the MENU rsrc is in this stack }
            HLock(params[2]);
            ZeroToPas(paramPtr, params[2]^, menuName); { Get the MENU rsrc name. }
            HUnLock(params[2]);
            if (result <> xresSucc) then      { set as a result of call to ZeroToPas }
              begin
                HandleError('Can''t convert the 2nd parameter to Pascal string.');
                goto 1;                        { If there is an error, exit PopUp }
              end;
            myHdl := GetNamedResource('MENU', menuName);{ Get a handle to the MENU rsrc. }
            if (ResError <> noErr) or (myHdl = nil) then
              begin                            { an error => the author passed in a container }
                if not CustomMenu then
                  goto 1;                      { If there is an error, exit PopUp }
              end
            else
              begin
                popUpMenuHdl := MenuHandle(myHdl);          { use type coercion to check if }
                if (popUpMenuHdl^^.menuProc = nil) then     {    GetMenu has been called }
                  begin
                    GetResInfo(myHdl, resourceID, menuType, menuName);   { get the ID of the MENU }
                    if ErrOccurred(ResError, 'GetResInfo') then
                      begin
                        ReleaseResource(myHdl); { clean up }
                        goto 1;                  { Leave the XFCN }
                      end;
                    popupMenuHdl := GetMenu(resourceID);    { Get the MENU from the rsrc fork of the stack }
                    if (popupMenuHdl = nil) then
                      begin
                        HandleError('GetMenu returned a nil handle.'); { inform user }
                        ReleaseResource(myHdl); { clean up }
                        goto 1;                  { Leave the XFCN }
                      end;                       { if popUpMenuHdl = nil }
                  end;                           { if menuProc = nil }
              end;                               { if ResError <> noErr }
          end;                                   { if paramCount = 2 }
      end;                                       { with paramPtr^ }


{ Display and handle the popup menu. }
InvertRect(theRect);                             { Highlight the target. }
{ Decide which item to check, if the lastItem = 0, don't check any item.  If }
{ the last item is too large, check the first item. }
if (lastItem <> 0) then
  begin
    { Ensure lastItem <= number of menu items (if not, set to 1) then check it. }
      if (lastItem > CountMItems(popupMenuHdl)) then
        lastItem := 1;                          { default to 1 if lastItem > # menu items }
      CheckItem(popupMenuHdl, lastItem, TRUE);  { check last item chosen }
```

```
      end;
    InsertMenu(popupMenuHdl, -1);              { Insert the menu into the menu list. }
    CalcMenuSize(popupMenuHdl);                { b/c PopUpMenuSelect bug: System 4.0 }
    with thePoint do                           { PopUpMenuSelect handles the pop up menu. }
      item := PopUpMenuSelect(popupMenuHdl, v + 1, h + 1, lastItem);
    menuID := popUpMenuHdl^^.MenuID;
    DeleteMenu(menuID);                        { Remove the menu from the menu list. }
    retStr := '';                              { Initialize the returnValue to ''. }
    if (HiWord(item) = 0) then                 { If no item is selected, then... }
      retStr := ',0'                           { text is empty and item # is 0. }
    else
      begin                                    { If an item is selected, then... }
        item := LoWord(item);                  { Low word contains menu item selected. }
        GetItem(popupMenuHdl, item, retStr);   { Get the text of the item selected. }
        NumToString(item, pascalStr);          { Convert the item chosen to text. }
        if (retStr[1] = Chr(0)) then           { special case for DA's }
          begin                                { strip out the leading null byte }
            for count := 2 to Length(retStr) do
              begin
                retStr[count - 1] := retStr[count];
              end;
            retStr[0] := Chr(Length(retStr) - 1);
          end;
        retStr := Concat(retStr, ',', pascalStr);  { Return the text,item selected. }
      end;
    InvertRect(theRect);                       { Set the highlight of the target to its original state. }

    { Clean up. }
    if NewMenuWasCalled then                   { see Inside Mac I-352 for an explanation }
      DisposeMenu(popupMenuHdl)                { Release the memory taken by the menu. }
    else
      CheckItem(popUpMenuHdl, lastItem, FALSE);    { uncheck item chosen }

    { Return retStr so that HyperTalk can access it as a result of the function. }
    paramPtr^.returnValue := PasToZero(paramPtr, retStr);

    SetPort(savePort);                         { Restore the port. }

1 :                                            { the end of the procedure PopUp }
  end;                                         { Procedure PopUp }
{--------------------------------------------------------------------------}
  procedure Main;
{ The procedure Main is the entrypoint and simply calls the procedure PopUp. }
  begin
    PopUp(paramPtr);                           { the call to the PopUp XFCN }
  end;
{--------------------------------------------------------------------------}
end.                                           { PopUp Unit }
{--------------------------------------------------------------------------}
```

29

A Serial Port XCMD

One of the largest untapped HyperCard stack categories is control of external devices. Into this category goes using HyperCard as a friendly front end to on-line information retrieval (through a commercial service or a networked mainframe computer). But there are also many opportunities for controlling devices that have serial ports on them. Such devices could be as simple as the X-10 style home light and appliance controller or as complex as manufacturing process controls. There may be a special purpose serial printer—like one that is sized to work with continuous feed, one-up mailing labels—that needs ASCII characters sent to it. A host of sophisticated laboratory test equipment can be accessed through serial communications. Before the end of 1988, we'll be able to control home versions of programmable laser videodisc players through a serial connection.

HyperCard, by itself, does not offer direct control of the Macintosh serial ports. The Comm XCMD in this chapter, however, adds that power to HyperCard.

What Comm Can Do

Before we get too far, I should explain that Comm is not intended to be a telecommunications terminal program. In other words, there is no interactive window into which you and a remote computer "converse." Instead, the Comm XCMD is to be used as a means of sending and receiving text information through the serial port behind the scenes. You then use a HyperTalk script to control the flow of information into and out of the Macintosh. When information comes in, your HyperTalk script can distribute it to various cards as needed. The script may also take text you typed earlier into an outgoing message kind of card, and send it through the serial port to the remote computer.

As the example stack in this chapter will show, you can design a stack around the Comm XCMD that logs onto a commercial service, retrieves specific bits of information, logs off the service, and distributes the information among cards so that the user can browse the information casually, when the Macintosh is not connected to the service. The more you can automate the information retrieval part of the exchange, the more quickly and efficiently it's retrieved. Connect charges are kept to a minimum, because there is no fumbling for commands to retrieve the data. Nor is the user distracted by the information as it rolls in. Only after the information is safely stored on familiar cards is he given access to it. And then it doesn't cost a cent to browse at will. You can even automate the process so that information is retrieved automatically overnight or while the user is at lunch. When he returns, the information stack is ready and waiting. Except for the time it takes to log onto the system and retrieve the information, the access to remote information is practically transparent to the user. It's almost as if the remote computer were part of the person's HyperCard stack.

The Stack

For our example I put together a simple communications front end to one of CompuServe's weather services. The stack is called The Weather Machine (Figure 29-1). Among the various services is one that gives you the National

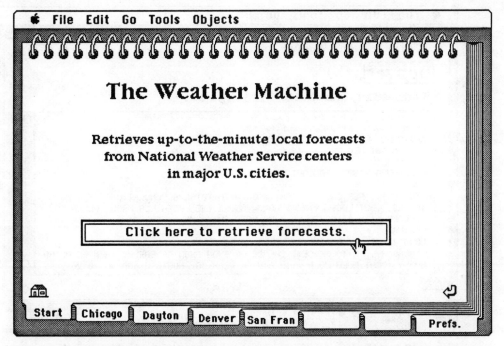

Figure 29-1 *The Start card of The Weather Machine provides a field that displays call progress messages as the stack logs on to the National Weather Service (via CompuServe) and retrieves forecasts for up to six cities.*

Weather Service local forecast for individual cities in the United States. As far as I can tell, these are the same forecasts that the radio and television stations and local newspapers get from the NWS. Forecasts for each city are prepared by meteorologists in each of the NWS offices and then made available to CompuServe subscribers.

To keep the complexity of the stack to a minimum, I've designed it with one particular applications scenario in mind. The setting is someone who likes to retrieve weather forecasts from a relatively stable list of one to six cities around the country, perhaps once or twice a day. Frequent business travelers or executives with branch offices in other cities may like to have this weather information handy or retrievable within a couple of minutes.

Information retrieval is so automatic in this stack that once a few Preferences card fields are set (they only need to be set once), the user simply clicks on one button. Call progress is displayed on the Start card. As each city's weather is downloaded from the service, its text is placed on a separate card for that city, along with the date and time the forecast was retrieved (Figure 29-2). A click on the city's tab of the on-screen flipbook brings up that city's card.

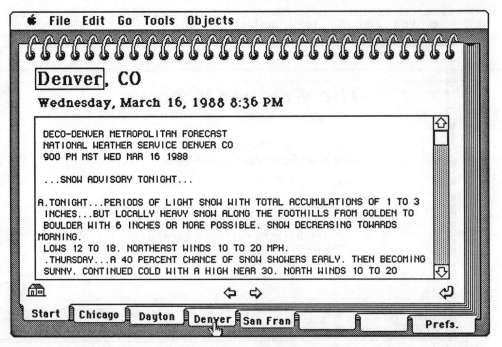

Figure 29-2 *After logging off, you may browse casually (and with no on-line charges) through the forecasts for the desired cities, each of which has been stored on its own card.*

Calling Conventions

This single XCMD acts as if it were four different XCMDs, depending on the first parameter sent along with the command. With one XCMD, we can open the serial port (as well as optionally specify whatever communications settings we like), close the port, read data that has come in through the port and write data out the port.

Before getting to the Comm command in your script, however, you must declare a global variable in all handlers that call Comm. This global must be named "commStorage." When Comm closes the serial port, commStorage is set to empty, but it is still declared. This global stores a few important values that Comm needs for reading and writing data. Unfortunately, HyperCard versions prior to 1.2 will not allow an XCMD to declare a HyperTalk global variable, but it may get and set the contents of a previously declared Hyper-Talk global. To accommodate users of older versions of HyperCard, the global must be declared "manually."

Opening and Closing Serial Ports

Opening the serial port is accomplished in one of two ways. If you are satisfied with the default communications settings (modem port, 1200 baud, 1 stop bit, no parity and 8 data bits), then you can open the port with this command:

```
Comm "open"
```

Alternatively, you can make other than the default settings by sending the entire string of settings along with the command, as in:

```
Comm "open","modem","300","1","even","7"
```

If you want to change only one setting from the default setting, you must include all the settings in the string.

Since this XCMD allows for only one port open at a time, you can close that port by sending the command

```
Comm "close"
```

when you're finished with the communications session. Always be sure to close the communications port when you're finished. Failing to do so may disrupt other serial functions later on.

Writing and Reading

To send text out the serial port, you issue the Comm "write" command along with the string you wish to write. The string may be in a container, such as a field or variable. Therefore, if you have an outgoing message in a field, you can send it with a command like:

```
Comm "write",field "Message"
```

Reading information into your stack requires a bit of explanation. While the serial port is open, any data that comes into it from outside is temporarily stored in a part of memory reserved for that purpose. That memory area is called a serial buffer, because it acts as a buffer between the information inflow and the eventual way in which you handle the information. The Comm XCMD is set up so that if the serial buffer begins to fill up, it sends a commonly recognized command to the sending party that it should stop (called XOFF, and pronounced *eks-off*).

The job of your HyperTalk script is to retrieve text from the serial buffer often enough so that incoming information may continue to flow into the buffer at an efficient rate. It doesn't do you any good to be connected to an on-line service that charges by the minute while your serial buffer is filled. The Comm XCMD, when accompanied by the "read" parameter, fetches data from the serial buffer. You may then see the data that was pulled from the buffer by using the HyperCard Result function. When the Result function is called immediately after a Comm "read" command, the current contents of the serial buffer are returned by the Result function. Therefore, you use Comm "read" and the Result function as a kind of scoop to take data from the serial buffer and put it into another container where it's safe from overflow (at least up to 32,000 characters). Each time you perform a Comm "read" command, the serial buffer is cleared, ready for further input. The Result function returns only that data taken from the buffer at the last Comm "read" command.

Basically, then, you need a loop in your stack that continually "listens" to what comes into the serial buffer. If your communications front end must wait for a particular prompt before sending the password, then you keep pulling data from the buffer and comparing it with the prompt that you expect. When the container holding all your data contains that prompt, then your script should know it's safe to send the password data.

Connecting to a Service

Telecommunications is not an easy subject for newcomers, because there are so many elements to worry about. There's making sure the computer can communicate with the modem. Then the computer must communicate with the telecommunications service, which has its own software interface of prompts and commands. This isn't the place to offer instruction about telecommunications services, so I'll have to assume that you are somewhat familiar with logging onto commercial services, like CompuServe.

Every communications program that ties into CompuServe requires user input of key information, such as the local telephone number that the computer dials to access the service. Then there are the account number and password. For the Weather Machine stack, these important settings are stored in fields of the Preferences card (Figure 29-3). There is also a field there for the modem string—the signal to the modem that makes it dial the phone number.

To keep the password somewhat private—at least hidden from casual viewers—the password you type into the apparent Password field on the card goes into a hidden field, while a series of asterisks go into the visible field. All this is triggered by a closeField handler attached to the Password Entry field:

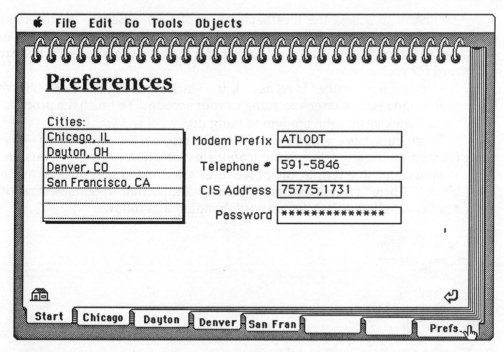

Figure 29-3 *A Preferences card lets you specify important log-on data and the names of cities.*

```
on closeField
   put card field "Password Entry" into card field "Password"
   put "**************" into card field "Password Entry"
end closeField
```

Now, if someone should happen upon this stack on your computer, the actual password is hidden from casual view.

The Communications Session

Before looking into how the Weather Machine scripts connect and retrieve the information, let's see what's involved in the process.

First, the stack must send a command to the modem to dial the phone. If the modem makes the connection with the service, then the stack must send a series of commands in response to prompts for the User ID (the person's CompuServe address) and the password. When that transfer is successful, the stack is officially logged onto CompuServe.

Since the purpose of this stack is to retrieve weather only, it sends the command to access the weather section of CompuServe. In response to prompts from CompuServe, it asks for weather forecasts for each city in turn. As the forecast comes into the Weather Machine, it stores the text in a separate card for each city.

Once all the weather is retrieved, the stack must log off CompuServe to prevent any extra charges accruing to your account. To finish the process, the stack then instructs the modem to hang up.

These three basic action blocks—log on, retrieve the data, log off—are the foundation for any telecommunications information retrieval. Thus, in the Weather Machine scripts, the procedures are divided into those same three blocks. There is one major background handler that triggers several other smaller handlers. That "outermost" handler is as follows:

```
on doSession
  set cursor to 4

  logOn
  getWeather
  logOff

end doSession
```

Each of the building blocks of a communications session has its own custom handler.

Dialing and Logging On

The logOn handler takes care of both dialing via the modem and logging onto the system. First, it gathers the field data from the Preferences card (storing the information in local variables) and then starts a series of sending and receiving.

The entire logOn handler is:

```
on logOn
  global commStorage

  put card field "Modem Prefix" of card "Preferences" ¬
  into modemString
  put card field "Fone Number" of card "Preferences" ¬
  into foneString
  put card field "Account Number" of card "Preferences" ¬
  into acctNo
```

```
    put card field "Password" of card "Preferences" ¬
    into password


    -- open serial port
    Comm "Open"

    -- reset modem (remove these lines for the Apple modem)
    Comm "Write","ATZ" & return
    listenFor "OK"

    -- dialing, handshaking, and logon
    put "Dialing service..." ¬
    into card field "Status" of card "Start"
    Comm "Write",modemString && foneString & return
    listenFor "CONNECT"
    put "Logging on to service..." ¬
    into card field "Status" of card "Start"
    wait 1 seconds
    Comm "Write",numToChar(3)
    listenFor "ID:"
    Comm "Write",acctNo & return
    listenFor "Password:"
    Comm "Write",password & return
    put "Log on process complete..." ¬
    into card field "Status" of card "Start"
end logOn
```

The receiving is done with a generic handler, called listenFor. As a parameter to the listenFor command, you may pass one or two possible prompts that the modem or communications service may send in response to the previous command. The listenFor handler is the one that retrieves data from the serial port buffer and transfers it to a local variable, called buffer. Even though I've used a similar name, this local variable is completely independent of the serial buffer, which you cannot access directly with this XCMD. Here's the listenFor handler:

```
on listenFor prompt1,prompt2
  global commStorage
  put empty into buffer

  repeat until buffer contains prompt1 or buffer contains prompt2
    comm "read"
    put the result after buffer
  end repeat
end listenFor
```

Notice that each time the listenFor handler is called, the local variable, buffer, starts fresh and empty. Each time through the repeat loop, the serial port's buffer is emptied into the local variable. This goes on until one of two possible prompts from the communications service come in through the serial port.

Back in the logOn handler, the Comm commands start with opening the serial port to its default settings. Then the handler sends the text "ATZ" and a carriage return. This is a modem command to reset the modem (although the Apple Personal Modem does not recognize this Hayes-standard command). If the modem has reset correctly, it sends back an "OK." That's what the first listenFor handler waits for.

The remaining sequences in the logOn handler continues by sending the dialing instructions to the modem and waiting for a CONNECT signal back from the modem. To make sure that your Macintosh and the remote computer are tied together, the handler waits for one second before sending the special signal that CompuServe likes to hear when you log on. That character is called a Control-C, which you cannot reproduce from the Mac Plus keyboard. That character turns out to be ASCII value 3. Hence the Comm "Write" command sends the function, numToChar(3), to pass that character to the XCMD. Finally, the handler listens for prompts for the user ID and the password, responding with data entered into the Preferences card.

Getting the Weather

The handler that leads the way for retrieving the weather data is:

```
on getWeather
  global commStorage
  put card field "Cities" of card "Preferences" into theCities

  -- go to Weather section of CompuServe
  listenFor "HELp!","number !"
  Comm "Write","go wea-1" & return
  put "Accessing National Weather Section..." ¬
  into card field "Status" of card "Start"

  listenFor "choice !"
  Comm "Write","LF" & return

  -- retrieve weather for each city and put into separate card
  listenFor "LF ID:"
  repeat with x = 1 to the number of lines of theCities
    get line x of theCities
    put "Getting weather for " & it ¬
```

```
            into card field "Status" of card "Start"
            Comm "Write",it & return

            set lockScreen to true
            go to card x of bkgnd "Forecasts"
            captureUntil "LF ID:"
            put it into field "Where"
            put the long date && the time into field "When"
            go to first card
            set lockScreen to false
        end repeat

        Comm "Write",return
        listenFor "choice !"

    end getWeather
```

The first few steps of retrieving the weather entail more waiting for prompts and issuing commands to enter the weather section of CompuServe. When you enter the National Weather Section of CompuServe, there is a menu that you would normally see on screen in a live telecommunications terminal situation. From the menu, you need to choose "LF" for the local forecast section.

This area has a special prompt, "LF ID:" that waits for the name of the city you wish to retrieve. After that first LF ID: prompt, the getWeather handler goes into a repeat loop for as many times as there are cities listed in theCities, a local variable containing the list from the Preferences card.

Inside the loop, the handler displays a status message with the city's name so you know what's going on. Then it sends the city name to CompuServe in response to the original LF ID: prompt.

To make sure that the data coming in from CompuServe goes into the right card, the screen is locked (so you only see the cover card during processing) and one of the cards from the background series with the large field is made the current card.

At the core of the retrieval is the captureUntil command, which calls another custom handler that is very similar to the listenFor handler. Here it is:

```
on captureUntil prompt1,prompt2
    global commStorage
    put empty into buffer

    repeat until buffer contains prompt1 or buffer contains prompt2
```

```
      comm "read"
      put the result after buffer
   end repeat

   delete line 1 to 3 of buffer
   put char 1 to (offset("$",buffer) -1) of buffer into field 2
end captureUntil
```

This handler retrieves data from the serial port buffer as it does in listenFor. But when the entire batch of data is read into the local variable, buffer, some leading lines and trailing characters are removed from the text, and the remaining text goes into field 2 of the current card. That's the large scrolling field on the city cards.

Back in the getWeather handler, the city name, date, and time are inserted into their respective fields. Before unlocking the screen, the handler returns to the first card. We must unlock the screen and return to the first card so that the next time through the loop the status message can be updated with the name of the next city.

After the repeat loop, the handler sends a carriage return, which returns CompuServe to the previous prompt level. From that level we may log off the service.

Logging Off

After all information is stored safely in its cards, the stack must officially log off CompuServe and hang up the modem. The logOff handler does this:

```
on logOff      -- tell CompuServe we're leaving
   global commStorage

   put "Logging off system..." ¬
   into card field "Status" of card "Start"
   Comm "Write","off" & return

   -- wake up modem for hang-up command
   Comm "Write","+"
   Comm "Write","+"
   Comm "Write","+"
   wait 2 seconds
   Comm "Write","ATH" & return

   put "Weather retrieval completed." ¬
   into card field "Status" of card "Start"
   wait 1 second
```

```
-- close serial port
Comm "Close"

put "Click here to retrieve forecasts." ¬
into card field "Status" of card "Start"
```

```
end logOff
```

Logging off the system is as simple as sending "off" at any CompuServe prompt. There's no need to wait for any further communication from CompuServe.

To hang up the modem, we must first send a signal to the modem that we're about to send it a command, as opposed to sending text through the modem. That signal is a series of three plus signs. In working with a Hayes 2400 modem, I found that writing three plusses as a single string did not work. In fact, modems prefer a more deliberately spaced series of plus signs. Making each sign go by way of its own Comm "write" command did the trick. The modem then likes you to wait a second or two before sending it the command. The command in this case is "ATH," which hangs up the modem.

A status message alerts the user that all is well. After a brief delay and the closing of the serial port, the status message returns to the one that prompts the user to retrieve the weather.

How the XCMD Works

This XCMD in Listing 29-1 is far more complex than the other two for a couple of reasons. The most obvious is that dealing with the serial port is not the easiest part of working with the Macintosh Toolbox. Secondly, the XCMD is doing the work of four XCMDs, depending on the parameters you send it.

Aside from the error handling procedure and function (identical to the same routines in the two previous XCMDs), most of the other procedures and function definitions in Comm help in communicating with the serial port— that is, between the XCMD and the serial port. Each of the four Comm operations (Open, Write, Read and Close) has its own procedure to keep the code more modular. Following the execution of the Comm source code should give you a good introduction to the workings of basic serial port communications on the Macintosh. If you plan to explore the subject further, *Inside Macintosh* is a must.

The LightSpeed Pascal project for Comm is the standard XCMD setup with the following files:

DA PasLib
MacTraps
XCMD Interface.p
XCMD Utilities.p
Comm.p

Comm.p is the source code file for the XCMD.

As a basic outline of the main procedure in the Comm XCMD, we have:

1. *Check parameters to make sure there is at least one sent along with the Comm message.*

2. *Inspect the first parameter and store it as a variable named controlStr.* This variable will be compared against each of four possible parameters. That, in turn, will direct execution to the appropriate procedure for opening, closing, reading, or writing through the serial port.

3. *Check first to see if the parameter is OPEN.*

4. *If so, then branch to the CommOpen procedure.*
   a. Be sure that either no additional parameters or five additional parameters were sent along with the command.
   b. Via the Clear_RefNums_SerBuffPtr function, initialize the HyperTalk CommStorage global variable to zero.
   c. Set the modem or printer port as the current serial port (via the PrinterOrModem function).
   d. Get the communications settings (via the UserConfig function)—either the default settings or the ones passed as parameters.
   e. Allocate memory space for the 2-kilobyte input buffer.
   f. Open both the input and output ports (even though at the HyperTalk level we see them together as one serial port), set their user configurations, and adjust handshaking properties of both ports.
   g. Cement the bond between the buffer memory space and the input serial port with SerSetBuf.
   h. Store the reference numbers in CommStorage (via Set_RefNums_SerBuffPtr).

5. *For Comm "write" branch to the CommWrite procedure.*
   a. Check to see there is a second parameter.

b. Send the data through the output serial port (Chris addresses the Device Manager for performance, rather than going through the File Manager).

6. **For Comm "read" branch to the CommRead procedure.**
   a. Be sure there are no additional parameters.
   b. Allocate memory for incoming data pulled from the input buffer.
   c. Read the data from the input buffer and store it in the newly allocated memory area.
   d. Go through text and strip out non-printing low value ASCII characters, as well as high-bit characters. This combination of conversions and stripping removes potentially troublesome characters of some communications services, while ensuring that packet switching networks (which often send high-bit characters) are received as readable text.
   e. Convert input data to a zero-terminated string, which is the type that must be passed back to HyperCard.
   f. Return the value of the buffer to HyperCard, so that it may read it with the Result function.
   g. Check for any errors that occurred in the serial driver during the data input.

7. **If call is Comm "close," then branch to the CommClose procedure.**
   a. Restore the serial input buffer to its original state.
   b. Set CommStorage to empty.
   c. Dispose of all handles and pointers.

One reason this XCMD isn't intended for use as an interactive terminal is that the data that is read from the serial buffer ends up coming into a HyperCard field in chunks—three or more characters at a time (depending on the communications baud rate). Terminal programs usually produce characters on the screen one at a time. Moreover, in a telecommunications window, the user can type outgoing text on the same line as, say, a prompt from a remote computer. The Comm XCMD is not set up for that kind of terminal emulation.

Further Ideas

The Weather Machine stack is rudimentary in its control over the communications process. If the stack were to become part of a real stack product, it would require substantial error detection within the HyperTalk section to accommodate unexpected delays from the remote computer, finicky modem responses, busy signals from the remote computer's telephone number and transmission errors that would corrupt prompts from the remote computer. These can all be added to the HyperTalk script, which is the advantage of running the front end in HyperTalk, with the XCMD handling the serial port part of the transaction.

Controlling serial devices other than communications services tends to be much easier. Such devices have a series of commands to which they respond, occasionally sending back data upon request. By dissecting the information that comes back from the device, you can display settings in various fields or buttons as your design dictates. Your script can also piece together whatever commands are necessary from a friendly controlling front end in HyperCard.

Listing 29-1

```
{   Title       :   Comm -- a HyperCard XCMD to control a communications session. }
{   Author      :   Chris Knepper }
{   Date        :   3/30/88 }
{   From        :   Danny Goodman's HyperCard Developer's Guide }
{   Publisher   :   Bantam Books, Inc. }
{   Copyright   © 1988 by Danny Goodman.  All rights reserved. }

unit CommUnit;

interface

  uses
    XCMDIntf,       { the data structures for the XCMD }
    XCMDUtils;      { the glue for the HyperCard callbacks }


  procedure Main (paramPtr : XCmdPtr);

implementation

  procedure Comm (paramPtr : XCmdPtr);
    label
      1;                        { the end of Comm }
    const
      BUFF_SIZE = $800;         { size of the input serial buffer -- 2K }
    var
      controlStr                { stores 1st param to Comm }
        : Str255;
      inRefNum,                 { Stores input reference number }
      outRefNum                 { Stores output reference number }
        : integer;
      err                       { stores the error codes of various Device Manager calls }
        : OSErr;
      count                     { stores the number of bytes to read/write }
        : longint;
      myBuffPtr                 { stores a pointer to the serial input buffer }
        : Ptr;
      myPBlock                  { Used in calls to PBRead and PBWrite. }
        : ParamBlockRec;
      myHdl                     { Stores handle 0-terminated string }
        : Handle;
{--------------------------------------------------------------------------}
    procedure HandleError (myStr : Str255);
    { HandleError sets the cursor to the arrow cursor and displays an error Alert }
    { informing the user of the error.  This procedure assumes that the ALRT & DITL }
    { resources with id = 3100 exist in HyperCard's resource fork. Although this is a }
```

```
      { valid assumption in HyperCard versions 1.1 and 1.0.1.  Calls to GetResource() verify }
      { that these resources do, in fact, exist.  If they don't, this procedure produces a beep. }
      const
        ERROR = 3100;                          { use a HC ALRT for error messages. }
      var
        whichItem : integer;                   { stores result of the Alert function }
      begin
        if (GetResource('ALRT', 3100) = nil) or (GetResource('DITL', 3100) = nil) then
          SysBeep(60)                          { beep if no ALRT or DITL resource }
        else
          begin
            InitCursor;                        { set cursor to the arrow cursor }
            ParamText(myStr, '', '', '');      { specify the ALRT's text }
            whichItem := Alert(ERROR, nil);    { display and handle the ALRT }
            SendCardMessage(paramPtr, 'set cursor to 4');   { set back to watch cursor }
          end;
      end;                                     { procedure HandleError }
{-------------------------------------------------------------------------}
    function ErrOccurred (errNum : OSErr;
                routineName : Str255) : Boolean;
    { ErrOccurred determines if an error occured by comparing errNum with NoErr. }
    { If equal, ErrOccurred returns FALSE indicating that no error occurred.  Otherwise, }
    { it returns TRUE, indicating that an error occurred and creates a string from }
    { errNum and routineName which it then passes to HandleError. }
      var
        errStr                                 { store error number as a Pascal string }
         : Str255;
      begin
        if (errNum = noErr) then
          ErrOccurred := FALSE                 { no error occurred -- return FALSE }
        else
          begin
            ErrOccurred := TRUE;               { oops, error occurred -- return TRUE }
            NumToString(errNum, errStr);       { convert error number to a string }
            HandleError(Concat(routineName, ' returned ', errStr, '.')); { inform user }
          end;
      end;                                     { function ErrOccurred }
{-------------------------------------------------------------------------}
    function Clear_RefNums_SerBuffPtr : boolean;
    { Clear_RefNums_SerBuffPtr sets the HyperTalk global "CommStorage" to empty }
    { and returns TRUE if successful, or FALSE if not successful. }
      var
        pascalStr : Str255;                    { stores message to send to HC }
      begin
        pascalStr := 'put empty into CommStorage';   { clear CommStorage with a... }
        SendCardMessage(paramPtr, pascalStr);  { ...HyperTalk command }
        if (paramPtr^.result = xResSucc) then  { test the callback }
          Clear_RefNums_SerBuffPtr := TRUE     { SendCardMessage succeeded }
```

```
      else
        begin
          Clear_RefNums_SerBuffPtr := FALSE;         { SendCardMessage failed }
          HandleError('SendCardMessage callback failed.');    { inform user }
        end;
    end;                                      { function Clear_RefNums_SerBuffPtr }
{--------------------------------------------------------------------------}
    function Set_RefNums_SerBuffPtr (output, input : integer;
                    buffer : Ptr) : boolean;
    { Set_RefNums_SerBuffPtr stores the input/output refnums and a pointer to }
    { the input buffer in a HyperTalk global called "CommStorage." If the function }
    { fails, it returns FALSE, otherwise it returns TRUE. }
      var
        pascalStr1,                           { converts LONGINTs, passed to PasToZero }
        pascalStr2                            { converts LONGINTs }
         : Str255;
    begin
        Set_RefNums_SerBuffPtr := TRUE;       { indicate that no error occurred }
        NumToString(output, pascalStr1);      { convert output refnum to Str255 }
        NumToString(input, pascalStr2);       { convert input refnum to Str255 }
        pascalStr1 := Concat(pascalStr1, ',', pascalStr2);   { a "," delimitted Str255 }
        NumToString(ORD4(buffer), pascalStr2); { convert the serial buf ptr to Str255 }
        pascalStr1 := Concat(pascalStr1, ',', pascalStr2);   { a "," delimitted Str255 }
    myHdl := PasToZero(paramPtr, pascalStr1);   { store Str255 in a handle }
    if (paramPtr^.result <> xResSucc) then
      begin
        Set_RefNums_SerBuffPtr := FALSE; { indicate that an error occurred }
        HandleError('PasToZero callback failed.');
      end
    else
      begin
        SetGlobal(paramPtr, 'CommStorage', myHdl);{ set the global }
        if (paramPtr^.result <> xResSucc) then
          begin
            Set_RefNums_SerBuffPtr := FALSE; { indicate that an error occurred }
            HandleError('SetGlobal callback failed.');
          end
      end;
    end;                                      { function Set_RefNums_SerBuffPtr}
{--------------------------------------------------------------------------}
    function Get_RefNums_SerBuffPtr (var output, input : integer;
                var buffer : Ptr) : boolean;
    { Get_RefNums_SerBuffPtr gets the refnums which have been stored in the }
    { HyperTalk global "CommStorage." If this global is empty, then an error }
    { has occurred and the function returns FALSE. Otherwise, the function }
    { gets the values in CommStorage and returns TRUE. CommStorage contains }
    { 3 items. Item 1 is the output refnum, item 2 is the input refnum, and item 3 }
    { is the address of the input buffer. }
```

```
      label
        5;                                    { the end of Get_RefNums_SerBuffPtr }
      var
        whichItem,                            { used as a for loop counter }
        scrInt                                { used when converting strings to nums }
         : Integer;
        scrLongint                            { scratch longint }
         : Longint;
        pascalStr,                            { used for local storage of Str255 }
        myExpr                                { used to pass a HyperTalk expression to HC }
         : Str255;
   begin
     Get_RefNums_SerBuffPtr := FALSE;         { return FALSE indicates errors }
     myExpr := 'CommStorage is empty';        { determine if the global CommStorage... }
     myHdl := EvalExpr(paramPtr, myExpr);     { ...is empty }
     if (paramPtr^.result <> xresSucc) then   { result is set by EvalExpr }
       begin
         HandleError('EvalExpr failed to test if CommStorage is empty.');
         DisposHandle(myHdl);                  { dispose of memory EvalExpr allocated }
         goto 5;                               { exit Get_RefNums_SerBuffPtr }
       end;
     HLock(myHdl);                             { lock handle before ZeroToPas }
     ZeroToPas(paramPtr, myHdl^, pascalStr);
     DisposHandle(myHdl);
     if (paramPtr^.result <> xresSucc) then   { result is set by ZeroToPas }
       begin
         HandleError('ZeroToPas failed while testing if CommStorage is empty.');
         goto 5;                               { exit Get_RefNums_SerBuffPtr }
       end;
     if pascalStr = 'true' then               { is CommStorage empty? }
       begin
         HandleError('CommStorage is empty.');   { inform user }
         goto 5;                               { exit Get_RefNums_SerBuffPtr }
       end;
     for whichItem := 1 to 3 do               { Get 3 items of CommStorage }
       begin
         NumToString(whichItem, pascalStr); { convert item to pascalStr }
         myExpr := Concat('item ', pascalStr, ' of CommStorage');
         myHdl := EvalExpr(paramPtr, myExpr);   { evaluate the expression }
         if ((myHdl = nil) or (paramPtr^.result <> xresSucc)) then
           begin { inform user of error }
             HandleError(Concat('Can''t get item ', pascalStr, ' of CommStorage'));
             DisposHandle(myHdl);              { dispose of memory EvalExpr allocated }
             goto 5;                           { exit Get_RefNums_SerBuffPtr }
           end;
         HLock(myHdl);                         { lock handle before ZeroToPas }
         ZeroToPas(paramPtr, myHdl^, pascalStr);
         if (paramPtr^.result <> xresSucc) then      { set by ZeroToPas }
```

```
                    begin
                      NumToString(whichItem, pascalStr); { convert item to string }
                      pascalStr := Concat('Can"t convert item ', pascalStr);
                      HandleError(Concat(pascalStr, ' of CommStorage to Pascal string.'));
                      DisposHandle(myHdl);              { dispose of the storage allocated by EvalExpr }
                      goto 5;                           { exit Get_RefNums_SerBuffPtr }
                    end;
                  DisposHandle(myHdl);                 { dispose of the storage allocated by EvalExpr }
                  StringToNum(pascalStr, scrLongint);  { convert to a number }
                  case whichItem of
                    1 :                                { the first item is the output refnum }
                      output := scrLongint;
                    2 :                                { the second item is the input refnum }
                      input := scrLongint;
                    3 :                                { the third item is the buffer pointer }
                      buffer := POINTER(scrLongint);
                  end;                                 { case statement }
                end;                                   { for loop }
            Get_RefNums_SerBuffPtr := TRUE;           { return TRUE indicates success }
5 :                                                    { the end of Get_RefNums_SerBuffPtr }
          end;                                         { function Get_RefNums_SerBuffPtr }
{-------------------------------------------------------------------------}
      function UserConfig (var serConfig : integer) : BOOLEAN;
      { This function gets the configuration specified by the user in the parameters to }
      { Comm.  3rd parameter is baud, 4th parameter is stop bits, 5th parameter is }
      { parity, 6th parameter is data bits.  If no parameters are passed (besides "Open") }
      { then the default configuration is returned.  If error occurs, UserConfig returns }
      { FALSE, otherwise it returns TRUE.  The configuration is returned in serConfig. }
        label
          7;                                           { the end of UserConfig }
        var
          pascalStr : Str255;                          { used when converting to pascal strings }
      begin
        UserConfig := TRUE;
        serConfig := 0;
        if (paramPtr^.paramCount = 1) then             { Assume the 1st parameter was "open". }
          serConfig := baud1200 + stop10 + noParity + data8  { Default configuration. }
        else
          begin
          { *** Get the third parameter -- Baud rate *** }
            HLock(paramPtr^.params[3]);
            ZeroToPas(paramPtr, paramPtr^.params[3]^, pascalStr);
            HUnlock(paramPtr^.params[3]);
            UprString(pascalStr, FALSE);
            if (pascalStr = '300') then
              serConfig := serConfig + baud300
            else if (pascalStr = '600') then
              serConfig := serConfig + baud600
            else if (pascalStr = '1200') then
```

```
            serConfig := serConfig + baud1200
        else if (pascalStr = '1800') then
            serConfig := serConfig + baud1800
        else if (pascalStr = '2400') then
            serConfig := serConfig + baud2400
        else if (pascalStr = '3600') then
            serConfig := serConfig + baud3600
        else if (pascalStr = '4800') then
            serConfig := serConfig + baud4800
        else if (pascalStr = '7200') then
            serConfig := serConfig + baud7200
        else if (pascalStr = '9600') then
            serConfig := serConfig + baud9600
        else if (pascalStr = '19200') then
            serConfig := serConfig + baud19200
        else if (pascalStr = '57600') then
            serConfig := serConfig + baud57600
        else
            begin                       { Error occurred in specifying baud rate. }
                HandleError('Error in specifying baud rate.');
                UserConfig := FALSE;
                goto 7;
            end;
{ *** Get the fourth parameter -- Stop bits *** }
        HLock(paramPtr^.params[4]);
        ZeroToPas(paramPtr, paramPtr^.params[4]^, pascalStr);
        HUnlock(paramPtr^.params[4]);
        UprString(pascalStr, FALSE);
        if (pascalStr = '1') then
            serConfig := serConfig + stop10
        else if (pascalStr = '1.5') then
            serConfig := serConfig + stop15
        else if (pascalStr = '2') then
            serConfig := serConfig + stop20
        else
            begin                       { Error occurred in specifying stop bits. }
                HandleError('Error in specifying stop bits.');
                UserConfig := FALSE;
                goto 7;
            end;
{ *** Get the fifth parameter -- Parity *** }
        HLock(paramPtr^.params[5]);
        ZeroToPas(paramPtr, paramPtr^.params[5]^, pascalStr);
        HUnlock(paramPtr^.params[5]);
        UprString(pascalStr, FALSE);
        if (pascalStr = 'NO') then
            serConfig := serConfig + noParity
```

```
              else if (pascalStr = 'ODD') then
                serConfig := serConfig + oddParity
              else if (pascalStr = 'EVEN') then
                serConfig := serConfig + evenParity
              else
                begin                          { Error occurred in specifying parity. }
                  HandleError('Error in specifying parity.');
                  UserConfig := FALSE;
                  goto 7;
                end;
            { *** Get the sixth parameter -- Data bits *** }
            HLock(paramPtr^.params[6]);
            ZeroToPas(paramPtr, paramPtr^.params[6]^, pascalStr);
            HUnlock(paramPtr^.params[6]);
            UprString(pascalStr, FALSE);
            if (pascalStr = '5') then
              serConfig := serConfig + data5
            else if (pascalStr = '6') then
              serConfig := serConfig + data6
            else if (pascalStr = '7') then
              serConfig := serConfig + data7
            else if (pascalStr = '8') then
              serConfig := serConfig + data8
            else
              begin                            { Error occurred in specifying data bits. }
                HandleError('Error in specifying data bits.');
                UserConfig := FALSE;
              end;
          end;                                 { if one or more than one parameter }
7 :                                            { label 7 is the end of UserConfig }
      end;                                     { function UserConfig }
{---------------------------------------------------------------------------}
    function PrinterOrModem (var outputStr, inputStr : Str255) : boolean;
    { PrinterOrModem determines whether the user is opening the printer or }
    { modem ports.  NOTE: cannot have BOTH the printer AND modem port open at the }
    { same time.  If the user calls Comm("Open") then default to modem port.  The }
    { name of printer or modem driver is returned in outputStr and inputStr. }
      var
        pascalStr : Str255;                    { used to convert args to upper case }
      begin
        PrinterOrModem := TRUE;                { TRUE indicates no errors }
        if (paramPtr^.paramCount = 1) then
          begin                                { assume 1st parameter was "open" }
            inputStr := '.AIn';
            outputStr := '.AOut';
          end
```

```
        else
          begin                                 { user specifies modem or printer port }
            HLock(paramPtr^.params[2]);
            ZeroToPas(paramPtr, paramPtr^.params[2]^, pascalStr);
            HUnlock(paramPtr^.params[2]);
            UprString(pascalStr, FALSE);        { Convert to upper case. }
            if (pascalStr = 'MODEM') then
              begin
                inputStr := '.AIn';
                outputStr := '.AOut';
              end
            else if (pascalStr = 'PRINTER') then
              begin
                inputStr := '.BIn';
                outputStr := '.BOut';
              end
            else
              begin                             { Error in specifying printer or modem. }
                HandleError('Comm expects Printer or Modem.');
                PrinterOrModem := FALSE;        { Inform user second param was bad. }
              end;
          end;                                  { If paramCount = 1. }
    end;                                        { function PrinterOrModem }
{-------------------------------------------------------------------------}
    function MySerShk : SerShk;
    { Returns the serial hand shake options and other control information. }
      var
        tempSerShk : SerShk;                    { stores the serial handshake settings }
    begin
      with tempSerShk do
        begin
          fXon := 1;                            { Enable XOn/XOff output flow control.  }
          fCTS := 1;                            { Enable CTS hardware handshake.        }
          xOn := CHR(17);                       { Set to control-q for continue.        }
          xOff := CHR(19);                      { Set to control-s for pause.           }
          errs := 0;                            { Errors which abort input requests     }
          evts := 0;
          fInX := 1;                            { Enable XOn/XOff input flow control.   }
        end;
      MySerShk := tempSerShk;
    end;                                        { function MySerShk }
{-------------------------------------------------------------------------}
    procedure CheckCumErrs;
    { This procedure checks the input and output serial ports for errors.  If an error }
    { occurred, then the Mac beeps. }
      var
        mySerStat : SerStaRec;                  { stores status information }
```

```
      begin
        err := SerStatus(outRefNum, mySerStat);
        If (mySerStat.cumErrs <> 0) then
          SysBeep(1);                         { beep if errors in output port }
        err := SerStatus(inRefNum, mySerStat);
        If (mySerStat.cumErrs <> 0) then
          SysBeep(1);                         { beep if errors in input port }
      end;                                    { procedure CheckCumErrs }
{------------------------------------------------------------------------}
      procedure CommOpen;
      { CommOpen opens the serial port to initiate communication. }
        label
          1;                                  { the end of CommOpen }
        var
          serConfig                           { Stores configuration info for the port }
           : integer;
          inputStr,                           { stores either '.AIn' or '.BIn'. }
          outputStr                           { stores either '.AOut' or '.BOut'. }
           : Str255;
      begin
      { Ensure that Comm("Open"...) was called correctly. }
        If (paramPtr^.paramCount <> 6) and (paramPtr^.paramCount <> 1) then
          begin
            HandleError('Error: Comm Open expects 1 or 6 parameters');
            goto 1;                           { exit CommOpen }
          end;

      { Init CommStorage to empty -- later store inRefNum/outRefNum }
      { and a pointer to the serial input buffer here. }
        If not Clear_RefNums_SerBuffPtr then
          goto 1;

        If not PrinterOrModem(outputStr, inputStr) then    { use the Printer or Modem port? }
          goto 1;                             { exit CommOpen }
        If not UserConfig(serConfig) then     { Get the configuration for the input/output ports. }
          goto 1;                             { exit CommOpen }

        myBuffPtr := NewPtr(BUFF_SIZE);       { Allocate memory for the input buffer. }
        If ErrOccurred(MemError, 'NewPtr') then
          goto 1;                             { exit CommOpen }
        err := OpenDriver(outputStr, outRefNum); { Open the output port. }
        If ErrOccurred(err, 'OpenDriver') then
          goto 1;                             { exit CommOpen }
        err := OpenDriver(inputStr, inRefNum);   { Open the input port. }
        if ErrOccurred(err, 'OpenDriver') then
          goto 1;                             { exit CommOpen }
        err := SerReset(outRefNum, serConfig);   { Configure the output port. }
```

```
        if ErrOccurred(err, 'SerReset') then
          goto 1;                              { exit CommOpen }
        err := SerHShake(outRefNum, MySerShk);{ set up output port handshake }
        if ErrOccurred(err, 'SerHShake') then
          goto 1;                              { exit CommOpen }
        err := SerReset(inRefNum, serConfig);  { Configure the input port. }
        if ErrOccurred(err, 'SerReset') then
          goto 1;                              { exit CommOpen }
        err := SerHShake(inRefNum, MySerShk);  { set up input port handshake }
        if ErrOccurred(err, 'SerHShake') then
          goto 1;                              { exit CommOpen }
        err := SerSetBuf(inRefNum, myBuffPtr, BUFF_SIZE); { Set up the input buffer. }
        if ErrOccurred(err, 'SerSetBuf') then
          goto 1;                              { exit CommOpen }

        { Save the input/output port refnums and serial input buffer pointer. }
        if not Set_RefNums_SerBuffPtr(outRefNum, inRefNum, myBuffPtr) then
          ;                                    { do nothing, since at end }
1 :                                            { the end of CommOpen }
      end;                                     { procedure CommOpen }
{-------------------------------------------------------------------------}
    procedure  CommWrite;
    { CommWrite writes data to the serial port. }
      label
        1;                                     { the end of CommWrite }
    begin
      if (paramPtr^.paramCount <> 2) then{ ensure Comm was called correctly }
        begin
          HandleError('Error: Comm Write expects 2 parameters');
          goto 1;                              { exit CommWrite }
        end;
    { Send the data out the serial port. }
      HLock(paramPtr^.params[2]);
      count := StringLength(paramPtr, paramPtr^.params[2]^);
      with myPBlock do
        begin
          ioRefNum := outRefNum;
          ioBuffer := paramPtr^.params[2]^;
          ioReqCount := count;
          ioPosMode := 0;                      { write from current mark }
        end;
      err := PBWrite(@myPBlock, FALSE);
      HUnlock(paramPtr^.params[2]);
      if ErrOccurred(err, 'PBWrite') then
        ;                                      { do nothing since at end }
1 :                                            { the end of procedure CommWrite }
      end;                                     { procedure CommWrite }
```

```
{--------------------------------------------------------------------------}
  procedure CommRead;
  { CommRead reads data from the serial port. }
    label
      1;                                       { the end of CommRead }
    var
      counter,                                 { For loop counter. }
      scratchInt,                              { Scratch integer necessary for BitAnd. }
      noLF_cntr                                { Counts good chars, ie. no line feeds. }
       : integer;
      myCharPtr                                { points to chars in the input stream }
       : Ptr;
  begin
    if (paramPtr^.paramCount <> 1) then{ ensure Comm was called correctly }
      begin
        HandleError('Error: Comm Read expects only 1 parameter');
        goto 1;                               { exit CommRead }
      end;

  { Look at the serial input buffer -- exit if there's an error in looking at it }
  { or if there are no characters in it. }
    err := SerGetBuf(inRefNum, count);
    if (ErrOccurred(err, 'SerGetBuf') or (count <= 0)) then
      goto 1;                                 { exit CommRead }
  { Allocate the storage area for the result of the read.  The size is equal to }
  { the number of characters in the buffer. }
    myHdl := NewHandle(count + 1);            { add 1 to ensure it's a 0-terminated string }
    if (ErrOccurred(MemError, 'NewHandle') or (myHdl = nil)) then
      goto 1;                                 { exit CommRead }
    HLock(myHdl);                             { lock it during the call to PBRead }
    with myPBlock do                          { set up the parameter block for PBRead }
      begin
        ioRefNum := inRefNum;                 { read from the input buffer }
        ioBuffer := myHdl^;                   { point to the storage area }
        ioReqCount := count;                  { read as many characters as are in the buffer }
        ioPosMode := 0;                       { read from current mark }
      end;
    err := PBRead(@myPBlock, FALSE);          { read ! }
    if ErrOccurred(err, 'PBRead') then        { any errors during read? }
      begin                                   { if so, then release the space... }
        DisposHandle(myHdl);                  { ...allocated to the handle. }
        goto 1;                               { exit CommRead }
      end;
  { Since some hosts transmit with the high-bit set, we'll turn off the high-bit for all }
  { incoming characters.  Also, we'll strip all non-printing characters (ASCII $00-$1F & $7F) }
  { except the carriage return (ASCII $0D). }
    noLF_cntr := 0;
    for counter := 0 to (myPBlock.ioActCount - 1) do
      begin
        myCharPtr := POINTER(ORD(myHdl^) + counter);
```

```
              scratchInt := BitAnd(Byte(myCharPtr^), $7F); { Turn off high-bit. }
              If ((scratchInt > $1F) or (scratchInt = $0D)) and (scratchInt <> $7F) then
                 begin
                    myCharPtr := POINTER(ORD(myHdl^) + noLF_cntr);
                    myCharPtr^ := Byte(scratchInt);
                    noLF_cntr := noLF_cntr + 1;
                 end;
              end;
        { make it a zero-terminated string }
          if (noLF_cntr = 0) then
             begin                              { if no good characters in the input... }
                DisposHandle(myHdl);            { ...then return nothing! }
             end
          else
             begin                              { make last byte a 0 }
                myCharPtr := POINTER(ORD(myHdl^) + noLF_cntr);
                myCharPtr^ := Byte(0);
                SetHandleSize(myHdl, noLF_cntr + 1);{ set the handle to the correct size }
                HUnlock(myHdl);                 { unlock it before passing it back to HyperCard }
                paramPtr^.returnValue := myHdl; { Return the string read from the input buffer. }
             end;
          CheckCumErrs;                         { beep if there are errors in the driver }
1 :                                             { the end of CommRead }
      end;                                      { procedure CommRead }
{-------------------------------------------------------------------------}
    procedure CommClose;
    { CommClose restores the input buffer to the default buffer and releases the }
    { memory used for Comm's input buffer. }
    begin
       err := SerSetBuf(inRefNum, nil, 0);      { restore the input serial buffer }
       if ErrOccurred(err, 'SerSetBuf') then
          ;                                     { do nothing }
       if not Clear_RefNums_SerBuffPtr then
          ;                                     { do nothing }
       DisposPtr(myBuffPtr);                    { dispose of the allocated buffer }
       if ErrOccurred(MemError, 'DisposPtr') then
          ;                                     { do nothing }
      end;                                      { procedure CommClose }
{-------------------------------------------------------------------------}
   begin                                        { procedure Comm }
    { Comm requires parameters, so check for at least one here. }
    if (paramPtr^.paramCount < 1) then
       begin
          HandleError('No parameters were sent to Comm.');
          goto 1;                               { exit Comm }
       end;
```

```
   { Get the first parameter -- this controlStr indicates what Comm should do. }
   HLock(paramPtr^.params[1]);
   ZeroToPas(paramPtr, paramPtr^.params[1]^, controlStr);
   HUnlock(paramPtr^.params[1]);
   UprString(controlStr, FALSE);            { Convert to upper case, strip diacriticals. }

   if (controlStr = 'OPEN') then
     CommOpen                               { open the communications session }
   else
     begin
       { If we get here, the communications session has already been established, so }
       { get the refnums for the input/output ports and serial input buffer pointer. }
       if not Get_RefNums_SerBuffPtr(outRefNum, inRefNum, myBuffPtr) then
         goto 1;                            { exit Comm }

       If (controlStr = 'WRITE') then
         CommWrite                          { write to the serial port }
       else if (controlStr = 'READ') then
         CommRead                           { read from the serial port }
       else if (controlStr = 'CLOSE') then
         CommClose                          { restore the serial port }
       else
       { If we get here, the first parameter to Comm doesn't match any of }
       { the control strings, so a bad control string was passed in. }
         HandleError('Comm doesn"t recognize the 1st parameter.');   { inform user }
     end;                                   { if }
1 :                                         { the end of Comm }
   end;                                     { procedure Comm }
{-----------------------------------------------------------------------}
   procedure Main;
{ procedure Main serves as the entrypoint and simply calls the procedure Comm. }
   begin
     Comm(paramPtr);                        { call the Comm XCMD }
   end;
{-----------------------------------------------------------------------}
end.                                        { UNIT CommUnit }
{-----------------------------------------------------------------------}
```

30

A Final Word

Even if you don't plan to jump into XCMDs right away (or ever), I believe it is very worthwhile to read through Chris Knepper's Pascal source code and comments for the three XCMDs in this book. It may appear to you that more lines of code were spent checking for errors that the computer or user might generate than in doing the actual work of the XCMD. There's an important message there for HyperTalk programmers.

The minute your stack leaves your machine and runs under someone else's keyboard and mouse, you lose control over how the person will be using your precious software. Just because you know that HyperCard likes the time of day entered as "3:15 PM" in the United States Macintosh System File doesn't mean that everyone will remember that.

They may try to enter it as just "3:15" or add periods after the letters, as in "3:15 P.M." It must be up to you, the stack developer, to anticipate all these formats and treat them in your scripts. For instance, you can reject all entries that aren't in the proper format, or try to adjust those that are close. In the time conversion stack of *Business Class*, for example, I strip out periods if the user adds them to a time entry (HyperCard chokes when you try to convert the time to seconds from an invalid format).

Overall, checking for errors and then guiding the user back with gentle messages contributes a great deal to the so called user-friendliness of software. You can't expect the user to be perfect, but the user expects you and your software to be.

Note, too, that much of the error checking is done in the form of functions. While most of the action in a function is the kind that you'd expect in a procedure (or a HyperTalk command handler), the item is placed in a function format so that it returns either true or false, depending on whether the action taken within the function was successful. If the action was successful, then the main procedure may continue; otherwise, an error message is needed or some other corrective action must be taken. A lot of the Macintosh Toolbox routines are written this way, as are the majority of the XCMD glue routines. I believe there is a lesson in this for us in HyperTalk as well.

Writing good HyperTalk takes practice and experimentation with timing traps to find the most efficient solutions. It also helps to read as many HyperTalk scripts as you can get your hands on. Not all of them will be poetry from Dan Winkler or his disciples, but you should still look at them and figure how you would improve every script you see. Make no assumptions about how good a script might be. Ninety-nine percent of the time it can be improved.

The same goes for stacks in general. Be critical, even of my stacks. But be critical to become better. My reward will be to see your stack winning praise from its intended users and admiration from the HyperCard corps. That you've pored through 1200 pages of HyperCard literature is a sign of your dedication. You certainly have the desire to become a good HyperCard stack developer.

If you can give it the necessary time, I'm confident you can do it.

APPENDIX

A

Sources

Here are the addresses of companies whose products are mentioned in this book:

Activision, Inc. (now Mediagenic)
3885 Bohannon Drive
Menlo Park, CA 94025 -1001

Addison-Wesley Publishing Co., Inc.
Route 128
Reading, MA 01867

AmandaStories
1025 Martin Road
Santa Cruz, CA 95060-9721

Apple Programmers and Developers Assn.
290 SW 43rd St.
Renton, WA 98055

CE Software
801 73rd Street
Des Moines, IA 50312

Farallon Computing
2150 Kittredge Street
Berkeley, CA 94704

Hayden Books
4300 West 62nd Street
Indianapolis, IN 46268

Heizer Software
1941 Oak Park Blvd., Suite 30
Pleasant Hill, CA 94523

HyperAge Magazine
108 E. Fremont Ave.
Suite 122
Sunnyvale, CA 94087

HyperNews
TRU, Inc.
31849 Pacific Hwy. South., Suite 115L
Federal Way, WA 98003

HyperPress Publishing Corp.
P.O. Box 8243
Foster City, CA 94404

Impulse, Inc.
6870 Shingle Creek Parkway, #112
Minneapolis, MN 55430

MacroMind, Inc.
1028 W. Wolfram St.
Chicago, IL 60657

Mainstay
5311-B Derry Ave.
Agoura Hills, CA 91301

Symmetry Corp.
761 E. University Dr.
Mesa, AZ 85203

Think Technologies
135 South Road
Bedford, MA 01730

The Voyager Company
2139 Manning Avenue
Los Angeles, CA 90025

Interactive Sound in HyperCard

By Tim Oren
Apple Computer, Inc.

Reprinted with permission of
HyperAge Magazine

Part One

Introduction

You can't use HyperCard without noticing the sound. From boings to clips of Beatles music, it seems to lurk under every button. What's not as obvious is that simple HyperTalk scripting can extend these sound fragments into full length synchronized sound and graphics shows. These shows achieve a feel similar to video production, and can be played straight through or interactively controlled, much like a VCR. You can use this technique to build presentations and training materials, create narrated tours of a HyperCard database, or design your own music videos. This is the first part of a two-installment article explaining the scripts which make this possible, and telling you how to set up your own HyperCard sound production studio. While writing I have assumed that you have a basic familiarity with Macintosh, HyperCard and HyperTalk.

HyperCard Sound Basics

First, some basics of Macintosh and HyperCard sound.

What is Sampled Sound? Mac sound is produced with a technique called digitizing or sampling. It's the same method used in compact discs and sampling keyboard instruments. In the digitizing process, the original sound waveform is examined many times per second (see Figure B-1). Each time the amplitude of the sound wave is recorded and stored in the computer, producing a data file. Later, the digitized sound is played back by fetching the data from the file at the same rate at which it was recorded, and driving a loudspeaker to the recorded amplitude for each instant. This will recreate a facsimile of the original sound waveform.

Any digitized sound has two characteristics: the frequency at which it was sampled, and the precision with which the sound level is recorded. The best quality sound from a Macintosh Plus or SE uses 22,000 samples per second (or 22 Kilohertz, written as 22 KHz) with a precision of one part in 256, corresponding to one byte per sample. Thus, sound digitized at this rate will

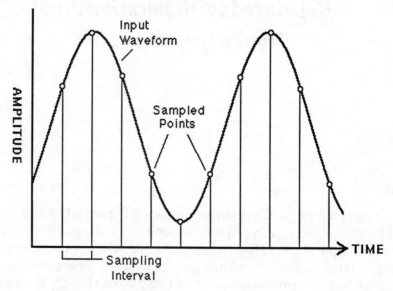

Figure B-1 *Digitizing a Sound Waveform*

consume 22 Kbytes per second of playing time. Compare this to compact disc audio, which samples at 44 KHz with 16 bits precision, producing 176 Kbytes per second for the two stereo channels.

HyperCard stores these digitized sounds in the resource fork of a stack file with resource type "snd." Each sound is given a name unique within the stack. If you are familiar with the use of ResEdit, try opening up a sound effects stack and examining the digitized resources. We'll worry about how the resources are created later — first a look at the HyperCard commands that use them.

HyperCard Sound Commands   The basic HyperTalk sound command is `play`. Its syntax is `play sName`, where sName is the name associated with an "snd" resource in the current stack, the home stack, or HyperCard itself. `Play` loads this piece of digitized sound into the Macintosh's memory (assuming there is room), and calls the Toolbox Sound Manager to begin the output. The Sound Manager is capable of queueing up sounds in memory, so you can issue multiple `play` commands, and the sounds named will be heard in order. Be warned that the `play` command issues no error warnings. If the sound named does not exist or there is insufficient room in memory, all you will hear is silence.

An important variant on `play` is `play stop`, which stops the current sound immediately and flushes it and any other queued-up sound resources from the Macintosh's memory. You should also enter play stop if you abort a sound using command-period, in order to flush any sound fragments from memory.

(The `play` command can also specify sequences of notes and duration. This is used in playing tunes with short, digitized samples of an instrument. This variant is not used in this article; see the Help Stacks for more information.)

A companion HyperTalk function is `the sound`. This returns the name of the sound resource that is currently being played. If there is nothing being played, the value `done` is returned. This allows your script to monitor the progress of a sound sequence.

All SCSI System   A requirement of HyperCard sound is use of a system with a SCSI hard disk. The sound stack, HyperCard, and the system itself must all be stored on a SCSI device. This is necessary because the Mac floppies and old-style HD20 hard disk are driven by the IWM "Integrated Woz Machine" chip. Due to timing requirements, the chip momentarily turns off the sound when accessing the disk. Sound played under these conditions will suffer from buzzes, clicks and dropouts.

Memory, Sampling, and Aliasing   HyperCard can play sounds which have been sampled at four different rates: 22, 11, 7.4, or 5.5 KHz. Lower sampling rates create fewer data points and use less memory for equivalent time. This lets you fit more sound in memory and on disks. As we'll see, minimizing the amount of data to be transferred between the disk and memory is also important in continuous play.

On the other hand, low sampling rates cannot reproduce high-pitched sounds. One-half the sampling rate is called the Nyquist frequency; sounds above this pitch are not reproduced accurately. So a sampling rate of 5.5 KHz will lose sounds above 2,750 Hertz. This amounts to losing everything from the middle of the third octave over middle C. Obviously, you don't want to use this rate for music, though it might serve for intelligible voice narration. Throughout my examples, I will use the 11-KHz rate, with a Nyquist frequency of 5,500 Hertz. This is adequate for most popular music and compares favorably to the audio fidelity of video equipment, though it's much poorer than CD sound.

Another sampling phenomenon you should be aware of is aliasing. Essentially, an incoming pitch above the Nyquist frequency will be played back falsely shifted down by the Nyquist number. For example, a steady tone at 5,600 Hertz would sound like a low hum at 100 Hertz when sampled at 11 KHz. With real music, aliasing creates an odd buzz or chirp when a high pitch should be present. To avoid this, you must remove the high frequency part of the audio before sampling. This is done with a low-pass filter or a graphic equalizer. I'll discuss these devices under hardware.

A Simple Slide Show Script

The basis for continuous sound is quite simple. We'll explore it first with a noninteractive, sound synchronized slide show.

Fundamentals of the Technique The essential trick is to use the `play` command to keep two sounds in memory at all times. One is playing, the other is waiting. `The sound` is called repeatedly to monitor progress. When the current sound changes, you know that the first sound has completed and play has moved to the second. A `play` is then issued to set up yet another sound for output, reusing the memory freed by completion of the first. In this fashion, a HyperTalk script can double buffer a continuous stream of sound resources through the Mac without overflowing its memory.

Synchronization is achieved as a side effect of the cuts between sound segments. During production, the break between sound resources is positioned just at the significant phrase or note. The playback script is set up to display the appropriate card when the sound notes this transition, just before loading a new sound.

Now look at the script "playIt" in Listing B-1. It takes one parameter, the name of a card of background type "PlayList." A sample PlayList is shown in

Figure B-2. Cards of this type associate sound cues with actions. The PlayList is read top to bottom. The leftmost column is a background field called "Cue," and holds the name of sound resources. Looking in the playIt script, you can see that a blank Cue line allows the PlayList to continue immediately, but a filled in Cue line causes the PlayList to pause until the sound named begins playing. The script also checks for the value "done" as a precaution, so that the PlayList does not hang if the sound was unable to load or was misnamed.

The second column in the PlayList is background field "Do." This may contain a single statement of HyperTalk which playIt will execute after waiting for the corresponding Cue. Typically, this line will assign a visual effect for an upcoming card transition, but you can also use it to perform animation effects such as hiding and showing a button or field, or invoking card level scripts that implement more complex actions. This field is also used to chain between multiple PlayLists, by including the statement "playIt nextList" as the last line on one card, where "nextList" is replaced with actual name of the following PlayList.

The third PlayList column is background field "GoToCard." If filled in with the number or name of a card, the playIt script will cause that card to appear after any HyperTalk statement from "Do" is executed. Numbering of cards has a slight performance edge over naming, but does require PlayList changes as slides are inserted or deleted.

On Cue	Do...	Go To Card...	and Play...
		22	BB1
			BB2
BB1	visual effect dissolve	23	BB3
	hide card field "Line1" of next card		
	hide card field "Line2" of next card		
	hide card field "Line3" of next card		
BB2	visual effect checkerboard	24	BB4
	show card field "Line1"		
	show card field "Line2"		
	show card field "Line3"		
BB3		25	BB5
BB4	visual effect dissolve	26	BB6
BB5	visual effect zoom open	27	
		28	
		29	BB7
BB6	hide card field "PopUp" of next card	30	BB8
	show card field "PopUp"		
BB7	playit "Blue Busters 2"		

Figure B-2 *Sample PlayList Card*

The final PlayList column is background field "NextUp." It is used for naming the next sound resource to be loaded. The load takes place after HyperTalk statement execution and card transition, if any. It is really this coordination of sound segment changes and new sound loads that keeps the whole system breathing.

The sample PlayList given is one scene from a lengthier production. No sound is playing when the scene begins. The first Cue is blank, so card number 22, the title, is immediately displayed and sound segment "BB1" is loaded and begins playing. On the next line the second sound segment is loaded into memory with no wait. On the third line we test that BB1 is playing (it should be), set up a visual effect and dissolve to the next slide. We also load the next sound segment; these particular sounds were cut so that three segments would fit in memory at once. The following three lines demonstrate a simple animation; three text fields are hidden on the next card. On seeing the transition to sound segment "BB2", the PlayList does a checkboard transition to the following card, leaves a short pause during the loading of the next sound segment and then exposes the hidden fields one by one. You can read through the rest of the PlayList, including its transition to a following scene.

Listing B-1. Basic Sound and Slide Show Script

```
on playIt script
  --How many lines in this Playlist?
  put the number of lines in bkgnd field "Cue" of card script ¬
  into cueTotal
  -- Loop over Playlist lines
  repeat with cueNo = 1 to cueTotal
    -- Wait for cue if necessary
    put line cueNo of field "Cue" of card script into Cue
    if Cue is not empty then
      wait until the sound is "done" or the sound = Cue
    end if
    -- Execute HyperTalk statement if present
    put line cueNo of field "Do" of card script into DoIt
    if DoIt is not empty then do DoIt
    -- Change card displayed if requested
    put line cueNo of field "GoToCard" of card script into GoTo
    if GoTo is not empty then go to card GoTo
    -- Queue up next sound, if any
    put line cueNo of field "NextUp" of card script into NextSound
    if NextSound is not empty then play NextSound
  end repeat
end playIt
```

Production Hardware and Software

The minimal system configuration for HyperCard sound is a Mac Plus with a SCSI hard disk. To get the sound into the Macintosh you will need an audio digitizer, a peripheral which performs the actual sampling of an analog signal under control of the CPU. Two competing models are available from Impulse of Minneapolis and Farallon of Berkeley.

Digitizing Hardware The Impulse Audio Digitizer with SoundWave has been available for some time at a retail price of $199. Discounts from dealers and mail order are common. The current model of the Digitizer itself is an anodized aluminum box with a level control, RCA jack for audio input and a nine-pin, D-style RS-232 connector for computer control and digital. The Digitizer requires a five-volt power supply. Since the Plus and later Macintosh models use a DIN-style RS-232 connection without five volts, you will need a power and cable adapter such as the PowerPort. The Digitizer can sample at all four Mac rates: 22, 11, 7.5 and 5.5 KHz. It does not delete higher frequency sounds before digitizing, so you will need to connect a graphic equalizer or low-pass filter in the audio line ahead of the Digitizer to avoid aliasing.

SoundWave is the name of the accompanying software. It provides the abilities to play the incoming sound in "oscilloscope" mode for leveling, and will then capture a segment of digitized sound up to the limits of your Mac's memory. The sound editor functions let you look at the sound wave in two resolutions and select and modify sections by point-by-point editing or effects such as amplification, ramp up or down, reverb and flange. Sound is stored in a special file format that must be converted to HyperCard resource format. SoundWave seems to be a reliable package with the bugs worked out. SoundWave and the Digitizer are available from Impulse, Inc., 6870 Shingle Creek Parkway #112, Minneapolis, MN 55430, (612) 566-0221. (Note: An earlier version of SoundWave called SoundCap may be available from existing users or dealers with slow turnover. This lacks many features of Sound-Wave, but does have a useful zoom in/out feature for examining the waveform. However, it will work only on a Mac Plus because of an incompatibility with the Desktop Bus system used on the SE and Macintosh II.)

The new kid on the block is the MacRecorder from Farallon, also priced at $199. The external hardware has all the features of the Impulse Digitizer and then some. A microphone is built in for direct voice input. The RS-232 connector will plug directly into the new Macintoshes and no external power is required. The unit also incorporates a low-pass filter, removing the need for an outboard filter or equalizer. The filter correctly switches characteristics for the different sampling frequencies.

Two pieces of software will be provided with the MacRecorder. Hyper-Sound is a stack that allows control of the Recorder directly from HyperCard. Sounds can be sampled in, manipulated and stored directly into a stack in "snd" resource form. It even generates buttons preprogrammed to play the sound clips. One warning: HyperCard uses a lot of memory itself and may limit the size of sounds that HyperSound can manipulate. You may find a need for two megabytes if you do extensive production.

SoundEdit is a companion standalone application that provides more sophisticated capabilities. It is memory based like SoundWave and includes similar editing capabilities, plus a full zoom in/out capability. Farallon claims that SoundEdit provides a more intuitive interface to the editing functions, allowing mouse-based specification of amplification envelopes, for instance. SoundEdit can also store its results directly into stacks in resource format. Farallon Computing can be reached at 2150 Kittredge, Berkeley, CA 94704, (415) 849-2331.

When the Farallon system emerges from vaporware, it will be the one to beat. For the same price it provides greater compatibility with HyperCard and does not require power and cable adapters or use of an equalizer. Like most new software and hardware, some first version bugs can be expected. In the meantime, the Impulse configuration is proven reliable and from personal experience does quite an adequate job.

Playback System Given the fidelity limits of the sampling process, the choice of audio components is not critical, so long as playback speed is accurate. A consumer grade cassette deck should be adequate; avoid "boombox" machines. Likewise any component turntable or CD player should suffice. If digitizing sound tracks from video tape, use HQ machinery only and expect some hiss; a professional 3/4-inch U-matic system is better. If you are using the Impulse Digitizer, you will also require a graphic equalizer to eliminate high frequencies. Again, consumer grade devices will serve since you are blocking out entire bands rather than achieving precision control.

Useful Software Finally, you will find some software items to be useful. If you are using the Impulse Digitizer, you will need a public domain stack called SoundCapConverter written by Bill Atkinson. This takes the files produced by SoundWave or SoundCap and inserts them into a stack in the required "snd" format. You can obtain this stack from most HyperCard user groups, bulletin boards, or on-line SIGs. A copy of the ResEdit program is also helpful for checking which sounds are present in a stack and moving or deleting them.

A good quality paint program is needed for touching up scanned images and trimming them to size. You want one that does a good job of handling larger than screen size images, so you can pick the part that looks best for your slide. My favorite is SuperPaint; FullPaint is also a good choice. Finally, you can keep short production plans and storyboards in your head or on scratch paper, but you may want some planning help as things get complex. I find More and Excel to be useful in structuring scripts and building production plans.

Production Techniques

Producing HyperCard sound shows is similar to video production. Before beginning work, you should prepare a storyboard containing the song lyrics or voiceover narration juxtaposed to a sketch of the corresponding images. This will be your guide for cutting the sound. The allowable time per image depends on system performance and is discussed below.

You should then digitize the sound, saving out segments which correspond to the slides in your storyboard. If you need more sound than will fit in memory during digitizing, you may need to do some splicing. Here is a crude but effective method: Successively select, save and delete segments from your large sample. Eventually you will be left with a residue at the end of the sound buffer. Display its first several hundred cycles on the screen (here's where zoom helps), and do a screen dump to the printer. Back up the sound input and digitize another buffer full. Select the same zoom level and match your printout to the new screen to find the corresponding start location for the next segment. This procedure is low tech, but amazingly accurate in avoiding pops and clicks when splicing.

After digitizing you should prepare a sound test PlayList, which simply sequences through the sounds in order without changing the screen. This lets you detect errors in the digitizing as well as any performance or memory overflow problems.

Now you are ready to paste up your original or captured images onto cards. Unless you are trying for special effects, use a blank background for these cards and make your entire graphic transparent. Selecting transparent saves HyperCard from loading an entire bit plane. Name the cards or record their number as you work. Referring to the storyboard, put the card designators onto the PlayList line that matches the associated sound cue, and retest the entire show.

Finally, add visual effects or animation scripts to the PlayList as desired. Remember that visual effects, particularly those specified as slow or very slow, consume CPU time and can affect sound performance, so retest once again. If everything works, you have completed your first HyperCard sound production!

Performance Considerations

As with many things, sound production and performance are not as simple as they first appear. Memory and CPU speed limits rear their ugly heads to complicate matters. You can follow some safe rules that I outline at the end of this section, but if you want to use special effects and fast cuts, you should be aware of the limits that follow.

All of these limits come from an inevitable fact: Sound playback burns 11 Kbytes per second (at my usual sampling rate). There must enough processor and disk bandwidth available to keep the data flowing at that rate, as well as to perform card flipping and script execution for the slide show. There must also be enough RAM available to store the sound while it is waiting to be played.

If these requirements are not met, the sound presentation will fail in one of two ways, both of which cause a break in the playback. If the data cannot be brought into memory fast enough, there will be a silent period while the Mac catches up, but the performance will resume without a loss of sound. If there is insufficient memory available, play will lose that sound segment, and a silent period with loss of material will result. Noting the type of failure will tell you which problem has occurred.

There are several factors to weigh in diagnosing and avoiding these problems. First, consider the speed of transfer from the SCSI drive to the Mac. Older disk drives, such as the Seagate ST225 movement used in many external hard disks, have a slower access and transfer rate than newer disks such as the Mac SE's internal drive. The model of Macintosh makes a difference also. A Mac II is fastest, of course, but the SE's SCSI transfer is markedly faster than the Plus, due to a rewrite of the SCSI ROM code in the newer model.

Because you are working through both HyperCard and the HFS File Manager, performance considerations enter at these levels. You should periodically choose the Compact menu option for any sound stack under production. This rearranges the stack for better performance. If you are doing large sound productions on a small hard disk, you should check the degree of disk fragmentation periodically, using a utility such as FEdit. A fragmented file structure will force the hard disk to perform a seek operation frequently, slowing the transfer of sound to memory. To fix this, copy the contents to another drive and reformat before copying back.

You should also consider the time and space requirements of your graphics and desired effects. Line and area graphics compress more efficiently than dithered images, and hence load more quickly. Script-driven animations and visual effects consume processor time.

Think about the effective memory size of the machines on which your presentation will run. There must always be room to buffer sound segments as specified by your PlayList. On a one-megabyte machine you may need to turn off the RAM cache. Also beware of large INIT resources that gobble up space in the system area without warning.

Distilling all of these considerations, here are some rules of thumb I have found to work on a base configuration of a one-megabyte Mac Plus using an older HD 20SC, playing sound digitized at 11 KHz: Plan on turning off the RAM cache. Cut your sound at six to eight-second intervals. You may need to vary outside the six to eight-second limit for dramatic purposes; do so sparingly. Sounds under four seconds take longer to load than to play; sounds over 10 seconds may overflow memory. Keep a regular cutting rate when possible. You can have faster image cutting rates, but not in synchrony with sound. Time them with HyperTalk wait commands, or base them on side effects such as the loading time of a sound segment.

The greatest influence on your production will be whether you can control the choice of playback system. If you can guarantee that your fancy boardroom presentation will be played only on a Mac II, then you can be very ambitious in choosing effects. If your production is for public release, you had better assume and test with the basic configuration.

I suggest following these rules for your first trial. Then you will want to try some special effects, so here are a few ideas. Try out all of HyperCard's visual effect palette. Experiment with `dissolve to black, wipe to inverse` and other variants.

You can create animation effects with buttons using the hide and show commands, or by changing their location under script control. A `show` command is the fastest to execute because it only causes the button to be drawn, while hiding and movement require redraws of several graphics planes.

Text fields can also be hidden, shown and moved. The same performance considerations apply. You can also have your script insert characters into a field, given the appearance of text flowing onto the screen. Each insertion causes a redraw, however. Often, an equally dramatic effect can be created by doing a slow wipe right to a card with graphic text, giving the impression of typing.

Dramatic card flipping animation can be achieved if the images are kept simple. Again, line art or block graphics work best. You can animate a small area of a complex image by putting the full image into the background and changing only the smaller area on each card. HyperCard is smart enough to load the large background only once. Finally, for blazing speed you can "prewarm" cards in memory by locking the screen and visiting each card, which forces it to be loaded into memory. Then return to the first card, unlock the screen, and step through the cards at maximum speed. Be aware that this trick competes heavily for the memory and CPU resources needed for sound, so use it sparingly. You can also use the "prewarming" technique if you require precise synchronization to a sound cut and are unwilling to wait for the card to load.

This concludes the first installment of the article. The conclusion will be presented in the next issue of HyperAge, and will describe scripting for interactive control of sound playback as well as ideas for using these techniques for realtime tours of HyperCard stacks.

Part Two

Introduction

The HyperCard sound stacks described in the first installment of this article are useful and entertaining, but not truly interactive. Their flow is linear — once begun, the only way to affect the play is to terminate it completely. However, more advanced HyperTalk scripting will let you use the same production techniques to create sound stacks which are controllable in a truly interactive fashion. Performances can be paused, scanned forward or back and resumed. While paused, the buttons on a displayed card are active, so that the viewer can branch into an underlying database, returning to resume the sound show later. In this issue of HyperAge, I conclude this two-part article by describing these scripting techniques, suggesting applications and opportunities for improvement, and considering the implications for the Macintosh interface and interactive media in general.

Interactive Sound Tours

Before jumping into the scripts, take a look at the card images in Figures B-3 and B-4. The first contains one of the images to be shown during a sound playback (it happens to be a picture of Bill Atkinson). At the bottom is a panel of control buttons. Each display card in the interactive sound stack contains this panel as a background element. The clear area above the panel is a "view screen" in which graphic elements, fields and buttons are pasted.

Stack and Background Structures　The control panel icons are meant to be suggestive of those used on tape or compact disc players, and the functions are similar. To flip forward or backward through the cards in the show, you click and press on the double right or left arrows, respectively. Clicking the left arrow with bar rewinds to the beginning of the show. When the single right arrow is clicked, it starts up sound playback at the passage associated with the

Figure B-3 *Sample graphic card with controls*

On Cue	Do...	Go To Card...	and Play...
		1	BILL1
		2	BILL2
	wait 30	3	
	visual effect dissolve	4	
BILL2	visual effect iris open	5	BILL3
	wait 60		
	visual effect wipe down	6	
BILL3		7	BILL4
	wait 30		
	visual effect zoom open	8	
BILL4		9	BILL5
	visual effect iris close		
	wait 90	10	
BILL5		11	BILL6
	wait 120	12	
BILL6		13	BILL7
BILL7		14	
done	visual effect dissolve slow	15	

Previous PlayList: Next PlayList:

Figure B-4 *Sample PlayList*

current screen. After the sound has begun, clicking anywhere on the screen stops the show and reactivates the control panel and any other buttons on the card in view. (The stop icon is present only to complete the visual metaphor.)

As with the linear sound productions, the flow of the presentation is controlled with one or more "PlayList" cards hidden at the end of the stack. A PlayList is shown in Figure B-4. As before, it contains columns of sound cues to wait for, HyperTalk commands to be executed, numbers or names of cards to be shown and sound resources to be loaded for playing. Actions following a cue read left to right, the whole show reads top to bottom. This PlayList card differs, however, in adding two new background fields, "Next" and "Previous." These fields will contain the names of PlayList cards that follow or precede this one in the production. If there are no next or previous PlayLists, the respective field is left blank.

Scripting These previous and next pointers are used to associate the various PlayLists of a production into one long bidirectional list which can be scanned forward and back. Looking now at the stack level scripts in Listing B-2, you will see that the loadPlayList handler takes the contents of a PlayList and stores them in global variables for faster access. An additional global, nowPlaying, is an index to the PlayList line which is currently active.

The changeCue routine implements the virtual bidirectional list using these globals. Given the current position and a command to move forward or backward, it will check if the intended movement will run off the front or back end of the current PlayList. If so, changeCue will chain to another PlayList as given by the next or previous pointer. If the intended movement cannot be completed, changeCue returns a function value of false, otherwise it is true.

The main loop routine during sound output is playThis. It is very similar to the previous linear playback script, except that changeCue is used to move between PlayList lines, and its failure is the signal to terminate the show. Holding the mouse button down also stops the presentation.

The real trickery comes in the playFrom script. This is activated when restarting the play in the middle of a show. It assumes that the PlayList which contains the desired graphic has already been found. The job of playFrom is to find the precise location of the restart graphic in the "GoTo" column, to figure out what sound is associated with that graphic, and to load and begin playing that sound and any other required sounds before fully activating the PlayList.

The bidirection PlayList list structure implemented by changeCue must be used, because the setup for a particular graphic might extend back to the preceding PlayList. Therefore, playFrom starts at the first line of the current PlayList and works forward until an exact match of the desired graphic card is found. Then it works backward to find the first non-blank sound cue. (Note that if there is no cue directly associated with the restart card, the show will actually resume with the preceding cue and its associated visual.) Having found this cue, `playFrom` continues backward until it finds where the sound was loaded. It loads and begins playing this sound. It then works forward, finding and loading other sound pieces which appear in the PlayList before the restart point. Notice that if `playFrom` runs off the beginning of the PlayList chain, it will simply start the show at its beginning.

Listing B-3 contains two of the control panel scripts. The play button uses HyperCard's find function to locate the PlayList that contains the number of the current graphic card, then turns control over to `playFrom` to figure out the exact restart sequence. (If you want to name rather than number your cards, some simple changes to this script will be needed.) Note that if a particular graphic card appears more than once in the presentation, this script will restart on its first occurrence given the order in which the PlayLists are stored in the stack.

The forward script flips through the graphic cards as long as the mouse is down. It stops at the last card of the control panel background type. A shortcut is provided to jump immediately to the last card when the control key is held down. (The backward button script can be generated from this script by replacing `last` with `first`, and `next` with `previous`.)

Listing B-2. Interactive Sound Script.

```
on idle
   set lockScreen to false
end idle

on loadPlayList script
   -- set up global values for PlayList card script
   global Cues,numCues,Does,GoTos,Nexts,NextPL,PrevPL
   put bkgnd field "Cue" of card script into Cues
   put number of lines in Cues into numCues
   put bkgnd field "Do" of card script into Does
   put bkgnd field "GoToCard" of card script into GoTos
   put bkgnd field "NextUp" of card script into Nexts
   put bkgnd field "Next" of card script into NextPL
   put bkgnd field "Previous" of card script into PrevPL
end loadPlayList

function changeCue forward
   -- move the current cue pointer
   -- forward is true to advance, false to go backward
```

```
          -- returns false if at end/beginning of Playlists, else true
          global Cues,numCues,Does,GoTos,Nexts,NextPL,PrevPL
          global nowPlaying
          if forward is true then
            -- Going forward.  At end of this PlayList?
            if nowPlaying is numCues then
              -- At end of all PlayLists?
              if NextPL is empty then return false
              loadPlayList nextPL
              put 1 into nowPlaying
              return true
            end if
            add 1 to nowPlaying
          else
            -- Going backward.  At beginning of this PlayList?
            if nowPlaying is 1 then
              -- At begin of first PlayList?
              if PrevPL is empty then return false
              loadPlayList prevPL
              put numCues into nowPlaying
              return true
            end if
            subtract 1 from nowPlaying
          end if
          return true
        end changeCue


        on playThis
          -- This one actually does the playing
          global Cues,numCues,Does,GoTos,Nexts,NextPL,PrevPL
          global nowPlaying
          hide menubar
          hide msg
          repeat
            -- Need to wait?
            put line nowPlaying of Cues into Cue
            if Cue is not empty
            then wait until the sound is "done" ¬
            or the sound = Cue or the mouse is down
            if the mouse is down then
              play stop
              exit playThis
            end if
            -- Any code to do?  (We keep reusing local variable Cue)
            put line nowPlaying of Does into Cue
```

```
      if Cue is not empty then do Cue
      -- Any card changes?
      put line nowPlaying of GoTos into Cue
      if Cue is not empty then go to card Cue
      -- Any sounds to load?
      put line nowPlaying of Nexts into Cue
      if Cue is not empty then play Cue
      -- More to the script?
      if changeCue(true) is false then exit repeat
    end repeat
end playThis


on playIt script
  -- A simple entry to start the beginning of a playList
  global nowPlaying
  loadPlayList script
  put 1 into nowPlaying
  playThis
end playIt


on playFrom script,cardNum
  -- A fancy script to start/restart in the middle of a playList
  -- Calling code must have found script where cardNum occurs
  global Cues,numCues,Does,GoTos,Nexts,NextPL,PrevPL
  global nowPlaying
  -- set up script
  loadPlayList script
  put 1 into nowPlaying
  -- find where the card is called
  repeat
    if line nowPlaying of GoTos is cardNum then exit repeat
    if changeCue(true) is false then exit playFrom
  end repeat
  -- Back up to the last cue.
  repeat
    if line nowPlaying of Cues is not empty then exit repeat
    if changeCue(false) is false then exit repeat
  end repeat
  put line nowPlaying of Cues into startCue
  if startCue is not empty then
    -- Back up to where the cue sound was loaded
    repeat while changeCue(false) is true
      if line nowPlaying of Nexts is startCue then exit repeat
    end repeat
    -- Load cue sound, and all other forward to start point
```

```
   repeat
      if line nowPlaying of Cues is startCue then exit repeat
      if line nowPlaying of Nexts is not empty then ¬
      play line nowPlaying of Nexts
      if changeCue(true) is false then exit playFrom
   end repeat
   end if
   -- Now positioned correctly - roll 'em!
   playThis
end playFrom
```

Listing B-3. Play Control Scripts

```
-- play button script
on mouseUp
   get the number of this card
   put it into thisNum
   set lockscreen to true
   go to first card of bkgnd "PlayList"
   find thisNum in bkgnd field "GoTo"
   if the result is "not found" then
      beep
      go to card thisNum
      set lockscreen to false
      exit mouseUp
   end if
   get the number of this card
   go to card thisNum
   set lockscreen to false
   playFrom it,thisNum
end mouseUp


-- forward button script
on mouseDown
   -- enhanced function
   if the commandKey is down then
      go to last card of this background
      exit mouseDown
   end if
   -- else step through stack to last display card
   repeat
      if id of this card is id of last card of bkgnd
      then exit mouseDown
      if not (the mouse is down) then exit mouseDown
```

```
      go to next card of this bkgnd
    end repeat
  end mouseDown
```

Trying It Out If you have already built a sound production using the earlier scripts, you can add interactivity by modifying your backgrounds as shown, and replacing the sequential play stack scripts with the more complex ones. There should be little variation in performance. If you would like to have an example to examine and modify, I have produced a small interactive stack called "BillSez." This contains a short audio message from Bill Atkinson and fits on one floppy disk. It is available from CompuServe, the Well and other networks, as well as through BMUG and many user groups. You are invited to copy, modify and redistribute this stack as you please (though not for profit).

Producing Graphics

The first installment of this article suggested that line and area graphics were the most efficient for disk storage and presentation speed. However, simple economics (and lack of artistic talent on some of our parts) mean that many of the pictures for sound shows must be scanned from existing art. The native HyperCard display format is the standard Macintosh screen size in 72 dot-per-inch black and white. Two choices are available for image input.

"Contact" scanners use a CCD array to digitize from a paper original. They come in feed-through and flat bed models and are capable of resolutions from 75 to 300 dots per inch. Generally, you should use a contact scanner when legibility of type or line art on the original is important. You may need to "magnify" the image using a higher resolution for the detail to show through.

A number of contact scanners are available for the Macintosh from companies such as Abaton, AST and Datacopy. Avoid feed-through models, as they make it nearly impossible to keep vertical and horizontal lines registered. Be sure to try a sample of your own material on the machine before buying, and choose one with local support, if possible. Look for the abilities to scan at multiple resolutions, and to produce a half-toned image. A scanner with a SCSI interface to the Mac will be faster than one which uses serial communications.

Video digitizers for the Mac Plus and SE produce a black and white dithered rendering of an incoming NTSC video signal. Video digitizing is required when the original material is in this form, and also works well in scanning original art with large half-toned or variable brightness areas. Art that is video scanned should be mounted on a well-lit camera stand. Use a good quality video camera, such as a Sony Pro 8 camcorder. Lesser equipment may degrade the image due to poorer optics, and may lack the "macro" capability necessary for closeup work.

There are two options for video scanning. The first is MacVision from PTI/Koala ($400 list — look for cheaper prices from discounters), which was originally created several years ago by Bill Atkinson.   It is slow, several seconds per scan, but still has the best dithering algorithm for representing pictures in black and white dots. Because of its low speed, MacVision can only be used with a still original, or with a videotape or videodisc player capable of generating a stable, smear-free freeze frame. A new MacVision software version, 2.0, was due to be released at the end of March. It will add gray-scale digitizing ability with no changes to the hardware. The upgrade will be available to owners of earlier versions for $80; current dealer stock includes a coupon good for a free upgrade. (PTI/Koala, 269 Mount Hermon Rd., Scotts Valley, CA 95066; 408-438-0946.)

An alternative to MacVision is MacViz digitizer, produced by Pixelogic. It is more expensive ($595 from factory or dealers) and produces a grainier image, but is capable of digitizing in near real-time — two video frames or 1/30th of a second. Choose this one if you need to capture from running video and don't have access to a freeze frame player. (Pixelogic, 800 West Cummings Park, Suite 2900, Woburn, MA 02180; 617-938-7711.)

Be aware that some original images may not work at all. Low contrast and fine detail can easily overwhelm the scanning and display capabilities of the basic Macintosh. If you cannot use the entire piece of art, see if there are scannable parts which still convey your message. A set of cardboard templates showing the screen rectangle at various scanning resolutions is a useful homemade accessory for framing and composing these excerpts.

A good quality paint program is needed for touching up scanned images and trimming them to size. You want one that does a good job of handling larger than screen size images, so you can pick the part that looks best for your slide. My favorite is SuperPaint; FullPaint is also a good choice. If you'd like to convert your scanned art into line and area graphics, take a look at Adobe Illustrator. It is expensive and requires some learning, but can produce stunning images which you may resize as desired before converting back to HyperCard bitmap format.   The most efficient graphics production setup uses MultiFinder with HyperCard, your digitizing program and a graphics editor all loaded at once, creating a true production line in one Macintosh. This gobbles memory, though. Plan on four megabytes or more to do all of these tasks at once.

Finally, while you can keep short production plans and storyboards in your head or on scratch paper, you may want some planning help as things get complex. I find More (an outlining program) and Excel (a spreadsheet) to be useful in structuring scripts, keeping notes and building production plans.

Applications

Linear sound shows can be used to build presentations or to create personal "MTV" productions that associate images with music. Interactive sound considerably extends this range of application. You can create lectures that display slides illustrating the point described, and which are also directly linked to database stacks from which a student can retrieve further information. A voice-over help system could describe the structure of a stack by bringing into view cards that exhibit the features being described. HyperCard educational "films" can be woven through reference material, using the attractive power of animation and music to draw students' attention to graphic and textual content which illustrate the curriculum. Industrial training applications might use these techniques to add life to exploded diagrams, textual instructions and parts lists. Audio sales presentations can be fleshed out with substantiating data and examples for the potential client to explore.

Possible Enhancements

There are many possible technical extensions of these techniques. For these examples I have kept within the framework of a single sound stack containing two background types. This has kept the complexity of the scripts and figures to a level manageable in a two-part article. However, there is no reason that these techniques cannot be extended to weave tours through multiple stacks, or create multiple sound shows within the scope of a single stack. To HyperCard can be added very simple XCMDs that use the Toolbox `Open-ResFile` and CloseResFile calls to allow a play command to access any sound file in the system. Other XCMDs can "float" a modal control panel dialog over any background type, manipulating the stack by calling back to HyperTalk as the user clicks on the controls.

Such extensions could be powerful enough to allow the construction of an "editing droid." Such a composing system would allow you to create and edit sound productions by fetching graphics and audio from any part of the system and combining the elements into a production by filling in a storyboard layout, rather than by manually creating and testing PlayLists.

HyperCard sound stacks get large very quickly. For anyone seriously contemplating commercial applications, distribution becomes an issue. CD-ROM (compact disc read-only memory) on the Macintosh may be a solution to this problem. At Apple we have created test CD-ROMs containing sound stacks such as I have described. We have found that the same production rules outlined in the first part of this article will generate a sound stack able to run directly from CD-ROM, even given its modest performance.

Conclusions

The uses of sound which I propose highlight a change in the style of Macintosh user interface which HyperCard has begun. The standard Mac interface is tool-like: the user is in control, the machine responds to external events, the focus of the designer is on giving the user transparent access to the task at hand, the appeal is cool and rational. In contrast, HyperCard sound exposes the Macintosh as a hot dramatic medium, capable of evoking response at an emotional level. The user becomes a viewer, the machine and its scripts must seize control of the pacing and content of the experience. The content is more art than engineering, and it cannot be created in the standard interface paradigm.

If Macintosh can operate at both ends of this spectrum, it should work in the middle also. But what is the middle? There are very few conventions for fluid exchange of initiative, control and direction between human and machine. Between the user-tool and viewer-player pairings of man and machine, there may be a place for both to be participants in a kind of conversation.

HyperCard will force this issue to be confronted. It is capable of spanning the range of interaction. It has been put into the hands of thousands of people who will begin experimenting in new media with a fresh eye, without requiring professional studios or budgets. My motive in describing these sound techniques is to provide the ingredients for some of these experiments-to-be. Go to it!

Writing XCMDs in LightSpeed Pascal

The folks at Think Technologies (publishers of the LightSpeed language series) have modified the interface and glue routines originally written for MPW by Dan Winkler so they work with the LightSpeed compilers. For LightSpeed Pascal, they put the definitions into two files. The definitions are in a file called "XCMD Interface.p" and the glue routines are in a file called "XCMD Utilities.p." Move these files into your LightSpeed Pascal folders. Within these files, you learn that the names of the Pascal units for these two sections of code are called "XCMDIntf" and "XCMDUtils."

If you plan to use these files "as-is" in compiling your XCMD, then the files must be added to the Project file in the order shown in Figure C-1. The DA PasLib and MacTraps library files must be listed for all XCMDs. XCMDs that call other parts of the Toolbox may need additional library files listed in the project.

Your LightSpeed Pascal XCMD source code must then include the names of the two units in the Uses statement of the XCMD's interface section. Also, LightSpeed code resources require that the main procedure be called Main. This is the procedure that has the parameter block pointer passed to it.

Thus, the basic outline of a LightSpeed Pascal XCMD is as follows:

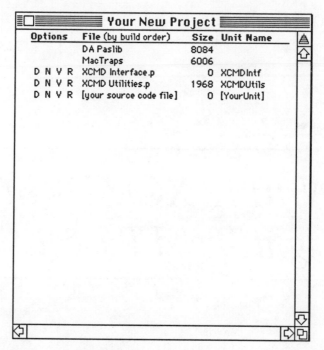

Figure C-1 *The minimum listing of files that must be put into a LightSpeed Pascal project. The order is important. Your XCMD code file would be listed at the end.*

```
unit  AnyUnit;  {any filler name will do}

interface
  uses
    XCMDIntf, XCMDUtils;

  procedure MAIN (paramPtr : XCmdPtr);


implementation
  procedure  myXCMD (paramPtr : XCmdPtr);
  begin
    {code for your XCMD here}
  end;

  procedure Main;
  begin
    myXCMD (paramPtr)
  end;


end.  (AnyUnit)
```

You are free to define other procedures and functions in the implementation section of your code, and then call them from the Main procedure.

When your XCMD source code is complete, be sure its file name is added to the Project list. Then choose Build & Save As from the Project menu and click on the Code Resource button in the standard file dialog. Whenever you click this Code Resource button, you'll see a Resource Information dialog box (Figure C-2) into which you may enter the Resource type (XCMD or XFCN), the ID (choose a number from 128 to 32767) and the resource name. The resource type you assign to your code determines how HyperCard treats the return value of your external code. The resource name is the name of the command or function you'll be calling from your HyperTalk scripts.

LightSpeed Pascal compiles a code resource to a disk file. As it compiles each unit, it performs error checking. If you haven't modified the XCMD interface and glue units, they should compile without a hitch. Any obvious bugs in your own XCMD source code will be pointed out to you by the compiler. During compilation, LightSpeed Pascal removes unneeded glue routines from the code. When the compile is successful, quit LightSpeed

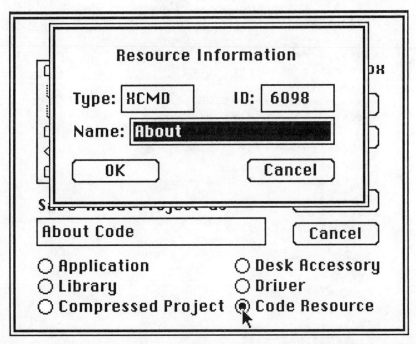

Figure C-2 *Building and Saving as a code resource brings up this dialog box. Specify the XCMD or XFCN type, assign it an ID number, and provide the name which you'll be calling from your HyperTalk script.*

Pascal and use ResEdit to move the resource from this code resource file to the stack of your choice.

With reprint permission from Think Technologies Division of Symantec Corp., here are the interface and glue units for LightSpeed Pascal:

File XCMD Interface.p

```
{ Hypercard XCMD interface unit for Lightspeed Pascal }

{ (c) 1987 Symantec Corp.  THINK Technologies Division }

{ Adapted for use with Lightspeed Pascal from information }
{ provided by Apple Computer, Inc. }

unit XCMDIntf;
interface
  const

  { result codes }
    xresSucc = 0;
    xresFail = 1;
    xresNotImp = 2;

  { request codes }
    xreqSendCardMessage = 1;
    xreqEvalExpr = 2;
    xreqStringLength = 3;
    xreqStringMatch = 4;

    xreqZeroBytes = 6;
    xreqPasToZero = 7;
    xreqZeroToPas = 8;
    xreqStrToLong = 9;
    xreqStrToNum = 10;
    xreqStrToBool = 11;
    xreqStrToExt = 12;
    xreqLongToStr = 13;
    xreqNumToStr = 14;
    xreqNumToHex = 15;
    xreqBoolToStr = 16;
    xreqExtToStr = 17;
    xreqGetGlobal = 18;
    xreqSetGlobal = 19;
    xreqGetFieldByName = 20;
```

```
      xreqGetFieldByNum = 21;
      xreqGetFieldByID = 22;
      xreqSetFieldByName = 23;
      xreqSetFieldByNum = 24;
      xreqSetFieldByID = 25;
      xreqStringEqual = 26;
      xreqReturnToPas = 27;
      xreqScanToReturn = 28;
      xreqScanToZero = 39;   {yes, it's 39}

  type

   XCmdPtr = ^XCmdBlock;
   XCmdBlock = RECORD
     paramCount : INTEGER;
     params : ARRAY[1..16] OF Handle;
     returnValue : Handle;
     passFlag : BOOLEAN;

     entryPoint : ProcPtr;    { to call back to HyperCard}
     request : INTEGER;
     result : INTEGER;
     inArgs : ARRAY[1..8] OF LongInt;
     outArgs : ARRAY[1..4] OF LongInt;
   end;

implementation

end.


==================================================
```

File XCMD Utilities.p

```
{ Hypercard XCMD utilities unit for Lightspeed Pascal }

{ (c) 1987 Symantec Corp.   THINK Technologies Division }

{ Adapted for use with Lightspeed Pascal from information }
{ provided by Apple Computer, Inc. }

unit XCMDUtils;

interface
```

```
uses
   XCMDIntf;

type
   Str31 = STRING[31];

function StringMatch (paramPtr : XCmdPtr;
                      pattern : Str255;
                      target : Ptr) : Ptr;

function PasToZero (paramPtr : XCmdPtr;
                    str : Str255) : Handle;

procedure ZeroToPas (paramPtr : XCmdPtr;
                     zeroStr : Ptr;
                     VAR pasStr : Str255);

function StrToLong (paramPtr : XCmdPtr;
                    str : Str31) : LongInt;

function StrToNum (paramPtr : XCmdPtr;
                   str : Str31) : LongInt;

function StrToBool (paramPtr : XCmdPtr;
                    str : Str31) : BOOLEAN;

function StrToExt (paramPtr : XCmdPtr;
                   str : Str31) : Extended;

function LongToStr (paramPtr : XCmdPtr;
                    posNum : LongInt) : Str31;

function NumToStr (paramPtr : XCmdPtr;
                   num : LongInt) : Str31;

function NumToHex (paramPtr : XCmdPtr;
                   num : LongInt;
                   nDigits : INTEGER) : Str31;

function ExtToStr (paramPtr : XCmdPtr;
                   num : Extended) : Str31;

function BoolToStr (paramPtr : XCmdPtr;
                    bool : BOOLEAN) : Str31;
```

```
procedure SendCardMessage (paramPtr : XCmdPtr;
              msg : Str255);

function EvalExpr (paramPtr : XCmdPtr;
              expr : Str255) : Handle;

function StringLength (paramPtr : XCmdPtr;
              strPtr : Ptr) : LongInt;

function GetGlobal (paramPtr : XCmdPtr;
              globName : Str255) : Handle;

procedure SetGlobal (paramPtr : XCmdPtr;
              globName : Str255;
              globValue : Handle);

function GetFieldByName (paramPtr : XCmdPtr;
              cardFieldFlag : BOOLEAN;
              fieldName : Str255) : Handle;

function GetFieldByNum (paramPtr : XCmdPtr;
              cardFieldFlag : BOOLEAN;
              fieldNum : INTEGER) : Handle;

function GetFieldByID (paramPtr : XCmdPtr;
              cardFieldFlag : BOOLEAN;
              fieldID : INTEGER) : Handle;

procedure SetFieldByName (paramPtr : XCmdPtr;
              cardFieldFlag : BOOLEAN;
              fieldName : Str255;
              fieldVal : Handle);

procedure SetFieldByNum (paramPtr : XCmdPtr;
              cardFieldFlag : BOOLEAN;
              fieldNum : INTEGER;
              fieldVal : Handle);

procedure SetFieldByID (paramPtr : XCmdPtr;
              cardFieldFlag : BOOLEAN;
              fieldID : INTEGER;
              fieldVal : Handle);

function StringEqual (paramPtr : XCmdPtr;
              str1, str2 : Str255) : BOOLEAN;
```

```
         procedure ReturnToPas (paramPtr : XCmdPtr;
                        zeroStr : Ptr;
                        VAR pasStr : Str255);

         procedure ScanToReturn (paramPtr : XCmdPtr;
                        VAR scanPtr : Ptr);

         procedure ScanToZero (paramPtr : XCmdPtr;
                        VAR scanPtr : Ptr);

         procedure ZeroBytes (paramPtr : XCmdPtr;
                        dstPtr : Ptr;
                        longCount : LongInt);

implementation

     procedure DoJsr (addr : ProcPtr);
     inline
        $205F, $4E90;



     function StringMatch;
     begin
        with paramPtr^ do
           begin
             inArgs[1] := ORD(@pattern);
             inArgs[2] := ORD(target);
             request := xreqStringMatch;
             DoJsr(entryPoint);
             StringMatch := Ptr(outArgs[1]);
           end;
     end;


     function PasToZero;
     begin
        with paramPtr^ do
           begin
             inArgs[1] := ORD(@str);
             request := xreqPasToZero;
             DoJsr(entryPoint);
             PasToZero := Handle(outArgs[1]);
           end;
     end;
```

```pascal
procedure ZeroToPas;
begin
  with paramPtr^ do
    begin
      inArgs[1] := ORD(zeroStr);
      inArgs[2] := ORD(@pasStr);
      request := xreqZeroToPas;
      DoJsr(entryPoint);
    end;
end;


function StrToLong;
begin
  with paramPtr^ do
    begin
      inArgs[1] := ORD(@str);
      request := xreqStrToLong;
      DoJsr(entryPoint);
      StrToLong := outArgs[1];
    end;
end;


function StrToNum;
begin
  with paramPtr^ do
    begin
      inArgs[1] := ORD(@str);
      request := xreqStrToNum;
      DoJsr(entryPoint);
      StrToNum := outArgs[1];
    end;
end;


function StrToBool;
begin
  with paramPtr^ do
    begin
      inArgs[1] := ORD(@str);
      request := xreqStrToBool;
      DoJsr(entryPoint);
      StrToBool := BOOLEAN(outArgs[1]);
    end;
end;
```

```
function StrToExt;
  var
    x : Extended;
begin
  with paramPtr^ do
    begin
      inArgs[1] := ORD(@str);
      inArgs[2] := ORD(@x);
      request := xreqStrToExt;
      DoJsr(entryPoint);
      StrToExt := x;
    end;
end;


function LongToStr;
  var
    str : Str31;
begin
  with paramPtr^ do
    begin
      inArgs[1] := posNum;
      inArgs[2] := ORD(@str);
      request := xreqLongToStr;
      DoJsr(entryPoint);
      LongToStr := str;
    end;
end;


function NumToStr;
  var
    str : Str31;
begin
  with paramPtr^ do
    begin
      inArgs[1] := num;
      inArgs[2] := ORD(@str);
      request := xreqNumToStr;
      DoJsr(entryPoint);
      NumToStr := str;
    end;
end;
```

```
function NumToHex;
   var
     str : Str31;
begin
   with paramPtr^ do
     begin
       inArgs[1] := num;
       inArgs[2] := nDigits;
       inArgs[3] := ORD(@str);
       request := xreqNumToHex;
       DoJsr(entryPoint);
       NumToHex := str;
     end;
end;


function ExtToStr;
   var
     str : Str31;
begin
   with paramPtr^ do
     begin
       inArgs[1] := ORD(@num);
       inArgs[2] := ORD(@str);
       request := xreqExtToStr;
       DoJsr(entryPoint);
       ExtToStr := str;
     end;
end;


function BoolToStr;
   var
     str : Str31;
begin
   with paramPtr^ do
     begin
       inArgs[1] := LongInt(bool);
       inArgs[2] := ORD(@str);
       request := xreqBoolToStr;
       DoJsr(entryPoint);
       BoolToStr := str;
     end;
end;
```

```
procedure SendCardMessage;
begin
  with paramPtr^ do
    begin
      inArgs[1] := ORD(@msg);
      request := xreqSendCardMessage;
      DoJsr(entryPoint);
    end;
end;


function EvalExpr;
begin
  with paramPtr^ do
    begin
      inArgs[1] := ORD(@expr);
      request := xreqEvalExpr;
      DoJsr(entryPoint);
      EvalExpr := Handle(outArgs[1]);
    end;
end;


function StringLength;
begin
  with paramPtr^ do
    begin
      inArgs[1] := ORD(strPtr);
      request := xreqStringLength;
      DoJsr(entryPoint);
      StringLength := outArgs[1];
    end;
end;


function GetGlobal;
begin
  with paramPtr^ do
    begin
      inArgs[1] := ORD(@globName);
      request := xreqGetGlobal;
      DoJsr(entryPoint);
      GetGlobal := Handle(outArgs[1]);
    end;
end;
```

```pascal
procedure SetGlobal;
begin
  with paramPtr^ do
    begin
      inArgs[1] := ORD(@globName);
      inArgs[2] := ORD(globValue);
      request := xreqSetGlobal;
      DoJsr(entryPoint);
    end;
end;

function GetFieldByName;
begin
  with paramPtr^ do
    begin
      inArgs[1] := ORD(cardFieldFlag);
      inArgs[2] := ORD(@fieldName);
      request := xreqGetFieldByName;
      DoJsr(entryPoint);
      GetFieldByName := Handle(outArgs[1]);
    end;
end;

function GetFieldByNum;
begin
  with paramPtr^ do
    begin
      inArgs[1] := ORD(cardFieldFlag);
      inArgs[2] := fieldNum;
      request := xreqGetFieldByNum;
      DoJsr(entryPoint);
      GetFieldByNum := Handle(outArgs[1]);
    end;
end;

function GetFieldByID;
begin
  with paramPtr^ do
    begin
      inArgs[1] := ORD(cardFieldFlag);
      inArgs[2] := fieldID;
      request := xreqGetFieldByID;
      DoJsr(entryPoint);
      GetFieldByID := Handle(outArgs[1]);
    end;
end;
```

```
procedure SetFieldByName;
begin
  with paramPtr^ do
    begin
      inArgs[1] := ORD(cardFieldFlag);
      inArgs[2] := ORD(@fieldName);
      inArgs[3] := ORD(fieldVal);
      request := xreqSetFieldByName;
      DoJsr(entryPoint);
    end;
end;


procedure SetFieldByNum;
begin
  with paramPtr^ do
    begin
      inArgs[1] := ORD(cardFieldFlag);
      inArgs[2] := fieldNum;
      inArgs[3] := ORD(fieldVal);
      request := xreqSetFieldByNum;
      DoJsr(entryPoint);
    end;
end;


procedure SetFieldByID;
begin
  with paramPtr^ do
    begin
      inArgs[1] := ORD(cardFieldFlag);
      inArgs[2] := fieldID;
      inArgs[3] := ORD(fieldVal);
      request := xreqSetFieldByID;
      DoJsr(entryPoint);
    end;
end;
```

```
function StringEqual;
begin
  with paramPtr^ do
    begin
      inArgs[1] := ORD(@str1);
      inArgs[2] := ORD(@str2);
      request := xreqStringEqual;
      DoJsr(entryPoint);
      StringEqual := BOOLEAN(outArgs[1]);
    end;
end;


procedure ReturnToPas;
begin
  with paramPtr^ do
    begin
      inArgs[1] := ORD(zeroStr);
      inArgs[2] := ORD(@pasStr);
      request := xreqReturnToPas;
      DoJsr(entryPoint);
    end;
end;


procedure ScanToReturn;
begin
  with paramPtr^ do
    begin
      inArgs[1] := ORD(@scanPtr);
      request := xreqScanToReturn;
      DoJsr(entryPoint);
    end;
end;


procedure ScanToZero;
begin
  with paramPtr^ do
    begin
      inArgs[1] := ORD(@scanPtr);
      request := xreqScanToZero;
      DoJsr(entryPoint);
    end;
end;
```

```
    procedure ZeroBytes;
    begin
      with paramPtr^ do
        begin
          inArgs[1] := ORD(dstPtr);
          inArgs[2] := longCount;
          request := xreqZeroBytes;
          DoJsr(entryPoint);
        end;
    end;
end.
```

Writing XCMDs in LightSpeed C

A version of the XCMD interfaces and glue routines have been converted to LightSpeed C (LSC) by Think Technologies. The disk of these files that Think offers seems not as polished as their Pascal version, but the pieces are there for you to compile XCMDs in C.

The interface file, HyperXCmd.h, needs to be included as a header in your C source code. Each of the glue routines has been broken out into its own file. To simplify inclusion of these files into your XCMD, you should combine these files into a separate project, with a name like XCMD.π (using π as a project file name extension is a convention used by the person who customized the XCMDs for LSC). You may then list that project as a file to be compiled with your own code as shown in the Project listing of Figure D-1.

Each of the XCMD glue files #includes the HyperXCmd.h file, so you don't have to list that in your project. The HyperXCmd.h file, itself, #includes MacTypes.h, which your code needs to access the Macintosh Toolbox. All #included files must be available on the disk before the XCMD may be compiled.

Given the idea of loading an XCMD.π project within your new project, here's a basic outline of a LightSpeed C XCMD:

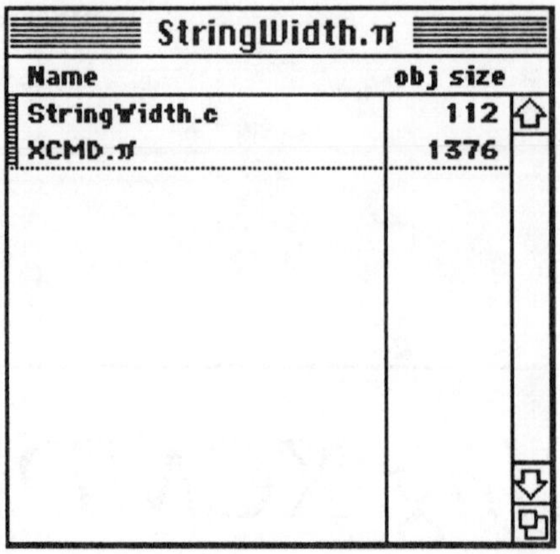

Figure D-1 *LightSpeed C XCMD projects may include another project, like the XCMD.π project. StringWidth.c is a source code file for an XFCN.*

Given the idea of loading an XCMD.π project within your new project, here's a basic outline of a LightSpeed C XCMD:

```
#include <QuickDraw.h>
#include "HyperXCmd.h"

pascal void
main(paramPtr)
XCmdBlockPtr        paramPtr;
{
        your code here
}
```

The program must be called "main," as LightSpeed assumes code resources are so named. If your XCMD needs other Macintosh libraries, then they may be #included with the rest.

Before building the code resource, you must make various setting about its name, type, and ID. Choose Set Project Type from the Project menu. The dialog box (Figure D-2) lets you specify a Code Resource, as well as the other important resource information. Assign an ID between 128 and 32767. The name of the resource is the name you'll be calling from your HyperTalk script.

Think Technologies has provided a small sample XFCN, called String-Width. It's the one whose project has been illustrated above. Its source code is shown in Figure D-3. This XFCN calls the TextWidth Macintosh Toolbox call, which returns the width in pixels of a string that is passed as a parameter.

XCMD.π	
Name	obj size
BoolToStr.c	52
EvalExpr.c	46
ExtToStr.c	46
GetFieldByID.c	60
GetFieldByName.c	58
GetFieldByNum.c	60
GetGlobal.c	46
LongToStr.c	46
NumToHex.c	54
NumToStr.c	46
PasToZero.c	46
ReturnToPas.c	46
ScanToReturn.c	40
ScanToZero.c	40
SendCardMessage.c	40
SetFieldByID.c	60
SetFieldByName.c	58
SetFieldByNum.c	60
SetGlobal.c	46
StringEqual.c	52
StringLength.c	46
StringMatch.c	52
StrtoBool.c	46
StrToExt.c	46
StrToLong.c	46
StrToNum.c	46
XCmdGlue.c	0
ZeroBytes.c	46
ZeroToPas.c	46

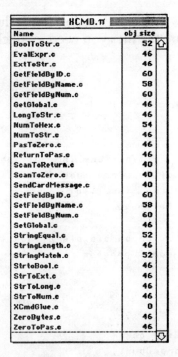

Figure D-2 *The XCMD.π project lists all the glue routines that your XCMDs might need.*

StringWidth.c

```
/*
    StringWidth -- a sample HyperCard user-defined command in C.
    ©THINK Technologies, Inc. 1987
    All Rights Reserved.

 */

#include <QuickDraw.h>
#include "HyperXCmd.h"


pascal void
main(paramPtr)
XCmdBlockPtr    paramPtr;
{
    long len;
    register char *str, *theStr;
    Str31 result;

    for (str = theStr = *(char **)paramPtr->params[0]; *str; str++)
        ;
    /* First param is string to return string-width of */
    len = TextWidth(theStr, 0, str - theStr);

    /* Convert the number to a string */
    NumToStr(paramPtr, len, result);
    paramPtr->returnValue = PasToZero(paramPtr, result);
}
```

Figure D-1 *A sample LSC XFCN application showsd that the program includes the HyperXCmd.h header file, as well as other librarires called by your external code. The main program must be called "main."*

Reprinted below (with permission from Think Technologies Division of Symantec Corp.) are the files you need to #include in your XCMDs.

File HyperXCmd.h

```
/*
        HyperXCmd.h  Definitions for calling all standard
        HyperCard callback routines from C.
        ƏApple Computer, Inc. 1987
        All Rights Reserved.

        See CFlash.C for an example of how to include this
        module in your C program.
*/

#include <MacTypes.h>

typedef struct XCmdBlock {
        short     paramCount;
    Handle  params[16];
    Handle  returnValue;
    Boolean   passFlag;

    void(*entryPoint)();      /* to call back to HyperCard */
    short        request;
    short        result;
    longinArgs[8];
    longoutArgs[4];
    } XCmdBlock, *XCmdBlockPtr;

typedef unsigned char Str31[32];
/*
typedef struct Str31 {
        char      guts[32];
        } Str31, *Str31Ptr;
*/

enum {
        xresSucc = 0,
        xresFail,
        xresNotImp
};
```

```
/* request codes */
enum {
      xreqSendCardMessage = 1,
      xreqEvalExpr,
      xreqStringLength,
      xreqStringMatch,
      xreqSendHCMessage,
      xreqZeroBytes,
      xreqPasToZero,
      xreqZeroToPas,
      xreqStrToLong,
      xreqStrToNum,
      xreqStrToBool,
      xreqStrToExt,
      xreqLongToStr,
      xreqNumToStr,
      xreqNumToHex,
      xreqBoolToStr,
      xreqExtToStr,
      xreqGetGlobal,
      xreqSetGlobal,
      xreqGetFieldByName,
      xreqGetFieldByNum,
      xreqGetFieldByID,
      xreqSetFieldByName,
      xreqSetFieldByNum,
      xreqSetFieldByID,
      xreqStringEqual,
      xreqReturnToPas,
      xreqScanToReturn,
      xreqScanToZero = 39    /* was suppose to be 29!  Oops! */
};


/* Forward definitions of glue routines.  Main program
      must include XCmdGlue.inc.c.  See XCmdGlue.inc.c for
      documentation of each routine.  */

typedef void (*MyProcPtr) ();

pascal void         SendCardMessage(XCmdBlockPtr, StringPtr msg);
pascal Handle  EvalExpr(XCmdBlockPtr, StringPtr expr);
pascal long         StringLength(XCmdBlockPtr, StringPtr strPtr);
pascal Ptr          StringMatch(XCmdBlockPtr, StringPtr pattern,
                    Ptr target);
```

```
pascal void          ZeroBytes(XCmdBlockPtr, Ptr dstPtr,
                       long longCount);
pascal Handle PasToZero(XCmdBlockPtr, StringPtr pasStr);
pascal void          ZeroToPas(XCmdBlockPtr,
                       unsigned char  *zeroStr,
                       StringPtr pasStr);
pascal long          StrToLong(XCmdBlockPtr,
                       unsigned char  * strPtr);
pascal long          StrToNum(XCmdBlockPtr, unsigned char  *str);
pascal Boolean StrToBool(XCmdBlockPtr,unsigned char  *str);
pascal void          StrToExt(XCmdBlockPtr,unsigned char  *str,
                       double *myext);
pascal void          LongToStr(XCmdBlockPtr, long posNum,
                       unsigned char  *mystr);
pascal void          NumToStr(XCmdBlockPtr, long num,
                       unsigned char  *mystr);
pascal void          NumToHex(XCmdBlockPtr, long num,
                       short nDigits,
                       unsigned char  *mystr);
pascal void          BoolToStr(XCmdBlockPtr, Boolean bool,
                       unsigned char  *mystr);
pascal void          ExtToStr(XCmdBlockPtr, double *myext,
                       unsigned char  *mystr);
pascal Handle GetGlobal(XCmdBlockPtr, StringPtr globName);
pascal void          SetGlobal(XCmdBlockPtr, StringPtr globName,
                       Handle globValue);
pascal Handle GetFieldByName(XCmdBlockPtr,
                       Boolean cardFieldFlag,
                       StringPtr fieldName);
pascal Handle GetFieldByNum(XCmdBlockPtr,
                       Boolean cardFieldFlag,
                       short fieldNum);
pascal Handle GetFieldByID(XCmdBlockPtr,Boolean cardFieldFlag,
                       short fieldID);
pascal void          SetFieldByName(XCmdBlockPtr,
                       Boolean cardFieldFlag,
                       StringPtr fieldName, Handle fieldVal);
pascal void          SetFieldByNum(XCmdBlockPtr,
                       Boolean cardFieldFlag,
                       short fieldNum,Handle fieldVal);
pascal void          SetFieldByID(XCmdBlockPtr,
                       Boolean cardFieldFlag,
                       short fieldID,Handle fieldVal);
pascal Boolean StringEqual(XCmdBlockPtr, unsigned char  *str1,
                       unsigned char  *str2);
```

```
pascal void          ReturnToPas(XCmdBlockPtr, Ptr zeroStr,
                     StringPtr pasStr);
pascal void          ScanToReturn(XCmdBlockPtr, Ptr *scanHndl);
pascal void          ScanToZero(XCmdBlockPtr, Ptr *scanHndl);
```

=====================================

File BoolToStr.c

```
#include "HyperXCmd.h"


 /* Convert a boolean to 'true' or 'false'.  Instead of returning
    a new string, as Pascal does, it expects you to create mystr
     and pass it in to be filled. */
pascal void
BoolToStr(paramPtr,bool,mystr)
register XCmdBlockPtr paramPtr;
Boolean              bool;
Str31 mystr;
{
     paramPtr->inArgs[0] = (long)bool;
     paramPtr->inArgs[1] = (long)mystr;
     paramPtr->request = xreqBoolToStr;
    (*paramPtr->entryPoint)();
}
```

=====================================

File EvalExpr.c

```
#include <MacTypes.h>
#include "HyperXCmd.h"

/* Evaluate a HyperCard expression and return the answer.
   The answer is a handle to a zero-terminated string.
 */
pascal Handle
EvalExpr(paramPtr,expr)
register XCmdBlockPtr paramPtr;
StringPtr       expr;
{
     paramPtr->inArgs[0] = (long)expr;
     paramPtr->request = xreqEvalExpr;
```

```
        (*paramPtr->entryPoint)();
          return (Handle)paramPtr->outArgs[0];
    }


    ==================================

    File ExtToStr.c

    #include "HyperXCmd.h"

    /* Original comment:
        Convert an extended long integer to decimal digits in a string.
        Instead of returning a new string, as Pascal does, it expects
        you to create mystr and pass it in to be filled. */

    /* My comment:
            I assume that an extended is supposed to be an 80-byte
            double, which is declared as double in LSC.  I've changed
    "extended" to "double" to reflect this
     */
    pascal void
    ExtToStr(paramPtr,myext,mystr)
    register XCmdBlockPtr paramPtr;
    double    *      myext;
    Str31 mystr;
    {
          paramPtr->inArgs[0] = (long)myext;
          paramPtr->inArgs[1] = (long)mystr;
          paramPtr->request = xreqExtToStr;
        (*paramPtr->entryPoint)();
    }


    ==================================

    File GetFieldByID.c

    #include "HyperXCmd.h"

    /* Return a handle to a zero-terminated string containing the
        value of the field whose ID is fieldID.  You must dispose
        of the handle.
     */
    pascal Handle
    GetFieldByID(paramPtr,cardFieldFlag,fieldID)
```

```
register XCmdBlockPtr paramPtr;
Boolean cardFieldFlag;
short fieldID;
{
      paramPtr->inArgs[0] = (long)cardFieldFlag;
      paramPtr->inArgs[1] = fieldID;
      paramPtr->request = xreqGetFieldByID;
    (*paramPtr->entryPoint)();
      return (Handle)paramPtr->outArgs[0];
}


==================================


File GetFieldByName.c

#include "HyperXCmd.h"

/* Return a handle to a zero-terminated string containing the
   value of field fieldName on the current card.  You must
   dispose of the handle.
 */
pascal Handle
GetFieldByName(paramPtr,cardFieldFlag,fieldName)
register XCmdBlockPtr paramPtr;
Boolean cardFieldFlag;
StringPtr      fieldName;
{
      paramPtr->inArgs[0] = (long)cardFieldFlag;
      paramPtr->inArgs[1] = (long)fieldName;
      paramPtr->request = xreqGetFieldByName;
    (*paramPtr->entryPoint)();
      return (Handle)paramPtr->outArgs[0];
}


==================================


File GetFieldByNum.c

#include "HyperXCmd.h"

/* Return a handle to a zero-terminated string containing the
   value of field fieldNum on the current card.  You must
   dispose of the handle.
 */
```

```
pascal Handle
GetFieldByNum(paramPtr,  cardFieldFlag,fieldNum)
register XCmdBlockPtr paramPtr;
Boolean cardFieldFlag;
short fieldNum;
{
     paramPtr->inArgs[0] = (long)cardFieldFlag;
     paramPtr->inArgs[1] = fieldNum;
     paramPtr->request = xreqGetFieldByNum;
    (*paramPtr->entryPoint)();
     return (Handle)paramPtr->outArgs[0];
}
```

===================================

```
File GetGlobal.c

#include "HyperXCmd.h"


/* Return a handle to a zero-terminated string containing the
   value of the specified HyperTalk global variable.
 */
pascal Handle
GetGlobal(paramPtr,globName)
register XCmdBlockPtr paramPtr;
StringPtr        globName;
{
     paramPtr->inArgs[0] = (long)globName;
     paramPtr->request = xreqGetGlobal;
    (*paramPtr->entryPoint)();
     return (Handle)paramPtr->outArgs[0];
}
```

===================================

```
File LongToStr.c

#include "HyperXCmd.h"


/*  Convert an unsigned long integer to a Pascal string.
    Instead of returning a new string, as Pascal does,
    it expects you to create mystr and pass it in to be filled.
 */
```

```
pascal void
LongToStr(paramPtr, posNum, mystr)
register XCmdBlockPtr paramPtr;
long          posNum;
Str31 mystr;
{
     paramPtr->inArgs[0] = posNum;
     paramPtr->inArgs[1] = (long)mystr;
     paramPtr->request = xreqLongToStr;
   (*paramPtr->entryPoint)();
}
```

=====================================

File NumToHex.c

#include "HyperXCmd.h"

```
/* Convert an unsigned long integer to a hexadecimal number
   and put it into a Pascal string.  Instead of returning
   a new string, as Pascal does, it expects you to create
   mystr and pass it in to be filled.
 */
pascal void
NumToHex(paramPtr, num, nDigits, mystr)
register XCmdBlockPtr paramPtr;
long          num;
short         nDigits;
Str31 mystr;
{
     paramPtr->inArgs[0] = num;
     paramPtr->inArgs[1] = nDigits;
     paramPtr->inArgs[2] = (long)mystr;
     paramPtr->request = xreqNumToHex;
   (*paramPtr->entryPoint)();
}
```

=====================================

File NumToStr.c

#include "HyperXCmd.h"

```
/* Convert a signed long integer to a Pascal string.  Instead of
```

```
        returning a new string, as Pascal does, it expects you to
        create mystr and pass it in to be filled.
  */
pascal void
NumToStr(paramPtr,num,mystr)
register XCmdBlockPtr paramPtr;
long           num;
Str31 mystr;
{
        paramPtr->inArgs[0] = num;
        paramPtr->inArgs[1] = (long)mystr;
        paramPtr->request = xreqNumToStr;
    (*paramPtr->entryPoint)();
}


====================================


File PasToZero.c


#include "HyperXCmd.h"


/* Convert a Pascal string to a zero-terminated string.
   Returns a handle to a new zero-terminated string.
   The caller must dispose the handle.  You'll need to
   do this for any result or argument you send from
   your XCMD to HyperTalk.  Note that if you use
   C-format strings, you won't need to do this from C.
  */
pascal Handle
PasToZero(paramPtr,pasStr)
register XCmdBlockPtr paramPtr;
StringPtr       pasStr;
{
        paramPtr->inArgs[0] = (long)pasStr;
        paramPtr->request = xreqPasToZero;
    (*paramPtr->entryPoint)();
        return (Handle)paramPtr->outArgs[0];
}


====================================
```

```
File ReturnToPas.c

*include "HyperXCmd.h"

/* zeroStr points into a zero-terminated string.  Collect the
   characters from there to the next carriage Return and return
   them in the Pascal string pasStr.  If a Return is not found,
   collect chars until the end of the string.
 */
pascal void
ReturnToPas(paramPtr,zeroStr,pasStr)
register XCmdBlockPtr paramPtr;
Ptr    zeroStr;
StringPtr      pasStr;
{
     paramPtr->inArgs[0] = (long)zeroStr;
     paramPtr->inArgs[1] = (long)pasStr;
     paramPtr->request = xreqReturnToPas;
    (*paramPtr->entryPoint)();
}


====================================


File ScanToReturn.c

*include "HyperXCmd.h"

/* Move the pointer scanPtr along a zero-terminated
   string until it points at a Return character
   or a zero byte.
 */
pascal void
ScanToReturn(paramPtr,scanHndl)
register XCmdBlockPtr paramPtr;
Ptr * scanHndl;
{
     paramPtr->inArgs[0] = (long)scanHndl;
     paramPtr->request = xreqScanToReturn;
    (*paramPtr->entryPoint)();
}


====================================
```

```
File ScanToZero.c

#include "HyperXCmd.h"

/* Move the pointer scanPtr along a zero-terminated
   string until it points at a zero byte.
 */
pascal void
ScanToZero(paramPtr,scanHndl)
register XCmdBlockPtr paramPtr;
Ptr * scanHndl;
{
     paramPtr->inArgs[0] = (long)scanHndl;
     paramPtr->request = xreqScanToZero;
   (*paramPtr->entryPoint)();
}


====================================


File SendCardMessage.c

#include "HyperXCmd.h"

/* Send a HyperCard message (a command with arguments)
   to the current card.  msg is a pointer to a
   Pascal-format string.
 */
pascal void
SendCardMessage(paramPtr, msg)
register XCmdBlockPtr paramPtr;
StringPtr      msg;
{
     paramPtr->inArgs[0] = (long)msg;
     paramPtr->request = xreqSendCardMessage;
   (*paramPtr->entryPoint)();
}


====================================
```

```
File SetFieldByID.c

#include "HyperXCmd.h"

/* Set the value of the field whose ID is fieldID to be the zero-
   terminated string in fieldVal.  The contents of the Handle are
   copied, so you must still dispose it afterwards.
 */
pascal void
SetFieldByID(paramPtr,cardFieldFlag,fieldID,fieldVal)
register XCmdBlockPtr paramPtr;
Boolean cardFieldFlag;
short fieldID;
Handle fieldVal;
{
      paramPtr->inArgs[0] = (long)cardFieldFlag;
      paramPtr->inArgs[1] =  fieldID;
      paramPtr->inArgs[2] = (long)fieldVal;
      paramPtr->request = xreqSetFieldByID;
    (*paramPtr->entryPoint)();
}


======================================


File SetFieldByName.c

#include "HyperXCmd.h"


/* Set the value of field fieldName to be the zero-terminated
   string in fieldVal.  The contents of the Handle are copied,
   so you must still dispose it afterwards.
 */
pascal void
SetFieldByName(paramPtr,cardFieldFlag,fieldName,fieldVal)
register XCmdBlockPtr paramPtr;
Boolean cardFieldFlag;
StringPtr    fieldName;
Handle fieldVal;
{
      paramPtr->inArgs[0] = (long)cardFieldFlag;
      paramPtr->inArgs[1] = (long)fieldName;
```

```
            paramPtr->inArgs[2] = (long)fieldVal;
            paramPtr->request = xreqSetFieldByName;
        (*paramPtr->entryPoint)();
    }


    ======================================


    File SetFieldByNum.c

    #include "HyperXCmd.h"

    /* Set the value of field fieldNum to be the zero-terminated
       string in fieldVal.  The contents of the Handle are copied,
       so you must still dispose it afterwards.
     */
    pascal void
    SetFieldByNum(paramPtr,cardFieldFlag,fieldNum,fieldVal)
    register XCmdBlockPtr paramPtr;
    Boolean cardFieldFlag;
    short fieldNum;
    HandlefieldVal;
    {
            paramPtr->inArgs[0] = (long)cardFieldFlag;
            paramPtr->inArgs[1] = fieldNum;
            paramPtr->inArgs[2] = (long)fieldVal;
            paramPtr->request = xreqSetFieldByNum;
        (*paramPtr->entryPoint)();
    }


    ======================================


    File SetGlobal.c

    #include "HyperXCmd.h"

    /* Set the value of the specified HyperTalk global variable to be
       the zero-terminated string in globValue.  The contents of the
       Handle are copied, so you must still dispose it afterwards.
     */
    pascal void
    SetGlobal(paramPtr,globName,globValue)
    register XCmdBlockPtr paramPtr;
    StringPtr       globName;
    HandleglobValue;
```

```
{
        paramPtr->inArgs[0] = (long)globName;
        paramPtr->inArgs[1] = (long)globValue;
        paramPtr->request = xreqSetGlobal;
    (*paramPtr->entryPoint)();
}
```

======================================

File StringEqual.c

#include "HyperXCmd.h"

```
/* Return true if the two strings have the same characters.
   Case insensitive compare of the strings.
 */
pascal Boolean
StringEqual(paramPtr,str1,str2)
register XCmdBlockPtr paramPtr;
unsigned char * str1;
unsigned char * str2;
{
        paramPtr->inArgs[0] = (long)str1;
        paramPtr->inArgs[1] = (long)str2;
        paramPtr->request = xreqStringEqual;
    (*paramPtr->entryPoint)();
        return (Boolean)paramPtr->outArgs[0];
}
```

======================================

File StringLength.c

#include "HyperXCmd.h"

```
/* Count the characters from where strPtr points until
   the next zero byte. Does not count the zero itself.
   strPtr must be a zero-terminated string.
 */
pascal long
StringLength(paramPtr,strPtr)
register XCmdBlockPtr paramPtr;
StringPtr        strPtr;
```

```
{
    paramPtr->inArgs[0] = (long)strPtr;
    paramPtr->request = xreqStringLength;
  (*paramPtr->entryPoint)();
    return paramPtr->outArgs[0];
}
```

==================================

File StringMatch.c

#include "HyperXCmd.h"


```
/* Perform case-insensitive match looking for pattern anywhere
   in target, returning a pointer to first character of the
   first match, in target or NIL if no match found.
   pattern is a Pascal string, and target is a
   zero-terminated string.
 */
pascal Ptr
StringMatch(paramPtr, pattern, target)
register XCmdBlockPtr paramPtr;
StringPtr        pattern;
Ptr   target;
{
    paramPtr->inArgs[0] = (long)pattern;
    paramPtr->inArgs[1] = (long)target;
    paramPtr->request = xreqStringMatch;
  (*paramPtr->entryPoint)();
    return (Ptr)paramPtr->outArgs[0];
}
```

==================================

File StrToBool.c

#include "HyperXCmd.h"


```
/* Convert the Pascal strings 'true' and 'false' to booleans.
 */
pascal Boolean
StrToBool(paramPtr,str)
register XCmdBlockPtr paramPtr;
```

```
Str31 str;
{
     paramPtr->inArgs[0] = (long)str;
     paramPtr->request = xreqStrToBool;
   (*paramPtr->entryPoint)();
     return (Boolean)paramPtr->outArgs[0];
}


====================================


File StrToExt.c

*include "HyperXCmd.h"


/* Original comment:
    Convert a string of ASCII decimal digits to an extended long
    integer.  Instead of returning a new extended, as Pascal does,
    it expects you to create myext and pass it in to be filled. */

/* My comment:  extended, as far as I know, is an 80-bit double,
    not a long integer.  Since LSC doubles are 80-bit,
    I've changed myext to a pointer to a double */
pascal void StrToExt(paramPtr, str, myext)
register XCmdBlockPtr paramPtr;
Str31 str;
double *myext;
{
     paramPtr->inArgs[0] = (long)str;
     paramPtr->inArgs[1] = (long)myext;
     paramPtr->request = xreqStrToExt;
   (*paramPtr->entryPoint)();
}
/*    FUNCTION StrToExt(str: Str31): Extended;
VAR x: Extended;
BEGIN
  WITH paramPtr^ DO
    BEGIN
      inArgs[1] := ORD(@str);
      inArgs[2] := ORD(@x);
      request := xreqStrToExt;
      DoJsr(entryPoint);
      StrToExt := x;
    END;
END;    */
```

```
=====================================

File StrToLong.c

#include "HyperXCmd.h"

/* Convert a string of ASCII decimal digits to
   an unsigned long integer.
 */
pascal long
StrToLong(paramPtr, strPtr)
register XCmdBlockPtr paramPtr;
Str31 strPtr;
{
      paramPtr->inArgs[0] = (long)strPtr;
      paramPtr->request = xreqStrToLong;
    (*paramPtr->entryPoint)();
      return (long)paramPtr->outArgs[0];
}


=====================================

File StrToNum.c

#include "HyperXCmd.h"

/* Convert a string of ASCII decimal digits to a signed
   long integer.  Negative sign is allowed.
 */
pascal long
StrToNum(paramPtr, str)
register XCmdBlockPtr paramPtr;
Str31 str;
{
      paramPtr->inArgs[0] = (long)str;
      paramPtr->request = xreqStrToNum;
    (*paramPtr->entryPoint)();
      return paramPtr->outArgs[0];
}
```

```
======================================

File ZeroBytes.c

#include "HyperXCmd.h"


/* Write zeros into memory starting at destPtr and going
   for longCount number of bytes.
 */
    pascal void
    ZeroBytes(paramPtr, dstPtr, longCount)
    register XCmdBlockPtr    paramPtr;
    Ptr dstPtr;
long  longCount;
{
     paramPtr->inArgs[0] = (long)dstPtr;
     paramPtr->inArgs[1] = longCount;
     paramPtr->request = xreqZeroBytes;
    (*paramPtr->entryPoint)();
}


======================================

File ZeroToPas.c

#include "HyperXCmd.h"

/* Fill the Pascal string with the contents of the zero-terminated
   string.  Useful for converting the arguments of any XCMD to
   Pascal strings.
 */
pascal void
ZeroToPas(paramPtr,zeroStr,pasStr)
register XCmdBlockPtr paramPtr;
unsigned char  *zeroStr;
StringPtr            pasStr;
{
     paramPtr->inArgs[0] = (long)zeroStr;
     paramPtr->inArgs[1] = (long)pasStr;
     paramPtr->request = xreqZeroToPas;
    (*paramPtr->entryPoint)();
}
```

Writing XCMDs in Turbo Pascal

All units that Turbo Pascal needs to compile a Macintosh program—other than your own source code—are actually inside the Turbo Pascal compiler program. When new kinds of units need to be added to the built-in library, you use a utility program called the Unit Mover (included with Turbo Pascal) to get the compiled unit into Turbo so you may call it from your source code.

To prepare Turbo Pascal for compiling XCMDs, you must compile the interface file (listed below) and move it into the Turbo Pascal compiler program. This file compiles into a unit called HyperXCmd, and will be listed with other units used by your XCMD. A separate glue file (the one with the routines) must be an Included file with your compilation. The glue file is the same one released by APDA for MPW Pascal, and is named XCmdGlue.inc. You must also add to Turbo two DHDR type resources with the resource moving abilities of ResEdit. These "driver headers" let you specify Turbo Pascal to compile and create programs other than standalone Macintosh applications. There is a DHDR resource for Desk Accessories, for example. Each style of external command, XCMD and XFCN, requires its own DHDR.

If you don't have access to the disk containing the DHDR resources, you can create them from scratch with ResEdit. Here's how to do it:

1. **Open ResEdit and the resource fork of Turbo Pascal until you open the DHDR type resources (be sure you are using a backup copy of Turbo Pascal for this).**
   You'll see that several DHDRs are already installed for creating INIT resources, desk accessories, and others.

2. **Choose New from the File menu.**
   ResEdit will create a new (empty) DHDR type resource, assigning it an ID number. The window is for entry of straight code (Figure E-1). Fortunately, the amount of code that goes into each DHDR is quite small, so you can enter it manually in less than a minute.

3. **Using the DHDR for XCMDs illustrated in Figure E-2, type the code that appears in the four central columns.**
   ResEdit will accept the characters you type and advance the cursor to the next position. These characters are in hexadecimal notation. Occasionally, the characters you type will shift a bit in anticipation of the next character you type, but by the end of the code, everything will even out.

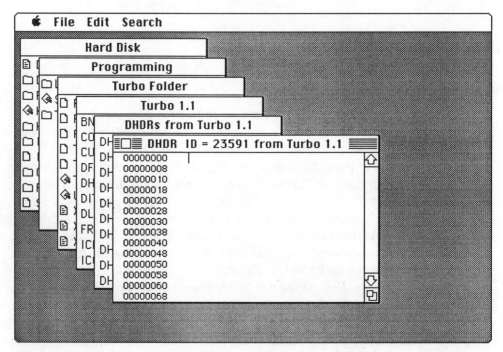

Figure E-1 *If you need to create the DHDR resources, start with a blank DHDR resource.*

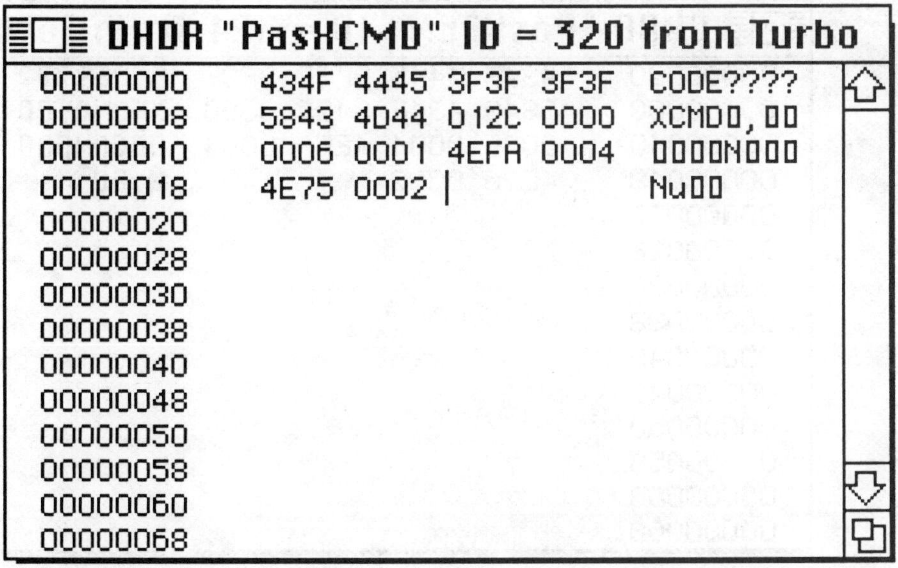

```
▤□▤ DHDR "PasHCMD" ID = 320 from Turbo
00000000    434F 4445 3F3F 3F3F    CODE????
00000008    5843 4D44 012C 0000    XCMD□,□□
00000010    0006 0001 4EFA 0004    □□□□N□□□
00000018    4E75 0002 |            Nu□□
00000020
00000028
00000030
00000038
00000040
00000048
00000050
00000058
00000060
00000068
```

Figure E-2   *Type the hexadecimal code (the middle four columns) of this XCMD DHDR into the blank resource. Assign the name and number via the Get Info dialog box for this resource.*

4. *Choose Get Info from the File menu*

5. *Name the DHDR for XCMDs "PasXCMD" and assign it the resource ID number 320.*

6. *Create the DHDR for XFCN as you did in steps 2 through 5 above, but use the DHDR illustrated in Figure E-3 as the model.* Also, name the XFCN driver header "PasXFCN" and assign it the resource ID number 321.

If you are writing an XCMD resource, then the following basic outline should be followed in structuring your Turbo Pascal code:

```
program xcmdtemplate;

{ change the name of the program}
{ to the name you want for the XCMD }

{$R-}
{$U-}
{$D PasXCMD}
```

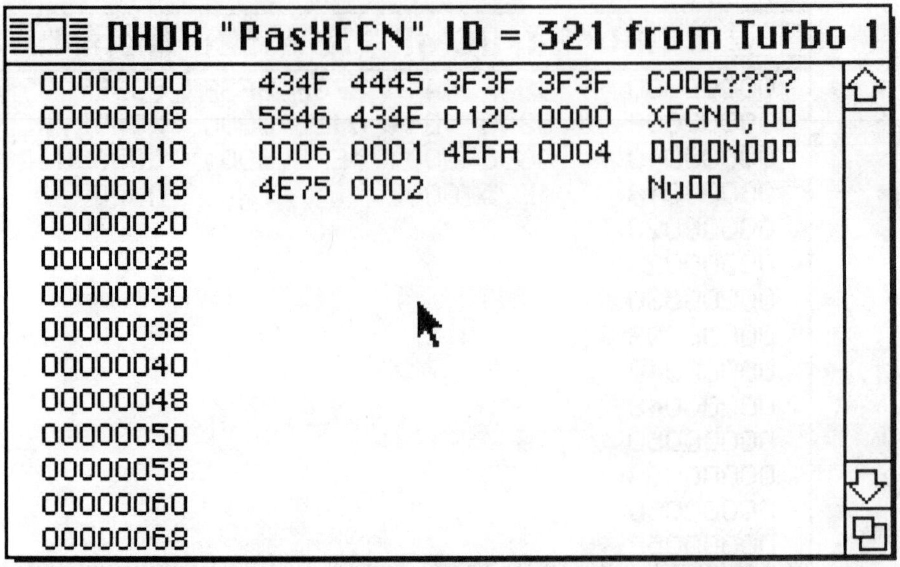

```
▤▢▨ DHDR "PasXFCN" ID = 321 from Turbo 1
 00000000    434F 4445 3F3F 3F3F    CODE????      ⬆
 00000008    5846 434E 012C 0000    XFCN◻,◻◻
 00000010    0006 0001 4EFA 0004    ◻◻◻◻N◻◻◻
 00000018    4E75 0002              Nu◻◻
 00000020
 00000028
 00000030                    ▶
 00000038
 00000040
 00000048
 00000050
 00000058                                         ⬇
 00000060                                         ▱
 00000068
```

Figure E-3   *Type the hexadecimal code (the middle four columns) of this XFCN DHDR into the blank resource. Assign the name and number via the Get Info dialog box for this resource.*

```
USES Memtypes,HyperXCmd;

PROCEDURE myXCMD(paramPtr: XCmdPtr);

{ this is the procedure that will be executed.}
{ the name must be myXCMD }

{$I XCmdGlue.inc}

  BEGIN

  { put your code here }

  END;

{ the BEGIN/END following this comment are }
{ a null program. don't delete it. }
{ it is required by Turbo. }

BEGIN
END.
```

For an XFCN, here's the outline to follow:

```
program xfcntemplate;

{ change the name of the program }
{ to the name you want for the XFCN }

{$R-}
{$U-}
{$D PasXFCN}

USES Memtypes,HyperXCmd;

PROCEDURE myXFCN(paramPtr: XCmdPtr);

{ this is the procedure that will be executed. }
{ the name must be myXFCN }

{$I XCmdGlue.inc}

  BEGIN

  { put your code here. don't forget to return a value }

  END;

{ the BEGIN/END following this comment are }
{ a null program. don't delete it. }
{ it is required by Turbo. }

BEGIN
END.
```

Note a few important things about Turbo Pascal implementations of XCMD and XFCNs. First, the program name must be the name you will be assigning to the resource—the same name you will be calling from HyperTalk to start the XCMD or XFCN.

Second, the $D compiler directive summons the appropriate DHDR type for the style of resource you are writing. Make sure you use PasXCMD for XCMDs and PasXFCN for XFCNs.

Third, the units that your XCMD code uses must include Memtypes and HyperXCmd at the least. Calls to many Macintosh Toolbox routines may require additional units. Consult the listing of Macintosh Interface units at the end of the Turbo Pascal manual, and see which units contain the Toolbox calls your XCMD makes.

Fourth, the main procedure must include (with the $I compiler directive) the XCmdGlue.inc file so your XCMD can communicate with HyperCard. If you need only one or two of these glue routines, consider placing them directly in your XCMD (in which case you won't have to include this file).

Finally, Turbo Pascal requires the last BEGIN/END construction, even though nothing goes into it. The outermost procedure (the one with the name of the XCMD) is the procedure that executes, and may call other local procedures and functions defined within it.

When you compile the program, Turbo Pascal creates a file containing your resource. Turbo Pascal automatically assigns the ID number of 300 to every XCMD or XFCN that it creates. Use ResEdit to change the ID number, assign the name (the name you'll be calling from HyperTalk) and move the resource to your stack.

Here is the listing for the interface file that you must compile (using Turbo Pascal) and move into the compiler with the Unit Mover:

```
UNIT HyperXCmd(-256);

{$U-}          { don't let Turbo give us anything we don't want }

{     HyperXCmd.p  Definition file for HyperCard
      XCMDs and XFNCs in Pascal.

      By Dan Winkler.  DO NOT call the author!

      ƏApple Computer, Inc. 1987
      All Rights Reserved.

      Modified for Turbo Pascal by Stephen Kurtzman
      Install this unit into the Turbo Pascal compiler
      using UNITMOVER
}

INTERFACE

USES MemTypes;     { necessary for Turbo interface }

CONST

    { result codes }
    xresSucc    = 0;
    xresFail    = 1;
```

```
         xresNotImp  = 2;

       { request codes }
       xreqSendCardMessage = 1;
       xreqEvalExpr       = 2;
       xreqStringLength   = 3;
       xreqStringMatch    = 4;
       xreqSendHCMessage  = 5;
       xreqZeroBytes      = 6;
       xreqPasToZero      = 7;
       xreqZeroToPas      = 8;
       xreqStrToLong      = 9;
       xreqStrToNum       = 10;
       xreqStrToBool      = 11;
       xreqStrToExt       = 12;
       xreqLongToStr      = 13;
       xreqNumToStr       = 14;
       xreqNumToHex       = 15;
       xreqBoolToStr      = 16;
       xreqExtToStr       = 17;
       xreqGetGlobal      = 18;
       xreqSetGlobal      = 19;
       xreqGetFieldByName = 20;
       xreqGetFieldByNum  = 21;
       xreqGetFieldByID   = 22;
       xreqSetFieldByName = 23;
       xreqSetFieldByNum  = 24;
       xreqSetFieldByID   = 25;
       xreqStringEqual    = 26;
       xreqReturnToPas    = 27;
       xreqScanToReturn   = 28;
       xreqScanToZero     = 39;  { was supposed to be 29.  Oops! }


   TYPE

     XCmdPtr = ^XCmdBlock;
     XCmdBlock =
       RECORD
         paramCount: INTEGER;
         params:        ARRAY[1..16] OF Handle;
             returnValue: Handle;
         passFlag:    BOOLEAN;

         entryPoint: ProcPtr;     { to call back to HyperCard }
         request:    INTEGER;
```

```
        result:       INTEGER;
        inArgs:       ARRAY[1..8] OF LongInt;
        outArgs:      ARRAY[1..4] OF LongInt;
    END;

{    include the types used by the interface routines
     in Xcmdglue.inc
}

    Str255 = string[255];
    Str31  = string[31];



IMPLEMENTATION      { necessary for Turbo interface }

END.
```

The XCmdGlue.inc file that you $Include in your XCMD source code is the same file you get from APDA in its HyperCard XCMD kit. This file is also readily available on most HyperCard or Turbo Pascal bulletin boards.

F

Writing XCMDs with Mainstay V.I.P.

The letters V.I.P. stand for Visual Interactive Programming, a graphical programming language published by Mainstay. Instead of writing lines of code, you select from a library of procedures. These procedures are assembled literally like building blocks in a window on the screen. Each procedure has one or more items that need to be filled in—the same as arguments you'd supply a written procedure in Pascal or C. Unlike Pascal or C Macintosh programming, however, you are essentially prompted for the arguments to any procedure or control structure.

V.I.P. is an interpreted language, but an optional accessory generates C code that may be compiled with MPW C or LightSpeed C. With release 2.5, the V.I.P.-to-C convertor also lets you write XCMDs for HyperCard. Before we go further, however, you should know that the C code generated by this conversion program is written to be compiled with a special V.I.P. library that contains a number of predefined procedures. Therefore, the C code may not look exactly like a "from scratch" C version of the XCMD.

Because everything you need to write XCMDs with V.I.P. comes in the required V.I.P-to-C package, there will be no files reprinted here (or on the companion disk). Instead, I'll show you a simple example of a V.I.P. XFCN, which demonstrates how an argument is passed from a stack to a V.I.P. XFCN and a return value is sent back to HyperCard. While you do have access to the XCMD parameter block from within V.I.P., you do not have the added commands of the glue routines shown in these appendixes for other programming environments. But for external functions and commands that don't require communication back with HyperCard midstream, V.I.P. is one way the novice programmer can get into the world of XCMDs.

Sample XFCN

The sample shown here was provided by Mainstay (with some minor changes I've made in variable names). While it replicates in V.I.P. what HyperTalk gives you automatically, you'll be able to follow what's going on without much difficulty. The XFCN returns the sine of a number passed to it as a parameter.

Figure F-1 shows the V.I.P. program for this XFCN as it appears in the window. The basic flow of the XFCN is: If the number of parameters sent with the XFCN is 1, then return the sine of that parameter; otherwise produce an alert box on the screen. Arguments for this "main" routine are set as follows:

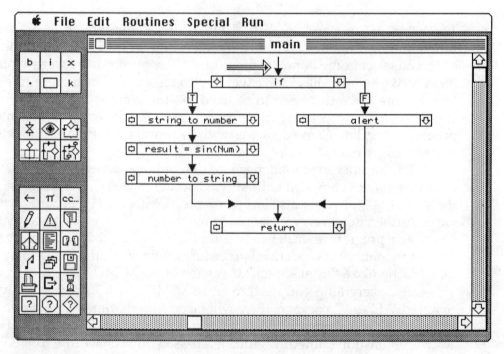

Figure F-1

Name	Dimensions	Type	Input/Output
paramCount	none	2	Input
returnValue	255	1	Output
params	16,255	1	Input

Because there aren't many procedures and structures in this code, I can show you the contents of them all. Figure F-2 artificially assembles the expanded procedures in the same order as they appear in their normal collapsed view (only one procedure may be viewed at a time in V.I.P.). To show the program in another way (along with all the variables declared), here is the listing as V.I.P. prints it out:

```
main (paramCount,returnValue,params)

-> integer paramCount
<- byte returnValue[255]
-> byte params[16,255]
```

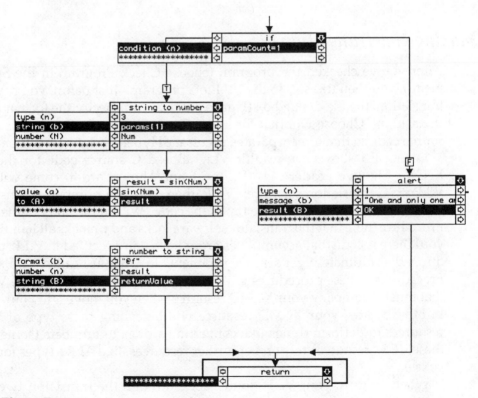

Figure F-2

```
byte
     OK

real
     Num
     result


if (paramCount=1)
     string to number (3,params[1],Num)
     assign (sin(Num),result)
     number to string ("@f",result,returnValue)
else
     alert (1,"One and only one argument is allowed",OK)
return
```

Making the Translation

After you've checked the program (choose Check Program in the Special menu), you then transfer to the V.I.PtoC program. Just before you save the translation, the file dialog box (Figure F-3) lets you specify the format of the translation. Choose External for HyperCard, as shown. This builds the C source code so that it incorporates necessary HyperCard parameter parsing.

Listing F-1 shows the resulting LightSpeed C source code for the sine XFCN. The two header files (VIPtoC.h and HyperCard.h) come with the V.I.P.-to-C translation software. V.I.P. then defines a number of constants, which are represented near the top of the code. Within the body of the main procedure (note that the translator software locks and unlocks all handles for you) there is code that accumulates arguments you specified in V.I.P. procedures that ultimately get sent as arguments to what are called V.I.P. Core Procedures. These procedures will actually "live" in resources (type VEPP) that must accompany your XCMD resource when you move it to your stack. In other words, your XCMD resource will be calling these type of VEPP resources to perform things like converting strings to numbers (sometimes these VEPP resources rely on yet further resources, like ALRT types for alert boxes).

When you run your V.I.P. source code through the translator, two files come out the other end: the C source code and a resource file, with the latter

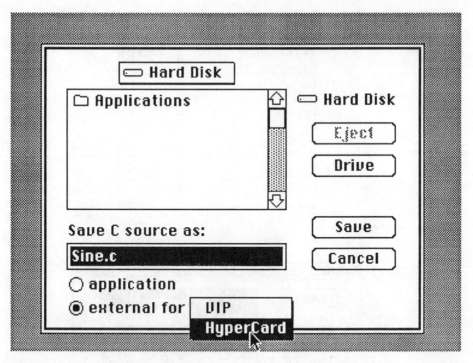

Figure F-3

bearing the name of the original source code file plus a .rsrc extension. Before compiling the C code in LightSpeed, you must change the name of the .rsrc file to the name of the intended LightSpeed C project name (NOT the source code file name), plus the .rsrc extension. A basic external code shell project, called VipCShell_CODE, is provided by Mainstay, and you may reuse this as often as you like. In that case, your .rsrc file would be named VipCShell_CODE.rsrc.

Figure F-4 shows the contents of the external shell project. CodeLink.proj is also provided by Mainstay. To this project, add your source code file. Choose Set Project Type from the Project menu to set the resource type (XFCN or XCMD), resource ID and resource name. Remember that the XCMD resource name is the command word you'll use from HyperTalk. Then compile, using the Build Code Resource choice from the Project menu.

Once the file is compiled, you may then use ResEdit or ResCopy to move all the resources in the freshly compiled file to the stack of your choice. Figure F-5 shows the resources that were created for the V.I.P. version of the sine XFCN. All of these resources must be copied to your stack.

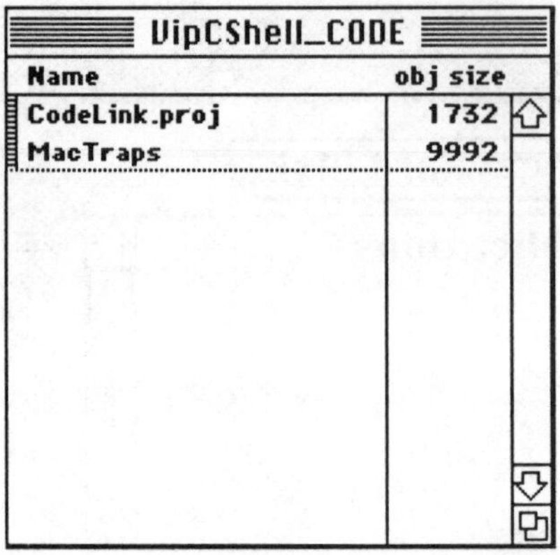

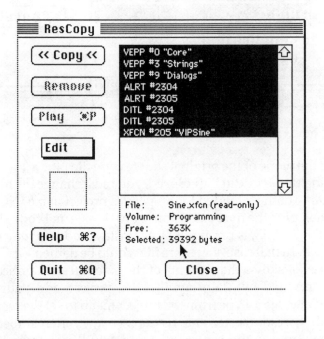

Figure F-4

Figure F-5

Listing F-1.

```
#include "VIPtoC.h"
#include "HyperCard.h"

/* Constants */
```

```
#define  v_ANY_FILE     "????"
#define  v_APPLE_MENU    "\24"
#define  v_BACKSPACE     '\10'
#define  v_CLOSE_EVT     '\4'
#define  v_CR    '\15'
#define  v_DLOG_EVT      '\5'
#define  v_DOWN  '\37'
#define  v_ENTER         '\3'
#define  v_ESC   '\33'
#define  v_EU    2.71828183
#define  v_FALSE         '\0'
#define  v_KEY_EVT       '\2'
#define  v_LEFT  '\34'
#define  v_MENU_EVT      '\1'
#define  v_MODEM         ".A"
#define  v_MOUSE_EVT     '\3'
#define  v_NULL_EVT      '\0'
#define  v_PI    3.14159265
#define  v_PRINTER       ".B"
#define  v_RIGHT         '\35'
#define  v_SINE_WAVE     "si"
#define  v_SIZE_EVT      '\6'
#define  v_SQR_WAVE      "sq"
#define  v_STDIO_WNDW    '\4'
#define  v_TRUE  '\1'
#define  v_UP    '\36'


/*
------- main -------
*/
pascal void main (paramPtr)
      XCmdBlockPtr paramPtr;
{


char v_OK;
real v_Num;
real v_result;


short k;
```

```
SetUpGlobalBase();
for (k = 0; k < paramPtr->paramCount; k++) HLock (paramPtr-
>params[k]);
paramPtr->returnValue = NewHandle (255L);
HLock (paramPtr->returnValue);
if (paramPtr->paramCount==1)
      {
      VIP_ExtArg[0].c = (char)(3);
      VIP_ExtArg[1].addr = (char *)*paramPtr->params[(1) - 1];
      VIP_ExtArg[2].addr = (char *)&v_Num;
      /* string to number */VIP_CoreProc(776);
      v_result = VIP_sin((real)(v_Num));
      VIP_ExtArg[0].addr = (char *)"@f";
      VIP_ExtArg[1].addr = (char *)&v_result;
      VIP_ExtArg[2].addr = (char *)*paramPtr->returnValue;
      /* number to string */VIP_CoreProc(777);
      }
else
      {
      VIP_ExtArg[0].c = (char)(1);
      VIP_ExtArg[1].addr = (char *)"One and only one argument is
allowed";
      VIP_ExtArg[2].addr = (char *)&v_OK;
      /* alert */    VIP_CoreProc(2313);
      }
return;
for (k = 0; k < paramPtr->paramCount; k++) HUnlock (paramPtr-
>params[k]);
HUnlock (paramPtr->returnValue);
RestoreGlobalBase();
}


vr_draw_port (v_wndwID)
      char v_wndwID;
{
}
```

Index

Special Software Offer!

Get a running start on HyperCard software development with the example programs from this book!

The stacks, interface routines, XFCNs and XCMDs featured in *Danny Goodman's HyperCard Developer's Guide* are available for only $9.95, plus $4.00 for shipping and handling.

Why spend hours typing? Send us your check, and we'll send you a 3 ½" diskette with all the scripts and source code from the book.

This disk is not for sale in any store; it can only be purchased directly from the publisher.

Use this coupon to order; mail your check or money order for $13.95 to:

     Bantam Books, Inc., Dept. HCD
     666 Fifth Avenue
     New York, NY 10103

Yes! Send me the *Disk to Accompany Danny Goodman's HyperCard Developer's Guide* (50055-4) for only $13.95 ($9.95 plus $4.00 for shipping and handling.)

Name _____

Address _____

City _____ State _____ Zip _____

My check or money order for $13.95 is enclosed. (Please make check payable to Bantam Books, Inc.)

About the Author

Danny Goodman has been an active participant on the editorial side of the personal computer and consumer electronics revolutions since the late 1970s. His articles have appeared in some of the most prestigious general audience publications, such as *Playboy*, *Science Digest*, *Chicago* and *Los Angeles* city magazines, and in-flight magazines for United, Eastern, PSA, TWA, and several other airlines. As Contributing Editor to *PC World* and *Macworld* magazines, he is frequently the first to report on the applications of new computer technologies. More recently, his computer magazine writing has focused on showing lay readers how to tailor advanced software tools to everyday business problems. In 1987, he won a PCW Communications award for the best hands-on article ("Four Secrets of Excel") appearing in any *Macworld* or *PC World* issue in 1986.

Danny is also the author of 10 personal computer books. His most recent book, *The Complete HyperCard Handbook*, published by Bantam Books in August 1987, has claimed honors as the best selling Macintosh book and fastest selling computer book in the history of our industry. In researching that book, he spent a year and a half working with the program's creator, Bill Atkinson, who acknowledges Danny's contribution to the design of *HyperCard*.

The term "software developer" is new to Danny's titles. In November 1987, Activision published his *Focal Point* and *Business Class* programs, the first HyperCard-based products to reach retail distribution. These two products received three Software Publishers Association awards for best products in three categories for 1987.

Danny, 37, was born in Chicago. He earned a B.A. and M.A. in Classical Antiquity from the University of Wisconsin at Madison. He moved to California in 1983, and now lives in a small San Francisco area coastal community, where he alternates views between computer screens and the Pacific Ocean.